CANADIAN

POLITICS

IN THE 1990s

CANADIAN
POLITICS
IN THE 1990s

Edited by **Michael S. Whittington**
and **Glen Williams**

16 0201

☑ Nelson Canada

I(T)P   An International Thomson Publishing Company

Toronto • Albany • Bonn • Boston • Cincinnati • Detroit • London • Madrid
Melbourne • Mexico City • New York • Pacific Grove • Paris • San Francisco
Singapore • Tokyo • Washington

I(T)P˙

International Thomson Publishing
The ITP logo is a trademark under licence

© Nelson Canada
A division of Thomson Canada Limited, 1995

Published in 1995 by
Nelson Canada
A division of Thomson Canada Limited
1120 Birchmount Road
Scarborough, Ontario M1K 5G4

Cover Illustration: Normand Cousineau

Canadian Cataloguing in Publication Data

Main entry under title:

Canadian politics in the 1990s

4th ed.
Includes bibliographical references and index.
ISBN 0-17-604247-4

1. Canada – Politics and government – 1963–1984.
2. Canada – Politics and government – 1984–1993.
3. Canada – Politics and government – 1993– .
I. Whittington, Michael S., 1942– .
II. Williams, Glen, 1947– .

| FC630.C35 1994 | 971.064 | C94–931210-X |
| F1034.2.C35 1994 | | |

Acquisitions Editor	Andrew Livingston
Production Editor	Bob Kohlmeier
Developmental Editor	Joanne Scattolon
Art Director	Liz Nyman
Design	Hania Fil

Printed and bound in Canada
   1 2 3 4 (WC) 98 97 96 95

Dedicated to the memory of
Joseph Saad, Julia Saad, Aline Shalhoub, and Ed Forrest

CONTENTS

PART THREE   LINKS BETWEEN SOCIETY AND STATE

PART FOUR   STRUCTURES OF CANADIAN GOVERNMENT

INTRODUCTION

It has now been thirteen years since the publication of the first edition of this book. While the contents have changed from edition to edition to reflect the changing realities of Canadian political life, we have tried to maintain the same "reader-friendly" format.

As in previous editions, contributors were asked to present a clear and uncluttered overview of their respective fields of specialization. Our objective here is not to dazzle the reader with extensive footnotes or elaborate theoretical frameworks. Rather, it is to explain in plain language the complex issues, institutional arrangements, and central processes that are part of the current Canadian political landscape. Our target audience is not our professional colleagues but students and other informed Canadians who are not professionals in economics or political science.

Since the publication of the third edition in 1990, the political scene in Canada has changed significantly. In its international relations, Canada's role has been forever altered: on this continent by the establishment of North American free trade and by the declining significance of NORAD; and, globally, by the disintegration of the former Soviet Union and the Eastern Bloc republics.

The national scene, too, has undergone dramatic change. The agenda of domestic Canadian political discourse has come to be dominated by items such as constitutional renewal, the growing demands of Quebec nationalists and aboriginal peoples, and a recognition by federal and provincial politicians that deficits must be reduced. Through all of this, the more familiar political issues based on race, gender, class, and region have not gone away.

More than the political scene has changed, however, for since our last edition the dramatis personae of Canadian politics have also been transformed. The party system and the composition of the House of Commons it gives rise to would be unrecognizable to a denizen of 1990. The cabinet has been radically restructured, the role of the judiciary continues to evolve as a result of the Charter, and even the bureaucracy is assuming a new mandate in state–society interaction.

Taking heed of these changes, we have included in this edition a number of new authors to cover new topics. Part One has been altered most radically. Of the six articles in the third edition that considered the political organization of regions within Canada, only Ken McRoberts's chapter remains. While we would have liked to include all of them again, the textbook editor's most formidable foe is limited space. New to this section are three chapters: Michael Whittington on aboriginal self-government, Laura Macdonald on Canada and the new world order, and Isabella

Bakker on the deficit and the debt. Glen Williams's chapter has been expanded to address the implications of Canada's participation in NAFTA.

Parts Two and Three will be recognizable to readers of previous editions. While all of the chapters have been rewritten or updated, most of the authors remain the same. There are also new chapters by Daiva Stasiulis on race and ethnicity and by Les Pal on the emerging "linkage" role of the federal bureaucracy. A new chapter on political parties by Nelson Wiseman looks at the new political alignments that emerged in the 1993 general election.

Part Four also features three new chapters. Roger Gibbins looks at the most recent developments (or nondevelopments) in constitutional renewal, Radha Jhappan discusses the Charter and the emerging role of the courts, and Reg Whitaker presents a new assessment of the relationship between politicians and bureaucrats in the policy process.

The editors are excited about the new and revised material brought together in this edition and believe that it will be as well received as the previous ones. Our thanks go out to those important contributors to the third edition who could not be included in this volume—Pat Marchak, Viv Nelles, Peter Boswell, Janine Brodie, Jane Jenson, David Milne, Jack Layton, Rick Van Loon, and Rick Schultz. Their chapters remain excellent reading. As in the past, the comments of our colleagues and students have been extremely useful in helping us to determine the nature and extent of the revisions required for this new edition.

CONTRIBUTORS

Michael M. Atkinson, Professor and Chair, Department of Political Science, McMaster University, Hamilton, Ontario

Isabella Bakker, Associate Professor, Department of Political Science, York University, North York, Ontario

David V.J. Bell, Professor and Dean of Environmental Studies, York University, North York, Ontario

Sandra Burt, Associate Professor, Department of Political Science, University of Waterloo, Ontario

Harold D. Clarke, Professor, Department of Political Science, University of North Texas, Denton, Texas

Frederick J. Fletcher, Professor, Department of Political Science, York University, North York, Ontario

Roger Gibbins, Professor and Chair, Department of Political Science, University of Calgary, Alberta

Radha Jhappan, Assistant Professor, Department of Political Science, Carleton University, Ottawa, Ontario

Laura Macdonald, Assistant Professor, Department of Political Science, Carleton University, Ottawa

Kenneth McRoberts, Director, Robarts Centre for Canadian Studies, and Professor, York University, North York, Ontario

William Mishler, Professor, Department of Government and International Studies, University of South Carolina, Columbia, South Carolina

Leslie A. Pal, Professor, School of Public Administration, Carleton University, Ottawa, Ontario

Jon H. Pammett, Professor and Chair, Department of Political Science, Carleton University, Ottawa, Ontario

Leo V. Panitch, Professor and Chair, Department of Political Science, York University, North York, Ontario

A. Paul Pross, Professor, Department of Public Administration, Dalhousie University, Halifax, Nova Scotia

David E. Smith, Professor, Department of Political Science, University of Saskatchewan, Saskatoon, Saskatchewan

Daiva Stasiulis, Associate Professor, Department of Sociology and Anthropology, Carleton University, Ottawa, Ontario

Garth Stevenson, Professor, Department of Politics, Brock University, St. Catharines, Ontario

Daphne Gottlieb Taras, Assistant Professor, Faculty of Management, University of Calgary, Alberta

Reginald A. Whitaker, Professor, Department of Political Science, York University, North York, Ontario

Michael S. Whittington, Professor, Department of Political Science, Carleton University, Ottawa, Ontario

Glen Williams, Professor, Department of Political Science, Carleton University, Ottawa, Ontario

Nelson Wiseman, Associate Professor, Department of Political Science, University of Toronto, Ontario

AGENDA TOWARD 2000

1 ABORIGINAL SELF-GOVERNMENT IN CANADA

Michael S. Whittington

The last decade has seen an expansion in the already arcane vocabulary of constitutional debate in Canada with the coming into common parlance of terms such as "inherency," "third order" of government, and "aboriginal self-government." This phenomenon is the outcome of a series of failed attempts to effect packages of constitutional reform from 1985 to the present. The impetus for much of this constitutional teeth-gnashing, which came largely from Quebec, was the result of the 1982 Constitution Act being viewed as "unfinished" in that the government of Quebec was not a signatory to the federal–provincial agreement that led to it (see Chapter 16). But neither had the issue of self-government for Canada's aboriginal "First Nations" been dealt with in 1982, and it was an issue that simply would not go away.

The first post-1982 approach to dealing with aboriginal demands was to establish a separate constitutional process to deal with aboriginal issues. A series of conferences that included the first ministers, the premiers of the two territorial governments, and representatives of four national aboriginal organizations were held over a three-year period, in an attempt to provide self-government rights through an amendment to section 35 of the 1982 Constitution Act. This round of negotiations foundered in March of 1987 when the provinces of Alberta, British Columbia, Newfoundland, and Saskatchewan could not agree to a package of self-government provisions because (despite three years of discussions) they claimed, "We don't know what self-government means." On the other side of the table, the Assembly of First Nations was not ready to agree with the package because it did not include an explicit recognition that self-government was an "inherent" or "free-standing" aboriginal right.

The federal and provincial governments, having made a "reasonable effort" to deal with aboriginal concerns, immediately embarked on a series of First Ministers' Conferences that ultimately produced the Meech

Lake Accord. This round of constitutional talks excluded the territorial governments and the aboriginal organizations and while there are many variables that contributed to the demise of the accord, such as the prime minister's ill-judged "roll of the dice" gaffe, the failure to deal with aboriginal issues was perhaps the fatal flaw. Elijah Harper's stand in the Manitoba legislature, which ultimately scuttled the deal, clearly would not have happened had aboriginal self-government provisions been part of the package.

The next paroxysm of constitutionalizing featured a series of conferences culminating in the Charlottetown Accord. But the lesson of Meech having been learned, this set of negotiations included not only the first ministers but the premiers of the Yukon and N.W.T. as well as the four national aboriginal organizations. That the astonishing and unprecedented achievement of a consensus among seventeen parties at the negotiating table was negated in a national referendum by a cynical and curmudgeonly populace is now simply an artifact of history. What has changed forever is that in the future such constitutional processes will likely have to include territorial governments and aboriginal leaders, and in the unlikely eventuality that an agreement is reached, that agreement will have to pass muster in a national referendum before the Constitution can be amended.

What has also changed forever is that the argot of constitutionalese featuring terms such as "Triple E," "distinct society," and "Canada clause" has been enriched with the new vocabulary of aboriginal self-government. Given that the self-government issue will not go away, we must ask ourselves what aboriginal self-government is and what it means for our political process in the decade leading up to the 21st century.

ABORIGINAL PEOPLE AND ABORIGINAL RIGHTS

The aboriginal people of Canada are the descendants of the people who were living on this continent when European explorers "discovered" it (although the aboriginal people continue to insist that they "knew it was here all along"). Canadian aboriginals include Indians, Inuit, and Métis, and make up 4–5 percent of the Canadian population.[1] While we tend to speak of aboriginal people as a discrete and identifiable segment of the Canadian population, there is in fact a very wide diversity of language, culture, and history among the various groups across Canada. What allows us to continue to use the general term is the fact that they have shared a common and usually unhappy historical relationship with non-Natives and non-Native governments.

Aboriginal rights are those rights that aboriginal people possess because they had them before contact with non-Native settlers. These rights continue to exist despite the fact that the continent has come to be populated by large numbers of "newcomers." According to the Canadian courts, aboriginal rights can be extinguished only by conquest, by treaty, or by explicit act passed by the Parliament of Canada. Moreover, even Parliament may not frivolously or casually enact legislation that affects aboriginal rights and must consult the people affected, minimize the impacts, and provide compensation.

Aboriginal rights were originally incorporated into the Constitution through the British Proclamation of 1763, which recognized the rights of the Indian nations and provided that their rights could not be taken away except according to the principles of British justice—in effect, by negotiated treaty. The obligations under this proclamation were automatically transferred to the Government of Canada by the British North America Act (Constitution Act 1967), section 91 (24) of which stipulates that only the *federal* government has the legislative authority to effect the surrender of any aboriginal rights. The Constitution Act of 1982 recognizes and affirms "the existing aboriginal and treaty rights of the aboriginal peoples of Canada," while section 25 of the Charter of Rights and Freedoms provides that the Charter cannot be construed so as to abrogate aboriginal or treaty rights. Thus, although the Constitution of Canada explicitly recognizes the existence of aboriginal rights and provides protection for those rights, it does not tell us what those rights are, nor whether they might have been surrendered or extinguished at some time in the past.

One way to come to grips with the nature and extent of aboriginal rights is to establish some understanding of the traditional or pre-colonial patterns of use and occupancy of the land. Indeed, because traditional aboriginal societies were largely based on hunting and gathering (in some cases supplemented by agriculture), the land is the foundation of the aboriginal economy, culture, and society. But the aboriginal concept of land is very different from the European one. Whereas our system is based on the notion of private *ownership*, aboriginal societies base their system on the notion of shared *use* of the land. The land belongs to everyone living today and to the unborn generations of the future, and while often there were informal understandings among communities or tribal groups that recognized each other's more or less exclusive use of certain territories for purposes of hunting and fishing, the land was owned only by the Creator, who put it there for the use of *all* people.

Thus, while aboriginal rights have not been exhaustively defined by the Constitution, statutes, or the common law, it is generally agreed that, at a minimum, such rights include the right to hunt and fish and to harvest plants, and the necessarily incidental rights of access and occupancy on the land upon which such potables are found. The significance of this is that unless there has been an explicit surrender of rights through a previous treaty or land-claim agreement in a given area, governments, both federal and provincial, must protect the aboriginal interests before they can sell or otherwise grant interests in public lands to individuals or corporations.[2] The thrust of the comprehensive claims process today, then, is to eliminate the uncertainty with respect to lands burdened by unextinguished aboriginal rights through negotiating a surrender of those rights in exchange for a set of rights defined in a "modern treaty" or land-claim agreement.

It is clear that aboriginal rights include at least a set of rights associated with the use and occupancy of the land, and that these rights remain alive and in effect until such time as they have been surrendered. The question (to which we turn now) that has not been answered by the courts is whether there is an aboriginal right to self-government.

THE RIGHT TO SELF-GOVERNMENT

Aboriginal people, as Canadians, currently govern themselves. Despite being denied the franchise in the past, and despite structural impediments to meaningful participation in the political process—such as lower levels of political, educational, and financial resources available to be spent on political involvement—aboriginal Canadians do vote, do run as candidates, and in fact do get elected in a smattering of federal, provincial, and territorial ridings.

The problem is that aboriginal people governed themselves long before the white man arrived in North America, and apparently did a fairly good job of it. When the settlers came, they brought with them their culture, language, and religion, and political institutions modelled after the ones they were accustomed to in Europe. Parliamentary democracy is, in fact, a fairly good system of governance by most measures, but it does not work very well for groups or individuals who are *not* included in the citizenry.

The aboriginal people of Canada were, from the outset, *subjects* of governmental policy and a *matter* of legislative jurisdiction. They were never fully enfranchised citizens. From the beginning "Indians" (and the Inuit considerably later) were simply another political problem or issue, and were part of the governmental process only as "subjects" of Her Majesty and as "wards of the state." And, as wards of the state, in a little more than a century aboriginal people were deprived of their traditional means of livelihood; their cultures and languages were wiped out; and their communities became socially dysfunctional. Thus, in the aboriginal view, the white man's government has messed up aboriginal lives for the past hundred years or so, and the First Nations are now saying, "Give us a crack at it—we certainly can't do any worse!" In sum, it is clear that the aboriginal people of Canada want a right to govern themselves that is greater than and different from the democratic rights that they already possess as Canadians in the 1990s.

There are a number of strategies that aboriginal people might employ in order to obtain a right to govern themselves, but the two most obvious ones are (1) to get the existing governments in Canada to specifically grant them self-government through legislation or negotiated agreements; or (2) to seek a recognition through the courts, through a political accord with governments, or through a constitutional amendment that such a right already exists or is *inherent*. Given their past experience in dealing with governments, it is not surprising that the aboriginal people of Canada would prefer a recognition that their right to self-government is inherent—one of the *existing* aboriginal rights affirmed in section 35 of the Constitution Act of 1982.

Although the right to self-government likely *is* an aboriginal right, a serious concern exists for aboriginal people who already have entered into treaties with the Crown. All of these treaties feature an "extinguishment clause" whereby the aboriginal people surrender their "aboriginal rights, titles, and interests" in exchange for explicit "treaty rights." The question is whether such a surrender includes the aboriginal right of Natives to govern themselves, in which case the groups with treaties would not have the inherent right enjoyed by groups in, for instance, B.C., the Yukon, and parts of the N.W.T., where there are few treaties.

While the courts have not rendered any decisions on this issue, it seems reasonable to assume that, given that the surrenders in the treaties were "in and to the land" only, the right to self-government is still alive. Governance involves authority in respect of people or citizens, and while most governmental jurisdiction is limited territorially, "land" per se is not what is "governed." But these issues may be moot, for the newly elected government of Jean Chrétien did not waste any time in stating uncategorically that their approach to negotiating self-government with aboriginal people is to start with the assumption that the right to self-government is inherent. This policy statement was not limited to nontreaty groups, but was clearly intended to apply to all First Nations in Canada.

In sum, it is probably safe to assert that there is an aboriginal right to self-government, and that because it is an *aboriginal* right it is by definition inherent. Having been burned before in their relations with government, the aboriginal people would still like to see a constitutional affirmation of the inherent right. However, there does not seem to be an abundance of enthusiasm among federal and provincial governments to return to the constitutional table in the near future. Instead, the proposal of the federal government is to proceed to negotiate self-government agreements with First Nations and the provinces and territories affected. As long as it is clear that these agreements would be without prejudice to the question of an inherent right to self-government, the aboriginal First Nations have nothing to lose by coming to the negotiating table.

SELF-GOVERNMENT AGREEMENTS

Having established that aboriginal people have a right to govern themselves, we have still addressed only a part of the issue before us in Canada. Whether that right is inherent, constitutionally affirmed, or merely a creature of statute, the practical realities are that the relationships between First Nation governments and the federal, provincial, and territorial governments that are already in place have to be defined. This is because, with the exception of a few First Nations such as the Mohawks, the aboriginal people of Canada generally wish to remain Canadians, and wish their governments to exist within the context, and under the protection, of the Constitution of Canada.

Most native people realize that it is unnecessary and impractical for them to attempt to take control of *all* the responsibilities of modern government in order to be self-determining. If they are to take control of their lives, it is essential that they have legislative authority over matters such as their lands and resources; social, community, and health services; education; economic development; and many aspects of the criminal-justice system. For the most part, they neither need nor want responsibility for matters such as national defence, navigation and shipping, banking and currency, bankruptcy, patents, and so forth. These are powers exercised by the federal government and involve matters that can generally be dealt with more effectively at the national level.

However, with respect to those areas under provincial control for which the First Nations *will* want to assume responsibility, there will be a need to work out the relationship between the aboriginal regimes and the affected province or territory. For example, while the aboriginal people will likely wish to take over matters such as community health services, in the case of most aboriginal communities it will be impractical to provide separate acute-care facilities—hospitals—for their people. In other areas such as municipal services, in cases where the Native community is adjacent to a municipality it may make financial sense to share the cost of a single fire department or sewage system.

Finally, there are very few First Nations today that possess the economic base or the fiscal resources to be able to assume responsibility for the programs currently being delivered by other governments. In a perfect world, the financing of aboriginal governments would be achieved entirely through First Nation taxation regimes. The First Nation government would finance its own programs and services, and would bear the same burden of fiscal responsibility in its spending practices as any other government. However, this level of self-sufficiency is unattainable even for most provincial governments today, and, as is the case with the poorer provinces, the First Nation governments will have to be supported by intergovernmental transfer payments until they can develop an economic base that will allow them to pay their own bills with their own tax revenues.

Thus, there is a clear need for negotiated agreements between the First Nations and the existing governments, first, to give practical effect to the right to self-government and, second, to define the new intergovernmental relationships that will evolve. These agreements need not be exceedingly lengthy or detailed. While it would seem critical that the matters of exclusive First Nation legislative authority and the areas of jurisdiction that are to remain exclusively in the hands of federal, provincial, or territorial legislatures be explicitly enumerated in the agreement, a large portion of the agreement will define *processes* for intergovernmental coordination, cost sharing, and the resolution of interjurisdictional disputes. Before returning to a discussion of some of the issues surrounding the contents of self-government agreements, we must first look at the broader question of the legal status of such agreements.

THE LEGAL STATUS OF SELF-GOVERNMENT AGREEMENTS

The legal status of First Nation self-government agreements is a matter of great concern to the aboriginal people. One issue involves the question of which governments should be party to the agreements, and while their experience with the federal government has not been particularly happy, most First Nations would prefer to deal with the "devil they know" than to get into three-party negotiations that include the province or territory. While the federal government does have the exclusive jurisdiction over status Indians and Inuit and their lands, the nonstatus or Métis people are largely subject to the provincial laws of general application. Hence, even if other things were equal, strictly bilateral federal–First Nation agreements could potentially exclude over half of Canada's aboriginal people. Moreover, other things are not equal.

Most significantly, the lion's share of the governmental powers that the First Nations wish to assume are those currently in the provincial or territorial sphere. In the absence of provincial or territorial participation in the agreements, there would be a high risk of creating many situations of conflict of law and overlapping enforcement regimes.

As well, for reasons of efficiency and economies of scale there will be many situations in which the First Nation and the provincial government will find it mutually beneficial to establish joint or shared-cost programs. Moreover, in a number of jurisdictions many of the services to aboriginal people off reserves (even status Indians) are currently delivered by the province or territory, with the costs recoverable from the feds through a "charge back" mechanism.

The key point is that the provinces and territories are already involved in a political relationship with aboriginal people, and whatever the constitutional niceties it simply would not work to exclude this order of government from the table. Besides, the current political reality in Canada is that the federal government, as a matter of policy, is unwilling to risk the ire of the provinces on this question when they need their cooperation in so many other areas of national concern.

The second and perhaps more troublesome concern about the status of the agreements is whether and how they will be given protection once they have been negotiated. The Indian Act has long provided for a form of limited local government on reserves through a system of elected band councils. Under this system, the band has bylaw powers on the reserve that are municipal in nature but not even as extensive as those enjoyed by most municipalities. While this system is flawed because of a too narrow range of powers ("Oh boy, we can pass bylaws dealing with stray dogs and beekeeping!"), the more important problem is that the powers are only delegated. This means that the Minister of Indian Affairs can veto any bylaws, and the department can replace the band council with an administrator if it is felt that the affairs of the band are not being well managed. Obviously this won't cut it.

Another possible means of protection is specific legislation for each self-government agreement. The Sechelt Band in the lower mainland of British Columbia has such a regime in place, and while most First Nations today would find the actual provisions of the agreement do not go far enough, the generic problem is that the legislation giving effect to the deal could be amended unilaterally at any time. The aboriginal people feel, understandably, that their governments must have more than statutory protection because statutes can be changed at the whim of the legislature that passed them.

Successive governments in Ottawa since 1987 have recognized this concern and have taken the formal position that negotiated self-government agreements should be given protection as "treaties" or land-claim agreements under section 35 of the Constitution Act of 1982. The Charlottetown Accord went still further by stating that the First Nation governments were to constitute a "third order of government"; this implied that their status would be constitutionally equivalent to that of the provinces.

While the federal government takes this brave position at the constitutional table, to date it has been unwilling to deliver on its promise. Four self-government agreements completed and ratified in the Yukon as part of the land-claim process are to be kept separate from the land-claim agreements that will be section 35 treaties. Despite the urging of the First

Nations involved and the Yukon government, Canada insists that the self-government agreements have to be treated separately and given effect only through ordinary statute. To be credible, self-government agreements must be solemn covenants among three orders of government, and must be amendable only with the consent of the parties that negotiated them. This can be achieved only through granting them constitutional protection, and it is to be hoped that in the near future some Minister of Indian Affairs will demonstrate the wit and political will to do so. In order to better illustrate the issues we have been discussing, let us now turn to an examination of the Yukon.[3]

LAND CLAIMS AND SELF-GOVERNMENT IN THE YUKON: THE PROCESS

Since 1973, the Council For Yukon Indians (CYI) has been engaged almost constantly in an attempt to negotiate a comprehensive land-claim agreement with the governments of Canada and the Yukon. In 1984, an agreement in principle (AIP) was negotiated and ratified by the governments of Canada and Yukon. Although the agreement was ultimately turned down by too many of the Yukon First Nations for it to be implemented, it did form the basic model for the successful negotiation of the four Yukon First Nation final agreements that were ratified by all parties in May 1993.

What was unique in the 1984 AIP was the fact that there were self-government provisions included in the land-claim agreement itself, even though the legislative powers granted to the aboriginal people were merely municipal in nature. The federal Comprehensive Claims Policy, dating from 1986, is quite explicit that land-claim agreements and self-government agreements should be separate because the latter are not to be constitutionally protected. A partial exception was made for the Yukon situation in the 1987 negotiator's *mandate*, in order to reconcile the precedent of the 1984 AIP with the new claims policy. The Government of Canada agreed that a "commitment to negotiate" self-government agreements with all fourteen Yukon First Nations, along with guidelines for such negotiations, could be included in the land-claim agreement and hence constitutionally protected. Moreover, while the feds continued to insist that the Yukon self-government agreements themselves could not be section 35 treaties, it was forced, through pressure from the CYI and the Government of the Yukon, to allow the self-government negotiations to proceed simultaneously with the land-claim process, and at the same table.

Thus, First Nation self-government agreements were ratified through the same process as the land-claim agreements in the Yukon; both agreements will come into effect simultaneously, and, in practical if not legal terms, they are completely interdependent. The First Nation institution that will bear the responsibility for taking on the obligations under the land claim will be not a corporation, as in previous claim settlements, but rather the First Nation government. It will also be the First Nation government that will manage and administer all of the rights and benefits of its citizens under the land claim.

It is not clear whether the Yukon process will form a precedent for the integrated negotiation of comprehensive claims and self-government in the future, but in those parts of Canada where there are still unsurrendered aboriginal rights, it doesn't make sense to separate the negotiation of the modern treaties from the negotiation of the system whereby the First Nations will implement those treaties.

SELF-GOVERNMENT IN THE YUKON: THE AGREEMENTS

It is worth talking about some of the features of the Yukon self-government agreements because these agreements go further than any other self-government arrangements negotiated to date. The Cree–Naskapi Act (which sets up a local government regime in the James Bay region of Quebec) and the Nunavut accord (which provides for the creation of a separate territorial government of Nunavut in the Eastern Arctic by the turn of the century) are idiosyncratic and unique to those specific situations.

Recent land-claim settlements with the Tetlit Gwitchin and the Sahtu of the N.W.T. include a commitment to negotiate self-government in the future, but those negotiations have not commenced. A mandate for the negotiation of land claims and self-government in B.C. has not yet been approved by the federal cabinet. Meanwhile, the current federal policy on self-government, almost a decade old, is quaintly entitled "Community Self Government" (the use of the term "community" is intended by Department of Indian Affairs and Northern Development [DIAND] minions to imply that such governments are only municipal in scope and status). Thus, while the Yukon self government model is still far from everything the aboriginal people would like, it does break some important new ground.

The First Nation self-government agreements in the Yukon obviously contain a lot of "boilerplate" legalese that sets out, among other things, general provisions about the processes for ratification, amendment, and dispute resolution, about the rules of interpretation, and remedies, and about the relationship between the land-claim agreement and the self-government agreement. There are five key sets of provisions in each agreement that define the status of the aboriginal governments vis-à-vis the federal and territorial regimes. Each of these requires some elaboration.

1. FIRST NATION CONSTITUTIONS

The Yukon agreements provide that the First Nation must have a constitution, which must contain a citizenship code, an amending formula, a system of financial accountability to citizens, and provisions recognizing the rights and freedoms of individual citizens. As well, the constitution must establish the basic governing institutions of the First Nation. However, the agreements do not require that the constitution be approved by the federal or territorial government, and essentially leave it to the First Nation to define the internal rules and regulations of governance. In this sense, the First Nation constitutions are freestanding and reflective only of the political values and traditions of the First Nation.

There is no explicit requirement that the First Nation be subject to the provisions of the Charter of Rights, but as long as the agreements are implemented by federal statute it is likely that the Charter provisions would apply to the laws passed by the First Nation. This may not be an issue, however, for the reality is that each of the First Nations with an agreement in place already has a constitution containing a charter of rights that, in all cases, goes beyond the Canadian Charter. Because the Yukon First Nations have had long and for the most part unhappy experience with governments, the strong protection of individual rights in their own constitutions tells us that they simply don't trust governments—even their own.

It is also significant that the First Nation constitutions do not have to provide for democratic elections as part of their institutional arrangements. While there was significant opposition from federal departmental officials to giving such free reign to the First Nations ("They might set up military dictatorships!"), the First Nation constitutions are, if anything, more democratic than ours. For the most part, aboriginal political traditions are based on consensus rather than majority rule; as such, the First Nation constitutions in the Yukon require important decisions to be taken by more than a simple majority. None of them has opted for a Queen.

2. FIRST NATION CITIZENSHIP

The agreements provide that the First Nation constitutions must contain a citizenship code. In the constitutions of the first four Yukon First Nations to conclude self-government agreements to date, the tendency has been for those codes to be very broad and inclusive. All beneficiaries under the First Nation land-claim agreement, all members of the pre–land claim

"Indian Act band," and any other individuals who are deemed (usually by the community elders) to have a longstanding involvement with the community are eligible to be citizens of that First Nation. The citizenship codes also provide that any First Nation citizen may renounce his or her citizenship at any time.

It is also stated explicitly in the Yukon First Nation self-government agreements that nothing in the agreements can be construed to take away any of the rights that an individual enjoys as a Canadian citizen. Hence, what is created in the Yukon model is a form of dual citizenship unique within Canada—individuals affected enjoy the benefits of both First Nation and Canadian citizenship.

Finally, the self-government agreements in the Yukon also provide that First Nation citizens who receive program benefits from the First Nation cannot demand benefits from similar or equivalent Yukon government programs. This is merely a practical provision to prevent enterprising First Nation citizens from "double dipping."

3. FIRST NATION JURISDICTION

The legislative authority of Yukon First Nations falls into three basic categories. First, the agreements provide for *exclusive* jurisdiction over all internal administrative matters and over all rights and obligations of the First Nation pursuant to the land-claim agreements.

A second category includes virtually comprehensive power to enact laws on First Nation land ("settlement land" under the land claim). The only significant limit to the exercise of these powers by the First Nation on its own territory is that the laws must be of a "local or private nature" and not trench upon federal jurisdiction in areas such as the Criminal Code, public health, and public safety. It is important to note that First Nation laws will apply to to all people on First Nation land, not just to First Nation citizens.

The third category of First Nation jurisdiction includes an extensive list of provincial-type powers, including health and social services, child welfare and adoption, education and training, solemnization of marriage, and general provision of a wide range of services to citizens. What is unique about this category of legislative jurisdiction is that it extends to First Nation's citizens anywhere in the Yukon, and not just on settlement land. If this completely untried experiment is to succeed, the Yukon and First Nation governments will have to cooperate. Should it prove workable, it may help to resolve the problem of providing self-government rights to aboriginal people who lack an extensive land base (e.g., the Métis in parts of western Canada).

Two areas of First Nation jurisdiction are dealt with as special cases because of their complexity and because of the need to carefully integrate

First Nation laws with the laws of general application in the Yukon. While the First Nations will have extensive powers to raise money by direct taxation, their tax system will have to be integrated with the federal and territorial systems, and collection agreements relating to First Nation income tax will probably have to be worked out with Canada. Hence, there is to be a three-year delay in the coming into effect of these tax powers to allow for a negotiated set of arrangements.

Second, while the First Nations must have the power to enforce their laws, the responsibility for the administration of justice (and particularly for the provision of judicial remedies) must be coordinated with the national and territorial justice system. There is thus to be a five-year delay in the coming into effect of the First Nation justice systems to allow for the negotiation of complementary processes.

Finally, it is important to recognize that while the Yukon First Nations are able to exercise a wide range of legislative powers that in some ways may exceed the powers of a province, they are in no way forced to assume any responsibilities until they are ready. The laws of general application and all of the governmental programs and services being delivered to First Nation citizens continue unchanged until the First Nation "occupies the field" by enacting its own legislation. When the First Nation law is given effect, the general law of the Yukon ceases to apply to the extent that it is inconsistent with the new First Nation law.

The beauty of this arrangement is that the First Nations are not rushed into taking on all the responsibilities of government for their people. Moreover, the fact that the general laws apply until explicitly superseded by a First Nation law means that there will be no hiatus in the transitional period—no period, in other words, in which *no* law is in effect in a given area. The end result of employing such a model is that the First Nations may decide *never* to occupy many areas of jurisdiction and choose instead to expend their limited resources on matters that are particularly culturally sensitive or affordable within the limited economies of scale of the First Nation communities.

4. FINANCING YUKON FIRST NATION GOVERNMENTS

As stated earlier, one of the main obstacles to effective aboriginal self-government in virtually all situations across Canada is the lack of a stable tax base. Clearly, the ultimate goal for aboriginal governments is that they be financially self-sufficient, financing their programs with their own revenue sources. However, the reality is that very few aboriginal communities have the economic base to support their governments without assistance.

Thus, the Yukon agreements provide for unconditional transfer payments from the federal government to the First Nation. These are calculated on the basis of fiscal need, taking into account the ability of the First Nation to raise its own revenues, the costs associated with diseconomies of scale, and the net savings to governments as a result of the First Nation taking over programs that are currently being delivered to First Nation citizens by the Yukon or Canada. There are also provisions for a separate Canada–Yukon agreement so that the net savings to the Yukon government resulting from First Nations taking over Yukon program responsibilities are recoverable by Canada.

As explained above, it is the hope that in the long run the First Nations can become completely self-sufficient; however, until that happy situation evolves, it is recognized that there is a need for the other two orders of government to help out. As well, the Yukon agreements provide that the First Nations must make a serious effort to raise their own revenues and to govern as efficiently as possible.

5. INTERGOVERNMENTAL RELATIONS

The Yukon agreements anticipate that the transition from the status quo to full aboriginal governance will be gradual and driven by the initiative of the First Nations. They are not forced to take on all of the burdens of modern government at a single moment in time, but will assume responsibilities as they feel ready and able to do so. As a consequence, there are many provisions in the agreements that identify processes for ongoing negotiation, consultation, and coordination among the First Nations, Canada, and the Yukon.

The agreements recognize that some programs can be delivered jointly, that others can be made compatible with First Nation interests by including First Nation representatives in their adaptation and development, and that some program responsibilities may be only partially taken over by the First Nation. The First Nations have the *legal* authority to "do it all," but precisely because they have that authority they also have the leverage to negotiate with the other levels of government the sharing of expensive program responsibilities in a mutually beneficial manner.

Finally, the Yukon agreements allow and even encourage the First Nations to delegate their powers to regional or Yukon-wide aboriginal bodies. It is hoped that the provision of some programs and services on a regional or territorial level will produce greater economies and efficiencies as well as higher-quality service for First Nation citizens.

CONCLUSION

The Yukon First Nation self-government agreements are by no means perfect and, in recognition of this fact, they also include opportunities for the first nations to renegotiate some provisions if the policies vis-à-vis self-government are made more favourable to other Canadian aboriginal interests in the future. In other words, in taking a leading role the First Nation of Nacho Nyak Dun, the Vuntut Gwitchin First Nation, the Champagne and Aishihik First Nations, and the Teslin Tlingit Council are not precluded from taking on new rights and benefits that may emerge through constitutional change or aboriginal policy developments elsewhere in Canada.

On the other hand, there are many features in the Yukon agreements that could be beneficially introduced elsewhere in Canada. What is required is that the federal government and the provinces build on these positive steps and extend the opportunity for aboriginal self-government across the country. There are indications that, while no government seems eager to return to the constitutional fray to deal with aboriginal concerns, there is some political will to move ahead on the *negotiation* of self-government—for instance, in B.C., Manitoba, and Ontario.

At the political level, the major difficulty in dealing effectively with demands that self-government is the cost. There is absolutely no way to disguise the reality that a third order of government is going to be extremely expensive. While nobody "does democracy" because it is cheap or efficient, huge annual deficits and growing national and provincial debts cannot be ignored. At a minimum, however, there is no reason governments cannot begin to transfer the resources they currently expend on aboriginal people to the First Nations themselves.

The main nonfinancial obstacle to effective aboriginal self-government is the refusal of the federal and some provincial governments to allow negotiated self-government agreements to have section 35 "treaty" status. This is merely a policy issue and can be achieved without constitutional change. The longstanding refusal of a succession of federal ministers to implement such a policy is the result of advice from the same unimaginative officials in DIAND and the Department of Justice. It is hoped that the ministers of both departments will be sufficiently moved to ignore their briefing notes and exercise political leadership in the near future. To be meaningful in the absence of an explicit constitutional guarantee, negotiated self-government agreements must be given at least the same protection as treaties.

Despite the obstacles and the oft-stated concern of politicians and bureaucrats that "we don't know what we are getting into," the demands for aboriginal self-government will continue to increase. The issue will not disappear, and its time has come in Canada. Doing the "right" thing instead of the "safe" thing (i.e., nothing) requires a modicum of political courage on the part of federal, territorial, and provincial politicians. After a couple of hundred years of neglect, the aboriginal peoples cannot be expected to wait much longer for justice to be done.

NOTES

1. It is difficult to establish a firm estimate of the aboriginal population because the aboriginal people define themselves by culture, lifestyle, and heredity, whereas under the Indian Act governments define them in terms such as "status." Only about three-quarters of a million Indians fall under the "status" category.

2. The courts have generally held that aboriginal rights have been extinguished on privately owned land. As a result of the 1982 affirmation of *existing* aboriginal rights, however, the government cannot dispose of Crown land that is burdened by underlying aboriginal rights unless the aboriginal people are accommodated or compensated.

3. It should be noted that from 1987 to 1993 the author served as the Chief Federal Negotiator in the Yukon, and participated in the negotiation of the Yukon-wide Umbrella Final Agreement as well as First Nation land-claim agreements and self-government agreements with Champagne-Aishihik, Nacho Nyak Dun, the Teslin Tlingit Council, and the Vuntut Gwitchin. After six years of intense engagement in this process, he does not claim to be totally objective.

FURTHER READINGS

Boldt, Menno. *Surviving as Indians: The Challenge of Self-Government.* Toronto: University of Toronto Press, 1993.

Cassidy, Frank, and R.L. Bish. *Indian Government: Its Meaning in Practice.* Halifax: Institute for Research on Public Policy, 1989.

Smith, Dan. *The Seventh Fire: The Struggle for Aboriginal Government.* Toronto: Key Porter, 1993.

2 REGIONS WITHIN REGION: CONTINENTALISM ASCENDANT

Glen Williams

An atlas portrays an uncomplicated image of the lines that divide northern North America: two colours, two nations; on one side of the border 49 states, on the other ten provinces and two territories. This seeming clarity obscures one of the most complex bilateral relationships in the world. In the 20th century, the informal evolution of our continental role in relation to the United States has parallelled along a number of important dimensions the formal incorporation of the Canadian colonies into the French and British Empires during the 17th to 19th centuries. Just as the evolution of modern Canada has been marked by the development of a dense system of interregional relations, so too have Canada's regions developed in relation to specific, often geographically adjacent, local areas in the United States. And, insofar as Canada is more than simply the sum of its southward-facing parts, over time the country as a whole has taken on many of the properties of a northernmost region of the United States.

The continental spatial structures that give meaning to Canada's North American regional identity are most readily visible within Canadian economic life: when investment, production, and trade are considered, the Canadian economy appears more like a *zone* within the American economy than a distinct national economy. For the last half-century, more than two-fifths of Canadian manufacturing and mining industries have been owned by foreign (mostly American) interests. Foreign control of key industrial sectors like transport equipment, machinery, chemicals, and electrical products is even more pronounced, ranging from two-thirds to four-fifths of total Canadian assests.[1] This imposing level of foreign ownership is not approached within any other advanced industrial nation.

Also outside of a typical national profile is the nearly exclusive territorial focus of Canadian trade. Over three-quarters of Canadian exports are destined for the United States, which is also the source of more than seven-tenths of Canadian imports. Not surprisingly, there is a direct link between high levels of American ownership of Canadian industry and Canada's extensive trade with the United States. Intrafirm trade between U.S. parent firms and their Canadian branch plants manifests itself in many cases as the essence of Canadian "international" trade. Foreign firms ship 75 percent of the exports of industrialized Ontario's 50 leading exporters. (These 50 firms are alone responsible for two-thirds of the province's exports.) Forty-four percent of the exports of Canada's 50 leading exporters comes from foreign-owned enterprises. This compares to less than 5 percent for France, Germany, Sweden, Japan, and the United States.[2]

Overall, the Canadian provinces ship a substantially greater proportion of their goods outside the country (mainly to the United States) than to one another. They also import more from outside the country—again, mainly the United States—than from one another.[3] Further, as Table 2.1 demonstrates, each of Canada's five geographic regions has developed its own intensive, deeply pervasive, north–south trading relationship with its closest American regional neighbour or neighbours. The spatial concentration of Canada–U.S. trade in many regional core commodities is even more pronounced than the table suggests. In 1987, for example, over 70 percent of Atlantic Canada's meat and fish exports to the United States was destined for just three Atlantic states, while over two-fifths of British Columbia's U.S. exports of crude and partially fabricated materials, including wood and metal ores, was destined for the five Pacific states. Just under half of Quebec's American wood and paper exports went to only six states, and over two-thirds of both petroleum and natural gas shipments to the United States from the prairies also went to six states. Two-thirds of Ontario's American-bound iron and steel, and 80 percent of that province's U.S. exports of transport equipment, was shipped to just five states.[4]

TABLE 2. 1 **Trade of Canadian Regions with United States Census Regions They Directly Border (percent of total trade with the U.S. for each Canadian region), 1992**

	Exports	Imports
Atlantic	78	51
Quebec	63	59
Ontario	77	58
Prairies	58	49
British Columbia	53	54

Note: Bordering U.S. census regions are Atlantic, Midwest, Mountain, and Pacific.

SOURCE: CALCULATED FROM CANADA, STATISTICS CANADA, MERCHANDISE TRADE, *EXPORTS*, 1992.

DEFINING A REGIONAL IDENTITY

Canada's regional identity within its continental space is not only visible from an economic perspective, but is also manifested at the focal points of Canadian politics, society, and culture. It was after World War II that Canadians were first warned that their nation had moved from "colony to nation to colony."[5] Similar sentiments are still being expressed, although it is hard today either to picture clearly our British colonial past or to understand fully the significance of this often repeated figure of speech. It is, however, helpful to realize that in the earliest part of this century, Canadians (especially English Canadians), were privileged members of the world's most powerful empire, and their identity and sense of "nationalism" grew out of that association. Colonial rather than indigenous symbols and institutions defined both Canadians' view of themselves and Canada's position on the international stage. For example, it was not until 1993 that Canada inaugurated its first ministry of *Foreign* Affairs. When its venerable predecessor, the Department of *External* Affairs, was created in 1909, it was the supremacy of the British Colonial Office in the conduct of our imperial and foreign relations that first designated Canada's international business as "external" rather than "foreign."

Today, mirroring our British colonial experience, more than two-thirds of our bilateral relations are conducted with one country, the United States.[6] Although the requirements of managing the extensive and complex continental economic relationship go a long way toward explaining this concentration, there are also important cultural and ideological factors at play. Just as most Canadians were content in the early part of the century to accept the primacy of Britain in defining the boundaries of imperial foreign policy, so now the United States is usually given the lead. Of course, deference is not to be confused with the abrogation of national sovereignty. If there was any cause for doubt on this question, periodic disengaged moments in the conduct of Canada's foreign policy serve to demonstrate to both American and Canadian audiences that Canada retains the capacity to be something more than a U.S. satellite. A list of such episodes would include Canada's maintenance of trade ties with China and Cuba during the Diefenbaker years; Prime Minister Pearson's 1965 call for a pause in the U.S. bombing of North Vietnam; the "third option" of the early 1970s, which called for reducing Canada's dependence on the United States by expanding its relations with other countries; and Canada's provision of development aid to Nicaragua during the Reagan presidency of the 1980s.

Living comfortably (for the most part) under the roof of U.S. foreign and defence policy while still asserting sovereignty is a position fraught with contradictions. One 1975 survey of some 300 members of Canada's foreign policy elites showed that nearly two-thirds saw the United States as Canada's best friend while one-half defined Canada as a "partner" in North America, suggesting that on most issues in international affairs Canadian and American interests are essentially the same. Even so, 52 percent also felt that the continental economy "significantly limited" Canadian autonomy in domestic affairs, while only 28 percent believed that, compared to most other countries, Canada acts independently in international relations.[7]

Elite opinions and mass opinions on this subject closely coincide. Seventy percent of Canadians in the 1980s viewed the United States as Canada's best friend, while one-half expressed "very great" or "considerable" confidence in the ability of the Americans to deal wisely with world problems.[8] When asked in the mid-1970s and again in the mid-1980s,[9] only one-quarter of Canadians were prepared to agree that we should withdraw from NATO and our defence agreements with the United States, and adopt a policy of neutrality. At least a plurality of Canadian public opinion usually backs controversial U.S. foreign policy initiatives such as Star Wars research in Canada, the 1986 bombing of Libya, or employing the American fleet to confront Iran in the Persian Gulf in 1987.[10] Even so, and reflecting the ambiguous approach of the state elite to this subject, two-thirds of Canadians in the mid-1980s believed that their government's views on international affairs were "unduly affected" by another country— three-fifths identified the United States as that country.[11] In 1990, 52 percent of Canadians believed that U.S. President Bush had too much influence on Prime Minister Brian Mulroney. Yet 58 percent favoured Canadian participation in the American-led 1991 Persian Gulf War against Saddam Hussein's Iraq, and 57 percent approved of Mulroney's handling of Canada's involvement in that war![12]

The gradual unfolding of Canada's status as a U.S. economic region, the virtual absence of a pre-existing anti-colonial tradition, and federalism have all played their parts in fostering relatively deferential international policies. Canada's politicians have no need to be reminded of the U.S. capacity to deliver economic rewards or punishments for Canadian behaviour in international affairs. Ultimately more decisive, however, has been the failure of Canadians to transmit through the generations enthusiasm for, or even knowledge about, their unique national experience.[13] This failure has been magnified by the way in which Canadians, throughout the 20th century, have eagerly absorbed U.S. popular culture during successive intensive bombardments from American print, radio, movie, and television media. Finally, the Canadian political system's obsessive promotion of domestic regional particularisms has also dampened possibilities for the articulation of pan-national voices and projects.

Canadians realize that volunteering to be an extension of the American political economy carries with it certain costs to national independence in world affairs. We earlier observed that both the foreign policy elite and the public agree on this point. However, this sense of realism and deference to U.S. leadership in the world does not carry over to the expression of what are perceived to be Canadian *regional* issues within North America. Here autonomy is jealously guarded. Territory is a good example of a subject where Canadian national sensibilities will readily engage American interests. Whether it is the Northwest Passage, Georges Bank, the southward diversion of rivers, or acid rain from the industrial states, Canadians display uncharacteristic enthusiasm in tracing the physical border between the two countries with some measure of precision.[14] Less than 10 percent would favour Canada becoming "a part of the United States of America," and in 1988 only one-quarter thought it would become so within the next 50 years. In 1990, only 13 percent of Canadians approved of their own province joining the United States.[15]

National identity as manifested through the preservation of images of distinctiveness in social culture or lifestyle is another no-go area. An important cultural legacy of the British colonial past has been the quiet conviction of many Canadians that they are more civilized than the avaricious and quarrelsome republicans to the south. However pronounced the similarity of the two national cultures in a world perspective, Canadians want very much to believe that they are different. In 1990, two-thirds of Canadians reported that they judged the Canadian way of life had been influenced too much by the United States.[16] Accordingly, Canadians continually define and measure (at least rhetorically) their social practices and policies against what is frequently perceived to be a negative American yardstick. Thus, in addition to territory, the Canadian region currently draws its sociocultural frontier by characterizing itself as possessing higher levels of societal order and urban cleanliness as well as a greater willingness to deliver goods and services collectively through the state.[17]

In contrast to their views on geographic or sociocultural territory, most Canadians have failed to recognize the economy as a terrain on which the promotion of a significant measure of national autonomy is necessary. Consistent with their behaviour in the foreign and defence fields, Canadians (especially Canada's business and state elites) have seemed mostly content to define their economic interests within the confines of empire. While accepting American economic leadership, Canadians have at times still been able to recognize specific points of divergence between their own and U.S. economic interests. Nonetheless, as we will now see, the development of Canada's economy as a *zone* within the U.S. economy has been facilitated by the relative weakness of economic nationalism within Canadian society during this century.

CONTINENTAL RESOURCE DEVELOPMENT

In the 20th century, countries reliant on natural resource production have been more vulnerable than manufacturing countries to upheavals in the world economy because resource products suffer from wildly irregular cycles of demand and competitors can readily replace traditional suppliers. Historically, Canada's response to these marketplace uncertainties has been to seek special concessionary trading relationships with its largest customers. Until the later half of the 19th century, Canadian fish, fur, lumber, and agricultural resources found shelter in Great Britain behind a system of imperial tariff preferences. When this privileged access was lost, many important Canadian business leaders signed a petition to annex Canada to the United States. The Reciprocity Treaty of 1854, which allowed relatively open American market access for resource products from the British North American provinces, was an attempt to forestall any growth in annexationist sentiment.

Although the Reciprocity Treaty was in effect only from 1854 to 1866, these years were subsequently romanticized by Canadian merchants and resource producers as "golden years" of prosperity. For many decades after the abrogation of reciprocity by the Americans, its memory was honoured in widespread and persistent calls for the renegotiation of a free-trade arrangement with the United States. As it turned out, however, through westward expansion and development of the wheat economy, Canada gradually re-established its pattern of resource staple export dependence on Britain. At the end of the first decade of the 20th century, nearly one-half of Canadian exports were agricultural exports destined for Britain.

With these renewed commercial links to Great Britain, it is perhaps not surprising that under a Canada–U.S. free-trade banner, Laurier's Liberals were unable to carry the country in the 1911 election. But this result marked only a setback, not a defeat, for the fuller integration of Canadian resource producers into the U.S. market. The growing sophistication of American industry was in part predicated on ready access to Canada's new staple resources: pulp and paper, minerals, and energy. It is hardly surprising that U.S. direct investment in Canadian resource industries sought to secure this access. As early as 1926, Americans owned one-third of Canadian mining and smelting. By 1963, they owned one-half.

After the Second World War, U.S. investment flowed into Canadian resource industries that complemented the U.S. manufacturing sector. Through investment and trade in Canadian natural resources, a continental division of labour was forged in which Canada's role became that of "a specialized (resource producing) adjunct to the American political economy."[18] The logic of profitability guided individual business decisions by private firms that cumulatively promoted the development of Canada's continental role as a resource storehouse. These decisions were also made within a supportive atmosphere fostered, on both sides of the border, by government officials who sought to establish resource security for the "free world" in the context of the Cold War of the 1940s and 1950s. Furthermore, Canadian politicians and bureaucrats were eager to promote an economic formula that, in their view, had stimulated the postwar economic boom.

Canadian producers of industrial raw materials have enjoyed remarkable success within this century's continental marketplace. Resource companies dominate the list of Canada's top exporters, and in 1992 supplied more than one-third of U.S. imports of copper, one-half of its imported nickel, three-fifths of its imported zinc, and nearly three-quarters of its imported aluminum. Canada also supplied all of the American imports of electricity and almost all of its imports of natural gas. As well, just under 10 percent of Canada's total export trade in 1992 was made up of wood and paper products destined for U.S. markets. Exports of these Canadian forestry commodities supplied four-fifths or more of U.S. imports of paper and paperboard, simply worked wood, and pulp and waste paper.[19]

CONTINENTAL INDUSTRIAL PRODUCTION

The other side of its impressive strength in resource industries has been Canada's relative weakness in manufacturing. It was not resource goods but manufactured products that established themselves as the most dynamic sector of world trade during the 20th century. Moreover, among manufactures, the most technologically advanced and highly finished categories have led the way. In the beginning of the 1980s, at least one-half of the exports of countries like Japan, West Germany, Sweden, and the United States were of such "finished" manufactures; Canada's proportion was only one-third.

By 1990, Canada's proportion of finished goods had risen to a more respectable 43 percent of its total exports. However, four factors have to be considered before we conclude that there has been any significant recent improvement in the international competitiveness of Canadian manufacturing. First, other countries have also been moving ahead; the new benchmark for Sweden and the United States is three-fifths of total exports.[20] It is also important to recognize that while most industrial countries are either in surplus or break even in their international trade in these strategic products, Canada is in perpetual deficit. Between 1970 and 1989, Canada's trade deficit in end products amounted to a staggering 310 billion (unadjusted) dollars. The first three years of the 1990s have added yet another 90 billion dollars to this total.[21] These deficits dramatically underline Canada's role as a mainly *resource-producing*, as opposed to *manufacturing*, zone in the U.S. economy.

A third factor that must be taken into account in assessing the surge in Canadian finished exports is the historical absence of the kind of innovative capacity in Canadian industry that would provide for the creation of internationally competitive products. Studies in the early 1960s first began to warn that Canada was near the bottom of the pile in industrial research and development (R&D). Little has changed. An Ontario government report noted that, at the end of the 1980s, Canada ranked "tenth out of twelve in total R&D intensity among the largest industrial economies." Even some newly industrialized economies such as Korea had higher R&D intensities than Canada.[22] In 1991, annual Canadian business expenditure on R&D was less than half the level of Swedish, American and Japanese R&D expenditures.

Finally, the special consequences of the 1965 Canada–U.S. Autopact must also temper any enthusiasm for recent apparent advances in the international competitiveness of Canadian industry. While massive in volume, the continental free trade in automobiles and parts made possible under the Autopact tells us very little about the ability of Canadian firms to develop and market internationally competitive products. The Autopact provides mainly for the intrafirm transfers of very similar goods between U.S. manufacturers and their Canadian subsidiary factories, which incidentally pass over an international frontier. As well, until the early 1980s, trade under the pact generally favoured the United States. It was only the radical devaluation of the Canadian dollar in the late 1970s and early 1980s, and the consequent lowering of Canadian labour costs, that made Canada attractive as a production site to American automakers. If, then, an adjustment is made to remove Autopact exchanges, Canada's proportion of finished manufacture exports falls to a dismal 27 percent of its remaining total trade in 1990; this is less than one-half the current Swedish level of finished exports.

As in the resource industries, the considerable structural anomalies of Canadian manufacturing can be explained only through a model of nonautonomous economic development and continental specialization. The base for Canada's modern industrial establishment was laid in the late 19th and early 20th centuries. This era marked the height of the British connection as expressed through the wheat economy and the sentiments of imperial nationalism. The politics and economics of Canada's location *within* the British Empire both contributed to the evolution of an autarkic industrial strategy and stifled the subsequent unfolding of a world competitive manufacturing. It was a strategy that provided for a modest industrial base unlikely to challenge British industry on its own turf; that, due to its relatively humble capital requirements, did not interfere with the massive investment program required to finance the wheat economy's transcontinental transportation infrastructure; and that even argued that it was strengthening the British Empire by transferring to Canada the production of "foreign" (U.S.) commodities.

The industrial strategy employed by early Canadian manufacturers, later known as "import substitution industrialization" (ISI), was characterized by unchallenged technological dependence—a dependence expressed in its nearly exclusive use of foreign machinery and production processes, and an interest in production only as it related to domestic consumption. State involvement took the form of setting tariff levels high enough to make feasible the domestic production of goods that would otherwise be imported. Canadian manufacturers, seeking a cheap and effective shortcut, licensed American industrial processes rather than develop their own. In contrast to the pattern in other countries whereby industrialists initially borrowed technology and then assimilated, adapted, and innovated from this knowledge base, the use of foreign machinery and production processes became a permanent part of the early Canadian industrial pattern, thus tying it in an important structural way to the evolution of industry in the United States.

With geographic proximity, a tariff-protected domestic market, and concessionary tariff privileges within the British Empire, Canada was an obvious location for the establishment of U.S. branch plants. By taking over existing Canadian manufacturing firms (to which they were often already linked through licensing arrangements) and establishing new subsidiaries, American industrialists consolidated a place of prominence in Canada's most dynamic industrial sectors by the 1920s. Canadian-owned manufacturing became concentrated in the technologically backward and less capital-intensive industries such as textiles, clothing and footware, food processing, and furniture manufacturing. Foreign control of Canadian manufacturing reached its peak in the early 1970s, and has since returned to its late 1940s level of somewhat more than two-fifths of total ownership.

Three production patterns have marked the seven decades of hegemony for U.S. manufacturing branch plants in Canada. None of these production patterns has broken the original mould that cast Canadian industries as mere ancillaries to staples resource extraction. All three have contributed to a spatial division within North American manufacturing that accounts for the failure of Canadian industry to become world competitive. The first period, from the 1920s to the late 1940s, consolidated the worst features of the previous import substitution behaviour of Canadian-owned industries. American firms established a Canadian presence in order to gain access to a tariff-protected market for products they would otherwise have shipped from their southern factories. There was no provision in their Canadian branch plants for the development of distinct product lines for world markets, save for the transfer of some export business from their U.S. operations to take advantage of the preferential tariff access that Canada enjoyed in Great Britain and the "white" dominions.

The second period, spanning the late 1940s to the mid-1970s, further institutionalized the import substitution model and with it Canada's industrial role in the continent. With the collapse of imperial preferences, Canadian branch plants ceased even this limited export role. Increasingly,

American firms viewed the Canadian market as part of their *domestic* operations. Typically, an administrative division of the North American market would establish a Canadian "satellite" plant to satisfy regional demand in this country, just as, say, a Chicago plant would fill demand in the U.S. midwest, while research and development as well as exports were centred in the U.S. parent plant.

Production in the contemporary period, roughly from the late 1970s to the mid-1990s, continues to be organized on a continental basis. However, instead of taking the form of "satellite" plants that produce a large range of miniature-replica lines for a limited territory, North American plants have become "rationalized." Following the relatively successful Autopact model, this means specialization in the production of a limited range of lines for the entire continent. Falling Canada–U.S. tariffs under the General Agreement on Tariffs and Trade (GATT) made rationalization possible, and increasing international competitive pressure made it necessary. Continuing investment in Canadian plant locations was made attractive by a radical program of currency devaluation that chopped nearly 30 percent of the value of Canada's dollar between 1976 and 1986. Devaluation created a marked Canadian labour-cost advantage over American plant locations in certain key industries such as automobiles. Nevertheless, it is important to recognize that continental rationalization did not fundamentally change the rules of the game. Most American-owned Canadian factories are no closer to becoming highly efficient and technologically advanced plants capable of autonomously generating world-competitive products. In both the miniature-replica satellite and continentally rationalized production models, managerial authority, research and development, and export marketing all remain the prerogatives of the U.S. parent firms.

POLITICS OF CONTINENTAL ECONOMIC INTEGRATION

The political climate remained consistently favourable to continental interests during the ongoing process that fashioned Canada's resource and manufacturing industries as regional extensions of the U.S. economy. In some measure, this was due to the growing ability of foreign investors to reward or punish Canadian politicians, whether directly (by providing funding for political parties and corporate directorships for retired politicians) or indirectly (by manipulating the levers of economic expansion or contraction). Politicians, even when they comprehended the structural limitations that hampered the performance of foreign firms in Canada, became understandably loath to threaten what they believed to be the motor of the economic growth on which their electoral fortunes depended.

Ultimately more decisive than the considerable power of foreign investors to promote or protect their own interests in the Canadian political system, however, was the nature of Canadian political discourse on continental economic integration. From the 1960s to the 1980s, two competing interpretations defined the context for the political management of this issue. While both interpretations originated in a general recognition of the inevitability of some extensive measure of Canadian integration into the continental economy, both proposed distinct sets of policy prescriptions that they believed should govern our association with the Americans. Significantly, more radical political options—annexation of Canada to the United States at one extreme or Cuban-style expropriation of all American interests in Canada at the other—had almost no impact on the course of the debate.

Continentalism favoured the elimination of trade and investment barriers between Canada and the United States. According to this view, the unhindered play of continental market forces would maximize Canadian prosperity. The continentalist school was unready to distinguish between Canadian and foreign-owned firms, and typically accorded the same Canadian "corporate citizenship" to both. *Nationalism* promoted greater Canadian control over the pace and extent of continental integration. Foreign investment, in this view, prevented Canada from reaching its considerable economic potential. The nationalist school would have had Canada's state system institute an industrial strategy to promote Canadian-owned enterprises and to coerce a better deal from American investors in Canada.

Continentalist assumptions went virtually unchallenged among Canada's economic, political, bureaucratic, and academic elites for almost two decades immediately following the Second World War. They were also hegemonic among the population as a whole. Canada–U.S. economic integration was championed by such dynamic political personalities as C.D. Howe, a Liberal cabinet minister during the 1940s and 1950s and the driving force behind taxation and investment policies designed to lure American dollars to Canada. Those few in this era who worried about the long-term consequences of foreign economic domination were accused of attacking the standard of living of ordinary Canadians and/or of trying to turn Canada into a "banana republic." Even prominent political personalities who dared champion a modest degree of economic or military nationalism (e.g., Prime Minister Diefenbaker or Liberal cabinet minister Walter Gordon) met a storm of public condemnation and were marginalized within their own political parties.

By the late 1960s, however, nationalist concerns were no longer easily dismissed. Reinforced by the publication of a number of widely publicized government and academic studies, public (and even a minority of elite) opinion had shifted. These studies documented the structural limitations imposed on Canada by continental economic integration, and even suggested that the capacity of Canadians to maintain themselves as a distinct social formation had been undermined. During the 1970s, two-thirds of Canadians thought there was sufficient U.S. capital invested in Canada and approximately one-half were prepared to countenance schemes to buy back majority control of U.S. companies in Canada *even if this were to reduce living standards*. It should nonetheless be noted that even during this peak of nationalist sentiment, popular misgivings about continental economic integration were far from universal, with approximately one-third disapproving of a buy-back.[23]

The public unease with the high level of American control over the Canadian economy had some limited resonance within the Trudeau cabinets of the 1970s and early 1980s. Following the 1971 publication of the widely discussed *Foreign Direct Investment in Canada* (Gray Report), the Foreign Investment Review Agency (FIRA) was created. This new agency was more an exercise in symbolic politics than a genuine effort to regulate foreign businesses in Canada. The massive existing stock of foreign investment that had originally sparked nationalist concerns was left undisturbed. The "new" foreign investment coming under the FIRA mandate typically enjoyed annual approval rates of 90 percent or greater. Nevertheless, from its inception, FIRA had to fight its way through a host of hostile and powerful critics. Foreign investors believed that the agency had established a dangerous precedent for future Canadian governments that might choose to be even more interventionist. Business leaders and conservative economists railed against the intrusion of state power into the free market. Provincial governments argued that the federal government was restricting their ability to pursue their region's economic development.

The high-water mark of nationalist influence occurred just after the 1980 federal election. In winning a number of key Ontario seats, the Liberals were helped by their promises of an industrial strategy for Canada and a tougher line on foreign investment. Discussed in cabinet were strong new proposals that significantly broadened the restricted FIRA mandate by ensuring that multinational manufacturers operating in Canada performed industrial R&D here and had export freedom. In the resource sector, the National Energy Program (NEP) sought to Canadianize ownership and control of the critical oil and natural gas industry through a far-reaching package of programs that discriminated against foreign investors. However, tough talk about "NEPing" other industrial sectors dissolved rapidly in the face of a determined onslaught led by continentalist cabinet ministers and senior civil servants supported by U.S. government officials and business interests. Key provincial governments and the federal Conservative Party also added forceful voices to the chorus of opposition.

The continentalist counterattack coincided with the severe economic recession of the early 1980s. Not only did this make any additional nationalist initiatives impractical, but it also had a critical effect on changing public attitudes toward continentalism. The percentage of Canadians wanting to see more U.S. capital in Canada increased after this recession while the 1970s majority favouring a "buy-back" became by the mid-1980s a majority who disapproved of this strategy.[24] With the 1984 election of a Conservative government committed not only to improving commercial relations with the United States, but to the immediate dismantling of FIRA and the NEP as well, the continentalist school triumphantly re-established its traditional political ascendancy in Ottawa.

THE CANADA–U.S. AND NORTH AMERICAN FREE TRADE AGREEMENTS

After the spectacular failure of the Canada–U.S. Reciprocity Agreement in the 1911 election, Canadian politicians avoided dealing so openly again with an issue obviously bonded to the electorate's fears of territorial surrender and/or loss of sociocultural distinctiveness. In the mid-1930s, Prime Minister William Lyon Mackenzie King established a pattern of de-politicizing continental commercial relations by presenting movement toward Canada–U.S. tariff liberalization as a disjointed series of technical, bureaucratic adjustments to tariff schedules. Under the post–Second World War General Agreement on Tariffs and Trade (GATT), this bureaucratic process of tariff reduction continued. Particularly through the 1967 Kennedy and 1979 Tokyo rounds of GATT negotiations, something very close to de facto Canada–U.S. free trade was established. By 1987, 95 percent of Canadian goods were to enter the United States with duties of 5 percent or less, while 91 percent of U.S. exports to the Canadian market were to be in an equivalent position.

After having been a deeply buried public issue for at least half a century, Canada–U.S. free trade was catapulted to the head of Canada's political agenda through a 1985 announcement by the Mulroney government that it would begin treaty negotiations with the Americans. Considering the already existing liberalized continental tariff regime, three factors seem to have been responsible for the surprising re-entry of the potentially explosive free-trade question into the Canadian political atmosphere: (1) the desire of the continentalists to consolidate their recent victories over the nationalists by seizing the policy initiative; (2) the rise of an American protectionism that threatened to disrupt, through the use of nontariff barriers, a Canadian resource and manufacturing production system that by the mid-1980s had become largely based on assumed low tariff access to U.S. markets; and (3) the particular partisan appeal of this initiative to both the neoconservative right and the populist western wing within the Conservative Party at a time when the party was demoralized by policy paralysis and petty scandals.

In the end, all three of these factors also figured in the resolution of this issue. The 1987 Canada–U.S. Free Trade Agreement (FTA), although it removed remaining tariffs between the two countries, achieved for Canada little more than cosmetic relief from the American nontariff barriers that had initially prompted Canadian business to press the Tories for the negotiations. Chapter 19 of the FTA established that each country retains its domestic antidumping and countervailing duty laws, although appeals on whether these laws have been properly applied may be made to binational panels. Of some significance as well for the trade side, Canada gave up the tariff safeguards, established under the 1965 Autopact, which obligated U.S. automakers to retain a base share of their North American production in Canada.

Of far more import than the sections of the FTA that specifically address tariff matters was the way in which the continentalists used the agreement to hobble politically their traditional Canadian nationalist opponents. The FTA entrenched a number of key continentalist policy positions in a transparent attempt to pre-empt institutionally any future Canadian challenge to the continentalist status quo from the nationalist school. In fact, the FTA was clearly designed to preclude future Canadian governments' considerations of the kind that took place in the 1980 Trudeau cabinet about an enhanced FIRA, with real policy muscle, and the NEP. Articles 105, 1402, and 1602 prohibited discrimination between foreign and Canadian firms in regard to establishment, investment, operations, and sale. Pertaining to manufacturing, article 1603 proscribed performance requirements such as export quotas or domestic sourcing for foreign firms. Pertaining to resources, Articles 408 and 409 forbade export taxes and export restrictions, and articles 903 and 904 restated these prohibitions with specific reference to the energy sector. At the conclusion of the negotiations, then Deputy Prime Minister Donald Mazankowski described the energy provisions to Calgary oil executives as "insurance against your own government," referring to the fact that they prevented the NEP from being re-introduced.[25]

The 1988 election was a direct confrontation over ratification of the FTA between forces carrying nationalist and continentalist banners. Business influence, as well as a highly favourable regional distribution of the Tory vote, delivered a narrow plurality victory to the Conservatives. Business and the media elite strongly supported the Tories, not because the FTA delivered secure access to the U.S. market (it did not) but because they feared that its defeat would allow the state-interventionist nationalists to seize the initiative. The remarkable strength of the nationalists in the free-trade debate stands in sharp contrast to their historically weaker position within Canadian political culture. Indeed, right up to the vote, public opinion was running against the trade agreement.

Two factors help explain the relative success of the nationalist forces. First, they were able to break out of their traditionally narrow leadership base in the cultural and intellectual elites and in the trade-union movement. The disadvantageous terms of the FTA fractured the continentalist camp, detaching from it the largest portion of the Liberal Party. Many of those who had previously strongly supported continental economic integration, and would have been themselves most unlikely to have sponsored a NEP or a strengthened FIRA, nevertheless believed that formally surrendering these powers unnecessarily weakened the capacity of the Canadian state system to bargain effectively with the Americans in the future.

Second, the nationalist forces enjoyed great success because they centred their attack on the FTA on precisely those two elements of the continental relationship where, as we earlier argued, Canadian autonomy has been jealously guarded: territory and the distinctiveness of the sociocultural milieu. In regard to territory, the nationalists repeatedly warned the public that Canada's political independence was at stake and that Canada was about to become the 51st state. It is no accident that one of the campaign's most effective television advertisements purported to show the FTA negotiators taking an eraser to the Canada–U.S. border on a map of North America. With respect to national identity, the nationalists argued forcefully that traditional Canadian cultural and social values were in jeopardy because the FTA posed direct threats to Canada's social-welfare programs as well as its regional and cultural subsidies. So powerful were these nationalist arguments that it was not enough for the continentalists to respond simply by stressing what they believed to be the FTA's considerable economic benefits. To hold their own in the debate, they were forced to protest vigorously that the nationalists were "liars," to extravagantly promise that social, cultural, and regional program would not be endangered by the FTA, and to produce television advertisements that pointedly redrew the Canada–U.S. border on a map of North America.

In the years immediately following the 1988 election, Canada's strained economic circumstances appeared to confirm the nationalist case against the FTA. During this period, an international economic recession hit Canada harder than most other developed countries. Many Canadian factories, both foreign and domestically owned, closed their doors and some even moved their operations to the United States. Employment in Canadian manufacturing was devastated, with 340,000 jobs lost between 1989 and 1992.[26]

Since tariffs between Canada and the United States had already been largely liberalized under the Autopact and the GATT regime *before* the FTA was implemented, nationalist claims that Canada's early 1990s economic woes embodied toxic FTA fallout were greatly overblown. In fact, Canada's post-FTA economic reverses were only indirectly related to the trade policies of the Mulroney Conservatives. Driven by an excess of rigid monetarist ideological zeal (see Chapter 4), and to the horror of the same business allies who had backed their 1988 re-election, the Tories forced up the value of the Canadian dollar by approximately 20 percent between 1987 and 1992. This revaluation had the immediate effect of making Canadian products far less competitive in American markets already shrunk by the force of a major economic recession. Ironically, the Tories' high–interest-rate/high-dollar policies worked at cross purposes with the FTA by seriously undermining one of Canada's principal locational advantages in the rationalization of continental production.

This is not to say that in the early 1990s many ordinary Canadians did not accept in some measure the nationalist argument that Canada's economic problems stemmed from Canada–U.S. free trade. As late as the summer of 1993, a plurality remained opposed to the FTA.[27] Yet many may have also concluded that transitional economic difficulties were the price Canadians had to pay for modernizing their special economic relationship with the Americans. As previously argued, in contrast to their views on geographic or sociocultural territory, most Canadians have failed to recognize the economy as a terrain on which the promotion of a significant measure of national autonomy is necessary. When, in the post-FTA years, it became apparent to nearly everyone that the nationalist electoral rhetoric had been overblown—that Canada's territorial borders were by no means about to disappear and that the nation's sociocultural distinctiveness had been retained—the emotional sting was removed from the 1988 nationalist crusade. The percentage of Canadians identifying U.S. trade relations as Canada's most important problem fell from 9 percent during the 1988 free-trade election to just 1 percent in 1992 and 1993.[28]

This decline was in spite of the opening of negotiations to include Mexico within the FTA framework in a North American Free Trade Agreement (NAFTA). As in the Canada–U.S. FTA, market access through tariff reduction was not the principal question. Mexico had already abandoned its highly nationalist investment and trade policies and became a signatory to the GATT during the 1980s. Nonetheless, important elements within U.S. and Canadian business judged Mexico to be an important complement to the FTA regime. Formally incorporating Mexico's Third World economy into the FTA zone could offer significant competitive advantages in the contemporary era of global manufacturing and international trade rivalry. Some even dreamed of a regional trading bloc composed of the nations of North and South America that could surpass the economic successes of the European Community. Canada's economic and political elites wanted to be stakeholders in this visionary enterprise, and feared the consequences of being left as spectators on the sidelines. They also saw NAFTA, and its possible South American extensions, in the light of the traditional Canadian foreign policy objective of filtering Canada's bilateral relationship with the United States through multilateral screens.[29]

With their 1988 momentum long abated, Canada's nationalist forces tried to regroup to fight NAFTA during the 1993 federal election. However, only the hapless NDP championed their cause. Continentalist and nationalist members of the Liberal Party had previously taken themselves off the field of battle by fashioning a compromise with each other around the vague notion of negotiating an improvement to the terms of the NAFTA if the party became the government. Going into the 1993 election, polls showed that three-fifths of Canadians were against the ratification of NAFTA. Still, the nationalists were not able to replay the successes of their 1988 campaign. Mexico, unlike the United States, could hardly be depicted as a tangible threat to Canada's geographic or sociocultural territory. Left to fight on the far less emotionally volatile terrain of economic nationalism, the nationalists' rhetorical assault against NAFTA was met by the public with polite, fatigued resignation.

CONCLUSION: MANAGING THE CONTINENTAL RELATIONSHIP

As a regional extension of a larger and more powerful political economy, the Canadian social formation faces special problems in self-management. The politics of issues such as the environment, economic expansion, social welfare, labour, and regional development have by necessity both a domestic and a bilateral dimension. This duality creates basic instability in the economic-management capacity of the Canadian political economy— an instability that is further exaggerated by the spatial dispersion of power within a federal structure of government. In the context of this instability, the Canadian state system is called upon to play the role of a point of balance by focusing, mediating, protecting, and developing the regional position of the Canadian social formation within the continental political economy.

Managing regional relations within the continent is far from easy. For one thing, the point of balance must continually shift to take account of the continuing changes that result from economic expansion and transformation. For another, finding balance within the political environment is also difficult because the fortunes of political ideas (e.g., nationalism and continentalism) and the parties that articulate them are constantly on the rise and fall. Finally, in the Canadian federation there are underlying centripetal and centrifugal forces at play with respect to continentalism.

The debates surrounding the FTA and NAFTA, as well as the Meech Lake and Charlottetown accords, have led many observers to place considerable stress on the centrifugal tendencies within the Canadian federation. It is said that if the movement within Quebec for sovereignty/separation is successful, there will be calls for political annexation to the Unites States from some of the remaining fragments of a Canada in disintegration. It is also said that the FTA and NAFTA have weakened the policy leadership capacity of the national government at the same time as provincial economies have been strengthening their already remarkably pronounced southward orientations. Indeed, these agreements leave provincial elites relatively free to pursue balkanizing regional economic-development strategies without having to measure them against any national program developed by the federal government. The provinces may increasingly find that political decisions taken in Washington have as much or even more relevance for their local economies as decisions taken in Ottawa. There could even appear in some areas demands for the direct political representation that would come with annexation.

Before succumbing to alarmism, a number of additional factors need to be considered. First of all, direct political representation in the U.S. political system would not necessarily be more effective than the current "special relationship." Without exception, the population of each of Canada's five regions is only a small fraction of the population of their contiguous American counterparts; representation in the U.S. Congress would be correspondingly small. Further, Canada's state system has given considerable advantage to Canadian elites over regional elites elsewhere in the continental economy, both by bringing Canadian elites together to recognize their joint interests and by providing them with a common vehicle for promoting these interests. Although the Canadian social formation is not electorally represented in the U.S. political system, Canada's state system has brought about the "external" political expression of its regional interests to the U.S. executive, Congress and state governments through diplomacy, treaties, and the advocacy of private interest groups. Although private advocacy is primarily energized by American businesses intent on fostering and protecting their Canadian investments, it may also include strategic alliances with indigenous forces within U.S. politics whose issue positions are similar to Canadian ones.

When it is remembered that all of Canada's regions share common interests in resource production and export to U.S. markets, the utility of constructing a common Canadian position through a separate federal order becomes clear. It should also be remembered that the burden of providing the highly expensive transportation infrastructure necessary for resource export has traditionally been shared by all of Canada's regions through the federal state. Weaker Canadian regions have also historically employed the federal state to capture some of the benefits of the uneven development of the continental economy from the stronger Canadian regions through equalization payments and social transfers. As well, while it may be shrinking in relative importance, the national market provided by trade between the Canadian regions will likely remain a factor of some significance for all the provinces. On this point, because of the exceptionally strong emotional commitment of Canadians to the integrity of their geographic territory, any province that, like Quebec, considered leaving the federation would have to consider the almost certain prospect of stiff retaliatory measures from the remaining provinces. These would likely include economic exclusion not only from the Canadian market but also from NAFTA.[30]

Some primary opinion-leading and agenda-setting sectors and groups—including the Canadian communications/media industries, the Canadian cultural and federal political elites, and academics who study Canada—strongly value a protected national market and could be counted on to oppose any siren call to annexation as if their livelihoods depended on it. Finally, and perhaps essentially, the maintenance of a federal state allows ordinary Canadians a means to affirm symbolically their autonomous national self-definition through the preservation of their territorial and sociocultural distinctiveness within the continent.

NOTES

1. Statistics Canada, Corporations and Labour Unions Returns Act, Part I, Corporations, *Annual Report, 1988,* October 1991.

2. Ontario, Premier's Council, *Competing in the New Global Economy,* vol. 1 (Toronto: Queen's Printer for Ontario, 1988), pp. 69, 73.

3. In 1988, 31 percent of provincial goods were exported, while 22 percent were sent to other provinces. Imports were the source of 32 percent of provincial goods, while 22 percent came from other provinces. Calculated from Canada, Statistics Canada, *The Daily,* April 29, 1992, p. 6.

4. Calculated from Canada, Statistics Canada, *Exports by Countries,* January–December 1987, March 1988.

5. H.A. Innis, "Great Britain, the United States and Canada," in Mary Q. Innis, ed., *Essays in Canadian Economic History* (Toronto: University of Toronto Press, 1956), p. 405.

6. P.V. Lyon and B.W. Tomlin, *Canada as an International Actor* (Toronto: Macmillan, 1979), p. 71.

7. Ibid., p. 85.

8. Canadian Institute of Public Opinion, *The Gallup Report,* July 4, 1985, and March 6, 1986.

9. Ibid., June 19, 1976, and May 26, 1986.

10. Ibid., July 8, 1985; June 5, 1986; and December 3, 1987. When the Americans downed an Iranian passenger airbus in the summer of 1988 (over 300 lives were lost), 49 percent of Canadians believed that "the U.S. acted in good faith to protect an American naval ship and lives," while only 31 percent felt that the U.S. military presence in the area made such an event "inevitable" (July 21, 1988).

11. Ibid., November 27, 1986.

12. Ibid., October 4, 1990; February 22, 1991; and June 28, 1991.

13. The classic study on this subject is A.B. Hodgetts, *What Culture? What Heritage? A Study of Civic Education in Canada* (Toronto: Ontario Institute for Studies in Education, 1968).

14. For a discussion of how Canadian territorial consciousness has been manifested in the conduct of Canada–U.S. environmental relations, see Glen Williams, "Greening the New Canadian Political Economy," *Studies in Political Economy* (Spring 1992).

15. Canadian Institute of Public Opinion, *The Gallup Report*, November 15, 1988, and June 7, 1990.

16. Ibid., June 7, 1990. In a 1993 (February 11) Gallup survey, just over one-third of Canadians identified themselves as "great, passive, friendly, or reserved," while a similiar number identified Americans as "self-centred, pushy, patriotic, ignorant or rude."

17. See S.M. Lipset, "Canada and the United States: The Cultural Dimension," in C. Doran and J. Sigler, eds., *Canada and the United States: Enduring Friendship, Persistent Stress* (Englewood Cliffs, N.J.: Prentice-Hall, 1985); and D. Bell, *The Roots of Disunity: A Study of Canadian Political Culture*, rev. ed. (Toronto: Oxford University Press, 1992).

18. M. Clark-Jones, *A Staple State: Canadian Industrial Resources in Cold War* (Toronto: University of Toronto Press, 1987), p. 11.

19. Calculated from United States, National Trade Data Bank, International Trade Administration, *U.S. Foreign Trade Highlights;* and Canada, *Summary of External Trade*, December 1992.

20. Calculated from United Nations, *Yearbook of International Trade Statistics*, vol. 1, various years.

21. Calculated from Canada, Statistics Canada, *Summary of External Trade*, various years.

22. Ontario, Ministry of Industry, Trade and Technology, *A Committment to Research and Development: An Action Plan*, January 1988, pp. 9–10.

23. Canadian Institute of Public Opinion, *The Gallup Report*, July 2, 1987, and June 16, 1988.

24. Ibid.

25. *The Globe and Mail* (October 17, 1987), p. A4.

26. Statistics Canada, *Historical Labour Force Statistics*, 1992, p. 158.

27. Canadian Institute of Public Opinion, *The Gallup Report* (August 31, 1993).

28. Ibid., January 31, 1994.

29. Roy MacLaren, soon after his appointment as Chrétien's first Minister of International Trade, reasoned that Canada would favour the entry into NAFTA of additional countries like Chile because it was in our interest to constrain U.S. domination of the smaller partners in the pact. *The Globe and Mail* (March 5, 1994), p. B2.

30. Article 2204 of NAFTA gives Canada, Mexico, and the United States a veto on the accession of new member states.

FURTHER READINGS

Clark-Jones, Melissa. *A Staple State: Canadian Industrial Resources in Cold War*. Toronto: University of Toronto Press, 1987.

Clarkson, Steven. *Canada and the Reagan Challenge*. 2nd ed. Toronto: James Lorimer, 1985.

Clement, Wallace, and Glen Williams. *The New Canadian Political Economy*. Montreal and Kingston: McGill-Queen's University Press, 1989.

Doern, G. Bruce, and Brian Tomlin. *Faith and Fear: The Free Trade Story*. Toronto: Stoddart, 1991.

Drache, Daniel, and Meric Gertler, eds. *The New Era of Global Competition: State Policy and Market Power*. Montreal and Kingston: McGill-Queen's University Press, 1991.

Grinspun, Ricardo, and Maxwell Cameron, eds. *The Political Economy of North American Free Trade*. New York: St. Martin's Press, 1993.

Hart, Michael. *A North American Free Trade Agreement: The Strategic Implications for Canada*. Halifax: Institute for Research on Public Policy, 1990.

Jenkins, Barbara. *The Paradox of Continental Production: National Investment Policies in North America*. Ithaca, N.Y.: Cornell University Press, 1992.

Williams, Glen. *Not for Export: The International Competitiveness of Canadian Manufacturing*. 3rd ed. Toronto: McClelland and Stewart, 1994.

3 CANADA AND THE "NEW WORLD ORDER"

Laura Macdonald

Out of these troubled times ... a new world order can emerge; a new era—freer from the threat of terror, stronger in the pursuit of justice, and more secure in the quest for peace, an era in which the nations of the world, East and West, North and South, can prosper and live in harmony.

... Today, that new world is struggling to be born, a world quite different from the one we have known, a world where the rule of law supplants the rule of the jungle, a world in which nations recognize the shared responsibility for freedom and justice, a world where the strong respect the rights of the weak.

— President George Bush, September 17, 1990

These are startling sentiments to come from a president of the United States, a country that until recently had been known for its unilateral rather than multilateral approach to international affairs. Mirroring how Canadians often see themselves, Bush's remarks evoke the traditional stereotypes of Canada's role in the world. Canadians like to think of themselves as polite, quiet, orderly, and cooperative people, distinct from their louder, more individualistic and assertive southern neighbours. Canada's foreign policy since World War II has traditionally been described in similar terms. According to this perspective, Canada has been uniquely suited to play the role of "helpful fixer" in the international system, with its commitments to upholding the international rule of law and promoting the principles of peace and cooperation in international organizations like the United Nations.

Although the extent to which Canadian behaviour actually conformed to these stereotypes has been exaggerated, Canada's position in the "old world order" led to the construction of an extraordinarily durable national consensus around the ideology of "middle-power internationalism." Since Canada was clearly not a superpower, Canadian policy-makers attempted to differentiate themselves from less wealthy and influential countries by carving out a role for "middle powers" in the international system. Despite the fact that Canadian foreign policy did not always conform to the ideals of "middlepowermanship," this self-image continued to shape the views of both supporters and critics of Canadian foreign policy throughout the Cold War period. It is doubtful, however, whether the "middle power" self-image can survive intact the recent dramatic changes in the world.

Since the fall of the Berlin Wall and the end of the Cold War, policy-makers, academics, and concerned citizens alike have been squinting into the horizon, attempting to glimpse the shape of the emerging structures of a rebuilt world order. International-relations analysts commonly focus on the sources of stability and instability related to given structures of world order. The new world order is thus variously portrayed as the dawning of either a new era of global cooperation, or of dangerous instability. Another way of looking at forms of world order, however, is to examine patterns of "inclusion in" or "exclusion from" global structures of power and prestige. While the Cold War period was hardly a phase of egalitarian participation, forces such as decolonization and multilateralism permitted at least the appearance of increased inclusion of lesser powers (e.g., the emerging countries of the Third World). This occurred largely because expanding competition between the superpowers throughout the world increased the geopolitical significance of areas outside the North Atlantic triangle. In contrast, the new world order appears to be characterized by greater concentration of economic, political, military, and ideological power in the hands of a few, and the construction of international institutions based on an exclusion of the many.[1] In this atmosphere of increased international economic and political polarization, the role of middle power has lost its erstwhile appeal as a source of even moderate power and prestige.

At the same time, Canada's changing relationship with the United States will affect the nature of Canada's international role. Despite the fact that the United States is Canada's closest ally, Canadian foreign policy has never been a simple reflection of U.S. policy. Throughout the post–World War II period, Canada pursued a two-track strategy, simultaneously expanding bilateral contacts with the United States in a so-called special relationship, while also vigorously pursuing multilateral contacts through membership in a wide range of international organizations. Multilateralism was, in fact, seen as a useful counterweight to U.S. power and influence over Canadian policy. In the last two decades, however, the international economic status of the United States has declined relative to that of Western Europe and Japan, while its influence in the Canadian economy and society has increased. These changes will inevitably have long-term repercussions on Canada's approach to multilateralism.

The nature of global hierarchies of economic and political power has fundamentally shifted. In the period following World War II, it was possible for countries like Canada to make a credible claim to middle-power status. However, in the new world order, power is increasingly polarized between a new "concert of powers," which attempts to collectively manage world affairs, and the countries excluded from this club. While in the past, Canada was widely perceived as playing an independent role and as an advocate for the less developed countries, it is now clearly aiming at full participation in this cartel of wealthy industrialized states. In the flux of the post–Cold War period, the Canadian government may have the opportunity to promote the establishment of a more inclusive, democratic structure of world order. However, it now seems that official attention is directed at inserting Canada into the inner circle of world power.

MIDDLEPOWERMANSHIP IN THE OLD WORLD ORDER

Prior to World War II, Canada retained preferential treatment within the British empire as a "white dominion." This special status, in addition to the country's geographical distance from European conflicts, meant that most Canadians, like most Americans, favoured a policy of international isolationism. Canada was considered a "fire-proof house," and foreign entanglements were seen as unnecessary and even potentially destabilizing, in light of the strong opposition of French Canadians to conscription during World War I. Canada's external relations were concentrated on managing its growing relationship with the United States and the declining colonial links with England. It is important to note, however, that while Canada was at the forefront of the pre-1945 struggle for autonomy in foreign policy matters within the British Empire, that struggle was waged on behalf of the "white" dominions only, not of the "nonwhite" colonies.

   The events of World War II convinced the Canadian foreign policy elite as well as the general public that isolationism was no longer a viable option. Both Canada and the United States were drawn into World War II, although Canada entered much earlier because of its ties to Britain.[2] The United States emerged as the hegemonic power after World War II, with the economic, military, political, and ideological weight necessary to exercise preponderant influence in shaping the postwar order. The new order was based on principles of economic liberalism and multilateralism, with the establishment of political and economic institutions designed to promote international peace and the opening of markets. It should be noted, however, that this version of multilateralism originally excluded most of the less developed parts of the world, which were still under colonial control. Only 46 states were present at the signing of the Charter of the

United Nations on June 26, 1945. As well, despite its openness to all existing nation-states, effective control of the United Nations remained in the hands of the great powers. The United States, the Soviet Union, England, France, and China were granted permanent seats on the Security Council and the right of veto over all its decisions.

In contrast to its previous semicolonial status, Canada emerged from World War II in a relatively strong position, and with a new commitment to international activism. According to John Holmes, "Canada went through a remarkably swift transition from the status of a wartime junior partner in 1945 to that of a sure-footed middle power with an acknowledged and applauded role in world affairs ten years later."[3] Canada had made an important contribution to the war effort, both in military and economic terms, and expected to be rewarded with an important position in the fledgling international organizations of the postwar order. The Canadian approach to these issues came to be known as *functionalism*—the argument that authority in international affairs should neither rest with the great powers only nor be distributed on an equal basis to all participants in the system, but rather that representation be awarded on a functional basis, with countries that are able to make a substantial contribution to the issue in question receiving disproportionate power.

For example, on the design of the United Nations Relief and Rehabilitation Agency (UNRRA), which was seen as a prototype for the new international organizations, Mackenzie King stated that

> ... *no workable international system can be based on the concentration of influence and authority wholly in bodies composed of a few great powers to the exclusion of all the rest. It is not always the largest powers that have the greatest contribution to make to the work of these bodies or the greatest stake in their success. In international economic organizations such as the Relief Administration representation on such bodies can often be determined on a functional basis and in our view this principle should be applied wherever it is feasible.*[4]

As a rich country with high levels of education and ample physical resources, Canada could be expected to do well if these became the rules of the game. Canada's eagerness to define a role for itself as a middle power was thus partly an attempt to maintain a relatively privileged position within a hierarchical system of world power. While Canada was clearly not a superpower, the policy was designed to explain to the world that "Canadians were of greater consequence than the Panamanians."[5] On the other hand, Canadian representatives at the United Nations and in External Affairs were clearly committed to the idea that stronger international organizations served the world community as a whole, and were not just a means of promoting Canada's national interests.

Canada did succeed in winning some international recognition based on the functional principle. For example, as one of the countries that had developed nuclear energy, it became a permanent member of the UN Atomic Energy Commission. As well, Canada and other middle powers successfully pressed for an amendment to article 23 of the UN Charter, which stated that, in electing nonpermanent members to the Security Council, "due regard" would be paid "in the first instance to the contribution of Members of the United Nations to the maintenance of international peace and security and to the other purposes of the Organization." While Canada hoped this would mean it and other middle powers would gain near-permanent representation on the Security Council, in practice allocation of the nonpermanent seats has been made on the basis of geographical representation rather than on functional grounds.

As the international system evolved, some of Canada's early hopes about the character of the postwar order dimmed. In particular, the escalation of Cold War conflict between the USSR and the United States eliminated early hopes that the United Nations could create an effective system of collective security.[6] Except for the Korean War, the collective-security provisions of the UN Charter were not used until the Persian Gulf War of 1990–91. During the Cold War, the potential power of the Security Council was paralyzed by the veto powers of both superpowers. As a result, and also because of the entry of the many new countries created by the rapid decolonization of the former territories of the European powers, the General Assembly and other bodies based on universal representation took on greater prominence in the UN system. However, because these more expansively defined bodies lacked any meaningful ways to check the behaviour of the superpowers, they too possessed only limited power.

With the intensification of the Cold War, the middle-power role shifted away from the corridors of international organizations and became focused on the relationship between the superpowers. The term "middle power" is perhaps misleading in this context, since it might seem to indicate that Canada sat as a neutral body halfway between the two contending powers. Instead, Canada was clearly aligned with the United States, and Canadian leaders shared their ally's anticommunist ideology. The rigid constraints imposed by the bipolar alignment of global forces left the so-called middle powers little room in which to manoeuvre. Canada's attempts at international mediation were designed not just to maintain global peace and stability, but also to curry favour in Washington. Canada's role as "middle power" was thus closely linked to its committed position in the Cold War alignment of forces and to its "special relationship" with the United States.

Canada had been increasingly integrated into U.S. plans for continental defence as early as the Ogdensburg agreement of August 1940. Canada's postwar defence commitments were partly based on geopolitical realities, particularly because if the USSR launched their long-range strategic bombers they would necessarily fly over Canadian territory. Early continental defence arrangements eventually led to the establishment in 1958 of the bilateral North American Aerospace Defense Command (NORAD) and the Defence Production Sharing Agreement (DPSA), which integrated continental defence production.

As we have already seen, it was Canada's desire to avoid U.S. domination of the continental relationship, together with frustration at the inability of the United Nations to promote collective security, that had led to the search for multilateral alternatives. Canada thus strongly supported the creation of the North American Treaty Organization (NATO) in 1949 on the grounds that it would insure against a U.S. return to isolationism, commit the United States to the defence of Europe, and, finally, balance the U.S. preponderance in the continental relationship. Canadian diplomats like Escott Reid hoped that NATO would promote the establishment of a North Atlantic community based on shared values and culture. Reid pushed for the inclusion of article 2 in the NATO charter, which stated that

> [t]he Parties will contribute toward the further development of peaceful and friendly international relations by strengthening their free institutions, by bringing about a better understanding of the principles upon which these institutions are founded, and by promoting conditions of stability and well-being. They will seek to eliminate conflict in their international economic policies and will encourage economic collaboration between any or all of them.[7]

The inclusion of this so-called Canada clause, like that of article 23 of the UN Charter, was more of a symbolic than a real victory, since it was never substantially acted upon.

Canada's continued claim to middle-power status thus did not rest upon an equidistant position between the two superpowers. Rather, the country took on the role as a mediator and "helpful fixer" not from a position of neutrality, but as a committed member of the Western alliance. Canada's mediation efforts were usually made with the approval of the United States, which recognized that unmitigated competition between the superpowers could be dangerously destructive. Even when, as in the 1980s, the United States was actively hostile toward multilateral organizations like the United Nations, Canada's attempts to bolster those organizations were probably in U.S. long-term interests in terms of international cooperation and stability. Canada was a good candidate for this role, since its lack of participation in direct colonial rule made its mediation more acceptable to the newly independent countries of the Third World, which were increasingly important theatres of superpower conflict. As peacekeeper and truce supervisor (participating in all UN-sponsored peacekeeping operations), Canada made a modest but significant contribution to maintaining international order in the perilous Cold War years.

In addition to its roles in peacekeeping, the United Nations, and NATO, Canada also participated actively in establishing and maintaining the organizations of the international financial system, the Commonwealth, la Francophonie, and a host of smaller international organizations. Canada thus became the international "joiner" *par excellence* out of a general philosophical commitment to international organizations and the continued hope of offsetting U.S. power with a diverse set of international linkages. All of these decisions were strongly influenced by the limitations and opportunities presented to Canada by the Cold War context and its close geographic, political, military, and economic relationship with the United States. As suggested, the middle-power role implied not a truly medium-level status, but rather a certain style of foreign policy activity in a world caught between the polarization of the Cold War and the formal universalism of the postwar international organizations. The end of the Cold War and changes in the role of the United States in the world system have left many of the fundamental tenets of Canadian foreign policy seriously outdated.

DECONSTRUCTING THE "NEW WORLD ORDER"

What is the shape of the "new world order"? The disappearance of the Soviet Union and the Warsaw Pact suggests to some analysts that the United States is now the world's only superpower. From this perspective Canada's position as close ally of the United States would seem to be highly advantageous. We will argue, however, that by focusing only on military dimensions of power this view of the new world order as a "unipolar moment" seriously exaggerates the relative position of the United States in the global hierarchy of nations. The economic power of the United States has clearly declined since the period after World War II when that country was virtually able to dictate the rules and norms of the postwar economic system. As the junior economic partner of the United States, Canada's position has also become much more precarious.

There is little debate over the claim that the demise of the former Soviet Union has led to objective changes in the structures of world order and a shift away from the postwar bipolar system. However, there is disagreement on the nature of the new system. Conservative U.S. political commentator Charles Krauthammer argues that the immediate post–Cold War world is unipolar, consisting of the United States at the apex of the industrial West:

American preeminence is based on the fact that it is the only country with the military, diplomatic, political and economic assets to be a decisive player in any conflict in whatever part of the world it chooses to involve itself. In the Persian Gulf, for example, it was the United States, acting unilaterally and with extraordinary speed, that in August 1990 prevented Iraq from taking effective control of the entire Arabian Peninsula.[8]

According to Krauthammer, the "pious talk" about a new multilateral world based on collective security confuses the United States with the United Nations: "In the Gulf, without the United States leading and prodding, bribing and blackmailing, no one would have stirred."[9]

There is some merit to this view. It is noteworthy that White House spokespersons soon abandoned the phrase "new world order" and its implied U.S. commitment to greater multilateralism. In fact, more recent U.S. foreign policy statements show a shift back toward unilateralism. In his inaugural speech, President Clinton stated that America would act militarily with others when possible, but "alone when we must." In contrast with the Canadian ideology of middlepowermanship, current U.S. Secretary of State Warren Christopher sees "multilateralism as a means, not an end."[10]

Krauthammer's discussion of the "unipolar moment" is thus a more realistic assessment of U.S. motivations and perspectives than those provided by most defenders of American policy. However, his exclusive focus on the importance of military might in assessing the nature of the international system leads him to overlook important changes in the global power equation. While the United States is now the world's only military superpower, the country's economic decline over the past two decades relative to other economic actors like the European Community and Japan precludes it from unilaterally imposing its will on the international financial and monetary system.

Richard Rosecrance provides a more apt image of the nature of the emerging world order, which he calls "a new concert of powers." He compares the current configuration of power with the 19th-century Concert of Europe, in which France, Britain, Russia, Austria, and Prussia collectively exercised direction for about 30 years after the Vienna Congress of 1815. This was a period of relative stability in Europe, one based on ideological consensus among the five major powers and aimed at the containment of liberal aspirations and the buttressing of autocracy. After the breakup of the Soviet Union, Rosecrance argues, five great powers (the United States, Russia, the European Community, Japan, and China) could again control the organization of the world order.[11] Ideological consensus around the principles of liberal democracy is a major factor fuelling cooperation among the great powers. While China continues to reject democracy, the country is moving closer toward integration into the global economy and thus does not pose a major challenge to the major principles of the system.

Moves toward an international concert system of more centralized decision-making are apparent in many directions. The most notable is in the nature of the United Nations. As noted above, the structure of the United Nations was originally designed to recognize the claims of the World War II victors to preponderant power in international decision-making. In the wake of the Cold War, and with the end of the veto stalemate, the Security Council has new capacity for action. This turn of events may seem to conform to traditional middle-power aspirations to strengthen international institutions. However, the events of the Persian Gulf War hold out less hope for greater effectiveness on the part of the Security Council. Many analysts, including Krauthammer, believe that UN actions in the crisis reflected the new capacity of the United States to manipulate the organization to achieve its foreign policy goals. In the absence of the "Communist menace," the United States requires a new source of legitimacy to justify its action. George Bush's rhetoric about the new world order and newfound belief in the United Nations were public-relations ploys designed to legitimize U.S. leadership in the Gulf.[12] Stephen Lewis, Canada's former ambassador to the United Nations, described the manipulation of the organization in these terms:

> ... the United Nations served as an imprimatur of legitimacy for a policy that the United States wanted to follow and either persuaded or coerced everybody else to support.... I cannot believe that the people who got together in San Francisco in 1945 intended that kind of inconsequential role for the United Nations—a role that sees the United Nations as a rubber stamp, as an organization that is manipulated on behalf of the foreign policy interests and priorities of a few very powerful states.[13]

There is no doubt that Iraq's illegal occupation of Kuwait warranted a strong response from the United Nations. However, there are many indications that the United States used its influence in the Security Council to override some of the rules and mechanisms established in the UN Charter. This may have forestalled the possibility of a peaceful resolution of the dispute. To illustrate, chapter VIII of the UN Charter encourages the use of "regional arrangements or agencies" in disputes and violations of peace and security, yet in this case the Arab diplomatic community was not given sufficient opportunity to resolve the crisis before the Security Council, under U.S. direction, moved in. On the question of the use of sanctions to respond to "threats to the peace, breaches of the peace, and acts of aggression," article 42, chapter VII states: "Should the Security Council consider that [such sanctions] would be inadequate or have proved to be inadequate" it may take such military action as may be necessary. Faced with the impatience of the United States and threats that it would act out-side the framework of the UN mandate if necessary, insufficient consideration of the effects of economic sanctions occurred before the decision to use force was taken. Moreover, the military forces that fought in the Gulf were under U.S. command rather than under UN command as the founders of the organization had intended.[14]

The events of the Gulf War thus indicate that the United States is now less constrained than previously in its capacity to display its military prowess. However, the United States did require the political and especially the financial support of other great powers in order to undertake its military action. The fact that the Persian Gulf War was financially underwritten by wealthy allies like Germany and Japan is just one indication of the U.S. decline in economic power, which, in turn, has important implications for its ability to maintain military predominance.

Following World War II, the fact that its economic power was unchallenged enabled the United States to exercise leadership in defining the character of the postwar economic system and in constructing international financial organizations such as the International Monetary Fund and the World Bank. However, since 1971, when the United States was forced to abandon the gold standard, international economic summitry has replaced unilateral U.S. leadership. Beginning in the mid-1970s, the leaders of the richest industrial states began meeting to try to coordinate macroeconomic policies in order to avoid international economic disorder. Canada was left out of the first meeting, in 1975, but was invited to attend the 1976 meeting by U.S. President Gerald Ford. The operations of what has come to be known as the Group of 7 (G7) are secretive and inherently exclusionary. Referring to the summits, Sir Shridath Ramphal, Secretary-General of the Commonwealth, wrote in 1988 that the global consensus about the interdependence of nations and the need for cooperation between weak and strong—a consensus that had emerged in the 1970s— "has become a casualty in the drift towards dominance and the ascendancy of unilateralism in world affairs." In Ramphal's view, "cooperation within a directorate of powerful countries is hardly the answer to the world's needs, the needs of all its nations. In fact, it could well have the result of reinforcing the dominance of the few over the many."[15]

The exclusion of the Third World from the central forums of international economic decision-making reflects the increased marginalization of the South in the evolving global economy. It is true that since the 1970s at least some countries in the South—the newly industrializing countries (NICs)—have benefited to some extent from the shift in industrial production away from the high-waged Northern economies. However, Northern states responded to this competitive threat by erecting protectionist barriers, including both tariffs and nontariff barriers. The emergence of regional trading blocs (the European Community, NAFTA, and the "yen bloc" centred on Japan) is yet another defensive response to increased international competition that excludes the majority of Southern countries. At the same time, the end of the Cold War has decreased the importance of the South to the geopolitical interests of the North, resulting in the decline of aid flows. A significant portion of the North's international economic assistance has also shifted from the marginalized countries of the South to the countries of the former Soviet bloc.

CANADA AND THE NEW MULTILATERALISM: BEYOND MIDDLEPOWERMANSHIP?

As we have seen, there have been substantial recent changes in the structure of the world system, the role of international organizations, and the relative position of the United States in the world system. Under the wing of its neighbour to the south, Canada has been an active participant in, and supporter of, all of these trends toward concentration of economic and political power in the new world order. According to John Kirton,

> [Canada's] traditional preoccupation with universalism, or at least ever broadening multilateralism, has been set aside in favour of plurilateralism, and particularly the plurilateralism of the plutocracy where Canada is grouped along with the great.[16]

As a result of this more elitist approach, the official rhetoric of middle-powermanship has been replaced by a view of Canada as a "principal power."

Although Canada does not have a permanent seat in the Security Council, it occupied one of the temporary seats at the time of the Gulf War. Canada played a leading role, along with some other members of the Security Council, in convincing the United States to gain a UN mandate for military action against Iraq. The Gulf crisis was seen as the first significant opportunity after the Cold War to revive the security role originally foreseen for the UN and to steer the United States away from its traditional unilateralism. Canadian support for the use of the Security Council to put pressure on Iraq was seen as a key factor in gaining support from Third World members of the Security Council who were particularly anxious to avoid the use of military force.[17]

Canada's traditional support for world order and international organizations was invoked repeatedly by the Canadian government to justify its role during the Gulf crisis. However, as seen above, the actions of the United Nations departed significantly from the UN mandate outlined in the provisions of its charter, and has reinforced the least democratic institution within the UN structure—the Security Council. As has occurred repeatedly in Canadian history, Canadian policy-makers focused more on the appearance of multilateralism than on its substance, encouraging the drift toward a concert-of-powers system.

The traditional peacekeeping role of the United Nations has also been expanded since the end of the Cold War, with active Canadian support. The end of the Cold War meant the organization's offices could be used to help resolve some of the most intransigent Third World conflicts, without superpower opposition. As a result, the United Nations was helpful in promoting peace settlements in Southern Africa, Cambodia, and Central America.

Nevertheless, Third World policy-makers and academics from a wide range of political perspectives are distinctly nervous about the implications of recent global realignments. Malaysia's president Mohamad Mahathir stated at the 1991 meeting of the nonaligned nations: "The new unipolar world is fraught with dangers of a return to the old dominance of the powerful over the weak. ... A new world order is propounded seemingly to legitimize interference in the affairs of independent nations."[18] After taking on an expanded "peacemaking" role in Bosnia, Somalia, and Cambodia, UN peacekeeping forces are increasingly perceived as intervening in local affairs without adequate resources, training, or knowledge of and sensitivity to complex political terrains. As a major actor in these operations (as well as supporting the Gulf War against Iraq), Canada risks being perceived as a participant in a global police force designed and led by the rich and powerful states to control unruly and disruptive upstarts in the South. Charges against several Canadian peacekeepers in the killing of a Somali prisoner in Canadian custody, and allegations of racism among Canadian troops, have contributed to the tarnishing of Canada's image abroad.

At the same time, changes in Canada's official development-assistance policies reinforce the view that the country is acting increasingly to promote its own self-interest at the expense of less wealthy and powerful nations. As part of its deficit-reduction strategy, the Mulroney government enacted repeated cuts in the budget of the Canadian International Development Agency (CIDA). In March 1993, bilateral aid to 14 African and Asian countries, among them some of the world's poorest countries, was eliminated or drastically reduced. The only region that did not have its aid budget cut was Latin America, which is more developed than most African countries, but which is also where Canada hopes to promote increased trade linkages. CIDA has also supported the imposition of neoliberal structural-adjustment programs in Third World countries in exchange for the granting of loans by the International Monetary Fund and the World Bank. These programs—which involve cutbacks in state funding for social services and subsidies, liberalization of trade and investment, and export promotion—have been widely criticized for contributing to prolonged economic hardship for the poor and middle classes in Third

World countries; at the same time, their long-term economic benefits have been questioned.

Canada has not only reduced its traditional commitment to a broad-based aid program, but it has also participated in the rise of the "new protectionism," which is directed primarily at Third World newly industrializing countries. Like other advanced industrialized countries, Canada has imposed new antidumping and countervailing duty actions against those Third World states that are perceived as threats to Northern market shares. It is true that Canada has followed the United States into a liberalized trading arrangement with one newly industrializing state—Mexico—in the North American Free Trade Agreement (NAFTA). Other Latin American and Caribbean states fear, however, that NAFTA will divert trade and investment away from them toward Mexico. While some of the strongest Third World states may thus be able to gain access to preferential trading arrangements through entrance into regional economic blocs, the more marginal and vulnerable states are likely to suffer continued exclusion from Northern markets.

CONCLUSION

What are the implications of a monopoly of power in the hands of a few states? The appeal of a concert-of-powers system is that it is believed to foster both economic and political stability. While it does not prevent wars (as the ongoing bloodbaths in the former Yugoslavia, Somalia, Angola, and elsewhere attest), it does represent a way of forestalling dangerous conflicts among the great powers, including the major nuclear powers. It may also forestall increased economic competition among the three centres of economic power: the European Community, NAFTA, and the Japanese yen bloc.

The costs, however, are great. Whatever the evils of the Cold War period, and they were many, the existence of a counterweight to U.S. power at least permitted the less powerful states a certain margin of autonomy to pursue alternative forms of political and economic organization. Moreover, it also required that the Northern countries develop a "humane internationalist" ideology, one that promoted assistance for the world's poorest, in order to gain influence in the South. According to Indian writer Rajni Kothari, what has taken place since the end of the Cold War is an "erosion of alternatives" at various levels. All countries are forced to follow the same liberal-democratic capitalist path, in the absence of alternative visions. Since Western economic and political models provide little hope for most Third World societies, however, this route is likely to lead to long-term political and economic instability, as well as ecological disaster, for all countries. For Canada, as well, the benefits of playing the role of social climber, of attempting to gain, or maintain, entrance to the most elite clubs, are dubious. The reorientation of Canadian foreign policy away from universalist traditions toward a more elitist stance may merely provide empty prestige to Canadian politicans and officials, rather than serve the interests of all Canadians. It may also blind policy-makers to the dangers of current global trends, and thus preclude them from calling forcefully for alternatives.

NOTES

1. For a similar argument focusing on Canada's role in the international economy, see David Black and Claire Turenne Sjolander, "Canada in the Transition: Prospects for a Re-constituted Multilateralism," paper prepared for presentation at the 65th annual meeting of the Canadian Political Science Association, Ottawa, June 6–8, 1993.

2. Although in an exercise of displaying Canada's new autonomy in foreign affairs, Mackenzie King waited ten days before declaring war on Germany.

3. John W. Holmes, *The Better Part of Valour: Essays on Canadian Diplomac* (Toronto: McClelland and Stewart, 1970), p. 5.

4. Quoted in Tom Keating, *Canada and World Order: The Multilateralist Tradition in Canadian Foreign Policy* (Toronto: McClelland and Stewart, 1993), pp. 31–32.

5. John W. Holmes, "Most Safely in the Middle," in J.L. Granatstein, ed., *Towards a New World: Readings in the History of Canadian Foreign Policy* (Mississauga, Ont.: Copp Clark Pitman, 1992), p. 90.

6. Under a collective security system, all members of the international community agree to respond automatically to violations against the sovereignty of any of them by imposing a set of agreed-upon measures (up to and including the use of force) to punish the aggressor.

7. Quoted in Keating, *Canada and World Order*, p. 89.

8. Charles Krauthammer, "The Unipolar Moment," *Foreign Affairs* 70 (America and the World 1990–91): 24.

9. Ibid., 25.

10. "U.S. Permanent Representative to the U.N. says U.S. to use diplomacy when possible, force when necessary," *Text*, U.S. Embassy, Ottawa, September 24, 1994.

11. Richard Rosecrance, "A New Concert of Powers," *Foreign Affairs* 71, no. 2 (Spring 1992): 64–82.

12. Phyllis Bennis, "False Consensus: George Bush's United Nations," in Phyllis Bennis and Michel Moushabeck, eds., *Beyond the Storm: A Gulf Crisis Reader* (New York: Olive Branch Press, 1991).

13. Stephen Lewis, "A Promise Betrayed," in Baha Abu-Laban and M. Ibrahim Alladin, eds., *Beyond the Gulf War: Muslims, Arabs and the West* (Edmonton: MRF Publishers, 1991), pp. 147–48.

14. Erskine B. Childers, "The Use and Abuse of the UN in the Gulf Crisis," in H.M. Amery, ed., *Shaping the Gulf: In Search of Order* (Toronto: Canadian Institute for Policy Research and Analysis, 1992).

15. Quoted in Robert W. Cox, "Multilateralism and World Order," *Review of International Studies* 18 (1992): 161–80.

16. John Kirton, "Further Challenges," in John Holmes and John Kirton, eds., *Canada and the New Internationalism* (Toronto: Canadian Institute of International Affairs, 1988), pp. 141–42.

17. Harald von Riekhoff, "Canada and Collective Security," in David Dewitt and David Leyton-Brown, eds., *Canada's International Security Policy* (Scarborough, Ont.: Prentice-Hall Canada, 1994).

18. Quoted in Deepa Ollapally, "The South Looks North: The Third World in the New World Order," *Current History* (April 1993): 175.

FURTHER READINGS

Cutler, Clare A., and Mark W. Zacher, eds. *Canadian Foreign Policy and International Economic Regimes*. Vancouver: University of British Columbia Press, 1992.

Dewitt, David, and John Kirton. *Canada as a Principal Power*. Toronto: John Wiley and Sons, 1983.

English, John, and Norman Hillmer, eds. *Making a Difference?: Canada's Foreign Policy in a Changing World Order*. Toronto: Lester Publishing, 1992.

Griffin, Keith. "Foreign Aid After the Cold War," *Development and Change* 22 (1991): 645–85.

Halliday, Fred. *From Kabul to Managua: Soviet–American Relations in the 1980s*. New York: Pantheon Books, 1989.

Holmes, John. *The Better Part of Valour: Essays on Canadian Diplomacy*. Toronto: McClelland and Stewart, 1970.

Langille, Howard Peter. *Changing the Guard: Canada's Defence in a World in Transition*. Toronto: University of Toronto Press, 1990.

Nossal, Kim Richard. *The Politics of Canadian Foreign Policy*, 2nd ed. Scarborough, Ont.: Prentice-Hall Canada, 1989.

Painchaud, Peter, ed. *From Mackenzie King to Pierre Trudeau: Forty Years of Canadian Diplomacy, 1945–1985*. Quebec: Les presses de l'université Laval, 1989.

4 THE POLITICS OF SCARCITY: DEFICITS AND THE DEBT

Isabella Bakker

INTRODUCTION

The past two decades have been marked by competing visions of the proper role of government in the economy. Government increasingly came to be seen as the problem, the market as the solution. As we approach the mid-1990s, Canada is firmly in the grip of a fiscal crisis that is propelling governments toward market methods and goals.

During the 1970s, the debate over the role of the public sector was generally dominated by two competing schools of thought: Keynesian and monetarist. The Keynesian school was the dominant influence in shaping Canada's post–World War II development strategy. Keynesians see a legitimate role for government intervention in the workings of the market. They recognize a need for government intervention in times of recession and unemployment in order to overcome shortfalls in aggregate demand. During the Great Depression and after the Second World War, Keynesians generally argued for active government, fiscal and monetary policies as well as regulations aimed at curbing the excesses of corporate concentration and abuses of consumers. In addition, some Keynesians embraced the proposition that redistributive measures such as social security and income supplements such as unemployment insurance were effective safeguards because they gave workers money to buy the goods the economy produced even during economic downturns.

Monetarists like University of Chicago economist Milton Friedman advocate a purely self-regulating market regime wherein all production, allocation, and distribution decisions, as well as the prices of goods, services, and income, are determined by the market. Public sector activity, including taxation, are viewed as disincentives to investment that distort the decision-making process of individuals and firms. Monetarists are strong advocates of the need for a sharply curtailed size and role for the public sector and for a strict control of the money supply. By the 1980s, the Keynesians had been chased from the spotlight, and the monetarists, champions of the free market, moved beyond their preoccupations with monetary policy to assume a new guise as neoliberals.[1]

A number of factors, domestic and international, contributed to Keynesianism's defeat. At home, a crisis in government finances fuelled anti-government sentiments and a sense that what had worked in the past could no longer offer a solution for the future. Up to the early 1970s, continuous economic growth had fostered a set of institutional arrangements and social policies that muted distributional conflicts between labour and capital. In a sense, the success of Keynesianism—continuous economic growth—was also its downfall. Once recession tested the Keynesian compromise between labour and capital, the way was paved for the monetarist resurgence. Part and parcel of this resurgence was the increasing visibility of the role of the state. With the breakdown of the Keynesian welfare state (KWS) compromise, distributional conflicts were exacerbated and the state became, once again, a subject and a site of struggle. This translated into a greater awareness and concern about the size and scope of government.[2]

The retreat from universal and redistributive welfare measures set the stage for the rise of new economic orthodoxies that rejected public intervention in the economy. This monetarist agenda, initially set by the Liberals in the mid-1970s, was accelerated by the Tories when they came to power under Brian Mulroney in 1984. During the 1980s, the federal government practised the "politics of scarcity" by reducing the revenue base while attempting to squeeze expenditures. The eventual downfall of this strategy was primarily due to the combined influence of two factors: (1) high interest rates that forced an ever larger share of government expenditure to service the national debt, and (2) strong public resistance to undermining the economic and social services provided by the KWS. The new Liberal government under Jean Chrétien appears to be caught in a contradictory position. On the one hand, it was elected on a platform of traditional mildly Keynesian policies; on the other hand, the pressures of the global economy, exacerbated by the Free Trade Agreement (FTA) and the North American Free Trade Agreement (NAFTA), diminish the effectiveness of such traditional domestic economic management policies by binding Canadians to international standards and agreements.

Not surprisingly, the amount of government spending continues to be identified as one key source of the country's economic woes, and has served to bolster the monetarist, market-based approach. This chapter will analyze Canadian expenditure trends, both in the international context and by the various levels of government (federal, provincial, and local), in light of these arguments. We will see that, from 1970 on, the share of Canadian government spending relative to the gross domestic product

(GDP) is not extraordinary when compared to that of other advanced capitalist countries. And when one examines all levels of government within Canada, it becomes apparent that provincial and local governments have realized a more rapid growth in expenditures than has the federal government. This in large part reflects the introduction of new layers of welfare programs (mainly in the jurisdiction of these subnational levels of government) in the late 1960s. The increasing share of federal transfers to the provinces is another indicator of the greater expenditure shift toward the provinces.

Public spending levels are frequently correlated with the size of deficits. The revenue section of this chapter will reject this argument. In large part, the Canadian deficit can be attributed to the failure of the federal government to bring its revenue-raising capacity in line with its expenditures. This is due to a number of factors, including increasing interest payments on the debt, increases in cyclical expenditures such as unemployment insurance, and various tax breaks and deferrals that have resulted in a significant loss of federal revenues relative to Canada's economic output. It is becoming clear that extra revenue gains promised by Conservative tax reforms in the 1980s are coming out of regressive consumption taxes rather than corporate taxes. The chapter concludes with the argument that negative trends on the revenue side, in conjunction with the free-trade initiative and its impetus toward harmonization (resulting in much lower levels of U.S. social spending), point to intensified pressures on Canadian social programs and the public sector in the 1990s. Efforts to reduce social spending represent an attempt by monetarist or neoliberal forces to emphasize economic efficiency over equity. Their arguments for spending cutbacks are particularly effective when federal deficits are at a high level. Rejecting government expenditures as the source of deficits, this chapter represents an attempt to clarify the high stakes of this political debate in the 1990s.

THE DECLINE OF POLITICAL REGULATION AND THE RISE OF THE NEW ORTHODOXY: TOWARD A NEW SYSTEM OF DISTRIBUTION

The recession of the early 1980s capped a decade of uncertainty for state policy-makers. The economic prosperity of the "golden era" came to a sudden halt in the early 1970s with the simultaneous appearance of high levels of unemployment and inflation (stagflation). Keynesian policies and the construction of the welfare state had been widely viewed as the foundation of this postwar prosperity and political compromise. However, Keynesianism represented more than an economic doctrine; it represented a *political regulation* of the market economy, and included state efforts to harmonize opposing interests through a series of economic and social policies. In the aftermath of the Great Depression and the Second World War, Keynesian principles of demand management and fiscal stabilization were harnessed to the traditional Canadian staples-led approach to economic development. When the underlying political and economic conditions that allowed Keynesian policies to flourish changed, the entire Keynesian approach came to be questioned. This was especially the case with the KWS.

The KWS was constructed to address the social policies and the pressures coming from a growing labour movement and the New Democratic Party. Although never warmly embraced in Canada, the KWS was tolerated as long as it was financed out of increased economic growth and higher marginal incomes; it was deemed acceptable, and muted distributional conflicts between capital and labour. The Canadian welfare state was to ensure the continuity of income over the ups and downs of the economy much in the same way as Keynesian macroeconomic policies were to secure the smooth flow of profits during economic upswings and downturns. Through this dual approach, Keynesianism managed to address the concerns of both labour and capital. The fiscal burden of the KWS was acceptable in the context of workers' rising standard of living and the rising profitability being stimulated by the high level of demand for Canadian resource exports in the international economy. However, the stable economic environment that had fostered this postwar development strategy began to crumble in the late 1960s and early 1970s. In addition, the tax burden of corporations and the wealthy was beginning to be reduced through a series of tax measures that shifted the increased cost of the KWS onto working-class and middle-income earners.

With the onset of recession in the early 1970s and the collapse of the postwar accumulation strategy, new economic orthodoxies that reaffirmed economic growth through market forces emerged. By 1975, with the governor of the Bank of Canada's announcement of reductions in the growth of the money supply and the advent of wage controls, monetarist principles were replacing earlier Keynesian-style approaches to macroeconomic policy. Constant attempts by the Bank of Canada to protect the value of the Canadian dollar meant high interest rates. In 1981, interest rates were at 20 percent; and by 1989, they had fallen only to 12.5 percent. High interest rates, reduced investment, and the federal government's withdrawal from direct job creation are part of the monetarist approach to federal government policy. The new monetarist economic orthodoxy also questioned the role of the state in harmonizing the production of wealth with its distribution by arguing that allocation and distribution should be left to the market.

State policy-makers were at the same time grappling with the declining international economic status of the United States. The position of the

United States has been affected by a decline in its share of world exports (from 22 percent in 1950 to 10 percent in 1980), reduced technological superiority, competition from the newly industrializing countries (NICs) in the Pacific Rim and South America, and the formation of powerful trading blocs such as the European Community (EC). This poses a particular problem for Canada because its postwar development had relied heavily on American investment in Canadian domestic manufacturing and resource development (see Chapter 2). Canada's branch-plant industrialization compounds the already difficult task for governments of coping with productivity declines and the accelerated application of technological innovation to production. Branch plants neither control their own technology nor undertake much research and development. As a result, many companies rely on responses to worldwide economic restructuring made south of the border. This, compounded by NAFTA and the FTA, makes it increasingly difficult to set a clear and independent economic policy direction in Ottawa.

Furthermore, the growth of provincial fiscal power has also complicated Ottawa's responses to international economic shifts. Canadian federalism, contrary to trends in other federal states, has been moving toward greater decentralization. In the 1970s, this was fuelled by the alternative vision that took hold among the premiers of the western, resource-producing provinces. Tired of servicing central Canada and having the status of an economic hinterland, the premiers began to emphasize market-driven economic development, greater North–South integration, and a decentralization of the federal government's economic prerogatives. They clashed with the central Canadian economic interests that sought to preserve existing Canadian manufacturing sectors and that advocated new state-directed development of the industrial and service sectors. However, the federal Progressive Conservatives had largely embraced the vision of the western premiers by the mid-1980s.

The Mulroney government came to power strongly supporting the pro-market liberalism of Ronald Reagan and Margaret Thatcher. In their early-1984 mini-budget and the May 1985 budget, the Tories set out their overall objective of "economic renewal," employing neoliberal policy instruments to realize that goal. This meant reorienting public policies to encourage entrepreneurship, investment, and risk-taking; rationalizing the management of government resources and programs; restoring fiscal balance in how Ottawa spent and taxed; and reducing both the size and role of the federal government.[3] By the late 1980s, the Bank of Canada and the Mulroney Conservatives had retreated from earlier commitments to balancing inflation (price stability) and unemployment in order to single-mindedly pursue a zero-inflation objective.

As the next section points out, the neoliberal view that associates high levels of welfare spending with negative economic performance has not been supported by the empirical evidence. Similarly, there is no simple correlation between government deficits and the KWS. While the Canadian government share of gross national product (GNP) has remained fairly static since 1975, the share of government expenditures for social programs dropped from 46 percent in 1976 to 40 percent in 1982.[4] This is precisely the period during which the deficit first became a source of economic and political concern. The source of the deficit lies in the reduced revenue-generating capacity of the federal government and the high interest rates that government was forced to pay due to the Bank of Canada's tight monetary policy.

THE INTERNATIONAL CONTEXT

Table 4.1 presents a series of economic indicators or characteristics, including government revenues and expenditures, for the seven largest economies in the Organization for Economic Co-operation and Development (OECD), the so-called Group of Seven (G7). As the table shows, growth in GNP/GDP[5] has been slow in the last few years in all of the G7 countries, with Canada experiencing growth below the average since 1988. GDP is used as a general indicator of the overall health of an economy because it measures the total output in money values of all goods and services produced within a given year. GDP is not, however, a measure of a nation's well-being since it takes into account not all work done (e.g., domestic labour and the underground economy) but only recorded transactions. The most sustained record of productivity growth over the 1983–92 period was experienced by Japan and West Germany. Turning to employment growth, Canada's record in the mid-1980s was fairly respectable, but began to drop off sharply with the implementation of the FTA and the recession of the early 1990s. The United States had the most vigorous performance in employment growth, but many of the new jobs it created over this period were in minimum-wage, nonstandard forms of employment. Indeed, in the 1980s many countries experienced a polarization of their labour markets, with a minority of workers in good jobs and a majority in bad jobs. This polarization was further marked by the increased gender and race segregation found in many national labour markets.[6]

Canadian unemployment rates have historically been higher than the OECD average, and the 1983–92 statistics confirm this tendency. Why does Canada have higher rates of unemployment? The Canadian economy's historical dependence on exports (in cyclically volatile natural resources) and its relatively small indigenous manufacturing sector (resulting in regional inequities in economic opportunities and rewards) have been offered as explanations for the higher levels of unemployment in Canada. In addition, some analysts point to the Bank of Canada's shift to monetarist policies in the 1980s as having redirected the attention of

TABLE 4.1 Recent OECD Economic Indicators, 1983–1992

	1983	1984	1985	1986	1987	1988	1989	1990	1991	1992
Growth in real GNP/GDP[1]										
United States	3.9	6.2	3.2	2.9	3.1	3.9	2.5	0.8	-1.2	2.1
Japan	2.8	4.3	5.1	2.7	4.3	6.3	4.8	4.8	4.1	1.5
West Germany	1.5	2.7	1.9	2.3	1.5	3.8	3.3	5.1	3.7	1.4
France	0.7	1.3	1.9	2.5	2.3	4.5	4.2	2.5	0.7	1.3
United Kingdom	3.7	2.3	3.8	4.1	4.8	4.4	2.1	0.5	-2.2	-0.6
Italy	1.0	2.7	2.6	2.9	3.1	4.1	2.9	2.1	1.3	0.9
Canada	3.2	6.3	4.8	3.3	4.2	5.0	2.3	-0.5	-1.7	0.9
Seven major countries	2.4	3.8	4.1	3.0	4.0	5.1	3.5	2.6	1.5	1.0
Employment growth										
United States	1.3	4.1	2.0	2.3	2.6	2.3	2.0	0.5	-0.9	0.6
Japan	1.7	0.6	0.7	0.8	1.0	1.7	1.9	2.0	1.9	1.1
West Germany	-1.4	0.2	0.7	1.4	0.7	0.8	1.5	3.0	2.6	0.8
France	-0.3	-0.9	0.5	0.3	0.4	1.0	1.4	1.0	0.1	-0.5
United Kingdom	-0.2	2.2	1.1	0.3	2.3	3.3	2.7	0.3	-3.2	-2.9
Italy	0.2	0.4	0.4	0.5	-0.2	1.1	0.1	1.8	0.9	-0.6
Canada	0.5	2.4	2.6	2.8	2.9	3.2	2.0	0.7	-1.8	-0.8
Seven major countries	1.2	3.2	1.7	1.9	2.2	2.1	2.0	0.8	-0.4	0.6
Unemployment rates[2]										
United States	9.6	7.5	7.2	7.0	6.2	5.5	5.3	5.5	6.7	7.4
Japan	2.7	2.7	2.6	2.8	2.9	2.5	2.3	2.1	2.1	2.2

(1) GNP numbers are reported for the United States, Japan, and West Germany, while GDP numbers are reported for France, the United Kingdom, Canada, and Italy.
(2) Unemployment rates are calculated on the basis of national definitions.

(Table continues next page.)

(Continued from previous page.)

	1983	1984	1985	1986	1987	1988	1989	1990	1991	1992
Unemployment rates										
West Germany	7.9	7.9	8.0	7.7	7.6	7.6	6.9	6.2	5.5	5.8
France	8.3	9.7	10.3	10.4	10.5	10.0	9.4	8.9	9.5	10.2
United Kingdom	11.2	11.4	11.6	11.8	10.4	8.2	6.2	5.9	8.3	10.1
Italy	10.0	10.1	10.2	11.2	12.1	12.2	12.1	11.1	11.0	10.7
Canada	11.8	11.2	10.5	9.5	8.8	7.8	7.5	8.1	10.3	11.3
Seven major countries	8.3	7.4	7.2	7.1	6.7	6.1	5.7	5.6	6.4	7.0
Consumer price index growth										
United States	3.2	4.3	3.5	1.9	3.6	4.1	4.8	5.5	4.2	3.0
Japan	1.8	2.3	2.0	0.4	-0.2	0.5	2.3	3.1	3.3	1.6
West Germany	3.2	2.4	2.2	-0.1	0.2	1.3	2.8	2.7	3.5	4.0
France	9.6	7.4	5.8	2.7	3.1	2.6	3.7	3.4	3.2	2.4
United Kingdom	4.5	5.0	6.0	3.4	4.2	4.9	7.8	9.5	5.8	3.7
Italy	14.7	1.8	9.2	5.8	4.8	5.0	6.3	6.5	6.3	5.2
Canada	5.9	4.3	4.0	4.2	4.3	4.0	5.0	4.8	5.6	1.5
Seven major countries	4.1	4.3	3.8	1.9	2.7	3.2	4.4	5.0	4.2	2.9
Growth of productivity										
United States	2.6	2.0	1.1	0.6	0.5	1.6	0.5	0.3	-0.3	1.5
Japan	1.0	3.7	4.2	1.8	3.1	4.4	2.8	2.7	2.1	0.2
West Germany	3.0	2.6	1.1	0.8	0.7	2.9	1.9	2.0	1.1	0.7
France	1.0	2.2	1.3	2.2	1.8	3.5	2.8	1.5	0.6	1.8
United Kingdom	3.7	0.1	2.7	3.8	2.5	1.0	-0.6	0.2	1.0	2.4
Italy	0.7	2.3	2.2	2.4	3.3	2.9	2.9	0.3	0.4	1.6
Canada	2.7	3.8	2.1	0.5	1.3	1.7	0.3	-1.2	0.1	1.7
Seven major countries	2.2	2.3	1.9	1.2	1.4	2.4	1.3	1.0	0.5	1.2

Note: Averages for the seven major countries are calculated by using weights based on the GNP/GDP respective shares in 1982.

SOURCE: DEPARTMENT OF FINANCE, ECONOMIC AND FISCAL REFERENCE TABLES, AUGUST 1993, TABLE 94.

policy-makers from unemployment to inflation. In recent years, structural unemployment, which refers to jobs lost due to changes in the structure of the economy (e.g., increasing automation, outdated skills), has been an important contributor to overall unemployment rates.[7]

Canadian expenditure and revenue trends demonstrate that Canada is slightly above the averages of the G7 countries but in the middle range of all the OECD countries, which include North America, Western Europe (including Scandinavia), Australia, New Zealand, and Japan. There are considerable variances in government expenditure and revenue levels across countries. Table 4.2 shows the share of total government revenues and expenditures as a percentage of GDP in the G7 countries from 1983 to 1992. In 1983, the level of revenues relative to GDP ranged from a low of 29.6 percent in Japan to a high of 48.5 percent in France. By 1992, Japan and the United States exhibited the lowest government share of revenues at 33.7 and 33.6 percent respectively, while France had the highest level at 48.3 percent of GDP. Canada has moved from 40 to 44.8 percent in government revenue share over this period.

The same extremes among the G7 countries are reflected in government expenditures. Japan is again at the low end of the scale, with expenditures at 33.2 percent in 1983 and 31.9 percent in 1992. This contrasts with France's expenditure share of almost 52 percent in 1983. In 1992, Italy's and France's government expenditures as a share of GDP stood at 53.9 and 52.2 percent respectively. Sweden, a non-G7 country well known for its high level of government expenditures (57 percent in the late 1980s) also had the highest level of government revenues (64 percent)—a decline, however, from the early 1980s and part of an overall trend in the OECD countries to slow the growth in government expenditures. The Canadian government share of expenditure relative to GDP is in the higher range of the G7 countries at 51.4 percent in 1992 compared with 38.4 percent for the United States, 44.1 percent for the United Kingdom, and 53.9 percent for Italy. For all countries over this period, revenues lagged behind expenditures. While the 1970–74 average shows a balance between revenues and expenditures, governments increasingly became net borrowers, and budget deficits became the norm by the early 1980s.

Several other significant changes in the public-sector activity of the OECD countries (including Canada) occurred in the period from the 1960s to the 1980s. First, there was a shift from defence and public administration to welfare-state expenditures on education, health, and income maintenance. With the onset of expenditure restraint in the 1980s, several common patterns emerged. As interest rates climbed, debt costs placed upward pressure on the expenditure ratio in most countries while social-security transfers contributed to a rise in government expenditures. Public consumption, mainly the public-sector wage bill, increased as a share of GDP in most of the countries listed in Table 4.2 (except Japan and

TABLE 4.2 Total Government Revenue as a Percentage of GNP/GDP

	1970–74	1975–81	1983	1984	1985	1986	1987	1988	1989	1990	1991	1992
United States	30.9	31.6	32.4	32.4	33.1	33.4	34.0	33.5	34.0	33.9	33.9	33.6
Japan	22.0	25.4	29.6	30.3	30.8	31.2	32.9	33.3	33.5	34.7	34.1	33.7
West Germany	41.1	45.1	46.0	46.2	46.5	45.8	45.5	44.8	45.6	43.9	NA	NA
France	39.4	44.0	48.5	49.5	49.6	48.9	49.3	48.6	48.1	48.5	48.7	48.3
United Kingdom	37.6	39.1	41.4	41.2	41.2	40.1	39.4	39.0	38.5	38.6	37.9	37.4
Italy	29.2	31.9	38.5	38.2	38.9	39.6	39.8	40.1	42.0	42.8	44.0	44.4
Canada	36.6	37.6	40.0	40.0	40.0	40.7	41.1	41.4	41.6	43.1	44.2	44.8
Weighted Average	31.7	33.7	36.0	36.2	36.6	36.7	37.3	37.0	37.4	37.6	NA	NA

Total Government Expenditures as a Percentage of GNP/GDP

	1970–74	1975–81	1983	1984	1985	1986	1987	1988	1989	1990	1991	1992
United States	31.5	32.9	36.5	35.3	36.2	36.8	36.5	35.5	35.5	36.3	37.3	38.4
Japan	21.3	29.5	33.2	32.4	31.7	32.1	32.4	31.8	31.0	31.8	31.1	31.9
West Germany	41.2	48.4	48.6	48.1	47.7	47.1	47.4	47.0	45.5	45.9	NA	NA
France	38.8	45.3	51.7	52.2	52.4	51.6	51.1	50.2	49.4	50.0	50.8	52.2
United Kingdom	38.3	42.8	44.7	45.2	44.0	42.5	40.7	38.0	37.6	39.9	40.8	44.1
Italy	36.1	42.2	49.2	49.8	51.4	51.3	50.8	50.8	51.9	53.7	54.2	53.9
Canada	35.9	39.9	46.9	46.5	46.8	46.1	44.9	43.9	44.5	47.3	50.5	51.4
Weighted Average	32.3	36.5	40.3	39.7	40.0	40.1	39.7	38.9	38.5	39.6	NA	NA

SOURCE: DEPARTMENT OF FINANCE, ECONOMIC AND FISCAL REFERENCE TABLES, AUGUST 1993, TABLE 99.

Germany), with only a minimal rise in Canada (less than in the United States). However, public-sector wages grew very little in real terms in most countries; the OECD suggests that public-sector wages for a wide range of countries, with the exception of the United States, have declined relative to the private sector. Employment growth in the public sector has also slowed substantially, and increasingly public-sector employment is characterized by precarious part-time positions and lower wage rates. As a long-term strategy, however, these substandard employment conditions may not be viable since they are likely to undermine the quality of services; an erosion in public-service quality reduces consumer willingness to pay for these services, which in turn leads to more cost pressures and a further reduction in wages.

Second, by 1990, government consumption in Canada, the United Kingdom, and the United States—in contrast to most European nations—was greater than transfer payments to individuals. This meant that spending on the goods, services, and labour consumed by government to carry out its various programs and activities (e.g., health care, police protection, and day care) surpassed transfers, which include subsidies, social security, welfare payments, and pensions. Some observers have pointed out that this particular policy mix has fuelled public resentment about the growth of government. Comparative studies confirm that welfare states that rely heavily on services rather than transfers open themselves up to a greater degree of public criticism about bureaucracy and public-sector wage demands.[8] If this is the case, Canada's public sector may garner relatively more negative reaction given that it is relatively generous in providing services such as health care and education, while less so in providing resources for programs that involve direct transfer payments to individuals.

Third, the move to privatize and deregulate the public sector gained momentum in many OECD countries, including Canada, in the 1980s. Canada has a long public-enterprise tradition that predates Confederation, reflecting activities (such as building the transcontinental railway) that were initially considered beyond the capacity of the private sector because of the scale and costs involved. The conversion of public enterprises to private ownership or the contracting-out of services to private firms reflected an ideological belief on the part of the Mulroney government that the market should be dominant. While Canada's limited yet important legacy of a public-enterprise culture, which found support in public opinion, slowed the government's privatization efforts, the Tories nonetheless proceeded with a modest program of privatization that included Air Canada, Teleglobe Canada, and CNCP Telecommunications.

GOVERNMENT SPENDING TRENDS IN CANADA

BY LEVEL OF GOVERNMENT

In order to fully understand the nature of government spending, it is necessary to disaggregate total government expenditures into federal, provincial, and local categories. Table 4.3 lists the expenditures of Canadian governments from 1951 to 1991 as a proportion of GDP.

Roughly three-fifths of the total increase in spending of subnational governments from 1961 to 1987 involved the direct purchase of goods and services, as opposed to transfer payments to persons. The growth in spending at the subnational levels of government is a reflection of the distribution of constitutional fields of governmental jurisdiction that were most significant to the KWS—education, health care, and social services. The provinces and municipalities also provided a disproportionate share of the personnel needed to deliver KWS services because these subnational levels of government became increasingly important as suppliers of new programs and services. The 1960s witnessed the introduction of the Canada and Quebec pension plans, national medicare, the Canada Assistance Plan (which provided an umbrella for various social-assistance programs), the progressive expansion of unemployment insurance and workers' compensation, and large public expenditures on schools, universities, and colleges.

This spending pattern fuelled a growing resentment on the part of the Trudeau governments of the 1970s. They had committed themselves to contributing to the cost of provincial social programs, but had received little political credit in the eyes of the electorate. Increasingly, the growth of government in the social field led to intergovernmental friction concerning federal intrusions into the provincial domain and discrepancies among provinces in their ability to provide services to their citizens. These concerns led to a complex set of federal–provincial fiscal agreements that are currently being renegotiated. Fiscal federalism promises to be one of the most controversial areas of federal–provincial relations in the mid-1990s as deficit pressures encourage the federal government to continue its retreat from many shared-cost arrangements.

Before a discussion of what is at stake in the next few years of federal–provincial fiscal relations can take place, a more detailed assessment of federal social-spending trends over the Conservatives' two mandates is warranted because: (1) social spending and government waste were seen as the major source of deficits, and (2) social policy has been transformed "by stealth,"[9] gradually undermining the egalitarian goals of the welfare state and with it the bonds of nationhood and citizenship. Combined with the FTA and NAFTA, these factors will have long-term implications for the

TABLE 4.3 **Expenditure as a Percent of GDP at Market Prices: All Levels of Government, 1951–1992**

	Current Expenditures on Goods and Services	Transfer Payments to Persons	Interest on the Public Debt	Transfers to Other Levels of Government	Total Current Expenditure
All levels of government					
1951	12.6%	4.6%	2.7%	—	23.5%
1961	15.1%	6.7%	2.9%	—	29.8%
1971	18.7%	8.5%	8.3%	—	36.2%
1976	19.3%	9.8%	4.1%	—	38.9%
1981	19.3%	9.8%	6.3%	—	41.3%
1986	19.8%	12.2%	8.5%	—	46.1%
1991	21.1%	14.5%	9.7%	—	50.5%
1992	21.5%	15.5%	9.4%	—	51.4%
Federal government					
1951	7.3%	2.6%	2.2%	1.2%	14.3%
1961	6.3%	4.9%	1.9%	2.8%	17.6%
1971	5.1%	4.8%	2.0%	4.4%	17.9%
1976	4.9%	5.8%	2.3%	4.3%	19.6%
1981	4.6%	5.2%	3.9%	4.0%	20.3%
1986	4.7%	6.6%	5.2%	4.2%	22.8%
1991	4.6%	7.4%	6.2%	4.1%	24.2%
1992	4.5%	7.7%	5.7%	4.3%	23.8%
Provincial government					
1951	2.1%	1.9%	0.4%	0.9%	6.3%
1961	2.6%	1.6%	0.4%	3.7%	9.7%
1971	4.9%	3.2%	0.9%	6.2%	17.0%
1976	5.5%	3.3%	1.2%	6.4%	18.1%
1981	6.1%	3.5%	1.7%	6.3%	19.5%
1986	6.3%	4.0%	2.6%	6.7%	21.7%
1991	6.9%	4.6%	2.9%	7.2%	23.3%
1992	7.1%	4.9%	3.1%	7.3%	24.2%
Local government					
1951	3.2%	0.1%	0.2%	0.1%	4.9%
1961	4.7%	0.2%	0.5%	0.1%	7.2%
1971	6.3%	0.3%	0.7%	0.1%	9.1%
1976	6.3%	0.2%	0.6%	0.0%	8.5%
1981	5.9%	0.1%	0.6%	0.1%	8.0%
1986	5.8%	0.2%	0.6%	0.0%	7.8%
1991	6.4%	0.4%	0.6%	0.0%	8.6%
1992	6.7%	0.5%	0.6%	0.0%	9.0%

SOURCE: DEPARTMENT OF FINANCE, ECONOMIC AND FISCAL REFERENCE TABLES, AUGUST 1993, TABLES 50, 52, AND 54.

viability of the Canadian economy and the Canadian polity. The fact that most Canadians are unaware of the extent to which the universality and long-term viability of many social policies have been weakened has implications for both the framework of Canadian parliamentary democracy and future responses to restructuring the economy. For example, in 1992, Ottawa cancelled the family allowance program, arguing against a universal system and supporting a targeted program of family assistance. The problem with targeted programs is that they are difficult to sustain because political support for them comes only from the small segment of the population that receives them; a universal program that benefits all members of society has a much stronger foundation of support. A comparative analysis of targeted versus universal programs suggests that the former tend to result in more unequal societies marked by greater poverty.[10]

IS GOVERNMENT SPENDING THE CULPRIT?

To what extent is social policy spending responsible for the increasing federal government deficits? First, it is important to highlight the fact that modern governments have grown for many reasons other than the emergence of the KWS. To illustrate, in the United States much of the increase in government deficits has been due to large military expenditures. As well, many services are not efficiently provided for on a pure market basis. In Canada, through the provision of public health care, governments reduce the costs to firms of private health insurance and ensure a healthy labour force. For example, the publicly run Canadian health-care system is more efficient and uses less resources than its American counterpart, which is privately financed and run. This is not to deny that there are no public services that are inefficient, but simply that privatizing these services is not the solution. In the American case, the higher administrative costs of a private system run by some 1,500 insurance companies result in per capita spending on health care of $2,354 U.S. compared to $1,683 U.S. in Canada. The policy challenge lies in providing high-quality, efficient services that benefit all income groups equally.

Canadian public enterprises and services have historically absorbed many of the expenses that private corporations did not wish to pay given the high start-up costs of infrastructural projects, such as the CPR and James Bay, or that otherwise would have to be paid by the private sector as part of its costs of production. In many instances, state spending on economic infrastructure (highways, mass transit, airports, electrical, gas, and water utilities, and the like) allows private companies to produce and market their goods efficiently. In a sense, the state provided enormous amounts of the risk capital that was needed for these investments, which in turn benefited the private sector through the provision of efficient transportation and cheaper power. A recent American study confirms the importance of government investment in infrastructure for economic growth. The study points to the slowdown in public capital growth as contributing significantly to the slowdown in that country's private productivity growth.[11] Several recent comparative public policy studies have found further evidence that the public sector may actually contribute to economic growth.[12]

In addition to establishing the economic infrastructure required for the private sector, there are a number of other necessary functions performed by the public sector that have contributed to increased spending over time. Government absorbs the costs of creating a well-educated and technically trained labour force, and although business bears part of the taxation and spending burden, the incremental cost to employers is frequently outweighed by the benefits of superior labour-force productivity.

The unique nature of Canadian economic development has also prescribed a vital role for the public sector. Canada is highly trade-dependent and has a weak manufacturing sector that is very reliant on American capital and technology. Empirical evidence, based on cross-national studies, suggests a strong relationship between the "openness" of an economy (measured by the proportion of GDP devoted to exports) and government spending. In open economies such as Canada's, changes in the international economy may lead to sudden adjustments in employment, production, and consumption, and this translates into a greater likelihood of government compensating the affected sectors, firms, and individuals.

A number of more general socioeconomic factors can also be identified as contributing to public expenditure growth. The growth in population and resulting demographic changes have been important determinants of public spending levels in all of the OECD countries, not just Canada. In particular, health care, education, and pension programs have simply expanded linearly with the size and age of the population. Aside from such natural growth, increases in service and benefit levels have also been a contributing factor. The degree to which coverage and benefit levels continue to expand will, aside from economic resources, depend on political factors such as the strength of organized labour and other social movements concerned with improvement in the standard of living of the working population, and on the extent to which the financing of social expenditures is centralized. In political systems where collective bargaining and the allocation of resources are relatively centralized (e.g., Austria and Sweden), social program coverage tends to be more generous and extensive.

Some have argued that government spending will increase over time because the demand for public expenditures rises with upward movement in real personal disposable income. Once basic needs are met, the argument goes, there will be an increase in public demand for "leisure" services (e.g., parks and cultural facilities) that require government spending. Inflation can also be identified as an influence on government spending levels. For example, if current dollars are "deflated" to take into account price increases, then the "real" rate of government expenditure growth declines significantly.

Finally, some analysts attribute the rise in public expenditures, and the resulting tax increases needed to pay for them, to the expansionary tendencies of the bureaucracy and the "empire-building" of individual bureaucrats. Such "public choice" theorists apply an abstract version of consumer and firm behaviour to voters, government, and political representatives (the political market) by arguing that political actors, much like economic actors, are guided by self-interest. This leads public choice theorists to conclude that, from the perspective of public budgeting, public servants' goals are related to maximizing the size of their budgets rather than to pursuing efficiency.[13]

What has happened to social spending in the last few years? Over the last decade, social spending has been constrained, frozen, or reduced as part of a broader neoconservative approach to public-sector management. Overall levels of social spending did not increase significantly from 1984 to 1991, and in fact decreased slightly in real terms from 1987–88 and 1990–91. As James Rice and Michael Prince note:

> *In relation to Canada's overall economic activity as measured by the gross domestic product (GDP), federal social spending rose in the early 1980s due to the 1981–82 recession, peaked in 1983–84 at 12.3 percent of GDP, then—over the Mulroney years—declined from 12.1 percent in 1984–85 to 10.7 percent in 1990–91, indicating social spending was growing more slowly than the Canadian economy.*[14]

The most significant change in the structure of federal social spending has actually occurred in the area of transfers to provincial welfare systems.

FEDERAL TRANSFERS TO OTHER LEVELS OF GOVERNMENT

Intergovernmental transfers serve several needs in a country like Canada with distinct levels of government and responsibility. First, transfers are the main mechanism for keeping the revenues and expenditures of each level of government approximately equal (vertical fiscal balance). As Richard Bird observes, "Central governments usually have greater revenue-raising capacity than subnational governments both because it is easier for them to tax mobile factors and for historical reasons such as the extreme centralization of revenue-raising in Canada during the Second World War."[15] Because of a continuing mismatch in revenues and expenditures between the different levels of government, intergovernmental transfers play an important role in balancing Canadian federalism.

Second, achieving horizontal fiscal balance among the provinces is an even more difficult and controversial policy objective. Equalization payments are unconditional grants given to the provinces by the federal government, and calculated on the basis of each province's ability to raise revenues. Equalization payments are currently about $8 billion, and their impact on provinces with weak fiscal capacities is significant. Equalization payments are a key part of Canadian fiscal federalism and are critical for reducing disparities among provinces and inequalities in income among individuals.

The two decades following the Second World War saw a proliferation of shared-cost programs in which Ottawa paid for half of the cost of provincially administered programs, provided that the minimal national standards were observed. Programs in such areas as health care and post-secondary education were established to ensure a fairly equal provision of services between the "have" and "have-not" provinces. In 1977, however, a new arrangement known as Established Programs Financing (EPF) replaced the old cost-sharing arrangements for health insurance and post-secondary education. This signalled the beginning of a diminished political and financial role for the federal government in funding these services.

Since 1984, the most notable change in federal social spending has been the 6.1 percentage point decline in transfers for social expenditures to other levels of government, which reflects the drive to a more decentralized system of fiscal federalism. Since the 1990 federal budget, the level of federal transfers to the provinces has been a source of friction and political confrontation due to Ottawa's decision to freeze EPF transfers, which support health care and postsecondary education, and to limit the Canada Assistance Plan (CAP) increases to 5 percent a year in the three "richest" provinces—Ontario, Alberta, and British Columbia. CAP (currently about $7 billion) is the social safety net of last resort, providing the federal share of welfare and social assistance to single-parent families, the unemployed, and people with disabilities. Currently, provincial governments like Ontario are lobbying hard against the freezes, which were instituted by Mulroney's Conservative government and extended by the new Liberal government. Ontario argues that approximately $20 billion has been lost over the last decade due to federal cuts in health, education, and welfare payments, $4.9 billion of which was offloaded since the New Democrats came to power in 1990.[16]

CAP and equalization arrangements will have to be renegotiated in the spring of 1994, and EPF in the spring of 1995. The outcome of these negotiations will have significant implications for Canadian federalism and for the future security of Canada's social programs. An overhaul of the current system is warranted given the imbalance between the growing costs of provincial program responsibilities (and the provinces' increasing inability to pay) and the diminishing contribution of the federal government as a result of its offloading policies.

As we have seen, Canada's level of social spending relative to that of the OECD countries is both fairly moderate and fairly stable. Michael Butler effectively sums up the situation:

> [I]f the charge—that excessively escalating program expenditures are the cause of Canada's fiscal predicament—does not withstand serious analysis, the basic question remains: what has impelled the federal government to take steps to restrict its transfers to provinces, a move which it must have known would greatly aggravate relations with the provinces and destabilize the federal-provincial fiscal balance?[17]

The answer lies in the nonprogram component of federal government spending—debt servicing.

THE DEFICIT, THE DEBT, AND SHRINKING REVENUES

The dramatic growth of debt-servicing costs has put considerable fiscal pressure on the federal government. In part, this trend reflects the revenue cuts initiated by the federal government in the 1970s and continued well into the 1980s. Also, since 1982, high interest rates have contributed to the rapid growth in public debt charges. Increasing interest costs were partly a reflection of the inability of federal policy-makers to intervene in international interest rates, especially those of the United States. The maintenance of high interest rates is one of the strategies that the Bank of Canada uses to keep inflation under control. However, higher interest rates have become a growing burden on government finances, absorbing a rising share of government budgets. By 1992, interest payments on the public debt took up some 30-odd cents of every expenditure dollar, with the total debt at about $460 billion.

Irwin Gillespie has referred to five "surges" or "waves" of debt creation in Canada, from Confederation to the present period.[18] The fifth wave of debt creation began in the mid-1970s; net debt as a percentage of GDP increased from 19.4 percent in 1975–76 to 62.6 percent in 1991–92. While most analysts apportion some of the blame to the 1981–82 recession, a number of tax policy changes originating from the 1970s, rather than federal government spending, are singled out as the key factors for rising deficits. These tax policy changes include the reduction in effective corporate income tax rates and the proliferation of tax expenditures.

Generally, the deficit is divided by observers into its structural and cyclical components. The term "structural deficit" refers to the deficit that would prevail if income corresponded to full employment, with full-employment tax revenue being collected. Cyclical expenditures are related to upswings or downswings in the level of economic activity. With the onset of a major recession in 1981, the cyclical component of the deficit rose dramatically. Falling incomes, high unemployment, and reduced trade all meant a loss of government revenues and increased government expenditures in social-welfare areas, especially unemployment insurance. This was compounded by historically high interest rates (thus, high debt-servicing costs) and a drop in petroleum revenues because of a decline in world prices. As table 4.4 illustrates, there was a significant jump in the cyclically adjusted deficit from 1981 to 1985. Explanations of the increase in the underlying structural or actual deficit must take into account the evolution of the revenue system over this period of time. There are a number of tax measures that to varying degrees can be blamed for revenue shortfalls. The partial indexation of the personal income tax system in 1974 resulted in a loss of federal revenues relative to GNP because indexed exemptions and tax brackets meant that the government could not capture income gains if they were attributable to inflation. Revenue decisions such as the introduction of a new lifetime capital gains deduction in 1984 and increased RRSP limits continued to weaken the federal government's revenue base in the 1980s and 1990s.

TABLE 4.4 **Actual and Cyclically Adjusted Federal Deficits as a Percentage of GDP, 1976–1992**

	Actual	Cyclically Adjusted
1976	1.7	1.8
1977	3.4	3.5
1978	4.5	4.5
1979	3.4	3.6
1980	3.4	3.3
1981	2.1	2.2
1982	5.4	4.1
1983	6.2	5.1
1984	6.8	6.5
1985	6.6	6.8
1986	4.7	4.9
1987	3.8	4.2
1988	3.2	3.9
1989	3.3	3.8
1990	3.8	3.7
1991	4.4	3.4
1992	3.7	2.5

SOURCE: DEPARTMENT OF FINANCE, ECONOMIC AND FISCAL REFERENCE TABLES, AUGUST 1993, TABLE 60.1.

A series of tax breaks or tax "expenditures" for individuals and corporate taxpayers have been singled out as a particularly significant drain on potential federal revenues. Tax breaks are in effect expenditures made by the government when it allows someone not to pay taxes that he or she would otherwise have to pay; it is not like a subsidy, which is a direct cash transfer. Rather, government gives up revenue and, in this sense, spends it. Tax deferrals were an additional way for corporations to reduce their tax burdens. Tax deferrals or credits refer to situations where government allows companies to deduct investment in plants, equipment, research, development, and exploration at a faster rate, thereby reducing profit levels for taxation purposes. Even when a tax break is deliberate government policy (e.g., small-business deductions and reduced rates for specified sectors), most of the debate over the measure is restricted to the narrow community of tax experts and their clients, businesspeople and investors. In addition to the hidden nature of tax expenditures, there is also the question of whom they benefit.

Allan Maslove, in a detailed 1979 study, concluded that the benefits of tax breaks received by upper-income Canadians were roughly 100 times greater than those received by low-income Canadians.[19] Such disparities have largely been kept out of the realm of public debate. Successive federal governments since the 1970s have limited direct spending on federal programs and Crown corporations, but little has been done to restrain tax expenditures. While government spending grew by 30 percent between 1976 and 1979, tax expenditures grew by 42 percent over the same period. By the late 1980s, tax expenditures were reported to cost the federal treasury at least $30 billion per year, a figure close to the size of the annual deficit. By using tax expenditures, governments could give the appearance of being fiscally responsible while still offering fiscal advantages to specific industries and individuals. At a time when concerns about "big government" were at the forefront of politicians' consciousness, tax expenditures were an acceptable form of hidden spending. In recent years, the Department of Finance has responded to demands that more careful scrutiny of tax-expenditure measures take place, and Ontario has started to introduce a policy-making framework around the budget process that could lead to more transparent tax expenditure decision-making.[20]

Finally, as Table 4.5 illustrates, there has been a significant reduction in the corporate tax contribution to government revenues since 1951. The resulting shift of the tax burden to individual Canadians may be one factor contributing to public resentment about the size and scope of government, since individual taxpayers are responsible for an increasing share of the burden of government financing. In several instances, Canada's lowering of corporate taxes was in response to a lowering of rates in the United States and general increased global competitiveness in manufacturing and production.

TABLE 4.5 Revenue as a Percentage of GDP at Market Prices: All Levels of Government, 1951–1992

All levels		Direct Taxes (Persons)	Direct Taxes (Corporations)	Indirect Taxes	Investment Income	Transfers from Other Levels of Government	Total Revenues
	1951	5.7%	6.4%	12.0%	1.3%	—	27.2%
	1961	7.2%	4.0%	12.5%	1.8%	—	27.7%
	1971	13.4%	3.4%	13.3%	2.9%	—	36.2%
	1976	14.4%	3.6%	12.5%	3.7%	—	37.1%
	1981	14.8%	3.6%	12.9%	5.1%	—	39.8%
	1986	16.8%	2.9%	12.7%	4.7%	—	40.7%
	1991	20.2%	2.1%	14.0%	4.9%	—	44.2%
	1992	20.4%	2.1%	14.3%	4.9%	—	44.8%
Federal							
	1951	5.2%	5.6%	6.7%	0.6%	—	18.7%
	1961	6.4%	3.3%	5.4%	0.9%	—	16.6%
	1971	8.5%	2.5%	4.6%	1.5%	—	17.8%
	1976	9.1%	2.6%	4.4%	1.3%	—	17.9%
	1981	8.2%	2.6%	5.3%	1.5%	—	18.3%
	1986	9.7%	2.0%	4.2%	1.6%	—	18.1%
	1991	11.3%	1.5%	4.5%	1.9%	—	19.6%
	1992	11.7%	1.4%	4.6%	1.9%	—	20.0%
Provincial							
	1951	0.5%	0.8%	2.6%	0.5%	1.2%	6.3%
	1961	0.8%	0.7%	3.1%	0.7%	2.7%	9.0%
	1971	3.7%	0.9%	4.7%	1.2%	4.4%	16.5%
	1976	4.1%	1.0%	4.6%	2.2%	4.2%	17.4%
	1981	5.5%	1.0%	4.3%	3.3%	3.9%	19.2%
	1986	5.9%	0.8%	5.2%	2.8%	4.1%	20.1%
	1991	7.3%	0.7%	5.6%	2.7%	3.9%	21.1%
	1992	7.1%	0.6%	5.7%	2.7%	4.2%	21.2%
Local							
	1951	—	—	2.7%	0.1%	0.9%	4.2%
	1961	—	—	4.0%	0.1%	2.1%	6.8%
	1971	—	—	4.0%	0.2%	3.7%	8.4%
	1976	—	—	3.5%	0.2%	3.7%	7.9%
	1981	—	—	3.3%	0.3%	3.7%	7.9%
	1986	—	—	3.3%	0.3%	3.7%	7.9%
	1991	—	—	3.9%	0.3%	4.0%	8.8%
	1992	—	—	4.0%	0.3%	4.2%	9.2%

SOURCE: DEPARTMENT OF FINANCE, ECONOMIC AND FISCAL REFERENCE TABLES, AUGUST 1993, TABLES 51, 53, AND 55.

Recent changes on the sales-tax side, notably the introduction of the Goods and Services Tax (GST), have not proven to be the steady and expanding source of government revenue as was first foreseen. In its final year of operation, the Manufacturers' Sales Tax (MST) brought in $18.5 billion; its replacement, the GST, produced $14.8 billion in 1992. Increased activity in the underground economy (partly attributable to avoidance of the GST) is estimated in the hundreds of millions of dollars, although accurate estimates are, for obvious reasons, difficult to obtain.

In the 1960s, discussions about taxation were motivated largely by the search for equity, fairness, and the redistribution of income. The most eloquent expression of these sentiments appeared in the 1967 Report of the Royal Commission on Taxation (the Carter Commission), which pressed for the elimination of tax breaks and special privileges. In the 1980s, tax reform regained a high public profile and became a key vehicle in Progressive Conservative efforts to control government spending by limiting the revenue side. In effect, the new spate of tax reforms made it increasingly difficult to finance existing programs because the burden of taxes has been shifted even more onto the middle and lower classes. There is, however, a limit to the amount of additional revenue that can be squeezed out of middle- and lower-income taxpayers. This holds important implications for social programs and the welfare state. With ballooning deficits and increasing fiscal restraint, a retreat from universal social programs will be the only "choice" open to a fiscally responsible government. The additional impetus of the FTA and NAFTA to harmonize tax rates and provision of benefits with the those in the United States will intensify pressures to cut back in the public sector in the 1990s.

In sum, the chronic deficits of the fifth wave can be largely attributed to changes on the revenue rather than the spending side. In addition, escalating debt-servicing costs had the effect of funnelling any revenue generated by new tax measures away from debt reduction.

CONCLUSION

As we approach the midway mark in the 1990s, many of the objectives of the neoliberal policy agenda have been put in place. The promise of the FTA and NAFTA to create "a level playing field" raises questions about the viability of differential tax levels across borders. In the face of competition with the United States and Mexico for investment in production and jobs, Canadians will be told that they have little choice except to follow the lead of their trade partners. The imperatives of the American level playing field will likely mean that the tax burden will continue to be shifted away from corporations. This means additional taxes for the individual taxpayer and/or drastic cutbacks in services. Canadians in the 1990s may be paying more taxes for fewer government services and transfers. The threat to our government's ability to tax is a threat to Canada's historically generous social welfare and regional assistance programs.

Free trade, as envisioned by the Macdonald Commission and the Mulroney government, harmonizes perfectly with the neoliberal political agenda and strategy for industrial restructuring, one that incorporates a market-driven approach to economic growth, continental rationalization, government cutbacks in social services, reduced rights for workers, and a diminished role for the state in the economy. Although the role of the Canadian state has not been curtailed, its focus has shifted from domestic policies of welfare, equality, and employment toward adapting the domestic economy to the exigencies of a global economy. Thus far, the federal government has pursued a strategy of adjustment that facilitates capital mobility through, on the one hand, a reduction in fiscal and regulatory burdens on industry, and, on the other hand, a lowering of expectations about social welfare, labour, and environmental standards.

From a domestic viewpoint, this strategy involves promoting the politics of scarcity: the belief that we can no longer afford the welfare state as it is a costly drain on our scarce resources. In an internationally competitive environment, the argument goes, we have no choice but to divest ourselves of these costs. In particular, this means decreasing the public debt load through cuts in KWS services and rolling back some of the social egalitarian gains (e.g., income redistribution, equal access to education and health services) that accompanied the rise of the welfare state. It also meant less funding for many of the transfers that were shared-cost programs between the provinces and the federal government. From the vantage point of debt reduction, this neoliberal strategy has not been effective. Debts and deficits are at an all-time high while, on a personal level, the costs of this strategy have manifested themselves in greater polarizations of income, market opportunities, and economic hardship.

Ironically, just at a time when governments are concertedly trying to follow their ideology and withdraw from the market, the market, propelled by the forces of international economic restructuring, is in turn making new and more strident demands. In the end, the 1990s may come to be characterized not by less government but by increased favouritism for the wealthy and for large corporations that benefit from market-oriented government. A continuation of the purely political solution of cuts and deregulation in the 1990s will likely contribute to a downward spiral of political conflict and economic hardship. The challenge for Canadians is to pursue a new strategy, one rooted in the productive potential of the new economy and the new political spaces within which democratic control over the regulation of a restructured economy can take place.

NOTES

1. Monetarists are now subsumed within the more general school of neoliberalism. The neoliberal umbrella includes a wide range of perspectives, all of which argue for the full liberation of the market from the fetters of almost all forms of government intervention. Neoliberals consistently argue that the growth of welfare-state expenditures necessitates higher rates of taxation, which in turn discourages productive investment and overall economic well-being. See Fred Block, "Rethinking the Political Economy of the Welfare State," in *The Mean Season: The Attack on the Welfare State* (New York: Pantheon, 1987), for a critical evaluation of this position. The earlier debates that pitted supporters of a proactive government against advocates of a particular type of inactive government have already been analyzed extensively. See Cy Gonick, *The Great Economic Debate* (Toronto: James Lorimer, 1987).

2. Also, people did not see a direct connection between the taxes that they were paying to government and the services and benefits that flowed from this. The pooling of taxes and the ministerial allocation of these funds is increasingly being challenged by calls for citizen choice and greater transparency in government resource allocations and decision-making. Calls to "reinvent government" or pressures for "democratic administration" reflect the lack of control, accountability, and visibility of government spending for services and programs.

3. Michael Prince, *How Ottawa Spends, 1986–87: Tracking the Tories* (Toronto: Methuen, 1986), p. 10.

4. David Wolfe, "The Politics of the Deficit," in Bruce Doern, ed., *The Politics of Economic Policy* (Toronto: University of Toronto Press, 1985).

5. GDP measures total amount of employment-created production activity within a country, whereas GNP measures the total income created by all factors of production (including investment income of factors of production owned by Canadians abroad).

6. OECD, "Controlling Government Spending and Deficits." *OECD Economic Studies* no. 17 (Autumn 1991). Follow-up to earlier article in *OECD Economic Studies* no. 4 (Spring 1985).

7. OECD, *Employment Outlook*, 1993.

8. Keith Banting, "Images of the Modern State," in Keith Banting, ed., *State and Society: Canada, A Comparative Perspective* (Toronto: University of Toronto Press, 1986), p. 6.

9. The phrase "social policy by stealth" refers to a heavy reliance on technical amendments to taxes and transfers that camouflage regressive changes in the rhetoric of equity and escape media and public attention because of their complexity. See Grattan Gray, "Social Policy by Stealth," *Policy Options* 11, no. 2.

10. See Linda McQuaig, *The Wealthy Banker's Wife*, Toronto: Penguin, 1993.

11. Alan Blinder, "Are Crumbling Highways Giving Productivity a Flat?" *Business Week* (August 29, 1988). See also Samuel Bowles, David Gordon, and Thomas Weisskopf, *Beyond the Wasteland* (New York: Basic Books, 1983).

12. Hugh Moseley and Gunther Schmid, *Public Services and Competitiveness*. Berlin: Wissenschaftszentrum, FS I 92-5, 1992.

13. See Donald Savoie, *The Politics of Public Spending in Canada* (Toronto: University of Toronto Press, 1990), for a discussion of the applicability of public choice to the Canadian case and critiques of the public-choice approach

14. Social spending refers to transfers to persons, cash transfers to other levels of government, other major social transfers, and transfers to Canada Mortgage and Housing Corporation and the CBC. See James Rice and Michael Prince, "Lowering the Safety Net and Weakening the Bonds of Nationhood: Social Policy in the Mulroney Years," in Susan Phillips, ed., *How Ottawa Spends, 1993–94* (Carleton University Press, 1993), for a detailed discussion.

15. Richard Bird, "Federal–Provincial Fiscal Arrangements: Is There an Agenda for the 1990's?" in R. Watts and D. Brown, eds., *Canada: The State of the Federation* (Kingston: Queen's University, Institute of Intergovernmental Relations, 1990), p. 168.

16. Harriet DeKoven, "Federal Provincial Transfers: Which Way from Here?" in *Policy Options* 14, no. 10 (Dec. 1993).

17. Michael Butler, "The Current Predicament of Fiscal Federalism," in *Policy Options* 14, no. 10 (December 1993). (The entire issue is dedicated to fiscal federalism.)

18. Irwin Gillespie, *Tax, Borrow and Spend: Financing Federal Spending in Canada*, 1867–1990. (Ottawa: Carleton University Press, 1991). See chapter 10.

19. Alan Maslove, "The Other Side of Public Spending: Tax Expenditures in Canada," in G.B. Doern and A. Maslove, eds., *The Public Evaluation of Government Spending* (Toronto: Butterworths, 1979).

20. Evert Lindquist, "Improving the Scrutiny of Tax Expenditures in Ontario: Comparative Perspectives and Recommendations," in Allan Maslove, ed., *Taxing and Spending: Issues of Process* (Toronto: University of Toronto Press, 1994).

FURTHER READINGS

Cox, Robert. "The Global Political Economy and Social Choice." In Daniel Drache and Meric Gertler, eds., *The New Era of Global Competition*. Montreal and Kingston: McGill-Queen's University Press, 1991.

Fair Tax Commission. *Searching for Fairness*. Toronto: Government of Ontario, 1993.

Gillespie, Irwin. *Tax, Borrow and Spend: Financing Federal Spending in Canada, 1867–1990*. Ottawa: Carleton University Press, 1991.

McBride, Stephen, and John Shields. *Dismantling a Nation: Canada and the New World Order*. Halifax: Fernwood Publishing, 1993.

Schmid, Gunther. *Women and Structural Change in the 1990s*. Paris: Organization for Economic Co-operation and Development, 1993.

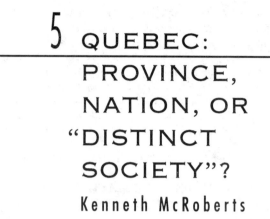

5 QUEBEC: PROVINCE, NATION, OR "DISTINCT SOCIETY"?

Kenneth McRoberts

In recent years, the term "distinct society" has assumed a central role in the continuing debate about Quebec and its place within Canada. For many English Canadians the term is anathema, as the collapse of both the Meech Lake and Charlottetown accords demonstrated (see Chapter 16). Yet, for most Quebec francophones, anything less than "distinct society" would not do justice to the reality of contemporary Quebec as they understand it. In fact, "distinct society" is only one among several different formulations of the same theme: *statut particulier, statut distinct, pas une province comme les autres,* and so on. There is, indeed, room for debate over the propriety and implications of inserting within the Constitution the statement that Quebec constitutes a distinct society. But it is difficult to dispute the underlying claim that the social and political reality of Quebec is that of a distinct society.

Clearly, Quebec is "distinct" in the sense of being "distinctive" or "different." Most obviously, it is different in terms of the first language of its residents: Quebec is the only province in which the population is primarily francophone. In 1991, 82 percent of its residents spoke French in the home. In New Brunswick, the province with the next largest francophone presence, only 31 percent spoke French at home. In Ontario, the figure was 4 percent; while in all other provinces it was 3 percent or less. In fact, Quebec contained 90 percent of Canadians who use French at home.[1] The specifically cultural distinctiveness of French Quebec may be less obvious than it was in the heyday of the Church when its leaders declared French Canadians to be a pre-eminently Catholic people with no less than a providential mission to preserve French, Catholic civilization. Now the French language is no longer *gardienne de la foi,* thanks to the pervasive secularization that Quebec society has experienced over the last 30 years. Nonetheless, subtle cultural differences clearly remain. Moreover, Quebec's political life is distinctive in a great many ways. In terms of political institutions, Quebec civil law is based on the Civil Code rather than on common law as in all the other provinces, and the symbols of the Crown have been markedly downplayed. Quebec provincial governments have pursued policies strikingly different from those of the other provinces. Concern with maintaining Quebec's cultural distinctiveness has led the provincial government to assume a much more important role than have the other provinces in selecting and settling immigrants and in supporting and regulating cultural activities such as book publishing and the distribution of films. Other areas of governmental activity also seem to reflect the impact of a distinctive balance of social forces. In labour relations, Quebec was the first government in North America to grant the right to strike in the public sector, and still remains the only government with an "anti-scab" law. Quebec pioneered in Canada the establishment of multifunctional public clinics, or Centres locaux de services communautaires, which seek to combine health and social services in a highly innovative fashion. During the 1960s, Quebec led the way among provincial governments in establishing a network of state enterprises; many observers claim that contemporary Quebec displays a distinctive form of collaboration among the state, capital, and labour.

Beyond differences such as these, Quebec is also distinct in terms of its separateness from the other provinces. This separateness is evident, for instance, in the sources of news and entertainment to which most of its population turns—French-language media that are institutionally separate from their English-Canadian counterparts. Even the public broadcasting system, ostensibly responsible to the Canadian Parliament and committed by statute to further national unity, has always been divided between the Montreal-based French-language system, Radio-Canada, and the Toronto-based English-language system, the CBC. But institutional separateness can be seen in areas other than culture. For instance, unlike their counterparts in the other provinces, most labour-union members belong to federations—the Confédération des syndicats nationaux (CSN) and the Corporation des enseignants du Québec—that are not affiliated with the Canadian Labour Congress (CLC). Relations between the CLC and the Fédération des travailleurs du Québec (FTQ), which groups together the Quebec union locals that are linked to the CLC, have always been difficult: FTQ leaders have regularly complained that the CLC's English-Canadian leadership cannot comprehend the distinctive concerns and needs of the FTQ's membership.

As one might expect, this manifest distinctiveness of Quebec society, and the sense of uniqueness associated with it, has encouraged distinct political loyalties. Quebec's political institutions command an allegiance among Quebec francophones that has no clear parallel in the other provinces. Underlying this allegiance is the simple fact that while the federal government is responsible to a predominantly anglophone electorate, the Quebec government is responsible to a predominantly francophone electorate. Thus, it has been commonly argued (and believed) in Quebec that only the Quebec government can be entrusted with the distinctive interests of Quebec francophones.

This argument, and the attachment to Quebec that it supported, has been most dramatically reflected in the movement to secure political sovereignty for Quebec. No other part of Canada has produced a serious movement calling for parity between it and the rest of Canada (as was proposed under sovereignty-association), let alone for independence. The contention that Quebec francophones must rely first and foremost on their provincial government has been a constant theme of Quebec politics since Confederation. Indeed, it was primarily because of French-Canadian fears that Confederation took a federal form, thereby affording Quebec French Canadians an autonomous government in which they could place their full confidence. Thus, one can trace back over the decades a strong commitment among Quebec's political activists to defend Quebec's provincial autonomy and to support the Quebec government over the federal government when the two are in conflict. By and large, Quebec provincial governments have themselves taken this stance.

In fact, so profound is this sense of Quebec's distinctiveness vis-à-vis the other provinces that by the 1970s the very term "province" had fallen into disuse. Some Quebec nationalists even claimed that it harkened back to the days of the British Empire when it was used to designate divisions within such other imperial holdings as India. But whatever its connotations, "province" served to equate Quebec with Canada's other territorial units when, at least in the eyes of nationalists, Quebec manifestly was not. Thus, the Quebec provincial government became "l'État du Québec." For the Quebec legislature, only the rather grandiloquent term "Assemblée nationale" would do.

This latter change goes to the nub of the matter: for many Quebec francophones, Quebec is not just a province with a difference, it's a *nation* and deserving of recognition as such. Since the early 19th century, nationalism has provided the set of assumptions through which francophone intellectuals have defined their collectivity and interpreted its historical fate. To be sure, over the decades, the dominant form of this nationalism has changed radically in terms not only of the geographical boundaries of the nation, but also of the nation's fundamental characteristics and goals. In part, these changes have reflected changes in the historical condition of the nation as a whole. But they also have reflected alterations in the balance of social forces within the nation, as members of different classes succeed in imposing their brand of nationalism—which invariably has reflected the particular preoccupations and ambitions of their class. If the central theme of this nationalism has been the necessity of maintaining cultural distinctiveness against British and English-Canadian threats, a recurrent theme has been the desire to break down the structures of anglophone economic and political domination. In each case, different nationalist leaderships have approached these themes in very different ways.

To understand why Quebec's society is distinctive, and how a "national consciousness" has developed out of this distinctiveness, we need to trace Quebec's historical development.

THE HISTORICAL ROOTS OF DISTINCTIVENESS AND NATIONALISM

Unlike the rest of Canada, Quebec society first emerged within the framework of the French Empire. This formative experience as the colony of New France established elements of distinctiveness that were to endure long after Quebec ceased to be a French colony. A common "Canadien" dialect was created out of the several French dialects that the colonists brought with them, predating the emergence of a national dialect in the mother country. The Catholic Church was afforded a privileged position within the formal institutions of the ancien régime, laying the basis for the central role that it was to play throughout so much of French Canada's history. And the Civil Code was entrenched within legal structures of the ancien régime. The colonists soon acquired a sense of collective identity (and destiny) as they faced the common challenges of a harsh climate and periodic threats both from Native peoples and the British colonies to the south. They began to call themselves "Canadiens" or "habitants" so as to distinguish themselves from the metropolitan French, as well as from English-speakers. In fact, they periodically expressed resentment against the metropolitan Frenchmen who were nominated to senior positions within the colony.

The colony was never the quasi-feudal society or theocracy that was later portrayed by historians. The bishop and his colleagues regularly had to spar with secular colonial authorities over policy. Commercial values and interests were actively pursued by some secular elites, who amassed considerable personal wealth through the fur trade. And the regularity with which the habitants challenged the authority of parish priests or resisted paying their tithes runs counter to images of a "priest-ridden" society. Thus, social tensions and conflict have marked French Canada from its beginning.

If Quebec emerged as part of the French Empire, it was a relatively unimportant and neglected one. In 1759, it fell under British control and lost forever its formal linkage with France. It was within the structures of the British Empire that the Canadiens would have to secure a future for themselves. If they were to maintain their distinctiveness, it would be on terms acceptable to the British authorities and to the English-speaking population that soon established itself within the colony. Moreover, it would be under the direction of a greatly shrunken Canadien leadership. With the Conquest, administrative and military structures fell into the hands of the British. And the replacement of France by England as Quebec's metropole ensured that the colony's trade would be controlled by the British rather than Canadiens. In short, all that remained by way of a viable leadership for the Canadiens was the Church and, to a lesser extent, the seigneurs—the two classes that had a strong interest in the Canadiens' defining their distinctiveness in the most traditional of terms.

Initially, British authorities were determined to destroy all forms of cultural distinctiveness for the Canadiens. The Royal Proclamation of 1763 was designed to do just that. However, the proclamation was not put into effect. With time, the colonial authorities determined that the imperial interest would be better served by winning the collaboration of the Canadien leadership and thus, presumably, of the Canadiens as a whole. Under the Quebec Act of 1774, the seigneurial system was re-established; the Church was once again empowered to collect tithes; Catholics were spared the need to renounce their faith to assume office; and French civil law was re-established. At the same time, out of deference to the Canadien clergy and seigneurs who feared a challenge of their own positions, a representative assembly was not created.

Ostensibly, the survival of Canadien society was assured. Yet, it was a particular *kind* of Canadien society that was so assured. In effect, the Quebec Act served to reinforce traditional structures and values within Canadien society. And it formalized a cultural division of labour that was to mark Quebec for the next two centuries. Canadiens could count upon being able to assume ecclesiastical and legal functions, at least to service the needs of the compatriots, but there was nothing to challenge the firm control over the colony's economic life that English-speakers had secured in the wake of the Conquest. Much of the history of the next two centuries, including the nationalist upsurge of the 1960s and 1970s, can be seen as a struggle by various groups to break French-Canadian society out of this mould—and out of the political and economic bonds that supported it— imposed by the British colonial regime in close collaboration with French-Canadian traditional elites.

It was in the early 19th century that French Canada's first nationalist movement took form. It was spawned by a new class of Canadiens, a petite bourgeoisie of liberal professionals and small merchants that coalesced in the legislative assembly that the Constitutional Act of 1791 had created (while at the same time dividing the British colony of Quebec in two). Within the new colony of Lower Canada, French Canadians were clearly preponderant, and even with an overrepresentation of anglophones in the assembly, the Canadiens still had a commanding majority. In part, the nationalism of this new Canadien petite bourgeoisie was a response to the continuing assimilationist projects of the colony's anglophone population. In part, it was a response to the English bourgeoisie's ambitious plans for development of the colonial economy; the Canadiens would not benefit directly from the projects even though they would have to assume part of the financial burden through taxation.

The petite bourgeoisie's nationalism also reflected its own class position. It was quite appropriate that this nationalist leadership should champion liberal political reforms and the rights of the representative assembly, given their own dominance of that assembly and relative exclusion from executive and administrative office within the colony. At the same time, the Canadien liberal professionals began to challenge clerical preeminence over the francophone population by sponsoring such projects as a secularized school system. Out of this protracted conflict emerged the "Patriote" movement, which championed an autonomous state for Quebec and, in 1837, staged an armed uprising to secure it. With overwhelming military superiority, the British authorities had no difficulty putting down the rebellion. For good measure, they had the vigorous support of the French-Canadian clergy, which had long been alarmed by some of the liberal notions that the Patriotes had been propagating.

With the defeat of the Rebellions of 1837, the more traditional forces within French-Canadian society, led by the Church, were able to secure a new ascendancy. The Church strengthened itself by importing priests from France (refugees from French liberalism), and by expanding the religious orders and educational institutions. In the process, a new, apolitical version of French-Canadian nationalism became hegemonic. In clerical hands, the essence of the French-Canadian nation became its Catholicism. National greatness was to lie in godliness and spirituality (best achieved in a rural setting) rather than in material accomplishments. For this, French Canadians were to rely on the institutions of the Church rather than on governments and politicians, corroded as they were by liberalism and corruption. By definition, within this worldview, anglophone dominance of Quebec's economic development was not a problem.

In the immediate aftermath of the rebellions, the very survival of French-Canadian society was placed in question by the British authorities. Under the Act of Union, inspired by the Durham Report, Lower Canada and Upper Canada were joined so as to encourage the assimilation of the troublesome Canadiens. However, French Canada survived yet another assimilationist threat as French-Canadian politicians from Canada East formed an alliance with English-Canadian reformers in Canada West and, on that basis, secured recognition of the French fact. In effect, duality became enshrined in the institutions of the United Canadas: French was made an official language along with English; hyphenated ministries were held by representatives of each of the two original colonies; and, to some extent, voting was based on a double-majority principle.

Eventually, this situation became unacceptable to many English Canadians, with the result that French Canadians in Quebec had to trade dualism for federalism. First, Canada West's population began to exceed Canada East's. In 1840, Canada East had been much more populous than Canada West; the two Canadas had been assigned an equal number of seats so as to prevent Canada East's dominance. By the 1860s, the residents of Canada West had become eager converts to "rep by pop." Second, the English-Canadian bourgeoisie found that its economic projects were being frustrated in the United Canadas assembly by French Canadians and their reformist allies. Thus, there ensued a campaign to join the several British colonies in a common union. There, French Canadians clearly would be in a minority and central political institutions would be dominated by English Canadians. To be acceptable to French Canadians, Confederation had to be based upon federalism, which would afford Quebec an autonomous state for certain purposes. That French Canadians could not entrust their distinctive interests to an English-Canadian majority was a central premise of Confederation.

Nonetheless, the notion of "distinctive interests" contained in the division of powers quite closely reflects the ascendancy of the Church within French-Canadian society. Along with the other provincial governments, Quebec was granted jurisdiction over matters that were central to its cultural survival (e.g., education) or that might affect the prerogatives of the Church and its institutions (e.g., health, welfare, and the solemnization of marriage). On the other hand, economic responsibilities were effectively lodged with the federal government along with exclusive access to the then primary source of government revenue—indirect taxes. In this sense, the terms of Confederation further formalized the cultural division of labour that underlay the Quebec Act of 1774. The same division of labour was reproduced within the federal government itself. In the cabinet, anglophones effectively monopolized the major economic portfolios. In the upper levels of the bureaucracy, francophones were seriously underrepresented.

THE ECONOMIC AND SOCIAL TRANSFORMATION OF QUEBEC: SEEDS OF POLITICAL CRISIS

By the turn of the century, Quebec was undergoing social changes that eventually would result in serious challenges to the political arrangements discussed above, and even to Confederation itself. Industrialization can be traced back as far as the 1870s. At that time, Montreal was producing as much iron and steel products as Toronto and Hamilton combined, and had a large number of manufacturing enterprises.[2] With the turn of the century, industrialization spread to other parts of Quebec. For its part, urbanization can be traced to the first part of this century. In fact, by 1921 half of Quebec's population as a whole was urban. The level of urbanization among francophones alone was not quite as high, but by 1931 it had reached 58 percent.

Until the 1960s, the full impact of these changes on Quebec's political life was delayed. Typically, industrialization entails an expansion of the role of the state to assist capital in its undertakings and to placate an expanded working class. And the social and economic problems of urban life usually raise demands for new government services. Moreover, one might well expect demands for state intervention to arise from the way in which English-Canadian and American capital dominated Quebec's industrialization. Not only were francophone enterprises marginal in industry (as they had been in commerce and finance), but to a large extent the growing francophone proletariat was employed by "foreigners."

Yet, especially when compared with the neighbouring province of Ontario, which was also being transformed through industrialization and urbanization, the economic and social role of the Quebec state remained limited. The provision of education and social services remained effectively under the control of the Church and its orders. Even the weakly developed public schools were subject to clerical domination through the Conseil de l'instruction publique; there was no Ministry of Education. As for the economy, the Quebec government played a largely passive role. Industrial development was encouraged primarily by making natural resources available to American and English-Canadian firms at nominal royalty levels. As one might expect, the administrative structures of the Quebec government remained poorly developed. Relatively few personnel had expertise in social sciences. By and large, they were political appointees.

There had been some significant reforms during the Liberal regime of Adélard Godbout (1939–44). The government made school attendance compulsory and granted women the right to vote, in both cases over the strong opposition of the clergy. It also established Hydro-Québec, through the nationalization of Montreal Light, Heat and Power Consolidated. But upon its return to power in 1944, the Union Nationale regime of Maurice Duplessis was little inclined to follow suit by further expanding the economic and social role of the Quebec government. It did, however, intervene vigorously in one area—labour relations. Through a variety of legislative measures and deployment of the provincial police, it sought to curtail the actions of unions.

In short, the Duplessis regime faithfully reproduced the historical cultural division of labour in Quebec's economy and did little to address the mounting need of the francophone population for higher levels of education and social services than the Church-related institutions were able, or willing, to provide. Needless to say, the Duplessis administration had the close support of English-Canadian and American capitalists, who highly prized Duplessis's ability to maintain labour peace and keep taxes low. However, by the 1950s, there had emerged within French Quebec two social groups that had a clear interest in changing this state of affairs.

First, the postwar years saw the emergence within French Canada of a "new middle class" of salaried professionals. Within the French-language universities, formally under Church control, the numbers of lay faculty had grown rapidly both in the physical sciences and the social sciences. Especially important in the development of a critical attitude toward the passivity of the Duplessis regime was the Faculté des sciences sociales at Université Laval, where lay faculty openly advocated a variety of reforms, earning Duplessis's bitter enmity in the process. Francophone intellectuals also gained a new base, and popular influence, as Radio-Canada began television broadcasting. At the same time, lay administrators and professionals acquired a new prominence in the Church-related institutions that provided health and social services. Finally, as it had for many years, l'École des hautes études commerciales continued to graduate accountants and business specialists.

Uniting these different strata of the "new middle class" was a common interest in greater state intervention, whether it be to attenuate clerical control of education and social services or to expand opportunity for francophones within the anglophone-dominated economy. This interest found expression in a variety of new middle-class movements and organizations. During the 1950s, proposals along these lines appeared in such publications as *Cité libre* and *Le Devoir*, and in the annual conferences of the Institut Canadien des affaires publiques. The Quebec Liberal Party, where influence of the new middle class was growing, adopted many of them. The Rassemblement pour l'indépendance national (RIN), the first Quebec *indépendantiste* party, was founded in 1960. Based within the francophone new middle class, the RIN called for state intervention on a variety of fronts. In 1960, francophone social workers formed a distinct professional organization in order to reduce clerical domination of their activities and carry on their lobbying for state intervention. And in 1961 many francophone academics and teachers joined in the Mouvement laïque de la langue française, which forthrightly advocated a secularization of Quebec's educational system.[3]

As well, from the 1950s, Quebec's union movements displayed a new militancy. Thanks to postwar prosperity, their memberships increased rapidly. The Confédération des travailleurs catholiques du Canada (CTCC), founded by the Church in 1921, came under a new leadership that was much more forthright in its advocacy of workers' interests and that began to distance the CTCC from the Church. Evidence of the CTCC's new militancy was a series of bitter strikes, including the celebrated

Asbestos strike of 1949, when the CTCC took on American mining interests as well as Duplessis and the Quebec provincial policy. This militancy was echoed by the Fédération des unions industrielles du Québec (FUIQ), which grouped together Quebec locals linked to the Canadian Labour Congress and the American CIO. The CTCC and the FUIQ regularly called upon the Quebec government not only to handle labour relations in a more even-handed manner, but to meet the needs of labour directly through a variety of initiatives such as public health insurance, improved social security, increased state involvement in education, stricter regulation of working conditions, and complete public ownership of hydro production and distribution in the province.

Finally, support for much more limited state initiatives came from the precarious francophone business class, which feared it would be further marginalized by American and English-Canadian capital. In the late 1950s, the Chambre de commerce du Québec began to call upon the Quebec government to establish an economic advisory council, with strong business representation. In particular, it was hoped that the Quebec state could help French Canadian firms to find much-needed capital.

With the death of Duplessis in 1959, the subsequent disintegration of the Union Nationale, and the election to power of the Liberals under Jean Lesage in 1960, the steadily widening demands for a major expansion of the role of the Quebec state finally found an outlet. The Liberal government was keen to project an image of progressive change, in contrast with the Duplessis regime. Moreover, unlike the Union Nationale, the Liberal Party was itself based primarily in urban Quebec. Elements of the new middle class had secured considerable influence in the Liberal Party, and the CTCC leadership had a good working relationship with Lesage and other party figures. In short, the conditions were right for what was to become a fundamental recasting of the Quebec state and Quebec politics in general. Over the next few years, Quebec underwent its "Quiet Revolution," a period of unprecedented intellectual and political ferment in which all the long-established assumptions about French–English relations and Quebec's place within Confederation were challenged.

THE QUIET REVOLUTION: STATE-BUILDING AND NATION-BUILDING

The Quiet Revolution represented first and foremost an ideological change, a transformation of mentalities. Within the new ideology, Quebec was to be clearly seen as the urban, industrial society that it had become. The state had to assume full responsibility for the social and educational functions that thus far the Church had been able to retain, just as it had to assume responsibility for planning the direction of the Quebec economy and undertaking the measures needed to modernize it and make it more competitive. In effect, the Quebec state was to assume the functions of a Keynesian state (see Chapter 4). But it was Keynesianism with a difference, since the Quebec state was also to be a "national state." With the 1960s, French-Canadian nationalism was recast into a more explicitly Québécois nationalism. The greatness of this Quebec nation was to lie not in the past, as represented by traditional French-Canadian nationalism's glorification of the ancien régime, but with the future, as represented by an urban, industrial, and secular society. Responsible to a primarily francophone electorate, the Quebec state was the one institution that could enable the Québécois to achieve these objectives. In particular, it was the indispensable lever to undoing the cultural division of labour within the Quebec economy, thereby making Québécois "maîtres chez nous"—"masters in our own house."

As with earlier formulations of nationalist ideology, the Quebec neo-nationalism of the 1960s bore the clear imprint of the class that fashioned and supported it—in this case, the francophone new middle class.[4] Qualified as its members were to assume managerial and technical positions, they could only be affronted by the anglophone dominance of the economy. By the same token, they had every interest in the transfer of responsibilities from the Church to an expanded Quebec state with a modern bureaucracy. And they had every reason to support the Quebec government in its struggles with Ottawa, where opportunities for the francophone new middle class were few and far between. Yet resentment over anglophone domination, the desire for better educational and social services, and mistrust of the federal government were shared by a great many francophones. The various initiatives of the Lesage Liberals enjoyed unwavering support not only from the new middle class but also from organized labour (especially the CSN), and, on a more qualified basis, from francophone business and traditional liberal professional nationalists. With steady propagation by the Quebec government and intellectuals, neo-nationalism acquired a certain degree of hegemony in Quebec. Thus, young francophones entering political life in the 1960s were massively socialized to it.

Beyond ideological change, however, the 1960s did witness real change in the structures and role of the Quebec state. In 1963, Quebec's private hydroelectric enterprises were nationalized so as to give Hydro-Québec a virtual monopoly over the production and distribution of electricity in the province. In 1968, a publicly owned steel mill, SIDBEC, was established. A Société générale de financement was created to inject capital into francophone-owned enterprises. On the basis of funds generated through the Quebec Pension Plan, the Caisse de dépôt et de placement du Québec became a major institutional investor and, when needed, purchaser of government securities. In 1964, a Ministry of Education was created, and over subsequent years many of the collèges classiques were transformed into secular, government-administered Collèges d'enseigne-ment général et professionnel (CEGEPs). Control over health and social services moved steadily from Church-related institutions to the Quebec bureaucracy.

Nonetheless, the overall effect of the Quiet Revolution reforms was uneven. Secularization of Quebec society progressed rapidly; as Church-held educational and social functions were transferred to the state, clerical influence in Quebec society declined at an astounding rate. However, much more limited progress was made in reversing the historical anglo-phone dominance of the Quebec economy, the expansion of Hydro-Québec notwithstanding. Moreover, by the mid-1960s the uneasy coalition of social forces that had supported the initiatives of the Lesage govern-ment had succumbed to its own contradictions. With the return of the Union Nationale to power in 1966, the government fell to a party that had a different social base. Financially, it was increasingly constrained. Thus, while the momentum of change in the Quebec state was not halted, it was markedly slowed. By the same token, mid-1960s relations between Quebec City and Ottawa became increasingly polarized. Initially, the fed-eral government had sought to accommodate Quebec's demands to oc-cupy its jurisdictions to the maximum, exemplified by the establishment of a Quebec Pension Plan in 1964 and other "opting-out" schemes. How-ever, misgivings arose in federal circles. With Pierre Trudeau's accession to power in 1968, the emphasis clearly shifted to other approaches to Quebec nationalism, including the extension of French-language rights outside Quebec.[5]

In sum, during the 1960s a great many Québécois had been con-verted to the Quiet Revolution conception of a dynamic, interventionist Quebec state. By the late 1960s, however, the Quebec state no longer seemed able to pursue the neonationalist agenda of economic and social change; it had reached its limits. Yet the original agenda was expanding as new concerns arose. Quebec nationalists began to fear that the con-tinuing anglicization of immigrants threatened francophone predominance in Montreal, if not all of Quebec, especially given the radical decline in the francophone birthrate. There arose new demands for restricting access to English-language schools. At the same time, the relative failure of the Quebec state to carve out new opportunities for francophones in the up-per levels of the Quebec economy fostered demands for state intervention to establish French as the language of work. These demands became all the more urgent as the 1960s expansion of the Quebec state structures wound down and fewer new positions were available to francophone university graduates. Finally, working-class organizations began to articu-late their own vision of an agenda for Quebec that was not bound by the preoccupations of the new middle class. The concerns acquired urgency as labour relations in the public sector became increasingly conflict-prone.

THE PARTI QUÉBÉCOIS AND QUEBEC INDEPENDENCE

All these forms of political frustration provided ready grounds for the cause of Quebec independence. Independence bore the promise of a Quebec state that would have the capacity and resolve to discharge this much larger agenda. Thus, it became the essential remedy for a wide variety of grievances. In addition, independence had more direct appeal. For the many francophones, especially among the youth, who had come to see themselves as pre-eminently *Québécois*, independence constituted the formal recognition of their own identity. As a result, the Quebec independence movement and its preoccupations were to colour, if not dominate, Quebec politics throughout the 1970s and early 1980s.

In 1968, the Parti Québécois (PQ), under the leadership of René Lévesque, emerged as the primary vehicle of the *indépendantiste* cause. The PQ proposed to repatriate the economic "centres of decision" through state enterprises and regulation of non-Quebec ownership in the financial sector. At the same time, this "technocratic" thrust was coupled with "populist" measures to help a variety of socially deprived groups. All this would be linked to the rest of Canada through a vaguely defined economic association, but Quebec would nonetheless achieve the full-fledged national status to which its centuries-old distinctiveness entitled it. Although members of the new middle class dominated the PQ leadership and the party program clearly bore their imprint, the Parti Québécois emerged as a broad-based coalition of social forces committed to Quebec sovereignty.[6]

The pressures to reinforce Quebec's distinctiveness only grew with the return of the Liberals to power in 1970, this time under Robert Bourassa. During the October Crisis of 1970, the Quebec government was effectively subordinated to Ottawa as the federal government proceeded with its hard-line response to the Front de libération du Québec (FLQ). The following year, efforts to revise the Canadian Constitution ground to a halt after the Bourassa government concluded that the Victoria Charter was insufficient to meet Quebec's needs. The government's efforts, through Bill 22, to satisfy nationalist demands for the pre-eminence of French within Quebec foundered over rejection of the bill by francophones and anglophones alike. At the same time, by retreating from state economic intervention, the government seemed to be playing down the issue of ownership within the Quebec economy. Dramatic confrontations between the Bourassa government and the union movement, especially with respect to public-sector workers, further served to weaken the legitimacy of the existing order. As the Parti Québécois dominated opposition forces, its option of Quebec sovereignty emerged as the logical remedy to all these problems. Accordingly, the PQ was able to win power in 1976.

The election of a party formally committed to sovereignty for Quebec served to demonstrate more clearly than ever before the distinctiveness of Quebec politics. Never before had a province elected a government committed to withdrawal from Canada (with the possible exception of the 1867 election of an anti-Confederation government in Nova Scotia). The PQ had not spelled out the precise nature of sovereignty; it remained committed to some notion of economic association. Moreover, the party had declared that a PQ government would first need to obtain popular approval in a referendum before it could proceed to secure sovereignty. Nonetheless, the mere evocation of sovereignty was sufficient to plunge the Canadian political system into its gravest crisis.

As it happened, the Lévesque government moved slowly on the question of sovereignty. Three years passed before the government fully defined its proposal; another year passed before it staged its referendum. Instead, the PQ became consumed with the task of running a provincial government. In both areas, the PQ's prudence reflected the new middle-class base of its leadership. Over the previous twenty years, this class had already made very substantial gains; thus, it was disinclined to take needless risks.

The Lévesque government first moved on the language front, with its Bill 101. In its final version, Bill 101 did not differ radically from Bill 22, but it did tighten nonanglophone access to English schools, and it was more stringent in requiring enterprises to francize their operations. Also, by requiring French-only commercial signs, it sought to give Quebec an unmistakably French face. Coming from an *indépendantiste* government, these measures carried much more credibility than had Bill 22. In addition, the Lévesque administration reformed electoral funding practices and passed a variety of social measures, such as public automobile insurance, labour-relations reform, a limited guaranteed-income scheme, and free medication for the elderly. In effect, the PQ went about providing "good" provincial government. In fact, when it came to routine federal–provincial relations, the PQ government agreed to a wide variety of joint programs with Ottawa.

This emphasis on providing "good government" was rationalized in terms of the PQ's *étapiste* strategy: as the population acquired confidence in the ability of the party to provide good provincial government, so it would be more prepared to support the party's option of independence. Yet this strategy carried risks common to all movements that, while committed to global change, assume office within existing structures. As party leaders and militants come to enjoy the concrete benefits associated with holding office, their own commitment to more radical change may be tempered. Party militants may become estranged from their leaders, who now have a separate base of power outside the party. Most important, efforts to provide good government may serve to make the existing system more tolerable to the discontented parts of the population, thus undercutting rather than reinforcing support for more radical change. All of these processes appear to have affected both the PQ itself and support for the independence option. Especially striking is the extent to which Bill 101 may have served to rehabilitate the existing federal order by appearing to resolve the language question to nationalists' satisfaction.

In addition, the PQ leadership applied *étapiste* logic to the goal of sovereignty itself, surrounding it with a very comprehensive economic association and committing the government to yet another referendum. In seeking to minimize the prospect of change, the government seemed to acknowledge that true independence would have catastrophic effects. On this basis, it could not address the fears of much of the population, which clearly believed that the PQ's real goal was independence. At the same time, the credibility of its option depended upon whether English Canada was likely to accept it; English-Canadian politicians spared no effort to convince Québécois that this would not be the case. Whatever the explanation, the PQ government was unable to broaden support much beyond its primary electoral clientele of younger francophones, especially those based within the public sector. Thus, with only 40 percent in favour (not quite 50 percent of francophones), the referendum proposition was soundly defeated.

QUEBEC IN THE 1980S: DISINTEGRATION AND RESURGENCE OF THE NATIONALIST MOVEMENT

The failure of the referendum had a devastating effect on the nationalist movement. Even though the Parti Québécois was able to secure re-election in 1981, what had once appeared to be an inexorable movement to Quebec independence now seemed to have come to a permanent halt.

The sense of defeat was only reinforced by the way in which the Canadian Constitution was revised in 1982. With the support of all provinces but Quebec, the federal government of Pierre Trudeau sent a formal request to the British Parliament to repatriate the Canadian Constitution. Until that time, Canada's primary constitutional document had been the British North America (BNA) Act, a statute of the British Parliament. The Canadian government requested that the BNA Act be replaced by the Constitution Act, which provided a procedure for amending the Constitution in Canada. At the same time, the Constitution Act would add a new element to the Canadian Constitution: a Charter of Rights and Freedoms.

The Quebec government of René Lévesque vigorously opposed the move. Although it supported repatriation as a general goal, Quebec claimed that the terms on which this was to be done ignored that province's particular concerns and diminished the powers of its government. The amendment formula did not provide Quebec with the veto it needed to protect its interests. The Charter in fact reduced the Quebec government's powers by limiting its prerogatives in such matters as the regulation of access to English-language schools and the restriction of access to government services by migrants from other provinces.

The Trudeau government derided this opposition as the predictable response of a "separatist" government. Yet the Quebec government's position was supported by a good number of Quebec federalists, including most of the Liberal members of the Quebec National Assembly. In fact, the Quebec government sought to have the federal move declared unconstitutional by the courts. It claimed that the initiative violated an established constitutional practice whereby Quebec, if not the other provinces, had enjoyed an effective veto over constitutional change. The Supreme Court rejected Quebec's claim, declaring that no such veto existed.

On April 17, 1982, the Constitution Act, 1982, was proclaimed by Queen Elizabeth. Canada's Constitution was repatriated over the objections of Quebec, but with the approval of all nine other provincial governments. Quebec's distinctive demands had been simply dismissed by the federal government and by a large proportion of English Canadians. In effect, not only had the dream of sovereignty been crushed, but within Canadian federalism Quebec was denied any particular status relative to the other provinces. The resulting bitterness extended beyond sovereigntists to include a significant proportion of Quebec's federalist ranks.

The Parti Québécois itself became badly divided over what strategy to follow in the wake of these successive defeats of the nationalist cause. In September 1984, René Lévesque even evoked the possibility of seeking an accommodation of Quebec within the federal system. He claimed that the new Progressive Conservative government of Brian Mulroney might be more receptive than the Trudeau Liberals to Quebec's claims for recognition. Lévesque acknowledged the risk that success in these negotiations might undermine the case for Quebec sovereignty, but he dubbed this "*un beau risque.*" Suck talk was anathema to leading PQ cabinet members, who resigned in protest. The impending disarray culminated in Lévesque himself resigning from office. Under his successor, Pierre-Marc Johnson, the PQ was soundly defeated by the Liberals, led once again by Robert Bourassa. Quebec appeared to be safely back in the federalist fold.

Despite the renewed dominance of federalist forces in Quebec, there were ample signs that most Quebec francophones continued to see Quebec as their primary political community. In terms of their political loyalties, nothing had changed. For instance, a 1988 survey asked Quebec residents how they identified themselves. The response of "above all Québécois" was selected by a full 49 percent of Quebec francophones (the same proportion that had voted "yes" in the 1980 referendum).

Another 39 percent defined themselves as "French Canadian," while only 11 percent said they were simply "Canadian."[7]

Yet it was not at all clear how this identity might give rise to new pressures for a change in Quebec's political status. For its part, the Parti Québécois renewed its commitment to Quebec sovereignty after the "neo-federalist" deviations of the mid-1980s. When Jacques Parizeau took over the leadership of the party in 1987, he promised to lead an all-out struggle for Quebec sovereignty. However, in the 1989 provincial election the Parti Québécois had to content itself with more seats in the opposition.

As it happened, a resurgence in nationalist fortunes did come about, but it was generated by a division among the forces for Canadian federalism rather than by a new mobilization of the forces for Quebec sovereignty. Quebec federalists found themselves isolated from their ostensible allies in the rest of the country, once again over the question of Quebec's distinctiveness. The division in federalist ranks, already manifest at the time of the constitutional repatriation, became much more pronounced, and was ultimately to push support for Quebec sovereignty to heights never seen before.

Upon their return to power, the Bourassa Liberals turned their attentions to the fact that Quebec was still not a signatory to the Canadian Constitution. In addressing this problem, the Quebec government announced five conditions that would enable Quebec to sign the document: (1) an expanded veto over constitutional change; (2) limitation of the federal government's use of the spending power in provincial jurisdictions; (3) participation in nominations to the Supreme Court; (4) recognition of Quebec's existing role in immigration; and (5) formal recognition of Quebec's status as a distinct society. Collectively, they represented an exceedingly modest package that fell well short of the constitutional demands that had been proposed by Quebec governments for decades.

Under the leadership of Prime Minister Brian Mulroney, the nine other premiers agreed to Quebec's demands contingent on one additional provision that was itself acceptable to Quebec: provincial participation in nominations to the Senate. This new document became generally known, of course, as the Meech Lake Accord.[8] At last, it seemed, Quebec would formally embrace the new constitutional order created in 1982. While there was no question that Quebec was bound by the Constitution Act, 1982 (even the Parti Québécois government tacitly acknowledged this), the Quebec government's failure to sign the new Constitution had severely limited its legitimacy in Quebec.

However, the accord soon came under heavy attack from federalists outside Quebec, who had a variety of grievances. Many claimed that negotiation of the accord had not involved sufficient popular consultation. Some feared that the federal government would be weakened as a result of certain provisions of the accord, such as the restriction on the federal spending power and the tying of Supreme Court and Senate nominations to provincial lists. But it is clear from analysis of public opinion that the most important basis of English-Canadian (and aboriginal) opposition was the clause declaring Quebec to be a distinct society.[9] The notion that Quebec was not simply a province like the others was at odds with the vision of Canada that was shared by a great many English Canadians.

Yet it is also clear that this formal recognition of Quebec's distinctiveness was the most important constitutional issue in the eyes of most Quebec francophones. For a great many of them—federalists as well as sovereigntists—English-Canadian rejection of the distinct-society clause amounted to rejection of Quebec itself.

English-Canadian opposition to the distinct-society clause was only exacerbated by the debate over Quebec's "sign law." In 1988, the Supreme Court struck down the provision of Bill 101 requiring that commercial signs be in French only, declaring that it contravened the protection of fundamental freedoms in the Charter of Rights and Freedoms. In response, the Bourassa government passed Bill 178, which drew upon the "notwithstanding clause" of the Charter to reinstate the sign law. Quebec francophones themselves were divided over the propriety of this law, but they appear to have rallied behind the Quebec government's action to defend the integrity of Bill 101 against the Supreme Court's application of the Charter. These events clearly demonstrated the precarious legitimacy of the new constitutional order in Quebec, just as they demonstrated the overwhelming legitimacy of the Charter in the rest of the country. Finally, in June 1990 time ran out for the Meech Lake Accord. Three years had elapsed since the accord received its first ratification by a legislature, Quebec's National Assembly. It still had not been ratified by all the provincial legislatures; Newfoundland had rescinded its ratification and Manitoba had yet to ratify it. Accordingly, under the terms of the Constitution Act, 1982, the accord died.

The collapse of the Meech Lake Accord triggered a deep reaction in Quebec. Not without reason, many Quebec francophones interpreted English-Canadian opposition to the accord as stemming from rejection of their claims for recognition of Quebec's distinct status. Rejection of the accord was seen as no less than rejection of Quebec itself. The resulting sense of resentment and humiliation raised support for Quebec sovereignty to unprecedented levels, from 44 percent in September 1989 to 56 percent in March 1990 to 64 percent in the following November, with only 30 percent opposed.[10]

Two different bodies produced documents that reflected the surge in Quebec nationalist sentiment. First, the 1991 Allaire Report, commissioned by the Quebec Liberal Party, proposed a radical reduction in the federal government's powers and responsibilities.[11] By the same token, it called for a referendum, to be held by autumn of 1992, that would ask Quebeckers either to approve an agreement with the rest of Canada modelled after the report's proposal, if there should be one, or to approve Quebec's accession to sovereignty, accompanied by an offer of economic association with the rest of Canada. With minor modifications, the report became Liberal Party policy in March 1991. Second, in March 1991 a final report was issued by the Bélanger-Campeau Commission, an all-party committee of the National Assembly.[12] The report saw only two available options for Quebec: a profoundly renewed federalism or Quebec sovereignty. It called for a popular consultation on Quebec sovereignty by October 1992.

For his part, Premier Robert Bourassa remained as committed as ever to Quebec's remaining within the Canadian federation. However, to assuage the nationalist feeling sweeping Quebec, he needed to offer a genuine prospect for a renewed federal system. To do that, he required the collaboration and support of Ottawa and the other provincial governments. This was to prove to be no small undertaking, given the popular sentiments in English Canada that had caused the Meech Lake Accord's demise.

After some false starts, in August 1992 the eleven first ministers, two territories, and four national aboriginal organizations did agree on a new scheme for constitutional revision—the Charlottetown Accord. While it retained the key elements of the Meech Lake Accord, this new document reflected a two-pronged strategy to satisfy English-Canadian concerns: to rein in the part of the Meech Lake Accord that had been objectionable and to incorporate a host of new provisions to respond to the many demands for constitutional change that English Canadians had been expressing. Thus, the infamous distinct-society clause was now only one of eight "fundamental characteristics" of Canada enumerated in a "Canada clause." Moreover, constitutional revision was now also to include Senate reform, a commitment to strengthen the social and economic union, recognition of the aboriginal peoples' inherent right to self-government, and reinforcement of some existing provincial jurisdictions.[13]

Nonetheless, this attempt at constitutional reform was also to fail—in large part over the issue of recognizing Quebec's distinctiveness. While recasting the distinct-society clause seemed to placate English Canada, another element in the Charlottetown Accord aroused a great deal of objection. In an attempt to mollify Québécois discontent with the Senate reform, which would have reduced Quebec's representation to the same as all other provinces, the accord increased Quebec's representation (along with Ontario's) in the House of Commons and guaranteed Quebec 25 percent of seats in perpetuity, even if its share of the Canadian population should fall below that mark. For many English Canadians, this new attempt to accommodate Quebec's distinctiveness was no less objectionable than the Meech Lake Accord's distinct-society clause. At the same time, this provision seems to have won few adherents to the Charlottetown Accord in Quebec, where attention focused on the relative insignificance of Quebec's gains vis-à-vis the division of powers. All these factors contributed to the resounding defeat of the accord in a national referendum held on October 26, 1992.[14] In Quebec, the vote split 45.7 percent for, 56.7 percent against; outside Quebec, it was 45.7 percent for, 54.3 against. The second attempt to secure Quebec's signature to the 1982 constitutional regime had ended in abject failure.

At the time of writing, the winter of 1994, nationalist forces are threatening once again to impose the Quebec question on the Canadian political agenda. The Bloc Québécois, a new political formation committed to Quebec sovereignty and closely linked to the Parti Québécois, secured no less than 54 of Quebec's 75 seats in the October 1993 federal election. In fact, with the collapse of the Progressive Conservatives, the Bloc Québécois was able to assume the role of official Opposition, edging out the Reform Party. For the first time, the argument for Quebec sovereignty is being made by a political party within the House of Commons. During the last three decades, the established federal political parties shared a clear consensus that the Quebec question could be resolved through such initiatives as official bilingualism and the Charter of Rights and Freedoms, combined with the maintenance of strong national institutions and an absolute equality among the provinces. With the arrival of the Bloc Québécois, the consensus has been broken; Canadian federal politics may never be the same.

However, it is the outcome of the impending Quebec provincial election that will really determine whether the Quebec question dominates Canadian politics once again. Opinion polls suggest that the election of the Parti Québécois is a distinct possibility. Should this occur, the PQ will hold a referendum on Quebec sovereignty. Moreover, it likely would pursue the objective of sovereignty in a much more resolute fashion than did the first PQ government—first, by holding the referendum more rapidly upon assuming power, and second, by presenting a referendum option that would focus on sovereignty for Quebec without linking it to economic association with the rest of Canada.

Whether the Quebec government would be able to win such a referendum is, of course, another matter. A multitude of factors could come into play in determining the vote, not the least of which would be voters' concerns about the economic costs associated with sovereignty. However, one argument that the federalist forces used to apparently good advantage in the last referendum will not be available—namely, that as an alternative to sovereignty, Quebec can secure its objectives through a "renewal" of the federal system. After the twin debacles of the Meech Lake and Charlottetown accords, this argument will have little credibility. In effect, the choice facing Quebec voters would be between Quebec sovereignty and the status quo. There is no viable "third way."

If the next provincial election should instead be won by the Liberals, under Daniel Johnson, then the Quebec government will be clearly committed to the federalist cause. Yet it will be saddled with a constitutional order that has limited legitimacy in Quebec. The likelihood that it would try to correct this by initiating new constitutional discussions is negligible. (Robert Bourassa's experience should discourage any federalist Quebec government from pursuing this route for many years to come.) Thus, the question of Quebec's place in Canada would remain as it has for the last three decades—unresolved.

In sum, there is every reason to believe that many, if not most, Quebec francophones will continue to see themselves first and foremost as Québécois. Thus, even if Quebec does remain part of Canada, its relationship with the rest of the country will be problematic in the eyes not only of Québécois but of many English Canadians as well. At a minimum, Québécois will continue to see Quebec as a distinct society, and Quebec will continue to be one.

NOTES

1. Figures taken from *Census of Canada*, 1991, 93–317.

2. John McCallum, *Unequal Beginnings: Agriculture and Economic Development in Quebec and Ontario until 1870* (Toronto: University of Toronto Press, 1980), p. 104.

3. These developments are traced in Michael D. Beheils, *Prelude to Quebec's Quiet Revolution* (Montreal and Kingston: McGill-Queen's University Press, 1985). See also Kenneth McRoberts, *Quebec: Social Change and Political Crisis*, 3rd ed. (Toronto: McClelland and Stewart, 1988), ch. 4.

4. he leading role of the new middle class within the Quiet Revolution coalition is discussed at length in McRoberts, *Quebec: Social Change and Political Crisis*, ch. 5. For a critique of this interpretation, see William D. Coleman, *The Independence Movement in Quebec, 1945–1980* (Toronto: University of Toronto Press, 1984).

5. This strategy and its consequences are analyzed in Kenneth McRoberts, *English Canada and Quebec: Avoiding the Issue*, Robarts Lecture in Canadian Studies (North York, Ont.: Robarts Centre, York University, 1991).

6. Competing approaches to classifying and explaining the ideology and class bases of the Parti Québécois are assessed in McRoberts, *Quebec: Social Change and Political Crisis*, pp. 242–59.

7. Among Quebec nonfrancophones the pattern was reversed: "Canadian" (75 percent), "Québécois" (10 percent), and "English Canadian" (10 percent). "Le francophone est Québécois, l'anglophone 'Canadian,'" *Le Devoir* (June 25, 1988), p. 1.

8. The Meech Lake Accord is analyzed in Peter W. Hogg, *Meech Lake Constitutional Accord Annotated* (Toronto: Carswell, 1988); Katherine E. Swinton and Carol J. Rogerson, eds., *Competing Constitutional Visions: The Meech Lake Accord* (Toronto: Carswell, 1988); and Patrick J. Monahan, *Meech Lake: The Inside Story* (Toronto: University of Toronto Press, 1991).

9. See André Blais and Jean Crête, "Pourquoi l'opinion publique au Québec a-t-elle rejeté l'Accord du lac Meech," in Raymond Hudon and Réjean Pelletier, eds., *L'engagement intellectuel: mélanges en l'honneur de Léon Dion* (Quebec: Les Presses de l'Université Laval, 1991), p. 398.

10. "Portrait des Québécois," *L'Actualité* (January 1991), pp. 13–16.

11. Rapport de Comité constitutionnel du Parti libéral du Québec, *Un Québec libre de ses choix* (January 28, 1991).

12. Quebec, *Rapport de la Commission sur l'avenir politique et constitutionnel du Québec* (March 1991).

13. See Kenneth McRoberts and Patrick J. Monahan, *The Charlottetown Accord, the Referendum, and the Future of Canada* (Toronto: University of Toronto Press, 1993); and "The Charter, Federalism and the Constitution," *International Journal of Canadian Studies* 7–8 (Spring–Fall, 1993).

14. McRoberts and Monahan, *The Charlottetown Accord, the Referendum, and the Future of Canada*, app. 3.

FURTHER READINGS

Balthazar, Louis. *Bilan du nationalisme au Québec*. Montreal: Les Éditions de l'Hexagone, 1986.

Behiels, Michael D., ed. *Quebec since 1945: Selected Readings*. Toronto: Copp Clark Pitman, 1987.

Coleman, William D. *The Independence Movement in Quebec, 1945–1980*. Toronto: University of Toronto Press, 1984.

Dion, Léon. *À la recherche du Québec, 1945–1980*. Quebec: Les Presses de l'Université Laval, 1987.

Gagnon, Alain G., ed., *Quebec: State and Society*. 2nd ed. Scarborough, Ont.: Nelson Canada, 1993.

McRoberts, Kenneth. *Quebec: Social Change and Political Crisis*. 3rd ed. McClelland and Stewart, 1993.

Monière, Denis. *Le développement des idéologies au Québec des origines à nos jours*. Montreal: Éditions Québec/Amérique, 1977. English-language version: *Ideologies in Quebec*. Toronto: University of Toronto Press, 1981.

THE SOCIO-CULTURAL MILIEU OF CANADIAN POLITICS

6 POLITICAL CULTURE IN CANADA

David V.J. Bell

NCE OF POLITICAL

nent of life because it affects how we per-
nteract with it. Culture provides a set of
lenses through which people view the world. Beliefs about the world and
individually held values shape both attitudes and actions. Culture also
provides a way of doing things, a common stock of knowledge about appropriate and inappropriate behaviour in different settings.[1] As we are socialized into a culture, we learn to behave in ways that others in the same
culture will find acceptable and comfortable. We learn what to wear, what
to say, and how to stand. We learn to distinguish between the public and
private, how to say "hello" and "goodbye," how to indicate pleasure or
unhappiness.

Political life is similarly affected by "political culture." Political culture consists of the ideas, assumptions, values, and beliefs that condition
political action. It affects the ways we use politics, the kinds of social
problems we address, and the solutions we attempt. Political culture
serves as a filter or lens through which political actors view the world; it
influences what they perceive as social problems and how they react to
them. Political perception and political action are mediated through language and speech. Political culture is the language of political discourse,
the vocabulary and grammar of political controversy and understanding.
Frequently, political values, beliefs, and attitudes are crystallized and represented by various symbols. In its simplest sense, a symbol is a kind of
shorthand, something that stands for something else. In politics, symbols
usually evoke both thoughts and feelings and reflect longstanding traditions to which individuals become strongly attached.

Canadian political culture includes a number of symbols. Some, such
as Parliament, the Crown, and Mounties in red coats, have been around

for a long time. Others, such as the Charter of Rights and Freedoms, the Meech Lake Accord, and NAFTA, are much more recent. Political symbols can evoke images of consensus and cooperation—as does the idea of helping the poorer provinces, or furthering Anglo–French partnership. But symbols can also catalyze negative emotions and hatred or distrust—as does the phrase "forcing French down our throats," angry references to Sikhs in turbans, or the bitter accusation of Eastern domination, symbolized by the phrase "freight rates" or by the National Energy Program. The variety and richness of these symbols demonstrate that Canadian politics simultaneously features harmony and disunity, conflict and cooperation. Politicians invoke symbols in their speeches in order to rally support for their parties and policies, to quiet discontent, or to inflame feelings of bitterness directed against their opponents. Members of the general public, for their part, often appear to need symbolic reassurances, to identify with the symbols that are manipulated in public debate by their political leaders, and to find gratification in the symbolic aspect of politics when more practical and material aspects are less than satisfactory.[2]

Because of its impact on individuals in their capacity as both citizens and subjects, followers and leaders, political culture (including symbols) affects the content and nature of what goes on in the "black box" that we call the political system. It helps transform the inanimate machinery of government into the living organic reality of politics. The foremost theorist of the systems approach, David Easton, points out that cultural inhibitors affect "what are to be considered culturally appropriate areas for political decision."[3] In any political system, the political culture demarcates the zone of appropriate action for government, and sets other areas beyond the realm of the legitimate. Thus, for example, Pierre Trudeau announced soon after his first election as prime minister in 1968 that "the state has no place in the bedrooms of the nation."[4]

Conversely, the political culture provides a range of acceptable values and standards upon which leaders can draw in attempting to justify their policies. Unless a politically viable justification can be attached to a controversial policy, it will not usually be adopted. The political culture sets the parameters within which debate over policy justification takes place. The political culture further affects what people view as appropriate areas of governmental action. It shapes the perception of politically relevant problems, thereby affecting both the recognition of these problems and the diagnosis of their various aspects. It influences beliefs about who should be assigned responsibility for solving problems, and what kind of solutions are likely to work. This aspect of political culture is, in turn, related to more general notions about the general purposes of government and the kinds of processes and substantive decisions that are acceptable and legitimate.[5]

The political culture greatly influences political discourse. In effect, the political culture serves as the language while political discourse constitutes speech. This language–speech metaphor is very helpful for understanding the day-to-day significance of political culture. It relates closely to the notion of "the universe of political discourse" developed by Jane Jenson:

> *What is the universe of political discourse? At its simplest it comprises beliefs about the ways politics should be conducted, the boundaries of political discussion, and the kinds of conflicts resolvable through political processes. In the vast array of tensions, differences, and inequalities characteristic of any society, only some are treated as "political." Thus, whether a matter is considered a religious, economic, private, or political question is set by this definition. Invisibility can exist for those questions that are, for whatever reasons, never elevated to the status of being "political."*
>
> *The universe of political discourse functions at any single point in time by setting boundaries to political action and by limiting the range of actors that are accorded the status of legitimate participants, the range of issues considered to be included in the realm of meaningful political debate, the policy alternatives feasible for implementation, and the alliance strategies available for achieving change. Thus, the universe of political discourse filters and delineates political activity of all kinds. Ultimately, its major impact is to inhibit or encourage the formation of new collective identities and/or the reinforcement of older ones. Within a given universe of political discourse, only certain kinds of collective identities can be forged; for more to be done, the universe itself must be challenged and changed.*[6]

When people talk about political issues and problems, they draw on symbols and concepts, embedded in the political culture, that provide shared definitions of the situation. The political culture privileges or favours one set of definitions over others. It thus helps establish a dominant discourse that, in turn, will favour the interests of particular groups in society. This allows political parties that support the status quo to articulate the dominant discourse. At the same time, it forces parties that wish to achieve significant reform to challenge the dominant discourse and attempt to gain legitimacy for an alternative discourse.

Over the course of its nine years in power, the Mulroney Conservative government largely displaced the neo-Keynesian discourse of the Trudeau Liberals with a neoconservative discourse of monetarism, deregulation, and privatization (see Chapter 4). Neither of these discourses pays much attention to class conflict and class divisions, matters deemed to be essential by class-based parties of the left. The dominance of neoconservative discourse was so complete that NDP governments elected in recent years in the provinces of Ontario and British Columbia were accused of adopting a neoconservative agenda! (The Ontario NDP formally lost the support of a number of major unions in retaliation for imposing "social contract" legislation that was considered by many critics to be "anti-working class.") It remains to be seen whether the election federally of Jean Chrétien's Liberals will result in any significant transformation of the dominant neoconservative discourse. According to Professor James Laxer, the Liberals appeared to be following the same course, giving Canadians "honest, small 'c' conservative government punctuated by populist gestures" that would fall into the category of symbolic reassurances to the contrary.[7]

In some instances, political values, attitudes, and beliefs cluster together in a particular constellation called an ideology. Ideologies are more or less coherent and explicit, and tend to be held by people whose political involvement is unusually high. Such activists find ideologies useful guides to political action. Ideologies have a programmatic aspect insofar as they provide a diagnosis of the problems facing society and a prescription of solutions for these problems. Indeed, ideologies in many instances amount to a way of viewing the world (*Weltanschauung*).

Ideologies are often derived from, or closely related to, more profound and sophisticated statements as set forth in works of political philosophy. In this respect, ideology is like the *Reader's Digest* paraphrase of a great work. Compared to political philosophies, ideologies are more simplified and less profound; they emphasize action over thought, and may stress emotions rather than cognitions. Most of the great works on ideology assume that ideologies rest on a set of underlying interests and predispositions, often derived from one's class position in society. Thus, one speaks of the ideology of the ruling class, working-class ideology, bourgeois ideology, and so on. This awareness of the connection between ideology and interests leads inexorably to a concern with "unmasking" ideologies in order to discover their material base in social relations.

It is evident that relatively few people have coherent and explicit ideas about politics that deserve the designation "ideology." Many individuals lack a clear, consistent set of political views. They react in an ad hoc fashion or simply avoid thinking about politics altogether. They may have low levels of information, hold contradictory opinions, misunderstand basic concepts, and so on. Still others do have politically relevant views, which are, however, either implicit or contradictory. At this point, the concept of political culture becomes useful. Indeed, an attempt to look at mass in addition to elite opinions and values regarding politics was a major consideration in developing the concept of political culture, which was viewed from the outset as a broader concept with wider application than ideology. A single political culture could comprise several ideologies; historically, the Canadian political culture has included the ideologies of conservatism, liberalism, and socialism.

These classical ideologies are being transformed by new issues, ideas, and political forces. The contours of these newly emerging ideologies are difficult to discern. Concerns about identity (including ethnicity and gender), participation, and quality of life are emerging alongside disenchantment with existing political institutions and leaders. The composition of the House of Commons following the 1993 federal election reflects these transformations. The traditional parties of the left (NDP) and the right (Progressive Conservative) were reduced to nine and two members respectively, too small to qualify for official party status. In their place (with over 50 members each) were elected the Western-based Reform Party, which espouses a peculiar mixture of populism and fiscal and social conservatism, and the Quebec-based Bloc Québécois, whose sole ideological commitment is to the dissolution of Canada and the attainment of sovereignty for Quebec.

In short, the political culture is invisibly interwoven into all aspects of politics and government. One can isolate the cultural variable for the purposes of analysis, but to do so requires a sensitive appreciation for the techniques that can render the often hidden assumptions, values, and beliefs visible and comprehensible. The study of political culture can, therefore, remain rather general and abstract, encompassing the broadly stated political values at their highest level; or it can be made much more specific and focused on beliefs and values related to particular issues or policies.

APPROACHES TO THE STUDY OF POLITICAL CULTURE

Most students of political culture seem to agree on one point: culture is a collective phenomenon, the attribute of a group, not an individual. An individual cannot make or possess a culture. However, she or he can learn a culture. For this reason, the components of a political culture—values, beliefs, and attitudes, among others—can be observed in the individual. Thus, one might refer to X's religious values or Y's attitudes to abortion as aspects of a culture. But what does it mean to talk about a *group* value or attitude? Is a group merely the sum of those individuals who belong to it, and its culture the average beliefs of its membership? Or is culture something different again from majority opinion or a statistical average? In grappling with these questions, social scientists tend to fall into one of two camps: some opt for a "holistic" approach, while others insist on "methodological individualism."

The *individualistic approach* to political culture assumes that values and beliefs exist only in specific individuals, who may or may not resemble one another. To generalize about the values of any group of people requires reliable information obtained from a large sample of individuals who are representative of the population as a whole. These data are almost always obtained by survey research. Once these individual-level survey data have been gathered, the problem of how to aggregate them in order to make judgments about the entire population involves the use of statistical "modal" characteristics. The term "mode" refers to that point along a continuum where the largest concentration of attitudes is found.

The first and most prominent example of the individualistic approach to political culture is Gabriel Almond and Sidney Verba's study of five countries: the United States, Britain, Mexico, Germany, and Italy.[8] The authors selected a sample of respondents from each country and administered a long questionnaire designed to elicit attitudes to the political system in general, and to the role of the individual as both a citizen (i.e., a participant in the decision-making process) and a subject (i.e., someone on the receiving end of the laws and regulations enforced by the system).[9] In analyzing their data, Almond and Verba introduced several categories that allowed them to generalize about the "modal" characteristics of each of the societies they studied. For example, they planned to use results of "citizen efficacy" and "subject competence" questions, together with questions about orientations to the system as a whole, to locate societies along a continuum, ranging from primitive political cultures, in which there is little awareness of the existence of the nation-state or of the individual's role in the national political system: through "subject" cultures, in which the individual responds positively to the system's outputs but has a low sense of personal citizen efficacy; to the most advanced "participant" cultures, which display high measures of both efficacy and competence. Their survey results proved somewhat disappointing. The neat distinctions between participant, subject, and primitive political cultures did not materialize. Instead, Almond and Verba found a mixture of attitudes encompassing elements from all three categories. Consequently, the term "civic culture" denoted the hybrid mixture of attitudes and values—some "modern," others premodern—found in what they believed to be the most highly developed democratic political system in their study: the United States.[10]

Although Almond and Verba did not include Canada in their five-nation study, their survey has been applied (at least in part) many times in this country. Virtually every major academic survey conducted since 1965 has included one or more items from the civic culture survey. Researchers have emphasized, in particular, the questions on "efficacy" and "trust." The questions measuring efficacy and trust include various versions of the following items:

Political Efficacy

1.   "Generally, those elected to Parliament (Congress) soon lose touch with the people."

2. "Sometimes politics and government seem so complicated that a person like me can't really understand what's going on."
3. "I don't think that the government cares much what people like me think."
4. "People like me don't have any say about what the government does."

Political Trust

1. "Do you think that people in government waste a lot of the money we pay in taxes, waste some of it, or don't waste very much of it?"
2. "How much of the time do you think you can trust the government in Washington (Ottawa) to do what is right?"
3. "Would you say the government is pretty much run by a few big interests looking out for themselves, or that it is run for the benefit of all of the people?"
4. "Do you feel that almost all of the people running the government are smart people who know what they are doing, or do you think that quite a lot of them don't seem to know what they are doing?"
5. "Do you think that quite a few of the people running the government are a little crooked, not very many are, or do you think hardly any of them are crooked at all?"[11]

The efficacy questions have been included in nearly every Canadian national election study since 1965. Some interesting trends emerge. Indicating their low feelings of political efficacy, one-half or more of Canadians have consistently agreed with statements such as "People like me have no say," and "Politics and government are too complicated to understand." (It should be noted that the same finding applies to many other developed democracies.) When measured, both efficacy and trust scores have been slightly higher for provincial as compared with federal governments, indicating that Canadians feel closer to their provincial government and trust it slightly more than the federal government.

One of the most useful and innovative applications of these concepts appears in the work of David Elkins and Richard Simeon. Instead of analyzing efficacy and trust responses separately, Elkins and Simeon combined them to form a new typology of orientations to politics, as shown in Table 7.1. Elkins and Simeon also used the typology to analyze political orientations in each of the ten provinces, separating out anglophones in Quebec and francophones outside of Quebec. Using data from the 1968 federal election survey, they obtained some rather surprising results. Only about one-quarter of the total sample of respondents fell into the "supporter" category, while fully one-third were classified as "disaffected." Striking provincial contrasts emerged. Only in Ontario, Manitoba, and British Columbia were there more supporters than disaffected; however, these provinces also had the largest number of "critics." In the Atlantic provinces, over half the respondents were disaffected. Nationally, and

TABLE 7. 1 Typology of Orientations to Politics (Elkins and Simeon)

		EFFICACY	
		High	*Low*
TRUST	*High*	Supporters	Deferentials
	Low	Critics	Disaffected

without exception in every province, the smallest group were the "deferentials."[12]

While these and similar survey results are clearly interesting and illuminating, they also have important limitations. Surveys provide a *direct* measure of political culture, and have the advantage of forcing people to make explicit what may be otherwise obscure or implicit. In doing so, however, these measures sometimes distort or twist reality in subtle ways. We cannot be sure that survey responses validly reflect what people really believe or value. Furthermore, surveys and interviews can be used only in the present or recent past, and thus do not illuminate the earlier periods of history that contain important clues to the development of political culture.[13]

Critical supplements to interviews and surveys are the *indirect approaches*, which are far more numerous and varied than individualistic approaches in their utility and validity. A number of techniques, usually involving content analysis, allow researchers to extract from written documents or speeches the values and beliefs that are implicit in them. In the case of the political values of the elite, a highly specialized "operational code" approach has been used to reconstruct the outlook and assumptions of key individuals.[14]

Biographies and autobiographies shed light not only on cognitive beliefs and values, but on life experiences that reflect how important those values are for behaviour. Indeed, by studying the behaviour of individuals, or the collective behaviour of institutions (i.e., their adoption of various policies), skilful students of political culture can excavate latent assumptions about politics and thus create a picture of the political culture of both the present and the past.

The latter kind of indirect approach often accompanies a "holistic" conception of political culture. In the holistic approach, political culture constitutes a kind of "ethos" that envelops and conditions a society.[15] Certain values and predispositions are, figuratively speaking, "in the air." For this reason, one sometimes speaks of a "climate" of opinion. Like climate, these values influence behaviour invisibly but effectively. The individual is born into this ethos and absorbs it through a kind of osmosis. Though people may vary in the degree to which they absorb the culture, everyone is exposed to these values to a great extent. An individual's departure from the prevailing ethos, or social deviance, in no way disproves the existence of the culture, because socialization is never complete.

Descriptions of the ethos of Canadian political culture are many and varied. Sometimes geography is credited with having produced a distinctive Canadian ethos. Two years after Confederation, for example, in a lecture about Canadian "national spirit" delivered to the Montreal Literary Club, Robert Grant Haliburton stressed the formative influence of Canada's "northern" geography and climate: "[M]ay not our snow and frost [he asked] give us what is of more value than gold or silver, a healthy, hardy, virtuous dominant race? [For Canada] must ever be ... a Northern country inhabited by the descendants of Northern races."[16] Haliburton regarded the superiority of northerners as a fundamental axiom of politics. Rhetorically he asked, "If climate has not had the effect of moulding races, how is it that the southern nations have almost invariably been inferior to and subjugated by the men of the north?" From the felicitous marriage of racial inheritance and northern environmentalism, there would emerge a Canadian people worthy of the ideals of "the true north, strong and free."

Not all efforts to define a Canadian ethos are infected by the virus of racial nationalism. Nor do they necessarily emphasize the formative impact of geography. Seymour Martin Lipset explicitly posits the existence of a national ethos in the following passage: "[V]alue differences between the United States and Canada suggest that they stem in large part from two disparate founding ethos."[17] But for Lipset (as we will see below), historical events rather than geographical factors account for the variation.

The approach presented in this chapter draws on both individualism and holism. We are interested in the pattern of individually held values and beliefs, and thus examine relevant survey results such as those discussed above. We are aware, however, that the individualistic approach alone is insufficient. To appreciate the importance of the larger whole within which individuals operate (without, however, arguing that values and beliefs are somehow preserved in an invisible ethos, a kind of social formaldehyde), we draw attention to certain distinctively Canadian political institutions, such as Parliament, the Constitution Acts, federal–provincial conferences, the CBC, elements of popular culture (novels, poetry, songs, films, etc.), that form part of Canada's political personality and illuminate the character of Canadian politics. In important respects, these institutions exist independent of the modal attitudes and values of individuals living in Canada at any particular moment in time. Some present themselves to the outside world as quintessentially Canadian, frequently with explicit authorization to speak or act on behalf of Canada. Notwithstanding the range of possible variation within the country, there are times and places where a single voice speaks, and it calls itself Canadian.[18] In these settings, the individual or group that presumes to speak for the collectivity, insofar as it is effective, becomes the collectivity. Individuals who hold a different outlook become irrelevant, at least until they are able to project a dissenting voice or image. The world, in short, contains significant "institutional facts" that assume a different character and exist apart from the individuals that surround and inhabit them. Canadians, whatever their individual conceptions of value and purpose, live and breathe to some extent in a common political space dominated by institutions whose very design and functioning evolves from, and gives shape to, the complexities of Canadian political culture. Thus, it is useful to examine the values promoted by, and embodied in, these institutions. Of particular interest are institutions that explicitly undertake a role in political socialization, and that are described in the title of a textbook as the "foundations of political culture."

POLITICAL SOCIALIZATION: THE LEARNING OF POLITICAL CULTURE

Political socialization is the process of transmitting political values and attitudes through time and across space. Agencies involved in the process include families, schools, churches, political parties, and, perhaps most importantly, the mass media. These and similar institutions consciously attempt to inculcate certain values and foster particular attitudes toward politics. Political socialization is especially effective during the "formative stage" in the development of the individual's values and orientations (the early teen years), but political socialization can continue beyond adolescence.[19]

Socialization and learning are not perfectly congruent. Socialization suggests a planned, controllable, linear pattern of acquiring knowledge and values. But people learn more than they are "socialized" to learn. They learn from unpredictable events in both the natural and the social environment. A flood can serve as a fundamental learning experience, as can a war, a hockey game, or even a federal election. People learn from introspection and self-education, often despite what their socializers would like them to learn instead. They learn as well from individuals and groups whose values run counter to the prevailing political culture. In short, learning, unlike socialization, is a dialectical process full of contradictions and unpredictable outcomes.

Furthermore, socialization is not always a benign process. The attempt to preserve and transmit a culture can have a nasty side. Although the following observation exaggerates the extent to which coercion is used to "socialize" people in our society, it serves to remind us that cultural continuity should never be taken for granted:

To maintain and transmit a value system, human beings are punched,
bullied, sent to jail, thrown into concentration camps, cajoled, bribed,

made into heroes, encouraged to read newspapers, stood up against a wall and shot, and sometimes even taught sociology. To speak of cultural inertia is to overlook the concrete interests and privileges that are served by indoctrination, education, and the entire complicated process of transmitting culture from one generation to the next.[20]

SOCIETAL ORIGINS OF POLITICAL CULTURE: FOUR VIEWS

We may surmise, therefore, that an individual acquires political culture traits through a learning process, part of which is controlled by various socializing agencies. But where do the political culture traits embraced by these socializing agencies originate? In attempting to answer this question, students of political culture have adopted differing interpretations. One theorist, Louis Hartz, argues that societies such as Canada and the United States, founded by immigrants from Europe, develop a political culture that reflects the values and beliefs of the groups that were dominant during the "founding period." Hartz contends that the "founders" are able to dominate the political culture of a "new society" by setting up institutions and myths that imbue their values and beliefs with a nationalistic flavour, thus making membership in the nation contingent on accepting the dominant ideology.[21]

Thus, new societies, "fragments" of Europe transported to the New World, tend to have a political culture that conserves and preserves the values, beliefs, and attitudes of the founders of that society. The "fragment theory" was first applied to the United States. Hartz describes the political culture of the United States as "bourgeois," and points to its origins in 17th- and 18th-century British society. Applying the fragment theory to Canada is complicated by the fact that ours is a "two-fragment" society. *La Nouvelle France* was founded by 17th- and 18th-century emigrants from feudal France. English Canada was founded by Loyalist refugees from the American Revolution, who were also largely bourgeois in outlook. Much of the present-day difference between Canadian anglophones and francophones can be traced back to the vast political culture differences between these two founding fragments.

Seymour Martin Lipset disagrees with Hartz's view that societies bear forever the cultural marks of their birth. In his view, cultural inheritance is less significant than the experiences that society undergoes. Indeed, he suggests that one can identify certain "formative events" in the history of a country that help mould or shape its values and consequently make a lasting impression on its institutional practices.[22] When he applies his fomative-events notion to English Canada, however, the differences between him and Hartz shrink. For Lipset, the most important formative event in Canada's history—the "counterrevolution" and subsequent migration north of the Loyalists—is the obverse of that in the United States; this event, he believes, affected Canada's political culture as significantly as the American Revolution moulded the United States.

Thus, both Hartz's fragment theory and Lipset's formative-events notion focus attention on the Loyalist experience as a major source of English Canada's political culture. Yet the cultural consequences of the Loyalist migration are a subject of considerable controversy among historians and social scientists. Much of the debate has turned on defining the ideological outlook of the Loyalists. The main issue has been to what extent the Loyalists presented an "organic conservative" alternative to the "liberal" worldview of the revolutionaries who expelled them and shaped the political institutions and culture of the new United States. Lipset himself speaks of the Loyalists as "counterrevolutionaries" who helped make Canada more elitist, ascriptive, and particularist (with greater emphasis on the collectivity) than the United States. To substantiate his claims, he examines not only survey results but also data comparing crime rates, educational practices, economic policies, popular culture, fiction, and even religious traditions in the two countries.

A number of scholars have criticized Lipset's interpretation of these data, and more fundamentally his failure to distinguish anglophones from francophones. Clearly, the two groups had different cultural origins and experienced different formative events. The French Canadians were relatively unaffected by the American Revolution. For them, the major formative event was undoubtedly the Conquest (described in their history books as the *Cession,* a term that reveals their profound sense of betrayal by France). French-language history books typically depict the events leading up to 1763 as a "catastrophe," and devote half of their space to the "golden age" that preceded it.

One advantage of Hartz's fragment theory is that it highlights the cultural uniqueness of the anglophone and francophone fragments. But despite a general consensus about the political culture of the francophone fragment, followers of Hartz have disagreed even among themselves about the impact of the Loyalists. Some have seen the Loyalists as primarily a bourgeois fragment, albeit "tinged with Toryism." Others have insisted that we not dismiss the "Tory touch," which is deemed to have had an important influence on both policies and institutions.[23] While both perspectives on the Loyalists (i.e., the "liberal" interpretation and the "conservative" view) contribute important insights, they tend to ignore effects of the Loyalist migration that go beyond the usual categories of ideology. Although undoubtedly Canada's unique brand of conservative liberalism probably can be traced back to our Loyalist origins, so too can our profound identity crisis, our fascination with the mosaic, and our willingness to use the state for "interventionist" purposes that most Americans would reject. Furthermore, one can regard the Loyalist experience as having produced an "anti-fragment" insofar as it encouraged a prolongation of emotional and cultural ties to Britain instead of leading to the kind of cultural isolation that is a precondition to the "freezing" of the fragment culture. Consequently, English Canada found no difficulty importing British-style parliamentary socialism in the 20th century, whereas both Quebec and the United States rejected it as "alien."

Although the fragment theory, enriched by the introduction of Lipset's formative-events notion, illuminates the otherwise baffling history of ideologies and political parties in Canada, political culture studies need not be confined by the categories of analysis that derive from the European ideologies of conservatism, liberalism, and socialism. Much of the experience of the New World lies beyond these categories, and, in any event, the study of political culture can and should embrace virtually every aspect of political practice. Similarly, Almond and Verba's concern with efficacy and trust is too limiting. They chose to focus on those aspects of political culture because they were primarily interested in the problem of democracy. But the problem of democracy is not the central political problem in Canada. Therefore, there is no reason to stick with their concepts and concerns either. Instead, as students of the Canadian experience, we need to examine values, attitudes, and beliefs that relate to more fundamental and pressing problems such as Anglo–French relations, regionalism, and American domination, not merely to the problem of democracy or the problem of class and ideology that animated the work of those who pioneered in the use of political culture.

Furthermore, we need to supplement Hartz's and Lipset's rather idealistic approaches to political culture with approaches that have a much firmer appreciation of the structural bases of culture. For culture never exists in a vacuum, nor does it have an all-determining effect on politics. Rather, culture and its structural underpinnings are interrelated and interdependent. To understand this aspect of culture and trace it back to its societal origins, we need to examine the work of two additional theorists, Harold Innis and Karl Marx.

Although he did not consider himself a student of political culture, Harold Innis offers important insight into the process of cultural transmission.[24] Unlike Hartz and Lipset, who seem to treat values and beliefs as determinants of social and political structures, Innis reverses the causal arrow by arguing that it is not culture that shapes society. For Innis, cultures are heavily affected by the technology of production and distribution of ideas. Hence the culture of society is transformed when new developments take place in the technology of communication. The invention of the printing press revolutionized Western culture, according to Innis. Recent revolutionary developments, dubbed "the third wave" by Alvin Toffler, include the discovery of radio and television, the introduction of inexpensive copying machines, and the still-emerging technology of the microchip, fibre optics, satellite relays, electronic mail, fax, two-way video communication, and other aspects of what has been called the "information highway."[25] Unfortunately, Innis died before most of these innovations had become widespread, and thus he did not assess how they have affected Canadian political culture. But his insight concerning the importance to culture of the underlying structure of communication remains fundamentally useful.

Innis's insights can be elaborated to explain much of the crisis of Canadian identity in the 20th century. Clearly, the means of distribution of culture (including popular culture) are important determinants of what ideas get transmitted to the general public. Canada, unlike virtually any other country in the world, has a cultural-transmission system that is almost entirely in the hands of foreigners. Most Canadian children pass into adulthood without, for example, ever seeing a Canadian feature-length film. They watch American television and even read school textbooks that are produced and written in the United States. They listen to American records and eat food produced by mass-distribution food outlets owned in the United States. They see American commercials and read American advertising. Little wonder then that they grow up with a very shaky sense of Canadian identity and relatively little knowledge about their own country and political institutions, much less any sense of what might constitute Canadian culture in the mass media, the arts, music, and letters. So extreme has been the domination of our cultural networks that, in a document prepared in 1977 to provide new directions for the Canadian Broadcasting Corporation, the then CBC president, Albert Johnson, commented, "Canada today faces its greatest crisis in history: the combination of national life-threatening arguments over our nationhood and the relentless American cultural penetration."[26] Whether this cultural domination leads to economic domination, or the reverse, is perhaps immaterial: the massive U.S. presence on the cultural scene is matched by an equally dominant U.S. presence in the economy, fully reinforced by the Free Trade Agreement and later consolidated under NAFTA. This leads us directly to Marxist and neo-Marxist analyses of the Canadian dilemma.

According to Karl Marx, the material conditions under which a society produces its wealth are a major factor in determining the nature of the political culture. In his view, there are relatively few "modes of production": primitive, feudal, capitalist, and socialist. Each limits the kind of political structures and culture that can exist. Within a given mode of production, however, variations will occur as a result of different patterns of external trade relations and internal control of production and distribution. Students of contemporary Canadian politics who have applied Marxist concepts to Canada emphasize the effect on our political culture of Canada's major economic structures. The fact that we are a capitalist country with a long history of economic dependence on foreign capital bears heavily on our current political difficulties.

Furthermore, the neo-Marxists have pointed out that within the dominant capitalist class are various "fractions" that have different perceptions of their interests and different orientations toward the economic system. They distinguish in particular between a mercantile/financial class fraction, which makes profits on the circulation rather than the production of goods and services, and a more entrepreneurial industrial capitalist fraction, which is focused on industrial development and expansion. Particularly in the crucial period of the late 19th century, the interests of these two class fractions were opposed. The mercantilists did not favour the development of an indigenous heavy industry in Canada, but instead sought to profit on the exchange of staple products from the hinterland for manufactured goods imported from the imperial centre (i.e., Britain and, at a later point, the United States). According to the neo-Marxists, the political culture of colonialism and imperial dependency was consciously fostered by the mercantile-class fraction to support its own economic interests. The dominant element of Canada's capitalist class, members of this group could not see themselves as rulers of a strong, independent nation-state. Burdened with a colonial mentality, they opposed any efforts to develop a true Canadian nationalism.[27]

Each of the above approaches to political culture sheds light on the social origins and development of culture. A comprehensive historical analysis must therefore take account of:

1. the cultural genes implanted by the founding groups (Hartz);
2. the kinds of formative events that affected cultural values and institutions (Lipset);
3. the nature of the technology of communication (Innis); and
4. the economic infrastructure of society (Marx).

These four perspectives complement one another. Any one of them alone is insufficient, yet together they illuminate the complexity and richness of a political culture. They show, as well, that a variety of institutions, including the family, schools, the mass media, and work experiences, play a part in transmitting political culture.

TRANSFORMATION OF POLITICAL CULTURE

Many critics of the political culture approach argue that political culture implies stability and stagnation because it is assumed to be an unchanging feature of the political system. But, clearly, political culture changes over time. To understand how and why it changes, we need to revisit the theoretical approaches that we invoked in looking at the origins of political culture. But additional factors need to be introduced as well.

Political culture might undergo a transformation in response to a formative event such as a revolution, major war, or other cataclysmic activity. Since the continuity of culture depends on political socialization, however, any interruption or transformation of the socialization process could have a transformative impact on political culture. Thus, new ideas about child rearing, or the introduction of new technologies of communication such as television, can change political culture. Each new generation presents a challenge for political socialization, and to some extent experiences a world different from the preceding one. A number of students of political culture have looked at intergenerational differences in fundamental values and orientations. This is precisely the approach underlying Ronald Inglehart's seminal work on the changes he associates with the transition from materialist to postmaterialist values. In his first work in this area, entitled *Silent Revolution*, he argued that "the values of Western publics have been shifting from an overwhelming emphasis on material well-being and physical security toward greater emphasis on the quality of life. The causes and implications of this shift are complex, but the basic principle may be stated very simply: people tend to be more concerned with immediate needs and threats than with things that seem remote or non-threatening."[28]

Inglehart's approach assumed that as the material conditions of advanced industrial societies improved, public attention would shift to nonmaterial values. The economic difficulties that have beset all industrial societies in recent years have certainly interrupted what he saw as a profound and irreversible change. Nevertheless, he has found a great deal of evidence for his hypothesis that material well-being allows generations to shift their focus and emphasis to other values. His later work, *Culture Shift*, presents considerable support for this hypothesis.

Another important influence on political culture is immigration and emigration. This insight follows clearly from the fragment theory and from other approaches that recognize that infusion of new groups of people with different values will have an effect on the societal value systems of the countries they enter or leave. A parallel hypothesis was developed around Karl Deutsch's concept of social mobilization. According to Deutsch, changes in values would come about through a combination of social changes that he called the subprocesses of social mobilization; these included education, urbanization, industrialization, growth of literacy, growing wealth, and exposure to mass media. Deutsch hypothesized that social mobilization was the central engine of modernization. Although his theory gave the impression that once countries had passed certain thresholds, the mobilization effects diminished or disappeared, his insights draw attention to the relationship between value change and changing aspects of the social structure of a society.

The social structures of advanced industrial societies are currently being transformed by forces of globalization in the economic sphere; new technology in communications and information transfer; shifting political identities and affiliations; and major developments in education and religion. This structural transformation has been accompanied by radical cultural changes involving values, attitudes, and beliefs. Central to the changing cultural outlook that has emerged in the latter part of the 20th century is a new perspective on the environment, one that represents a paradigm shift as profound as the change that occurred at the dawn of the modern age. Nature was then viewed as fully explainable and controllable by human science and technology. It appeared to be a rich storehouse of virtually limitless resources to be harvested or exploited for the benefit of people. This outlook minimized or ignored at least two problems: the possibility of exhausting nature's "storehouse" and the danger of doing irreparable and irreversible environmental damage in the course of extracting riches from nature. Though some spoke out to warn of these dangers, their cries went largely unheeded until the last 30 years.

The discovery by scientists and others that ecological systems are fragile and profoundly threatened by human incursions has reverberated throughout modern society, resulting in a re-evaluation of policies at all levels. Legislation and new agencies devoted to "environmental protection" have brought a new range of considerations and additional levels of complexity to the policy-making process of both government and industry. Environmental degradation has profound consequences for human health. Changed consumer behaviour and preferences have transformed the marketing of products as well as the techniques for producing them. Concerns with pollution and the deteriorating quality of the basic resources of air and water have led to new subfields and journals in various academic disciplines, new industries concerned with environmental technology, and the new social movements and political parties.

A driving force behind the new perspective on the environment has been the environmental movement, which is but one of several new social movements that deliberately set out to change fundamental attitudes in such areas as gender, environment, and ethnicity. In many respects, these social movements have captivated public attention and added to the political agenda a whole new range of concerns and issues that are themselves evidence of transformations occurring in our political culture and political discourse. Canadian political discourse features a vocabulary uncontemplated 20 or 30 years ago, with concerns like aboriginal self-government, gay rights, environmentalism, sovereignty-association, and women's issues well placed in the vocabulary and high on the political agenda.

SUMMARY

It is possible to analyze the development of Canadian political culture in more detail using the four insights mentioned above. From the Hartzian perspective, we realize that Canadian political culture developed from the cultural genes implanted by the two major founding groups, the English and the French. These two groups embodied contrasting ideologies that would never easily mix together. The absolutism and feudal tendencies of the French fragment led to a preservation of that culture and an antipathy toward the modernizing impulses of the anglophones. The anglophones, for their part, were a very strange mixture of elements. Irrespective of how important the Tory touch was, the anglophone bourgeois culture had the ironic and paradoxical characteristic of being simultaneously liberal and anti-American. Because the United States had made liberalism into its national culture, the anglophones were prevented from doing so—hence the origin of Canada's never-ending identity crisis and the peculiar combination of celebration of the British connection and antipathy toward a culture that was ideologically very similar to that of English Canada. Furthermore, because of the failure to nationalize the political culture of the anglophones, and because of the pattern of settlement that led to a direct importation into the Canadian West of founding groups from Europe that did not become socialized either to English- or French-Canadian culture before settling there, the Canadian West featured what some have called a process of "subfragmentation" in which new groups brought with them ideologies that reflected their European origin and that were much more progressive than those of the older fragments. Thus socialism arose in Saskatchewan. The Alberta subfragmentation reflected the influence of the United States, from which many of the founding settlers of Alberta came. In general, the political culture of the Canadian West has shown noticeable differences from that of the older parts of the country, and has featured the appearance of at least two ideological variants not found in much strength elsewhere: socialism and social credit.

The Lipset emphasis on formative events is similarly revealing. Canada had no single great nationalizing formative event. The significant events in our history show the strong influence of the colonial powers, because in almost every instance they were the outcome of struggles taking place between England and France or England and the United States. These events include the Conquest of New France in 1763, the American Revolution in 1776, and the War of 1812. Two other significant events, ones with more of an indigenous flavour, were the uprisings in 1837 and the passage of the British North America Act in 1867. But even the latter event took place in England as a statute of the British Parliament, a fact that continued to bedevil (until 1982) attempts to patriate the Constitution. A second insight from the formative-events notion is that different regions and different cultural fragments have had a different perspective on these formative events and, in effect, a different kind of history.

The Innis approach suggests how important it is to have a national communications network capable of binding the community together. This system would have to offset cultural fragmentation between anglophones and francophones and the enormous cultural influences from south of the border. But in several respects we have failed to carry out this task successfully. Despite the setting up of a national broadcasting network in the 1930s, the CBC has proved incapable of bringing together francophones and anglophones or of offsetting infusions of American culture. Furthermore, other important socializing agencies were not left in the hands of the federal government. Responsibility for education was assigned to the provinces, and political party organizations developed into quasi-autonomous provincial organizations with a very loose federal alliance at the top. Thus, two of the most critical socializing agencies have been under provincial control and have contributed to the development of provincial political cultures, in some cases at the expense of a national culture. In the early 1990s, Canada was facing a severe crisis over the control of new communications systems such as Cablevision, pay-TV, and satellite broadcasts. The provinces, aware of the potential of the communications system to control the thoughts and minds of the public, are determined not to let this control pass to the federal government.

Finally, from the Marxist perspective, we see immediately the important impact on our political culture of foreign dependency and the different alignment of capitalist groups around the dominant capitalist forces in the country. We see as well the effect that uneven economic development has had on the country in fostering regionalism and leading to the growth of regional economic interests and regional perspectives. Paradoxically, however, class divisions (supposedly the major determinants of political culture in a modern society) have had only a minor effect on Canadian politics, in part because the party system and the electoral system enhance sectional cleavages.

CONCLUSION

Political culture consists of individually held values, attitudes, and beliefs concerning politics; symbols that catalyze sentiments and beliefs about politics and political action; politically relevant knowledge and perceptions, including perceptions of historical experiences and notions of identity; and, finally, ideologies as aggregations of values and beliefs that have coherence and internal cohesion. Political culture must be examined historically, and therefore one must use both direct and indirect techniques to measure it. Political culture serves as an important filter that affects political action by constraining perceptions about politics, notions of what constitute political problems, and prescriptions for resolving these problems.

Political culture is historically derived. It is affected by the cultural baggage brought to a society by immigrants, especially first settlers. It is moulded by the formative events a society undergoes in the course of its modernization. It is conditioned by such structural underpinnings as class relations, trade patterns, the flow of transportation, and communications. It changes as a result of contact with other cultures.

Political culture can be seen as the "language" of politics. Political discourse is its "speech." Through political discourse, contending groups in society attempt to shape both public perceptions and governmental responses. They proffer competing conceptions of problems that embody their interests and preferences, and privilege the outcomes they wish to see achieved. In effect, these conceptions entail both a diagnosis of the nature of the problem and a prescription concerning the appropriate response to it. Political discourse is not always manipulated in such a conscious, deliberate manner. Sometimes the discourse reflects assumptions and values that are no longer obvious or explicit—historical viewpoints that have sunk beneath the surface of conscious awareness but that are potent forces nonetheless. To achieve social change, these implicit conceptions must be "excavated" and made apparent.

NOTES

1. Cf. Clyde Kluckhohn, *Culture and Behaviour* (New York: Free Press, 1962), p. 42: "Culture is—among other things—a set of ready-made definitions of the situation that each participant only slightly re-tailors in his idiomatic way." Cf. also Clifford Geertz's definition of culture as "an historically transmitted pattern of meanings embodied in symbols, a system of inherited conceptions expressed in symbolic forms by means of which men communicate, perpetuate, and develop their knowledge about and attitudes toward life." *The Interpretation of Cultures* (New York: Basic Books, 1973), p. 89. Quoted in S.M. Lipset, *Continental Divide: The Values and Institutions of the United States and Canada* (New York: Routledge, 1990), p. 8.

2. For a discussion of symbolism in politics, see the several books by Murray Edelman, including *The Symbolic Uses of Politics* (Urbana, Ill.: University of Illinois Press, 1964); and Lowell Dittmer, "Political Symbolism and Political Culture: Toward a Theoretical Synthesis," *World Politics* 30 (1977).

3. David Easton, *A Systems Analysis of Political Life* (New York: John Wiley and Sons, 1965), p. 101.

4. The boundaries of legitimate political activity, like other elements of the political, can and do change over time. Responding in part to the growth of neo-conservatism in Britain and the United States, and in part to an indigenous concern that government had become too big and too interventionist, the Mulroney government began to "privatize" a number of Crown corporations and to "deregulate" some aspects of the Canadian economy. See Janine Brodie and Jane Jenson, *Crisis,*

Challenge and Change: Party and Class in Canada Revisited (Ottawa: Carleton University Press, 1988), ch. 10.

5. See, among others, David V.J. Bell, "The Political Culture of Problem-Solving and Public Policy," in David Shugarman and Reg Whitaker, eds., *Federalism and Political Community* (Peterborough, Ont.: Broadview, 1989).

6. Jane Jenson, "Changing Discourse, Changing Agenda: Political Rights and Reproductive Policies in France," in Mary F. Katzenstein et al., eds., *The Women's Movement of the United States and Western Europe: Consciousness, Political Opportunity and Public Policy* (Philadelphia: Temple University Press, 1987). See also Brodie and Jenson, *Crisis, Challenge and Change*.

7. James Laxer, "A healthy dose of heresy for unbending orthodoxy," *Toronto Star* (January 2, 1994). For theoretical discussion of these issues, see, among others, Brodie and Jenson, *Crisis, Challenge and Change*, ch. 10; and contributions by Janine Brodie, Jane Jenson, Neil Bradford, and Duncan Cameron to Alain G. Gagnon and A. Brian Tanguay, eds., *Canadian Parties in Transition: Discourse, Organization, and Representation* (Scarborough, Ont.: Nelson Canada, 1988).

8. Gabriel Almond and Sidney Verba, *The Civic Culture* (Princeton: Princeton University Press, 1963).

9. The distinction between citizen and subject was first discussed by Jean Jacques Rousseau in his famous book *The Social Contract*, trans. W. Kendall (Chicago: Henry Regnery, 1954). Rousseau says (p. 21): "The members of a body politic call it 'the state' when it is passive, 'the sovereign' when it is active, and 'a power' when they compare it with others of its kind. Collectively they use the title 'people' and *they refer to one another individually as 'citizens' when speaking of their participation in the authority of the sovereign, and as 'subjects' when speaking of their subordination to the laws of the state*" (emphasis added).

10. Carole Pateman and many other scholars sharply criticized Almond and Verba's interpretation of their results. Faced with evidence that large numbers of Americans were apathetic, and that apathy correlated highly with low socioeconomic status, Almond and Verba counselled complacency, apparently in the belief that modern democracy requires apathy to ensure stability. This viewpoint left Almond and Verba (and others who shared their outlook) unprepared for the "participation explosion" that erupted in the United States in the late 1960s. See Pateman's "Political Culture, Political Structure and Political Change," *British Journal of Political Science* 1, no. 3 (July 1971):291–306.

11. As summarized in Nathaniel Beck and John Peirce, "Political Involvement and Party Allegiances in Canada and the United States," *International Journal of Comparative Sociology* 18 (March–June 1977):28.

12. In a follow-up study, Jon Pammett analyzed the 1984 data, this time separating federal from provincial citizen types. Significant changes appeared. The percentage of both supporters and deferentials had risen considerably to nearly 60 percent. Critics and disaffecteds fell to about 40 percent. Harold Clarke and Allan Kornburg, in their book *Citizens and Community: Political Support in a Representative Democracy* (New York: Cambridge University Press, 1992), developed a similar typology of Supporters, Oppositionists, Discontented, Instrumentalists, and Alienated (Partial and Total). They too applied this typology to different regions of the country, distinguishing Quebec anglophones from francophones. Using data from the 1988 election survey, they found significant differences between Quebec francophones and other Canadians with respect to Alienated and Supporter

groups. Only 15 percent of Quebec francophones were Supporters while 35 percent were Alienated. These figures were nearly reversed among other groups. The closest pattern to that found among Quebec French was in the Prairies, where Alienated outnumbered Supporters 24 percent to 22 percent (see pp. 253–63, and particularly table 8.1). Note that in 1983, the similarity between Quebec French and Prairies was even greater; over 30 percent of Prairie respondents were classified as Alienated.

13. For an insightful critique of the use of polling and surveys, see F.J. Fletcher, "Polling and Political Communication: Lessons from the Canadian Case." Conference paper available from *International Association for Mass Communication Research*, 1990.

14. See, among others, Ole Holsti, "The 'Operational Code' Approach to the Study of Political Leaders: John Foster Dulles's Philosophical Beliefs," *Canadian Journal of Political Science* 3 (1971).

15. The most extensive discussion of "ethos theory" has occurred in the literature on urban politics. In 1963, Edward Banfield and James Q. Wilson in *City Politics* (New York: Vintage Books) wrote about "two fundamentally opposed conceptions of politics" (p. 234), "two mentalities" (p. 46) found in U.S. cities. These two conceptions accounted for a great deal of political behaviour in urban settings. For a critique, see Timothy M. Hennessy, "Problems in Concept Formation: The Ethos 'Theory' and the Comparative Study of Urban Politics," *Midwest Journal of Political Science* 14 (November 1970).

16. Quoted by Carl Berger, "The True North Strong and Free," in Peter Russell, ed., *Nationalism in Canada* (Toronto: McGraw-Hill, 1966), p. 6.

17. S.M. Lipset, *Revolution and Counterrevolution* (New York: Anchor Books, 1970), p. 55.

18. By the same token, however, a number of important institutions are provincial, and they help foster and maintain a provincial outlook.

19. For a discussion on a related theme, see Jon Pammett and Jean-Luc Pepin, eds., *Political Education in Canada* (Montreal: Institute for Research on Public Policy, 1988).

20. Barrington Moore, *Social Origins of Dictatorship and Democracy* (Boston: Beacon Press, 1966), p. 486. To validate Moore's point, one need only review the history of cultural contact between whites and Natives in Canada. The coercion that sometimes accompanies political socialization indeed proves, as Moore argues, that cultural inertia is not inevitable. But it also shows how difficult it is to engineer cultural change. This difficulty complicated attempts to inculcate the "official" political culture in countries such as Poland and Czechoslovakia where values from an earlier era continue to dominate. See Archie Brown and Jack Gray, eds., *Political Culture and Political Change in Communist States* (London: Macmillan, 1977). To some extent, the collapse of communist regimes in the former Soviet Union and Eastern Europe is testimony to the strength of national political cultures, even in the face of determined policies of cultural transformation pursued relentlessly by the communist governments that controlled these countries for decades.

21. Louis Hartz et al., *The Founding of New Societies* (New York: Harcourt Brace, 1964). Hartz is well aware that the so-called founding groups in all cases impose themselves on a society already in place. His work discusses the interac-

tion between the "fragments" and aboriginal groups that truly constitute the "first nations."

22. Lipset, *Revolution and Counterrevolution*. See also Lipset, *Continental Divide*.

23. See especially Gad Horowitz, *Canadian Labour in Politics* (Toronto: University of Toronto Press, 1967).

24. See, for example, the following works by Harold Innis: *Canadian Economic History* (Toronto: University of Toronto Press, 1956); *The Fur Trade in Canada*, rev. ed. (Toronto: University of Toronto Press, 1970); *Empire and Communications*, rev. by Mary Q. Innis (Toronto: University of Toronto Press, 1972). See also James W. Carey, "Harold Adams Innis and Marshall McLuhan," *Antioch Review* (Spring 1967); and William H. Melody et al., eds., *Culture, Communication and Dependency: The Tradition of H.A. Innis* (New Jersey: Ablex Publishing, 1981).

25. See David V.J. Bell, "Global Communications, Culture and Values: Implications for Global Security," in David Dewitt and John Kirton, eds., *Building a New Global Order* (Toronto: Oxford University Press, 1993).

26. Albert Johnson, *Touchstone for the CBC* (mimeo, 1977), p. 2. See also John Redekop, "Continentalism: The Key to Canadian Politics," in John H. Redekop, ed., *Approaches to Canadian Politics*, 2nd ed. Seventeen years later, little has changed despite (1) a revision to the Broadcasting Act (1991) that removed mention of "contributing to the development of national unity" from the mandate of the CBC, and (2) cutbacks in funding that have threatened the CBC's viability as an agency of cultural public policy. For a discussion of these issues, see Colin Haskins and Stuart McFadyen, "The Mandate, Structure and Financing of the CBC," *Canadian Public Policy* 18 (1992); and Marc Raboy, *Missed Opportunities: The Story of Canada's Broadcasting Policy* (Montreal and Kingston: McGill-Queen's University Press, 1990).

27. Gary Teeple, ed., *Capitalism and the National Question* (Toronto: University of Toronto Press, 1972). For a critique, see Glen Williams, "The National Policy Tariffs: Industrial Underdevelopment through Import Substitution," *Canadian Journal of Political Science* 12 (June 1979).

28. Ronald Inglehart, *The Silent Revolution: Changing Values and Political Styles among Western Publics* (Princeton, N.J.: Princeton University Press, 1977), p. 3.

FURTHER READINGS

Bell, David V.J. *The Roots of Disunity: A Study of Canadian Political Culture.* Toronto: Oxford University Press, 1992.

Brodie, Janine, and Jane Jenson. *Crisis, Challenge and Change: Party and Class in Canada Revisited.* Ottawa: Carleton University Press, 1988.

Carroll, William K., ed. *Organizing Dissent: Contemporary Social Movements in Theory and Practice.* Toronto: Garamond Press, 1992.

Clarke, Harold, and Allan Kornburg. *Citizens and Community: Political Support in a Representative Democracy.* New York: Cambridge University Press, 1992.

Gagnon, Alain, and A. Brian Tanguay, eds. *Canadian Parties in Transition: Discourse, Organization, and Representation.* Scarborough, Ont.: Nelson Canada, 1988.

Hartz, Louis, et al. *The Founding of New Societies*. New York: Harcourt Brace, 1964.

Inglehart, Ronald. *Culture Shift in Advanced Industrial Society*. Princeton, N.J.: Princeton University Press, 1990.

Lipset, Seymour Martin. *Continental Divide*. New York: Routledge, 1990.

Merelman, Richard M. *Partial Visions: Culture and Politics in Britain, Canada, and the United States*. Madison, Wis.: University of Wisconsin Press, 1991.

Pammett, Jon, and Michael Whittington, eds. *Political Socialization: Foundations of Political Culture*. Toronto: Macmillan, 1976.

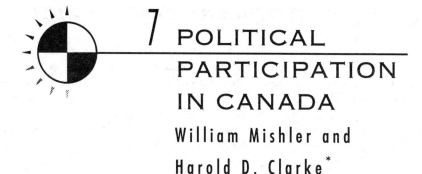

7 POLITICAL PARTICIPATION IN CANADA

William Mishler and
Harold D. Clarke*

Few aspects of Canadian government reveal as much about its political character as the way in which citizens participate in the political life of the country. Widespread, informed, and effective participation is a hallmark of democracy. Participation provides citizens a means with which to influence the selection of political leaders, to communicate their needs and aspirations to government, and hold public elected officials accountable. It also enables citizens to express dissent and vent their grievances with government, thereby regulating societal conflict and promoting political stability. Thus, participation is healthy for society.

Democratic theory holds that political participation is important also for the health of individual citizens. Liberal democrats have long believed that citizens' ability to participate effectively in the important decisions affecting their lives contributes to their sense of self-esteem. It enhances human dignity and self-respect, and contributes to the individual's civic education and moral development. To a substantial degree, therefore, the quality of democracy in Canada is revealed by the nature and extent of citizen participation in the political system. How do Canadians participate in politics, and how extensively? Who participates, and in what activities? Why do some people participate, but not others? What is the quality of citizen participation? How effective is participation in influencing the course of government action? And what are the prospects for promoting higher levels of better-informed and more effective participation in the years ahead? The answers to these questions reveal a great deal about the health of democracy in Canada in the 1990s and beyond.

* The authors wish to thank Donley T. Studlar for graciously sharing his data on the nomination and election of women to the Canadian Parliament.

HOW DO CITIZENS PARTICIPATE?

Political participation consists of those voluntary activities by citizens that are intended to influence the selection of government leaders or the decisions they make. In an open society such as Canada's, there are many ways in which citizens can attempt to influence government, directly or indirectly, individually or in groups, legitimately or illegitimately.

Voting in periodic elections, whether at the national, provincial, or local levels, is among the most common and widely recognized avenues for citizen participation in Canada, as in other western democracies. Although Canada does not hold as many elections as some countries (most notably the United States), the federal structure of the Canadian polity, combined with parliamentary norms that require federal and provincial governments to resign and call elections whenever they are defeated on fundamental issues, provides citizens with opportunities to vote in federal, provincial, or municipal elections on an average of almost once a year. Canadians also have occasional opportunities to vote in referendums where they make direct decisions on important issues. Although rare, referendums can generate considerable political interest and activity and have significant effects, a dramatic recent illustration being the public rejection of the Charlottetown Accord in October 1992.

Voting, however, is only the most visible means of individual political action. Canadian federal and provincial election campaigns are invariably expensive and labour-intensive contests. As a consequence, campaigns provide manifold opportunities for voluntary activity such as ringing doorbells, canvassing neighbourhoods, mailing campaign literature, distributing posters, telephoning potential voters, and the like. Moreover, parties and candidates are always willing to "allow" citizens to participate with their pocketbooks by contributing money to help finance campaigns.

Political parties also depend heavily on volunteer labour between elections. For a small minority of citizens, parties provide opportunities to engage in significant and oftentimes exciting activities such as screening candidates for party nominations, developing party policies, and attending party conferences and national or provincial leadership conventions. Larger numbers confine their party work to a myriad of routine and frequently boring tasks such as organizing party files, updating membership lists, and stuffing envelopes.

Citizen participation is not confined to the electoral process, however. Citizens frequently have interests that cannot be expressed adequately through the simple choices that voting for one of several political parties provides or interests that they want addressed before the next election. Moreover, although elections can be effective instruments of citizen influence on government in the aggregate, the act of voting provides citizens relatively little influence individually. Thus, some citizens attempt to increase their influence on government between elections by participating directly in the political process. One way they do this is by contacting public officials to express an opinion on a pressing public issue or to request assistance with a problem. Government officials at all levels receive a steady flow of letters, telegrams, and telephone calls. Citizens also visit the offices of their federal MPs, provincial MLAs, and local councillors, or approach them at shopping centres, hockey games, restaurants, or wherever else they may encounter their representatives in day-to-day life. Elected officials, for their part, are generally quite receptive to such communication and in fact regularly make themselves available in locales where it is likely to occur.

Some people find it more comfortable, or think it more effective, to try to influence government as part of a group. Some are members of formal organizations or interest groups, such as the Canadian Labour Congress or the Canadian Federation of Agriculture, which regularly employ full-time professionals to lobby government on behalf of member interests. Others belong to informal groups such as neighbourhood associations that pressure government for group or community concerns or take direct action to solve a problem themselves—for example by cleaning up a neighbourhood park.

The most direct means for Canadians to influence government is to become part of it by running for elected office or by seeking an appointed post. Opportunities to hold elected office are severely limited, however, by the small number of available positions, by the time and money required for successful campaigns, and by the practical necessity of securing a party's nomination and, ultimately, the approval of the electorate. Appointive offices also are relatively few in number, and prestigious ones historically have been used to reward political "influentials" who have rendered long and faithful party service. Nevertheless, although the ascent to public office is a slippery slope, there are always ample volunteers to attempt the climb.

Despite having many ways to engage in election-related and other conventional forms of political activity, some Canadians choose to employ more forceful and dramatic means to register their opinions or protest government actions. Such unconventional or protest activities may be individual or collective, legal or illegal, violent or passive. People may march in peaceful demonstrations to protest public policies; they may disobey specific laws in an effort to have them changed; or they may even attempt to stop government actions directly through the use of force or violence. During the past 50 years, protests have run the gamut from bombings, kidnapping, and murder by the radical Front de libération du Québec to the passive resistance of the Greenpeace conservation group attempting to stop government-sanctioned hunting of baby seals.

HOW EXTENSIVELY DO CANADIANS PARTICIPATE?

Opinions vary on the extent of public political participation in Canada.[1] Some argue that Canadians are political "spectators" who are generally quite content to observe the political spectacle from the sidelines. Others maintain that Canadians are relatively active in comparison to the residents of most other democratic countries. Few deny, however, that opportunities for participation far exceed actual levels of involvement.

Those who hold that Canadians are relatively active usually point to the level of voter turnout in federal and provincial elections. Given a chance to vote, most citizens do. In elections since World War II, an average of 75 percent of those on the voters' lists have cast a ballot in federal elections. During this period, turnout was lowest in the 1953 and 1974 elections, which were held during the summer months when many citizens were away on vacation and unable to get to the polls. Turnout was slightly below average again in 1980 and in 1993. In the latter cases, however, turnout is probably underestimated due to the use in these elections of voters' lists from the 1979 federal election and the 1992 referendum on the Charlottetown Accord, respectively. Use of older lists increases the number of citizens on the lists who have died, migrated from Canada, or otherwise become ineligible to vote in the interim. When the effects of these outdated lists are taken into account, the average turnout in federal elections increases to more than 75 percent. A similar percentage of citizens turned out in 1992 to vote on the referendum on the Charlottetown Accord, and turnout in provincial elections is roughly the same level as well, although it can vary significantly from province to province and from one election to the next.[2]

Excluding nations such as Australia, Belgium, and the Netherlands, where voting is compulsory and enforced by legal sanctions, turnout rates among other democratic countries vary between 60 and 90 percent.[3] Canada ranks behind several of these countries, but compares favourably with others such as Japan, Switzerland, India, and particularly the United States, where fewer than two-thirds of eligible citizens are registered to vote and only about 70 percent of those who are registered turn out for presidential elections. Even fewer Americans vote in congressional and state elections, and turnout in all U.S. elections, unlike that in Canada, has been declining for several decades.

Electoral turnout in Canada is even more impressive when individual participation is examined over time. There are many reasons that a person may fail to vote in a particular election: bad weather, illness, or the need to be out of town on business. However, voter surveys suggest that fewer than one person in ten is a habitual nonvoter in federal or provincial elections. Another quarter occasionally fail to cast a ballot, but nearly two-thirds report voting whenever they get a chance.

Underlying these national averages, turnout in both federal and provincial elections varies substantially among the provinces. These differences can be explained in part by special circumstances such as the presence in one province, or in one election, of an especially controversial issue or unusually popular (or unpopular) leader. Differences in weather and geography also have some impact. However, the effects of such idiosyncratic factors are probably quite modest. More important in explaining differences in turnout among the provinces appear to be such considerations as the relative organizational effectiveness of the parties, the levels of competitiveness among them, and public perceptions of the importance of the issues at stake. Competition among the parties makes elections interesting and gives voters a sense that their ballot is meaningful and more likely to make a difference. Moreover, political competition increases party efforts to mobilize their supporters and get them to the polls on election day. It also contributes to the vitality of party organization more generally.

Among other forms of political activity, most Canadians express at least a spectator's interest in political campaigns. As indicated in Table 7.1, for example, more than 80 percent of citizens interviewed during the 1993 federal election campaign indicated that they were are least "fairly interested" in the campaign, and similar percentages said they had discussed politics with friends or watched election-related programs on television during the campaign. Nevertheless, although most Canadians follow the campaign and vote in elections, very few engage in more demanding campaign or election activities. In 1993, only about one citizen in five said he or she tried to influence the vote of a friend, only about one in ten attended a pol itical meeting or rally, and only about one in twenty worked for a political party or candidate. Political parties appear even less successful in attracting workers between elections. At most, only 5 percent of the public are even sporadically active in party organizations, and even then devote an average of less than an hour a week to party affairs.[4]

Part of the reason that Canadians do not participate more extensively in party organizations or electoral campaigns may be that many are unaware of the opportunities that exist. Surveys indicate that greater numbers would be willing to contribute both time and money if they were asked. In Canada, however, political parties are loosely knit organizations that are not very efficient in recruiting or mobilizing members, particularly in the periods between elections. Except at the highest echelons, party organizations "hibernate" between elections. They lack public visibility and do very little to stimulate citizen activity or involvement until the "spring thaw" provided by a new election writ.

In addition to election-related activities, Canadians also enjoy abundant opportunities to participate in noncampaign activities, from writing

TABLE 7.1 **Participation in the 1993 Federal Election Campaign**

	%
Voted in 1993 Federal Election	71
Percentages who "often" or "sometimes":	
Discussed politics with others	81
Watched TV programs about the election campaign	80
Read about the election campaign in newspapers	79
Listened to radio programs about the election campaign	51
Tried to influence friends' vote	23
Attended political meeting or rally	12
Worked for political party or candidate	7
Interest in 1993 federal election: Very interested	52
Fairly interested	31
Slightly interested	14
Not at all interested	3

Note: Weighted national sample, N=1496, missing data removed.

SOURCE: HAROLD D. CLARKE AND ALLAN KORNBERG, THE DYNAMICS OF SUPPORT FOR NEW PARTIES AND NATIONAL PARTY SYSTEMS, STUDY.

their elected officials to working with others in the community to solve local problems. Of these activities, citizens are somewhat more likely to work with others in their community. About a third of all citizens report that they have done so on at least one occasion during their lives. In contrast, only about 20 percent of citizens report that they have ever contacted a public official. What makes this all the more surprising is that an overwhelming majority of Canadians—more than 75 percent, according to some surveys—believe that MPs, MLAs and other public officials would pay attention and respond if contacted by the citizen about a problem.

About 60 percent of Canadians are members of one or more voluntary organizations or groups such as labour unions, professional associations, and church or fraternal groups. Many of these groups are involved in political affairs and thereby enable citizens to participate indirectly in politics by becoming involved in group affairs. However, only about one person in four ever plays an active role in the groups to which they belong. Still fewer express interest in, or are even aware of, the political activities of their groups. Most join groups for social, economic, or professional reasons rather than as a means of political expression. Thus, the number of citizens who can be said to engage in politics indirectly through the involvement of voluntary groups is quite small.[5]

Political protest and violence, though not unknown in Canada, traditionally have been much lower than in many other countries, including the United States. During the 1960s, a period of relatively high political ferment in both countries, Canada experienced an estimated 40 significant protest demonstrations, which resulted in nearly ten deaths. In the United States, by comparison, the 1960s witnessed more than 700 riots and demonstrations resulting in more than 250 deaths. Controlling for the difference in population size, Canada experienced less than a quarter as many protests and demonstrations during that decade of discontent.[6]

Nevertheless, for a minority of Canadians, protest, is or can be, an important avenue of political expression. In separate surveys in 1983 and 1988, for example, 68 percent of Canadians indicated having signed a political petition at some point during their lives. Nearly 40 percent of citizens in both surveys reported having participated in a politically motivated boycott, and 20–25 percent reported having participated in a protest march or rally (see Table 7.2). Even among citizens who have not engaged in these activities, however, majorities believe that such activities are legitimate and potentially effective. This suggests that even larger numbers of Canadians would be willing to take part in such activities given sufficient cause. In sharp contrast, very few citizens have ever taken part in more extreme or confrontational protest activities such as sit-ins or demonstrations where the potential for violence is substantial. Still, the potential for confrontational protests is very real given the evidence that upwards to a quarter of the public think that such activities are legitimate, with significant numbers believing that these activities can be effective as well.

The portrait of the Canadian public that emerges from an examination of any single political activity is not encouraging. There are few activities other than voting in which as many as half of the adult population participates even on an occasional basis. It is important to realize, however, that different political activities appeal to different individuals. The 20 percent of citizens who write letters to public officials are not necessarily the same 20 percent who participate in protest rallies or who try to influence how their friends will vote. Different activities require different resources and skills, and appeal to different types of individuals.

When the entire range of political activities is considered, the picture of the public that emerges is one of a moderately, if sporadically, active citizenry. It is true that upwards of 10 percent of the public appear completely disengaged politically. Such individuals rarely if ever read or talk about politics, and they seldom participate in any discernible way. It also is the case that another 25–30 percent confine themselves exclusively to voting and talking about politics. What is impressive and widely overlooked, however, is the fact that between 50 and 65 percent of adult

TABLE 7.2 Attitudes toward and Participation in Political Protest Activities

	Approve	Effective	Participate	
	1983	1983	1983	1988
Activity	%	%	%	%
Sign petitions	85	71	68	68
Boycott goods or services	64	61	38	38
March or rally	53	52	20	24
Sit-in	26	35	5	8
Potentially violent demonstration	11	23	4	8

Note: Weighted national samples, 1983 N=2117, 1988 N=2215, missing data removed.

SOURCE: HAROLD D. CLARKE AND ALLAN KORNBERG, *SOURCES, DISTRIBUTION AND CONSEQUENCES OF POLITICAL SUPPORT IN CANADA; SUPPORT FOR DEMOCRATIC POLITICS: THE CASE OF CANADA,* STUDIES.

Canadians not only vote but also engage at least occasionally in some form of higher-intensity political activity. When confronted with an issue about which they feel strongly, sizable minorities of citizens become more intensively involved in the political process, choosing avenues of political expression compatible with their personal abilities, needs, and resources.

WHO PARTICIPATES?

Because of the likelihood that the interests of less active citizens will be overlooked by government, democratic theory emphasizes the importance of high levels of involvement by all segments of society. Although opportunities for political involvement are widely distributed in Canada, certain groups of citizens enjoy greater political opportunities, possess superior resources, and are exposed to more intense political stimuli, all of which result in unequal levels of participation.

As indicated in Table 7.3, the largest and most consistent differences in political activity in Canada are those associated with citizens' positions in society. In Canada as elsewhere, the higher a person's social status, the more like it is that he or she will participate in virtually all types of

TABLE 7.3 Who Participates in Selected Political Activities

	Discuss Politics	Party Work	Sign Petition	March/ Rally	Sit-in
	%	%	%	%	%
Age					
18–25	73	4	67	26	14
26–35	78	4	75	30	13
36–45	82	6	77	34	8
46–55	86	10	67	19	3
56–65	81	8	63	17	3
66 and over	82	9	51	9	1
Education					
elementary or less	68	9	34	14	5
some secondary	75	4	57	18	6
completed secondary	82	8	69	19	6
some university	82	7	78	32	10
completed university	86	7	86	45	13
Gender					
Males	81	8	69	26	9
Females	81	6	67	23	6
Income					
Less than $20,000	70	5	54	21	7
$20,000–$39,999	80	5	69	24	8
$40,000–$59,999	82	7	77	30	9
$60,000–$69,999	87	9	76	27	10
$70,000 and over	87	12	79	30	7
Occupation					
Professional/managerial	86	9	78	37	10
White collar	89	6	76	26	7
Blue collar	75	4	71	26	9
Farmer	85	15	53	15	2
Homemaker	76	7	59	13	4
Student	73	3	74	28	16
Unemployed	84	12	51	17	9
Retired	79	8	55	11	2

Note: The "discuss politics" and "party work" percentages are those who reported performing the activities "often" or "sometimes" in the 1993 federal election campaign; the "march/rally" and "sit-in" percentages are those in 1988 who reported ever engaging in the activity.

SOURCES: SEE TABLES 7.1 AND 7.2.

political activity. In addition to determining the social and economic resources available for political investment, social status influences citizens'
perceptions of their personal stakes in politics and their ability to influence government decisions. Higher-status persons also are more likely to
be strategically placed in informal communication networks: they are
more likely to be the neighbours and curling partners of public officials,
high-ranking party officials, and other members of the political elite; they
are more likely to know and be known by political decision-makers, and
to be viewed by the public and politicians alike as community opinion
leaders.

In advanced industrial societies like Canada, social status is determined by a variety of factors, but especially by occupation, income, and
education. Since work is a central experience of adult life, it is not surprising that occupation has important consequences for citizen participation.
Generally, individuals in higher-status occupations participate more than
those with lower-status jobs. Although this relationship holds broadly for
all types of political activity, differences based on occupation are most
pronounced for the more intensive and time-consuming forms of participation. This is illustrated most graphically for the highest-level political activities—seeking and holding elected public office. Lawyers, business
executives, and other professionals constitute less than 20 percent of the
work force, yet they dominate the political arena, occupying as many as
three-quarters of the seats in Parliament and the provincial assemblies.[7]

Income and education reinforce the political advantages of occupation. Education in particular increases political interest, expands awareness of opportunities to participate, and nurtures many of the skills
necessary for effective involvement. The university experience is especially important in this respect. Given their idealism and free time, university students are particularly likely to engage in protest activities.
Involvement in protests declines as individuals grow older, but the excite-
ment generated by the protest activities frequently whets the appetite for
participation in more conventional political activities later in life.

Similarly, although money may not "buy" political power, it does
provide access to political opportunities and resources, which give the affluent decided advantages in political life. Money purchases the leisure
time necessary to pursue politics either as a hobby or career; it buys political information, which increases both political interest and awareness;
and it facilitates contacts with party leaders and public officials, which enhance both political communication and influence. Consequently, wealthy
citizens participate more extensively in all forms of political activity. The
wealthy enjoy only marginal advantages with respect to voting and community work, which are not as resource-intensive as some other activities.
However, they are considerably more active in party-organizational and
election-campaign activities, and virtually monopolize elected office. Interestingly, they also are somewhat more likely to sign petitions or engage in

other protest activities. For example, student protestors tend most often to be sons and daughters of the wealthy. Similarly, the leaders of protest movements, such as the separatist movement in Quebec, also traditionally have been drawn disproportionately from the upper strata of society.[8]

Although occupation, income, and education are the principal social forces structuring participation, other factors such as ethnicity, region, religion, age, and gender also are widely believed to influence both the nature and extent of political activity. However, in Canada the importance of these other social characteristics is substantially less than that of social status, and frequently disappears when status differences between groups are taken into account. With regard to region and ethnicity, for example, although there are significant differences in voter turnout between provinces and among regions, there is relatively little regional variation in party or campaign work. Although residents of the Atlantic provinces rank near the bottom with respect to virtually every type of political activity, this can be attributed almost entirely to the relative poverty of the region and the lower-than-average educational levels of persons living in these provinces. Similarly, francophone residents of Quebec participate less in most electorally related activities than do their anglophone neighbours. However, these differences, which are small in the first place, vanish in most cases when the educational and income advantages of anglophone Quebeckers are controlled.[9]

One trait that is important irrespective of social status is age. Politics traditionally has been the preserve of the middle-aged. Younger people, especially those 18 to 25, tend to be preoccupied with school and the demands of starting jobs and families. As a consequence, they are slow to take advantage of the political opportunities available to them—a phenomenon known as the "start-up" effect. In contrast, older citizens are subject to a "slow-down" effect. They participate somewhat less than middle-aged persons (but more than the youngest citizens) not only because of the increasing burden of poor health that often accompanies advancing age, but also because older Canadians have somewhat less formal education on average than do younger generations. The principal exception to this pattern occurs with respect to political protest, where activity rates are highest among students and those 26 to 35, and decline among older groups.

GENDER AND PARTICIPATION

Traditionally in Canada as in other western democracies, some of the most consistent differences in political participation have been those based on gender. Politics traditionally has been a "man's game" from which women were excluded, or at least discouraged from entering. This is illustrated most dramatically by the denial of women's suffrage in

Canadian federal elections until 1918 and in some provincial elections until 1940. However, even after legal barriers to the participation of women were eliminated, a variety of informal obstacles continued to make political involvement more difficult for women than for men.[10]

Explanations for male–female differences in participation are numerous. Some believe that women traditionally were less involved in most political activities because of discrimination (the reluctance of party leaders to select women candidates for public office, or of voters to cast ballots for women). Others think the problem originated with the definition of women's roles in society. Where once women were handicapped by the expectation that they had the principal, if not the exclusive, responsibility for child rearing and homemaking, now women who want to "have it all" may be expected to "do it all," adding the burdens of building a career to the traditional responsibilities of home and family. Still others argue that the problem stems from the socialization process wherein women learned (or were taught) as children that politics is a man's preserve and that women should be politically passive and deferential.[11]

Frequently overlooked in the debate about causes of gender differences in political activity is the fact that male–female differences in many political activities have declined substantially in recent years. Data from a 1993 election survey indicate that no more than three percentage points separate men's and women's participation levels in any of the political activities examined (see Table 7.3). Moreover, most of these small differences disappear when occupation and education are controlled. As demonstrated in Table 7.4, for example, gender differences among college-educated men and women, and among men and women with similar professional occupations, are virtually nonexistent. Interestingly, high-status women actually participate slightly more in protest activities than do their male counterparts, although the differences are very small and insignificant. In contrast, among men and women without college educations or with middle- to low-status occupations, gender differences in participation are more pronounced. This suggests that gender differences in most conventional political activities, as well as in protest activities, stem more from early socialization experiences than from overt discrimination or even role differences. It also suggests that women's early socialization can be reversed by later life experiences. In this regard, access to a university education may play an especially critical role in liberating women from traditional political roles. Unfortunately, only a minority of women attend college, and the percentage has increased only slightly since the early 1970s.[12]

Although gender differences in both conventional and protest activities are fairly small and probably do not reflect overt discrimination, gender differences in more elite political activities remain pronounced; moreover, they are difficult to explain in terms of socialization alone. Regarding participation in political parties, for example, women tend to be

TABLE 7.4 **Mean Number of Political Activities of Men and Women Controlling for Occupation and Education**

		Men	Women
		$\bar{X}$	$\bar{X}$
A.	Conventional Participation[1] by occupation		
	Professional, managerial	3.19	3.14
	Other, none	2.98	2.80
B.	Conventional Participation by Education		
	Attended university	3.19	3.17
	Secondary school or less	2.96	2.74
C.	Protest Participation[2] by Occupation		
	Professional, managerial	1.73	1.92
	Other, none	1.36	1.24
D.	Protest Participation by Education		
	Attended university	1.91	1.92
	Other, none	1.25	1.17

[1]Conventional activities include voting in the 1993 federal election, voting in the 1992 constitutional referendum, and "often" or "sometimes" discussing politics, trying to influence friends' votes, attending political meetings, and working for parties or candidates in the 1993 federal election campaign.

[2]Protest activities include signing petitions, boycotting goods or services, and engaging in marches or rallies, sit-ins, and potentially violent demonstrations.

SOURCES: SEE TABLES 7.1 AND 7.2.

relegated to the bottom of the organizational hierarchy, where they do much of the time-consuming and tedious organizational maintenance work, but have little influence on candidate selection or party policy. The proportion of women involved in the party declines sharply at successively higher levels—a phenomenon sometimes called the "law of increasing disproportion." Thus, for example, approximately 70 percent of local constituency association riding secretaries are women, but women constitute only about 30 percent of party convention delegates.

Women also continue to be a small, if growing, minority of candidates for public elective office. Overall, the percentage of women nominated as parliamentary candidates by the three traditional national parties has increased rather steadily, if slowly, over the past twenty years.[13] The NDP has led the way in providing women with opportunities to run for Parliament. In fact, in 1993 the NDP committed itself to a quota of 50 percent female candidates for Parliament, a goal the party came close to reaching. However, many of the women NDP candidates have run in ridings where the NDP has had little prospect of victory. As a result, the percentage of NDP women elected to Parliament has lagged well behind the percentage nominated. This was especially evident in 1993; only one of the nine successful NDP candidates for Parliament was a woman. The Liberal and Progressive Conservative parties also have gradually increased the number of women they have nominated for Parliament, although even in 1993 male candidates for Parliament continued to outnumber female candidates in both parties by a ratio of more than three to one. The proportion of women candidates nominated in 1993 by the Reform Party and the Bloc Québécois was even smaller.

For most of the past twenty years, the percentage of women candidates actually elected to Parliament also has grown quite slowly. As recently as 1988, only thirteen women were elected to Parliament out of 295 seats. This changed dramatically in the 1993, however, with the election of 53 women MPs, an increase of more than 500 percent. Whether the sudden increase in women MPs represents the beginning of an important new trend in Canadian politics, or whether it is a serendipitous and possibly short-term result of the tumultuous 1993 elections, is at this point uncertain. What is clear is that women continue to be underrepresented in Parliament despite substantial recent gains. They also continue to be underrepresented in the federal cabinet. Historically, very few women have been cabinet ministers, and fewer still have held important portfolios. Unfortunately, women have not fared appreciably better in provincial politics—male dominance of provincial legislatures and cabinets remains pervasive.

In sum, although the ranks of the political activists in Canada include representatives from all segments of society, certain types of people participate more than others. The wealthy and well educated—men and the middle-aged in particular—are disproportionately represented in the ranks of the politically active. Importantly, as well, the differences are greatest for the highest level, most influential activities.

WHY DO SOME CITIZENS PARTICIPATE MORE THAN OTHERS?

The extent of citizen participation in political life is determined by the interplay of motivation and opportunity. People become involved politically when they want to be involved and when they possess both sufficient opportunity and adequate resources to translate motivation into action. Although political opportunities in Canada once were severely circumscribed by laws restricting the participation of women, the poor and those without property, Native peoples, and members of certain religions, most legal barriers to participation have been eliminated.[14] It remains true, of course, that politically relevant resources vary substantially between individuals and groups, thereby impeding the participation of some citizens more than others. This is particularly true with regard to public officeholding. However, if most Canadians do not have sufficient resources to become full-time politicians, they do have the wherewithal and opportunities to perform a wide range of political activities. Therefore, the differences observed in most types of political activity today are probably better explained by differences in motivations.

The motivation to participate in politics is an amorphous concept whose level is determined by a complex set of attitudes and beliefs about politics, society, and self. Among the more important of these are the individual's awareness of, interest in, and concern about government and public affairs. It should come as no surprise that political participation varies with political interest. Although even a passing interest in politics usually is sufficient to motivate most people to vote, interest of a more absorbing kind is required for other types of activity. Few persons possess an abiding interest in politics. Predictably, interest in politics is highest during political campaigns. As noted in Table 7.1, about half of all citizens reported being very interested in the 1993 federal election. Between election campaigns, however, only about one in five citizens indicate they closely follow politics on a daily basis. Political interest also probably increases somewhat during periods of crisis or in response to highly visible events, but for many citizens government and politics during ordinary times seem irrelevant and remote.

Compounding the problem of low levels of political interest is the fact that many citizens are poorly informed about politics, and do not understand how government works. Political interest and knowledge are closely related and mutually reinforcing. Just as people who are interested in politics attend more closely to public affairs and are likely to be better informed, those who understand government are more sensitive to the political messages around them and are more likely to acquire the incentive to participate. The latter also are more likely to acquire the resources needed for effective participation, and to comprehend, as well, the range of opportunities available. Most citizens, however, possess only a superficial understanding of their country's government and politics. Although virtually everyone can identify the prime minister and most recognize the name of their member of Parliament, knowledge of the policy stances and more general ideological positions espoused by leading politicians and the major parties is much more limited.

Low levels of political information have important consequences not only for the extent or quantity of participation but also for its quality. With respect to voting, for example, the classic view is that the democratic citizen studies political issues, evaluates parties' programs and platforms, and then votes for the party whose positions on important issues are closest to the voter's own. Although election surveys indicate that most voters cast their ballots for the party they think is closest to them on a few highly salient issues, these studies also indicate that most voters are concerned only with one or two leading issues, and that their understanding of these issues is often vague, superficial, and poorly informed. Moreover, the positions voters express on issues often are either rationalizations or projections based on partisanship or feelings about party leaders or local candidates. Although issues do influence electoral choice, their role frequently is overshadowed by party loyalties or by public reactions to the images of the party leaders and candidates.[15]

For many citizens, therefore, the motivation to participate stems from general feelings—"likes" or "dislikes"—for parties, leaders, or candidates rather than from a commitment to specific issues or broader political ideologies, philosophies, and ideals. Partisanship, or a sense of identification with a political party, is an especially powerful motive for numerous political activities, especially those related to elections. Persons with strong psychological attachments to a party are more likely to vote and to engage in the variety of campaign activities. They also are the ones on whom the burdens of party work disproportionately fall, since they are more likely to volunteer their services or to be easily recruited when an election is in the offing.

Although few citizens hold intense opinions on political issues or possess well-developed ideologies, those who do are among the most active members of the polity. However, because political parties in Canada typically favour pragmatism over ideological consistency, citizens with strong ideologies frequently encounter difficulties finding appropriate outlets for expressing their views. Persons motivated by ideology often identify with one of the smaller, more radical or programmatic parties such as the Co-operative Commonwealth Federation (CCF) or Social Credit during the 1930s, or the Reform Party, the New Democratic Party (NDP), or Bloc Québécois today. Those who cannot find appropriate parties for their points of view sometimes express their frustrations through protest activities or by rejecting politics and abstaining from participation altogether.

Whatever the impetus for political activity, citizens are unlikely to act on that impulse unless they also are convinced that their involvement holds reasonable prospects for success. Political efficacy, the belief that one can influence political decisions through personal action, is a necessary if not sufficient condition for nearly all forms of participation. Although it appears that many Canadians believe that voting is a civic obligation to be performed regardless of its likely impact, few are willing to take part in more demanding activities unless they believe not only that opportunities for effective participation exist but also that they personally are capable of exploiting those opportunities. Even the discontented must be convinced that dissent will make some difference before they are likely to express their dissatisfaction through protest.

For many citizens, however, government appears too large, complicated, and remote for them to understand much less influence its operations and policies. In 1993, two-thirds of those interviewed in a national survey complained that politics was too complicated for them to understand. Similar proportions indicated that people like themselves had no say about what government did, and that government doesn't care about their opinions. Even more impressive, fully 80 percent thought that persons elected to Parliament in Ottawa soon lose contact with their constituents. Such feelings of political powerlessness are not novel; studies conducted over the past quarter-century consistently show that large numbers of Canadians think they are politically inefficacious or powerless (see Figures 7.1 and 7.2). Nevertheless, beliefs that government is unresponsive have become increasingly common over time. As Figure 7.1 illustrates, the percentages of people who think "MPs lose touch" with voters and that "government doesn't care" about their opinions have trended significantly upward since at least the mid-1960s. Studies also show that feelings of political powerlessness and incompetence are widespread. Moreover, they are not confined to certain regions of the country or focused on one level of government but are commonplace in every region of Canada and apply to provincial as well as federal politics.

Feelings of political incompetence frequently are products of more generalized feelings of powerlessness, cynicism, and distrust. These feelings of alienation appear to be linked in turn to the frustration many people feel at being excluded from significant opportunities to participate in important nonpolitical decisions that affect their everyday lives at home, in school, and on the job. Participation in nonpolitical institutions, it appears, provides training for political life. Citizens who are reared in homes where family decisions are shared, and who are educated in schools where student opinions are solicited and taken seriously, acquire confidence in themselves. This confidence increases feelings of personal competence and efficacy, and enhances political involvement later in life. Opportunities to engage in decision-making at work appear to be even

FIGURE 1 **Percentages Agreeing That MPs Lose Touch and Government Doesn't Care, 1965–1993**

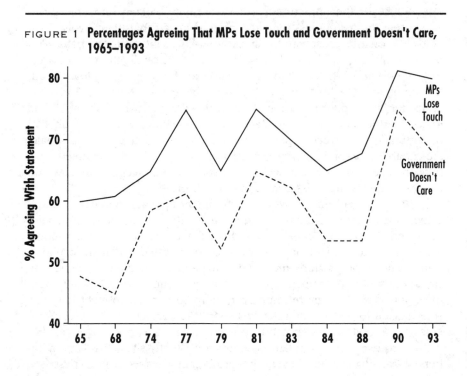

FIGURE 2 **Percentages Agreeing That Politics Too Complicated and People Like Them Have No Say, 1965–1993**

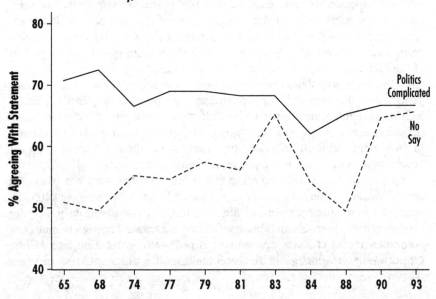

more important in this respect. Even limited involvement in workplace decisions appears sufficient to increase political interest and efficacy, to promote tolerance, and thus to enhance both the quantity and quality of citizen participation.

HOW EFFECTIVE IS PARTICIPATION?

Underlying all that has been said thus far is the assumption that citizen participation matters—that who participates, how, and how extensively have real consequences for the selection of political leaders and the substance of public policy. Democratic theory, we have noted, is predicated on the belief that participation is the most effective means for citizens to express their interests to government. Consequently, inequalities of political participation can distort the representation of public interests and undermine the fundamental basis of political equality. Unfortunately, very little evidence is available regarding the consequences of participation for leadership selection and public policy in Canada. What information is available, however, suggests that participation does matter; government is most responsive to the interests of those who participate most extensively and in the most demanding political activities.

Although opportunities for citizen participation are numerous, the effectiveness of certain forms of political activity is tenuous at best. This is particularly the case for election-related activities. Despite widespread public involvement, the practical value of voting and campaign work is severely limited by the absence of effective competition in many elections combined with the fundamental agreement of the major parties on many of the most basic political issues. Because the major parties often fail to offer Canadians meaningful choices even where competition is robust, elections too often are little more than civic rituals. They permit people to participate symbolically but provide ordinary Canadians with little real influence in the selection of political leaders or the development of public policies. Moreover, because of the large number of ballots cast (even in local elections), the probability that any one individual's vote will decide who wins an election is so small as to be virtually nil. This has led some theorists to conclude that voting is not a rational use of one's resources, and that people would be better advised to devote the time and energy spent in voting on more productive political activities.

One problem with this logic, however, is that many of the more demanding and influential political activities are effectively monopolized by social and economic elites. Political parties, for example, play obvious and important roles in leadership selection and policy development. However, despite periodic attempts to expand their memberships and encourage wider participation by the rank and file, the major parties have been careful to ensure that the nomination of candidates, the selection of party leaders, and the formulation of party programs are dominated by high-ranking party officials and party insiders who differ significantly from ordinary party members in social background and political opinion.[16]

Interest groups also have substantial influence in Canadian government and politics. Even more than parties, however, interest groups are dominated by elites whose backgrounds and interests may be very different from those of the average group member. This is true even of groups, such as labour unions, that represent working-class interests. Despite the formal trappings of democracy in their organizations, interest-group leaders often are only nominally accountable to their membership for actions taken on the organization's behalf.[17]

Nor does political protest necessarily provide a viable alternative to elite-dominated activities. Protests frequently are exciting, even dramatic, departures from what constitutes "normal politics" in Canada. As such, they often receive widespread attention from the mass media, who are hungry for a good story to "spice up" an otherwise dull news day. Although it is arguable that the publicity surrounding protests can heighten public consciousness of neglected interests and thereby lay a foundation for gradual, long-term changes in government policy, in the short run the usual response of government has been to suppress (sometimes forcefully) protest and to resist taking actions that might be interpreted as capitulation to the demands of highly visible protest groups.[18]

Given the relative ineffectiveness of voting combined with the domination of more demanding and effective activities by social and economic elites, it is not surprising that the composition of Canada's political leadership continues to be upper-status (and male) dominated or that the tenor of public policy appears to many observers to manifest an elite bias. At the same time, however, although the composition of Canada's political leadership has changed very little in this century (despite broad changes in the nature and extent of citizen participation), even relatively modest changes in the configuration of the politically active strata of society have been sufficient to stimulate significant changes in government policies and priorities. In particular, it appears that the gradual expansion of opportunities for working-class participation in political life has focused somewhat greater attention on the interests of the disadvantaged, especially in those provinces where political competition has been comparatively high and where the working-class oriented CCF/NDP has enjoyed its greatest success. The point is contentious, but a case can be made that the increasing numbers of women who have been nominated for and elected to public office over the past quarter-century not only have resulted from, but also have resulted in, increased attention and concern for women's issues in Canada.

On balance, the available evidence suggests that the nature and extent of public participation do have important consequences for political accountability and responsiveness—albeit consequences that sometimes work to the disadvantage of the majority of Canadians. There also is increasing evidence that political participation has intrinsic value for individual citizens, enhancing their self-esteem and fostering more democratic personalities. The problem, however, succinctly stated by Robert Presthus, is that

> [i]n the context of democratic participation, the going system produces some questionable consequences. Participation tends to be restricted to those groups that possess the greatest amounts of resources ... The majority are unable to compete effectively in the political arena, for lack of such resources ... which tend to be monopolized by those we have defined as political elites. Government in responding to the elites is placed in the somewhat anomalous position of defending the strong against the weak.[19]

DEMOCRATIC IDEALS AND CANADIAN REALITIES

Perhaps inevitably, assessments of the democratic character of political participation in Canada depend on one's perspective. Although it is obvious from this brief discussion that the structure of citizen participation in political life falls considerably short of the democratic ideal, it also is the case that Canada approaches this ideal more closely than all but a handful of the world's nation-states. Indeed, it is doubtful that any country provides significantly greater opportunities for participation than are enjoyed in Canada. Moreover, opportunities for participation in Canada continue to expand and to make the structure of participation more egalitarian.

In many respects, the structure of citizen participation in Canada is wider and deeper than often assumed. The great majority of citizens regularly accept the responsibility to vote, and substantial numbers take part (at least from time to time) in more demanding political activities as well. Moreover, although many citizens display little interest in politics and are poorly informed about both the structure of government and pressing issues of the day, there are good reasons to believe that both the quantity and quality of public participation would increase if political competition were strengthened and if more people were accorded even more effective opportunities to become involved in political life, and especially, in such basic social institutions as the family, school, and workplace.

Political participation is a tonic. It is healthy for the individual and therapeutic for the state. Increased political activity in Canada would enhance citizen interest in and knowledge of government and public affairs, promote subjective political competence, and strengthen historically fragile feelings of membership in the community of Canada. Increases in the political activity of working-class persons—especially women—and of other politically disadvantaged groups also would foster more equitable representation of all social and economic interests as well as strengthen political equality.

It is highly unrealistic, of course, to expect everyone to engage intensively in every facet of political life. The number of citizens who can hold elected office in any year is limited, and widespread resort to certain forms of political protest would threaten the continuing existence of the democratic order. Notwithstanding such limits, there remain abundant opportunities to increase public participation in a wide variety of conventional and less conventional political activities, thereby increasing the quality of democratic citizenship in Canada in the 1990s and achieving a closer approximation of the democratic ideal.

NOTES

1. Early works on participation in Canada that offer contrasting perspectives include, Richard J. Van Loon, "Political Participation in Canada," *Canadian Journal of Political Science* 3 (September 1970): 376–99; Léon Dion, "Participating in the Political Process," *Queen's Quarterly* 75 (Autumn 1968): 437–38; and William Mishler, *Political Participation in Canada* (Toronto: Macmillan, 1979).

2. For comprehensive data on Canadian federal and provincial elections, see Frank Feigert, *Canada Votes: 1935–1989* (Durham, N.C.: Duke University Press, 1989).

3. Ivor Crewe, "Electoral Participation," in David Butler, Howard R. Penniman, and Austin Ranney, eds., *Democracy at the Polls* (Washington, D.C.: American Enterprise Institute, 1981), pp. 234–37.

4. Allan Kornberg, Joel Smith, and Harold D. Clarke, *Citizen Politicians— Canada: Party Officials in a Democratic Society* (Durham, N.C.: Carolina Academic Press, 1979).

5. On interest-group membership and participation, see Robert Presthus, *Elite Accommodation in Canadian Politics* (Toronto: Macmillan, 1973); Robert Presthus, *Elites in the Policy Process* (London: Cambridge University Press, 1974); A. Paul Pross, *Group Politics and Public Policy* (Toronto: Oxford University Press, 1986).

6. Ronald Manzur, *Canada: A Socio-Political Report* (Toronto: McGraw-Hill Ryerson, 1974), pp. 74–84. See also Harold D. Clarke, Allan Kornberg, and Marianne C. Stewart, "Active Minorities: Political Participation in Canadian Democracy," in Neil Nevitte and Allan Kornberg, eds., *Minorities and the Canadian State* (Oakville, Ont.: Mosaic Press, 1985), ch. 16.

7. Harold D. Clarke et al., "Backbenchers," in David Bellamy et al., eds., *The Provincial Political Systems* (Toronto: Methuen, 1976), pp. 216–19; Allan Kornberg and William Mishler, *Influence in Parliament: Canada* (Durham, N.C.: Duke University Press, 1976).

8. Kenneth McRoberts and Dale Posgate, *Quebec: Social Change and Political Crisis*, rev. ed. (Toronto: McClelland and Stewart, 1980), pp. 185–89.

9. Regional differences in attitudes such as political efficacy and interest, which are conducive to political participation, also largely disappear when educa-

tional and income differences are controlled. See, for example, Allan Kornberg, William Mishler, and Harold D. Clarke, *Representative Democracy in the Canadian Provinces* (Scarborough, Ont.: Prentice-Hall Canada, 1982), p. 83.

10. Catherine L. Cleverdon, *The Women's Suffrage Movement in Canada* (Toronto: University of Toronto Press, 1950).

11. See, for example, Jerome H. Black and Nancy McGlen, "Male–Female Political Involvement Differentials in Canada, 1965–1975," *Canadian Journal of Political Science* 12 (September 1979): 471–98; Kornberg et al., Citizen *Politicians—Canada*, ch. 8; and Barry Kay et al., "Gender and Political Activity in Canada, 1965–84," *Canadian Journal of Political Science* 20 (December 1987), 851–63.

12. Alfred A. Hunter, *Class Tells: On Social Inequality in Canada*, 2nd ed. (Toronto: Butterworths, 1986), p. 122.

13. Sylvia B. Bashevkin, *Toeing the Lines: Women and Party Politics in English Canada* (Toronto: University of Toronto Press, 1985); and M. Janine Brody, *Point of Entry: The Election of Women in Canada* (Toronto: University of Toronto Press, 1985).

14. Terrance H. Qualter, *The Election Process in Canada* (Toronto: McGraw-Hill Ryerson, 1979).

15. Harold D. Clarke, Jane Jenson, Lawrence Le Duc, and Jon H. Pammett, *Political Choice in Canada* (Toronto: McGraw-Hill Ryerson, 1979), chs. 5, 7, and 11.

16. Kornberg et al., *Citizen Politicians—Canada*, chs. 7 and 8.

17. Presthus, *Elite Accommodation in Canadian Politics*, pp. 286–87.

18. Judith Torrance, "The Response of Canadian Governments to Violence," *Canadian Journal of Political Science* 10 (December 1977): 473–96.

19. Presthus, *Elites in the Policy Process*, p. 461.

FURTHER READINGS

Bashevkin, Sylvia B. *Toeing the Lines: Women and Party Politics in English Canada*. Toronto: University of Toronto Press, 1985.

Clarke, Harold D., Jane Jenson, Lawrence LeDuc, and Jon H. Pammett. *Absent Mandate: The Politics of Discontent in Canada*. 2nd ed. Toronto: Gage, 1988, ch. 2.

Clarke, Harold D., and Allan Kornberg. *Citizens and Community: Political Support in a Representative Democracy*. Cambridge: Cambridge University Press, 1992, ch 7.

Crewe, Ivor. "Electoral Participation," in David Butler, Howard R. Penniman, and Austin Ranney, eds., *Democracy at the Polls*. Washington, D.C.: American Enterprise Institute, 1981.

Kornberg, Allan, Joel Smith, and Harold D. Clarke. *Citizen Politicians—Canada: Party Officials in a Democratic Society*. Durham, N.C.: Carolina Academic Press, 1979.

Mishler, William. *Political Participation in Canada*. Toronto: Macmillan, 1979.

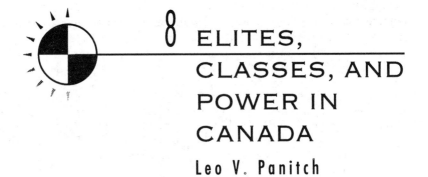

8 ELITES, CLASSES, AND POWER IN CANADA

Leo V. Panitch

"In Toronto there are no classes ... just the Masseys and the masses." This little ditty, perhaps reflecting a centralist bias characteristic of Canadian politics itself, captures graphically the way political scientists have often approached the study of power in Canadian society. Inequalities of political and economic power are rarely denied and indeed are frequently a direct object of study. In general, however, political scientists have operated with a somewhat impoverished—and misleading—set of concepts in trying to understand these inequalities. As in the case of "the Masseys and the masses," they have tended to categorize society in terms of a gradation of rich, middle, and poor, and to examine politics in terms of elites with power and masses without. In employing such imprecise and oversimplified generalizations, social scientists have obscured and mystified the real links between social, economic, and political power in Canada.

Who, then, are these "elites" and "masses"? Occasionally, and most usually in the context of voting behaviour studies, the "masses" are divided into statistical classes grouped together on the basis of income, occupational status, or the "common-sense" self-perception of individuals themselves in class terms. Insofar as actual socioeconomic collectivities of people are dealt with, this has usually been done in terms of the concept of "interest groups"—formal organizations of farmers, workers, businesspeople, and the like. Those who lead such organizations are usually designated as "elites" and differentiated from the "non-decision-making" mass of their members. In this view, *power* is seen in terms of *relations among elites*. It is extended to the study of relationships between elites and masses only through the highly structured contexts of elections, opinion polls, and interest group "demands."

The problem with this approach is not that it sees politics as isolated from socioeconomic structure. On the contrary, the behaviour of elites is very much seen as conditioned by the socioeconomic "background" of the individuals who compose them, and by the highly structured demands coming through voting or interest groups from society. As in the celebrated political system approach, which serves as a conceptual framework for Canada's most widely used introductory political science text,[1] the determinant of politics is seen as "demands" coming from the "environment" of politics.

It is often alleged that what is wrong here is that the political system is a "black box" that reveals little of the inner workings of government, where the most salient elites make their decisions. There is something in this argument, but what is even more striking is the "black hole"—the environment. We are told that scarcity prevails here and that demands are generated by conflicts over resources, but a systematic examination of the way in which our economy is structured to cope with material scarcity, of the social relations that result between people, and thus of the concrete material clash of social forces that goes on is seldom undertaken. References to individual competition or intergroup competition, as with rich and poor, elite and mass, may give us clues, but because of their "grossness" as categories, because of their abstraction from concrete social relationships between people in a capitalist society such as Canada, they do not contribute enough to our understanding of what is acknowledged to be the determinant element of politics—the socioeconomic system in which politics is embedded.

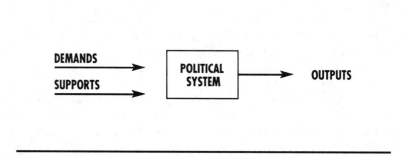

To properly understand the relationship between society and politics involves taking an analysis of society seriously, which itself entails going beyond categories such as elite, mass, and group. It involves getting down to the material social relationships between people, their common experiences in terms of these relationships, and the actual collectivities they form and the struggles they enter into handling these experiences. This is what a *class analysis*, as opposed to an *elite analysis*, of society and politics is designed to do. In Canada—and even in Toronto—there *are* classes, and it is their history of contradictory relations to one another, and the balance of power that results at given periods and instances, that establishes the foundation of politics, including setting the extent and limit of the power of the Masseys, or that of any other "elite."

ELITE ANALYSIS IN CANADA

There is fairly widespread agreement among political scientists that what is meant by the term "democracy" as applied to a contemporary political system is "that institutional arrangement for arriving at political decisions in which individuals acquire the power to decide by means of a competitive struggle for the people's vote." The people themselves do not decide, and therefore power does not immediately reside with the people, but rather "the people have the opportunity of accepting or refusing the men [*sic*] who are to rule them."[2] This is an "elitist" conception of democracy that does not require or expect high citizen participation in public affairs beyond the act of choosing between competing teams of leaders. A degree of *elite-pluralism* is guaranteed in this system, at least with a view to elections and formal parliamentary opposition, by a two-party or multi-party system. Moreover, in the case of a federal system like Canada's, the elite-teams compete for votes in various jurisdictions, and this further tends to multiply the extent of elite-pluralism. Finally, insofar as freedom of association prevails, it is recognized that the decision-making elites may be subject to a process of interest-group competition for influence upon them.

This system of elite-pluralism, however much it may be demarcated from broader, more mass-participatory conceptions of democracy, is not to be sneezed at as a minimal description of "actually existing" liberal democracies. It captures, albeit in too formal and nonhistorical a fashion, some of the basic differences between a polity such as ours and an authoritarian regime. Yet serious students of power in Canadian society have understandably not been willing to rest content with minimal descriptions of this sort. They have wanted to know *who* these competing teams of leaders are in socioeconomic terms and the extent to which they reflect in their competition and decision-making a narrow or broad range of approaches to public issues and concerns. They have wanted to know the relationship between the democratically elected political elites and those decision-makers in institutional spheres, such as the private corporations that dominate our economy, that are not democratically elected. To speak of elite-pluralism properly, they have recognized, entails examining the degree of *autonomy* political elites have from, at least, the elites that exercise power (in this sense of decision-making) in the economic sphere.

John Porter's *The Vertical Mosaic*[3] is the classic Canadian study that asks these questions within the elite-pluralist conceptual framework, and it is for the most part better than similar studies of other liberal-democratic societies. Porter began with an examination of the broad social differentiations between people in Canada in terms of demographic patterns, occupational and income distribution, and ethnic and educational inequalities. Although he discerned persistent "class" inequalities in Canada, in keeping with the elite–mass dichotomy of his conceptual approach, he tended to treat class as merely a "statistical category" imposed on society by the researcher rather than an actual collectivity of people with real social cohesion and power. Instead, he reserved the study of social cohesion and power only to the "elites"—to those identifiable individuals who occupied decision-making positions at the top of all the major institutional orders that might be said to perform "essential tasks" for Canadian society. Society is seen to be composed of institutional power centres in the state, the economy, and the ideological sphere, with a set of elites in each (political and bureaucratic; corporate and labour; mass media, educational, and religious) that have power by virtue of the necessity of institutions to be "directed and coordinated," itself entailing "the recognized right to make decisions on behalf of a group of people." Thus turning the question of power into a matter of "authority," Porter went on to isolate the principal authority roles in each institution, to locate the individuals who filled these roles, to examine their social backgrounds, and to study the degree of elite cohesion within each power centre and among them. His test of Canada's claim to democracy rested, then, not on popular involvement in, or resistance to, the exercise of power, but rather on whether the elites came from different social backgrounds and whether they were autonomous from, and competitive with, one another.

Porter's findings, covering the 1940–60 period, substantially undermined the conventional wisdom of treating Canada as an "elite-pluralist democracy." Examining the boards of directors of the 183 corporations that dominated the Canadian economy in terms of assets and sales, he found an internally cohesive and concentrated elite characterized by extensive interlocking directorships between corporations, recruitment on the basis of "upper-class" family ties and exclusive private-school education, common ethnic (Anglo-Saxon) origins and religious (Anglican) affiliations, common membership in exclusive social clubs, and a shared commitment to a "free-enterprise" capitalist value system.

In contrast, the political and bureaucratic elites (federal cabinet ministers, provincial premiers, Supreme Court and provincial chief justices in the first case, and highly paid civil servants in the second) were somewhat less exclusive in terms of social backgrounds, although still drawn from a narrow "middle class" excluding some 90 percent of most Canadians. The political elite was characterized by a high degree of co-option from other elites and lacked a discrete internal career structure; cabinet membership itself often served as a stepping stone for entry into the corporate elite. In terms of values it was ideologically cohesive, but with an obsession with national unity ("From Sea to Sea" as the formative credo of politics) that was innately conservative in that it failed to express substantive values ("Liberty, Equality, Fraternity," "All Power to the People") that could challenge the economic elite's dominant value system. As such, Porter saw Canada as burdened with an "avocational" political elite, particularly weak as a base for guaranteeing pluralism. As for the ideological elite, neither the mass media nor religious leaders or intellectuals had the independence or the inclination to challenge the power of the economic elite.

Porter concluded that the Canadian system of power relations was best seen as a "confraternity of power" rather than as a set of competing, autonomous elites. The various elites were "operating more or less within the same value system, a condition brought about in part by the establishments of kinship and class. Any examination of career interchanging, the membership of boards, commissions and councils, and the structure of political parties would probably show the dominance of the corporate world over the institutional systems."

Labour was the one elite Porter studied that was marked off from this "confraternity." Alone in being drawn from "lower-class" social backgrounds, the labour elite was questionably an elite at all in that it operated in the economic sphere as an oppositional element, excluded from decision-making positions. In any case, its role did not much extend beyond collective bargaining in the economic sphere, since it "rarely shared in the informal aspects of the confraternity of power." It was on "the periphery of the overall structure of power, called in by others when the 'others' consider[ed] it necessary, or when the labour leaders demand[ed] a hearing from the political elite." Defining democracy as entailing equality of opportunity for individuals, and competition among elites, Porter concluded: "Canada ... has a long way to go to become in any sense a thoroughgoing democracy."[4]

Subsequent studies have produced similar conclusions. Wallace Clement's examination of the corporate (and mass-media) elites in the early 1970s[5] found a greater degree of corporate concentration (with 113 firms now dominant in the economy), even more extensive interlocking directorships among them, and a higher degree of social exclusiveness in terms of "upper-class" family background than there had been twenty years before. Clement stressed the greater structural differentiation within the corporate elite, distinguishing between a dominant fraction of Canadian-controlled corporations in the financial, utilities, and transportation sectors, and a predominance of foreign-owned corporations in the manufacturing and resource sectors, with Canadian corporate executives located there as "compradors." But the interlocks between these "fractions" were extensive, as Canadian bankers were allied with American multinational capital. As for the mass-media elite, Clement showed that it functioned as part of the corporate sphere. And he demonstrated that some 40 percent of the corporate elite themselves had, or had close relatives who had, occupied positions in the important political and bureaucratic offices.

Dennis Olsen's *The State Elite*, covering the 1961–73 period, found marginal changes from what Porter had described, particularly pertaining to greater French and "other ethnic" representation. In the case of the political elite, he found that the elite had changed only "very slowly and not at all in some respects," in that it was still dominated by those from a narrow band of middle- and upper-middle-class origins and still lacked a discrete political career structure. As for the bureaucrats, he found that "the new elite is more open, more heterogeneous and probably more meritocratic, than the old," but that "the overall pattern is one of the marked persistence of both social class and ethnic preferences in recruitment." He concluded that the "middle class state elite sees itself in alliance with business, or at least not in any fundamental opposition to its general interests."[6]

Robert Presthus's study of the accommodation between political, bureaucratic, and interest-group elites in Canada, although more oriented to a survey of the attitudes of the elites, is not in sharp variance with the above findings of elite analysis in Canada with regard to socioeconomic backgrounds or general ideological disposition. He too found an absence of institutional cohesion within the political system that would facilitate it acting as a counterelite to business. He demonstrated that it is difficult for new or substantively weak interest groups to penetrate the decision-making process, because "functional ties and established clientele relationships tend to crystallize existing power relationships." Significantly, he found that the senior bureaucrats showed a marked lack of enthusiasm for state welfare activities, although he still contended that the state elite "plays an equilibrating role in welfare areas." But "much of its energy is also spent in reinforcing the security and growth of interests that already enjoy the largest share of the net social product." Of particular note, in terms of the continuity of findings of elite studies, is that organized labour still "fails to enjoy the legitimacy imputed to other economic groups" and remains "marginal" vis-à-vis established elite arrangements.[7]

More recent studies continue to confirm these findings. Sometimes, following in the journalistic tradition of Peter C. Newman, these studies are directed at a more popular audience and are more anecdotal, but they contain valuable statistical data as well. Thus, Diane Francis's *Controlling Interest* demonstrates that 32 wealthy families, alongside five conglomerates, control about one-third of Canada's nonfinancial assets. Members of this tiny "power elite" had a combined income among them in 1985 of $123 billion, whereas the federal government's total income was around $80 billion. Francis's conceptual analysis of what she calls Canada's "financial feudalism" is rather weak and unelaborated, however, as is her proposed solution, which is merely to call for new rules and tax breaks that will allegedly encourage more entrepreneurial competition. Indeed, Linda McQuaig's excellent study of Canada's tax policies, *Behind Closed Doors*, shows conclusively how tax breaks operate to promote the concentration of wealth and power in Canada. She shows how the rich consistently are able to veto progressive reform of the tax system and to use their political influence and the leverage that their control over the economy gives them to ensure that lower- and middle-income Canadians pay for the tax breaks for the economic elite.

These exercises in elite analysis, while not gainsaying the value of liberal-democratic institutions, are valuable for piercing the myths that tend to accompany these institutions, such as equality of opportunity, competitive pluralist power relations, and the state as autonomous from corporate capital or neutral between "interest groups." But while useful in this sense, the very mode of analysis also obscures many aspects of power that require study, and tends toward either viewing power as monolithically exercised at the top of our society or suggesting that more equality of opportunity would resolve the problem of power. The mode of analysis, sometimes against the inclinations of the researchers themselves, is thus both too radical and too liberal in the conclusions it tends to produce.

There is an implicit tendency in elite analysis toward seeing power in terms of a metaphor of "representation." Social groups are spoken of loosely as being "represented," not in the sense of election, accountability, and control by the groups in question, but rather in the sense of elites having similar social backgrounds to the groups that are thus "represented." Yet, there is no *necessary* link between someone who comes from a particular class or ethnic background and the behaviour he or she will exhibit as a member of the elite. Only if a person has a social base in a given collectivity, and only if her or his position in the elite is dependent upon this base and accountable to it in some significant respects, can we properly speak of representation. Much less valid is the notion that, by virtue of state personnel being more or less recruited from "middle-class" social origins, we can speak of the middle class as a social force engaging in alliances or conflict with other classes on the basis of state elite behaviour. This is a form, not so much of "class reductionism" as of "class substitutionism," in that it substitutes individuals of certain social backgrounds for a class that is not even specified in terms of its own social relations, associations, and struggles.

Turning to the tendency for elite analysis to treat social, political, and economic power in relation to equality of opportunity, it should be apparent that problems of domination and subordination are not reducible simply to patterns of recruitment. Even a perfect meritocracy implies a social division of labour, with people in authority and people subject to their authority. Authority positions, positions of control, set structural limits to what individuals can do in occupying decision-making roles within these institutions. If the president of INCO were to change places with a hard-rock miner, the structural position of the *place* occupied by each individual would strongly condition her or his behaviour. Elite analysis, in general, gives too much credence to the autonomous ability of "elites" to make unconstrained decisions. An awareness of individual social backgrounds and values is not unimportant in trying to understand behaviour. But neither should one overestimate their importance. Replacing one set of politicians or bureaucrats or capitalists with another is just that, unless the *social base and purpose* of the institutions in which they are located change simultaneously.

It may be said that the main shortcoming of elite analysis is that it tends to ascribe *too much power*, indeed exclusive power, to those at the top. Restricting the concept of power, by definition, to authority in institutions obscures the fact that *power is a fluid social process* that, if stopped dead and anatomized in institutional terms, constantly evades analysis. The very private property market economy that corporate elite members seem to dominate by virtue of their institutional authority and cohesiveness is at the same time a limit on their authority and cohesiveness. Their positions are dependent on maintaining a rate of profit relatively high in relation to other corporations. Even if corporation executives don't lose their positions by the corporation going bankrupt, capital will flow from the less profitable corporations to the more profitable, and thus those in the less profitable will lose a good deal of their power. It is less institutional control than control over capital, a much more fluid thing, that is the foundation of the power of the corporate elite.

Similarly, by looking for power only among the elites one is forced to treat the masses as inert political clay, without self-activity (except perhaps in the highly structured context of elections). Yet the ways in which collectivities outside the "confraternity of power" engage in struggles to further their interests both limit and influence the decisions of institutional officeholders. Indeed, in the very definition of democracy that introduced this section it may be noted that the political elites' power finds its source in "the people's vote." This already implies that the power in question cannot be atomized only by examining the elites but must instead be seen in terms of a relationship between masses and elites. This would mean paying attention to the social collectivities that make up the "masses," inquiring whether these have modes of activity, of exercising power, outside of the electoral process—as indeed they do. If would also mean examining whether and where the relations between the collectivities intersect and overlap within and between the spheres of economy, state, and culture that the elite theorists look at only in terms of those at the top.

It is one of the ironies of elite theory that it often takes its intellectual root in the argument that Marxist class analysis assumes an all-powerful ruling class that does not fit 20th-century reality. Yet elite theory ends up seeing power much more monolithically than class analysis ever does, for class analysis entails seeing power as a *relational* concept, involving the necessity of tension, conflict, and struggle between social classes. The economy, the state, and culture are not seen here merely as hierarchically structured institutions (with the rational bureaucracy becoming the model for society as a whole), but rather as fields of competition and struggle among the social classes that compose a society such as ours. It is an approach that, despite the metaphor "ruling class," does not see power as the unconstrained prerogative of certain individuals at the top, but as a quality of conflictual social relationships that runs through society as a whole.

CLASS ANALYSIS

The concept of class which finds the significant determinant of social and political behaviour in the ability or inability of labour—one's own and others'—demonstrated its value in nineteenth-century historical and sociological analysis, but has been rather scorned of late years. No doubt it is inadequate in its original form to explain the position of the new middle class of technicians, supervisors, managers, and salaried officials, whose importance in contemporary society is very great; yet their class positions can best be assessed by the same criteria: how much freedom they retain over the disposal of their own labour, and how much control they exercise over the disposal of others' labour. Nor is this concept of class as readily amenable as are newer concepts to those techniques of measurement and tabulation which, as credentials, have become so important to modern sociology. Yet it may be thought to remain the most penetrating basis of classification for the understanding of political behaviour. Common relationship to the disposal of labour still tends to give the members of each class, so defined, an outlook and set of assumptions distinct from those of the other classes.

This does not necessarily mean that the members of a class, so defined, are sufficiently conscious of a class interest to act mainly in terms of it in making political choices. Nor need it mean that their outlook and assumptions are a conscious reflection of class position or needs as an outside observer or historian might see them.

These words by C.B. Macpherson, from *Democracy in Alberta*,[8] are as relevant today as when they were written 30 years ago. The central notion here is that it is people's *relationship* to property, to the ownership and control of the means of production, that is the main guide to the social composition of society and to the power relations that pertain therein. Macpherson has noted in another context that a "somewhat looser conception of class, defined at its simplest in terms of rich, middle or poor, has been prominent in political theory as far back as one likes to go."[9] It is this looser definition of class that is employed in elite analysis in Canada. Insofar as the object of attention is the elite and its characteristics, the 80–90 percent of the population that is excluded from the upper or middle class (defined by elite family backgrounds, private-school or university education, fathers with professional occupations, or an income above a certain level) remains an undifferentiated "mass." Thus, even though Olsen and Clement insist that "class is defined objectively by relationships to the ownership and control of capital and other valued resources,"[10] this definition stands external to their elite analysis, which rests on the categories of upper, middle, and "below middle" (the rest) as defined above. While this is appropriate to gaining a sense of limited mobility in our society, it runs counter to the way they say classes must be objectively defined. Unfortunately, they sometimes slip into referring to those who are in the "below-middle" category as "working class," and it is thus often confusing to the student which operative definition of class they are working with at different points in their analysis.

A class analysis always begins with *social relationships* that people enter into, or are born into, in producing their material means of livelihood. For production to take place in any society—and without it no society can exist—three elements are necessary: producers—the people doing the work themselves; objects of labour—the natural materials to work on (land, mineral, fish, etc.); and means of labour—instruments to work with (hoes, nets, tractors, boats, machines, computers, etc.).[11] These elements may be owned by the producers themselves (collectively as in many primitive tribal societies, or individually as in the case of the family farm or the craftsperson's workshop) or by someone else who is a nonproducer. In a slave society, all the elements—including the producers—are predominantly owned by slaveholders. Under feudalism, the most important object of labour—the land—is predominantly owned by landlords. In a capitalist society, the means of labour—the machines, factories, offices, etc.—are predominantly owned by capitalists, individually or as groups of capitalists (as in the modern corporation).

Thus, the relationships between owners and nonowners, producers and nonproducers, vary in different modes of production. Under slavery, the direct producers are in a position of servitude to the nonproducers and can be bought and sold or born into servitude. Under feudalism, the peasants are not themselves owned and possess their own tools, but are legally tied to the land and required to pass over a portion of their produce to the landlord. Under capitalism, the producer is free, in the sense of having a proprietary right over his or her own labour, but is disposed of proprietary holdings of the objects and means of labour. In order to obtain the wherewithal to exist, therefore, the producer must sell his or her labour for a wage or salary to those who own the means of production and who control this labour directly—or indirectly through managers—in the production process. On this basis we can locate the predominant social classes of each society.

Classes are large groups of people, differing from each other by the
places they occupy in a historically determined system of social produc-
tion, by their relation (in most cases fixed and formulated in law) to
the means of production, by their role in the social organization of la-
bour, and consequently by the dimensions of the share of social wealth
of which they dispose and the mode of acquiring it. Classes are groups
of people one of which can appropriate the labour of another owing to
the different places they occupy in a definitive system of social
economy.[12]

It will be seen immediately that classes thus approached are not ordered
in a higher and lower fashion, as rungs on a ladder, but rather in terms of
people's *relationship* to one another. While it is a multidimensional relationship in that people are dependent on one another (the elements must
be brought together in order for production to take place), it is unequal
dependence in that one class appropriates the labour of another. Because
the mutual dependence is therefore one of dominance of one class and
subjection of another by the appropriation of labour, the social relationships is a *contradictory* one, entailing the potential of antagonism, of conflict, between the classes. This is not to say that the permanent condition
of society is one of strikes, demonstrations, revolts, and revolutions. These
are but the more explosive outcomes of the contradictory relations in
question. But in the sense of an irreconcilable *basis* of conflict, over how
much and under what specific conditions labour will be appropriated
from the direct producers, the system is a conflictual one. This has historically been expressed in struggles over control of the labour process, over
the length of the working day, and over remuneration, over new machines that displace labour and/or require labour to work more
intensively.

But if these kinds of struggles have been more common than struggles
to "change the system" itself, this reflects the balance of power between the
classes. Class analysis is precisely about assessing that balance of power.
This does not mean that those who sell their labour to others—the working
class in capitalist society—have power only at the moment of social
revolution. For it will be seen that what is operating in the relations between
classes is never all power on one side and the lack of it on the other. Because
the classes are constituted in terms of their mutual, contradictory
dependence on one another, both sides always have power. The balance of
power may be unequal, and may structurally favour those who own and
control the means of production, but depending on given economic,
cultural, and political conditions, the balance may change. This may alter the
terms and conditions of the appropriation of labour, and it may give rise to
struggles over changing the historically structured relations between classes
themselves. But all this is the object of inquiry within a class analysis.

It should be stressed that in talking about classes in this way, we are talking about actual historical groups, real collectivities of people, who therefore cannot ever be examined in terms of economic categories alone. Classes, as societies, are constituted on a material basis in terms of producing the material means of livelihood, but they exist simultaneously in terms of culture, ideology, politics, consciousness. Insofar as we speak of classes in terms of statistical economic categories (so many owners, so many workers, etc.), we miss the point that we are dealing with real men and women. This is usually seen to be important—and it is—in terms of assessing the degree to which class relations as defined above are expressed in cultural, political, and ideological differentiations and conflicts. But it is important as well in terms of understanding the basis of social cohesion and stability of a society in the face of the inherently contradictory relations between classes, since the maintenance and reproduction of the relations of production is itself dependent not only on economic relations but on the degree of cultural, political, and ideological homogeneity that keeps these contradictory relations in check. This too, then, is part of the balance of power, which means that to undertake a class analysis of society we do not just map out economic relations, but rather examine the totality of cultural, ideological, and political, as well as the economic, relations between classes as the relevant "variables" in the overall balance of power.

Elite studies have certainly provided us with a window on the constitution of the capitalist class in Canada (albeit only the most dominant fractions of it) as a social force along all of these dimensions. However, recent work in Canadian labour history has begun to reclaim for contemporary students of Canadian society the fact that it is not the "corporate elite" alone that is an active historical actor, with the "masses" but mere statistical categories. In a study of the formation of the working class in Hamilton in the latter half of the nineteenth century, Bryan Palmer has written:

> Class is inseparable from class struggle. The process of confrontation conditions an understanding of class and of people's place in the larger social order, an understanding mediated by a particular cultural context. Class is thus defined by men and women as they live through the historical experience. It is class struggle and culture, not class itself, as an analytic category, that are the primary concepts upon which classes themselves arise and assume importance. One task of social history ... is to address the class experience in such a way as to force consideration of the central place of conflict and culture in any historical and/or theoretical discussion of class.[13]

Palmer's study shows that through baseball clubs, firehalls, benevolent societies, and above all the union halls, skilled workers created for themselves an associational network and a discrete culture that both grew out of and sustained the conflicts they engaged in with their employers. These struggles, taking place both in industry and politics, were about the very organization of workers into their own unions, about control over the labour process, about the ten-hour working day, about wages and conditions—in short, about how much and under what conditions labour would be appropriated from the workers by the capitalists.

Labour history has, moreover, increasingly been sensitive to the way that gender relations and class relations intertwine. Elite studies have often counted the (very small) number of women who have been "represented" in Canada's boardrooms or cabinet rooms or even legislative chamber, but recent attention has also been given to the way in which women have been either marginalized from direct participation in the economy (while engaged in reproduction in the domestic sphere) or concentrated, as "working women," in particular spheres of the economy, while continuing to do a double-day's work in the home. The importance of women's work, in either sphere, in generating the surplus appropriated by the capitalist class has been increasingly stressed. Research by Pat and Hugh Armstrong, Marjorie Cohen, Meg Luxton, and Heather Jon Maroney might be cited here, but perhaps the most important contribution to the study of the way in which the changing pattern of class relations over the past century has changed the role of women—in a different way within each class—has been Dorothy Smith's remarkable class analysis of women's inequality and the family. It demonstrates how the changing role of women in the economy and the family has changed the internal structure of each class.

Studies such as these provide an antidote to other recent accounts of Canadian history that, while freely and loosely employing the term "class," in fact have more in common with the tradition of elite analysis than with class analysis proper. In particular, Tom Naylor's *History of Canadian Business*[14] sought to locate the roots of Canada's limited and dependent industrialization in the dominance of financial capitalists over other fractions of capital and the state. Characterized by an ideology that impelled them toward making profits through commercial transactions, rather than by appropriating labour directly through industrial production, these capitalists are seen to have frozen out Canadian industrial capitalists and constructed a National Policy that encouraged resource exports and branch-plant industrialization, with the Canadian banks as a source of loan capital. Yet in concentrating on the values and political power of one fraction of the capitalist class, Naylor replicates the shortcomings of elite analysis in his one-sided perception of power. And, somewhat surprisingly, so do those recent important studies that offer critiques of Naylor by stressing not the value of capitalists, but rather the structural dynamics of global capital competition, concentration, exploitation, and accumulation in their analysis of Canada's capitalist class. They emphasize the development and role of

Canada's own multinational corporations (Jorge Niosi); and/or they recognize that American investment has actually encouraged the development of the industrial sector in Canada, and identify the rise of a Canadian class, not of *financial capitalists* who are uninterested in industry but of a *finance capitalism* based on interlocks between finance and industry (William Carroll). But like Naylor, they look very little at relations between classes as opposed to relations among capitalists. By looking at interclass relations, especially by examining the extent of class struggle between workers and capitalists in industry we may discern discrete limits to the accumulation potential of Canada's indigenous manufacturers, apart from those allegedly imposed by the values and machinations of the bankers (many of whom invested in industrial production, where it was profitable to do so, and thus became industrial capitalists themselves).

Given Canada's late start toward capitalist industrialization (relative to the United States), and given our more limited domestic market, the only way capitalists could have competed successfully with American capitalists was through a higher degree of exploitation of the working class than was practised in the United States. Thus, the very struggles of Canadian workers, emboldened by the ready possibilities of migration to the United States and by the example of relatively high incomes in Ontario farming, put limits on the potential competitiveness of Canadian capitalists. These limits were constantly tested in struggles by both sides, but given this balance of power (as opposed to the presumed monolithic power of capitalists alone), it was scarcely surprising that Canadian capitalists (industrial and financial) and politicians turned to tariff barriers, new staple resource exports, *and* foreign investment in industry as a means of promoting economic growth in Canada. Insofar as this entailed a clear strategy at all, it emerged more through the push and pull of contending social forces than from the heads of a fully conscious and cohesive class of mercantile capitalists, and its development was conditional upon its ability to mediate between interests of the full array of class forces in Canada, including those of the working class (who after all had an interest in obtaining jobs in Canada at as low a rate of exploitation as possible). If Canada's entry to the modern world of capitalist industrialization has proved to be based on the shifting sands of resource-export dependence and foreign ownership, a class analysis of the roots of this sorry state of affairs has to go beyond the mercantile mentality of our leading capitalists.

This example will perhaps help to dispel one of the major misconceptions that commonly pertains to what class analysis is about in political science—that it is a sectarian attempt to confirm Marx's famous aphorism that the state is but "the executive committee of the whole bourgeoisie." Apart from the fact that what Marx may have written on any given occasion can scarcely be taken as the last word on anything (either by proponents or detractors of class analysis), the charge is unfounded.

Because capitalism is a competitive system, and because capitalists are competing with one another, for the state to pursue policies in the interest of the *whole* capitalist class it must have a degree of *autonomy* from the dictation of particular capitalists.

But the state's "relative autonomy" from the capitalists entails more than this. It will be recalled that, whereas in a slave or feudal system class relations are *legally* constituted and hence *directly* dependent on the state's coercive force, in a capitalist society individuals are free and classes are constituted on the ability to dispose of labour in the economy. This separation of the state from the constitution of classes and from the economy is also the basis of the state's "relative autonomy." To speak of the state in a capitalist society as a capitalist state means only that, to use Porter's phrase, the "essential task" of the state is to maintain the necessary social conditions for economic growth and the reproduction of classes in a way consistent with the dynamics of an economy that is capitalistically structured. This will mean the promotion of the profitable accumulation of capital, for economic growth is *dependent* on how much capitalists invest, but also on the containment and mediation of the contradictory class relations that might give rise to disruptive social conflict. This does *not* mean that the state is to be conceived of as a perfect planner, an all-seeing "collective capitalist" that balances the provision of favourable conditions for profit against the necessity of throwing the occasional crumbs to the working class. Rather, because the state is not the preserve of one class, it means that *the state is a field of class struggle itself.*

The capitalists are a "ruling class" only in the sense that the condition for the economy's growth is conditional on private profit, on the capitalists' structural position as investors and organizers of production on which all other classes and the state are dependent. But the degree to which the state is "relatively autonomous" from the capitalist cannot be given in the abstract. It can be assessed only through a concrete class analysis. And such an analysis of the balance of class forces must look not only at the political field directly (in terms of parties, interest groups making demands on the state, etc.) but also at the economy and culture, for the balance of forces here also constrains, limits, and provides guidance to the possible choices of the state in any particular instance.

A second misconception that often arises regarding class analysis is that it produces only a bipoloar, two-class model of society: workers–capitalists, peasants–landlords, etc. For the sake of exposition in relation to the bipolar elite-mass distinction of elite analysis, I have myself given this impression. But it is incomplete. Because societies are products of history, not of analytic models, the various ways in which people are related to one another in material production allow for a wide variety of relationships. Although one may still discern the predominant social relationships that mark off one stage of history from another, each stage contains within it older forms of such relations and newer developing ones.

Thus, in Canada it is commonplace to observe that for a very large part of our history, and to some extent even today, extensive groups of people have neither sold their labour nor directly appropriated the product of other people's labour through employing them, but have rather been independent producers—owning their own means of production and working on it themselves, engaging in commodity and credit exchange relations with the other classes. This is the traditional middle class, the old "petite bourgeoisie" of independent craftspeople, family farmers, etc. It is sometimes alleged that such a class exists only as an analytic category, not as a real historical actor through culture and struggle, because the independent nature of the activity begets no common bonds between these producers. Yet history, and above all Canadian history, demonstrates the contrary. From the Rebellions of 1837–38 to the Prairie radical farmer movements of this century, we have seen that this class was significant in the overall balance of social forces, with its own culture, institutions, and ideologies whose effects were very strongly felt historically and whose influence can still be felt today.

To be sure, the development of capitalism, entailing as it does an increasing concentration and centralization of production as the forces of competition tend to squeeze out the weak and less capital-intesive units, orientates class relations more and more toward a worker–capitalist dimension. In Canada, as elsewhere, the working class has been drawn, apart from immigration, from the displaced members of the class of independent producers. But Canada's history over the past century was distinctive in that the very industrialization of the country was in good part dependent on the successful exploitation of the wheat staple, which historically involved the growth of the petit bourgeois farmer class in the western frontier simultaneously with the development of the working class (primarily located in industrial Ontario in terms of manufacturing, although more widely dispersed in relation to mineral and forest resource extraction). This multidimensionality of class in 20th-century Canada, characterized as it was by uneven regional location and salience of the various classes, produced a cacophony of interlocking but distinct struggles in the economy, polity, and culture. Whereas an identity of class opponents sometimes united the farmers and workers, their different class experiences also divided them, as the farmers focused on conditions of credit, commodity prices, transportation costs, and the tariff itself, rather than on wages and conditions of employment or control of the labour process, as the main terrains of conflict. Thus, even on those occasions when farmers and workers went so far as to identify the capitalists, the capitalist parties, and even the capitalist system as their common enemy, the concrete struggles of each revealed a far more complex and ambiguous pattern of relationships at work.

At first glance it might appear that this situation has now changed, that today a bipolar set of class relations more nearly obtains. With the decline of the importance of Prairie wheat in the economy as a whole, and with the stark decline in the number of independent producers over the century, wage and salary employees now constitute over 80 percent of the economically active population. But not all wage and salary earners can be unambiguously identified as working class.[15] This is not primarily due to differences in income and status between white-collar salaried employees and manual wage workers, as the stratification approach of elite analysis would have it. These differences have more and more proved ephemeral and temporary, as the clerks in the office and the steelworkers in the mill are increasingly aware. Nor is it so much because many white-collar workers are located in the state and in commercial sectors that are not directly a source of the profits on which the economy continues to depend for its dynamism.

For here as well, the main criterion is the ability to dispose of labour that is at issue, and this criterion traverses the industrial, commercial, and state sectors of the economy. Indeed, the extensive unionization and militancy of so many white-collar employees would seem to suggest increasingly that they are indeed well into the process of class formation along the dimensions of culture and struggle that compose real social classes. But in terms of the disposition of labour, it is also clear that within both the private corporations and the public sector there has developed over this century a stratum of employees who, without ownership or control of the means of production, neverthless dispose of labour in terms of managing, supervising, and controlling the labour of others. Although there is some theoretical disputation regarding the "class position" of such employees, it does seem that in the terms within which we have been speaking these people might be properly conceived of as a (for want of a better word) "new middle class," who by virtue of their function in the labour process stand in a contradictionary relationship both to capital and labour, as salaried technocrats, managers, and professionals.[16]

It has indeed become one of the favourite themes of contemporary political science in Canada to identify many political changes in terms of this "new middle class" as a social force. In particular the "new middle class" has been seen as a dominant force underlying the expansionary political and economic projects of provincial states, especially those that took shape within the governments of Alberta and Quebec. However suggestive these analyses, it must be said that there tends to be a rather cavalier attitude toward clearly delineating this class. To take the example of Alberta, in John Richards and Larry Pratt's *Prairie Capitalism* this class is variously referred to as an "arriviste bourgeoisie" and an "upwardly mobile urban middle class," which includes not only "upper-income" professionals and managers but also indigenous Alberta entrepreneurs (capitalists) and a "state-administrative elite." Operative here is a vague set of criteria that borrows rather indiscriminately from elite analysis and class analysis proper. It is possible that, in terms of the culture and struggle that bind these groups together, one might find the basis of a cohesive social force in class terms. But much more needs to be done in this respect before the case is convincing, not least involving the attempt to define more clearly the common social relationships with other classes that give this disparate "new middle class" its unity.

CLASS AND PARTY

There is a tendency in much "new-middle-class" analysis, moreover, to posit a very close identity between class and party. This has, to be sure, long been a bane of class analysis in Canada, revealing an inclination to think that class analysis has relevance only if it receives an unequivocal party political expression. A number of points may be made in this regard. Although it is easy to locate the social backgrounds of a party's leading personnel, one must be careful to avoid the trap of "sociological representation" that we saw in elite analysis. Without representation in the sense of social base, control, delegation, and accountability in the expression of common class interests, the socioeconomic origins of leaders may be quite misleading as indicators of class interests. *If* the party is one of the places through which the class is united as a social and cultural entity, one may speak of it properly as a party of a certain class.

But one should still be careful of treating the party *as* the class. Precisely because parties aim at state office (and even when they get there are only a part of the state as governing parties) their project entails a relative autonomy from specific classes, since a political party, as Gilles Bourque puts it, "poses the question of power amidst the whole process of the class struggle. ... By definition, it cannot assert itself as the unilateral, unequivocal instrument of just one class or class fragment. The struggle between parties, in liberal democracies, is not a tournament with as many teams as there are classes or fragments."[17] Bourque goes on:

> *Involved in a party is social space in its totality. A party undertakes not only the promotion of specific, multiple and heterogeneous interests, but also the reproduction of the totality of the social formation. In it unfolds the whole domain of hegemony, alliances and compromises. A party seeks to create those political and ideological conditions which are most favourable to the promotion of the economic interests it defends, whether or not these interests are dominant within the social formation. While it is true that a party does not enjoy the same autonomy vis-à-vis its hegemonic class, or even subordinate classes and fragments in its midst, as the state vis-à-vis the totality of classes, a party is less directly controlled than is a corporative organization by the short-term economic interests of its members. The program of a party, much*

less the policy of a government, cannot be unequivocally identified with the specific interests of its hegemonic class. While the legislation of a government may be used as an indication of the class interest defended by a party in power, this is not a demonstration of the operating social force.

This issue has relevance to a broader one in the domain of class analysis. It is often argued that class analysis is irrelevant *in Canada* because there is no major working-class party (often defined as Bourque warns us not to) on the national scene, or because voting behaviour does not exhibit a distinct pervasive cleavage along class lines. But it is a major mistake to arrange parties along ideological or policy dimensions of "left" and "right" and then hypothetically assign classes to them in a bifurcated fashion. If voters are found not to conform with this procedure, this may say as much about the brittleness of the analytical construct as about the flexibility of the voters. As Bourque suggests, every party seeks to contain within it the totality of social relations in a society.

Thus, when John A. Macdonald's Conservative Party constructed a "Tory–Producer" alliance around the tariff and mildly progressive industrial relations legislation, it did so not by ignoring class (although certainly by decrying class conflict) but by incorporating working-class demands, interests, and leaders in their project, mediating them in a way consistent with the hegemony of the capitalists in the party. When the Mackenzie King Liberals constructed their industrial relations and welfare state program in 1944–45, they did much the same thing. How far a simple voting-behaviour test of the relevance of class in Canadian politics departs from capturing reality may be noted in the fact that the Communist Party supported the Liberals rather than the Co-operative Commonwealth Federation (CCF) in the 1945 election. And Pierre Trudeau, seeking to end his dependence on the New Democratic Party (NDP) in a minority government, and faced with the opportunity of the Stanfield Conservatives' calling for an incomes and prices freeze, went to Sudbury during the 1974 election campaign and shouted, "So what's he going to freeze? Your wages! He's going to freeze your wages!"[18] Here again was the incorporation of class, the expression and mediation of working-class interests, within the framework of the Liberal Party.

To be sure, the way in which politicians employ language and symbols is enormously important to whether the electorate itself explicitly perceives politics, and elections in particular, to be about class. People who have but recently engaged in militant and protracted strikes may very well fail to perceive that a subsequent election is about class struggle, much less connect either their strike or the election to the question of "socialism versus capitalism." It is parties, not voters, that structure the symbols of the electoral battle (although the concrete promises contained within these symbols are certainly shaped by the balance of class forces).

As Jane Jenson and Janine Brodie have argued in an analysis that applies as much to the CCF/NDP as to the Liberals and Conservatives:

> *From the beginning, mass political parties have integrated voters into a system of partisan relations but in this process of integration, parties have also provided voters with a* definition of politics. *They define, for the electorate, the content of politics and the meaning of political activity. In other words, at the level of ideology,* political parties shape the interpretation of what aspects of social relations should be considered political, how politics should be conducted, what the boundaries of political discussion most properly may be and what kinds of conflicts can be resolved through the political process. *From the vast array of tensions, differences, and inequalities characteristic of any society, political parties choose which will be treated as political alternatives in the electoral process and, thereby, how the electorate will divide against itself. This role of parties is profoundly important because before electoral cleavages come into being, a definition of what is political must exist. Whether a social problem is considered to be a religious, economic or political question is something that is set by this definition. A conspiracy of silence can exist around matters which parties, for whatever reason, choose not to elevate to the level of partisan debate.*[19]

It can certainly be appreciated that the ability of a party to catalyze the working class around a class definition of politics, and reciprocally for the working class to construct a party in which it is the hegemonic class while successfully integrating other classes, is something that contributes very much to the cohesion and strength of the working class in society. But here we have to return to the balance of class forces. The inability to do so does not invalidate class analysis but rather necessitates it all the more to cut through the veil of appearances that confronts the social scientist. (The sun *looks* like it is moving around the earth, even though we know that not to be the case. Indeed, we explain why it looks that way through scientific analysis.) It is only when class analysis is thought to be a teleological exercise that involves the claim that the working class exists only when it has full consciousness and political expression of its "revolutionary destiny" that class analysis is invalidated. But this precisely fails to grasp that class analysis entails not only imposing abstract categories (whether statistical categories or pristine parties) on real social relations but rather concerns actually examining the many ways in which contradictory social relations between people take historical expression, through culture and struggle.

In Canada it has usually been the case that the struggle of the working class finds direct expression more in the arena of work and in union struggles than in electoral politics or in the "elite accommodation" of interest groups. Although this is not immediately promising in terms of replacing capitalism with socialism, neither is social-democratic electoral politics or the elite accommodation of labour leaders. For in those countries where labour leaders have indeed been assimilated to the "confraternity of power" through these mechanisms, this has often not carried the class struggle to a higher plane, but weakened it as labour leaders, as a condition of their entry into the confraternity of power, have acted as agencies of social control over working-class demands "in the national interest." If it appeared in the 1950s that such integration foretold the final "end of ideology" and the "embourgeoisement" of the working class, the resurgence of industrial militancy after the mid-1960s (of which Canada was one of the most prominent examples) belied such predications. In Europe, this rendered social-democratic parties' "consensus" politics unstable. In Canada, given the lesser importance of such parties, this particular effect of industrial militancy has been less visible. But it has nonetheless had real political effects.

POLITICAL SCIENCE AND SOCIAL CHANGE

The study of politics is not just the study of parliaments or bureaucracies or even a broader study of the most powerful decision-makers in all spheres of society. It must be a study as well of the social forces "from below." Some will say that is the proper field of sociology, especially insofar as the activities of those below, even if they influence the decision-makers, do not have enough power "to change the system." But this is an impoverished view of political science. Indeed, as Antonio Gramsci wrote half a century ago,

> If political science means science of the State, and the State is the entire complex of practical and theoretical activities with which the ruling class not only justifies and maintains its dominance, but manages to win the active consent of those over whom it rules, then it is obvious that all essential questions of sociology are nothing other than questions of political science.[20]

There is another important dimension to political science, of course, which precisely has to do with "changing the system"; which is not just about analyzing what the state and ruling class do, criticizing it on this basis, or even coming forward on the basis of this analysis with "public policy" proposals for enabling the state to manage the system better. Rather, this other dimension of political science is about developing analyses of the processes and strategies involved in changing the system from one based on class competition, exploitation, and conflict to a different system based on the elimination of classes and the development of as fully a democratic, egalitarian, and cooperative society as possible. Here we begin to raise larger questions about what "science" is really all about. And Gramsci is again a valuable guide:

> *Is not science itself "political activity" and political thought, in as much as it transforms men, and makes them different from what they were before? ... If science is the "discovery" of formerly unknown reality, is this reality not conceived of in a certain sense as transcendent? And is it not thought that there still exists something "unknown" and hence transcendent? And does not the concept of science as "creation" then mean that it too is "politics"? Everything depends on seeing whether the creation involved is "arbitrary," or whether it is rational—i.e., useful to men in that it enlarges their concept of life, and raises to a higher level (develops) life itself.*[21]

We can see, in this sense, the importance of a political science that is trying to know more than how to uncover how the power elites rule the world, but that also has an understanding that the majorities subjected to that rule also have power capacities, and is trying to discover how those capacities might be enhanced—not just to criticize the elites or ruling classes, not just to influence their decisions through struggles "from below," but to "transcend" the present system of power relations entirely. This is less a matter of constructing utopian visions of a "good society" than of discovering the means whereby the subordinate classes have increased their power historically, and of trying to discover further and better means. Political science has a role to play in demonstrating that most people are not just passive recipients of someone else's power, that they currently exercise some power even if just in relation to the greater power of the dominant classes. It could have a larger and more creative role to play by discovering the limits to the ways in which subordinate classes have organized so far, and by trying to think through and offer advice on how to organize for a fundamental challenge to the powers that be. This will, above all, be a matter of discovering the kind of political organizations that enhance the intellectual capacities of working people themselves, so that they can become leaders and educators in their own communities and develop their capacities to run society and state in a fully democratic manner. To be a political scientist, in this conception, is to be someone who knows how to do more than criticize the power elite. It is to be someone who is orientated to discovering how to help those who have the potential power to change the system to realize that they have that potential—and then actually to act upon that potential. Philosophers, a great social scientist once said, have always tried to understand the world, but the point of this understanding, he appropriately insisted, was to change it.

NOTES

1. R.J. Van Loon and M.S. Whittington, *The Canadian Political System*, 2nd ed. (Toronto: McGraw-Hill Ryerson, 1976).

2. J.A. Schumpeter, *Capitalism, Socialism and Democracy*, 5th ed. (London: George Allen and Unwin, 1976), pp. 269, 285.

3. J. Porter, *The Vertical Mosaic: An Analysis of Social Class and Power in Canada* (Toronto: University of Toronto Press, 1965). For two useful critiques of Porter's approach, especially his conception of class and power, see J. Heap, "Conceptual and Theoretical Problems in *The Vertical Mosaic*," *Canadian Review of Sociology and Anthropology* 9 (May 1973), and J. Hutcheson, "Class and Income Distribution in Canada," in R.M. Laxer, ed., *(Canada) Ltd., The Political Economy of Dependency* (Toronto: McClelland and Stewart, 1973).

4. Porter, *The Vertical Mosaic*, pp. 532, 539–40, 557.

5. W. Clement, *The Canadian Corporate Elite: An Analysis of Economic Power* (Toronto: McClelland and Stewart, 1975).

6. D. Olsen, *The State Elite* (Toronto: McClelland and Stewart, 1980), pp. 82, 124.

7. R. Presthus, *Elite Accommodation in Canadian Politics* (Toronto: Macmillan, 1973), pp. 348–49, 169.

8. C.B. Macpherson, *Democracy in Alberta: Social Credit and the Party System* (Toronto: University of Toronto Press, 1st ed., 1953; 2nd ed., 1963), p. 225.

9. C.B. Macpherson, *The Life and Times of Liberal Democracy* (Oxford: Oxford University Press, 1977), p. 11.

10. Clement, *The Canadian Corporate Elite*, p. 10.

11. See J. Harrison, *Marxist Economics for Socialists* (London: Pluto, 1978), p. 30.

12. V.I. Lenin, "A Great Beginning" (1919), *Selected Works*, vol. 3 (Moscow: 1971), p. 231.

13. B.D. Palmer, *A Culture in Conflict: Skilled Workers and Industrial Capitalism in Hamilton, Ontario, 1860–1914* (Montreal and Kingston: McGill-Queen's University Press, 1979), p. xvi; cf. G.S. Kealey, *Toronto Workers Respond to Industrial Capitalism 1867–1892* (Toronto: University of Toronto Press, 1980).

14. T. Naylor, *The History of Canadian Business, 1867–1914* (Toronto: James Lorimer, 1975).

15. See L.A. Johnson, "The Development of Class in Canada in the Twentieth Century," in G. Teeple, ed., *Capitalism and the National Question in Canada* (Toronto: University of Toronto Press, 1972).

16. For important attempts to "map" the contemporary class structure in these terms see: G. Carchedi, "On the Economic Identification of the New Middle Class," *Economy and Society* 4 (1975): 1; G. Carchedi, *On the Economic Identification of Social Classes* (London: Routledge and Kegan Paul, 1977); and E.O. Wright, *Class, Crisis and the State* (London: New Left Books, 1978). For a good example of the cultural dimension entailed in the relation between this new middle class and the working class, see A. Gorz, "Technical Intelligence and the Capitalist Division of Labour," *Telos* 12 (Summer 1972), especially pp. 34–35.

17. G. Bourque, "Class, Nation and the Parti Québécois," *Studies in Political Economy* 2 (Autumn 1979): 130.

18. Quoted in *The Toronto Star* (October 18, 1975).

19. M.J. Brodie and J. Jenson, *Crisis, Challenge and Change: Party and Class in Canada* (Toronto: Methuen, 1980), p. 8.

20. Q. Hoare and G. Nowell Smith, eds., *Selections from the Prison Notebooks of Antonio Gramsci* (London: Lawrence and Wishart, 1971), p. 244.

21. Ibid.

FURTHER READINGS

Armstrong, Pat, and Hugh Armstrong. "Beyond Sexless Class and Classless Sex." *Studies in Political Economy* 10 (Winter 1983).

Carroll, William K. *Corporate Power and Canadian Capitalism*. Vancouver: University of British Columbia Press, 1986.

Clement, Wallace. *Continental Corporate Power*. Toronto: McClelland and Stewart, 1977.

Cohen, Marjorie. *Women's Work, Markets, and Economic Development in Nineteenth-Century Ontario*. Toronto: University of Toronto Press, 1988.

Cuneo, C. "Corporate Power in Canada." *Studies in Political Economy* 27 (Autumn 1988).

Fox, J., and M. Orenstein. "The Canadian State and Corporate Elites in the Post-War Period." *Canadian Review of Sociology and Anthropology* 32, no. 4 (1986).

Francis, D. *Controlling Interest: Who Owns Canada?* Toronto: Macmillan, 1986.

Hunter, Alfred A. *Class Tells: On Social Inequality in Canada,* 2nd ed. Toronto: Butterworths, 1986.

Maroney, Heather Jon, and Meg Luxton, eds. *Feminism and Political Economy: Women's Work, Women's Struggles*. Toronto: Methuen, 1987.

McQuaig, Linda. *Behind Closed Doors: How the Rich Won Control of Canada's Tax System ... and Ended Up Richer*. Toronto: Penguin, 1987.

Miliband, R. *Marxism and Politics*. Oxford: Oxford University Press, 1977.

Niosi, Jorge. *Canadian Multinationals,* trans. Robert Chodos. Toronto: Between the Lines, 1985.

Palmer, Bryan D. *Working-Class Experience: The Rise and Reconstitution of Canadian Labour, 1800–1980*. Toronto: Butterworths, 1983.

Panitch, Leo. "Capitalism, Socialism and Revolution." In R. Miliband et al., eds., *The Socialist Register, 1989*. London: Merlin Press, 1989.

Panitch, Leo, ed. *The Canadian State: Political Economy and Political Power*. Toronto: University of Toronto Press, 1977.

Panitch, L., and D. Swartz. *The Assault on Trade Union Freedoms*. Toronto: Garamond Press, 1988.

Porter, John. *The Vertical Mosaic*. Toronto: University of Toronto Press, 1965.

Smith, Dorothy. "Inequality and the Family." In Alan Moscovitch and Glenn Drover, eds., *Inequality: Essays on the Political Economy of Social Welfare*. Toronto: University of Toronto Press, 1981.

9 RETHINKING CANADIAN POLITICS: THE IMPACT OF GENDER

Sandra Burt

THE SUCCESSES (?) OF THE 1990S

The status of Canadian women has changed dramatically since the turn of the century, and even since the Royal Commission on the Status of Women submitted its report to Parliament in 1970. Most apparent has been the gradual improvement in women's legal position. The 1982 Charter of Rights and Freedoms stands as a symbol of Canadian women's *legal equality* with men. In section 28 of the Charter, women are guaranteed the same rights and freedoms as men, and section 15 guarantees women equality both before and under the law. These equality guarantees replaced the 1960 provision in the Canadian Bill of Rights that simply instructed the courts to apply all Canadian laws equally to women and men, without imposing any restrictions on discriminatory provisions within such laws. Following 1982, the federal government reviewed its existing legislation to correct for unequal provisions, and in 1985 passed the Statute Law Amendment Bill to remove such inequalities.

The Charter also made provision for remedial measures that might violate the equality principle in the short term, in order to correct past inequalities and produce a fairer distribution of rights and freedoms in the longer term. In the wake of this provision both federal and provincial governments have passed some affirmative-action laws. These laws fall short of establishing quotas, but do encourage the hiring or promotion of female candidates who are as qualified as male applicants.

Pay-equity laws, based on the principle of similar rewards for work of similar value, also have become more common, with five provinces (Manitoba, Ontario, Nova Scotia, Prince Edward Island, and New Brunswick) passing different versions of such laws between 1985 and 1989. These laws differ from preceding equal-pay provisions in two important respects. First, they place the responsibility for ensuring equal pay for women on the employer rather than on the female employee. This is particularly important in view of women's historical record of insecurity in the labour market. Second, they take into account the fact that women and men are not always in the same or similar occupations, but may be carrying out equally valuable jobs. And while the federal government has reduced its commitment to providing affordable, accessible child care (in particular between 1986 and 1993, when privatization and pro–family values took over the federal Conservative agenda), new union agreements in the automobile industry suggest that the unions may in the future take more responsibility for this issue.

Beginning in the 1980s as well, the problems of *sexual harassment* and *violence against women* became policy concerns of both federal and provincial governments. For example, the federal government began a four-year family violence initiative in 1988, and later extended it to 1995. As part of this initiative, the Panel on Violence was set up in August 1991, with representatives from women's groups and aboriginal communities included as members. The members of this panel broke new ground in federal policy circles by insisting on feminist-inspired and informed research on the issue. In their report, the panel members reflected on those characteristics that set their activities apart from those of other government agencies or commissions. First, the panel members had nonpartisan and feminist backgrounds, and many had considerable experience in anti-violence work. Second, the panel adopted an interactive, community-based approach, meeting with women in their own surroundings. Third, the panel experimented with interaction between an advisory committee and an aboriginal circle. It was forced to work within government-set criteria and structures, but sought to adapt both to serve women's needs.[1] The members grappled as well with the fact that the panel "had no identity separate from the Government,"[2] and spoke openly about the problems associated with this constrained legal and political situation.

In 1992 the federal government passed a sexual-assault bill (Bill C-49) to provide guidelines for determining when a victim's past sexual history can be admitted as evidence in a court case, and to define, for the first time, the legal meaning of consent to sexual activity. Stricter gun-control legislation was passed by the federal House in December 1991, partly in response to pressure from women seeking to control the proliferation of wife abuse.

There was evidence as well, in the 1993 federal election, of women's continued movement into the more visible arena of *electoral politics*. Two of the national parties were led by women, and the proportion of female legislators moved upward from 13 percent in 1988 to 18 percent in 1993. Thirty-six of the 53 women elected in 1993 represent the governing

Liberal Party, which gives them greater potential access to decision-making than their opposition counterparts. One of the key Liberal Party election strategists in the 1993 federal campaign is a former President of the National Action Committee on the Status of Women, a feminist umbrella group that claims to represent over 470 women's groups. In the postelection speculation, *The Globe and Mail* referred to the increase in female representation as a "surge" that "raises activists' hopes."[3]

THE REAL WORLD OF GENDER POLITICS

However, optimism about changes in women's status must be tempered with concern about the narrow limits of Charter-based equality rights decisions for women in the courts; the weaknesses in some of the legislative reforms intended to improve women's economic status, combined with the failure of Canadian governments to deal effectively with the increasing feminization of poverty; and the persistence of violence against women. A closer look at the "successes" of the past twenty years reveals some serious flaws in successive governments' commitment to improving women's status, even within the fairly narrow confines of equal-rights feminism, which is predicated on the belief that women should be granted access to the public sphere (both politics and the labour force) in the spirit of equal opportunities for all.

WOMEN AND THE COURTS

In 1981, when the federal Liberal government introduced a Constitution bill to patriate the British North America (BNA) Act and provide Canadians with constitutionally entrenched rights, Canadian feminists who were part of the organized women's movement became mobilized around the equal-rights issue for the first time in their history. Before 1981 they had concentrated on winning specific legislative reforms such as equal pay for work of equal value, affordable and accessible child care, abortion on demand, and improved access to all sectors of the labour market. But the possibility of a constitutionally entrenched declaration of rights that excluded women mobilized some of the older groups, and gave rise to the creation of some new ones, to ensure that women were well represented at the bargaining table.

Following a mass rally of women on Parliament Hill early in 1981, members of the newly created Ad Hoc Committee on the Constitution and the somewhat older (1974) National Association of Women and the Law (NAWL) negotiated with Jean Chrétien—then Minister of Justice in the Trudeau Liberal government—for meaningful legal equality clauses in the

Charter. Women's demands were based on the resolutions passed at that 1981 rally. Most of the women who participated in that lobbying process were elated with their successes. They were convinced that the revised Charter would improve women's access to substantive equality with men; allow for the creation of affirmative-action programs as necessary; and make it impossible for provincial governments to override the sex-equality provisions. One activist expressed her enthusiastic response to the process in these terms: "This process has strengthened the idea that women can move and they can be heard. They can be taken seriously. Women's groups feel that they are more powerful now, they are bolder and more confident. The government has recognized that women are a significant force."[4]

The constitutional entrenchment of equality rights for women resulted in the creation of another new group, the Legal Education and Action Fund (LEAF), composed primarily of feminist lawyers and human-rights professionals. LEAF sponsors selected cases involving women's rights, and at the same time engages in the process of legal education and legislative lobbying.[5] Its emergence has marked a new reliance on women's groups—especially the National Action Committee on the Status of Women and the Canadian Abortion Rights Action League—as well as on advice from feminist legal experts.

These experts have adopted two principal strategies in their court work. First, in the tradition of the wording of the sex-equality clause in the Charter, they have tried to pressure the courts to think in terms of *substantive* rather than *formal* equality. Beverley Baines summarizes the distinction between these two interpretations of equality rights this way:

> *"Formal equality" is simply another name for the Aristotelian theory of equality, the theory that assumes equality is achieved when the law treats likes alike. Sometimes it is appropriate for the law to treat women and men as alike or formally equal—the right to vote being a prime example. However, since women and men are not identically situated much of the time, mostly "the formal equality model breaks down; in fact, it is inherently discriminatory." Formal equality is inadequate because it fails to encompass or even to acknowledge that "Women's conditions are worse than men's: they are disadvantaged, exploited, degraded, and brutalized."[6]*

LEAF's second and related goal has been to convince the courts to listen to women's stories, to develop a contextual understanding of court cases as they relate to women, and to place women's equality claims within the context of their past experiences as a subjugated group.

The equality provisions of the Charter did not take effect until 1985. Thus, we have less than ten years of judicial reasoning to consider when evaluating the success of feminist legal claims. But the early signs are not encouraging. In 1989, Shelagh Day and Gwen Brodsky reviewed the first three years of Charter litigation and concluded that the courts were basing their decisions on the formal interpretation of equality rights. They noted as well that the equal-rights provisions were used more frequently by men than by women, and primarily in child-custody cases. In other words, the equal-rights clause in the Charter has worked against rather than for women's interests, resulting in an increase in the number of men winning child-custody cases.

The problem here is that women and men have been treated by the courts as if they are "the same," without concern for the historical legacy of workplace discrimination against women and unequal pay. When the economic profiles of women and men are compared, women are consistent losers. On the question of context, women's hopes for the Charter also have been dimmed. In 1991 the Supreme Court nullified section 276 of the Criminal Code, which had removed the right of an accused rapist to introduce the alleged victim's sexual history as evidence. In other words, the courts seemed to accept the feminist argument that context matters, but only in a situation that most women have deemed unfair. In 1993 the Court refused to allow self-employed women to claim child-care expenses as a business-related deduction for income-tax purposes. While groups like the National Action Committee applauded the court's decision on the grounds that this deduction would help only privileged women, it could be argued that the Court was assigning greater value to business entertainment than to child care, even if only for this small group of self-employed women and men.

Baines sees cause for qualified optimism about the potential for more decisions based on a vision of substantive equality in some Supreme Court decisions that have not been based on the Charter. In *Brooks v. Canada Safeway* (1989), the Supreme Court took the position that discrimination on the basis of pregnancy could be sex discrimination, and thus recognized that one of the characteristics that makes women different from men (pregnancy) could impose unfair costs on women only. In the Lavallee case of 1990, the Court was willing to take into account a woman's history of battering when assessing her action of shooting her partner in the back. Baines's optimism is tempered by her observation that "in the context of the Charter it is impossible to ignore the Supreme Court's record of avoidance when the sex-equality provisions are invoked."[7]

One possible explanation for the failure of the Supreme Court to accept a broad interpretation of equality is that most of the judges are men. Madame Justice Bertha Wilson was the first female appointee. She sat on the bench from 1982 to 1991. Madame Justice Claire l'Heureux-Dubé was appointed in 1987, and Madame Justice Beverley McLachlin in 1989. A gender split has not been apparent in all decisions. But it *was* Madame Justice Wilson who articulated the issue of substantive equality rights in 1985, in *Operation Dismantle v. The Queen*. In that case, she raised the question of "whether fundamental justice is entirely procedural in nature or whether it has a substantive impact as well."[8] Again in 1988, Madame Justice Wilson called on the concept of substantive equality when the Supreme Court struck down Canada's abortion law. She argued that "the more recent struggle for women's rights has been a struggle to eliminate discrimination, to achieve a place for women in a man's world, to develop a set of legislative reforms in order to place women in the same position as men."[9] Most recently, in the 1993 judgment on the eligibility of child-care expenses as a business deduction, the two women on the bench dissented from the majority opinion and supported the request.

It should also be noted that even when women are successful in the courts, this does not always result in improved conditions for the majority of those affected by the legal decisions. William Bogart makes this point in his review of the limitations of litigation in Canada. The Supreme Court's decision in 1988 to render invalid the 1969 provision of the Criminal Code (s. 251) that sets out specific conditions for legal abortions was hailed by many women as a victory for choice. Section 251 restricted abortions to women who, in the view of a therapeutic abortion committee of at least three physicians, were at risk for their health through the continuation of the pregnancy. In this decision (*R. v. Morgentaler*), the Court drew on section 7 of the Charter, which guarantees "life, liberty and security of the person and the right not to be deprived thereof except in accordance with principles of fundamental justice." The therapeutic abortion committees required by section 251 were not available in all communities, and the Court ruled that this posed a restriction on some women's right to security. In the judgment, Justice Brian Dickson wrote:

> *Section 251 clearly interferes with a woman's bodily integrity in both a physical and emotional sense. Forcing a woman, by threat of criminal sanction, to carry a foetus to term unless she meets certain criteria unrelated to her own priorities and aspirations is a profound interference with a woman's body and thus a violation of security of the person.*[10]

A victory for women? Bogart draws on the American experience in sounding a note of caution. In the United States, the landmark decision in *Roe v. Wade* opened the door to legal abortions. But that decision placed no responsibility on the state "to provide safe and accessible abortion, to curb the growth of private abortion clinics whose interest is profit, to provide counseling, or pre-natal education and nutrition, and child-care after the birth of a continued pregnancy."[11] In Canada as well, there is no evidence that the favourable court decision has resulted in greater access to abortion for those women living in remote northern or rural communities, or in cities where the majority of the physicians in residence are not prepared to offer the service.

WOMEN AND LEGISLATURES

Some would argue that it is inappropriate for the courts to advance women's claims. This is the position adopted by Wayne Mackay, who notes that there are limits to the expertise of the judges on the bench, and that, in any case, Canadians prefer their elected representatives to make judgments about appropriate courses of action.[12] But here too the evidence from the past twenty years suggests that legislative reforms have been formulated within the concept of formal legal equality of opportunity, with only occasional, albeit significant, forays into the discourse of substantive equality.

Since the early 1970s, Canadian governments have been committed, in rhetoric at least, to this principle of legal equality rights for women. Undoubtedly, even this shift in thinking represents a significant movement away from the earlier protective vision of legislators that guided their actions throughout the 19th century and into the 20th. The exigencies of running wartime economies in the first half of the 20th century, when the Industrial Revolution was already well under way, were instrumental in convincing legislators that women were needed in the public world of commerce and industrial labour. But without the pressure exerted by strong women's groups, such as the Federation of Women Teachers and the Young Women's Christian Association, it is unlikely that governments in Canada would have introduced, beginning in 1954, a series of legislative measures that have eased women's access into some areas of the economy. Largely as a consequence of the groundbreaking work performed by the Women's Bureau in the Department of Labour, successive Liberal and Conservative governments have adopted equal-pay laws, maternity-leave legislation, and some limited child-care measures.[13] Their rationale has always been that of promoting equal opportunities for women to assume most or all of the jobs currently performed in the economy and in public life. At times, this rationale has even included affirmative-action (or substantive equal-opportunity) measures that reflect women's historical disadvantages. These past disadvantages, it is recognized, have appeared both as role expectations that would consign women to the private sphere of the home and family, and as structural obstacles imposed by men to restrict women's access to the public sphere.[14]

In 1979, the federal Liberal government issued its first formal plan of action for women following the appearance in 1970 of the landmark *Report of the Royal Commission on the Status of Women*. The authors of the plan wrote about the need to help women achieve economic independence. They targeted five areas of policy concern: rape; wife battering; sexual harassment; women in the media; and pensions.[15] This early plan is typical of both the federal and provincial governments' strategies for women. It reflects the significant role played by government bureaucrats in status-of-women positions in setting the government agenda, thereby bypassing the many women's groups across the country. It also illustrates the equal-opportunity framework within which most "women's issues" policy initiatives have been undertaken.

The 1979 plan, worked out primarily by Status of Women Canada, a federal government department led by the minister responsible for the Status of Women, did not reflect the predominant concerns of the many women's groups pressuring governments for change. This may have been due partly to poor record-keeping on the part of government. Although Status of Women Canada is a repository for group submissions to government, its records in 1979 were in disarray and there was no central listing of the demands of women's groups.[16] At that time, the agenda of the women's movement included all five areas in the federal government's plan. But equally important were demands for affirmative-action strategies, pay equity, and accessible, affordable child care. For without a safe place to leave one's children during working hours, economic independence could not become a reality for most Canadian women. And the feminization of poverty was already well under way in 1979, so group proposals included attempts to deal with this growing problem.

Subsequent federal policy initiatives have included some limited and voluntary affirmative-action measures for the federal civil service and large companies doing business with the federal government. For example, the 1990 report of a federal task force on barriers facing women in the public service encouraged managers "to pursue the objectives of employment equity."[17] Pay-equity legislation means that, for the first time, women's jobs are compared with men's in the same establishment on the basis of criteria such as qualifications required, responsibilities involved, and the nature of the duties performed. Only female job classes (i.e., jobs in which between 60–70 percent of the holders are female) qualify for assessment.

Ontario's legislation is the most progressive, since it applies to both private and public employees. Furthermore, Ontario's act "permits a job class to contain only one person, while Manitoba's, Nova Scotia's, and New Brunswick's legislations require that there be ten people before a group of positions can be a job class, and thus qualify to be involved in the pay equity exercise."[18] However, even Ontario's legislation reveals the limits of state action on issues affecting women. Sue Findlay worked as a consultant to the Pay Equity Commission in Ontario, and writes about her experience in a collection of feminist analyses of pay-equity policy. She notes that almost one-half of the women in workplaces covered by the act cannot claim pay-equity adjustments under it. Women for whom there is no comparative male group in the same workplace are excluded. Although special provision was made for women in this situation in the early drafting of the Ontario law, subsequent policy directives have not corrected the problem. Section 33 of the Ontario legislation includes the proviso that the Pay Equity Office would conduct a study of the problem and make recommendations within one year of the commencement of the program. Findlay concludes that structural constraints have retarded action, and notes that

> *in the struggle to define ways for women in predominantly female establishments to achieve pay equity adjustments, it was clear that our reforms were shaped in three major ways: one, by the balance of power at the political level where public issues are translated into political commitments; two, by the presentation of our interests in the policy-making processes of the state bureaucracy where the implementation of these commitments is organized; and three, by the institutionalization of our own political practices as we participated in these processes.*[19]

Patricia McDermott also concludes that the Ontario legislation will do little to reduce the wage gap between women and men. Indeed, in 1991 Ontario women working full-time for a full year were still earning only 69.8 percent of what men were earning. Furthermore, women who see their wages increase minimally as a result of the legislation "will be told that they now have 'pay equity' and will, therefore, have no recourse but to engage in undoubtedly lengthy and expensive litigation over the issue of gender neutrality."[20]

Nonetheless, Ontario's pay-equity legislation, even with its flaws, was written with women in mind. Even more serious problems arise when governments adopt economic strategies that obviously fail to take women's needs into account. The federal government's position on free trade is a good example of such a policy. In 1993, the Ontario government prepared a study of the impact of the North American Free Trade Agreement (NAFTA) on women. The authors of the study point to women's special vulnerability to the effects of NAFTA, and conclude that "the cumulative and indirect effects of the agreement will likely result in greater economic inequality for women."[21] They estimate that the earlier (1989) Free Trade Agreement contributed to the loss of 55,000 jobs for women in the manufacturing sector, and that the disproportionate effects of NAFTA will be even greater.[22]

In the 1990s we have a much better sense of what is needed to create a fairer world for women, even within the context of the equal-opportunity principle. Women's labour-force participation patterns demonstrate clearly the areas of need for women seeking access to, or appropriate remuneration for, participation in the work world. Since 1951, when the Women's Bureau in the federal Department of Labour first began publishing its annual report on women in the labour force, women's participation rate has jumped from 24 percent to 58 percent in 1989. But even this dramatic increase doesn't capture the extent of the changes that have occurred in Canadian women's lives, for the proportion of what were called "working wives" in 1951 has increased from 11 percent in that year to 59 percent in 1988, and in 1988 "about two-thirds (65.9 percent) of women whose children were under 13 years of age participated in the labour force."[23]

In spite of affirmative-action programs at both levels of government, women remain concentrated in five occupational groups: clerical, medical, health, teaching, social sciences, and service.[24] The difficulties facing immigrant and visible-minority women are even more severe. The work force is still highly segregated by gender, with women making up 72 percent of the workers in the ten lowest-paying jobs, and only 20 percent of those in the highest-paid occupations.[25] In addition, while women's participation in full-time employment has increased, so too has their involvement in the part-time economy. In 1989, for example, 72 percent of all part-time workers were women. Women's share of the unemployed work force has also increased, to 46 percent in 1989 (although women then constituted only 44 percent of the total labour force). In her review of the special problems of immigrant women, Roxana Ng concludes that for essentially "unskilled and dead-end" jobs, these women "must have a variety of general, interchangeable skills that they have developed from housekeeping and childrearing." The jobs are short-term and insecure, with irregular and long working hours and few labour-standard protections.[26]

Studies of earlier legislative changes have revealed the significance of women's presence on elected bodies for gender-sensitive laws. For example, at the federal level, even the pro-family stance of the ruling Conservative Party could not keep Barbara McDougall from speaking out in the House of Commons in support of freedom of choice on the abortion question. She called upon women's individual intellect and spirit in the struggle to deal with the abortion question, arguing that "women make the right choice, a far better choice than you or I or all the pageantry of institutions that have been invented."[27] Much earlier, women like Agnes Macphail and Grace MacInnis helped to break down existing stereotypes of women's appropriate roles. MacInnis was particularly instrumental in winning maternity-leave legislation for women in 1970. As the only female member of the NDP in the federal House in 1965, she was instrumental in pressuring the minority Liberal government for the Royal Commission on the Status of Women.

Provincially, the record of female legislators is just as impressive. Irene Parlby, representing the United Farmers of Alberta in the government they formed in 1921, worked in the Alberta legislature for a minimum wage for women, property rights for married women, and mothers' allowances.[28] Linda Trimble has reviewed the significance of female legislators in contemporary Alberta politics, and concludes that women have been more likely to engage in debates on the basis of their issue positions than on their partisan identification in the legislature. Opposition women in particular are prepared to work across party lines.[29]

So women's presence in the legislatures seems to make a difference even when party ideologies are taken into account. It is not yet clear if recent increases in the proportion of women elected to legislatures are part of a new trend in women's involvement. Undoubtedly, important obstacles remain, including the high cost of campaigning, the problem of combining electoral careers with child rearing, and the continued presence of party gatekeepers who prefer male candidates. A combination of personal and structural obstacles continues to limit both the desire and the opportunity of women to seek elected office in ridings where winning is within reasonable reach.

THE LIMITS OF EQUAL OPPORTUNITY

Even with these provisos, it is clear that the push for equal opportunity has resulted in some improvements in the legal and economic status of Canadian women during the past twenty years. Today, slightly more than twenty years after the royal commission made its report on the status of women in Canada, many of the problems the commissioners noted have either diminished or, more rarely, disappeared. While equality of condition is still an elusive goal for most women, many of the barriers to equal opportunity have been removed.

But is equal opportunity enough? One of the most serious problems facing women today is the proliferation of violence. Funding programs initiated by Health and Welfare Canada, or by the Women's Programme in the Secretary of State, have contributed to the creation of shelters for battered women. As noted above, federal initiatives to deal with the issue of violence have resulted in the development of impressive research programs. However, recent survey evidence demonstrates the continued severity of the problem, in spite of these initiatives. Early results from the first national survey on violence were published in November 1993. Of the 12,300 women interviewed, almost one-half (45 percent) reported that they had at some time been assaulted by dates, boyfriends, husbands, friends, family members, or other men familiar to them. Violence was reported across all socioeconomic groups, and 60 percent of those assaulted reported more than one attack.[30]

Equal-opportunity measures cannot control this pattern of violent behaviour, because they do nothing to alter existing gender power relations. Evidence from available research on the problem of violence underlines the need to restructure Canada's legal, economic, health, and social institutions so that "new options—which will *not* be based on aggressiveness, competition, and autonomy—will be made possible through the support and reinforcement of our social institutions."[31]

Much of the work undertaken by groups that are part of the contemporary women's movement in Canada is based on such a vision of a society no longer governed by patriarchal, competitive, and acquisitive value systems. While a significant minority of the organized women's movement in Canada has set equal opportunity as its main goal, there is a diversity of theoretical perspectives critical of liberal thinking among the remaining groups. In a 1984 survey, only about one-quarter of the participating women's groups (21 percent of 153) described themselves in equal-opportunity terms. The remaining majority supported a wide variety of positions. A few (8 percent) were working in the social-feminist tradition of spreading the message of social concern and equality from a strong family perspective. Most (54 percent) were working to change existing conditions for women in the home, in society, and in the workplace. Their visions of change included two streams of thought that have been significant in the development of second-wave feminist thinking both in Canada and internationally.

One of these streams is generally referred to as *socialist feminist*, although it must be noted that feminists with different worldviews are commonly united on many issues. The socialist-feminist position is based on the premise that women's inequalities are grounded in the class relationships that are part of the capitalist system. Early socialist-feminist thinkers believed that women's emancipation could be achieved through the overthrow of the capitalist system and its replacement by a collectivist-inspired system based on the principle of equality of condition. Later thinkers saw patriarchal relations as a secondary system of power relations that could persist in a socialist society. They argued that class and gender interact in the present system to produce women's inequality, and that significant transformations in both are necessary for women's emancipation. Further refinement of the socialist-feminist position has taken place within the past few years, as feminist theorists have tried to come to terms with the different experiences of women of different races. In her review of the modern Marxist position, Valerie Bryson concludes that "Marxism can, in principle, point to the historical specificity of the situation experienced by different groups of women and show the ways in which racism, like sexism, is not simply a question of individual wickedness or injustice, but the product of particular historical situations which have become embedded in the structures of society."[32] Calls for fairness and justice, then, will remain empty rhetoric without the removal of those situations.

A different attack on existing power relations has come from feminists who have adopted what has been called a radical position. They argue that patriarchy, as a subjugating force, is more powerful than any economic system. *Radical feminists* see the state and state action as manifestations of male power. They argue that the family as a social institution serves this patriarchy, and that true emancipation for women will not come without the overthrow of the family, at least in its present form. As with socialist feminism, the term "radical" includes a variety of positions that attribute the exploitation of women to sexual relations. But like the socialist-feminist position, this set of views is also predicated on the need to transform fundamentally the existing nature of social relations and the state that regulates these relations.

Carole Pateman categorizes these positions as transformative in nature, as opposed to the accommodative vision of many liberal feminists, and most of the policy-makers, who have been prepared to grant some of the demands made by women within the past twenty years. Canadian policy-makers have begun to take women into account, particularly in areas they have classified as part of a "women's issues" package—some social services, employment opportunities, legal rights, and, from time to time, child care. But their reform initiatives are limited ideologically by the boundaries of liberal-democratic thinking, in which the values of scarcity, competition, and aggressiveness prevail. They are limited as well by their continued adherence to the belief that policy issues can be neatly packaged into categories reflecting women's concerns or men's concerns. Feminist writers have been eloquent during the past twenty years in their call for a rejection of traditional categories "that are derived from male priorities and that are dissolving in the light of women's needs and experiences."[33] While they are not agreed on a blueprint for the good society, they are persuasive in their insistence that the new world of Canadian politics must take women into account in a fundamental restructuring of priorities and values.

NOTES

1. The Canadian Panel on Violence Against Women, *Changing the Landscape: Ending Violence, Achieving Equality* (Ottawa: Supply and Services, 1993), pp. B2–B4.

2. Ibid., B4.

3. *The Globe and Mail*, "Surge in female MPs raises activists' hopes" (October 28, 1993), p. A11.

4. Interview with member of the Ad Hoc Committee on the Constitution, March 10, 1983.

5. For a good review of the origins and operation of LEAF, see Sherene Razack, *Canadian Feminism and the Law* (Toronto: Second Story Press, 1991).

6. Beverley Baines, "Law, Gender, Equality" in Sandra Burt, Lorraine Code, and Lindsay Dorney, eds., *Changing Patterns*, 2nd ed. (Toronto: McClelland and Stewart, 1993), p. 269, with quotations from Gwen Brodsky and Shelagh Day, *Canadian Charter Equality Rights For Women: One Step Forward or Two Steps Back?* (Ottawa: Canadian Advisory Council on the Status of Women, 1989), p. 148.

7. Baines, "Law, Gender, Equality," p. 272.

8. *Operation Dismantle Inc. v. The Queen*, [1985] 1 S.C.R. 49–51, as quoted in A. Wayne Mackay, "Fairness after the Charter: A Rose by Any Other Name?" *Queen's Law Journal* 10 (1985): 301.

9. *R. v. Morgentaler,* [1988] 1 S.C.R. 172.

10. *R. v. Morgentaler,* Reasons for Judgment by the Rt. Hon. Brian Dickson, 16.

11. W.A. Bogart, *Courts and Country: The Limits of Litigation and the Social and Political Life of Canada* (Toronto: Oxford University Press, 1994). In chapter 5 Bogart examines the relations between women and the courts.

12. Mackay, *Queen's Law Journal,* 296.

13. For an analysis of the early work of the Women's Bureau, see Sandra Burt, "Organized Women's Groups," in William D. Coleman and Grace Skogstad, eds., *Policy Communities and Public Policy in Canada* (Toronto: Copp Clark Pitman, 1990), pp. 191–211.

14. For a full discussion of the implications of the public/private gender split, see Jean Bethke Elshtain, *Public Man, Private Woman* (Oxford: Martin Robertson, 1981).

15. Canada, Status of Women, *Towards Equality for Women* (Ottawa: Supply and Services, 1983).

16. This observation is based on interviews I conducted with representatives of Status of Women Canada between 1982 and 1986.

17. Canada, Department of Multiculturalism and Citizenship, *Convention on the Elimination of All Forms of Discrimination Against Women, Third Report* (August 1992), p. 31.

18. Patricia McDermott, "Pay Equity in Canada: Assessing the Commitment to Reducing the Wage Gap," in Judy Fudge and Patricia McDermott, eds., *Just Wages: A Feminist Assessment of Pay Equity* (Toronto: University of Toronto Press, 1991), p. 23.

19. Sue Findlay, "Making Sense of Pay Equity: Issues for a Feminist Political Practice," in Fudge and McDermott, "Pay Equity in Canada," p. 104.

20. McDermott, "Pay Equity in Canada," p. 28.

21. Ontario, Women's Directorate, *The North American Free Trade Agreement: Implications for Women* (Toronto, 1993), p. 7.

22. Ibid., p. 2.

23. Canada, Department of Labour, Women's Bureau, *Adapting to a Changing Work Force,* prepared by Judith L. MacBride-King (Ottawa: Supply and Services, 1992), p. 3.

24. Canada, Department of Labour, Women's Bureau, *Women in the Labour Force* (Ottawa: Supply and Services, 1990–91), pp. 3–7.

25. National Action Committee on the Status of Women, *Our Lives: Excerpts from the Review of the Situation of Women in Canada, 1993* (Toronto, 1993).

26. Roxana Ng, "Racism, Sexism and Immigrant Women," in Sandra Burt, Lorraine Code, and Lindsay Dorney, eds., *Changing Patterns: Women in Canada,* 2nd ed. (Toronto: McClelland and Stewart, 1993), p. 289.

27. Barbara McDougall, as quoted in Janine Brodie, Shelley A.M. Gavigan, and Jane Jenson, *The Politics of Abortion* (Toronto: Oxford University Press, 1992), p. 76.

28. Alison Prentice et al., *Canadian Women: A History* (Toronto: Harcourt Brace Jovanovich, 1988), pp. 281–82.

29. Linda Trimble, "A Few Good Women: Female Legislators in Alberta 1972–1991," in Randi Warne and Cathy Cavanaugh, eds., *Standing on New Ground: Women in Alberta* (Edmonton: University of Alberta Press, forthcoming), p. 41.

30. "Attacks on women widespread, study finds," *The Globe and Mail* (November 19, 1993), p. A4.

31. Linda MacLeod, *Battered But Not Beaten ... Preventing Wife Battering in Canada,* study prepared for the Canadian Advisory Council on the Status of Women (Ottawa, June 1987), p. 119.

32. Valerie Bryson, *Feminist Political Theory: An Introduction* (London: Macmillan, 1992), 255–56.

33. Ibid., p. 267.

FURTHER READINGS

Bryson, Valerie. *Feminist Political Theory: An Introduction.* London: Macmillan, 1992.

Burt, Sandra, Lorraine Code, and Lindsay Dorney, eds. *Changing Patterns: Women in Canada.* 2nd ed. Toronto: McClelland and Stewart, 1993.

The Canadian Panel on Violence Against Women. *Changing the Landscape: Ending Violence, Achieving Equality.* Ottawa: Supply and Services, 1993.

Fudge, Judy, and Patricia McDermott. *Just Wages: A Feminist Assessment of Pay Equity.* Toronto: University of Toronto Press, 1991.

Pateman, Carole, and Elizabeth Gross, eds. *Feminist Challenges: Social and Political Theory.* Sydney: Allen and Unwin, 1986.

10 "DEEP DIVERSITY": RACE AND ETHNICITY IN CANADIAN POLITICS

Daiva Stasiulis*

[On June 23, 1985,] 110 miles off the southwest coast of Ireland, 329 passengers and crew of Air India Flight 182 were blasted from the skies by a bomb presumably planted in Vancouver. ... Upon receiving news of the crash, the Prime Minister of Canada telephoned the Prime Minister of India offering Canada's condolences for India's loss, although more than ninety percent of the victims were Canadian citizens.[1]

The above response demonstrates how a public perception of an event as foreign or non-Canadian can be shaped by the nondominant ethnicity and race of its central figures—in this case, Canadians with origins in India. In his rush to demonstrate concern, the prime minister failed to recognize that the victims were mostly Canadian citizens, and thereby negated the right of their families to have their loved ones mourned by their nation. Mocking our claims to a multicultural society, Canada's initial response to the Air India disaster is a prime instance of *nonrecognition* of the "equal dignity of all citizens," or the "politics of universalism" to which liberal democracies are said to be committed.[2]

In January 1994, Gurbax Malhi, a Sikh-Canadian Liberal MP, became the first person to wear a turban in the House of Commons. According to section 17 of the Commons Standing Orders, an MP must be "uncovered" when he or she rises to speak in the chamber. Aware of the widespread

* The author wishes to thank Radha Jhappan and Yasmeen Abu-Laban for their valuable comments and suggestions.

controversy regarding the wearing of turbans by Sikh members of the RCMP and in Royal Canadian Legion halls, Malhi sought the opinion of the government House leader. The subsequent ruling by the Clerk of the Commons was that while MPs were prohibited from wearing hats while speaking in the House, the turban was not a hat.[3] Through recognition of the legitimacy of a turban in one of the most august chambers in Canada's democratic system, Canadian parliamentary politics reflected a notion of the "politics of difference" with which most multiethnic societies are now grappling. As Charles Taylor argues, within culturally diverse democracies the "politics of equal recognition" is constructed out of two seemingly contradictory principles—(1) *universalism*, which often requires being "blind" to ethnic, racial, and other differences among citizens; and (2) *difference*, which recognizes and indeed values distinct ethnic and other identities.[4]

There are, however, many forms of ethnocultural and racial "difference" in Canada. Canadian political scientists have generally been allergic to analyses of ethnic and racial difference, with the notable exception of the French–English cleavage. They have preferred to view "real" politics as shaped by regional, class, or federal–provincial relations.[5] The Canadian political-science literature has consequently ignored a number of formative and dynamic features of Canadian government and politics. The absence of any significant body of knowledge or debates in the discipline of political science on the management and representation of racial and ethnocultural diversity is particularly striking in light of the changing and increasingly heterogeneous ethnic and racial character of Canada's population.

Beginning in the 1970s and accelerating in the 1990s, Canadian immigration and demographic trends have brought about an absolute decline in Canadians of European origin and an increase in the population of people with origins in the Caribbean, Central and South America, Africa, the Middle East, and, especially, Asia. Whereas 30 years ago, more than 80 percent of immigrants came from Europe or were of European origins, currently 70 percent come from Asia, Africa, and Latin America, with 43 percent coming from Asia alone.[6] Approximately 90 percent of these immigrants have settled in the country's eight largest metropolitan areas.[7] Whereas residents of British heritage made up the majority of Vancouver's population as recently as 1961, in the 1991 census barely 24 percent acknowledged British origins. In contrast, nearly 30 percent of Vancouverites in 1991 were of Asian origin, with fully 22 percent of Chinese origin.[8] Similarly, social demographers predict that as a result of the large influx of immigrants, Toronto's population by the turn of the century will be one-third black and Asian.[9]

The growing diversity of urban Canada raises in a dramatic fashion a number of questions about cultural and racial pluralism that a monochromatic Canadian political science, with its narrow conception of "relevant ethnicity" (i.e., French–English divisions), has been ill-prepared to address. How have race and ethnicity been represented in Canadian state institutions and policies, and in the visions and practices of those at the helm of Canadian development? What success have ethnocultural groups had in enlisting the state in support of particular projects? How accessible have Canadian political institutions been to ethnic and racial minority groups and their concerns? For their part, what role have ethnic minorities played in Canadian politics? To what extent should Canadian public institutions accommodate ethnocultural diversity?

Many social scientists, Marxist and otherwise, are uneasy about referring to "race" when the concept has no scientific or biological validity. "'Races' are social constructs, not objectively identifiable physical realities, for there is much genetic variation within so-called races that are superficially similar in physical appearance."[10] The fact that the very belief in the objective existence of "race" spawned the eugenics policies of the Nazis and the fear that it could legitimate new racist policies have led to the convention of placing the term in quotation marks. Similarly, public policy-makers in Canada have invented the euphemism "visible minorities" to refer to peoples who are "non-Caucasian in race or non-white in colour," thus escaping accusations that public authorities are perpetuating racism by making reference to the discredited notion of race.[11]

Like race, the notions of "ethnicity" and "ethnic" or "ethnocultural group" are contested and elusive concepts among social scientists and in society at large. According to the original meaning of the term "ethnicity," which derives from the Greek *ethnos* (people or nation), all 28.3 million Canadians can be said to be "ethnic." In its popular contemporary and social scientific usage, however, ethnicity is ascribed only to nondominant immigrants and their descendants—Canadians who are perceived to deviate from an assumed norm (white, English- or French-speaking, northern or western European). Thus, British and French Canadians are misleadingly assumed not to be "ethnic," whereas Canadians born or with origins in Italy, China, Jamaica, and the Ukraine are considered as such.

Some anthropologists and sociologists have defined ethnicity as a "primordial" phenomenon, as something given or ascribed at birth and associated with a number of "givens" such as kinship ties, "being born into a particular religious community, speaking a particular language ... and following particular social practices."[12] Ethnic groups are shaped historically through the emergence of a sense of common origin and feelings of loyalty toward members of the ethnic collectivity. Individuals' identification with their ethnic group or community is facilitated by a number of common features such as ancestry, distinct language, religious beliefs, and cultural and political traditions. However, some authors argue that the cultural resources of ethnic groups are less significant than the external forces that construct and activate ethnic sentiments and solidarity, as well as produce particular "ethnic traits."[13]

State institutions play a central role in drawing the external boundaries of ethnic groups through population censuses that ask (or fail to ask) questions about ethnic origins, through state funding of ethnic community organizations, and through other forms of official sanction (or suppression) of ethnic organizations.[14] When state authorities wish to downplay the political importance of ethnic or racial divisions, official census-taking may simply omit questions about ethnicity or race. The politics of constructing the ethnic categories for the census question on ethnic origin also involves lobbying on the part of particular groups in order to bolster official recognition of their distinctness, numerical weight, and potential political significance.[15]

A definitional issue that has sparked heated debate is whether there is a clear distinction to be made between the concepts of "race" and "ethnicity."[16] The view that there is a significant difference between what in Canada have been referred to as "visible minorities" and "invisible (or white) minorities" is based on the assumption that discrimination and exclusion are exclusively linked to "nonwhite" skin colour.[17] Unlike the liabilities of "invisible minority" immigrants (e.g., lack of fluency in official languages), which can disappear over time, the physical differences of visible minorities from the white majority continue to define them as "other" and inferior across many generations. This distinction is built into recent public policies meant to ameliorate inequalities. Employment-equity policies, for example, have existed for visible but not invisible minorities in the federal government since 1986,[18] and since December 1993, when Bill 79 was enacted, in the Ontario government. As elaborated below, the view that visible minorities face greater discrimination than white ethnic minorities in Canadian politics wins some support insofar as the non-Anglo, non-French groups best represented in political parties, Parliament and cabinet are white, northern, and eastern European groups that migrated early to Canada.[19]

One need not deny the unique histories of racism experienced by Canadian blacks, Asians, and other visible minorities in order to argue that racism can also be directed against groups that share the same (white) skin colour as the dominant racial/ethnic group. Different racisms have developed as waves of European and non-European migration have brought to Canada people who do not conform to Anglo-Saxon culture and physical appearance. Language, religion, and other cultural markers have made diverse groups targets of racist scorn, intolerance, and unequal treatment—groups including the Catholic Irish in the 19th century, the European Jews who unsuccessfully sought refuge in Canada from the Holocaust in the 1930s, and southern Italians who migrated to postwar Toronto. In the latter case, for example, a 1941 Anglican Church report opposed the immigration to Canada of southern Italians on the grounds that they were "'amenable to the fallacies of dictatorship,' 'less versed' in democratic traditions and better suited for the hot climate of 'fragile' political structures of Latin American nations."[20]

Moreover, for racial minority groups, it is not skin colour per se that produces racism, but rather their structural location in concrete as well as historically specific social and economic conditions, as well as the discourses that aid in the processes of denigration and exploitation of non-white peoples. For Jamaican-Canadians and for recent Somali refugees in Canada, it is not only their black skin that has evoked racism. What is more important is the residue of a historical vision of Canada as a white country, as well as the contemporary portrayal of these groups by the media and politicians as criminals and welfare defrauders.

Whether it is anti-aboriginal, anti-black, anti-Italian, or anti-French, each racism can be viewed as having a specific history that arises from a particular set of historical, material, and cultural circumstances, and that is reproduced through particular systemic, institutional, and ideological mechanisms. But specific racisms are also found in particular relationships to each other. Thus, while French Canadians and Aboriginal peoples in Quebec can both be said to have had histories of colonization and economic marginalization at the hands of the British and English Canadians, the particular nature of anti-French and anti-aboriginal racism situates these groups differently within Canadian society. As part of the white settler groups that viewed aboriginal peoples as "uncivilized" and without legitimate claim to territory or self-government, French Quebeckers have been placed in a dominant position vis-à-vis Aboriginal peoples. Thus, Daniel Salée observes, "by an ironic twist, Quebecers, who have ... long been cast in the role of oppressed but courageous victims of historical circumstances, appeared in the wake of the Oka crisis as the intolerant and unsympathetic oppressors, [a depiction that dealt] a shattering blow to the image Quebecers have of themselves."[21] This illustration conveys a sense of the importance of understanding the different and fluid positions of different racisms with respect to one another, in place of the more commonplace racial ranking.[22] It accounts for how a particular political project such as nationalism, which is fuelled by a sense of injustice within an ethnocultural collectivity, can result in the exclusion or subordination of other oppressed or marginalized groups.

Feminists have drawn attention to how all forms of social relations, whether based on global inequities, class, race, or ethnicity, are also *gendered*. This gendered aspect of racism was a critical dimension of the historical project to build a "white Canada" from the mid-19th century to the 1960s, a project that relied on immigration as well as the marginalization of Aboriginal peoples. Although political elites wished to limit the entry of Asians and blacks through restrictive immigration laws, business actively recruited cheap migrant labour from Asia. Legislation was more effective, however, in preventing male or female migrants from bringing in and establishing their families in Canada. Moreover, the disempowerment of many immigrant women who currently enter the country as part of the "family class" category of immigrants is accomplished through assigning female immigrants inferior entry status as dependents of husbands and fathers. In conjunction with the rules governing entitlement to other state policies such as government-assistance schemes and official-language/job training, a dependent immigration status has allocated many immigrant women to vulnerable, low-paid, and dead-end positions in the service sector, or in competitive or declining industries such as the garment trades. Differences among racial/ethnic groups in terms of their political concerns and actions have been shaped by such historical patterns of state-led discrimination in immigration as well as by other policies that drew upon an intersection of racial/ethnic, gender, and class relations.

RACIAL AND ETHNIC HIERARCHIES IN STATE POLICIES

Canada's position within the British Empire meant that two sets of conflicting principles were played out in the formation of policies such as immigration, foreign affairs, and governance of Aboriginal peoples. On the one hand, the imperial philosophy of a nonracial empire, influenced by 19th-century liberal humanitarianism, proclaimed that all subjects were equal before the law, regardless of race, creed, or colour. On the other hand, a sense of the racial superiority of all things Anglo-Saxon, including the special capacity for political self-governance through a constitutional system, led to the impulse among British settlers to build a country that was as white and as British as possible.[23] These two contradictory principles were played out in the policy debates among Canadian politicians over the immigration and citizenship rights of Asian and black immigrants, who were perceived as being inherently incapable of assimilation to British-Canadian culture without injury to British civilization.

The idea that only certain "kindred races" can successfully intermingle was rooted in the pseudo-scientific race theories popular in Europe during the 19th century. In 1885, this view was elaborated in a speech by Canada's first prime minister, Sir John A. Macdonald, as he introduced legislation to deny the federal franchise to persons of Chinese descent:

> [A]ll natural history, all ethnology, shows that while the crosses of the Aryan races are successful—while the mixture of all those races which are known or believed to spring from common origins is more or less successful—they will amalgamate. If you look around the world you will see that the Aryan races will not wholesomely amalgamate with the

Africans or the Asiatics. It is not desired that they should come; that we should have a mongrel race; that the Aryan character of the future of British America should be destroyed by a cross or crosses of that kind. ... Let us encourage all the races which are cognate races, which cross and amalgamate naturally, and we shall see that such amalgamation will produce, as the result, a race equal if not superior to the two races which mingle. But the cross of [Aryan and non-Aryan] races, like the cross of the dog and the fox, is not successful; it cannot be, and never will be. ... We are in the course of progress; this country is going on and developing, and we will have plenty of labor of our own kindred races, without introducing this element of a mongrel race to disturb the labor market, and certainly we ought not to allow them to share the Government of the country.[24]

While Macdonald employed eugenics ("race betterment") arguments and the fear of miscegnation ("race-mixing") to justify the exclusion of Asians from the rights of universal British citizenship, it is significant that some other politicians were unconvinced by his arguments. For instance, L.H. Davies, a former premier of Prince Edward Island, argued for a consistent, unrestricted approach.

If a Chinaman becomes a British subject it is not right that a brand should be placed on his forehead, so that other men may avoid him. As a member of this House, and as a Radical, I enter my protest against this reactionary proposal. It is especially unfair ... that the Chinaman, who has become a British subject, who is an honest and hardworking man, and has made up his mind to work in this country, should be excluded from taking part in the politics of the country. ... I am in favor of any one who has become a British subject and has the necessary qualifications having the right to exercise the franchise.[25]

The failure of nonwhite British subjects to gain open access to Canada by employing the rhetoric of universal-empire citizenship suggested that the drive to maintain the racial purity of Canada was more decisive than a British sense of "fair play." Thus, one of the historical discourses that designated immigrants from outside northern Europe as unsuitable settlers in Canada was their assumed inability to adapt to British civilization and democratic political traditions. In 1928, Prime Minister R.B. Bennett expressed his anxiety over the threat of non-British immigrants to British civilization.

[W]e are endeavouring to maintain our civilization at that high standard which has made the British civilization the test by which all other civilized nations in modern times are measured. ... We must still

*maintain that measure of British civilization which will enable us to
assimilate these people [immigrants] to British institutions, rather than
assimilate our civilization to theirs.*[26]

Two decades later, Prime Minister Mackenzie King affirmed before
Parliament the desire by Canada's political elites to use immigration policy
to maintain Canada as a white, European country:

*There will, I am sure, be general agreement with the view that the
people of Canada do not wish, as a result of mass immigration, to
make a fundamental alteration on the character of our population.
Large-scale immigration from the Orient would change the fundamental composition of the Canadian population.*[27]

Racist and restrictive immigration policy from the 1880s until the
1960s conformed to the intent of Canadian prime ministers and generations of immigration ministers and top immigration officials to develop
Canada as a "white settler colony." The unease felt by at least some politicians about formulating explicitly racist policies, however, meant that in
order to preserve appearances, immigration policies denied entry through
bizarre orders-in-council and administrative regulations. These included
the imposition of head taxes to deter Chinese immigrants, a "direct passage" regulation to prevent South Asian immigration, and reference to the
challenges posed by Canada's "temperate" climate to exclude Caribbean
blacks and southern Italians.

Denial of the franchise through provincial and federal legislation reinforced the political marginality and subordination of Asians, and made it
harder for them to build links to party and electoral systems. The Canada
Elections Act of 1920 accepted provincial racial restrictions (except for
war veterans) in determining who was qualified to vote in federal elections. Since legislation had been passed in several provinces to disenfran-
chise the Chinese (as early as 1872 in British Columbia, and 1908 in
Saskatchewan), they were barred from voting in federal elections until
1947.

Similar legal bases for discrimination existed for (East) Indians and
Japanese-Canadians, regardless of whether they were Canadian- or foreign-
born. In British Columbia, such laws remained until the late 1940s. Exclusion from the provincial voters' list barred Asian-Canadians from election
to the provincial legislature, from nomination for municipal office, and
from school-trustee positions and jury service.[28] In British Columbia,
where the majority of Asians resided, politicians tried to outdo one another in promising to limit the economic and political involvement of
Asians in Canada. Other European groups, labelled "enemy aliens" during
the two world wars, also faced disenfranchisement and isolation from
party, electoral, and parliamentary politics, except as objects of control.

The segregated school systems, employment, and housing and public facilities that existed for blacks in Canada (in the Maritimes and Ontario until the 1960s) undoubtedly gave rise to this group's alienation and mistrust of mainstream, white-dominated political institutions.[29] Aboriginal peoples have experenced the most profound sense of isolation from the Canadian polity, an isolation stemming from external paternalistic control (via the Indian Act and the Department of Indian Affairs), the reserve system, and ongoing destruction of their traditional economies and cultures.

Not surprisingly, the political marginalization of non-British, non-French groups came to be reflected in their extreme underrepresentation in mainstream political institutions. For example, in the House of Commons between 1867 and 1964, only 97 MPs were from ethnic minorities, with 40 of these being of German origin. Only two visible minorities (one Chinese and one Lebanese) made it to the House of Commons during this period.[30] As early as the turn of the century, parties would court the "ethnic vote," and, at times, ethnic minorities were even nominated as candidates. However, those few elected MPs from non-British, non-French origins typically represented "ethnic constituencies" such as the predominantly Ukrainian ridings of Vegreville in Alberta or the heavily Jewish ridings in cities like Montreal, Toronto, and Winnipeg.[31] Even when ethnic minorities attained office in the House of Commons, they had limited impact in shaping policies in a manner favourable to the ethnic groups they represented. Lacking a critical mass in either their parties or the House of Commons, minority politicians had limited power to shape government policy in directions favourable to the interests of their communities.

CONTEMPORARY POLITICAL REPRESENTATION AND PARTICIPATION OF ETHNIC AND RACIAL MINORITIES

While there have been some improvements, the historical pattern of underrepresentation of ethnocultural and especially visible minorities in political parties and the House of Commons persists to the present day.[32] The representation of ethnic minorities in the House of Commons increased "from 9.4 percent in 1965 to 16.3 percent in 1988. The increase was smaller for visible minorities, however, varying from 0.8 percent in 1968 to 2.0 percent [or only 6 members out of 295] in 1988."[33]

The severity of underrepresentation is greater for visible minorities than for ethnic minorities (which include visible minorities). Thus, while 16.3 percent of MPs were non-British, non-French Canadians in 1988, these groups accounted for 23.6 percent of the general population; this meant that ethnic minorities achieved 70 percent of the mark of proportional representation. In contrast, visible minorities constituted 6.3 percent of the total Canadian population but held only 2 percent of the seats in the House of Commons. Thus, visible minorities had achieved only 32 percent of the mark of proportional representation.[34]

Women from ethnic and visible minorities are particularly unlikely to become members of Parliament. Between 1965 and 1988, only 5 percent (or 6 of 120) of MPs of minority ethnic origin were women. In 1988, only 2 percent (or 1 of 48) of minority ethnic MPs were female.[35] Although women of all ethnic origins were underrepresented in the House of Commons (constituting 13.5 percent of MPs but 52 percent of the population), women from ethnic minorities, and especially racial minorities, face particular obstacles to participation in party and parliamentary politics.

In the October 1993 federal election, according to the media, "historic breakthroughs" were made by women, visible minorities, and aboriginal candidates, all of whom increased their representation in the House of Commons. Still, only 9 of 295 or 3 percent of the seats were won by visible-minority candidates; an additional three MPs are aboriginal. Only two of the visible-minority and one of the aboriginal MPs are women. Viewed in the context of all 54 women elected to Parliament, less than 4 percent of female MPs are from visible minorities. The Canadian Ethnocultural Council also reported that the results of the 1993 election produced a record number of ethnic-minority MPs, most of them Liberals.[36]

The increased ethnic/racial diversity and presence of women in the House of Commons was not reflected in the first Liberal cabinet of newly elected prime minister Jean Chrétien. Chosen primarily on principles of cronyism and experience, the 1993 cabinet consisted mostly of white men. Indeed, only Immigration Minister Sergio Marchi and House Leader/ Solicitor General Herb Gray, just two out of 23 members of the cabinet, are of non-British, non-French descent. Clearly, it was not a Liberal priority to change the "very white," male face of the Canadian cabinet. The prime minister's neglect of racial/ethnic minority representation in the cabinet is consistent with a trend, evident under the previous Progressive Conservative government, to downplay the cultural diversity of the Canadian population.

Why do ethnocultural and visible minorities continue to be underrepresented in key political institutions such as the cabinet and federal Parliament? One explanation focuses on the immigrant status of ethnic minorities and the presupposition that immigrants are less likely to have knowledge about or participate in the political process. They are less likely than nonimmigrants to have Canadian citizenship, which is a basic criterion for exercising the right to vote and to run for political office. They are also more likely to face barriers to political participation (e.g., language difficulties). Depending on the recency of their arrival and their social class, they may be more preoccupied with economic and social survival than with political issues.

There is some evidence to support the view that immigrant status rather than minority ethnic origin affects the levels of political activism and subsequent political representation. In a 1983 Toronto-based survey, Jerome Black found in comparing the patterns of participation of four categories of minority groups—South, North, and East Europeans, and British West Indians—to those of the British majority group, that immigrant status rather than ethnicity per se accounted for lower levels of political activity.[37] In 1988, the proportion of House of Commons members with minority ethnic origins was slightly higher than the proportion of immigrant members—16.3 and 15.4 percent, respectively.[38] Furthermore, while the Liberal Party is perceived by ethnic minorities to be the party that is most open to ethnic pluralism, the Conservatives had the largest number of members of non-British, non-French origins elected between 1965 and 1988. Pelletier attributes this to the fact that most of the Conservative Party's ethnic-minority MPs are from Northern and Eastern Europe. Since immigration from these countries took place much earlier than did immigration from the countries of those ethnic minorities attracted to the Liberals and the New Democrats, these members have more completely integrated into Canadian society.[39]

However, the significance of not having citizenship status should not be overstated in attempting to explain the small numbers of ethnic and especially racial minorities in the House of Commons. First, groups such as the Chinese, African-Canadians, Japanese, and South Asians have had a presence in Canada since the 19th century and earlier. Second, among the visible-minority groups with origins in Asia, Africa, and Latin America, whose major waves of immigration date from the beginnings of the 1970s, nearly one-third were born in Canada and three-quarters are Canadian citizens.[40]

Moreover, an explanation that focuses on the immigrant status of ethnic and visible minorities deflects attention from the numerous cultural, organizational, and structural barriers to participation that exist within the workings of Canada's parties and society at large.[41] The culture of political parties may be unfamiliar or alienating to new immigrants and to people from non-British traditions. Howard McCurdy, an African-Canadian and former MP for Windsor–St. Clair, has commented on how the informal culture of Canadian political parties (e.g., their social activities, type of music played at parties, etc.) has made people from diverse cultures feel unwelcome and alienated. Another barrier lies in the conventional means of recruiting volunteers and activists, which are heavily reliant on personal networks within which trust and loyalty are built. It is ironic that much of the criticism of recent ethnic activism in regard to the recruitment of candidates for the Liberal Party has centred on the purported abuse of ethnic community networks. Networks of participants within the main parties have tended to follow traditional patterns of recruitment from white and, depending on the region, also British and French communities. Women from ethnic and racial minorities must also contend with the disadvantages of being excluded from the "old boys' network."

Structural hurdles to minority inroads within the party system include the "incumbency" factor, an unwritten rule that holds that challenges without due cause to the renomination of incumbent members of Parliament are unacceptable. This informal rule has proven to be a barrier to the placement of minority candidates within winnable or "safe" seats. Thus, the majority of ethnic-minority candidates (71 percent) and an overwhelming number of visible-minority candidates (90 percent) who ran in the 1988 federal election did so in ridings where the parties had not won in 1984.[42]

Another barrier faced by minorities is the reluctance among those who now have power to share it with those who are defined as outsiders by virtue of their ethnicity or race. Several party officials and activists have described the fear among the political establishment that ethnic and visible minorities are "taking over" the riding associations.[43] The perception of both minorities who have made it into the system (e.g., as MPs) and those seeking entry into the political establishment is that the political gatekeepers hold negative, stereotyped views of ethnic and visible minorities. Albina Guarnieri, Liberal MP for Mississauga East since 1988, and the first Italian-Canadian woman to become a member of Parliament, stated that party officials underestimated the political maturity of ethnic communities:

> *I think that they are baffled about ethnics. They lack some understanding that they have to include us. They lack sensitivity. What the [Liberal] party finds is that the old lines don't work anymore. The ethnic communities won't be hoodwinked any longer. I find that there is an arrogance among the traditional members.*[44]

The Canadian mass media have also played a key role in creating and perpetuating negative stereotypes about the political participation of ethnic and visible minorities. They have provided lurid coverage of events such as nomination meetings with "ethnic candidates," and the practice of recruiting new Liberals from ethnic communities. In interviews conducted with minority candidates and MPs in 1990, many expressed concern with the biased and/or marginal coverage of their campaigns, in contrast with the coverage accorded candidates of British or French origin. The media delegitimated minority candidates by straitjacketing them with the designation "ethnic candidate." In part this was done by reporters who assumed that these candidates had competency only to address "ethnic issues" (e.g., multiculturalism, immigration, and employment equity), thereby discounting their considerable expertise in other policy areas.

For ethnic/racial minorities, and for Asian and African-Canadians in particular, a marginal political status has been linked to severe curtailment of the growth of these communities through restrictive immigration policies. While restrictions on immigration and the denial of the franchise and other basic citizenship rights affected some racial and ethnic minority groups more harshly and for longer periods of time than others, one feature of the Canadian party system that has affected all minority groups has been the pre-eminence given to the French–English question by all three major parties.

The hegemonic vision of Canadian society reflected within party discourse has, at best, reflected biculturalism and, at worst, Anglo-conformity.[45] This has meant that the collective identities, aspirations, and symbols of the British and (to a lesser though significant degree) the French have been legitimized within party and state discourse, agendas, and policies. In contrast, those of the non-British, non-French groups have been suppressed. Both the failed Meech Lake Accord and the defeated Charlottetown Accord (which sought protection for Quebec's "special status") gave credence to the view that French–English relations formed Canada's most significant ethnocultural cleavage.

Since the 1970s, multiculturalism has been added to the kaleide-scope of ethnic policies endorsed by the parties as a means of accommodating the symbolic aspirations of non-British, non-French communities. Indeed, in the 1980s there were concrete moves to provide multiculturalism with a constitutional and statutory base. The concept of multiculturalism became entrenched in section 27 of the 1982 Canadian Charter of Rights and Freedoms. The Canadian Multiculturalism Act of 1988 provided for the first time a legislative basis for the existing multiculturalism policy and programs. Nevertheless, the ancillary position of multicultural rights within the Charter and the low status of the federal multiculturalism bureaucracy show that multiculturalism has never seriously challenged the pre-eminent position of a national politics centred on the French–English cleavage.

In sum, the underrepresentation of ethnic and visible minorities within the major parties can be explained in terms of a variety of structural, cultural, and organizational obstacles. For recent immigrants lacking official-language skills, linguistic barriers intersect with lack of familiarity with the Canadian political culture and system. Racial minorities confront discrimination practised at the highest levels of party structures and within the mass media. For women of colour and ethnic-minority women, the barriers are gendered as well as based on race, ethnicity, and (often) class. And for all marginalized groups, there is a legacy of exclusion that is reinforced by the hegemonic bicultural discourse of party politics, by patterns of recruitment through networks, and by party traditions such as the incumbency factor within the electoral process.

The alienation from political parties and electoral and parliamentary politics has not meant that ethnic minorities have withdrawn from all types of political involvement, however. On the contrary, it has meant that the political activism of minorities has been channeled into different forums that are perceived to provide greater means for self-empowerment and the pursuit of substantive gains.

ALTERNATIVE MINORITY POLITICS

One common form of politics pursued in ethnic communities is "homeland" politics, which concerns itself with providing support for political conflicts waged in the originating countries of immigrants and their descendants. Many immigrant and ethnic collectivities conceive of themselves as diasporas (i.e., as communities uprooted by physical compulsion or economic coercion) and retain the idea of return to the homeland. This is precisely the type of politics that is assumed by some critics to breed "ethnocentric hatreds," "tribalization," and a "resurgence of racism." Homeland politics, it is said, is an outgrowth of immigration, multiculturalism, and/or citizenship policies that encourage "divided loyalties."[46] Fuelled by the stereotypes of "dangerous foreigners" held by Anglo-Celtic and French elites, the political activism of ethnic minorities in pursuit of foreign causes and "foreign ideologies" was historically met with the deportation of leaders, for example, to stem the "alien Bolshevik menace" between 1910 and the 1930s. It has also attracted excessive surveillance by security agencies such as the RCMP and the Canadian Security Intelligence Service (CSIS). This was evidenced in the responses to the Black Power movement in Canada during the 1970s and by the harassment of Arab-Canadians during the 1991 Gulf War.

There is little question that homeland politics plays a major role in the political life of many ethnic communities, even those such as the East European communities (Ukrainian, Polish, Lithuanian, etc.) where there are third and fourth generations born in Canada. This form of politics in ethnic communities has been either polarized along left-to-right divisions that correspond to different waves of migration or else factionalized according to support or opposition to homeland regimes.

In some instances, the absorption of leadership and other resources of ethnic communities in politics abroad has deflected energies away from mobilization around political issues in Canada. Thus, the waning of the spirited fight of Sikh-Canadian associations against racism in Canada in the 1970s coincided with the mobilization of some Sikh organizations around the goal of establishing a separate Sikh state in India ("Khalistan"). However, there is little evidence that an ethnic community highly politicized on homeland issues cannot simultaneously participate in Canadian politics. As Jean Burnet and Howard Palmer observe, in the 1950s Ukrainian-Canadians, many of whom were keenly interested in the liberation of the Ukraine from the Soviet Union, took great pride in the growing number of Ukrainian-Canadian elected officials, an increase that signalled their growing acceptance in Canadian society.[47]

Moreover, it should be borne in mind that the homeland politics taken up by diasporan communities often address questions regarding the foreign policies of the Canadian government on whether to support a boycott of South Africa, a peacekeeping force or air strikes in Bosnia, or aid for the Palestinians in the Middle East, and so forth. The political activism of ethnic minorities in homeland causes often takes the form of lobbying Canadian politicians and senior bureaucrats in federal departments such as External Affairs.

The extent to which the Canadian government takes up particular causes and positions put forward by ethnic groups is largely dependent on Canada's position within the international political economy (including its subordination to its southern neighbour) and its pre-established diplomatic relations with other countries. Thus, despite intense lobbying by East European groups, the Liberal government of Louis St. Laurent in the 1950s refused to support the liberation of their homelands. An apparently decisive factor in this refusal was the need to avoid the appearance of interference in the internal affairs of the Soviet Union.[48] This concern faded with the crumbling of the Soviet Union in the early 1990s, when prominent Conservatives such as International Trade Minister Michael Wilson publicly supported the independence of the Baltic states.

While the influence of minority ethnic groups on Canadian foreign policy has generally been limited, the increasing cultural and racial diversity of Canadian society has had a decisive impact in reshaping the politics of major Canadian social movements. In the 1920s and 1930s, the presence of "Red" Ukrainian, Finnish, Jewish, and other European workers in a variety of resource and manufacturing industries radicalized labour unions and spawned networks of grass-roots foreign-language cells in the Communist and Socialist parties. Since the 1970s, visible-minority workers have formed an increasing proportion of trade-union members in unions within sectors such as steel, auto, and the garment trades. They have challenged the traditional white (and male) leadership to take up issues such as affirmative action and racism within unions, power-sharing with an ascendant minority leadership, and the construction of organizational models more appropriate to the conditions of minority workers.

Faced with discrimination in major institutions such as the labour market, policing, and education, racial- and ethnic-minority communities have engaged in prolonged and varied strategies to reform racist policies and practices. The creation of pioneering human-rights legislation in Ontario is owed largely to the political work of black and Jewish activists working within the labour movement and community organizations in the 1930s and 1940s.[49] Numerous police shootings of blacks in Toronto and Montreal since the 1970s have kindled a sense of solidarity as well as vigorous protests against police racism within black communities. In the late 1970s, the sustained work by black and South Asian community organizations resulted in the Toronto Board of Education's adoption of an innovative antiracist policy that sought to "de-institutionalize" racism in Toronto's public school system.[50] In the 1980s and 1990s, foreign domestic workers from the Philippines and the Caribbean have been militant in contesting coercive Canadian immigration policies and substandard provincial employment standards.

In 1988, the Japanese-Canadian community won an unprecedented victory in the redress settlement reached with the federal government to compensate individual Canadians of Japanese ancestry for their internment, dispossession, and abrogation of rights by the federal government during World War II. The redress issue was not simply an isolated injustice perpetrated against one ethnic/racial community but rather a wider Canadian human-rights issue. The campaign received the active support of a variety of interests, including human-rights organizations, church groups, ethnocultural associations, aboriginal groups, and the three major federal parties. The compensation package included legislation (which has since been tabled) to create a Canadian Race Relations Foundation with a mandate to fight racism, and was accompanied by the repeal of the War Measures Act, which had legalized the repressive actions taken against the Japanese-Canadians during the 1940s.[51]

Perhaps the social movement that has been most profoundly shaken by racism and by racial and ethnic diversity has been the women's movement. Outside Quebec,[52] especially in provinces with large racially heterogenous populations, the questions of racism and racial diversity have transformed feminist politics. The experience of dealing with racism within the ranks of white-dominated women's organizations has been described as traumatizing and silencing by both women of colour and white women, and has led to major organizational splits in key feminist institutions such as the Toronto-based Women's Press.[53] It has also led, however, to the building of a more inclusive feminist movement that has recognized the need for numerical and substantive representation of women of colour.[54]

The appointments of Glenda Simms, a Jamaican-born black woman, as President of the Canadian Advisory Council on the Status of Women, and of Sunera Thobani, a Tanzanian-born woman of South Asian origins, as President of the National Action Committee on the Status of Women (NAC) are profoundly symbolic of the growing diversity of Canadian women. Of equal significance, the leadership of women of colour in "mainstream" feminist organizations has defined fighting racism as a feminist issue rather than simply as a human-rights issue supported by feminists. This has meant taking up issues and state policies previously thought outside the purview of women's issues, as exemplified by the recent involvement of NAC in refugee policy aimed at providing asylum for abused women. It has also meant fundamentally rethinking some of the central categories and analyses of "old" issues such as reproductive rights, the workplace, violence against women, as well as the contradictory relations among women defined by race, ethnicity, class, and sexuality. For instance, as Sunera Thobani observes, women of colour have highlighted the inadequacy of the pro-choice movement's focus on individual "choice," in that "women are pitted against women by technologies which enhance the fertility [and choices] of affluent, white women, and which severely curtail the reproductive capacities of poor women and of women of colour."[55]

CONTEMPORARY STATE POLICIES OF CULTURAL DIVERSITY AND RACIAL EQUITY

While at least segments of the women's movement have come to accept that the "fundamental character" of the Canadian population is becoming more racially and culturally diverse, many other forms of politics and state policies are resisting, downplaying, or regulating such diversity. The key federal government policies at the centre of debates over support and containment of ethnic and racial diversity have been immigration and multiculturalism. Other government provisions that address issues of racial/ethnic inequality and racism are employment equity and the Charter of Rights and Freedoms.

The politicization of ethnic and racial issues in Canadian politics and the mass media is guaranteed by the presence in the current federal Parliament of two opposition parties holding over 50 seats each. The Bloc Québécois, whose agenda is to take Quebec out of Canada, views multiculturalism policy as detracting from Québécois sovereignty. The Reform Party, on the other hand, boasts an explicitly anti-immigration, antimulticulturalism platform. Outside Parliament, the resurgence of white-supremacist organizations such as the Heritage Front is only the extreme end of a growing backlash against racial minorities. The results of recent national surveys indicate that there is increased popular purchase to the ideas of returning to a "white Canada" immigration policy and abandoning government multiculturalism policies. An October 1993 national poll revealed that 41 percent of respondents believed that current immigration policy allows "too many people of different races and cultures coming into Canada."[56] A January 1994 poll found that 45 per cent of Canadians want

Canada to take in fewer immigrants. Only 11 percent favoured an increase in immigration, the lowest number recorded since 1982.[57]

In this volatile climate, the February 1994 announcement by the new Liberal government of immigration levels replicating those of recent years was predictably met by strong condemnation. The major opponent in the House of Commons was the Reform Party, which argued that immigration should be half of the proposed 250,000 target set by the government and reproduced unsubstantiated claims about immigrant illiteracy and economic insolvency. Such claims fuel anti-immigrant and anti-Third World sentiments. They are supported by the ideological work of right-wing, pro-business think tanks such as the Fraser Institute and the C.D. Howe Institute, both of which have recently commissioned works arguing for lower levels of immigration, particularly of the "nontraditional" (i.e., nonwhite) variety.

Ironically, it will be the Liberals, previously known for their relative openness toward immigrants, that will be forced to mediate increasingly hostile debates on Canada's "absorptive capacity" in relation to new Canadians who are "culturally and racially different." Given the effects of the Green Paper on Immigration Policy (public consultations preceding the enactment of the 1978 Immigration Act encouraged the public articulation of racist sentiment), the Liberal government should be wary. The Progressive Conservatives, during their nine years in power, were able to sidestep this minefield through an immigration policy that reflected an implicit depoliticization of race questions. However, the Tories also introduced encroachments on the freedoms of new immigrants and refugee claimants in the 1993 Immigration Act (Bill C-86). Their policies deepened fiscal restraint in the administration of immigration and settlement, and shifted the costs of immigrant integration not only onto other beleaguered levels of the state but also onto the groups most vulnerable to racism and other forms of disadvantage.

While some state policies (such as immigration) have contributed to racial/ethnic disadvantage and inequities, other state policies reflect an official recognition of the central role the state must play in eradicating racism in a pluralist society. The problems of discrimination based on race, national or ethnic origin, colour, and a number of other characteristics were explicitly recognized in section 15(1) of the 1982 Charter of Rights and Freedoms. However, the utility of the Charter as a tool for fighting racism is limited. Given that it protects individuals only from the actions of governments, it does not cover the majority of discriminatory practices (e.g., by employers in the private sector). Section 15(2) allows for but does not require affirmative-action programs for disadvantaged groups. Most cases of discrimination continue to be directed to provincial and, to a lesser degree, federal human-rights commissions, where procedures for investigating complaints are notoriously slow and cumbersome, and where the penalties against discrimination are mild and ineffectual.

Alain Cairns predicts that as Canadians become more racially and ethnically diverse and as the proportion of the population with British and French origins declines, minorities will increasingly focus on constitutional politics to protect and further their interests. He suggests that the Charter of Rights and Freedoms gave ethnic minorities "constitutional identities," and identifies certain clauses in the Constitution that these minorities had fought to include and that are specifically theirs.[58] For ethnocultural minorities, Cairns is referring to section 27, which provides that "[t]his Charter shall be interpreted in a manner consistent with the preservation and enhancement of the multicultural heritage of Canadians." Clearly, section 27 is only a very general interpretive clause (unlike the clauses in the Charter that guarantee substantive rights such as freedom of speech or minority language rights), and it is difficult to see how it could be enforced. Moreover, antidiscriminatory protections (s. 15.2 of the Charter), to which racial minorities might lay claim, are subject to the provincial override clause (see Chapter 17).

One federal government policy protected by section 15.2 of the Charter is the Employment Equity Program (enacted in 1986 by the Mulroney government), whose purpose is to redress systemic discrimination against disadvantaged minorities—women, aboriginal peoples, visible minorities, and persons with disabilities. The legislation, although it requires employers under federal jurisdiction to prepare an annual employment-equity plan with goals and timetables, does not require them to submit this plan to the government. Since its inception, the program has drawn fire from visible-minority–rights advocates. Criticisms have centred on its lack of specific goals and timetables, of systematic monitoring mechanisms, and of effective sanctions linked to the nonimplementation (as opposed to mere reporting) of employment-equity measures. The assumption that "public scrutiny" will provide the mechanism for enforcing the act has been called "fanciful" by human-rights activist Shelagh Day, as it places the burden of action on the victims of discrimination.[59]

The federal multiculturalism bureaucracy has made race-relations programs an increasing component of its activities since the early 1980s. By 1990–91, 27 percent of the funding for federal multiculturalism was allocated to programs dedicated to the improvement of race relations. The major emphasis of the race-relations program has been to provide support for education and training within institutions in the areas of policing and justice, education, media and the arts, health and social services, and the workplace. In many instances, such support has been limited to one-time workshops and conferences, and thus is unlikely to bring about antiracist institutional reform.

Katharyne Mitchell argues that the antiracist program in multiculturalism was given its impetus by the increased racial tensions in Vancouver that followed the influx of wealthy Hong Kong Chinese through the "investor" stream of immigration policy. Canadian politicians and capitalists were eager to attract the several billion dollars in investment brought into Canada by the Hong Kong Chinese. However, the link between the influx of wealthy immigrants and the rapid inflation in real estate and aesthetic changes (e.g., "monster houses") in affluent Vancouver neighbourhoods gave rise to anxiety among the established European-Canadian population. The perceived threat of Hong Kong Chinese immigrants prompted the federal government to step up both its promotion of better race relations within its multiculturalism program and its propaganda on the economic benefits of multiculturalism. In this manner, Mitchell maintains, multiculturalism discourse has been politically appropriated by real-estate companies and other corporations to facilitate international investment and the spatial integration of Vancouver into the global economy in the interests of multinational capitalism.[60]

Judging from a number of measures, federal multiculturalism policy has been less than successful in convincing Canadians that harmony and other desirable goals can be reached through government support of cultural diversity. Since its establishment as official federal government policy in 1971, the central tenet of multiculturalism has been the promotion of racial/ethnic harmony and equality through respecting individuals' fundamental cultural and racial differences. Yet some critics of the federal multiculturalism policy have argued that far from smoothing racial tensions, multiculturalism *creates* and *deepens* ethnocentrism and racial hatreds. As novelist Neil Bissoondath expresses this sentiment, "In stressing the differences between groups, in failing to emphasize that this is a country with its own ideals and attitudes that demand adherence, the [multiculturalism] policy has instead aided in a hardening of hatreds."[61]

Although the arguments for rejecting multiculturalism are themselves diverse, there is little question that increasing numbers of Canadians are willing to discard government policies that promote a "cultural mosaic." About 72 percent of respondents in an October 1993 national survey stated their agreement with the view that "the long-standing image of Canada as a nation of communities, each ethnic and racial group preserving its own identity with the help of government policy, must give way to the U.S. style of cultural absorption."[62] What this suggests is that Canadians are yearning for simpler solutions, for policies that "melt away" troublesome differences and promote cultural homogeneity. How unrealistic such hopes are can be seen in the failure of the U.S. "melting pot" to deal with the deep racial divisions between African-Americans and white America, in the growing trend toward bilingual (Spanish/English) states such as California, and in the continued prevalence of ethnic enclaves in American cities. In light of the limitations of alternative models for Canadian national integration (e.g., two or even three nations, liberal individualism, and so on), multiculturalism allows for a more inclusive framework in an increasingly ethnically and racially diverse political community.

FUTURE CHALLENGES

The ease with which parliamentary rules were recently interpreted to permit turbans in the House of Commons was one small but significant symbolic change that reflected how Canadian political institutions are adapting to the politics of difference. Widespread racism, which deprives visible minorities equal rights to full recognition as Canadians, is a reminder that individuals and institutions continue to view racial distinctions as reasons to deprive people of their universal rights.

The challenge posed by ethnocultural and racial diversity—a challenge facing Canadian politicians and society as a whole—is greater than the challenge of finding a balance between the contradictory principles of *universalism,* which treats all citizens equally regardless of differences, and *difference,* which respects and promotes collective rights. Currently, there are different collective interests that correspond to ethnic/racial divisions—Quebec francophones, Aboriginal peoples, non-Anglo, non-French minorities—each fuelled by its own sense of collective origins, injustice, and destiny, and each vying for protection and enhancement through diverse political strategies and state instruments. The model of diversity pursued by each of these collectivities submerges the "special" claims, for symbolic recognition and for state and material resources, that are advanced by the other collectivities. How, then, can such divergent ethnocultural claims be integrated into the same political, institutional, and constitutional framework?

Charles Taylor has recently suggested that "deep diversity is the only formula on which a united federal Canada can be rebuilt."[63] Canadians must accept the existence of two types of diversity. A "first-level" diversity corresponds to "great differences in culture and outlook and background in a population that nevertheless shares the same idea of what it is to belong to Canada."[64] For Canadians of non-Anglo, non-French, and non-Aboriginal origins, their sense of belonging is associated with feeling "Canadian as a bearer of individual rights in a multicultural mosaic," and does not "pass through some other community." In contrast, first-level diversity is insufficient for most French Canadians and for most Aboriginal peoples, and must be accommodated by "second-level" or "deep" diversity. For these collectivities, their sense of belonging to Canada occurs through "being members of their national communities."[65]

Taylor's belief that the sense of belonging experienced by Canadians "of, say, Italian extraction in Toronto" does not "pass through some other community" is contradicted by the sociological reality of large, institutionally complete ethnic communities in Canadian urban centres. As described by Robert Harney in 1981, Toronto is a "metropolitan area with upwards of half a million Italian immigrants and their descendants. It is also a city with visible and massive Italian neighbourhoods and with healthy ethnocultural institutions that afford an Italian Canadian the opportunity to live and die within an immigrant Italian *ambiente.*[66] "New Canadians" and those who date their migration to Canada back several generations are unlikely to accept models of "deep diversity" that resuscitate exclusionary concepts such as "two founding nations." Deep diversity thus relegates "the others" to the status of second-class citizens just as it relegates questions of the representation of ethnic/racial minorities to a much lower rank of importance than representation of "charter groups."

Deep diversity also cannot make sense of the new patterns of ethnic and racial pluralism in Canadian cities where new and wealthier immigrants are setting their own terms for integration into Canada. There now exist in Vancouver's residential and commercial districts Asian enclaves where store owners are known to observe with unconscious irony, "We do not see many foreigners here," referring to Canadians of European extraction.[67] The Hong Kong Chinese immigrants to Canada are more likely to identify themselves as "global citizens," to speak several languages, and to feel more comfortable with many different cultures than with any limited "first-level" diversity model of Canadian citizenship. Moreover, their capacity to influence Canadian state policies has less to do with preestablished patterns of ethnic power within Canada than with the power of international capital and the potential for investment in Canada that they represent.

But global migration and Canadian immigration policies have also brought to Canada's shores Third World migrants (foreign domestic workers, garment workers, agricultural seasonal workers, refugees) who are less privileged in class terms. The subordinate labour-market position and political marginality of these groups have much in common with oppressed Third World peoples, and have spawned an activist and more global form of "ethnic politics." As we approach the 21st century, the notion of Canadian citizenship must be recast. It must become attuned to Canada's position within the global economy, to international migration, and to developing forms of ethnic/racial stratification that dovetail with relations of power based on class and gender. It must be inclusive and equitable enough to undercut old forms of ethnic and racial hierarchy, and to prevent new ones from emerging.

NOTES

1. Clark Blaise and Bharati Mukherjee, *The Sorrow and the Terror: The Haunting Legacy of the Air India Tragedy* (Markham, Ont.: Penguin, 1988), pp. x–xx.

2. For a discussion of the "politics of equal recognition," see the essay by Charles Taylor, *Multiculturalism and "The Politics of Recognition"* (Princeton, N.J.: Princeton University Press), 1992.

3. Geoffrey York, "Turban no bar to speaking in House," *The Globe and Mail* (January 29, 1994), p. A4.

4. Charles Taylor, *Multiculturalism and the "Politics of Recognition,"* pp. 37–39.

5. See Yasmeen Abu-Laban and Daiva Stasiulis, "Ethnic Pluralism under Siege: Popular and Partisan Opposition to Multiculturalism," *Canadian Public Policy* 18 (1992): 365–86; Alan Cairns, "Political Science, Ethnicity, and the Canadian Constitution," in Douglas E. Williams, ed., in *Disruptions: Constitutional Struggles from the Charter to Meech Lake* (Toronto: McClelland and Stewart, 1991), pp. 168–69; V. Seymour Wilson, "The Tapestry Vision of Canadian Multiculturalism," *Canadian Journal of Political Science* 26, no. 4 (December 1993): 645–59.

6. Canada, Employment and Immigration Canada, "Immigration to Canada: A Statistical Overview" (Ottawa: Minister of Supply and Services Canada, 1989), p. 8.

7. V. Seymour Wilson, "The Tapestry Vision of Canadian Multiculturalism," pp. 647–48.

8. Andrew Phillips, "Lessons of Vancouver," *Maclean's* (February 7, 1994), p. 30.

9. Lois Sweet, "Racism: 'As Canadian as the maple leaf,'" *The Toronto Star* (February 22, 1992), p. A8.

10. Rick Ponting, "Racial Conflict: Turning the Heat Up," in Dan Glenday and Ann Duffy, eds. *Canadian Society: Understanding and Surviving in the 1990s* (Toronto: McClelland and Stewart, 1994), p. 89.

11. Daiva Stasiulis, "Symbolic Representation and the Numbers Game: Tory Policies on 'Race' and Visible Minorities," in F. Abele, ed., *How Ottawa Spends: The Politics of Fragmentation, 1991–1992* (Ottawa: Carleton University Press, 1991), pp. 233–36

12. Clifford Geertz, "The Integrative Revolution: Primordial Sentiments and Civil Politics in New States," in C. Geertz, ed., *Old Societies and New States* (New York: Free Press, 1963). For further elaboration of the primordial view of ethnicity, see Harold Isaacs, "Basic Group Identity: The Idols of the Tribe," in N. Glazer and D.P. Moynihan, eds., *Ethnicity: Theory and Experience* (Cambridge, Mass.: Harvard University Press, 1975).

13. Fredrik Barth's work on ethnic-group boundaries has been influential in the development of approaches to ethnicity that downplay ethnic culture and highlight the construction and mobilization of ethnic groups. See Fredrik Barth, *Ethnic Groups and Boundaries* (Boston: Little Brown, 1969).

14. Daiva K. Stasiulis, "The Political Structuring of Ethnic Community Action: A Reformulation," *Canadian Ethnic Studies* 12, no. 3 (1980); Audrey Kobayashi, "Representing Ethnicity: Political Statistexts," in Statistics Canada and U.S. Bureau of the Census, eds., *Challenges of Measuring an Ethnic World: Science, Politics and Reality* (Washington: U.S. Government Printing Office, 1993).

15. Audrey Kobayashi describes the efforts on the part of the Canadian Hispanic Congress to convince Statistics Canada to include "Hispanic" as one of the ethnic categories in the ethnic-origin question in the 1991 census. She argues that the organization sought an opportunity to advance its influence and future potential for state funding at a time when its constituency was expanding "as a result of refugee immigration from Central and South America." See Kobayashi, "Representing Ethnicity," p. 520.

16. The confusion over the boundaries between ethnic and racial groups is highlighted by the use in Canadian census-taking—up to and including the 1941 census—of a question on "racial origin," which at the time meant mostly European

origins. Also indicative of the conflation between the two terms is the (until recently) common reference to the French and English in Canada as the "two founding races." An anomaly in the 1986 and 1991 censuses for a government that purports to reject "racial" categories; is the existence of "black" as one of the mark-in entries for the "ethnic origin" category; this entry assumes that respondents of African origin identify with a black community. See Pamela M. White, Jane Badets, and Viviane Renaud, "Measuring Ethnicity in Canadian Censuses," in Statistics Canada and the U.S. Bureau of the Census, *Challenges of Measuring an Ethnic World,* p. 223. The fact that differences in skin pigmentation and other physical differences between collectivities become a means of transcending racism (through political mobilization, affirmative-action measures, and group identification) undermines efforts by well-meaning social scientists and politicians to transcend racial differences. See Kobayashi, "Representing Ethnicity," p. 519.

17. The insistence on the enduring liability of race or skin colour also draws attention to the origins of racism in European colonialism and the continued imperialism of the First World in Third World countries with nonwhite populations.

18. However, the program to make the federal civil service bilingual subsequent to the Royal Commission on Bilingualism and Biculturalism was, in effect, an employment-equity program for francophones. Indeed, this program is the most successful Canadian affirmative-action program to date.

19. Alain Pelletier, "Politics and Ethnicity: Representation of Ethnic and Visible-Minority Groups in the House of Commons," in K. Megyery, ed., *Ethnocultural Groups and Visible Minorities in Canadian Politics: The Question of Access* (Toronto: Dundurn Press, 1991), pp. 132–33.

20. Franca Iacovetta, *Such Hardworking People: Italian Immigrants in Postwar Toronto* (Montreal and Kingston: McGill-Queen's University Press, 1993), p. 22.

21. Daniel Salée, "Identifies in Conflict: The Aboriginal Question and the Politics of Recognition," unpublished manuscript, School of Community and Public Affairs, Concordia University, 1994, p. 6.

22. The conceptualization of racisms in terms of "differential positionality" is taken from Atvar Brah, "Difference, Diversity, Differentiation," *International Review of Sociology* 2 (April 1991): 62.

23. Robert A. Huttenback, *Racism and Empire: White Settlers and Colored Immigrants in the British Self-Governing Colonies, 1830–1910* (Ithaca: Cornell University Press, 1976), pp. 13–25.

24. House of Commons, *Debates* (May 4, 1885), p. 1588, cited in Daiva Stasiulis and Glen Williams, "Mapping Racial/Ethnic Hierarchy in the Canadian Social Formation, 1860–1914: An Examination of Selected Federal Policy Debates," paper presented at the Canadian Political Science Association meetings, Charlottetown, University of Prince Edward Island, June 1992. "Aryan" is a linguistic term that was used to denote the family of Indo-European languages related to Sanskrit. The word took on quite a different meaning when it was used in the 1850s and 1860s by Joseph Arthur Gobineau to identify a group of people who produced a refined civilization, in contrast to the lowly ones created by the black and yellow races. See Michael Banton, "Aryan," in E. Cashmore, ed. *Dictionary of Race and Ethnic Relations* (London: Routledge, 1984), p. 21.

25. House of Commons, *Debates* (May 4, 1885), p. 1583, quoted in Stasiulis and Williams, "Mapping Racial/Ethnic Hierarchy."

26. House of Commons, *Debates* (June 7, 1928), pp. 392ff.

27. House of Commons, *Debates* (May 1, 1947), p. 2645.

28. See Peter S. Li, *The Chinese in Canada* (Toronto: Oxford University Press, 1988), pp. 2, 27–30, 86; and Ann Sunahara, *The Politics of Racism: The Uprooting of Japanese Canadians during the Second World War* (Toronto: James Lorimer, 1981), pp. 7, 17, and 151.

29. As recently as 1964, a run-down all-black school operated in a rural area near Windsor; white children from the area were bused out to a newly constructed school. The City of Windsor, Ontario, was reportedly the last municipality to desegregate its public facilities, in 1975. The exclusion of blacks from public facilities continues to take place in the present day. In 1991, the barring of blacks from a nightclub in Halifax resulted in street violence. See Daniel Hill, *Human Rights in Canada: A Focus on Racism* (Ottawa: Canadian Labour Congress, 1977), p. 11; Frances Henry and Carol Tator, "Racism in Canada: Social Myths and Strategies for Change," in R.M. Bienvenue and J.E. Goldstein, eds., *Ethnicity and Ethnic Relations in Canada*, 2nd ed. (Toronto: Butterworths, 1985); and Ponting, "Racial Conflict," p. 95.

30. Pelletier, "Politics and Ethnicity," p. 127.

31. Jean Burnet and Howard Palmer, *"Coming Canadians": An Introduction to a History of Canada's Peoples* (Toronto: McClelland and Stewart, 1988), p. 162.

32. Pelletier, "Politics and Ethnicity." See also Daiva K. Stasiulis and Yasmeen Abu-Laban, "The House the Parties Built: (Re)constructing Ethnic Representation in Canadian Politics," and Carole Simard et al., "Visible Minorities and the Canadian Political System," in K. Megyery, ed., *Ethnocultural Groups and Visible Minorities in Canadian Politics: The Question of Access* (Toronto: Dundurn Press, 1991).

33. Pelletier, "Politics and Ethnicity," p. 129.

34. Ibid., pp. 128–29.

35. Ibid., p. 130.

36. *Ethno Canada*, vol. 16 (Ottawa: Canadian Ethnocultural Council, forthcoming).

37. Jerome H. Black, "Ethnic Minorities and Mass Politics in Canada: Some Observations in the Toronto Setting," *International Journal of Canadian Studies* (Spring 1991): 129–51.

38. Pelletier, "Politics and Ethnicity," p. 129.

39. Ibid., p. 133.

40. Ibid., p. 114.

41. The following discussion of barriers to participation of ethnic minorities in political parties is an adapted version of Stasiulis and Abu-Laban, "The House the Parties Built," pp. 11–13 and 41.

42. Pelletier, "Ethnicity and Politics," p. 141.

43. Stasiulis and Abu-Laban, "The House the Parties Built," p. 66.

44. Author interview with Albina Guarnieri, MP for Mississauga East, October 16, 1990, Ottawa.

45. See Janine Brodie and Jan Jenson, *Crisis, Challenge and Change: Party and Class in Canada Revisited* (Ottawa: Carleton University Press, 1988); and Karl Peter, "The Myth of Multiculturalism," in J. Dahlie and T. Fernando, eds., *Ethnicity, Power and Politics in Canada* (Toronto: Methuen, 1981).

46. See Gilles Paquet, "Multiculturalism as National Policy," *Journal of Cultural Economics* 13, no. 1 (June 1989): 17–33; and Neil Bissoondath, "A Question of Belonging: Multiculturalism and Citizenship," in W. Kaplan, ed., *Belonging: The*

Meaning and Future of Canadian Citizenship (Montreal and Kingston: McGill-Queen's University Press, 1993).

47. Jean Burnet with Howard Palmer, *"Coming Canadians": An Introduction to a History of Canada's Peoples* (Toronto: McClelland and Stewart, 1988), pp. 174–75.

48. Burnet with Palmer, *"Coming Canadians"*: pp. 171–72.

49. H. Sohn, "Human Rights Legislation in Ontario: A Study of Action," unpublished doctoral dissertation, School of Social Work, University of Toronto, 1975.

50. Daiva Stasiulis, "Minority Resistance in the Local State: Toronto in the 1970s and 1980s," *Ethnic and Racial Studies* (January 1989): 63–83.

51. Audrey Kobayashi, "The Japanese-Canadian Redress Settlement and Its Implications for 'Race Relations,'" *Canadian Ethnic Studies* 24, no. 1 (1992): 1–19.

52. The Quebec women's movement reflects a distinctive linguistic and cultural milieu of Quebec feminists who are almost exclusively francophone. They combine feminist goals with nationalist ones of an empowered majority in Quebec pursuing the furtherance of *la nation canadienne-française* in a larger North American anglophone context. Racial and cultural differences within Quebec feminism have thus not been addressed to the same extent as they have in the Canadian women's movement outside Quebec.

53. Daiva Stasiulis, "'Authentic Voice': Anti-Racist Politics in Canadian Feminist Publishing and Literary Production," in S. Gunew and A. Yeatman, eds., *Feminism and the Politics of Difference* (Sydney: Allen and Unwin, 1993).

54. The distinctive conditions of Aboriginal women have also until recently eluded the meaningful support of a non-Aboriginal women's movement that failed to see how issues such as land claims and self-government were "feminist issues." White feminists, far removed from First Nations' battles over sovereignty, were quick to recognize the sexist character of the old Indian Act. But they have been less comprehending of the role of women in Aboriginal self-determination and nation-building. Within the context of forging a position on the Charlottetown Accord (defeated in a 1993 national referendum), the issue of protection of equality rights of Aboriginal women was at the forefront of the National Action Committee on the Status of Women's (NAC) highly publicized opposition to the accord.

55. Sunera Thobani, "Making the Links: South Asian Women and the Struggle for Reproductive Rights," *Resources for Feminist Research* 13, no. 1 (Fall 1992): 19–20.

56. Jack Kapica, "Canadians want mosaic to melt, survey finds," *The Globe and Mail* (December 14, 1993), pp. A1–A2.

57. Geoffrey York, "Liberals to let in 250,000 this year," *The Globe and Mail* (February 3, 1994), p. A1.

58. Cairns, "Political Science, Ethnicity, and the Canadian Constitution," p. 173.

59. Shelagh Day, "Cries and Statistics: The Empty Heart of Federal Employment Equity," *Our Times* 9, no. 2 (April 1990): 22–25.

60. Katharyne Mitchell, "Multiculturalism, or the United Colors of Capitalism?" *Antipode* 25, no. 4 (1993): 263–94.

61. Neil Bissoondath, "A Question of Belonging," p. 376. For analyses of the diverse criticisms of multiculturalism policy, see Abu-Laban and Stasiulis, "Ethnic Pluralism under Siege," and Wilson, "The Tapestry Vision of Canadian Multiculturalism."

62. Kapica, "Canadians want mosaic to melt," p. A1.

63. Charles Taylor, "Shared and Divergent Values," in R.L. Watts and D.M. Brown, eds., *Options for a New Canada* (Toronto: University of Toronto Press, 1991), p. 76.
64. Ibid., p. 75.
65. Ibid, pp. 75–76.
66. Robert F. Harney, "Toronto's Little Italy, 1885–1945," in R.F. Harney and J.V. Scarpaci, eds., *Little Italies in North America* (Toronto: The Multicultural History Society of Ontario, 1981), p. 41.
67. Phillips, "Lessons of Vancouver," p. 28.

FURTHER READINGS

Abu-Laban, Yasmeen, and Daiva Stasiulis. "Ethnic Pluralism under Siege: Popular and Partisan Opposition to Multiculturalism." *Canadian Public Policy* 18, no. 4: 365–86.

Black, Jerome H. "Ethnic Minorities and Mass Politics in Canada: Some Observations in the Toronto Setting." *International Journal of Canadian Studies* 3 (Spring 1991): 129–51.

Breton, Raymond. "The Production and Allocation of Symbolic Resources: An Analysis of the Linguistic and Ethnocultural Fields in Canada." *Canadian Review of Sociology and Anthropology* 21 (1984): 123–44.

Burnet, Jean R., and Howard Palmer. "Ethnicity and Politics." Chapter 8 in *"Coming Canadians": An Introduction to a History of Canada's Peoples.* Toronto: McClelland and Stewart, 1988.

Cairns, Alan. "Political Science, Ethnicity and the Canadian Constitution." In David P. Shugarman and Reg Whitaker, eds., *Federalism and Political Community.* Peterborough, Ont.: Broadview Press, 1989.

Dahlie, Jorgen, and Tissa Fernando, eds. *Ethnicity, Power and Politics in Canada.* Toronto: Methuen, 1981.

Megyery, Kathy, ed. *Ethnocultural Groups and Visible Minorities in Canadian Politics: The Question of Access.* Toronto: Dundurn Press, 1991.

Stasiulis, Daiva, and Yasmeen Abu-Laban. "Ethnic Minorities and the Politics of Limited Inclusion in Canada." In Alain-G. Gagnon and James P. Bickerton, eds., *Canadian Politics: An Introduction to the Discipline,* Peterborough, Ont.: Broadview Press, 1990.

LINKS
BETWEEN
SOCIETY
& STATE

11 POLITICAL PARTIES

Nelson Wiseman

Political parties are ubiquitous throughout the Western world, and it is difficult to imagine a modern society without them. In Canada, as in Europe and the United States, they emerged with the growth of representative and popular government, and are a central feature of the political system, serving as transmission belts that help convert public opinion into public policy and vice versa. Parties mobilize voters around issues, offer policy alternatives, and as governing instruments lead and direct the bureaucratic machinery of state in transforming philosophical dispositions and policy pronouncements into concrete programs.

When we examine parties collectively and comparatively, and search for patterns of interaction among them, we are studying the *party system*. We may analyze the party system's performance by asking a number of theoretical questions. How do the parties operate? How do they relate to one another in Canada's federal system? Who and what do they stand for? By answering these questions, and by examining party preference in recent elections, we can discern the salient features of the contemporary Canadian party system.

THE DEMOCRATIC IMPULSE

One of the hallmarks of a democratic society is the competition of political parties for power. Paradoxically, the parties need not function as democratic organizations themselves. However, as the democratic impulse has grown in the land, so too has the parties' response to manage and finesse it. As such, parties reflect the trends in the society at large. Thus, in the early years of Confederation—when the franchise was restricted, when balloting was public rather than secret, when bribery and corruption guided public policy—a putrid odour pervaded party politics.

In those years, the Liberal and Conservative parties were loose coalitions of diverse interests, factions, and personalities. The coalition government of the first prime minister, John A. Macdonald, is best labelled

Liberal–Conservative. Sporting labels such as the Clear Grits in Ontario, Bleus and Rouges in Quebec, and Tories and Reformers elsewhere, the parties of the immediate pre- and post-Confederation period were not the coherent or disciplined forces they are now. Even more so than today, these embryonic organizations, were lorded over by their leaders, men who attained their position by virtue of their forceful personalities, their brokering, bullying, and speechifying. Around them huddled their intimates, parliamentary cliques, and financial backers. Mass-based party membership, and the democratic system it hinted at, was inchoate, an idea still to take form.

It is misleading to discuss the national party system before 1896, for one barely existed. The parties had virtually no life or organization outside of Parliament and barely coherent identities within it. Many MPs were identified not as party men but as "loose fish," "shaky fellows," or "ministerialists." These men, rather than run for a party, were elected as independents by trading on their reputations as local notables. They were keen to embrace the government of the day, and any government would do. Further, they condemned and distanced themselves from the opposition, whatever it might be. Party affiliation was anathema not only to them but to those who voted for them: to many citizens an acclamation was preferable to an election because their MP could then agree to support the strongest party in the House in exchange for favourable patronage terms and government largesse for the constituency. Thus, antipathy to party politics was driven by the fear of limiting the bargaining power of the local MP with the government.

The evolution of recognizable modern parties was aided, ironically, by the government's cynical manipulation of the electoral process. Voting was staggered rather than simultaneous: elections were first held in safe ridings to build a sense of momentum and impending victory for the government coalition; then they were held in constituencies where the government had a reasonable chance of success; and, lastly, they were conducted in ridings considered impossible to win. These tactics induced a bandwagon effect; voters in unsafe ridings could opt for government candidates rather than "loose fish" independents, because the overall results were already discernible.

These features of the early electoral and party systems in Canada no longer exist. Society has changed and the franchise is universal. Not only are all women and aboriginals now enfranchised but the electorate includes members of dozens of diverse ethnic groups that immigrated over the course of more than a century, and that currently outnumber one of the founding national groups (the French). The economy has also changed; a simple rural agricultural society has been replaced by a complex industrial, urban, better-educated, and technologically advanced one. People now look to governing parties and the state, rather than to charitable and religious institutions, for health care, education, and social assistance. Most important, the concept of democracy has blossomed. In the 19th century, this concept was suspect; in the 20th century, it has become *the* ruling ideology. To harness it, new parties have come into being, and, not to be swept away by it, old parties have changed their ways.

Consider party leadership. While in the old days a parliamentary caucus anointed one of its own, the leadership selection process today has been stretched much closer to the outer limits of what the democratic principle might entail. Partly under the influence of the neighbouring American model, Canada became the first country with a British parliamentary system to choose its leaders via special conventions called for that purpose. At first, when the Liberals tentatively initiated the convention process in 1893, about half the delegates were *ex officio*; they were MPs, senators, MLAs, party officeholders, and defeated candidates. Over time, more and more of the delegates to party conventions were selected by constituency associations, and the first "modern" leadership conventions were held by the Liberals and Conservatives in 1919 and 1927, respectively. In 1984, the Parti Québécois, with little forethought, decided to open its leadership selection process still wider by giving each party member a vote. Since then, many more provincial parties have followed suit and the federal Liberals have promised to do the same when their next leader is selected.

The logic of democracy calls for deliberation. Simple electoral democracy—one person, one vote—is difficult to resist and politically incorrect to assault. The filtration mechanism that is the party system is being short-circuited. It is imperative to ponder the unfettered workings of contemporary democratic party practice, so that the negative features of party politics in the distant past not be reproduced under a new guise in the future. Technological advances such as telephones connected to computers have made it possible for party members to choose their leaders without actually meeting, debating, or exchanging views with each other. Most parties do not require citizenship for membership, and some have no age limit, so that tourists, children, recent immigrants, and even foreigners awaiting deportation may participate in selecting Canada's party leaders and future prime ministers. The ultra-modern, stripped-down model of leadership selection has arrived. In Alberta, in 1992, anyone buying a Conservative membership card for five dollars could participate in determining the future premier, and candidates could purchase party memberships and give them away, even on voting day. Does this process lead to the selection of better leaders? Is there more openness and accountability and less manipulation than in the procedures of the past, and has democracy truly been served?

The spread and increasing popularity of the democratic principle clearly has weighed on how parties operate and how they see themselves and the polity. Let us consider two current examples. Until recently, referendums and plebiscites were relatively rare in Canadian practice, but increasingly in the 1990s, beseeched by their memberships, parties have become keen to employ them. Another good example can be drawn from the 1993 federal election campaign, which two dramatically contrasting views served as subtexts with respect to what democratic citizenship means in Canada. The Bloc Québécois, which ran only in Quebec, posited that Canada was a failed binational experiment, that the Confederation bargain, a solemn pact between two equal, founding peoples, had gone awry. The right of one of these peoples—the French—to self-determination, to sovereignty, should be settled through a referendum expressing their will. This was presented by the Bloc as just and unassailable—indeed, as the ultimate democratic exercise. The Reform Party, which offered candidates everywhere but Quebec, held out an antithetical view, but one similarly based on a claim to democratic legitimacy. In contrast with the Bloc, Reform advocated the equality of individuals and provinces, not linguistic and cultural groups, and insisted that no special or distinct status be conferred on any group or government. It denounced officially imposed and financed bilingualism and multiculturalism, but did not denounce Quebec's right to secede. Like the Bloc, Reform wants referendums to express the public will. But while the BQ pursues a single cathartic vote on the cardinal issue of Quebec's identity and destiny, Reform wants multiple referendums to offset the power of governments and party elites. It proposes American direct democracy, rather than British parliamentary democracy, as a political model in which citizen initiatives and referendums determine major policy questions. Moreover, the Reform Party wants MPs to vote according to their consciences or their constituents, not their party whips, whereas the BQ intends to impose strict party discipline on its backbenchers.

MASS AND CADRE

Party democracy is related to how leaders and followers understand their roles and how they behave toward each other. Let us employ a model, or paradigm, of polar opposites. All parties may be placed on a continuum between the two poles. At one end is the cadre party; at the other extremity is the mass party. However, in reality, all parties are a mix of both elements. The cadre–mass distinction is clear in theory but muddled in practice. All parties might insist that their leaders are servants of their followers, but their behaviour reveals that leaders in cadre parties count for more than those in mass parties. As we describe their structure and operation, let us think of how Canada's parties—the Liberals, Bloc Québécois, Reform, NDP, and Conservatives—may be characterized. Where are they situated on the continuum, and what is their relationship to one another?

A cadre implies a group of trained personnel who form the nucleus of an organization. Cadre parties look up to and rely on their leaders, who are distinguished, influential, or otherwise noteworthy. The number of party members is not as critical as the character of the leader. Leadership tends to be inherited rather than captured. The cadre party has a small number of large private or corporate contributors. It engages experts to manage and massage public opinion, to organize election campaigns, and to manipulate the media for political advantage. Party policy is what the leadership, rather than the members, proclaims it to be. In short, the party is run from the top down.

Mass parties are the opposite of cadre parties. Whereas cadre parties stress the few and the select, mass parties focus on the many—the rank and file. Some would say that the cadre party searches for quality, while the mass party seeks quantity. For a mass party, membership recruitment—facilitating mass political education and funding—is a core activity. Leaders are democratically elected rather than oligarchically determined. Party policy is what the members, voting on resolutions in conventions, say it is rather than what the leader divines it to be. The leader is perceived as the party's mouthpiece, not its shepherd. Mass parties put principles before personalities and are preoccupied with issues rather than charisma. Financed from the bottom up, the mass party seeks modest sums from large numbers of people and from other mass organizations such as unions and cooperatives.

At different times, Canada's parties have appeared at different points on the cadre–mass continuum, and from different angles we may draw different inferences. The Conservatives and Liberals began as cadre parties. Both were born within Parliament and developed extraparliamentary organizations afterward. As the democratic principle spread, these parties reached out to recruit newly enfranchised voters and a corps of reliable partisans to act as foot soldiers in the campaign trenches. The old cadre parties set out to remodel and refurbish themselves in an effort to gain the support of a mass base. The Liberals succeeded in appealing to new citizens and minorities, and they introduced leadership conventions. In the 1970s, the Conservatives pioneered the mass direct-mail campaign as a means of accumulating more funds. The registration of parties through the Election Expenses Act of 1974 fostered the mass party model by providing income-tax rebates for party supporters who make modest contributions. Simultaneously, the law appeared to reinforce the cadre party model by requiring party leaders to sign the nomination papers of candidates who sported the party label on the ballot.

Parties born outside of Parliament—such as the Progressives in the 1920s, the Co-operative Commonwealth Federation (the NDP's forerunner), and Social Credit in the 1930s—presented themselves as mass parties. In some respects, however, they acted like cadre parties, especially when in power. The CCF–NDP has held a leadership vote at every one of its biennial conventions. But real challenges have been rare, and when a leader's resignation begets a contest, it often appears to be a coronation rather than a conquest. With the Liberals and Conservatives, death or resignation was understood to be required before a race took place. This pattern was shattered only by the Conservatives in the 1960s, when party leader John Diefenbaker was undermined by the party president.

FIGURE 11.1 **Possible Party/Regional Placements on Cadre–Mass Continuum, 1993**

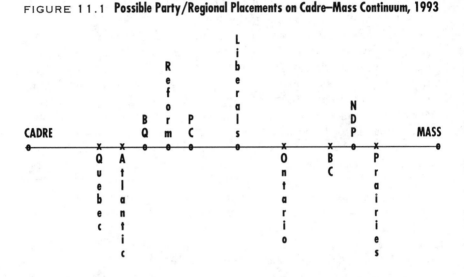

Parties in Atlantic Canada have tended toward the cadre model, while those in the West have inclined to the mass model. Leadership selection in Prince Edward Island was left to a party caucus until the 1950s (although the first convention-chosen leader to become a premier was selected there in 1903). Newfoundland's Liberals had no formal party organization until the late 1960s, and Nova Scotia's Conservatives had no constitution until 1975. The various United Farmers'/Progressive parties in Alberta, Manitoba, and Ontario were among the most democratic in the history of political parties. The Progressives and Social Credit offered the rhetoric and some features of the mass party model, but the federal Progressives' leaders were co-opted into the federal Liberal cabinet, and Social Credit's founder, "Bible Bill" Aberhart of Alberta, personally chose his party's candidates. His followers were submissive.

The newest parties in Parliament, the BQ and Reform, also exhibit a mix of cadre and mass features. The BQ deliberately refused to call itself a party in the 1993 election, and Reform began its campaign with the populist motto "Let the People Speak." These are not in themselves, however, cadre and mass characteristics; Jeffersonian Democrats were a *populist* mass party and Lenin's Bolsheviks were an *elitist* mass party. Despite their cultivation of the grass roots, Lucien Bouchard and Preston Manning towered over their parties during the 1993 campaign, much more so than the other leaders loomed over theirs. In Bouchard's case, this was consistent with Quebec's cultural tradition where the dominant party's leader—Maurice Duplessis, René Lévesque, and Robert Bourassa are examples—has been not only a partisan chieftain but a societal leader as well. English-Canadian premiers have no such status because their societies are not distinct and not surrounded by a foreign language and culture. Manning appeared in 1993 as a populist in the U.S. mould—folksy, homespun, evangelical, and on a crusade.

It was difficult in 1993 to imagine the BQ or Reform having a life or identity independent of their leaders. The Bloc, like a cadre party, was born in Parliament as a breakaway fragment of disenchanted Conservatives and Liberals. It did not begin as a mass party, although it aspired to be one. Reform, like a mass party, was born outside Parliament. It is a modern reincarnation of the social conservative philosophy espoused by its leader's father, Ernest Manning, who served as Aberhart's successor and Alberta's premier for a quarter-century. Like Aberhart, Preston Manning promises to subject his MPs to recall by their constituents. Aberhart, it should be remembered, scrapped this principle when his constituents attempted to recall him.

FEDERAL AND PROVINCIAL

Canada has twelve party systems, one federal, ten provincial, and one territorial (Yukon). As citizens of a federal state but residents of specific provinces, Canadians exhibit dual loyalties. They vote for, follow, and identify with parties in two arenas. Let us employ another abstract model, one that reflects party relations in a federal system. At one polar extreme is the *integrated* party, at the other the *confederal* party. The poles of the paradigm are pure types; in practice, all the parties and provinces reflect some aspects of both integrated and confederal party systems.

The poles of our model are defined by six criteria. The first is voter support or electoral dependence. An integrated party draws on the same body of voters in both federal and provincial elections. Shifts for and against the party follow closely in elections at both levels. The analysis applies to individuals as well as to groups of voters such as youth, francophones, farmers, and so on. If the youth vote swings to the Liberals in a federal election, for example, it then swings to them in the subsequent provincial election as well, and vice versa. In a confederal party system, in contrast, common voter allegiances are uncommon. Changes in voter support for a party at one level are not parallelled at the other level. Some observers have posited a "balance theory"—that Canadians, on the whole, consciously choose to vote for different parties federally and provincially. In support of this contention, note that in 1984, the last year of the

Trudeau Liberal regime, there were no provincial Liberal governments; and in 1993, the last year of the Mulroney Conservative administration, there were only two provincial Conservative governments.

The second, third, and fourth criteria differentiating integrated from confederal parties are organization, careers, and finances. In the integrated party there are common organizational structures, and the same machinery is used to nominate federal and provincial candidates and to run campaigns. In contrast, a confederal party has separate and autonomous federal and provincial organizations and mechanisms for candidate selection, policy determination, fundraising, and campaigning. In an integrated party, officials and personalities move easily from a career at the federal level to the provincial level, or vice versa. Three Ontario examples are Bob Rae, Sheila Copps, and Allan Lawrence, each of whom served as MPs and MPPs for their respective parties at the other level of government. Two of many possible Nova Scotia examples are premiers Gerald Regan and Robert Stanfield, while Quebec examples are Jean Lesage and Raymond Garneau. Three NDP examples—all premiers and MPs—are British Columbia's Dave Barrett, Saskatchewan's Tommy Douglas, and Manitoba's Ed Schreyer. Conversely, in a confederal system, party careerists would serve exclusively at one level, examples being Robert Bourassa, Pierre Trudeau, Bill Davis, Ernest Manning, and Roy Romanow. In an integrated party, financial contributors subscribe to the party as a whole, and intraparty mechanisms distribute the funds between the party's federal and provincial wings. In contrast, in a confederal system, contributions are specifically earmarked for either the provincial or the federal party, and the two levels of the party are financially independent. Disparate federal and provincial election finance legislation often compels the parties to operate in a confederal manner, as in Ontario where provincial tax credits are available only to provincial party contributors, while federal tax credits are reserved for federal party contributors.

The fifth and sixth criteria in our model are ideology and party symmetry. The federal and provincial wings of the integrated party offer common positions and principles, and a single and distinctive ideology distinguishes the party from its competitors. In contrast, in a confederal system, the federal and provincial parties of the same name often offer dissimilar positions. In an integrated party system, there is symmetry when, in a given province, the same parties contest and have comparable levels of success in both federal and provincial elections (e.g., Ontario, Saskatchewan, and Nova Scotia before 1993 with their Liberals, Conservatives, and NDP). In a confederal system, exemplified by British Columbia and Quebec, the configuration of parties in federal and provincial elections is asymmetrical. In British Columbia, Social Credit and the NDP were the major provincial parties from the 1960s through the 1980s, a period in which the provincial Conservatives and Liberals were relatively dormant; during the same period, in federal elections in British Columbia, Social Credit was a relatively minor player, while the Liberals and Conservatives were major ones. Quebec's asymmetrical party system was reflected in the presence of the Union Nationale and the Parti Québécois, neither of which had federal counterparts from the 1930s through the 1980s.

Where are parties and provinces located on our integrated–confederal continuum? As with the cadre–mass dichotomy, different parties and provinces stand at different points at different times. Of the three older parties—the Liberals, Conservatives, and NDP—the NDP is the most integrated and the Conservatives the most confederal. It is impossible, for example, to be a federal NDP member unless one joins the provincial party—membership is totally integrated. Similarly, all NDP provincial headquarters serve as federal and provincial party offices during campaigns at both levels. In contrast, the Conservatives have separate federal and provincial membership lists, financing efforts, and party offices in most provinces. The Liberals are less integrated than the NDP, but more so than the Conservatives. This ranking of the parties in terms of integration—NDP-Liberal-Conservative—is buttressed by the federal parties' constitutions, which provide for relations between federal and provincial wings.

FIGURE 11.2 **Possible Party/Regional Placements on Integrated–Confederal Continuum, 1993**

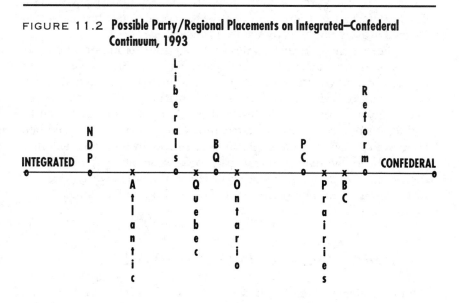

As for provincial/regional differences, the Atlantic region has the highest levels of party integration. Quebec, followed by British Columbia, exhibited the most pronounced confederal tendencies in recent decades. In the Atlantic provinces, campaign efforts by all three of the traditional parties are most likely to feature the same party activists, contributors, and organizations at both the federal and provincial levels. Ontario, with its separate Liberal and Conservative federal/provincial offices, has a some-what less integrated system. The Prairie pattern is more confederal than Ontario's, but less than British Columbia's. There the NDP is integrated as elsewhere, but the provincial Social Credit operated for four decades as an alliance of federal Liberals and provincial Conservatives. Consider two prominent provincial Social Crediters elected to the same caucus in 1986—Bill Vander Zalm and Kim Campbell, the former a federal Liberal, the latter a federal Conservative. Quebec had the most distinctly confed-eral party system for over a half-century, as we noted, with nationalist provincial parties—the UN and the PQ—having no federal counterpart until the BQ's recent debut. The PQ–BQ alliance in 1993 has left Quebec's party system more integrated.

Sometimes a provincial party makes a show of officially severing its links with its fraternal federal party, almost always when the latter is in power. Below the surface, however, the party's very name and traditions are ties that continue to bind. Saskatchewan's provincial Liberals, for ex-ample, made much of breaking their bond with the unpopular Trudeau Liberals, but the rift did not stop the provincial Liberal leader, Davie Stu-art, from accepting a seat in the Senate. Similarly, in 1991, Alberta's Con-servatives voted to break with the unpopular federal Conservatives, but in the 1993 federal election the Conservative premier and his party cam-paigned actively for the party's federal candidates.

The two new federal parties—the BQ and Reform—may also be placed on the integrated–confederal continuum. The Bloc is the more in-tegrated of the two in that its campaign machinery in 1993 and almost all of its organizers were drawn from the provincial PQ. One Bloc MP served as a PQ minister and two others served as PQ MNAs. Furthermore, the BQ and PQ share a common commitment to Quebec's sovereignty, and both claim to be social democratic (a claim shared only by the NDP). Reform is confederal in that its constitution has, to date, prohibited provincial Re-form wings. When one examines its electoral support, however, one finds that many of Reform's voters—including its leader—are former federal Conservative voters.

IDEOLOGY AND CLEAVAGES

Another continuum on which we may position parties has to do with what they stand for and whose interests they espouse. Let us therefore employ an ideological model in which the polar extremities are *left* and *right*. A leftist party champions the interests of the less privileged, the downtrodden, the dispossessed, and those generally less well off. Leftist parties identify with the working and lower classes; conversely, a rightist party defends the upper classes. Both leftists and rightists are concerned with the global welfare of society, but they offer different strategies for achieving it: leftists want to move toward equality through the redistribution of wealth, while rightists want to improve conditions and expand opportunities by creating more wealth and letting it "trickle down" to the less well off. Leftists are sympathetic to, and in solidarity with, the struggles of workers and oppressed minorities, while rightists support entrepreneurs and corporations that can mobilize capital and labour in ways that expand the economy.

Among the positions of Canada's parties, there is policy convergence and obfuscation. All of them defend social programs such as medicare and unemployment insurance, and all of them decry government deficits and burgeoning public debt. To disentangle the parties' positions, we must undertake a subtle approach, for as we shall see, it is the rationale *behind* a policy, more than the policy itself, that reveals ideology. Historically, the spectrum featured the Conservatives on the right, the NDP on the left, and the Liberals in the centre. Social Credit and the Communists were further out on the right and left, respectively. The centrist Liberal Party was frequently successful at moving either left or right as pressures and circumstances dictated. It alternately appeared as a leftist force (introducing medicare and pension legislation in the 1960s) and as a rightist force (imposing wage controls in the 1970s). Sometimes it upheld the banner of welfare or reform liberalism, which means using the instrumentality of the state to provide minimal standards of health, education, and social assistance to all individuals, and promoting equality of opportunity through the construction of a social safety net. At other times, the Liberal Party unfurled the banner of business liberalism, which means decrying state intervention as an infringement on private choice, and advocating the invisible hand of the market as a means to achieve efficiency in allocating scarce resources.

Where do Reform and the BQ sit on the left–right spectrum? Reform is a party of business liberalism, of the right, like America's Republicans and Margaret Thatcher's Conservatives. Reform denounces subversion of market forces via state subsidies for regional development programs. It wishes to rein in the welfare state. The Bloc's ideological position is less certain, more confounding. It labels itself social democratic, and a number of its MPs have been associated with the labour movement. The party's leader, however, is a former Conservative, as are most of its veteran MPs. In retrospect, they were not "real" Conservatives—as Bouchard puts it— but temporary, tactical members of the Mulroney caucus, ones devoted primarily to Quebec nationalism. The Bloc's economic policies have won the endorsement not only of Quebec's unions but also of the right-wing Conseil du Patronat, the province's major employers' lobby. The corporatist tradition of unions and employers forging common cause is an old one in Quebec, reflected in the Catholic union movement. In Quebec, the left–right dynamic is overwhelmed by the national question. Cross-national surveys in the 1980s confirmed this: after university students in Canada, Britain, the United States, New Zealand, and Australia classified themselves as leftist or rightist, this served as a more powerful predictor than their citizenship of attitudes to the state's role, equality, and minorities. Only with francophone Quebeckers was this left–right self-classification not a particularly helpful predictor. So too with the Bloc: its personnel and ideas are a mix of left and right in which the most powerful common thread is nationalism.

FIGURE 1 1 .3 **Possible Party Placements on Left–Right Continuum, 1993**

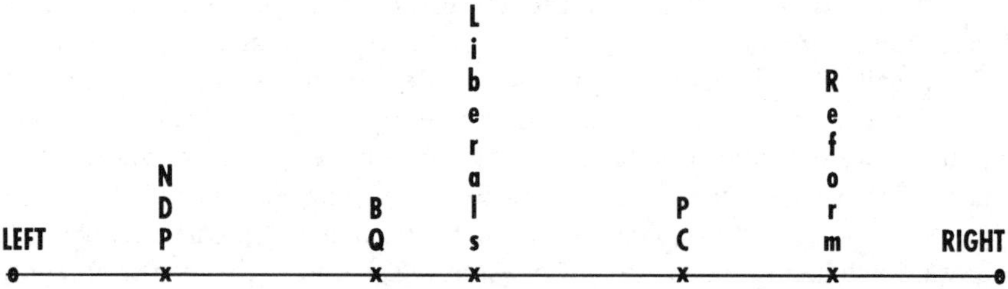

```
                    L
                    i
                    b                   R
                    e                   e
                    r                   f
         N          a                   o
         D       B  l         P         r
LEFT     P       Q  s         C         m        RIGHT
●──────────x──────────x────x──────────x──────────x────────●
```

The success of Reform, largely at the expense of the Conservatives in the 1993 election, suggests some ideological realignment in the party system. It has become *the* party of the right, certainly in most of English Canada. At the same time, the decline of the NDP helped the Liberals appear less ambivalently leftist in the election campaign. The fact that the Liberals manifested themselves as centrists or rightists does not detract from their "leftist" appearance in 1993, just as the Ontario NDP's social contract—imposing wage reductions in the public sector in 1993—did not reposition it to the right of the provincial Liberals and Conservatives. Many traditional Conservatives flocked to the Reform banner, while many traditional NDP supporters moved to the Liberal one. Crossovers from the NDP to Reform, especially in western Canada, reveal that the "protest" vote against the establishment is to some extent situational, not monopolized by leftist or rightist considerations. Similarly, in Quebec, the BQ represented an outlet for protest against federalists as well as sovereigntists.

We may also analyze the parties according to their philosophical outlooks or worldviews—how do they see society and the state? Once upon a time, Canadian conservatism, like British toryism in the late 19th century, posited an organic-collectivist view of society. For social stability, tories looked to the state to enforce order and authority; and for national development, the state guaranteed economic infrastructure. Consider Conservative initiatives in the 1870s: creation of a national police force—(the future RCMP) and the National Policy of imposing tariffs and underwriting the Canadian Pacific Railway. The first ensured the peaceful, orderly settlement of the West, while the latter created a national economic community. On both counts, this was quite a contrast to America's "wild West," where vigilantes and gunslingers roamed and where private lands, rather than Crown lands, prevail to this day. Although all of Canada's parties borrowed from traditional tory ideology in some way, by the 1990s it was largely a spent force. After the defeat of Diefenbaker conservatism in the 1960s, Conservatives more than Liberals unabashedly gave higher priority to liberal individualism than to collective community efforts. Surveys of party activists confirmed these outlooks. At the beginning of the century, the Liberals had been the leading advocates of free trade with the United States; by late century, the Conservatives had displaced them. Conservatives who had once looked to Britain as a social model increasingly looked to the United States, the traditional model for the Liberals.

Canadian socialism synthesized antithetical aspects of liberalism and toryism. It combined the rationalist-egalitarian outlook of classical liberalism with the organic-collectivist outlook of classical conservatism or toryism. The CCF–NDP was founded, led by, and voted for by turn-of-the-century British-born immigrants carrying Fabian socialist and labourist ideological baggage. Like the early Conservatives, they rejected America's model of "rugged individualism," and like the post–Second World War Liberals they embraced Keynesianism and welfare liberalism. They urged Canadian emulation of the Scandinavian welfare state model, something neither Liberals nor Conservatives cared for.

FIGURE 11.4 **Defining Principles and Linkages among Classical Ideological Traditions**

TORYISM ←——— *antithesis* ———→ LIBERALISM

- TRADITION
- AUTHORITY/ORDER
- HIERARCHY
- COMMUNITY PRIORITY
- COOPERATION

- REASON
- FREEDOM
- EQUALITY
- INDIVIDUAL PRIORITY
- COMPETITION

- COMMUNITY PRIORITY
- COOPERATION

- REASON
- FREEDOM
- EQUALITY

synthesis

SOCIALISM

Tories, liberals, and socialists may all support the same policy, (e.g., universal medicare), but for quite different reasons. To identify ideological dispositions, rationale is more critical than policy, for it deals with the "why" rather than merely the "how," with values rather than procedures or mechanics. A classical conservative might endorse medicare out of a sense of noblesse oblige. A liberal might do so in the cause of providing equality of opportunity, so that misfortune unrelated to an individual's skills or ambitions—such as illness—not be a penalty in the rat race of the market economy. A socialist would justify medicare in terms of equality of condition, as a redistributive mechanism: from each according to his abilities to each according to his needs.

Looking at a party's social base of support, rather than the superstructure of its ideas, we detect another factor in Liberal success. After the failure of the Conservative Macdonald–Cartier alliance that had created Canada's duality, the Liberals enjoyed massive support among French Canadians (and still do outside Quebec) until 1984. The support was not so much ideological in the sense of left versus right as it was cultural, rooted in historical experience and leadership. The Conservatives were perceived by the French as the party of the English, the executioners of Louis Riel, as the party of British racism and imperialism, conscription and antipathy to the spread of the French language and culture. The Liberals, in contrast, offered French-Canadian leaders—Laurier, St. Laurent, Trudeau—and were the party espousing bilingualism and respect for Canadian dualism. While English Canadians divided their support more equally between the two major traditional parties, Quebec offered a bedrock base of support for the Liberals.

Regional, religious, ethnic, and linguistic divisions play prominent roles in party fortunes. With an eye to Europe's experience, Canadian social scientists looked for the eclipse of these traditional cleavages as determinants of party support. They anticipated—some eagerly—the triumph of class voting. According to a "modernization thesis" proffered by social scientists, the maturation and development of society and economy over time should induce class consciousness. Class divisions would then overshadow the traditional cleavages, feeding the rise of a modern party system with rival left and right parties engaged in a democratic class struggle, and offering creative, principled, political choices to replace tribal and sectional ones. Although evidence of class politics was to be had here and there—in Winnipeg and Vancouver, for example—in the overall national scheme the class variable appeared highly problematic.

A long-established interpretation of Canada's parties sees them as brokers, as mediating agents bringing together and accommodating diverse interests and regions. According to the "brokerage theory," successful parties downplay ideology and build a coalition of forces that cut across societal cleavages—East–West, English–French, labour–capital, rural–urban, and so on. Canada, so brokerage party logic goes, is too heterogeneous a state to sustain the kind of ideologically driven configuration of parties found in the relatively homogeneous states of Britain and Western Europe. In the 1980s, Conservatives succeeded in cobbling together an entente of Quebec nationalists and English-Canadian (especially western Canadian) social and fiscal conservatives. Lengthy Liberal success before that was similarly but somewhat differently constructed, combining

Quebec's votes with those of English Canada's metropolitan centres and those of the non-Charter (non-British, non-French) ethnic minorities.

BEFORE AND BEYOND THE 1993 ELECTION

The 1993 election simultaneously crystallized regional tendencies in the party system and demonstrated the continuing strength of the brokerage party par excellence, the Liberals. Reform won the overwhelming majority of seats in Alberta and British Columbia, while the BQ won the overwhelming majority of francophone ridings in Quebec. The Conservative axis that had secured majority voting support in both Quebec and Alberta in the 1980s was dead. Once again, the modernization thesis proved wanting. The outcome was concurrently traditional (a Liberal victory with regional cleavages reflected in the strength of regionally based parties) and postmodern (reflected in the emaciation of the traditional left and right, the NDP and the Conservatives). What accounted for the astonishing outcome? What does it tell of the past and portend of the future?

The Liberal victory—winning 60 percent of the seats with 41 percent of the popular vote—was a sign of continuity and constancy. As have most elections since 1921, the first-past-the-post electoral system produced a stable majority government built with only a plurality of votes. The Liberal victory was consistent with the pattern of the past; the Liberals have been the natural governing party for two-thirds of the past century. There is, moreover, an apostolic flavour to their party leadership, suggestive of the cadre model: Jean Chrétien served in the cabinet of Trudeau, who served in the cabinet of Pearson, who served in the cabinet of St. Laurent, who served in the cabinet of King, who served in the cabinet of Laurier, who served in the cabinet of Mackenzie, the first Liberal prime minister in the 1870s. The Liberal triumph was also consistent with an apparent cyclical pattern. In 1984, the unpopular governing Liberals replaced Trudeau with Turner, who overnight took his party to first in the polls. He called an election, and the Liberals were reduced to their worst-ever showing. In 1993, the unpopular governing Conservatives replaced Mulroney with Campbell, who overnight took her party to first in the polls. She called an election, and the Conservatives too were reduced to their worst-ever showing. The lesson is an old one: opposition parties are not so much elected on their platforms as governing parties are defeated on their stewardship.

But what caused the severe jolt to the party system as manifested in the rise of the BQ and Reform? The "free trade" election of 1988 demonstrated that parties may stake out unambiguously clear policy distinctions in some areas. It simultaneously demonstrated that parties may adopt congruent positions in other areas. In that election's aftermath, the national political agenda was dominated by a constitutional-reform enterprise that had gone unquestioned and undebated during the election. The failure of the Meech Lake and Charlottetown accords was devastating to the long-established party system because the long-established parties had refused to divide on the issue, to provide any kind of sharp alternatives. Those who objected, for whatever reasons, had no outlet in the traditional parties and the established party system. The only parties that spoke against the ill-fated constitutional misadventure—and for quite different reasons—were the BQ and Reform. Ironically, their popularity in the polls did not rise during the 1992 referendum campaign. Nevertheless, they firmly established their ground and their profile. In contrast, *none* of the first ministers who were signatories to the 1987 Meech Lake Accord were still in power in the spring of 1994.

The 1993 election proved to be Round Two of the referendum. The Conservatives paid in both Quebec and the West for their failed attempt to appease Quebec's nationalism. The NDP paid for being in league with the major parties, indicating that it no longer offered a clear alternative to the Tweedledum Conservatives and Tweedledee Liberals. It tumbled from its best-ever showing, in 1988 (over 20 percent of the vote and 43 seats), to its worst-ever showing (less than 7 percent and 9 seats). Many NDP supporters, determined to defeat the Conservatives, defected to the Liberals, with whom they were ideologically closest in English Canada, and to the BQ in Quebec, where the NDP vote collapsed, falling from 14 percent in 1988 to a paltry 1.5 percent. The Liberals won so decisively not so much on their own merits but because the rise of Reform and the BQ undermined the Conservatives, the only other party that could win.

At the start of the 20th century, Canada had a simple and straightforward two-party system: the Liberals and Conservatives captured 99 percent of the votes and all of the seats in the 1900 election. As the century draws to a close, the continuing ability of the two old parties to draw *half* the votes and *half* the seats will be in doubt. The federal Conservatives may not disappear, but they may never regain their former glory. What will contribute to sustaining them are their well-ensconced provincial kin and their senators. The federal NDP also appears to be on the edge of irrelevance; at least until 1995, however, the party continues to govern 52 percent of Canadians at the provincial level. The contributions of the Conservatives and the NDP, moreover, are now deeply embedded in the national political culture. While it may turn out that the 1993 election was an aberration, more likely it represented a fundamental realignment of the Canadian party system and national politics.

FURTHER READINGS

Brodie, Janine, and Jane Jenson. *Crisis, Challenge and Change: Party and Class in Canada Revisited.* Ottawa: Carleton University Press, 1988.

Carty, R. Kenneth, Lynda Erickson, and Donald E. Blake, eds. *Leaders and Parties in Canadian Politics: Experiences of the Provinces.* Toronto: Harcourt Brace Jovanovich, 1992.

Christian, William, and Colin Campbell. *Political Parties and Ideologies in Canada.* 2nd ed. Toronto: McGraw-Hill Ryerson, 1983.

Duverger, Maurice. *Political Parties: Their Organization and Activity in the Modern State.* 2nd ed. trans. B. North and R. North. London: Methuen, 1959.

Gagnon, Alain G., and A. Brian Tanguay, eds. *Canadian Parties in Transition: Discourse, Organization, and Representation.* Scarborough, Ont.: Nelson Canada, 1989.

Horowitz, Gad. "Conservatism, Liberalism, and Socialism in Canada: An Interpretation," *Canadian Journal of Economics and Political Science* 32, no. 2 (May 1966).

Perlin, George, ed. *Party Democracy in Canada.* Scarborough, Ont.: Prentice-Hall Canada, 1988.

Thorburn, Hugh G., ed. *Party Politics in Canada.* 6th ed. Scarborough, Ont.: Prentice-Hall Canada, 1991.

Wearing, Joseph. *Strained Relations: Canadian Parties and Voters.* Toronto: McClelland and Stewart, 1988.

Althoug   of recent times,
the noti   ancient one. In
the Athens of 500 B.C., an assembly of citizens elected generals and voted
on numerous policy questions. Republican Rome operated an elaborate
system of voting assemblies that elected consuls, tribunes, and many other
officials. Medieval city-states such as Florence and Venice developed very
complex structures of government in which officials were chosen by a
combination of election and selection by lot.[1]

One of humanity's most ancient political institutions, elections have
become virtually omnipresent in nations of the modern world, popular
because they serve a multiplicity of functions for almost everybody connected with them, as well as for the political system that sponsors them.
Whatever complaints are registered about the time they take, the expense
they involve, the choices they present, or the results they produce, elections are vital to the image that almost every country wishes to present to
the rest of the world. Whether they are perceived to be "meaningful" or
not, few would truthfully wish to do away with them altogether.

Impressive catalogues of functions performed by elections may be
compiled on all levels of analysis. For the *political system,* elections fulfill
at the outset a recruitment function by providing an orderly way to choose
the rulers or elites that govern the society. By facilitating grouping within
the political system, elections participate in the creation and maintenance
of political parties. We have already mentioned that elections operate as
symbols through which a country signals to the rest of the world its democratic nature. This legitimation function is also important within the bounds
of the political system, in that elections generate support for that system
(providing the result is seen as having been fairly arrived at) as well as a
certain amount of legitimacy for the resulting government. Elections also
perform an important political socialization function by focusing attention
on the political system and thereby providing citizens with opportunities to
learn about it. An election is one of the few genuine communal experiences shared by people in a diverse country, and simple participation in
the same activity can be integrative for the system as a whole.

Political parties, for their part, are served by elections, which provide a ready-made occasion for a party to build or renew its internal orga-

nization. In some cases, elections may perform the function of allowing competing party elites to resolve internal power relationships and strategic conflicts within the party.[2] Elections can also provide the parties with policy guidelines or parameters, depending on how politicians interpret the impact of particular issues on the election result. The messages to be gleaned from elections range from very specific policies that were accepted or rejected along with the party, to more general philosophical or ideological approaches to governing. Finally, the result of an election legitimizes the status of a party, whether it be that of victor, official Opposition, major or minor party.

For *individuals*, elections serve the function of forging a link between them and the political system. This connection can foster a sense of support for the system and a sense of voter efficacy. It has been suggested that elections protect individuals by giving them control over those in power and a "voice in their own affairs." Elections facilitate the socialization function by educating and informing individuals about politics, as well as by affecting the partisanship they hold. Elections can also give individuals an opportunity to make a political statement, and to boost their egos by impressing others with their political knowledge or cynicism.[3] Finally, political participation, stimulated by the election context, may advance a variety of functions, ranging from direct personal gain and advancement, to ego-identity formation, to satisfaction derived from working with other people.[4]

In keeping with the foregoing division of the functions of elections, analysis by political scientists takes place at both the level of the individual and the level of the political system, and includes as well a considerable number of studies on the internal operations of political parties. The individual-level analysis attempts to explain voting behaviour, more precisely how individuals arrive at their decision to support one party or another at a given time. Researchers in this field have carried out numerous surveys in order to amass the data they need to test their theories. The less common system-level studies are generally of two types. The first involves intensive study of the "context" of a particular election—the party platforms and activities, the media coverage, the events of the campaign, the patterns of the results, and so on.[5] The second involves the use of survey data to explain the outcomes of particular elections. We will explore this subject further after examining some aspects of individual voting behaviour in Canada.

VOTING BEHAVIOUR IN CANADA

The fact that elections perform a variety of functions for the individuals who vote in them would lead us to expect considerable diversity in their reasons for casting ballots in any given election. All indications we have from the National Election Studies, which are conducted after Canadian federal elections, are that this expectation is easily met.[6] The evidence from these studies shows that virtually any shorthand explanation of why Canadians vote is bound to be correct for only a portion of the electorate. Thus, one should be highly suspicious of the generality implied by such interpretations as "Canadians rejected wage and price controls in 1974," "Pierre Trudeau's unpopularity led to the Liberal defeat in 1979," "Brian Mulroney won the 1984 election," "Canadians provided a mandate for free trade in 1988," or "Voters rejected traditional politics in 1993." None of the factors underlying each of these interpretations produced the election result by itself, or even came close to doing so.

Rather than being some monolithic entity, the Canadian electorate comprises subgroups of people who vote for a myriad of different reasons. Some people say they are voting for some the party as a whole, either because of a longstanding loyalty or a newfound conviction that it is time to give a new lot of politicians a chance to run the country. For some voters, the comparative evaluation of party leaders is a major factor in their decision to vote, whereas for others the decisive factor is the candidate from the local riding. Voters cite a wide variety of different issues, some of longstanding concern (e.g., unemployment), others specific to certain elections (free trade in 1988 but not in 1993).

The question of the importance of issues to individual voting decisions has long interested political scientists. Because the electoral process involves decisions made by the general public, and therefore by many people who score low in political information or interest, there has always been scope for charges that voting decisions are not being taken for the "right reasons." Voters are accused of deciding on the basis of personality or image, or unthinking party loyalty, rather than on "the issues." This kind of debate often includes questions about the extent of "rational voting," that is, voting on the basis of a reasoned consideration of the issues important to the voter. It does not seem profitable to engage here in a discussion of whether Canadians vote rationally or not (it would seem even less advisable to take a position on just what constitutes a rational motive for voting choice in the first place). It is possible to state, however, that in Canada a considerable amount of voting does take place for issue-related reasons.

The extent to which voting choice is motivated by issue concerns can be seen more clearly if we look at how voters rank four factors— leaders, candidates, parties, and issues—in terms of their importance to their vote decisions. To avoid setting up a direct choice between issues and these other factors in people's minds (we felt that the number citing issues might be artificially high since voting on the issues is a more socially approved answer), survey respondents were asked to choose among the three factors of party, leader, or candidate, and then asked whether or not there was an issue basis to their choice. The percentage of people who ranked the four factors as important in the last three federal elections is shown in Table 12.1. As the table indicates, the party as a whole emerged as the most important factor in all three elections. Interestingly, choice of this factor is increasing with time, while the party leader factor has become less important to voting choice in recent years. Although the table does not go back that far, earlier data show that the importance of party leader to voting choice was much greater during the Trudeau years, when it rivalled the party factor for top spot.[7]

TABLE 12.1 **Most Important Factors in Voting**

1993 Election

Party Leaders		Local Candidates		Party as a Whole	
22%		21%		57%	
Issue	Personal	Issue	Personal	Issue	General
Basis	Qualities	Basis	Qualities	Basis	Approach
62%	38%	52%	48%	54%	46%

1988 Election

Party Leaders		Local Candidates		Party as a Whole	
20%		27%		53%	
Issue	Personal	Issue	Personal	Issue	General
Basis	Qualities	Basis	Qualities	Basis	Approach
71%	29%	57%	43%	57%	43%

1984 Election

Party Leaders		Local Candidates		Party as a Whole	
30%		21%		49%	
Issue	Personal	Issue	Personal	Issue	General
Basis	Qualities	Basis	Qualities	Basis	Approach
56%	44%	46%	54%	37%	63%

Note: Population weights applied.

SOURCES: 1993 INSIGHT CANADA RESEARCH POST ELECTION SURVEY; 1984 NATIONAL ELECTION STUDY; AND 1988 REINTERVIEW OF 1984 NATIONAL ELECTION STUDY SAMPLE.

There is a certain amount of variation between elections, as well, in the number of people who declared there was an issue basis to their choice of party. While less than half of those citing party as the most important factor in their voting choice declared there was an issue basis to this choice in 1984, more than half did so in 1988 and 1993. This reflects the enhanced importance of issues in recent elections, particularly free trade in 1988 and job creation and deficit reduction in 1993. Similarly, the number of people reporting an issue basis to choice of leader or candidate as most important to them rose substantially in 1988, and stayed high in 1993. In Canadian elections, a majority of the electorate now reports an issue basis for their voting decision, a finding that refutes glib assertions that elections are nothing more than popularity contests between the leaders.

Academic surveys on voting behaviour show that a large proportion of reasons for voting are distinctly short term in nature. Leaders and candidates are subject to frequent change; indeed, in 1993 Reform leader Preston Manning was the only holdover from the previous election, and a large majority of elected MPs were new to the House of Commons. Issues can also vary considerably, both in substance and urgency, from one election to, the next. Although Canadians are by no means bereft of general images of, and loyalties to, the political parties, a majority claim to make up their minds at each election on the basis of short-term factors operative at the time.

This picture of the Canadian electorate is supported by research findings on the nature of partisanship in this country. A majority of voters develop party loyalties that are either weak, changeable over time, or different at the two levels of the federal system. All of these factors contribute to the *flexible* partisanship that characterizes the link between about 60 percent of Canadian voters and the federal political parties. Thus, the question "To which party do you feel closest?" may elicit different answers from the same respondent if repeated at various intervals over a period of time.

Several facets of the political culture contribute to the flexibility of voter ties to political parties. The most basic is that Canadian political culture is relatively apolitical. While Canadians are moderately interested in politics, this interest does not translate for most into substantial political involvement. The amount of detailed political information possessed by the average Canadian is low. Studies of children's political learning, or socialization, show a relatively weak transference of preference for a political party from parent to child. Such transmission of enduring partisan ties from generation to generation is not the norm because these feelings may not be strongly or persistently held in the adult "socializer." As a result, children are less likely to develop such feelings for themselves, and, in turn a culture is perpetuated in which partisanship is not strongly held or is changeable.

Canadians are not often content with being apolitical; in many cases they are downright antipolitical. In the 1974 national survey interview, the respondents were handed a blank map of Canada and asked to "write in five words or phrases which best describe politics in Canada." The replies revealed a considerable degree of negativism toward almost everything associated with the political system.[8] In particular, the public feels negatively about political parties and politicians; ratings of them after the 1988 election were lower across the board than at any time since such surveys began. Given such an atmosphere, it is no wonder that large numbers of people are unwilling to stick with "their party" in perpetuity. When those people who changed their partisanship were asked their reasons for doing so, more talked of the negative qualities of the party they were changing from than mentioned the positive qualities of the party they were changing to. It was not hard to foresee that when 1993 presented an opportunity to choose new parties, many voters would do so.

Because of the conflicts and regional loyalties associated with its founding and development as a nation, Canada is governed by an extremely complex federal system. While most people have a basic understanding of the constitutionally established functions performed by the various actors of the federal system, it would be unrealistic to expect detailed knowledge of intergovernmental relations on the part of the mass public. Lack of knowledge begets lack of interest. Further, the image of conflict surrounding the Canadian federal system contributes to the general public mood of exasperation with, and cynicism about, the political process.

Every Canadian except for those resident in the Northwest Territories is a member of a political community that possesses two systems of political parties. This situation does not necessarily further complicate the individual's political world, since in some areas those party systems are for all intents and purposes the same. For example, the provincial Liberals and Conservatives in Nova Scotia are really the same parties as their federal namesakes. In several provinces, however, this is not the case. In British Columbia and Quebec, political parties that have no counterpart at the federal level have, in recent years, formed governments. In other provinces, such as Ontario, parties have different competitive positions at the two levels, and there are different strategic choices involved in casting votes.

Those whose ties to political parties are flexible are more likely to shift their votes from one election to the next, though only a minority of them do so in normal times. The factors that influence such partisans, particularly those who switch their votes, are predominantly short-term in nature—liking a political party at a particular time, positive (or negative) feelings toward a leader or candidate, concern about a particular issue, or some combination of these factors. We can pinpoint further types of flexible partisans who will be influenced by different factors if we subdivide them on the basis of their political interest. About one-third of the electorate are flexible partisans who have a low degree of interest in politics, while just over one-quarter are flexible partisans with a high degree of political interest. It is this flexible higher-interest group that gives relatively heavy weight to political issues in determining its voting choice; the parties aim to appeal to this group with their issue-oriented campaigns. The flexible lower-interest group, on the other hand, pays less attention to issues and more to general images of leaders and parties; the personal appeal of leaders tends to influence this group.

The flexibility of partisanship in Canada and the tendency for voting decisions to be determined by short-term considerations relating to parties, issues, leaders, and candidates active at any given time has meant that the social cleavages sometimes thought to form enduring loyalties in the population have relatively little influence over how people vote. One of these cleavages—religion—can still be discerned in voting patterns (e.g., in the tendency of Roman Catholics, particularly those outside Quebec, to vote Liberal). Overall, however, analysts see the relationship between religion and voting decisions as weak (and continuing to decline) or as impossibly difficult to explain in modern circumstances.[9] Studies have consistently found that another important cleavage—social class—has very little relationship to voting choice in Canadian federal elections, though there is more connection between the two variables in some provincial elections.[10] The votes of Canadians, then, are not heavily "preordained" by social or demographic factors, just as they are not predetermined by durable party loyalties.

One major consequence of this situation is that election campaigns can be of major importance in affecting election outcomes. Over half the electorate claims to arrive at a voting decision during the campaign period, while about one-fifth say they decide during the last week of the campaign or on election day itself. Given the short-term nature of the factors that influence many voting decisions, and the potential impact of the campaign and its events, the Canadian electorate is highly volatile. The potential for dramatic swings in election results is always present. However, it takes a particular constellation of factors to make them occur; it is to this subject that we now turn our attention.

ELECTION OUTCOMES

It may seem anomalous that a political system in which the electorate is characterized by such volatility appears so stable at the aggregate level of federal election results that it has at times been referred to as a one-party dominant system. The Liberal Party, or "Government Party" as it has been called, has been in power for much of the 20th century, with the Conservatives forming governments only under Borden (1911–20, part of which was a wartime Unionist government), Meighen (1926), Bennett (1930–35), Diefenbaker (1957–63), Clark (1979–80), and Mulroney (1984–93). With the collapse of the Conservative Party in 1993, observers are already talking about a Liberal dynasty stretching into the next century.

The resolution of the apparent paradox between individual volatility and aggregate stability lies in our ability to differentiate between the effects of electoral conversion and electoral replacement, and to plot the patterns of the "vote flows" related to them. *Conversion* involves the extent of vote switching among those who are members of the "permanent electorate," that is, people who are already eligible voters and who can be counted on to vote every time. All parties, through their campaign appeals, try to persuade those who voted for some other party in the previous election to switch their allegiance in this one. We have seen that the potential for such conversion is high, since the incidence of durable party loyalty is relatively low. *Replacement,* in contrast, is the impact on the result that is brought to bear by newly eligible voters, as well as by "transient" voters who do not turn out in every election. The impact of the transient vote will be determined by the difference in behaviour between those leaving the electorate and those returning to the electorate following a past abstention. The overall success of the federal Liberal Party has been achieved because, whatever the patterns of conversion in any given election, the party has usually gained through the process of electoral replacement.

Canadian elections held in the last two decades illustrate how conversion and replacement frequently operated to the Liberals' benefit.[11] In 1974, the Liberals were able to increase their overall popular vote from 1972 and win enough seats to form the majority government that had eluded them two years earlier. However, if conversion had been the only process operating, the result of the 1974 election would actually have been *worse* for the Liberals than the 1972 one. This is because vote switching from 1972 to 1974 among members of the permanent electorate favoured the Conservatives. The process of electoral replacement, however, worked quite differently from 1972 to 1974. The Liberals won the bulk of the young voters who became newly eligible in 1974, and also the majority of support from transient voters who had not gone to the polls in 1972. Thus, because those who did not vote in the previous election (either through choice or lack of eligibility) favoured the Liberal Party by a wide margin, the party's losses through vote switching were more than offset.

In determining the outcome of the 1979 election, in which the Conservatives came close to forming a majority government, conversion and replacement again operated differently. Over 8 percent of the 1979 electorate switched from the Liberals to the PCs, whereas only 1.5 percent went the other way. In addition, the Conservatives gained slightly from switches between their party and the NDP, a better performance than they had managed in 1974. Once again, however, electoral replacement was the PCs' Achilles' heel. They did manage to win a slight plurality of the transient vote, important because of the high turnout in 1979. Newly eligible voters, on the other hand, still favoured the Liberals by a substantial margin, and this new-voter group was particularly large in 1979 because of the five-year interval since the previous election. Because of the effects of the high post–World War II birthrate, almost 2.5 million new voters had come of age since the previous election. The Liberals' ability to retain their appeal to this group, therefore, reduced the magnitude of their 1979 defeat; conversely, the Conservatives' unpopularity with the same group denied that party not only majority-government status but also the opportunity to renew their support among the young.

In the 1980 election held a scant few months later, the processes of conversion and replacement worked in the same direction, favouring the Liberals. The Liberals showed a net benefit in vote switching with the PCs and the NDP, and also regained their edge among transient voters moving into the electorate from a nonvoting stance in 1979. Similarly, since voting turnout in 1980 was down from 1979, it is relevant to note that the Conservatives suffered disproportionately from the 1980 abstention of voters who favoured them a year earlier.

By 1984, voter dissatisfaction with the Trudeau and Turner regimes finally caught up with the Liberal Party. The factors of electoral conversion and replacement both operated strongly in the same direction, away from that party. The proportion of the total electorate switching to the Conservatives from a 1980 Liberal vote was almost as high as that remaining with the Liberals (13.4 percent versus 15 percent). Similarly, transient voters entering the electorate following a 1980 abstention favoured the Conservatives by a wide margin, as did newly eligible voters by a narrower margin. The resulting landslide gave the Conservative Party one of its few solid majority governments in the 20th century.

The 1988 election presented a different scenario. As often happened when the Liberals were in power, vote switching went against the Conservative government. Although the differences between those abandoning the Tories and those attracted to them were not overwhelming, they were consistent. The Tories lost voters to the Liberals, the NDP, and the new Reform Party. The Conservatives managed to win the 1988 election because their margin of victory in 1984 had been so overwhelming that they could afford to lose votes through electoral conversion and still survive comfortably. Second, however, the PCs were able to win a plurality of transient and newly eligible voters, suggesting a tendency for these groups to support incumbent governments unless the overall electorate is in a mood for massive change.

Table 12.2 documents the patterns of electoral conversion and replacement that occurred between the 1988 and 1993 federal elections. As the summary indicates, over 40 percent of the total electorate consisted of those who changed their votes between these two elections. Conservatives who stayed with their party from 1988 to 1993 were fewer in number than former Tories who switched to the Liberals, or those who chose to vote Reform. In Quebec, a further substantial percentage switched their vote from Conservative to Bloc Québécois. Nationally, the NDP lost slightly more of their 1988 voters to the Liberals than they retained for themselves, and another sizable group to the Reform Party. The strong Bloc and Reform showing meant that the proportion of people changing their behaviour between 1988 and 1993 was likely the largest in Canadian history.

TABLE 12.2 Canadian Electoral Behaviour, 1988–1993

1993 Voting Behaviour

1988 Vote/ Status	Liberal	PC	NDP	Reform	BQ	Other	Did Not Vote
Liberal	18.2	1.3	.7	2.2	1.5	.3	1.8
PC	9.5	7.8	1.2	8.5	4.9	.4	3.7
NDP	4.2	1.3	4.1	2.3	.9	.8	2.2
Reform	—	.1	—	.9	—	—	—
Other	—	.1	.1	.2	.5	.3	.1
Did Not Vote	1.8	.5	—	1.3	.4	.1	4.8
Not Eligible	3.6	.6	.3	1.2	1.1	.1	4.0

100%

Note: The entire table adds to 100%. N= 934

Summary

Voted Same Party	Switched Vote	Previous Voters Not Voting	Previous Non-Voters Voting	New Voters
31.3%	49.9%	7.7%	4.4%	11.0%

SOURCE: INSIGHT CANADA RESEARCH POSTELECTION SURVEY.

The table also shows a reduced voter turnout in 1993. It can be seen that 1988 Conservative and NDP voters who decided not to vote in 1993 were more numerous than 1988 Liberal voters who did the same. Of the three major parties that contested the election, only for the Liberals was there an approximate equivalence between 1988 voters who decided not to vote this time and previous nonvoters who did vote in 1993; the Liberals were thus able to neutralize the turnout factor. Finally, that party gained substantially from the voting choices made by newly eligible, mostly young, voters in 1993. More new voters went to the Liberals than to all the other parties combined.

A major reason for the electoral success of the federal Liberals in this century has to do with the kind of political issues that emerge in Canadian elections. More than any other party, the Liberals have managed to develop political issues that can affect an election *outcome,* as opposed to simply affecting a number of individual voters. This distinction may not be immediately apparent, but it is extremely important if elections are to be analyzed as political events. An issue can affect an individual's vote simply by being important to that particular voter. To affect an election outcome, however, an issue must meet three conditions. First, an issue must be salient to an appreciable number of people—if few people think it is important they are not likely to act on it. Second, an issue must have a "skewed" distribution of opinion, which is to say people must be generally for or against it; if voters are split on the general desirability of something like the Free Trade Agreement, as they were in 1988, then any shift of votes to one party on the basis of that issue is likely to be offset by a countervailing shift away from that party of those who are opposed to its position. Third, an issue position must be disproportionately linked to one party in the electorate's perception. If no one party is preferred overall on an issue, then even if the voters consider the issue to be important to their individual decisions, their voting behaviour will be unlikely to benefit any one party. In this case, even a very important issue may not produce an electoral victor.

Political parties have difficulty finding economic issues that meet the above three criteria and that can therefore influence the outcome of an election in their favour. When general economic problems are raised as election issues—such as inflation (1974), the energy supply (1980), and unemployment (1984)—many voters recognize their importance, but no one party is seen as having all the solutions. When parties propose specific policies, such as wage and price controls (1974) or the Free Trade Agreement (1988), strong contingents of voters array themselves on each side. The Liberal Party has managed, however, to meet the three conditions on a series of constitutional issues, including national unity and bilingualism. In the 1993 election, the Liberals were seen (particularly outside Quebec but also by a significant number of voters in Quebec) as the party that could best keep Canada together. The Liberals also managed to create a specific economic issue in 1993—the "jobs plan"—which influenced the election outcome in their favour. The future of the Liberal Party will be closely linked with its ability to persuade the public that it is the one party that can appeal to both English Canada and French Canada, that can find solutions to constitutional problems, and that can be trusted with the stewardship of the economy. The demonstrated volatility of the Canadian electorate will make this a difficult task.

CONCLUSION

If we return to consider some of the major functions of elections referred to at the beginning of this chapter, it is apparent that federal elections in Canada perform some of these functions much better than others. Recruitment, for example, is reasonably well served; each election produces the requisite number of leaders to operate the ministries. However, the fact that the strength of the parties is often highly variable across regions can affect their performance of another function—namely, creating support for the political system and legitimizing it in the eyes of its citizens. The 1993 election result leaves the federal government open to charges that it represents certain parts of the country at the expense of others. Those who supported the Reform Party and the Bloc Québécois were not all protesting either the operations of the federal system or the viability of the country; however, there is no doubt that the election allowed many negative sentiments to be expressed about both. Those concerned about the survival of Canada as a federal country sometimes find it difficult to summon up the act of faith that allows them to argue that the system support and continuity implied in the simple conduct of federal elections is more important than the pattern of particular results.

We have also noted that elections perform functions for the political parties themselves. They give parties opportunities to revive and reestablish their organizations; since many of them exist primarily for the purpose of contesting elections these events are a *sine qua non*. With regard to the proposed function of establishing policy parameters for the parties, or sorting out the specific policies they will have a mandate to enact, the Canadian election system does not perform very well. This is partly because parties often seek to avoid specific policy stands during election campaigns, for these positions usually alienate as many voters as they attract. Even if specific policies are proposed, recent Canadian history shows that parties rarely feel bound by them. During the 1974 campaign, for example, the Liberals fought strenuously against the idea of wage and price controls, and then promptly introduced them once reelected. On free trade, the Mulroney government turned from opponents to proponents in the 1984–88 period, and one of the first acts of the new Liberal government in 1993 was to accept the free trade-legislation it had battled so fiercely a short time before. This tendency of parties in power means that elections provide little opportunity for the public to affect policy; it damages the credibility of politicians and increases political cynicism among the population.

Finally, with regard to serving functions for individuals, elections also produce mixed results. We can agree only partially to the suggestion that elections give people a sense of control over their own affairs and a sense of efficacy in their dealings with government. Most Canadians are not very confident that they can understand and influence the political system, and many are quite cynical about the possibility of producing any significant change through elections (see Chapters 6 and 7). This situation may be mitigated somewhat by the feeling on the part of most Canadians that neither their general well-being nor their standard of living is greatly affected by government. Thus, the feeling that elections accomplish little manifests itself not in rage and destructiveness, but rather in a bemused detachment from the whole political process—a symptom of the apolitical political culture we noted earlier. Some observers have argued that this situation is, on balance, beneficial in that elites are free to govern and to implement policies that might have been more vigorously opposed in a more politicized society. That may be true, but in a country that depends heavily on politics to negotiate solutions to its numerous problems there are also inherent dangers in having a public so divorced from, and cynical about, the political process.

NOTES

1. These and other examples of ancient elections are discussed in Jon H. Pammett, "A Framework for the Comparative Analysis of Elections Across Time and Space," *Electoral Studies* 7, no. 2 (1988): 125–42.

2. Primary elections in the United States are an obvious example of this; however, it also takes place in other contexts. See Jane Jenson, "Strategic Divisions within the French Left: The Case of the First Elections to the European Parliament," *Revue d'integration europeene/Journal of European Integration* (September 1980).

3. Norman D. Palmer, *Elections and Political Development* (Durham, N.C.: Duke University Press, 1975), p. 87.

4. Jon H. Pammett, "Adolescent Political Activity as a Learning Experience: The Action-Trudeau Campaign of 1968," in Jon H. Pammett and Michael Whittington, eds., *Foundations of Political Culture: Political Socialization in Canada* (Toronto: Macmillan, 1976), pp. 160–94.

5. See Alan Frizzell, Jon Pammett, and Anthony Westell, *The Canadian General Election of 1993* (Ottawa: Carleton University Press, 1994). Other books, on the 1988 and 1984 elections, by the same authors are included in this series. For an influential early study, see John Meisel, *The Canadian General Election of 1957* (Toronto: University of Toronto Press, 1962).

6. Large national surveys have been conducted after or during all Canadian federal elections since 1965, with the exception of 1972. Extensive use is made of this data in two books by Harold D. Clarke, Jane Jenson, Lawrence LeDuc, and Jon H. Pammett: *Political Choice in Canada* (Toronto: McGraw-Hill Ryerson, 1979); and *Absent Mandate: Interpreting Change in Canadian Elections* (Toronto: Gage, 1991). For the 1988 federal election, see Richard Johnston, André Blais, Henry E. Brady, and Jean Crête, *Letting the People Decide: Dynamics of a Canadian Election* (Montreal and Kingston: McGill-Queen's University Press, 1992).

7. Clarke et al., *Political Choice in Canada*, p. 334.

8. The replies are analyzed in considerable detail in ch. 1 of ibid.

9. See William Irvine, "Explaining the Religious Basis of Partisanship in Canada," *Canadian Journal of Political Science* 7 (1974): 560–63; John Meisel, "Bizarre Aspects of a Vanishing Act: The Religious Cleavage and Voting in Canada," in John Meisel, *Working Papers in Canadian Politics*, 2nd rev. ed. (Montreal and Kingston: McGill-Queen's University Press, 1975), pp. 253–84; and Richard Johnston, "The Reproduction of the Religious Cleavage in Canadian Elections," *Canadian Journal of Political Science* 18 (1985): 99–114.

10. For a survey analysis of class and vote, and an extensive bibliography, see Jon H. Pammett, "Class Voting and Class Consciousness in Canada," *Canadian Review of Sociology and Anthropology* 24, no. 2 (1987): 269–90.

11. More complete analyses of the voting patterns in these elections may be found in Clarke et al., *Political Choice in Canada* and various editions of *Absent Mandate* by the same authors.

FURTHER READINGS

Beck, Murray J. *Pendulum of Power.* Toronto: Prentice-Hall, 1968. Gives accounts of Canadian election campaigns to 1968.

Clarke, Harold D., Jane Jenson, Lawrence LeDuc, and Jon H. Pammett. *Political Choice in Canada.* Toronto: McGraw-Hill Ryerson, 1979, and abridged edition, 1980. An extensive treatment of Canadian voting behaviour and partisanship.

———. *Absent Mandate: Interpreting Change in Canadian Elections.* Toronto: Gage, 1991. An analysis of voting behaviour and election outcomes through 1988. A new edition is forthcoming.

Courtney, John C., Peter MacKinnon, and David E. Smith, eds. *Drawing Boundaries: Legislatures, Courts and Electoral Values.* Saskatoon: Fifth House, 1992. Considers legal and ethical factors involved in constructing Canadian electoral boundaries.

Frizzell, Alan, Jon H. Pammett, and Anthony Westell. *The Canadian General Election of 1993.* Ottawa: Carleton University Press, 1994. Analyses of party strategy, media coverage, and voting behaviour in the 1993 election. Companion volumes on the 1988 and 1984 elections are also available in this series.

Gidengil, Elizabeth. "Canada Votes: A Quarter Century of Canadian Election Studies." *Canadian Journal of Political Science* 25 no. 2 (1992): 219–48. A thorough and balanced review of the use of election surveys in Canada. Numerous references make it very useful for students.

Johnston, Richard, André Blais, Henry E. Brady, and Jean Crête. *Letting the People Decide: Dynamics of a Canadian Election.* Montreal and Kingston: McGill-Queen's University Press, 1992. A detailed study of the 1988 election that focuses on the campaign dynamics.

Meisel, John. *Working Papers on Canadian Politics.* 2nd enlarged ed. Montreal and Kingston: McGill-Queen's University Press, 1975. A series of perceptive empirical essays on Canadian elections.

Regenstrief, Peter. *The Diefenbaker Interlude.* Toronto: Longmans, 1965. Based on the author's own polling during the Diefenbaker years. Many of the conclusions about Canadian voting behaviour in this book have stood the test of time.

Wearing, Joseph, ed. *The Ballot and Its Message: Voting in Canada.* Toronto: Copp Clark Pitman, 1991. A collection of important articles on Canadian voting behaviour by many leading authors in the field.

13 PRESSURE GROUPS: TALKING CHAMELEONS

A. Paul Pross

The most difficult of all government's tasks is communicating with the public. Despite the millions of words expended in public debate every day, modern governments have great difficulty finding out what the public wants and needs, and what it feels about the work that the state is already doing. Equally, although its payroll is laden with press officers, writers, and others skilled in the arts of communication, government has immense problems explaining itself to the public, reporting back to it, and persuading and leading it.

Pressure groups are one of three communications systems used by most modern states to overcome these problems. The other two are the internal apparatus of the government itself, such as the press officers and writers mentioned above, and the party system. Political parties are best equipped to transmit the demands and views of individuals and groups of individuals concerned about specific localities. This is because political parties tend to be built around an electoral system created to fill a legislature that is territorial or spatial in orientation—that is, each member represents the people who live in a specific area or constituency.

Pressure groups have become prominent because they are effective where parties fail. They can identify and articulate the views and needs of individuals who may live far apart but who share common interests. In modern society, with its interdependent economy, its multinational corporations, and its very large and specialized government bureaucracies, this sectoral approach of pressure groups is an essential complement to the spatial orientation of political parties. Even so, as we shall see later, the rapid growth and rising influence of pressure groups troubles many observers, some of whom feel that democratic government is threatened thereby.

Pressure groups are organizations whose members act together, attempting to influence public policy in order to promote their common interests.[1] Unlike political parties, they are not interested in directly wielding the power of the state, though sometimes a group representing a particularly large socioeconomic block will decide to transform itself into a political party, such as the Bloc Québécois. In general, pressure groups are interested in exerting influence and in persuading governments to accommodate the special interests of their members.

To achieve this, pressure groups have to be more than mere assemblages of people. Their members have to be organized, brought together in structured relationships with one another and dragooned into identifying and expressing their common interests. Pressure groups are consequently distinct, clearly identifiable elements in the body politic. While their chief role, as far as the political system is concerned, is to provide a network for policy communication, in the following paragraphs we shall see that they have several other functions as well.

Pressure groups are also very adaptable members of the polity—so adaptable, in fact, that we can use their structure and behaviour as a guide to charting the policy process in a particular political system. We cannot look at this aspect of pressure group life in great depth here, but we shall try to use it to draw some comparisons between the manner in which policy is made in Canada and the United States. Furthermore, we shall use our understanding of the adaptive behaviour of pressure groups to set out a theory that explains the day-to-day relationship between pressure groups and the policy system. Finally, we shall look at a couple of the very large issues raised by the growing influence of pressure groups in the policy system.

THE FUNCTIONS OF PRESSURE GROUPS

Whenever we try to set down precisely what it is that pressure groups do, we have to remember that, like most institutions, they are different things to different people. Leaving aside for the moment those who feel that pressure groups are a curse and an abomination, let us look briefly at the ways in which government officials and group members relate to them.

Most of us are unaware of the number of pressure groups we belong to. Because we join many associations in order to share our interests and concerns with others, we tend not to think of them as pressure groups. Each September, as Canadian universities resume classes, thousands of students pay dues to their campus student associations. Most of that money supports local campus activity that has nothing to do with politics, but some of it is channelled to provincial and national federations of student associations, which in turn devote considerable time and money to lobbying governments on such matters as tax breaks for students, university funding, tuition fees, student loans, and national or international issues that have pricked the conscience of the university community. Acquiring a university degree is a serious business, and, if government is to be deeply involved in education, we should expect student associations to act as pressure groups.

We do not expect our leisure associations to camp as regularly on the doorsteps of government, yet they are among the most active pressure groups to be found in Canada. For instance, many a rural politician has trembled as provincial legislatures have debated hunting and fishing legislation; game laws have often been the most hotly contended items on legislative agendas, and provincial associations of hunters and anglers have been slow to forget the transgressions of politicians who opposed their ideas. Similarly, associations of camping enthusiasts, naturalists, bird watchers, and wilderness buffs have a surprising degree of influence with government agencies, such as the Canadian Parks Service, that cater to their interests. In fact, the wilderness orientation of Canada's national parks system is in large part a reflection of the strength of this lobby.

These examples illustrate a basic point: very few pressure groups exist simply to influence government. Their members have joined to obtain some special benefit that each organization alone can offer. Yet, because government intrudes so much upon our daily lives, these associations become a very convenient vehicle for communicating with government. While most associations inevitably develop some capacity in this role, the members often only very grudgingly allow this to happen—lobbying governments is an expensive business. But as the need to express their views becomes more urgent, they hire consultants, undertake studies, appoint "government liaison officers," meet with officials and politicians, and generally join the babble of tongues that surrounds the policy process.

From the group members' point of view, then, the lobbying activities of their associations are first and foremost intended to communicate. People in government also see pressure groups in this light, though not always happily. Communication may take many forms, some of them violent, many of them distinctly noticeable to the general public—and therefore usually embarrassing. However, most communication is unobtrusive, involving the careful negotiation of technical and regulatory details of policy. Although often unwelcome—after all, no official or politician likes to be told that a pet project or policy is faulty—pressure groups are frequently the most reliable and best-informed link between government agencies and those segments of the public that they serve. Indeed, so important is this function that governments have often gone out of their way to encourage the creation of special-interest groups. In the Maritime provinces, the federal and provincial governments did exactly this in the late 1970s when they encouraged independent fishers to form bodies able to participate in developing policies for managing Canada's newly expanded fishery. "If I had to write the manual for dealing with government," federal Fisheries Minister Romeo LeBlanc told one group, "I would put two main rules of the road: carry a flag—that is, have an organization—and sound your horn. Let people know you are there."[2] Similarly, core funding from the federal government was an important factor in developing the political capacity of the aboriginal peoples.[3]

Nor does communication flow in only one direction. Most lobbying organizations present governments with a convenient means of reaching a special audience. Annual meetings can be addressed by ministers and senior officials intent partly on flattering and winning over a special clientele or constituency, but also on conveying various messages: a hint at policy change, an explanation of action, warnings, encouragement, and so on. Eyes watering from cigar and cigarette smoke, perspiring under the television lights, wondering whether they can be heard above the clatter of coffee cups and the hum of comment, guest speakers drone through their after-dinner jokes, their compliments, and their pious reminders, knowing that alert minds in the audience will soon have interpreted the speech's central message and passed it on to the less discerning. Similarly, organization newsletters, regional meetings, and informal get-togethers offer government spokespersons networks for the rapid transmission of information.

If communication is the primary function of pressure groups, legitimation is not much less important.[4] That is, pressure groups play a very significant part in persuading both policy-makers and the general public that changes in public policy are worthwhile, generally desired, and in the public interest. Because pressure groups frequently speak for a significant proportion of the public that will be affected by a change in policy, governments find it reassuring to have their proposals endorsed by the relevant groups. As Romeo LeBlanc told fishers in the speech we previously quoted, "Push the officials ... they like it." Cabinet ministers know how helpful it is to have a pressure-group leader tell a legislative committee, as one did in 1975, that "we provided extensive comments ... with respect to the first draft. When we saw the new bill most of the corrections, changes or criticisms we had found with the first draft had been corrected, modified or vastly improved."[5] In a similar way, group leaders sell their members on the desirability of policy changes.

On the other hand, officials are aware that a disaffected group can use its many connections with the media, the opposition parties, and perhaps other governments to attack policy and so undermine its legitimacy. The mining industry did this between 1967 and 1972 when it disagreed with the federal government over tax reform. Using a combination of general appeals to the government and behind-the-scenes lobbying with provincial governments, the mineral industries eventually forced the federal government to revise its proposals. One of the reasons for their success lay in their ability to persuade the public and the provinces that the new laws would discourage investment in the mining industry and thus hurt the economy. In other words, they undermined the legitimacy of the proposed changes.[6] More recently, finance ministers in Ottawa, Fredericton, and Edmonton have developed elaborate programs of consultation with group representatives and the general public in order to enhance the acceptability—the legitimacy—of their budgets.[7]

Administrative and regulatory activities are much less prominent functions than communication and legitimation, but they occur often enough to deserve mention. Provincial administration of social services is often supplemented by the work of voluntary groups. In the years when Canada was receiving large numbers of immigrants, voluntary associations provided many facilities that helped newcomers move to and settle in their destinations. Children's Aid societies often administer child welfare programs. The Victorian Order of Nurses provides home care. The John Howard and Elizabeth Fry Societies undertake many services for prisoners. In most rural communities, volunteer fire departments perform a service that in urban areas is a municipal government function.[8] Today, as tight budgets constrain governments' ability to pay for services we once took for granted, we have begun to revive the practice of encouraging voluntary associations to provide supplementary services, particularly those in support of food banks and home care for the elderly. Often the groups involved in these activities are not thought of as pressure groups, but because they often do contribute to the development of policy in their areas of interest, we are justified in thinking of them in this way.

Pressure groups perform administrative functions for several reasons. Often, as we have suggested, governments cannot afford to offer the services that groups provide through a combination of volunteer and paid help. Sometimes governments are not willing, for policy reasons, to provide special services, though they are willing to help voluntary associations provide them. The community is so divided over many issues related to birth control, for example, that some governments prefer to support birth-control counselling indirectly, through general grants to organizations like Planned Parenthood, rather than directly advocate one position or another. Finally, many groups administer programs that could as easily be carried out by government officials, simply because they have traditionally offered such services.

Regulatory functions are delegated to groups for quite different reasons. Lawyers, doctors, chartered accountants, and other professional groups have been given considerable authority to govern themselves through their associations, largely because governments are reluctant to thrust themselves into the complicated and often treacherous debates that surround professional accreditation and ethics. As well, though, some professional groups have a great deal of influence that in all likelihood has been exerted to keep government at arm's length. Even so, we see governments increasingly cutting back on this autonomy, for instance, by forcing the medical profession to accept publicly approved fee schedules, or, as in Quebec, by imposing a high degree of regulation on all professional groups.[9]

In summary, we have argued that as far as the political system is concerned, pressure groups serve four functions: they communicate, legitimate, administer, and regulate, though to their members these are often the least important roles that they play. We have suggested that the communications function is the most important. In the following section, we shall concentrate on this aspect of pressure group life, looking especially at the way in which factors such as the need to communicate with government, the amount of resources available for communication, and the level of understanding of policy systems combine to affect both the structure and behaviour of such groups.

STRUCTURE AND BEHAVIOUR

The functions that pressure groups perform have much to do with both the organizational form they take and the way they behave. We might be tempted to claim that their form follows their function were it not for the fact that structure is also greatly influenced by such things as the kind of resources made available by the group's members, their determination to promote their common interest through exerting influence, and the characteristics of the political system itself. We shall return to these influences after we have looked at the more fundamental aspects of pressure group structure and behaviour.

Earlier, we defined pressure groups as "organizations whose members act together, attempting to influence public policy in order to promote their common interest." The fact that they are organizations is crucial. In political life, there are many interests, and over time a considerable number exert influence in the policy process. But unless these interests have access to more resources than do most individuals and the majority of companies, they lack the ability to sustain their influence. Unaggregated demand, as political scientists call the political demands of individual persons and corporations, tends to occur sporadically and on a piecemeal basis. Often it is sufficient to achieve or avert specific decisions, such as a spot rezoning in a city plan, but this rarely influences public policy because the process of policy formation is extremely complex, involving many participants, taking place over a long period of time, and usually consisting of innumerable decisions.[10] For most of those who want to take part in this process, the only feasible way to do so is to band together, to share costs, to deploy at appropriate times the different talents that participation requires, even simply to maintain continuity as the process unfolds—in other words, to organize.

Not all pressure groups organize in the same way or to the same extent. Much depends on what they want to achieve by engaging in the policy process, on the resources they can put into lobbying, and on their understanding of the mechanics of policy-making. Since the way in which all these factors come together has a lot to do with the policy consequences of the work of pressure groups, it is important to try to understand the relationship between the levels of organization pressure groups attain and their behaviour in the policy process.

Our goal here is not simply to explain the behaviour of pressure groups; the way in which they behave can also tell us a great deal about policy-making in specific political systems and even about the political system itself. For example, as the introduction to this chapter implied, studies of Canadian pressure-group behaviour have led some students to conclude that administrators in Canadian governments have a far greater influence in policy-making than our earlier work on political parties, parliamentary institutions, and legal frameworks had led us to believe.

To understand these aspects of pressure-group life we must arrange what we know about them in meaningful patterns. There are various ways to do this. One used by many scholars is to classify all groups according to the kinds of causes they promote. This usually results in two broadly defined lists: (1) groups that pursue the self-interest of their members; and (2) groups that pursue more general, public interests. Some important insights have come from using this approach. For example, as a result of the debate triggered by studies like *The Logic of Collective Action*[11]—which argues that interest groups survive only if they can offer their members advantages (selective inducements) that can be obtained nowhere else—we now know a great deal about the internal forces that motivate pressure-group behaviour, and appreciate more than ever the problems that beset public interest groups. A practical consequence of this improved understanding has been the trend in several countries toward giving public interest groups special assistance in arguing for the public interest before regulatory and policy-making bodies.[12]

Useful though this approach is, it has serious weaknesses. In the first place, the classification system itself is "messy," for there are far too many groups that work simultaneously for both selective benefits and the public interest, and it is often difficult to categorize them; there is often a very fine line between self-interest and public interest.[13] More important, however, this method takes a one-sided view of the relationship between pressure groups and governments. Although it admits that pressure-group activity is often triggered by government action, such as the creation of a new program or the termination of an old one, it tends to explain the subsequent behaviour of such groups either in terms of competition between rival groups or in terms of what one writer has called their "interior life." In other words, the approach focuses on the effort group members are willing and able to make to convince policy-makers of the rightness of their cause. This concern is very necessary, but it has to be put in perspective. The other partner in the relationship—government—affects pressure-group behaviour just as much as does membership commitment, organizational sophistication, and so on. In fact, most pressure groups are chameleons: those that take their lobbying role seriously adapt their internal organizations and structure to suit the policy system in which they happen to operate. That is why pressure groups working only at the provincial level in Canada are often quite different from those that concentrate their efforts at the federal level, and why both differ dramatically from their counterparts in eastern Europe, the Third World, and even the United States.[14]

Several years ago, this writer developed a conceptual framework that tries try to look at pressure groups from the perspective of the influence of government as well as from that of the internal dynamics of groups. This approach starts with the assumption that pressure groups have functions to perform that are as necessary to the development of government policy as those performed by political parties, bureaucracies, executives, and courts. However, the way in which they perform those functions is as much determined by the shape of the policy system as it is by knowledge, enthusiasm, financial capacity, and other internal characteristics of individual groups.[15] For example, a policy system like Canada's, in which legislatures do not have a large say in policy development, will encourage pressure groups to develop quite differently from those that emerge in a system such as found in the United States, with its emphasis on congressional power.

Institutionalization, this approach argues, gives us the key to understanding pressure group behaviour. If we can come to understand how it is that some groups survive in a political system and become both influential and organizationally sophisticated while others quickly disappear, then we can learn a great deal about their interior life and about their particular policy environment.

An institution is a sophisticated entity, one that not only works to achieve the goals laid down for it, as any organization should, but that actually embodies the values on which it is built. Like any organization, it begins life as a collection of individuals gathered to achieve certain objectives. Sometimes such groupings have organizational shape—the members have structured relationships with one another that permit them to carry out specialized tasks—but often they are simply a group of people who want to accomplish something. Gradually (if they stay together), they elaborate an organizational structure, and if they are successful their organization develops into an institution, "a responsive, adaptive organism" that, to its members and many of those it deals with, has a philosophy, a code of behaviour, and sense of unity related to the values it has come to embody. The Greenpeace Foundation is a good example of such an organization. It is not only sophisticated as an organization with an international structure, but it stands very firmly for certain beliefs and acts accordingly. As a pressure group, it is highly institutionalized even though it is not popular with governments.

When we apply the concept of institutionalization to pressure-group analysis, we must be very aware of a point made by an early student of institutions, Philip Selznick. "As institutionalization progresses," he maintains, "the enterprise ... becomes peculiarly competent to do a particular kind of work."[16] In the case of pressure groups, this means that they must become "peculiarly competent" to carry out the four functions we have already discussed, especially the function of communication. The institutionalized group knows what government is thinking about, what it needs to know, and how to get that information to it at the right time, in the right place, and in the most acceptable form.

This means a great deal more than simply buttonholing politicians at cocktail parties. It means the group must have an expert staff—or a helpful, well-informed membership—able to communicate with government officials at bureaucratic as well as elected levels, on a continuing basis. The need for this particular competence has led this writer to claim that one of the defining characteristics of institutionalized pressure groups is "an extensive knowledge of those sectors of government that affect them and their clients." In its entirety, that definition describes institutional pressure groups as:

> groups that possess organizational continuity and cohesion, commensurate human and financial resources, extensive knowledge of those sectors of government that affect them and their clients, a stable membership, concrete and immediate operational objectives associated with philosophies that are broad enough to permit [them] to bargain with government over the application of specific legislation or the achievement of particular concessions, and a willingness to put organizational imperatives ahead of any particular policy concern.[17]

We cannot explain this definition completely here, but we should note several things about it. First, it is very unlikely that any real group could be described in these particular terms. It is an idealized version of a certain kind of group—a model with which to compare the various types of groups we come across. Second, because the idea of institutionalization suggests a progression, and because this particular model can be used as a benchmark against which other groups can be compared, it becomes possible to think of pressure groups as falling along a continuum. At one extreme we can place institutional groups like those in our model, and at the other we can put those groups that have the opposite characteristics. These, we would argue:

are governed by their orientation toward specific issues ... [and have]
limited organizational continuity and cohesion, minimal and often
naive knowledge of government, fluid membership, a tendency to en-
counter difficulty in formulating and adhering to short-range objec-
tives, a generally low regard for the organizational mechanisms they
have developed for carrying out their goals, and, most important, a
narrowly defined purpose, usually the resolution of one or two issues or
problems, that inhibits the development of "selective inducements" de-
signed to broaden the group's membership base.[18]

Nascent groups of this sort are often called "issue-oriented" and we can readily identify them. They spring up at a moment's notice, usually in reaction to some government action or a private-sector activity that only government can change. (They are often seen in city politics confronting developers, highway builders, and planners.) Usually, they disband when their goals are either won or convincingly lost, but occasionally they keep on playing a part in politics and slowly become recognized voices in policy-making. In order to do this, they have to become more highly organized, developing their "peculiar competence" to communicate their policy views to government, in effect engaging in the process of institutionalization. Greenpeace and Pollution Probe, like many environmental groups, developed in this way.[19] So did the Canadian Federation of Independent Business, which grew out of a small-business tax revolt in the 1970s. Such groups do not, of course, become institutionalized overnight. In fact, very few achieve that status, and most could be described as either fledgling or mature, depending on how closely they seem to conform to the models at either end of our continuum.

Figure 13.1 sets out a visual guide to this continuum by showing how the organizational development of each kind of group helps define its relationship to the policy process. For example, the issue-oriented group with its supporters participating out of concern for a particular issue usually has a small membership that tries to make up in devotion to the cause what is lacks in resources or staff. Lack of staff is this type of group's most serious deficiency, at least in the Canadian setting, because it generally means that the group does not have expert knowledge about what government is doing or thinking about the issue concerning them. Its members tend, therefore, to work in an information vacuum. Not only do they not know what government is thinking, they tend not to know who in government thinks about their particular issue. Their reactions, therefore, tend to be gut reactions directed at the most likely figure in sight, usually a politician, and expressed vociferously through the media. The majority of protest groups do not outlive this "placard-carrying" stage. Even if they win their immediate objective, group members may find that they lack the resources and the commitment to keep the new organization going. Those groups that do survive this stage generally do so by changing their relationship with their members and by adapting to the policy system.

FIGURE 13.1 **The Continuum Framework**

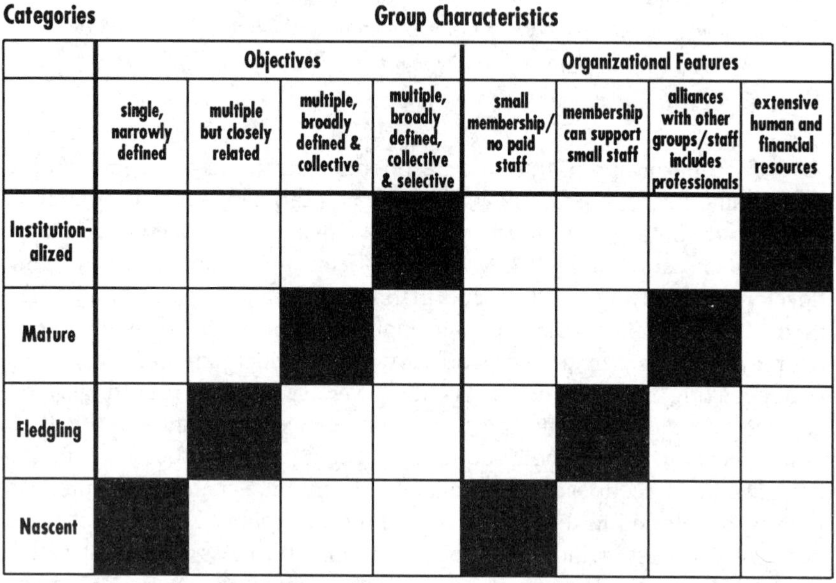

Categories   **Group Characteristics**

	Objectives				Organizational Features			
	single, narrowly defined	multiple but closely related	multiple, broadly defined & collective	multiple, broadly defined, collective & selective	small membership/ no paid staff	membership can support small staff	alliances with other groups/staff includes professionals	extensive human and financial resources
Institution-alized				■				■
Mature			■				■	
Fledgling		■				■		
Nascent	■				■			

One of the first steps in this adaptation is that the organization must stop being concerned with only one issue and instead take up several causes. Many environmental groups took this route, first establishing themselves to prevent the destruction of a particular natural amenity, then switching their concern to large issues. With a broader range of interest the group attracts a wider membership. While the new members may lack the fervent sense of commitment of the group's founders, and may be less inclined to sound a strident ideological note when the group tries to communicate with government, a wider membership base usually broadens the group's financial resources, bringing stability and a strengthened capacity to engage in the information game.

Here again, group-oriented and policy-oriented developments may take place in tandem. With a steady budget the group may take on a modest staff, a move that usually ensures that finances are better managed and that the members are served more consistently. Financial capacity usually also means that the group can afford to hire professionals—lawyers, public policy experts, public relations specialists—who can help it acquire the information it needs to participate in the policy process. These are the first steps in institutionalization, and from this point on the organization does not change a great deal. It simply becomes more complex, more ca-

pable of adapting to changes in the policy system, and, to the disappoint-
ment of founding members, more remote and professional, guided
increasingly by its paid staff.

PRESSURE GROUPS IN THE POLICY PROCESS: THE ROLE OF POLICY COMMUNITIES

Once started on the road to institutionalization, the pressure group more
readily wins the attention of government officials, and at the same time, is
more likely to adapt to shifts in government policy processes. This largely
follows from the decision to hire professionals. Because they are familiar
with the way in which policy is made, professional analysts, managers,
and lobbyists guide the group away from some lines of action and encourage others. Traditionally, in Canada, this meant that groups became
more and more intimate with the details of bureaucratic decision-making
and less and less inclined to use the media except when formal hearings
necessitated the presentation of rather general briefs intended to create an
image rather than promote a specific policy.

This approach to policy-making was a product of the policy system
that Canada used for the first half of this century. Because debate in Parliament was tightly controlled by the government, the basic form of public
policy could be worked out between the political executive and senior
administrators. Consequently, lobbyists, and others wishing to influence
public policy had to do so by approaching and persuading civil servants
and cabinet ministers rather than parliamentarians. Innumerable consequences stemmed from this—some affecting pressure groups, others the
policy process itself—most of which we cannot discuss here. Suffice it to
say that the end effect of this system was that "legitimate, wealthy, coherent interests, having multiple access to the legislative process, would tend
to be more influential than less legitimate, poor, diffuse interests, having
few sources of access to the legislative process."[20]

Since the early 1970s, however, this pattern of behaviour has
changed significantly as policy-making in Canada has become increasingly complex and at the same time more public. It used to be said that
government officials, protected by administrative secrecy and the limited
opportunities given groups to formally participate in policy-making, could
simply by withholding vital information undermine any group too inclined to publicly attack policy. Information control thus made government agencies the dominant partner in their relations with pressure
groups, and forced protest groups trying to survive to follow a pattern of
institutionalization that took them very rapidly from the placard-carrying
stage to the collegial and consultative relationship favoured by government.

When we look at group–agency relations today, it is much more difficult to say categorically that government agencies are the dominant partners. There are two different sets of reasons for this. First, changes within government—such as the diffusion of power that occurred at the federal level during the 1970s and the reduction of policy capacity that appears to have taken place in recent years—have limited the ability of agencies to control their relations with groups.[21] Diffusion means, for example, that groups dissatisfied with one agency can often find support at another. Second, outside government the electronic media and interest groups have created an environment that supports public participation. Interest groups alert the media to issues, supply protagonists for news show dramas, and help keep stories alive, either by feeding the media with new information or by creating newsworthy events. These activities not only promote groups' policy objectives but also attract new members and supporters, all of them important assets in the business of negotiating with officials. The influence of the media—together with changes in Parliamentary procedure, in the structure of policy-making, in the availability of government information, and in our constitutional framework—has modified our system of pressure-group politics, making groups less dependent on bureaucracy and more capable of engaging in open and public debate.[22]

We sometimes think of pressure groups in the singular: acting alone to bring off a policy coup or to thwart some scheme cooking in the "policy shops," as government policy analysis units are often called. At other times, they are described en masse: collaborating, competing, and generally rampaging across the policy stage. In general, however, their participation in the policy system is continuous, discreet, and multifaceted.

The first responsibility of any pressure group is to attend to the immediate needs of its clients. This usually means dealing with quite routine problems: alleviating the too stringent application of regulations, negotiating a minor shift in policy, bringing about the slight extension of a service. Such minor irritations along the public-sector–private-sector interface occasion daily contacts with government officials that serve to familiarize pressure-group representatives with the subtle changes in administrative routine and attitude that eventually crystallize into a change in policy.[23] When formal policy discussions begin, the understanding developed through these routine contacts is of immense value.

The policy process itself is hard to define; the origins of policy are often obscure, and the roles of those who take part are seldom exactly the same from debate to debate. Even so, we do have some general notions as to how the key policy actors—politicians, bureaucrats, and lobbyists—relate to one another, and this helps us develop a rough picture of the part pressure groups play in the process.

The first point that we must bear in mind is that the entire political community is almost never involved in a specific policy discussion. Specialization occurs throughout the policy system. The existence of pressure groups gives us the most obvious evidence of this, but specialization occurs elsewhere as well. Government departments, however large and multifaceted they may appear to be, are confined to a precisely defined territory. Even the political executive finds that only the really big issues are discussed by the entire cabinet. All the rest are handled by individual cabinet ministers or by specialized cabinet committees. Richard Crossman, once a member of the British Cabinet, remarked in his diary that "we come briefed by our departments to fight for our departmental budgets, not as Cabinet ministers with a Cabinet view."[24] Only prime ministers and presidents play roles that encourage them to consider policy in the round, and they live with such tight schedules that only the most urgent and significant issues come to their attention.

Out of specialization come what we call "policy communities"— groupings of government agencies, pressure groups, media people, and individuals, including academics, who, for various reasons, have an interest in a particular policy field and attempt to influence it. Most policy communities consist of two segments: the subgovernment and the attentive public. To all intents and purposes, the subgovernment is the policy-making body in the field. It processes routine policy issues and when doing so is seldom successfully challenged by interlopers. The subgovernment is what has been called "the durable core of any policy arena."[25] It consists of the government agencies most directly engaged in setting policy for and regulating the field, and a small group of interests— generally associations, but occasionally major corporations—whose power guarantees them the right to be consulted on virtually a daily basis. Their power wins them a place at the policy table, but government also needs their expert knowledge of the technical aspects of policy.

The power of the inner circle is used to limit the participation of others in policy debate. Those who are excluded congregate in the "attentive public." This outer circle includes those who are interested in policy issues, but who do not participate in policy-making on a frequent, regular basis. The academic community often plays this role, as do journalists working for specialized publications and, of course, a range of organizations and associations whose interest is keen but not acute enough to warrant breaking into the inner circle.

The attentive public lacks the power of the subgovernment, but it still plays a vital part in policy development. Conferences and study sessions organized by professional and interest associations offer opportunities for officials at various levels to converse with the grass roots of their constituency and with journalists and academics who have been studying public policy. Most have views on government performance and are quick to put them forward. Though most are greeted sceptically, sometimes patronizingly, they contribute to the process through which government and people gradually amend, extend, and generally adapt policies and programs to the changing needs of the community. Similarly, the newsletters, professional journals, and trade magazines that circulate through the policy community give both the subgovernment and the attentive public plenty of opportunity to shore up, demolish, and generally transmogrify the existing policy edifice. In this turmoil of theories and interests, officialdom—which is almost never monolithic, nearly always pluralistic, and seldom at peace with itself—discerns the policy changes government must make if it is to keep abreast of circumstances. The main function of the attentive public, then, is to maintain a perpetual policy review process.

Figure 13.2 illustrates the kind of policy community that might be active in a field in which the federal government is prominent. At the heart of the community are the key federal bodies involved: the agency primarily responsible for formulating policy and carrying out programs in the field; cabinet with its coordinating committees and their support structures—the Privy Council Office, the Treasury Board, the ministries of state, and so on. None of these are located at the very centre of the figure because no agency is ever consistently dominant in the field. On average, though, because so much of policy-making is routine, the lead agency tends to be most influential over time. Clustered around it are the pressure groups and provincial government agencies, to which we have already referred, keeping a sharp eye on "the feds" and generally participating in the subgovernment. Also involved are other federal agencies whose mandate overlaps that of the lead agency. These usually review agency policy, working through interdepartmental committees to do so, and often greatly alter it. For example, even in the midst of the catastrophic collapse of cod stocks off the East Coast, Canada has been slow to force international fishing fleets to stop fishing in international waters beside the Grand Banks. This may reflect the influence of the Department of Foreign Affairs, which worries about our general relations with trading partners who fish there.[26]

Hovering on the edge of the subgovernment is Parliament—perennially interested, intermittently involved, sometimes influential—and a further cluster of provincial government agencies. Some of these may wish to be part of the subgovernment but lack the resources to maintain a presence; others are simply not interested and are content to observe the activities of the subgovernment, interfering when necessary. In the final analysis, they may be no more influential than some of the major pressure groups active in the community. Some of the pressure groups are depicted as overlapping one another, because in fact they do overlap. They share membership, are often put together on advisory boards, and frequently combine their efforts to present a common stand to government and the public.

Finally, we should note that foreign governments must also be included in Canadian policy communities. The reasons for this are diverse. On the one hand, Canadian politicians and officials are great travellers, always aware of changing trends and conditions abroad—sometimes more

FIGURE 13. 2 **The Policy Community**

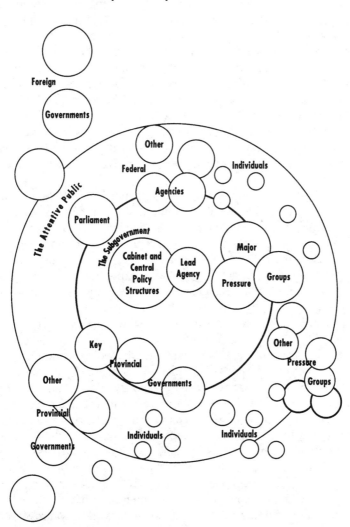

alert to developments elsewhere than to developments in parts of Canada—and ready to import new ideas and approaches to the Canadian scene.[27] More significantly, foreign government interest in our policies is a reflection of our participation in a global economy. The American pharmaceutical industry, which has branch plants in this country, has taken a continuing interest in our drug patent laws, and is said at times to invoke American government intervention in our debates over the amount of patent protection that should be given to major drug companies. The British and French have been similarly interested in our defence-procurement policies. Other countries track Canadian immigration and refugee policy closely.

Figure 13.2 suggests an orbital movement around the lead agency and the federal executive, but that would be too static. Rather than revolving around the key agencies, the other members of the policy community are in constant motion. As governments and key personnel change, provincial government participation varies, or changing economic factors compel provincial agencies to retreat or advance into the subgovernment. Similarly, pressure groups come and go from the centre. In the debate over tobacco product regulation, for example, Ottawa has been prominent for many years, but the participation of individual provinces and groups has varied. Recently Ontario and Nova Scotia have actively supported tough regulation, but New Brunswick and Quebec have been less engaged, even backing away from policies—such as prohibitively high taxation of tobacco products—which have been favoured by health activists and tax officials.[28]

Pressure groups, along with individual members of the attentive public, are the most mobile members of the policy community. With their annual meetings, their newsletters, their regional organizations, and, above all, their informal networks, they have an ability to cross organizational lines that is denied more formal actors such as government departments. They can, therefore, act as go-betweens, provide opportunities for quiet meetings between warring agencies, and keep the policy process in motion. These services, together with their ability to evaluate policy and develop opinion, make pressure groups integral members of the policy community.

Before we conclude our comments on the policy community, we have to remember that the most prominent of its members are not primarily interested in making or reformulating policy. For them, the policy community is a protective device, limiting rather than expanding the opportunities for the public at large to achieve major policy changes. Thus, it is the goal of the subgovernment to keep policy-making at the routine or technical level. If it achieves this, the subgovernment can keep interference to a minimum. Often, however, circumstances outside its control—economic changes, the development of new technologies, changing public concerns—are more than the subgovernment can handle through its system of formal communications and informal networks. Controversy develops, new issues emerge, and more and more interests want to take part in policy-making. Policy debate broadens as levels of conflict rise, so that eventually central issues are taken out of the hands of the subgovernment and policy community and resolved at the highest political levels—by cabinet and by the First Ministers' Conference.[29] When this occurs, the policy community, as well as policy, is often vastly altered.

PRESSURE GROUPS AND DEMOCRACY

Many people feel that pressure groups are a threat to democratic government. They distrust special-interest groups, arguing that their special pleading circumvents the legitimate authority of elected representatives and unfairly competes with the average citizen who approaches government as an individual. Robert Stanfield, as leader of the Progressive Conservatives, was one of the first politicians to express concern about the rise of interest groups. "It is one thing," he argued in 1977,

> *for individuals to pursue their own interests as they always have: it becomes a qualitatively different kind of society when individuals organize to pursue their individual interests collectively. National life has become a struggle for advantage among large and powerful organizations—not simply corporations and trade unions. Organized pressures abound.*[30]

By 1993, party activists had become bitter critics of the rise of interest groups, convinced that democracy itself was suffering because powerful groups were winning concessions for their members while the country was losing "the only organizations whose nature forces them to work towards a national consensus,"[31] Party antipathy to interest groups is to some extent reflected in a number of government decisions. Government funding of groups has been cut back. The charitable status of advocacy groups has been questioned. Attempts have been made to limit advertising by groups during elections. Salaried group representatives must register under the Lobbyists Registration Act. It would be misleading to interpret all of these steps as motivated entirely by an urge to "get" interest groups. Most are overdue adaptations to changes in the policy process. Nevertheless, taken together they represent less tolerance of groups on the part of politicians, and some, such as the attempt to ban election advertising, reflect a distinctly antagonistic approach.[32]

This approach was given voice at the 1993 Tory leadership convention when Kim Campbell drew "enthusiastic applause" from delegates when she suggested that, as prime minister, she would cut government support to special-interest groups.[33] She was appealing to a widespread conviction among party members that interest groups are no longer simply useful adjuncts to the political system, but rivals of the parties themselves. Like Stanfield 26 years earlier, they see pressure groups supplanting political parties as the citizen's chief vehicle for communicating with government. However, the decline of the political party as an instrument for developing policy has come about because government itself has changed, not because of weak party leadership, rapacious pressure-group activity, or a declining sense of community among the public. The modern state delivers innumerable services, manages vast resources, and attempts to direct complex economies, and to do all of these things it has organized itself into massive, functionally oriented, specialized bureaucracies. These agencies have great difficulty dealing with human beings. They deal with cases, with the partial needs of individuals. To develop policy they must talk with the public—not the public in general, but with the public they serve: their special public. What could be more natural than to persuade this public to organize itself, to adapt to the structure of modern government in order to communicate more effectively with it?

As a result of this bureaucratic need, in Canada and elsewhere, governments have encouraged the growth of interest groups. They have given them moral encouragement and financial assistance. They have made places for them on advisory boards and regulatory agencies. They have created regulations that intentionally push those who are regulated into associations, and they have made many groups a part of the administrative process. None of these steps have been taken in order to destroy democracy, and although some challenged political patronage, they attacked corruption, not the party system.

Nor does the trend to special–interest representation stem solely from the growing complexity of modern government. Equally important are the changes that have taken place in the economy over the last two centuries. The world of small enterprises whose fortunes were associated with the fortunes of particular places gave way during this century to a world economy vastly influenced by the giant corporation. Whether it is a multinational or not, the giant corporation is not very interested in what happens in specific localities. It has plants in many places, draws its resources from around the world, and markets its products everywhere. In its own way it is just as concerned with specialized issues as are government agencies, and it is no accident that these two forms of human organization have achieved complexity together.

Similarly, it is no accident that as these structures have evolved, political parties have declined. Political parties in most western nations, at least, have a territorial basis. They are designed to win control of legislatures and thus political power, and because most legislatures are based on territorially demarcated constituencies, party organization must follow suit. This is in many ways anachronistic, for the reasons we have outlined: governmental bureaucracies and their clients deal with sectoral issues, not the local concerns that disturb constituency organizations. Hence the decline of party influence. Yet the party system is not as outdated as it may seem. Despite decades of organizational conditioning, human beings still exhibit tremendous attachment to specific places. Consequently, the spatial basis of political party organization provides an important antidote to the sectoral bias of the administrative arm and the machinery of the economy. Unfortunately, political parties have not yet found a way to give the grass roots a role in the formation of public policy that is comparable to that played by interest groups as they work with, and through, the bureaucracy. Until Canadian political parties successfully meet that challenge, the increasingly bitter rivalry between groups and parties is likely to continue.

To the extent that the quarrel between parties and groups is over political roles—a turf war—it can be readily understood and best addressed through party reform. Recent criticisms of pressure groups, however, point to a more deep-seated problem. Many observers believe that pressure groups are fragmenting our political communities into mere coalitions of interests and undermining existing longstanding political institutions.

There is no doubt that, for many Canadians, pressure-group politics is the politics of a new age, offering not only access to a political system traditionally dominated by established elites, but also the means of achieving a new social order. Clearly, too, many other Canadians find this threatening. The sentiments of some of these Canadians were captured by a Reform Party official when he wrote in triumph to a defeated Tory candidate:

> Gone are the days of catering to radical women's groups, minority groups, etc. Gone are the days of protecting these and other parasites of society ... Gone also are the days when people like you will be able to treat some people better than others and justify it by saying that people like me have got to make up for past injustices to these groups.[34]

Although the Reform Party disavowed this official's views, his opinion— expressed in more moderate terms—reflected a significant part of recent public debate. Thus, while many hailed the contributions of aboriginal, women's, and minority groups to the 1992 constitutional discussions, others were profoundly threatened by the reordering of social power that was portended by the Charlottetown Accord. Jeffrey Simpson of *The Globe and Mail* called the accord "the apotheosis of interest group politics," a sad reflection of today's reality, but "hardly ... a vision for Canada."[35] Some commentators concluded that "far too many" voted against the Charlottetown Accord "because of their affiliation with, or dislike of, any one of many minority interest groups."[36]

This burgeoning debate over fragmentation is extremely important. It addresses the nature—and future—of our political community. It is unfortunate, however, that it begins by associating fragmentation only with those groups that saw in the constitutional debate an opportunity to seek a redistribution of power in the political system. After all, women's groups, aboriginal groups, and minority groups were only following in the footsteps of other, more established interests. Accompanying the rise of pressure groups has been a tendency for institutionalized groups—the majority representing business interests—to dominate debate within policy communities. As William Coleman has pointed out, because policymaking has become so diffuse, it is difficult to compel these interests to consider the general welfare or to be accountable to the public. Equally, it is extremely difficult for other interests to participate effectively—let alone on equal terms with business—in public debate.[37] These developments, too, threaten democratic discourse and have played their part in persuading minority groups to become more militant.[38]

With the legitimacy of government rooted in a spatial orientation to political communication, and its effectiveness depending on sectoral organization, the modern democratic state contains a tension that is an increasingly disturbing feature of modern political life. For Canadians, it has led to the decline of the political party and the rise of the pressure group, the ideal instrument for sectoral, specialized communication. It has also contributed an important dimension to our concerns for the capacity of our political institutions to deal with the cleavages that beset the country. As we approach the end of the century, those concerns will intensify the public debate over the proper role of Canadian pressure groups.

NOTES

1. This definition was first presented in "Pressure Groups: Adaptive Instruments of Political Communication," in A. Paul Pross, ed., *Pressure Group Behaviour in Canadian Politics* (Toronto: McGraw-Hill, 1975), pp. 1–26, and has been elaborated in A. Paul Pross, *Group Politics and Public Policy* (Toronto: Oxford University Press, 1992).

2. Lunenburg *Progress-Enterprise* (April 5, 1978), p. 16.

3. J. Hugh Faulkner, "Pressuring the Executive," *Canadian Public Administration* 25 (1982) 2: 240–44, 248.

4. See David Kwavnick, *Organized Labour and Pressure Politics* (Montreal and Kingston: McGill-Queen's University Press, 1972), for a useful discussion of this aspect of pressure-group life.

5. W. L. Canniff, Technical Director, Canadian Chemical Producers' Association, House of Commons, Standing Committee on Fisheries and Forestry, *Minutes of Proceedings and Evidence* (April 17, 1975), p. 18:4. (Re: "An act to protect human health and the environment from substances that contaminate the environment.")

6. See Arthur Drache, "Improving the Budget Process," *Policy Options* 3 (1982) 5: 15–19; and Douglas Hartle, *The Revenue Budget Process of the Government of Canada* (Toronto: Canadian Tax Foundation, 1982).

7. Evert Lindquist, "Rethinking Budget-making: The Salience of Ideas and Research in Retrospect and Prospect," in Susan D. Phillips, ed., *How Ottawa Spends 1994–95: Ideas and Innovation* (Ottawa: Carleton University Press, 1994).

8. Freda Hawkins, *Canada and Immigration: Public Policy and Public Concern* (Montreal and Kingston: McGill-Queen's University Press, 1972), p. 301; and National Council of Welfare, *In the Best Interests of the Child: A Report by the Na-*

tional Council of Welfare on the Child Welfare System in Canada (Ottawa: The Council, 1979). Other examples are derived from interviews conducted as part of a study of Canadian public interest groups being carried out by the author and Iain S. Stewart.

9. See René Dussault and Louis Borgeat, "La reforme des professions au Quebec," *Canadian Public Administration* 17 (1974): 407.

10. For example, in June 1983 officials in Ottawa sat down with representative of the Canadian Chamber of Commerce, the Business Council on National Issues, and the Canadian Manufacturers' Association to discuss revisions to federal competition legislation. On six previous occasions since 1971, government proposals to change the legislation had been set aside in the face of fierce opposition from business groups (Kingston *Whig-Standard*, June 21, 1983). The story of the long attempt to reform competition policy can be found in W.T. Stanbury, *Business Interests and the Reform of Canadian Competition Policy* (Toronto: Carswell/Methuen, 1978); and Irving Brecher, *Canada's Competition Policy Revisited: Some New Thoughts on an Old Story* (Montreal: Institute for Research on Public Policy, 1981).

11. Mancur Olson, *The Logic of Collective Action* (Cambridge, Mass: Harvard University Press, 1965).

12. See Peter H. Schuck, "Public Interest Groups and the Policy Process," *Public Administration Review* 37, no. 2 (1972): 132–40.

13. Terry M. Moe, *The Organization of Interests* (Chicago: University of Chicago Press, 1980).

14. Clive S. Thomas, ed., *First World Interest Groups: A Comparative Perspective* (Westport, Conn.: Greenwood, 1993).

15. A similar view is put forward by Henry W. Ehrmann, ed., in *Interest Groups on Four Continents* (Pittsburgh, Pa.: University of Pittsburgh Press, 1958).

16. Philip Selznick, *Leadership in Administration* (New York: Harper and Row, 1957), p. 139.

17. A. Paul Pross, "Canadian Pressure Groups in the 1970s: Their Role and Their Relations with the Public Service," *Canadian Public Administration* 18, no. 1 (1975): 124.

18. Ibid.

19. See Gregor Filyk and Ray Cote, "Pressure from Inside: Advisory Groups and the Environmental Policy Community," and Jeremy Wilson, "Green Lobbies: Pressure Groups and Environmental Policy," in Robert Boardman, ed., *Canadian Environmental Policy: Ecosystems, Politics and Process* (Toronto: Oxford University Press, 1992), pp. 60–82 and 109–25.

20. Fred Thompson and W.T. Stanbury, "The Political Economy of Interest Groups in the Legislative Process in Canada" (Montreal: Institute for Research on Public Policy, Occasional Paper No. 9), p. viii.

21. In *Interests of State: The Politics of Language, Multiculturalism, and Feminism in Canada* (Montreal and Kingston: McGill-Queen's University Press, 1993), Leslie A. Pal concludes, for example, that despite receiving a large proportion of their funding from the Department of the Secretary of State, a number of language, multicultural and feminist advocacy groups were able to act autonomously, even to the point of vigorously criticizing departmental policies (pp. 262–64, 271–76). The tendency of Canadian groups to "bite the hands that feed them" is not confined to the groups studied by Pal, and frequently leaves officials puzzled and resentful.

22. The recent evolution of the Canadian policy process has caused a good deal of debate, which probably can best be followed in the journals *Canadian Public Administration, Governance,* and *Policy Options.*

23. There are useful descriptions of these relationships in Kwavnick, *Organized Labour and Pressure Politics.*

24. Quoted in J.J. Richardson and A.G. Jordan, *Governing Under Pressure: The Policy Process in a Post-Parliamentary Democracy* (Oxford: Martin Robertson, 1979), p. 26.

25. John E. Chubb, *Interest Groups and the Bureaucracy: The Politics of Energy* (Stanford: Stanford University Press, 1983), pp. 8–10, quoted in William D. Coleman, *Business and Politics: A Study of Collective Action* (Montreal: McGill-Queen's University Press, 1988), p. 277. Coleman presents case studies of a number of policy fields in which the workings of the policy community can be discerned. For an elaboration of the concept itself, see my *Group Politics and Public Policy.* Susan McCorquodale and I have looked at a specific policy community in *Economic Resurgence and the Constitutional Agenda: The Case of the East Coast Fisheries* (Kingston: Queen's University, 1987).

26. Frustration over foreign fishing led fishers to prevent a Russian trawler from leaving Shelburne harbour in the summer of 1993 (Kevin Cox, "Little fish become big issue in fight against foreign vessels," *The Globe and Mail,* July 28, 1993). Although the government promised stronger action against foreign fishing ("Pact that ended fishermen's blockade outlined," Lunenburg *Progress-Enterprise,* August 4, 1993), Canada remains committed to a diplomatic approach to resolving the issue (Eric Reguly, "Canada pushes plan to save fish," *Financial Post,* July 17, 1993) and continues to be thwarted by other governments (Deborah Jones, "Foreigners to continue fishing cod," *Financial Post,* September 11, 1993).

27. For example, Canadian minimum-wage policy has been influenced by the experience of other countries and by the work of international organizations. See Chris Parke, "The Setting of Minimum Wage Policy in the Maritimes" (Halifax: Dalhousie Institute of Public Affairs, 1980).

28. Paul Pross and Iain S. Stewart, "Organized Interests, Attentive Publics and Policy Ideas," in Susan Phillips, ed., *How Ottawa Spends, 1994–95: Ideas and Innovation* (Ottawa: Carleton University Press, 1994).

29. This paragraph applies to the Canadian scene concepts developed in E.E. Schattschneider, *The Semi-Sovereign People: A Realist's View of Democracy in America* (New York: Holt, Rinehart and Winston, 1960). The Canadian variant is looked at more fully in Pross, *Group Politics and Public Policy.*

30. Robert L. Stanfield, Fifth George C. Nowlan Lecture, Acadia University (February 7, 1977), mimeo.

31. Ibid.

32. For a discussion of the regulatory environment of interest groups, see A. Paul Pross and Iain S. Stewart, "Lobbying, the Voluntary Sector and the Public Purse," in Susan D. Phillips, *How Ottawa Spends, 1993–94: A More Democratic Canada ...?* (Ottawa: Carleton University Press, 1993), pp. 109–42. Politicians' views on election advertising by interest groups can be sampled in the comments of Peter Milliken on Bill C-114, An Act to Amend the Canada Elections Act in Canada, House of Commons, *Debates* (daily edition) (March 8, 1993), p. 1665.

33. Shawn McCarthy, *The Toronto Star* (June 13, 1993).

34. "Women, minority groups called 'parasites' by Reform official," *The Globe and Mail* (October 29, 1993).

35. "Reforms beyond the worse nightmares of Meech Lake critics," *The Globe and Mail* (June 11, 1992). For a more sympathetic view, see Linda Hossie, "Grassroots groups altered content of unity debate," *The Globe and Mail* (February 25, 1992).

36. Editorial, "An opportunity to reverse the tides," Lunenburg *Lighthouse Log* (November 2, 1992) commenting on the referendum and an article in *The Economist* (October 17, 1992).

37. Coleman, *Business and Politics*, pp. 261–65.

38. See, for example, John Sawatsky, *The Insiders: Government, Business and the Lobbyists* (Toronto: McClelland and Stewart, 1987); and Hyman Solomon, "Business got its feet wet in public policy," *Financial Post* (December 5, 1988).

FURTHER READINGS

Atkinson, Michael, and W.D. Coleman. *The State, Business and Industrial Change in Canada.* Toronto: University of Toronto Press, 1989.

Coleman, W.D. *Business and Politics: A Study of Collective Action.* Montreal and Kingston: McGill-Queen's University Press, 1988.

Coleman, W.D., and Grace Skogstad, eds. *Policy Communities and Public Policy in Canada.* Toronto: Copp Clark Pitman, 1990.

Dion, Léon. *Société et Politique: La Vie des Groupes.* Quebec: Les Presses de l'Université Laval, 1971.

Kwavnick, D. *Organized Labour and Pressure Politics: The Canadian Labour Congress, 1956–1968.* Montreal and Kingston: McGill-Queen's University Press, 1972.

Lang, Ronald W. *The Politics of Drugs: The British and Canadian Pharmaceutical Industries and Governments—A Comparative Study.* Farnborough: Saxon House, 1974.

Ng, Roxana, Gillian Walker, and Jacob Muller, eds. *Community Organization and the Canadian State.* Toronto: Garamond Press, 1990.

Pal, Leslie A. *Interests of State: The Politics of Language, Multiculturalism, and Feminism in Canada.* Montreal and Kingston: McGill-Queen's University Press, 1993.

Presthus, Robert. *Elite Accommodations in Canadian Politics.* Toronto: Macmillan, 1973.

———. *Elites in the Policy Process.* Toronto: Macmillan, 1974.

Pross, A. Paul. *Group Politics and Public Policy.* Toronto: Oxford University Press, 1992.

Razack, Sherene. *Canadian Feminism and the Law.* Toronto: Second Story, 1991.

Seidle, F. Leslie, ed. *Equity and Community: The Charter, Interest Advocacy and Representation.* Montreal: Institute for Research on Public Policy, 1993.

Stanbury, W.T. *Business–Government Relations in Canada.* Scarborough, Ont.: Nelson Canada, 1992.

Thomas, Clive S., ed. *First World Interest Groups: A Comparative Perspective.* Westport, Conn.: Greenwood, 1993.

Thorburn, Hugh G. *Interest Groups and the Canadian Federal System.* Toronto: University of Toronto Press, 1985.

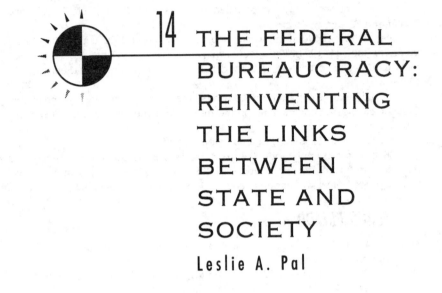

14 THE FEDERAL BUREAUCRACY: REINVENTING THE LINKS BETWEEN STATE AND SOCIETY

Leslie A. Pal

The 1993 Liberal election policy book, *Creating Opportunity,* had a short chapter entitled "Governing with Integrity." It noted that "cynicism about public institutions, governments, politicians, and the political process is at an all-time high," and that Canadians were fed up with the high cost and inefficiency of government services. With respect to appointments and elections, the party promised that vacancies on boards and commissions would be filled on the basis of competence. At the same time, new appointees would "better represent women, visible minorities, Aboriginal peoples, and people with disabilities."

As short as it was, the chapter captured both the broad public sentiment that government bureaucracy must change to be more efficient, and the ambivalence over how to combine that new efficiency with the broader purposes that the bureaucracy serves in contemporary society. Bureaucracy does not merely deliver public services; indeed, the Ottawa bureaucracy, given the division of powers in Canadian federalism, delivers fewer services than do most continental European central governments. Government bureaucracies are also expected to reflect a wide range of democratic purposes, from employment equity to managing consultative processes in order to facilitate public input into policy-making.

The pressures for change over the last decade have become overwhelming. The level of disaffection with bureaucracy and public institutions has been steadily rising in Canada. The referendum defeat of the Charlottetown Accord in 1992, the crushing defeat of the Conservative government in 1993, and the election of a sizable Reform Party caucus that actively campaigned against government inefficiency and waste together revealed a strong public demand for change. Other countries around the world have undertaken radical reforms, and "reinventing government" has become the watchword for major changes in the way in which public organizations, from Washington to Whitehall, operate. Ottawa has undertaken its own reforms in the guise of Public Service 2000 (PS 2000), an attempt to change the corporate culture of bureaucratic Ottawa while at the same time streamlining the administrative machinery. The Chrétien government carried forward promised Conservative reforms to reduce the number of departments, the size of the cabinet, and the budget deficit.

The problem is that these pressures for change focus almost exclusively on efficiency; the responses to these pressures (initiatives such as PS 2000) have been couched largely in these terms as well. This focus on efficiency tends to underplay the three other great forces that will drive debates about governance in the 1990s. The first is the demand for more participation, greater democracy, and more public input in the policy process. The second is the unabated expectation that Canadian public bureaucracies will not merely be competent and efficient, but that they will be instruments of equity and fairness. In theory, efficiency and equity need not be contradictory; in practice, they are sometimes difficult to achieve simultaneously. The third is the need for "societal steering" in an age of globalization. Falling trade barriers and new technologies are often thought to undermine the nation-state and the traditional purposes of government, but they also create substantial pressures for new and even increased levels of government activity to help cushion the negative effects of global competition. The Liberal government elected in 1993 will take Canada to the threshold of the next millennium, and it is ideologically committed to a more activist vision of Ottawa's role in both economy and society. These conflicting pressures and expectations will be the backdrop for continued efforts to reinvent the ways in which bureaucracy connects the political system to Canadian society.

THE REINVENTION RAGE

One of the most widely read books on public management in 1992 was *Reinventing Government* by David Osborne and Ted Gaebler. This book possessed remarkably good timing, since concerns about government inefficiency have been building for years in the United States, as reflected in the anti-government rhetoric of just about every politician, starting with President Reagan himself. The anger over inefficiency was driven by more than the conventional wisdom that the private sector could, by definition, do everything better than the public. It was also impelled by a growing fiscal crisis at both the state and national levels, as deficits increased and all but eight American states passed versions of California's Proposition 13, restricting revenue sources for government. The issue had become bipartisan, however, and the newly elected Clinton administration promised to deal with government red tape as well. Osborne became an adviser to the President, and in 1993 the administration launched a National Performance Review headed by Vice President Al Gore.

Osborne and Gaebler spent five years researching their book, travelling around the United States, and examining small-scale innovations at the local and state level. The book is filled with concrete illustrations of how governments can act differently. The most important aspect of the book's argument was its rejection of the hierarchical architecture of most government bureaucracies. In the Canadian political system, a minister sits atop a department. Policy is designed at this apex and filtered down the system until finally delivered as services. Accountability is conceived exclusively in terms of the political accountability of the minister as an elected official. The bureaucracy is simply a huge, finely calibrated machine designed to fulfil the minister's and the government's policy objectives. But it is a machine of hundreds and sometimes thousands of people who have to be managed and organized if they are to contribute precisely to the larger objective. In this model, discretion is minimized through the use of a variety of management systems: personnel systems, budgetary systems, procurement and planning systems.

The result very often is inflexible, costly, lumbering organizations that are driven by rules rather than results. Creativity is stifled, problem-solving is discouraged in favour of following routine, and significant resources are devoted to managing people within the system rather than to achieving policy goals. Osborne and Gaebler distilled ten principles of reinventing government from the cases they reviewed. These principles are grounded in the assumption that government, although necessary, does not necessarily have to act like government.

Most entrepreneurial governments promote competition *between service providers. They empower citizens by pushing control out of the bureaucracy, into the community. They measure the performance of their agencies, focusing not on inputs but on* outcomes. *They are driven by their goals— their* missions—*not by their rules and regulations. They redefine their clients as* customers *and offer them choices—between schools, between training programs, between housing options. They* prevent *problems before they emerge, rather than simply offering services afterward. They put their energies into* earning *money, not simply spending it. They* decentralize authority, *embracing participatory management. They* prefer *market mechanisms to bureaucratic mechanisms. And they focus not simply on providing public services, but on* catalyzing *all sectors—public, private, and voluntary—into action to solve their community's problems.*[1]

While the United States is just embarking on its reinvention, Britain has implemented radical changes in the organization of its central government, to the point that two-thirds of "government employees" work not for traditional departments, but for executive agencies that have been contracted to provide certain services. This wide range of reforms has been underway since Margaret Thatcher's prime ministership, but two initiatives—the Next Steps Program and the Citizen's Charter—illustrate the organizational revolution that has taken place.[2]

Next Steps had its origins in the Financial Management Initiative of 1982, which tried to underscore the importance of management in government by introducing better practices and by giving managers greater autonomy over budgets and operations as long as they met certain performance and output targets. By the late 1980s, the reforms had bogged down, and so efforts were redoubled to take the "Next Steps" of the original Financial Management Initiative in decentralizing government services. The plan called for as many agencies as possible to be converted into "departmental executive agencies" that would essentially act as businesses delivering public services. The chief executive officer of each Next Step agency was to negotiate with the department a contract specifying performance goals and targets, but would then have substantial freedom to operate the "business" as he or she saw fit.

The Next Steps program had Margaret Thatcher's strong approval and was launched in 1988. In a little over a year, eight agencies were created. By April 1993, there were 89 such agencies employing almost two-thirds of the civil service. Among them were the Central Statistical Office, the Employment Service, the Prison Service, the Royal Mint, and the Social Security Benefits Agency. These are not privatized agencies; they remain parts of government and their employees are still civil servants. The key change is the introduction of substantial managerial autonomy. Each agency has a framework document or agreement that is negotiated between the parent department and the Treasury, and is subject to some renegotiation later by the chief executive officer. The framework document differs for each agency, though all of them outline the agency's objectives and targets, resource-management guidelines, and the pattern of agency–department relations.

The result is the provision of government services in markedly new ways. The Next Steps agencies, for example, no longer need to follow general government guidelines on expenditures as long as they work within their framework agreement. Agencies can set salary levels and classify jobs as they see fit. Managers can take risks, be more entrepreneurial, and the agency as a whole can respond more effectively to its "customers." One of the most difficult things to change in government is the organizational culture within bureaucracy. The Next Steps initiative has been defended on the grounds that by forcing organizational changes it has brought cultural changes as well to the way in which civil servants see their role. It has encouraged them to be more "market sensitive" and competitive, since the program is joined to initiatives that compel regular reviews of agency performance and evaluations of whether services can be provided more efficiently through the private sector.

The U.K. Citizen's Charter was introduced by John Major in 1991 after he had assumed the prime ministership from Margaret Thatcher. The charter's principles, however, are entirely consistent with the Next Steps project of remaking the way that government works. Whereas Next Steps introduced fundamental organizational changes, the charter is designed to alter bureaucratic practices in order to raise the quality of public services. The charter was launched with a White Paper that laid out four key themes: (1) the improvement in the *quality* of public services; (2) the introduction, wherever possible, of greater *choice* through competing providers of public services and consultation with citizens about the type of services they wanted; (3) the clear statement of *standards* of services, to enhance accountability; and (4) the assurance that taxpayers would receive *value* for their money. In addition, the White Paper listed seven principles of public service: clear standards, openness, ease of access to information, choice, nondiscrimination on the basis of race or sex, accessibility to suit the needs of the public rather than civil servants, and responsiveness when things go wrong. The Citizen's Charter applies to all central government agencies and departments, nationalized industries, local governments, the health service, courts, police, and private and publicly regulated utilities.

Each agency is to publish its own charter, and they can be remarkably detailed. The Employment Service Job Seeker's Charter, for example, gives a list of the services the agency provides, and their sequence. Standards are posted, with performance results, for the number of people the agency has helped find a job, the time clients have to wait for an interview, and the time it takes to answer the phone and send people money. British Rail's charter has similar provisions stipulating standards of service, but also provides compensation, through reduced ticket prices, for passengers who have suffered delayed arrivals of more than an hour. Though clear standards like this are often used in the private sector, statements of output measures and performance levels run against the grain of public bureaucracy. It has been argued that the Citizen's Charter forces organizations to be clearer about the goods and services they are providing to the public, and indeed to think of the public as "customers" and "clients." Designing a charter can be a catalyst to rethinking goals, redefining the organization's mission, and clarifying relationships both to client groups and to other service-delivery organizations.

Reinventing Government, the Next Steps program, and the Citizen's Charter are examples of the managerial revolution taking place in public administration. Similar reforms have been undertaken in Australia, New Zealand, and elsewhere with the same goal of introducing radically new forms of service delivery by government. The key point is that all of these reforms accept that some services must be provided through the public sector much of the time, but that the way in which these services are provided must change. Government organizations have to become more like private-sector companies; they must be internally flexible to respond to change, responsive to their clients, clear about their goals, and, above all, efficient. The focus on performance, vision, entrepreneurship, and market responsiveness sometimes obscures the equally important if not dominant concern with efficiency. As Osborne and Gaebler point out, government has to reinvent itself because it is running out of money (the U.K. initiatives were first launched as part of a financial management reform).

REINVENTING GOVERNMENT OTTAWA-STYLE

The approach to reinventing government discussed above clearly takes the market and private enterprise as its model. The attack on bureaucratic waste and inefficiency has, unsurprisingly, been led by Conservative governments, though by the early 1990s, as the opening quote from *Creating Opportunity* showed, it was broadly accepted across the political spectrum. When the Conservatives were elected in 1984, however, their approach to public-sector restructuring was far less subtle. During his campaign for the Tory leadership, for example, Brian Mulroney promised that if the Conservatives won office they would hand out "pink slips and running shoes" to hundreds of civil servants. He played on the small-business prejudices of his party by joking about the insensitivity and arrogance of Ottawa bureaucrats.

Public-sector reform under the newly elected Tory government rested on four key principles. The first was the elimination of inefficiency, waste, and duplication in government programs. Upon being elected, Mulroney appointed Erik Nielsen to head a Program Review Task Force. With the help of a private-sector advisory group and public/private-sector review teams, the task force conducted an inventory of all federal programs (the first time this had been done in Canada). The review cost $3.7 million and produced 21 volumes of analysis and recommendations. The task force's approach was light years away from the reinventing government view that government services should be provided, but provided differently. The Nielsen report was concerned about waste, duplication, excessive spending, general inefficiencies, and program effectiveness.

Assessments of its impact vary, from the view that it was minimal to Nielsen's own judgment that it saved 135 times its cost within the first year.

The second principle was the importance of eliminating the deficit. In 1984, the federal deficit was $38 billion and budgetary policy throughout the nine years of Tory rule aimed (unsuccessfully) at reducing the debt. The deficit thus became the rationale for a host of strategies to reduce the public service and cut back programs. Given the magnitude of the federal deficit, public-service cuts could contribute relatively little compared to reductions in social programs, cuts to provincial transfers, or increases in revenues. Nonetheless, the symbolic importance of cutting any government fat was behind consistent attempts to reduce the size of the federal public service. The third principle was linked to the deficit, but on the expenditure-control side. The Conservatives argued that deficit reduction was more than merely a matter of cutting programs, it was a matter of establishing control over the complex expenditure budget process. To this end, they tinkered with the cabinet committee system, and in 1989 revised it substantially so that the prime minister himself chaired an Expenditure Review Committee that would regularly review all government expenditures and ensure that they were consistent with the fiscal framework.

The fourth principle was joined to the others, since cutting government fat and reducing the deficit might mean actually getting rid of some government operations. The first Mulroney government therefore established an Office of Privatization and Regulatory Affairs to guide the divestiture of Crown corporations and to conduct reviews of regulatory frameworks. The privatizations eventually included such large and visible companies as Air Canada and Petro-Canada, but also included others such as de Havilland Aircraft and Teleglobe Canada. Deregulation would not reduce the cost of government noticeably, but it would theoretically enhance efficiencies in the private sector if the dead hand of bureaucracy were removed.

The effects of these initiatives on actual government spending and the deficit are debatable (by 1993, the annual deficit had hit a record high of $45 billion, and Statistics Canada figures suggested that the number of federal civil servants had actually increased by 12,000 since 1984), but they had a powerfully negative effect on public-service morale. The unceasing rhetorical attacks on government inefficiency and waste throughout the first Mulroney government were dispiriting enough, but they were compounded by the lack of upward mobility for the middle ranks of managers. The civil service had grown quickly through the 1970s and early 1980s under a succession of Liberal governments, but had slowed by the 1980s. Many of the talented people who had been recruited in the boom period suddenly found their career paths blocked by a stagnant bureaucracy headed by relatively young senior managers, who were likely to be around for a long time. PS 2000, announced by the prime minister in December 1989, tried to respond both to the specific problems that afflicted the Canadian public service and to the broad perspectives that underlay the reinventing government movement.

According to Paul Tellier, who was then the Clerk of the Privy Council and responsible for launching PS 2000, the program had three core objectives. The first related to better service to the Canadian public, which would be achieved through decentralization and delegation so that deputy ministers, line managers, and regional staff would have the authority they needed to respond to public needs. The result would be that "jobs of public servants across Canada will be enriched, individual motivation will be increased, and the public service as a whole will do a better job for all Canadians."[3] The second objective was clarified responsibilities for personnel management. The current system did not encourage initiative, often impeded the proper delegation of authority to people who needed it, and was so unclear that managers often took refuge in control systems rather than empowering their employees to get results. The third objective was increased flexibility; the federal bureaucracy was to become a supple, responsive organization that could quickly adapt to external changes and demands. Together these objectives would shift public-sector thinking from a philosophy of control to one of empowerment.

Rhetoric aside, the PS 2000 exercise was very much an internal affair for the public service itself. It did not engage the broader public (indeed, outside of Ottawa and the academic community, it was unlikely that many ordinary Canadians had even heard of it) and lacked the high profile of either the Next Steps or Citizen's Charter initiatives. PS 2000 established ten task forces consisting of deputy and assistant deputy ministers who addressed the following issues: classification, the structure of the management category in the public-sector classification system, salaries and benefits, staffing, staff relations, staff training, adaptation of the work force to external changes, resource management, administrative policies and services common to departments, and service to the public. This list may have sent hearts aflutter among the Ottawa mandarinate, but it was hardly the stuff to stir the public imagination. The focus was inward, and the reviews undertaken by the various task forces were designed to address arcane organizational issues largely incomprehensible to the public at large.

The Task Force on Service to the Public was an exception in that it was the only task force to deal directly with what was alleged to have been the goal of the entire initiative. Changes in staff classification and common service might yield more flexibility over the long term and change the bureaucracy's corporate culture, but they were unlikely to have any immediate impact on service. The role of the Service Task Force was to review "best practices" in the public service and develop a "template for the model of the ideal service organization."[4] Though it found that individual public servants were keen to provide good service, the system as a whole did not encourage it. Classification and budget systems encourage a control mentality rather than a service culture. The system was built not to serve the public but to avoid mistakes.

Improved service to the public, the Service Task Force reported, would come only if there were strong leadership at the top and a commitment to empowering the front-line public servants who deal directly with clients. Along with empowerment, there was a need to decentralize wherever possible, and to ensure that the bureaucracy actually valued high service achievement by recognizing and rewarding it. Staff reviews in the public service are often ritualistic rather than informative, and many public-sector managers fail to see as one of their responsibilities the creation of a work environment that will motivate employees to achieve better service levels to the public. While the report was upbeat and, in general terms, called for many of the kinds of changes in public management that inform the reinventing-government perspective, the focus was less on structural changes to the bureaucracy itself than on management practices that might in the end lead to a change in culture. Whereas Next Steps called for a radical restructuring of government departments and agencies, on the assumption that organizational change would lead to new behaviour, the PS 2000 approach, even in an area like service to the public, was to avoid recommendations about structure in favour of recommendations about management and culture.

The ten PS 2000 task force reports submitted over 300 recommendations, many of which dealt with minor administrative changes. Some of the others followed the pattern of the recommendations coming from the Task Force on Service to the Public: broad statements of principle that called primarily for changes in the way that people think. By 1992, the entire process had bogged down. Paul Tellier had left his post as Clerk of the Privy Council, and the government became preoccupied with constitutional and other policy issues, as well as the impending election. Another problem was the way in which PS 2000 had been managed. The use of internal task forces headed by senior officials to review their own practices was unlikely to be perfectly objective. Public-sector employees also wondered how the PS 2000 recommendations on changing current senior management practices would in fact be implemented if the current senior management were retained. The public-sector unions had not been happy with the exercise either, claiming that they had not been truly consulted in the process, and that the senior mandarinate had controlled the terms of reference of the reviews as well as the scope of changes to be undertaken. In short, what had started with all the fanfare of a radical rethinking of the public service had fizzled into a relatively conservative, managerially oriented exercise in tinkering at the margins. The 1992 progress report on PS 2000 showed very thin results across the federal public service. Defenders could argue that since the intent had been less to change organizational structures than to modify organizational culture, it would take some years for the PS 2000 revolution to occur. Hearts and minds are notoriously brittle, and cultural change requires greater commitment and leadership than organizational change does. By 1993, PS 2000 seemed to have been orphaned to a few specialized agencies and smothered by organizational routine.

PS 2000 ebbed, but organizational changes of another type were being undertaken in 1993. In January, Prime Minister Mulroney shuffled his cabinet and promised to restructure government departments. The plan was drawn up by Robert de Cotret, but when Mulroney resigned in February it languished until midsummer. Glen Shortcliffe, who succeeded Paul Tellier as Clerk of the Privy Council, presented the plan to Kim Campbell after she assumed the prime ministership. Campbell had campaigned for the Conservative leadership on a platform of political renewal, of responding to demands for more citizen participation and a political system that was more responsive to the citizenry. A radical restructuring of government departments fit the bill nicely, and she gave Shortcliffe the authority to proceed. Unlike PS 2000, which had focused on organizational culture, the Shortcliffe reorganization was structural. Once more, the issue was efficiency and effectiveness, but this time it was to be achieved through a radical reduction (from 32 to 23) and recombination of federal government departments. Much like Next Steps, changes in behaviour would flow from changes in structure: "The idea behind the restructuring is to force government to re-examine what lines of business it should be in and, within those lines, what the priorities are."[5]

The plan was launched on June 25, 1993, with the announcement of a new federal cabinet consisting of only 25 ministers. A dozen departments were left as before, but a key element of the restructuring was the creation of five new "superministries": Human Resources and Labour, Canadian Heritage, Public Security, Industry and Science, and Government Services. The new Ministry of Human Resources and Labour, for example, has a staff of 27,000 and a budget of close to $70 billion, accounting for over half of Ottawa's direct program spending. It includes most of the functions and programs of the former departments of Labour, Employment and Immigration, Health and Welfare, and educational spending under the Secretary of State. The streamlining of ministries and departments suddenly made some deputy and assistant deputy ministers redundant. Shortcliffe was severely criticized for the manner in which the plan was implemented. On the morning of the cabinet announcement, he invited the survivors to a breakfast meeting in Ottawa and gave them their new assignments; those who were not invited would be pressured to leave. At least 40 assistant deputy ministers were on the chopping block, and initially Shortcliffe hoped that he could work out severance packages and let them go quickly. But Robert Giroux, president of the Public Service Commission, which has authority over appointments below the level of deputy minister, wrote to all 325 assistant deputy ministers promising that a special-hearing process would precede any dismissals.

Reorganization of government along these lines had been recommended from various quarters (including Gordon Osbaldeston, a former Clerk of the Privy Council), but Shortcliffe's methods were roundly criticized. He had moved brutally and without consultation, had demanded departmental redesign in an impossibly short time, and had devastated morale among the senior management ranks by dangling a sword over everyone's head. There had also been complaints that the reorganization disproportionately affected female senior managers. Despite these attacks (Shortcliffe himself took the rare step of responding publicly to them), the reorganization went ahead and was accepted in all but a few details (for example, immigration was moved out of Public Security) by the newly elected Chrétien government in October 1993. Indeed, Chrétien weighed in with an even smaller cabinet (23 instead of Campbell's 25, though he also appointed eight secretaries of state who would be paid less than full ministers and not sit at the cabinet table). The Liberals also eliminated the post of chief of staff, a political appointment at the deputy-minister level that the Mulroney Conservatives had invented in 1984 to ensure their new ministers would not get captured by the Ottawa mandarins and their agendas.

Reinventing government Ottawa-style has been a curious affair over the past decade. Until 1989, it was driven almost exclusively by a strong antipathy to the public sector, and by an assumption that the point of government reorganization was to get rid of as much government as possible. Public-sector employment freezes, privatization, deregulation, program review—all of these together would reduce in absolute terms the role and scope of Canadian government. After 1989, with the introduction of PS 2000, public-sector reorganization took on a calmer and more nuanced tone. Now the purpose was to take a battered and abused public service and revitalize it with a new corporate culture of empowerment, client service, and flexibility. The sudden and massive reorganization undertaken in 1993 was supposed to complement PS 2000 by streamlining departments and reducing the number of decision-making units, but this was clearly only a rationalization. PS 2000 and the Shortcliffe restructuring had nothing in common; one echoed the fashionable nostrums of reinvention through changing organizational culture, while the other was driven by the view that nothing would change unless organizations were completely redesigned.

BEYOND REINVENTION

Why reinvent government? There are essentially two answers that, while they have very different implications, are often combined in proposals to redesign the public sector. The first is that traditional government is inefficient and expensive. Public bureaucracies are organized so rigidly and consumed by so many rules, regulations, and procedures that they inevitably spend more than they should to achieve even mediocre results. They are insulated from the types of signals that guide private companies in the market, and so will often oversupply goods and services. The second answer is that we need to reinvent government because it is unresponsive. This is an argument about democracy rather than costs. It might be possible, for example, to have a perfectly "efficient" bureaucracy that was nonetheless closed and unresponsive to the public. This approach therefore focuses less on what governments spend than on how governments and bureaucrats relate to society. The classic bureaucratic structure of hierarchy, strict control, and accountability to the minister results in highly inaccessible government structures.

Most of the debate over reinventing government has focused on the first answer—on redesigning systems and structures so that they will do some of the same things, but with less money. Fiscal constraints figure prominently in Osborne and Gaebler's analysis, as they did in the United Kingdom's Next Steps program. When reinvention rhetoric does focus on participation and bureaucratic responsiveness, it usually does so by conceptualizing people as "clients" rather than as citizens.[6] There is nothing inherently wrong with this, and the U.K.'s Citizen's Charter demonstrates its potential for forcing agencies to be both clearer about their goals and more accountable to the public. But it does recast the issue from an inherently political issue to a quasi-market one. If people are defined as clients and consumers, then responsiveness almost automatically gets defined in terms of decentralization, small operating size, flexibility, transparency, and visibility—the government agency as a firm operating in a public-sector "market." When citizens complain about government unresponsiveness, however, they often have more fundamental political concerns in mind. They do not see government merely as a provider of services, but as a reflection of society's broader purposes. The bureaucracy, in short, is not simply an instrument of the state, but is a link between state and society.

This point can be illustrated with reference to three fundamental forces that will call for the reinvention of government, but not merely reinvention in the sense of efficiency. The first is the unabating demand from the public for *consultation and real participation* in the policy process. The first tremors in this earthquake were felt during the Meech Lake Accord constitutional process from 1987 to 1990, and then again during the process involving the Charlottetown Accord and the 1992 referendum. As many commentators have observed, the adoption in 1982 of the Charter of Rights and Freedoms appears to have galvanized Canadians to defend "their" Constitution directly. The Citizens' Forum on Canada's Future (the Spicer Commission) pioneered a wide variety of consultative mechanisms, from 1-800 telephone lines to organizing thousands of discussion groups on the Constitution. Parliamentary committees and special conferences on the Constitution were visible evidence of a new thirst for more democratic and more participatory forms of policy-making. This has spread well beyond the constitutional arena, and Ottawa has elaborate guidelines for departmental consultations with the public. But real consultation and participation is something qualitatively different from responding to people as clients and consumers of services. It means sitting at tables, jointly developing agendas, and politicizing a range of traditional "management" decisions. It also requires of citizens and citizens groups a substantial degree of discipline and skill. The current evidence suggests that a consultative culture is still absent from most Ottawa departments, and the 1993 reorganization into larger ministries may make public participation in decision-making even more difficult to achieve.

A second force that promises to complicate attempts at reinvention is the sense that government agencies and bureaus should reflect a *commitment to social justice*. One aspect of this is the concept of equal entitlement to programs based on citizenship. Canada Post, for example, has discontinued door-to-door delivery in new subdivisions and closed post offices in sparsely populated areas. It undertook these changes only once it had been converted from a department to a Crown corporation, and it has encountered substantial resistance from people who claim that postal services should be uniformly available to all citizens, no matter where they live. Canada Post was reinventing its services in ways perfectly consistent with a market-driven approach. The reaction was grounded in a political logic that views all citizens as fundamentally equal and therefore entitled to similar levels of service.

Another aspect of social justice is equity. Bureaucracy is both an instrument through which services are delivered and a *catalyst for social change*, one that reflects and validates public values. Government agencies often pioneer employment standards not simply because they can afford to waste taxpayers' money, but because they are expected to demonstrate leadership. Employment and pay equity, for example, started in the public sector. Policies and programs against racism and sexual harassment are usually more elaborate and comprehensive in public-sector agencies than in the private sector. Many initiatives considered to be on the cutting edge of social-justice concerns, such as same-sex marriages and spousal benefits, have been undertaken first in the public-sector. As well, a host of agencies are designed not merely to reflect but to enforce these public standards. Human-rights commissions and broadcasting regulators demonstrate that citizens in a political community expect government to reflect and enforce standards of conduct as well as provide services.

The final force that will complicate reinventing our government is globalization and the concomitant pressure for strong national policies to steer the Canadian economy and society. Globalization is a complex phenomenon that encompasses falling trade barriers, changing technologies of communication and transportation, and international competition and sourcing of products. In Canada these forces are joined by the North American Free Trade Agreement (NAFTA), which creates a continental economy with the United States and Mexico. Globalization is usually seen as having two categories of effects: it exposes national economies to global competition and at the same time, given the fluidity of capital and investments, makes it increasingly difficult for governments to use traditional policy instruments to manage those economies. This perception is true but incomplete. Globalization does affect domestic economies, but precisely because of that it compels governments to react both defensively and offensively to position their societies in the new global order.

The ways in which Canadians expect the national government to react to the pressures of globalization make simplistic forms of reinvention for pure efficiency's sake difficult. For instance, as the 1993 federal election demonstrated, Canadians place a high priority on job creation and programs that will facilitate adjustment at the regional and sectoral level. The Liberal election policy book, *Creating Opportunity,* listed a host of initiatives to deal with Canada's economic challenges: increased federal–provincial cooperation, apprenticeship programs, a Youth Services Corps, literacy and workplace training, a national child-care strategy, a defence conversion program to move industries from military production to high-tech civilian purposes, and the famous infrastructure program. The important point about these promises is that they imply a strategic stance by the federal government, something that is considerably more complex and far-reaching than the simple delivery of services.

CONCLUSION

Citizens in the Anglo-American democracies have been intensively questioning the form and functions of their governments for more than a decade. Public bureaucracy has become emblematic of the problem; it has been attacked as distant, insular, expensive, inefficient, and unresponsive. The reaction to this attack—cut costs, decentralize, delegate, empower front-line officials, and even restructure in such a way that public bureaucracies become hybrids of private and public enterprise—has been remarkably similar in systems as different as the United States and Britain, though the pace of reform has varied.

Canada has barely begun to consider seriously this potential revolution in the public sector. The PS 2000 initiative anticipated many of the themes and ideas of the reinventing-government movement, but it was essentially a managerial exercise aimed at changing organizational culture. Its impact to date has been quite modest. The Shortcliffe departmental reorganization was another "top-down" undertaking, but one that emanated directly from the Prime Minister's Office without the approval, or even knowledge, of the senior management in the public service. Its rationale was virtually the direct opposite of PS 2000: rather than change hearts and minds and hope that behaviour and organization would come to reflect that change, it operated on the organizational side. With the amalgamation of programs and services into several "superministries," bureaucrats would be forced to ask themselves about their programmatic missions, their expenditures, and possible overlaps and conflicts within departments.

Both of these projects respond in some measure to the widely perceived pathologies of the public sector reviewed in this chapter. For the remainder of the decade, there will be continued pressure to make the Canadian bureaucracy more efficient, less costly, more flexible and more consumer-oriented. This chapter has argued that the focus on efficiency, while laudable, misses another important dimension of bureaucracy. Bureaucracy delivers goods and services and at the same time expresses and reflects the public purpose and the public good. The first type of relationship between state and society lends itself quite well to disaggregation, decentralization, and a quasi-market organization. The second is more ambiguous, but it sees bureaucracy as a more cohesive link—one that treats people as citizens as well as clients, that exemplifies certain standards of social justice, and that can act strategically to steer the society and economy as a whole. Canadian bureaucracy will continue to be reformed and reinvented in the 1990s, and the challenge will come in reconciling these two visions.

NOTES

1. David Osborne and Ted Gaebler, *Reinventing Government: How the Entrepreneurial Spirit Is Transforming the Public Sector* (Reading, Mass.: Addison-Wesley, 1992), pp. 19–20. Reprinted by permission of Addison-Wesley Publishing Co., Inc., Reading, Mass.

2. The rest of this section borrows heavily from Bill Jenkins and Andrew Gray, "Reshaping the Management of Government: The Next Steps Initiative in the United Kingdom," in F. Leslie Seidle, ed., *Rethinking Government: Reform or Reinvention?* (Montreal: Institute for Research on Public Policy, 1993), pp. 73–109; and G. Bruce Doern, "The UK Citizen's Charter: Origins and Implementation in Three Agencies," *Policy and Politics* 21 (1993): 17–29.

3. Paul M. Tellier, "Public Service 2000: The Renewal of the Public Service," *Canadian Public Administration* 33 (Summer 1990): 126.

4. Bruce Rawson, "Public Service 2000 Service to the Public Task Force: Findings and Implications," *Canadian Public Administration* 34 (Autumn 1991): 491.

5. Giles Gherson, "Top Bureaucrat Defends Shakeup," *The Globe and Mail* ([Toronto] July 17, 1993), p. A2.

6. I am indebted to Denis St.-Martin for this insight.

FURTHER READINGS

Canada. *Public Service 2000: A Report on Progress*. Ottawa: Minister of Supply and Services, 1992.

Canada. *Public Service 2000: The Renewal of the Public Service of Canada*. Ottawa: Minister of Supply and Services, 1990.

Doern, G. Bruce. "The UK Citizen's Charter: Origins and Implementation in Three Agencies." *Policy and Politics* 21 (1993): 17–29.

Kernaghan, Kenneth. "Empowerment and Public Administration: Revolutionary Advance or Passing Fancy?" *Canadian Public Administration* 35 (Summer 1992): 194–214.

Osborne, David, and Ted Gaebler. *Reinventing Government: How the Entrepreneurial Spirit Is Transforming the Public Sector*. Reading, Mass.: Addison-Wesley, 1992.

Seidle, F. Leslie, ed. *Rethinking Government: Reform or Reinvention?* Montreal: Institute for Research on Public Policy, 1993.

15 THE MASS MEDIA: PRIVATE OWNERSHIP, PUBLIC RESPONSI-BILITIES[1]

Frederick J. Fletcher and

Daphne Gottlieb Taras

The mass media have become in modern industrial societies the primary communicators of politically significant images. The capacity of these media—newspapers, magazines, radio, film, and television—to reach large audiences and to select which ideas and images will have wide popular currency gives them great potential influence. In large part, the media form our psychic environment, especially with respect to matters beyond our direct personal experience, a realm into which most aspects of politics fall. The average Canadian adult spends more than three hours watching television each day, a little less listening to radio and more than 50 minutes reading a daily newspaper. Television viewing takes up more of the average Canadian's time than anything but work and sleep, and nearly half our population say that they stay informed by watching television news.[2]

The mass media are a multibillion dollar industry, and their business is attracting audiences to sell to advertisers. While informing and entertaining us, and capturing us in order to increase their market share, "the media ... define what is normal and respectable in a society, what is debatable and what is beyond discussion by decent, respectable citizens," as Anthony Westell put it.[3] In choosing among the vast array of available drama scripts, news items, and other materials, key media personnel have great influence on the beliefs and perspectives presented to the citizenry. These choices help to determine the available role models, images of reality, and definitions of what is political. Exposure to the media not only provides information on a wide range of subjects but also generates topics of conversation and things to worry about (from environmental issues to advertiser-generated concerns about dandruff and bad breath).

MEDIA EFFECTS: GATEKEEPING, FRAMING, AGENDA-SETTING, PRIMING

Thousands of potential news stories are caught in the news net and fed into an ever-narrowing funnel known as the newsroom, where news-workers decide what stories will become news. Many will be missed because the news net tends to focus its attention on official sources, elite countries, and easily accessible locations. The importance of this *gatekeeping* function[4] derives in large part from the fact that gatekeepers tend to share assumptions about what makes appropriate media content. These assumptions can be traced to cultural norms, government regulations, policies of media organizations, training of media personnel, current fashion, and the requirements of media technologies. Within the boundaries of acceptability, the gatekeepers are primarily concerned about attracting audiences. While each medium has its own requirements, they all tend to prefer the immediate, the personal, and the concrete to long-term social processes or abstract ideas. Topics that are complex, technical, and difficult to research, as well as those that fall outside mainstream ideas and institutions, rarely became news, regardless of their significance.[5] Media consumers are conditioned to accept these standards as well, making it difficult for messages that do not fit the media mold to get a hearing.

The news selection criteria—that the story be immediate, involve conflict, concentrate on personalities, require little background research, and, for television, have good visual properties, to name the most influential—affect presentation as well as selection. Reporters are sent out to interview personalities, camera crews seek out sensational shots, and the stories that are written highlight any inherent drama. This shaping of the news story for entertainment value is one aspect of *framing*,[6] a process that influences the way issues come to be viewed.

The effects of gatekeeping and framing on our political life are hotly debated. To paraphrase an early study of newspapers, the media may not be successful much of the time in telling people what to *think*, but they are stunningly successful in telling people what to *think about*.[7] It is becoming increasingly evident that the items that receive prominent attention on the national news, especially the leading items or those items that appear frequently, become the problems the public regards as the nation's most important. This is known as *agenda-setting*.[8] By concentrating on free trade and polls during the 1988 federal election, the media were able to influence the agenda of public debate without necessarily having a direct effect on opinions or voting intentions. Over the long run, the effects of agenda-setting also contribute to the "generation gap": adults over 40 remember a time when they were consumed by worries about the Cold War and nuclear weapons, whereas those under 20 are "programmed" for environmental issues. Societal agendas change, and the media are instruments of these transformations. Other prominent issues today are jobs, the deficit, the economy, and child abuse.

Television is a particularly powerful shaper of values, not only because of its popularity but also because people tend to use it nonselectively, watching whatever attracts them most at the time they want to relax. A leading American communication researcher has concluded that television viewing is a "ritual" that crosses social, religious, generational, and class lines in an unprecedented manner. Most viewers come to "share a great deal of cultural imagery," so that "the most recurrent patterns of the ritual tend to ... become the assumptions we make about the world."[9] These patterns include the stereotyping of minority groups, a great exaggeration of the amount of crime and violence in society (ten times that of the real world), and an unwarranted emphasis on conflict and risk. Portrayal of less industrialized nations' issues is almost always characterized by natural calamities, riots, scandals, and political violence, with little attention given to longer-term problems and achievements. Coverage emphasizes the differences among peoples, not their similarities. The line between news and entertainment shows is increasingly blurred by television. Generally speaking, entertaining us is more profitable than informing us. Indeed, a training manual for CBC television producers states bluntly that "news is theatre."[10] The risk is that even public broadcasters will turn from providing the news we need to make informed choices to the news we want for relaxation and diversion.

Although many experts believe that television newscasts are at best a distorted mirror of society, their visuals and eyewitness quality give them great credibility. Audiences appear generally unaware of the medium's limitations (a 30-minute newscast contains less information than the front page of the *The Globe and Mail*) and beguiled by the illusion of access to newsmakers that television news provides. A 15-second clip from a 20-minute speech is not real access. Despite its limitations, most media consumers sincerely believe that television is the most "believable" news medium.[11] The tendency to view television news as accurate, objective, and impartial means that audiences are more receptive to influence from that source, and helps to explain the attention that politicians give it.

There is growing evidence that television not only has substantial influence on the public agenda but also helps to set the standards by which governments, policies, and candidates for public office are judged. It appears that media consumers evaluate political figures based on the information they have most recently and most frequently been exposed to on the news, a process called *priming*.[12] During the 1993 federal election, voters probably were primed by media coverage of unemployment and cutbacks, which heightened the saliency of deficit management as a campaign issue. The fall of the NDP in 1993 may have been accelerated due to repeated inferences conveyed in the media that because the NDP was failing in the polls, NDP votes would be "wasted." In media interviews, even traditionally loyal NDP voters admitted to altering their votes in order to make them "count." The emphasis of the national news on party leaders has primed many voters to evaluate parties based on leaders—their charm under fire, their "telegenic" attributes such as warmth and sincerity, and their delivery of campaign speeches—rather than local candidates or even party platforms. The question is no longer whether the media affect our lives, but rather in what ways?

SCHOOLS OF THOUGHT

In attempting to understand the role of the media in Canadian politics, analysts generally draw upon two competing schools of thought: the liberal-democratic and neo-Marxist approaches. The two perspectives share the view that the mass media, though for the most part privately owned, have important political functions. Both believe that the media have significant social power and reject the argument advanced by some media people that they merely reflect the values and tastes of their audiences.

In liberal democracies like Canada, the media are seen by many as a "fourth branch of government" that meets the needs of citizens by presenting the information necessary for effective political participation and by providing a forum for debate on public issues. In this process, they are expected to help governments disseminate vital information about public services and government accomplishments while providing opportunities for opposition parties to criticize government and propose alternative policies. Ideally, they provide commentary on public affairs from a wide variety of perspectives, including those of unpopular minorities. An important tradition in the Anglo-American democracies holds that the news media should serve as watchdogs, sniffing out abuses of power—especially by governments—and barking out the alarm. In a detailed study of the Canadian media, Richard Ericson and his colleagues argue that "deviance is *the* defining characteristic of what journalists regard as newsworthy. ... Journalists act as watchdogs, policing organizational life for deviations from their conceptions of the order of things."[13] In short, news organizations have a duty to "help keep democracy alive in societies too populous and too complex for face-to-face exchange."[14]

An alternative view, drawing on neo-Marxist thinking, sees the media as an important part of an ideological system that effectively promotes the dominant ideology of society, providing a justification for the economic and political status quo and thus serving the interests of the rich and powerful. By establishing the limits of debate, the media screen out radical critiques and reinforce existing values, values defined by the powerful and communicated from the top down. In North America, the mass media are seen as promoting consumerism, which supports the economic system, and the myth of "middle-classness," which holds that society's advantages are equally available to all. Critics of the system are presented as failures, with only themselves to blame, or as promoters of "foreign" ideologies.[15] Private ownership of property is presented as an inviolable norm. The inefficiencies, wrongdoings, and mismanagement of private corporations are hidden in shadow while the media searchlight is trained on corrupt or ineffectual individuals in the public sector. When criticisms of the economic and political system are presented, the approach is generally reformist rather than radical. The media are seen as "a powerful ideological weapon for holding the mass of people in voluntary submission to capitalism."[16]

It has been demonstrated many times that those who control the mass media are a powerful segment of Canada's economic elite. Class analysts argue, therefore, that the owners and thus the media have a stake in the perpetuation of the existing power structure. "Freedom of the press," as the American media critic A.J. Liebling said, "is guaranteed only to those who own one."[17] The extent to which corporate control of media organizations actually influences content is examined below.

THE CANADIAN MASS MEDIA SYSTEM: EVOLUTION

The mass-media system in Canada has undergone great change in audience penetration, operating philosophy, technology, and ownership over the years. From their earliest beginnings in the 18th century, Canadian newspapers were highly political, with close ties to government or opposition parties. In the 19th century, they often served as personal vehicles for editor-politicians like George Brown, William Lyon Mackenzie, Étienne Parent, Joseph Howe, and Amor de Cosmos. During the upheavals of the late 1830s, the press was a thorn in the side of those in power, and the reformist strain of Canadian journalism was firmly established along with a tradition of press freedom. After the Rebellions of 1838 in Upper Canada, Attorney-General John Beverley Robinson lamented the principle of a free press, but could do little about it:

> *It is one of the miserable consequences of the abuse of liberty that a licentious press is permitted to poison the public mind with the most absurd and wicked representations, which the ill-disposed, without inquiry, receive and act upon as truths.*[18]

In the 19th century, newspapers were small operations, locally owned and highly partisan, often relying on government patronage or party financial support. They engaged in vociferous competition and denounced political opponents with vigour, contributing much to the vitality of political debate but often little to public enlightenment.

By the 1870s, the growth of urban centres and the emergence of new technologies—mechanized printing, cheap newsprint, the telegraph for rapid newsgathering—contributed to the proliferation of newspapers and the creation of a mass press that emphasized social issues of broader interest than strictly political matters. Newspapers tried to extend their appeal to serve two distinct but related markets: readers and advertisers anxious to reach them. Newspapers were no longer primarily vehicles for political debate among competing elites, and advertisers freed the press from financial dependence on politicians. In the competition for mass audiences, many publishers fell by the wayside, and, by the turn of the century, successful publishers were buying out those in financial difficulty. For example, the Southam family purchased *The Ottawa Citizen* (1897), the *Calgary Herald* (1908), *The Edmonton Journal* (1912), and the *Winnipeg Tribune* (1920). The Southam and Sifton chains were well established by 1920, and the trend toward concentration of ownership has continued to accelerate, with a handful of large corporations now controlling most daily newspapers and many weeklies, magazines, and privately owned radio and television outlets, as well as cable systems.

The quest for mass audiences, the growth of newspaper chains and absentee ownership, and the advent of wire services selling news to a wide range of clients all contributed to the decline of the partisan press. More interested in profits than politics, the larger publishers moderated their partisanship to appeal to broader audiences. Wire services were founded to sell newspaper copy across the country and throughout the world. Their reports were kept as neutral as possible, especially with regard to domestic politics, so they could appeal to newspapers of all partisan stripes. Publishers were delighted to subscribe to news services and to purchase syndicated features because they were so much cheaper than staff-written material. The costs were shared by many clients. For these reasons, the era of so-called objective journalism emerged, spreading gradually in the years following the Depression.

The major Canadian wire service, the Canadian Press (CP), was founded in 1917 as a national cooperative owned collectively by the major daily newspapers. Set up as a clearing house for news gathered by Canada's dailies, CP has provided an effective and inexpensive mechanism for exchanging news among member papers and for bringing in up-to-date foreign news. CP remains today the primary source of nonlocal news for all but the largest Canadian dailies. With its own staff of reporters, it covers major stories within Canada and provides limited foreign coverage. It has been criticized, however, for relying too heavily on the central Canadian media and for importing most its foreign news from the world's major news services. Because of its heavy reliance on American sources—especially its U.S. counterpart, the Associated Press (AP)—Canadians continue to see the world "through U.S. eyes."[19]

Radio and television newsrooms, most of which lack the resources to do much newsgathering on their own, also rely on CP and its subsidiaries. Television news uses the U.S. networks as well as Visnews, which is dominated by the British Broadcasting Corporation (BBC). The French media rely on these same sources, with a heavy dose of material from Agence France-Presse (AFP), the Paris-based service. While the CBC makes a real effort at independent foreign coverage, with bureaus in a few major world centres and a number of excellent foreign correspondents, its limited resources compel it to rely heavily on local feeds or news services, using voice-overs to give a Canadian slant on an agenda set by the sources of its pictures, usually U.S. networks.

From the beginning, the development of Canada's magazine and motion-picture industries was hindered by competition from the United States. Since the 1930s, the Canadian government has employed tariffs, tax measures, subsidies, and government agencies, including Crown corporations, to help Canadian enterprises survive competition from large and well-funded American corporations that regarded Canada as a convenient secondary market. The consistent view of Canadian governments has been that to permit American-based media to dominate Canadian markets would threaten Canada's cultural identity and siphon off revenues needed by Canadian enterprises to perform their public duties. Countervailing measures included the creation of the award-winning National Film Board in 1939 and a variety of subsidy schemes that have had only limited success in staunching the flood of American movies and television shows. The Broadcast Fund of Telefilm Canada has recently been quite successful in promoting Canadian drama on television. In the 1970s, new legislation helped *Saturday Night* to survive and created room in the advertising market for *Maclean's* to become a weekly newsmagazine. In recent years, Canadian magazines have flourished, but their finances remain precarious given their relatively small market.

PRESERVING THE INTEGRITY OF THE CANADIAN BORDER

Canadian radio and television services were founded in direct response to the spillover of American signals. Government intervention was made necessary not only by the need to allocate frequencies and to negotiate an agreement with the U.S. government for a share of the airwaves, but also by the high cost of reaching Canada's scattered population. Faced with a choice between a government-owned system and a U.S.-dominated commercial one (with little Canadian content) that would serve only the major cities, the Conservative government of R.B. Bennett opted in 1932 for a Crown corporation, which became the CBC and which now provides nationwide signals in both French and English. The radio network was joined by a television service in the 1950s. In 1958, the Board of Broadcast Governors (BBG) was created to regulate both the CBC and the growing private sector. It oversaw the end of the dream of a single integrated broadcasting system and the growth of parallel public and private systems. The most important product of this evolution was CTV, a national private English-language television network formed in 1961. Since the early 1970s, a number of independent stations and regional networks have been licensed.

The year 1968 saw passage of a new Broadcasting Act that changed the name of the regulatory agency to the Canadian Radio-Television Commission (later the Canadian Radio-television and Telecommunications Commission, or CRTC) and set out some ambitious objectives for the broadcasting system:

> ... the Canadian broadcasting system should be effectively owned and controlled by Canadians so as to safeguard, enrich and strengthen the cultural, political, social and economic fabric of Canada; the programming provided by the Canadian broadcasting system should be varied and comprehensive and should provide reasonable, balanced opportunity for the expression of different views on matters of public concern, and the programming provided by each broadcaster should be of a high standard, using predominantly Canadian creative and other resources.

Both public and private broadcasters were expected to contribute to these goals, and the CRTC was to implement them. The new act, it was hoped, would "help maintain the existence of a broadcasting system intended to serve Canadian needs despite the influence everywhere of American television and films." Federal government objectives have also included provision of coast-to-coast service in both official languages, reflecting the diversity of Canadian cultural and social values, and, for the CBC, contributing to the development and maintenance of national unity and Canadian cultural identity.[20]

In attempting to fulfil these objectives, the CRTC has promulgated Canadian content regulations for both radio and television, and has required cable systems, which came into being to deliver clear U.S. signals, to give priority to Canadian stations.[21] U.S. border stations have complained that Canadian regulations removing tax deductions from Canadian businesses advertising on non-Canadian stations, and requiring cable systems to carry only the Canadian station when a program is broadcast simultaneously on a U.S. station, are interfering with the free flow of information. It must be noted that the border stations do not pay program suppliers for the right to broadcast shows in Canada, while Canadian stations do pay. Yet another cross-border concern is financial compensation for U.S. stations when their signals are distributed via cable in Canada. These types of issues are likely to come up in future free-trade negotiations.

Station owners are primarily concerned with their own profits. The cost of Canadian content relative to its revenue potential is a sore point with private broadcasters. Private broadcasters argue that they generate most of their revenues (about 70 percent) from U.S. imports, while Canadian shows absorb most of their program expenditures.[22] The American imports are usually proven winners, already promoted by the U.S. networks, and much cheaper than homegrown shows of comparable quality because their costs have already been covered in the U.S. market. It is this economic fact of life that has limited CTV to producing dramatic series only as coproductions with U.S. networks, resulting in shows that have little direct relevance to Canada.

The conflict between open borders and cultural sovereignty is not unique to Canada, of course, and in the Canadian case virtually no U.S. network programs are denied entry to Canada. The objective is not to shut out U.S. programming, but rather to preserve a place for Canadian content. Because cultural "products" are a major U.S. export, the open borders versus cultural sovereignty issue has been a source of conflict in free-trade negotiations. In both the Free Trade Agreement with the United States and the North American Free Trade Agreement (NAFTA), Canadian negotiators held out for modest exemptions from free-trade rules for measures designed to protect and promote Canadian productions (books, magazines, films, television programs, and so on). These exemptions, though quite limited, have become a model for other countries seeking to preserve a space for their own cultural creations. In the recent negotiations under the General Agreement on Tariffs and Trade (GATT), France cited the Canadian example in its successful efforts to protect its own program of regulation and subsidies. These exemptions recognize that books, art, music, drama, and especially television and film are important aspects of a nation's sense of identity and have consequences quite apart from their commercial value.

Canadian audiences demonstrate an interesting ambivalence on the issue. While showing a strong preference for U.S. entertainment programs, they generally prefer Canadian documentaries and news and public affairs shows. Moreover, there is clear evidence from public-opinion surveys that Canadians want to have a substantial amount of Canadian programming available, even if they reserve the right not to watch it.[23] The regulations have encouraged the development of good quality news and public affairs shows that are now popular moneymakers. In addition, the CBC has in recent years been able to improve its audience share with an increasingly Canadian lineup, including some shows with very high ratings.

When the CRTC licensed pay-television in 1982, having resisted cable-company lobbying for a decade, it also sought to promote Canadian content through stringent requirements regarding the allocation of broadcast time, revenues, and program acquisition budgets to Canadian productions.[24] Despite the financial difficulties of the pay services, few of which survived, the CRTC quickly licensed a number of other specialty services, including MuchMusic, The Sports Network, and narrowcasters such as TeleLatino and ChinaVision, and permitted the cable systems to import the Cable News Network (CNN) and Arts and Entertainment (A&E). In 1988, Youth TV and Vision TV were approved as new Canadian services to be offered on cable, along with a new pay-television service, the Family Channel. In 1989, the CBC, with private-sector partners, introduced an all-news channel, "Newsworld," a nondiscretionary cable service that has added important new dimensions to Canadian political journalism (including live coverage of major events and more detailed coverage of provincial politics).[25] In 1994, the CRTC plans to license a maximum of six new services, from among 48 applications. The goal has been to provide a wide range of choice on cable so that most Canadians will not feel the need to turn to U.S. satellite services, which provide little Canadian content. The emergence of pay-per-view and interactive services in subsequent years almost certainly will lead to dramatic changes in the advertising-driven, mass-audience television Canadians are accustomed to viewing. The long-term political consequences of these developments are not yet clear.

Despite the regulatory efforts of the CRTC and the promises of private broadcasters, Canadians continue to be inundated with the values of American commercial television. Even on Canadian stations, U.S. programs dominate prime time.[26] English-speaking Canadian children spend more than 80 percent of their television viewing time watching U.S. programs. The effect upon Canadians is both subtle and profound. The Caplan-Sauvageau Task Force on Broadcasting lamented in 1986 that "English Canadians ... are virtual strangers in television's land of the imagination."[27] American images crowd out Canadian ones, and Canadians who do not pay close attention can easily become confused about our political institutions, many of which have similar names but differ markedly in theory and practice from their U.S. counterparts. Many believe, as John Meisel puts it, that television "has contributed significantly to the loss of regional and national identities" and to the Americanization of Canada.[28] This pattern of communication reduces our capacity to come to grips with our own particular problems and to preserve our distinctive values such as civility, order, compassion, and community responsibility. How far can the American occupation of the Canadian imagination go without threatening the foundations of Canadian society?

CANADA'S INTERNAL DIVISIONS: REGIONALISM AND DUALISM

The extent to which the mass-media system can contribute to promoting national unity and identity is also affected by two other enduring issues in Canadian politics: regionalism and cultural dualism. Canada's dispersed and culturally diverse population has always presented a formidable barrier to the development of national consensus. The Caplan-Sauvageau Task Force on Broadcasting concluded in its 1986 report that the broadcasting system was woefully inadequate in promoting Canadian national identity. The task force identified as major causes insufficient funding for the CBC and other public outlets by successive governments, the unimpressive performance of the privately owned media in explaining Canadians to one another, the CRTC's inability to pursue these objectives vigorously as a result of legislative and political constraints, and the system's insensitivity to regional differences. In its wide-ranging recommendations on the future of Canadian broadcasting, the task force attempted to find ways to promote Canadian cultural identity and the Canadian broadcasting industry without requiring unrealistic levels of government funding. The main thrust of the recommendations was to encourage increased Canadian programming through new services—such as an all-news channel and a new, noncommercial satellite-to-cable service in both official languages—and increased funding derived from mandatory cable subscription fees and a variety of tax measures. The task force also recommend tax incentives for advertisers sponsoring Canadian entertainment programming and decentralization of the CBC and the CRTC to encourage regional input.[29] While various aspects of these recommendations have already been implemented, others have fallen by the wayside or were put on hold awaiting the long-heralded 1991 Broadcasting Act. Almost simultaneous with the act's passage, however, was a series of deep budget cuts to the CBC, which eliminated local-level broadcasting and severely traumatized the CBC as an institution.

The 1991 act explicitly directs the Canadian broadcasting system as a whole to "serve the needs and interests, and reflect the circumstances and aspirations, of Canadian men, women and children, including equal rights, the linguistic duality and multicultural and multiracial nature of Canadian society and the special place of aboriginal peoples within that society." Thus, where the act now specifies the many stakeholder groups to be served, at the same time the capacity of the CBC to deliver this broad mandate is diminished by its budgetary restrictions. It remains debatable whether the Broadcasting Act can be used to compel the private broadcasting industry to meet the new obligations enumerated in the act—and, if so, how.

Canada's cultural dualism has been a barrier to effective national communication. The two language groups tend to live in separate media worlds. Attempts over the past twenty years to integrate the CBC's French and English services have been largely ineffective, and the Caplan-Sauvageau Task Force recommended that they be permitted to focus on serving their culturally distinct audiences.[30] Section 3(1)(m) of the 1991 Broadcasting Act tries to strike a balance between CBC's "contributing to shared national consciousness and identity" and a separation of English and French programming "reflecting the different needs and circumstances of each official language community." Until recently, most Quebec outlets concerned themselves primarily with Quebec issues, and few had correspondents beyond Ottawa. In the late 1970s, interest in the rest of Canada increased and coverage improved, as English media coverage of Quebec had a decade earlier.

Frequently, major political events are given sharply different interpretations in French and English media. The most striking differences occur with respect to issues involving the preservation of Quebec's distinct society: issues of language policy, constitutional issues such as the Meech Lake Accord and 1992 constitutional referendum, and clashes between collective and individual rights in Quebec. This distinctiveness is found in all types of programming that reflect and promote Quebec's own social perspectives.[31] The overwhelming Conservative victory in Quebec in the 1988 federal election reflected an elite consensus, communicated by the media to the voters, that both the Free Trade Agreement and the Meech Lake Accord were in the best interests of the Quebec community. The debate over free trade in English Canada was not mirrored in the French-language media. The 1993 election issue in Quebec was the emergence of the Bloc Québécois (eventually to the status of official Opposition) while western Canada lived in a media world that emphasized the Reform Party's meteoric rise. French and English seem to be experiencing separate but parallel media events.

There are important issues within the English-Canadian media system as well. Although major advances in cross-regional communication have been made in recent years, primarily through improved regional coverage by *The Globe and Mail*, the seventeen Southam dailies through Southam's news service (SN), and the CBC, the news still tends to originate in the Ottawa–Toronto–Montreal triangle. The news services and national syndicates, which distribute news and features, tend to draw heavily on the Toronto papers and broadcast outlets. The reporters in the regional bureaus of the *Globe*, SN, and CBC write for Toronto- or Montreal-based editors. The national media—the *Globe, Maclean's*, CBC Radio, and the television networks—remain few in number and are limited in their penetration. The system's combination of parochialism (with most news outlets locally oriented) and central-Canadian domination of national coverage has not done very much to strengthen the ties of Confederation.

CBC's "Newsworld," by originating newscasts in Calgary during prime time (4 p.m. to 9 p.m.) may help to redress regional imbalances in coverage, but the show's modest audience makes such decentralization more of a symbolic gesture than an instrument of statecraft.

OWNERSHIP AND CONTROL[32]

Fascination with the media's entertainment and public-service functions often obscures the financial importance of this industry and its role as a major employer of highly skilled workers. The trend to large-scale corporate ownership of the media is widespread and accelerating, at a time when media employment is shrinking as media giants deliver their services using fewer and fewer workers. Most of the country's approximately 110 dailies are owned by a handful of media conglomerates. In most provinces, ownership of major media is concentrated in very few hands. In the English daily press, two major chains, Southam and Thomson, own some 55 dailies with more than half the daily circulation. The French daily press is dominated by three chains that control most of the circulation.

The central features of the dominant media chains in Canada are: (1) both vertical and horizontal integration, with in-house production capabilities combined with distribution facilities and ownership of outlets in more than one medium; (2) mass-media holdings that form only a portion of the conglomerates' total operations; (3) a pattern of co-ownership among the communication giants, including media and nonmedia holdings; and (4) the development of specialized markets so that competition among dailies (and other media) is limited. Southam, with the largest total circulation and corporate assets of almost $900 million (Cdn.), illustrates these patterns well. In addition to its seventeen dailies and 56 weeklies, it owns a majority of the Angus Reid polling company, and the largest retail bookstore chain in Canada (Coles). Both the Vancouver *Sun* and *Province* are Southam papers, as are the Montreal *Gazette, The Ottawa Citizen, The Calgary Herald,* and *The Edmonton Journal.* Since 1993, Southam has been partially owned by Conrad Black's international media conglomerate, Hollinger, and another major Canadian holding company, Power.

Thomson Newspapers Ltd. is a true multinational conglomerate, with over $7.9 billion (U.S.) in assets. It has interests in 108 newspapers, 124 magazines, over 39,000 books and directories, 190 on-line services, 161 CD-ROM products, and over 9,600 other products. It owns a travel group that, among other activities, operates Britannia Airways, Britain's leading leisure airline. In Canada, it owns *The Globe and Mail* and the *Winnipeg Free Press,* and 36 dailies in smaller centres. Until recently, it also owned The Bay, Simpsons, and Zellers.

Business conglomerates now house "communications" divisions for which any informational or entertainment product or technology is a potential investment. Cross-media ownership (e.g., owning the city's news-paper plus its radio and television stations) carries with it potential for abuse, as it is possible that an entire point of view, advertising campaign, or political candidate could be frozen out of all media in a particular com-munity. The Irving group is frequently accused of failing to give appropri-ate coverage to events that might prove detrimental to the Irving family or their business interests in New Brunswick.[33]

Another cause for concern is absentee ownership. In the three most western provinces, all of the major daily newspapers are owned by chains with headquarters in Ontario. Indeed, almost all of Canada's smaller dai-lies are controlled from Toronto and Montreal. The extent to which this pattern influences local coverage depends largely on the policies of the owners. Chain ownership can bring the benefits of shared resources, in-cluding national and foreign coverage far beyond what smaller, locally owned dailies could afford. It can also produce homogenization of cover-age and insensitivity to local concerns.[34]

Over the past few decades, direct competition among daily newspa-pers has been declining rapidly. At this writing, only Canada's largest cities enjoy any form of competition among dailies published in the same lan-guage. In all but three of these, the second paper trails substantially in cir-culation, so that such papers as *The Calgary Herald, The Edmonton Journal,* and the *Winnipeg Free Press* dominate their markets. In Vancouver, both dailies are owned by Southam. Only in Toronto and Montreal (and, to a lesser extent, Quebec City) is there full competition, which survives mainly because the newspapers have been able to find distinct audiences.

Until 1980, two major chains—Southam and FP—competed vigor-ously across Canada. They had competing dailies in Vancouver, Calgary, Winnipeg, Ottawa, and Montreal, and operated competing news services based in Ottawa. Not long after the Thomson interests purchased FP in January 1980, there occurred a series of manoeuvres that ended the com-petition. Several newspapers were closed (in Montreal, Ottawa, Winnipeg, Calgary, and Victoria), and ownership was consolidated. While there may have been sound business reasons for these transactions, they clearly marked the end of meaningful newspaper competition for most of English Canada, and alarmed politicians and interested citizens to the point that the Royal Commission on Newspapers (Kent Commission) was set up and a parallel investigation was begun under the Combines Act.[35]

Charges of conspiring to lessen competition and unlawful merger were subsequently laid against Thomson and Southam in 1981. Although court testimony made it clear that the two giant chains had exchanged in-formation and discussed the future of the newspapers to be closed, the court found no public detriment and the charges were dismissed in late 1983. It has proven exceedingly difficult to demonstrate harm under the act, and, in practice, there is no real legal barrier to concentration of me-dia ownership.[36]

The Kent Commission was given a tight ten-month deadline, in the hope of heading off further takeovers, and produced a detailed report and eight volumes of research. The commission viewed conglomerate ownership as a powerful threat to the public-service functions of newspapers, fearing that concern for return on investment would reduce editorial quality and that corporate leaders would not live up to their promises to the commission to take a hands-off approach to their newsrooms. The commission recommended a series of measures to restrict concentration and to limit the influence of corporate owners in the editorial offices of the newspapers they owned. A number of indirect measures designed to encourage editorial quality were suggested, including guarantees of autonomy for editors and more self-policing mechanisms, such as press councils. When the commission's report was released on August 18, 1981, the industry response was hysterical denunciation. The head of the commission later described the outcome of the investigation: "[It] came to nothing except the production of useful material for journalism students."[37]

Whatever the role of corporate ownership, there is little doubt that the media present a rather similar picture of society. Observers agree that the media tend to reinforce the dominant institutional and cultural patterns of authority. By setting the limits for public debate, the media generally exclude serious challenges to the status quo, whether from the left or the right. Even as mild a challenge as that mounted by the New Democratic Party (NDP) is too much for most editorial boards. Editorial endorsements for the NDP are so rare as to be newsworthy. Most newspapers are reluctant to challenge in any direct way the dominant interests in their communities. However, there is a reformist thrust in the media, both private and publicly owned, that angers some conservatives. Both business and labour tend to feel aggrieved about their coverage and can cite evidence of bias.[38] Certainly, both sides in the free-trade debate of 1988 complained of biased coverage.

There is some evidence that journalists as a group see themselves as slightly left of centre,[39] yet editorial endorsements of the NDP are rare. One explanation for the status quo orientation is that all major private media are owned by members of the business community and that it is unreasonable to expect "the owners of watchdogs to let them loose on their own friends," or to provide succor for their enemies.[40] In a discussion of the Irving chain, Alden Nowlan suggests that while the Irving family may not interfere directly in editorial operations, they can hardly be expected to mount campaigns against themselves.[41] It seems that journalists do learn the limits of tolerance in their newsrooms and therefore avoid submitting materials likely to be rejected.[42]

The argument that the media elite use their outlets in any direct way for propaganda purposes under normal circumstances is discounted by many observers, who claim that return on investment is the dominant motive of the media barons. According to this explanation, the media cling to the "extreme middle" of the political spectrum, not so much because their owners and managers are closely affiliated with the country's power structure as because their profits depend upon attracting mass audiences to sell to advertiser and mass values tend to be middle-of-the-road. By reflecting these values, the mass media reinforce them, a cycle that is most frustrating to those who seek change.

NEWS COVERAGE OF GOVERNMENT AND POLITICS

Much of what Canadians know about the political process comes from the day-to-day news coverage of government. The news and commentary from Ottawa, the provincial capitals, and city hall are important for the quality of public debate. Parliamentary debates and Question Period would be empty rituals without the media to tell the country about them. Opposition parties are rarely able to mobilize support to modify government policies without media attention.

The largest and most important group of political reporters is in the parliamentary press gallery in Ottawa. The gallery has about 400 members, the majority from the electronic media. As an "adjunct of Parliament," in Mackenzie King's words, gallery members are given special access to government documents and the activities of Parliament.[43] They have access to cable coverage of the House of Commons and press coverage, as well as clipping services and other information not readily available to the public. Gallery correspondents are a vital link between the federal government and the electorate. Through their selection of events to cover, they help to determine the national political agenda. Political columnists are particularly influential because they provide interpretations of events that colour the way we view the political process.

The gallery's growth and the arrival of a new generation of better-educated journalists have helped the gallery provide more (and improved) coverage of federal politics than it did two decades ago. Yet much government activity goes unreported as the majority of reporters concentrate on Question Period and government announcements (with opposition reactions). Because most editors give priority to routine coverage, reporters rarely have time to dig behind the scenes for the real story of how decisions are made. As Anthony Westell has observed, "The question period ... is almost a perfect media event. *Public personalities* come into *Conflict* over current *Controversies*, providing in one neat package the basic ingredients of a news story."[44] These stories meet the standard criteria of news, but provide little information about policy development or the philosophical differences between parties. The courts, regulatory agencies, and inner workings of the public service and cabinet are rarely covered adequately.

The gallery often operates according to a kind of "herd instinct," partly because many reporters lack expertise and partly because editors complain if their staff coverage differs in significant ways from that provided by the wire services. In fact, some of the major news organizations—CP, SN, *The Globe and Mail, The Toronto Star, La Presse,* the CBC, and one or two others—do have specialists on such subjects as finance and economic affairs, energy policy, social issues, federal–provincial relations, and so on. However, what few specialists there are tend to lead the herd in their areas of expertise. The major stories of the day are generally identified collectively and often given a common interpretation.[45]

An important aspect of political reporting is the mutual dependence of reporters and their sources. Politicians need publicity to promote themselves and their programs, while reporters need information and quotes for their stories. Even prime ministers need media attention to maintain their political popularity, which is an important resource when dealing with cabinet, negotiating with provincial premiers, or trying to persuade a private group to support government initiatives. On the other hand, as Ottawa's chief newsmaker, the prime minister has considerable capacity to manage the news, by timing announcements and by rewarding sympathetic journalists with interviews, for example. He or she can also bypass the gallery by requesting network television time. Other prominent political figures, including premiers, cabinet ministers, and opposition party leaders, have similar resources, but none can match the "clout" of the prime minister.[46] In all news-management situations, the government has the advantage of being able to act, while opposition parties can only react or suggest. Governments often use the media to test public opinion by leaking proposals to a reporter who will value the "scoop." A positive public response often strengthens the position of those in government supporting the policy, while a negative reaction might kill it.

The introduction of the electronic *Hansard* into the House of Commons in October 1977 reduced the dependence of radio and television reporters on direct access to the prime minister and other leading politicians. While such access is still sought for various reasons, reporters can now obtain clips for their stories from the audio- and videotapes. Politicians can expect more media exposure, but, except for the relatively few citizens who watch the proceedings on cable, the focus remains on Question Period. Television in the House has increased the visibility of the opposition party leaders and critics, putting them on a more equal footing with the prime minister and cabinet.

Especially when the stakes are high, governments have turned to advocacy advertising to bypass the gallery. Using mainly television, governments have employed spot commercials to promote everything from energy conservation and physical fitness to national unity, constitutional reform, and free trade.[47] An ancillary objective, it seems clear is to improve the government's image at public expense. Advertisements played a major role in the 1980 Quebec referendum campaign, the 1988 free-trade debate, and what proved to be a futile effort to support the "yes" side in the 1992 constitutional referendum. (On the other hand, as we saw in the 1992 referendum battle, advocacy ads are also an attractive and effective vehicle for coalitions who oppose government platforms.) The line between government information and partisan propaganda is hard to draw. The 1991 Royal Commission on Electoral Reform and Party Financing recommended a ban on advocacy advertising during election campaigns.[48]

While some observers feel that the gallery is credulous and easily manipulated, others feel that too many journalists have come to see themselves as commentators and critics rather than as reporters, with a mandate to render judgments as well as report the arguments of the contending parties. One study of the 1984 campaign found that most of the time devoted to coverage of the two major party leaders (127 stories in all) on the CBC national news was taken up with description and commentary by reporters; only 12 percent of the time was taken up by the leaders speaking for themselves, a total of 42 minutes over eight weeks.[49] Perhaps responding to this study, CBC's "The National" provided considerably more direct quotes during the 1988 campaign, but of course the "sound bites" remained relatively short.

Some see the automatic hostility to authority expressed by many gallery members as an unjustified extension of the appropriate stance of scepticism; others say that politicians have given reporters much to be cynical about. Westell argues that the parliamentary system has an institutionalized opposition and does not need an adversarial press: "The central business of the press is to facilitate communication between the institutions which do the business of democratic society and the publics which are supposed to oversee them."[50] There is a concern that journalistic cynicism and emphasis on conflict create a sense of continuing crisis that alienates citizens from the political process. However, Marxist critics argue that the conflicts emphasized are not the significant conflicts in society, and that the adversarial approach to government is superficial and personalized rather than aimed at the real issues of class conflict.

MEDIA AND ELECTIONS

From a liberal-democratic perspective, election coverage is particularly important. Modern campaigns depend upon extensive media coverage. Although many daily newspapers continue to endorse candidates and parties on their editorial pages, overt partisan bias is now rare. Nevertheless, reporters and editors, through their selection and presentation of news, clearly prime the electorate by shaping the images of party leaders, defining campaign issues, and influencing the tone of the coverage.

In many respects, campaigns are contests in which media attention is the prize. In both Canadian and American elections, the roles of "media handlers" (who manage relations between politicians and media) and "spin doctors" (who try to channel media coverage of leaders, events, and policies in favourable directions) have become more and more central to election campaigns. The increasingly overt activities of these new professionals underscore the preoccupation of parties with managing the media, especially during the critical weeks of an election campaign.[51]

The dominant role of television has become particularly evident in recent campaigns, primarily because party strategists believe that it is the best medium for reaching uncommitted voters. The party leaders' tours are tailored for television, with speeches written to produce a brief clip (usually three to twelve seconds) for the television news and cameras given the best vantage point at rallies. The commitment to "image politics" also shows up in the increasing use of television advertisements (mainly 30- or 60-second spots), which provide time to communicate symbols, not arguments. In 1988, the three largest parties spent well over $30 million on the campaign, more than one-third of which was spent on television advertising (which is permitted only during the final four weeks of an electoral campaign).[52]

The main consequence of television's dominant role is that style tends to overwhelm substance. Campaigns become contests of television performance, favouring some leaders over others on attributes irrelevant to the capacity to govern. Liberal leader John Turner is a good example of a politician who was initially glorified by the media (having become something of a political legend while he was out of public life and the glare of media scrutiny) but whose weaknesses—probing stare, nervous cough, and brittle delivery—were magnified by television. It seems likely that his "image problem" was a major factor in his two electoral defeats. Former Conservative leader Joe Clark was also victimized by a media that would not tolerate a nontelegenic leader.[53] As Clive Cocking has put it,

> *the normal journalistic reaction is not to praise but to criticize. There is a tacit understanding among journalists that to write favourably about events or people is, if not perverse, at least gutless and certain to harm one's career. Criticisms, charges and accusations produce the most jolts on television news and the biggest headlines in the papers.*[54]

Politicians these days are a self-selecting group who take on the risk of unleashing journalistic investigations of their personalities, past decisions, and private lives. Every perceived flaw is magnified and broadcast. Prime Minister Mulroney described this "absolutely extraordinary phenomenon" in a Maclean's interview:

You turn on a television set and there is someone describing you and your wife. And I say, "Honey, who is this guy?" She says, "I don't know." This is the latest expert on Brian Mulroney.[55]

Kim Campbell was the subject of at least a handful of biographies during the brief months between her rise to power and swift electoral execution. Few individuals with the talents and commitment necessary to step into the highest public offices would tolerate (or, indeed, withstand) the media's relentless scrutiny.

Yet the emphasis placed on national leaders by the national media means that voters tend to see relatively little of local candidates or potential cabinet ministers during campaigns. The local MPs for whom we are actually casting our votes generally are out of the glare of the media spotlight, and are desperately dependent upon the performance of party leaders. The 1993 electoral humiliation of "Kim's team" is ample evidence of the diminishing role of MPs relative to their leaders.

In the end, the campaign presented in the media is a product of the interaction of media and parties. As long as the parties play by the media rules, focusing on the leaders and a few central issues and presenting their appeals in brief and dramatic fashion, they can set the campaign agenda.[56] Only a few of the major news organizations have made any real effort to get the leaders to address issues they might wish to ignore. The 1988 election was fought almost entirely on the issue of free trade, an agenda set largely by the parties, and one that tended to crowd out other issues of interest to significant numbers of Canadians. The 1993 campaign and election drama focused on the suspense provided by the pincer movement flanking the victorious Liberals—namely the Bloc Québécois in Quebec and the Reform Party in the West.

The actual effect of media coverage on election outcomes remains a matter of controversy. While it seems clear that the media cannot deliberately swing elections, there is also evidence of significant effects. For example, though there was a consistent drift of editorial support away from the Liberals after 1972, the Trudeau government was returned to office in 1974 and 1980, when only two major dailies endorsed it. The Mulroney Conservatives were returned to office in 1988 despite four previous years of almost unabated negative coverage of patronage, cabinet-level scandals, and policy problems. On the other hand, the 1993 election saw the implosion of the Conservatives under Kim Campbell, perhaps due to the lingering desire to obliterate the vestiges of the Mulroney years. Given the substantial numbers of undecided voters at the outset of any campaign in Canada, it seems plausible to suggest that the agenda-setting and priming effects of the media do trigger voting decisions for a good number of citizens. While only a minority of voters will acknowledge the direct effects of the media on their vote choices, most will admit that they make their judgments of leaders and party platforms at least in part on the basis of information gleaned from the media. It is difficult to separate the possible effects of long-term media coverage from the consequences arising from the compressed and carefully orchestrated campaign period. Mulroney's PCs in 1988 were able to recover electoral support largely because of their excellent campaign, while Campbell's 1993 campaign compounded disaster on disaster. Virtually overnight after the election results, members of her campaign team savaged her (and each other) in the media.

In addition to the media's direct effects on voting, there are other important outcomes of media coverage. For example, campaign contributions, public endorsements, and expressions of support such as lawn signs, the recruitment and enthusiasm of campaign volunteers, and internal party morale are all affected by the tone of coverage.[57]

THE POLITICAL SIGNIFICANCE OF MEDIA PATTERNS: IMAGES AND ISSUES

Because the effects are often long term or obscured by other influences, media effects on individual attitudes and behaviour are frequently hard to trace, as we saw with voting. Nevertheless, most observers agree that the media set the agenda for public discussion and influence the basic value system of society. Over time, the priorities of the media tend to become the priorities of the public. These priorities are largely byproducts of the media quest for audiences and profits. Conspiracy theories attributing vast malevolent influence to the media, in the form of subliminal advertising and deliberate slanting of the news, have had to give way to theories that view the process as a form of social interaction. Media priorities emerge from the organizational needs and interests of the media and from their interaction with political parties, interest groups, advertisers, boards of directors, and government regulators, as well as audiences. The political bias that excludes radical criticism of the status quo is as much a function of the perceived limits of public tolerance as it is of the preferences of corporate owners. The relative absence of tough-minded investigative journalism can be explained more readily by the unwillingness of publishers to spend the necessary funds and risk libel suits than by corporate ideologies.[58]

As we have seen, there exist in our media system certain systematic biases that may well have significant political effects. For reasons of both convenience and ideology, journalists prefer official sources and established images to more unconventional approaches. While it is true that effective mass communication is difficult without reference to widely known personalities and ideas, the resulting status-quo orientation means that audiences are rarely asked to question society's basic assumptions.[59]

The media's focus on public- rather than private-sector abuses of power lends support to the popular notion that governments by nature are fraught with mismanagement and incompetence, while the private sector, despite its own share of turmoil and ineptitude, is given greater (and perhaps undeserved) deference. These tendencies, which are found in entertainment programming as well as news and public affairs, probably promote political stability at the expense of social progress. Canadians are now more cynical than Americans about government.

Other patterns, such as the weaknesses in communication across regional and linguistic lines, together with the stress on conflict and on the personal side of politics, may well damage the fabric of Confederation. The denigration of political leaders and institutions in the quest for media jolts may hamper their capacity to cope with the strains in the system. The desirability of public office certainly has been diminished in the eyes of many potential leaders. The crowding out of Canadian images on television by popular American programming appears to be weakening our sense of ourselves. The scarcity of journalists with the genuine expertise to gain credibility with policy-makers impoverishes public policy debate in Canada. While the individual-level effects of these patterns are difficult to demonstrate, the larger effects seem clear enough. As we look ahead to the 21st century, we must consider the implications for Canadian identity and democracy of new technologies and global concentration of ownership. The simultaneous development of small-scale alternative media and vast international conglomerates presents us with an important set of choices, choices that will help to determine the nature of our political community.

Their power and important public function make it imperative that the media be carefully monitored by both regulatory agencies and an informed citizenry. Yet direct interference with the media is problematic for democratic nations. As Christopher Dornan aptly observes,

> *The problem of accountability persists because the press is answerable to no higher authority. But the press cannot be so answerable without compromising its essential freedom. This may be an uncomfortable fact, but it is also a fact of democracy.*[60]

Each of the issues raised in this chapter is an enduring challenge to Canadians. The unsettling terrain between interference and freedom, between the interests of the public and those of the media industry, must be explored. Because of its role and impact on the political life of Canadians, it is obvious that the media industry is not merely a business like any other.

NOTES

1. This chapter is an extensively revised and updated version of "Images and Issues: The Mass Media and Politics in Canada," which appeared in the third edition of this volume.

2. Leonard Kubas et al., *Newspapers and Their Readers,* Royal Commission on Newspapers, research studies on the newspaper industry, vol. 1 (Ottawa: Supply and Services Canada, 1981), pp. 11–12. See also the *Report of the Task Force on Broadcasting Policy,* hereinafter cited as Caplan-Sauvageau Report (Ottawa: Supply and Services Canada, 1986), pp. 82–87; and Michael Adams and Jordan A. Levitin, "Media Bias as Viewed by the Canadian Public," in Robert J. Fleming, ed., *Canadian Legislatures: 1987–88* (Ottawa: Ampersand, 1988), p. 5.

3. Anthony Westell, *The New Society* (Toronto: McClelland and Stewart, 1977), p. 73.

4. A useful discussion of gatekeeping and the factors affecting it may be found in Walter C. Soderlund, Walter I. Romanow, E. Donald Briggs, and R.H. Wagenberg, *Media and Elections in Canada* (Toronto: Holt, Rinehart and Winston of Canada, 1984), pp. 31–35.

5. Coverage of the Meech Lake Accord by television news is an excellent example of that medium's tendency to focus on the clashes and human-interest aspects of the story's main characters rather than on the dry technical information necessary for citizens to assess the content of the accord. See David Taras, "Meech Lake and Television News," and Elly Alboim, "Inside the News Story: Meech Lake as Viewed by an Ottawa Bureau Chief," in *Meech Lake and Canada: Perspectives from the West* (Edmonton: Academic Printing and Publishing, 1988), pp. 219–46.

6. Todd Gitlin, *The Whole World Is Watching* (Berkeley: University of California Press, 1980), p. 7.

7. Bernard Cohen, *The Press and Foreign Policy* (Princeton, N.J.: Princeton University Press, 1963), p. 13.

8. Shanto Iyengar and Donald R. Kinder, *News That Matters: Television and American Opinion* (Chicago: University of Chicago Press, 1987), pp. 16, 112–14. The authors recruited more than 1,000 respondents who were shown subtly altered versions of national television newscasts. In a series of rigorous experiments, their responses to different news formats were measured and compared. The work is considered a significant advance in research on media effects. For some Canadian evidence, see Frederick J. Fletcher, "Mass Media and Parliamentary Elections in Canada," *Legislative Studies Quarterly* 12, no. 3 (August 1987): 361–64.

9. George Gerbner, "Television: a new religion?" *The London Free Press* (January 24, 1981). For a more detailed account of Gerbner's views, see G. Gerbner and L. Gross, "The Scary World of TV's Heavy Viewers," *Psychology Today* (April 1976), pp. 41–89, and a series of articles in *Journal of Communication*. In a provocative essay entitled *The Age of Missing Information,* Bill McKibben challenges the reader to consider whether the "information age" is cramming viewers with relatively useless factoids while allowing audiences to retreat from authentic first-hand experiences (New York: Plume, 1993).

10. Quoted in Richard V. Ericson, Patricia M. Baranek, and Janet B.L. Chan, *Visualizing Deviance: A Study of News Organization* (Toronto: University of Toronto Press, 1987), p. 51.

11. Adams and Levitin, "Media Bias as Viewed by the Canadian Public," pp. 10–11. See also "TV Is Most Believable Medium," *Marketing* 93, no. 7 (February 15, 1988): 5.

12. Iyengar and Kinder, *News That Matters*, pp. 63, 114–33. See Matthew Mendelsohn, "Television's Frames in the 1988 Canadian Election," *Canadian Journal of Communication* 18, no. 2 (Spring 1993): 149–72.

13. Ericson et al. *Visualizing Deviance*, pp. 4–5.

14. John Westergaard, "Power, Class and the Media," in James Curran et al., eds., *Mass Communication and Society* (London: Edward Arnold, 1977), p. 97. Westergaard sets out this view to debunk it. For a more sympathetic treatment, see Fred S. Siebert, Theodore Peterson, and Wilbur Schramm, *Four Theories of the Press* (Urbana: University of Illinois Press, 1956), pp. 39–103. For an examination of these theories in a Canadian context, see Ross A. Eaman, *The Media Society: Basic Issues and Controversies* (Toronto: Butterworths, 1987), pp. 63–90.

15. See the arguments presented by Linda McQuaig in *The Wealthy Banker's Wife* (Toronto: Penguin, 1993) about the forces moving Canadians to accept a conservative agenda of social welfare cuts and the dismantling of the universality concept.

16. Ralph Miliband, quoted in Denis McQuail, "The Influence and Effects of the Mass Media," in Curran et al., *Mass Communication and Society*, p. 89. The general argument is taken from Wallace Clement, *The Canadian Corporate Elite: An Analysis of Economic Power* (Toronto: McClelland and Steward, 1975), pp. 270–86.

17. Clement, *The Canadian Corporate Elite*, pp. 325–43. The quotation is from p. 343.

18. This discussion of the development of the Canadian media draws on Paul Rutherford, *The Making of the Canadian Media* (Toronto: McGraw-Hill Ryerson, 1978), and W.A. Kesterton, *A History of Journalism in Canada* (Toronto: McClelland and Stewart, 1967). The quotation is from Rutherford, p. 1.

19. Arthur Siegel, *Politics and the Media in Canada* (Toronto: McGraw-Hill Ryerson, 1983), p. 194. See also Royal Commission on Newspapers, *Report* (Ottawa: Supply and Services Canada, 1981), pp. 119–33, hereinafter cited as Kent Commission; Joseph Scanlon, "Canada Sees the World through U.S. Eyes: A Case Study in Cultural Domination," *The Canadian Forum* (September 1974), pp. 34–39; and Joseph Scanlon and Al Farrell, "No Matter How It Sounds or Looks, It's Probably Not Canadian," paper presented at the Conference on Media and Foreign Policy, University of Windsor, October 29, 1983. It must be noted that the CBC, Southam News service (SN), and *The Globe and Mail* maintain a number of foreign correspondents of their own and devote significant resources to overseas coverage.

20. Frank Peers, *The Public Eye: Television and the Politics of Canadian Broadcasting* (Toronto: University of Toronto Press, 1979), p. 409. See also Martha Fletcher and Frederick J. Fletcher, "Communications and Confederation: Jurisdiction and Beyond," in R.B. Byers and R.W. Reford, eds., *Canada Challenged: The Viability of Confederation* (Toronto: Canadian Institute of International Affairs, 1979), pp. 171–72; and David Taras, "Defending the Cultural Frontier: Canadian Television and Continental Integration," in Helen Holmes and David Taras, eds., *Seeing Ourselves: Media Power and Policy in Canada* (Toronto: Harcourt Brace Jovanovich, 1992).

21. For details, see Rowland Lorimer and Jean McNulty, *Mass Communication in Canada* (Toronto: McClelland and Stewart, 1987), pp. 217–19 and 224–25, and the second edition, published in 1991.

22. For further discussion of these issues, see John Meisel, "Escaping Extinction: Cultural Defence of an Undefended Border," *Canadian Journal of Social and Political Theory* 10, nos. 1–2 (1986): 20. See also Caplan-Sauvageau Report, Parts 1–5; and David Taras, *The Newsmakers* (Scarborough, Ont.: Nelson Canada, 1990).

23. See the discussion in Lorimer and McNulty, *Mass Communications in Canada*, pp. 171–73 and 322–23.

24. The major services were required to: (1) devote a minimum of 30 percent of total broadcast time to Canadian content, rising to 50 percent in later years; (2) allocate 50 percent of total revenues and 50–60 percent of total expenditures to acquisition of or investment in Canadian productions; (3) obtain certification from government officials for content claimed as Canadian. In addition, they were forbidden to show commercials or produce their own programs. Canadian Radio-television and Telecommunications Commission, "Statement by Chairman John Meisel on CRTC Decision 82-240 (Pay-Television), Ottawa, March 18, 1982. For details of the decision, see CRTC, "Decision 82-240," Ottawa, March 18, 1982. For a useful summary, see Udo Salewsky, "Pay TV, Canadian Style," *Cable Communications Magazine* 48 no. 4 (April 1982): 11–17.

25. The CRTC requires cable companies to carry some services (nondiscretionary), and permits them to offer others as part of the basic service (for which subscribers must pay if they wish any cable service) or as optional to subscribers for an additional fee.

26. While anglophone Canadians spend about five hours per week watching CBC television, they still spend more than 75 percent of their viewing time watching non-Canadian programs. But then more than 75 percent of the programs available to Canadian households are non-Canadian. See Pierre Juneau, "A Report to Shareholders," notes for an address to the Broadcast Executives Society, Toronto, January 18, 1984. The demand for Canadian programs is discussed extensively in the Caplan-Sauvageau Report. See the summary on p. 691.

27. Caplan-Sauvageau Report, p. 81.

28. John Meisel, "Five Steps to Survival," speech at Conference on Mass Communication and Canadian Nationhood, York University, Toronto, April 10, 1981.

29. Caplan-Sauvageau Report, pp. 341 and 696.

30. Ibid., p. 217.

31. Many of the relevant studies are summarized in Andre H. Caron and David E. Payne, "Media and Canadian Politics: General and Referendum Applications," paper presented at the Duke University Conference on Political Support in Canada: The Crisis Years, November 1980. On the Quebec press, see Dominique Clift, "French Journalism in Quebec: Solidarity on a Pedestal," in Walter Stewart, ed., *Canadian Newspapers: The Inside Story* (Edmonton: Hurtig, 1980), pp. 205–18. See also Lysiane Gagnon, "Journalism and Ideologies in Quebec," and Florian Sauvageau, "French-Speaking Journalists on Journalism," in *The Journalists,* Royal Commission on Newspapers, research studies on the newspaper industry, vol. 2 (Ottawa: Supply and Services Canada, 1981), pp. 19–52; and Caplan-Sauvageau Report, pp. 205 and 207. The task force found that Quebec, with one-tenth the population, produces more programs than France.

32. See Kent Commission, pp. 1–14 and 87–103; and Siegel, *Politics and the Media in Canada*, pp. 110–24.

33. Alexander Bruce, "Lords of the Atlantic," *The Globe and Mail* (February 21, 1987), pp. D1–D2. See also Alden Nowlan, "What About the Irvings?" in Walter

Stewart, ed., *Canadian Newspapers: The Inside Story* (Edmonton: Hurtig, 1980), pp. 63–72.

34. For discussions of "Thomsonization," see Frederick J. Fletcher, *The Newspaper and Public Affairs*, Royal Commission on Newspapers, research studies on the newspaper industry, vol. 7 (Ottawa: Supply and Services Canada, 1981), pp. 36–40; Eaman, *The Media Society*, pp. 104–5; and Stewart, *Canadian Newspapers*, pp. 17–18.

35. For more details, see Fletcher, *Newspaper and Public Affairs*, ch. 1; and Kent Commission, chs. 1 and 3.

36. See Kent Commission, pp. 57–60. The charges against Southam and Thomson were dismissed on October 28 and December 9 in judgments handed down by Mr. Justice William Anderson of the Supreme Court of Ontario.

37. Tom Kent, "The Times and Significance of the Kent Commission," in Holmes and Taras, *Seeing Ourselves*, p. 21. Murray Campbell, "Requiem for the Kent Report," *The Globe and Mail*, (November 15, 1984), p. 9. For a summary of industry response, see Donald C. Wallace, "The Kent Commission: The Fourth Estate Under Attack," in R.B. Byers, ed., *Canadian Annual Review, 1981* (Toronto: University of Toronto Press, 1982).

38. See E.R. Black, *Politics and the News* (Toronto: Butterworths, 1982), pp. 54–56 and 140–45, for a penetrating discussion of these issues. One observer has suggested that there is an implicit agreement between reformist journalists and generally conservative publishers that newspapers may take a reformist stance on social issues as long as economic matters are treated conservatively. Conrad Winn, "Mass Communication," in C. Winn and J. McMenemy, *Political Parties in Canada* (Toronto: McGraw-Hill Ryerson, 1976), p. 132.

39. For example, in 1982 a survey of the Ottawa press gallery found that 37 percent of journalists felt closest to the NDP, compared to 17 percent who cited the Liberals and 11 percent the Conservatives. Peter Desbarats, "Eye on the Media," *The Financial Post* (July 13, 1985), p. 7, and "Media Influence on the Political Process," in Fleming, *Canadian Legislatures*, p. 20.

40. Ericson et al., *Visualizing Deviance*, p. 38.

41. Nowlan, "What About the Irvings?" p. 68.

42. Special Senate Committee on the Mass Media, *The Uncertain Mirror*, vol. 1 of the *Report* (Ottawa: Queen's Printer, 1970), p. 87. For a recent description of newsroom dynamics and the values and socialization of reporters, see Ericson et al., *Visualizing Deviance*.

43. For example, when the Minister of Finance makes his budget speech, reporters are locked up with advance copies and given full briefings by government officials in an attempt to improve the quality of reporting.

44. Anthony Westell, "Reporting the Nation's Business," in Stuart Adam, ed. *Journalism, Communication and the Law* (Scarborough, Ont.: Prentice-Hall Canada, 1976), p. 63.

45. Allan Levine, *Scrum Wars: The Prime Minister and the Media*. (Toronto: Dundurn Press, 1993).

46. See Frederick J. Fletcher, "The Prime Minister as Public Persuader," in Thomas A. Hockin, ed., *Apex of Power*, 2nd ed. (Scarborough, Ont.: Prentice-Hall Canada, 1977), pp. 86–111; and David Taras, "The Prime Minister and the Press'" in *Prime Ministers and Premiers* (Scarborough, Ont.: Prentice-Hall Canada, 1988), ch. 9.

47. Jonathan Rose, "Government Advertising in a Crisis: The Quebec Referendum Precedent," *Canadian Journal of Communication* 18, no. 2 (Spring 1993): 173–96.

48. Canada, Royal Commission on Electoral Reform and Party Financing, *Reforming Electoral Democracy*, vol. 1 (Ottawa: Supply and Services Canada, 1991), pp. 417–18.

49. Mary Anne Comber and Robert S. Mayne, *The Newsmongers: How the Media Distort the Political News* (Toronto: McClelland and Stewart, 1986), p. 92. The reliability of this study is difficult to assess because no details on methodology are given.

50. Anthony Westell, "The Press: Adversary or Channel of Communication?" in Harold D. Clarke et al., eds., *Parliament, Policy and Representation* (Toronto: Methuen, 1980), p. 49. Other important roles of the media are described by David Taras in "The Mass Media and Political Crisis: Reporting Canada's Constitutional Struggles," *Canadian Journal of Communication* 18, no. 2 (Spring 1993): 131–48.

51. These media managers even have their own professional journal, *Campaigns and Elections*, published in Washington, D.C., in which they exchange trade secrets. For details on the role of campaign consultants, see Gerald Caplan, Michael Kirby, and Hugh Segal, *Election: The Issues, the Strategies, the Aftermath* (Scarborough, Ont.: Prentice-Hall Canada, 1989); and John Laschinger and Geoffrey Stevens, *Leaders and Lesser Mortals: Backroom Politics in Canada* (Toronto: Key Porter Books, 1992).

52. Royal Commission on Electoral Reform, *Reforming Electoral Democracy*, vol. 1, pp. 348–50.

53. For an overview of media treatment of recent prime ministers, see David Taras, "Prime Minister and the Press," Comber and Mayne, *The Newsmongers*, pp. 43–53; and Levine, *Scrum Wars*.

54. Clive Cocking, *Following the Leaders: A Media Watcher's Diary of Campaign '79* (Toronto: Doubleday, 1980), p. 111.

55. *Maclean's* (March 8, 1993), p. 39.

56. Fletcher, "Mass Media and Parliamentary Elections in Canada," pp. 341–72.

57. Fred Fletcher and Bob Everett, "Television and the 1988 Campaign: Did It Make a Difference?" *Scan* (January 1988). See also *Maclean's* (December 8, 1988). For a general perspective on voting in Canada, see Harold D. Clarke et al., *Absent Mandate: The Politics of Discontent in Canada* (Toronto: Gage, 1984), esp. pp. 84–89 and 117–23. See also Richard Johnston, André Blais, Henry E. Brady, and Jean Crête, *Letting the People Decide: Dynamics of a Canadian Election* (Montreal and Kingston: McGill-Queen's University Press, 1992), especially chs. 3 and 7.

58. The proposition that the absence of hard-hitting (and costly) investigative journalism is more a reflection of tight editorial budgets than political timidity as such is supported by a wide range of anecdotal evidence. See "No Virginia, There Is No Lou Grant," in Stewart, *Canadian Newspapers*, pp. 17–18. In the end, the entire FP news service was closed down. See also Ericson, *Visualizing Deviance*. There are, of course, notable exceptions, such as the 1988 series of stories in *The Globe and Mail* on land developers and development issues in communities surrounding Toronto, which consumed more than a year and cost more than $200,000.

59. For a survey of evidence on the status-quo orientation of the media in the United States see Doris Graber, "Media Impact on the Political Status Quo: What Is the Evidence?" in Robert J. Spitzer, ed., *Media and Public Policy* (Westport, Conn.: Praeger, 1993), pp. 19–30.

60. Christopher Dornan, "Free to Be Responsible: The Accountability of the Print Media," in Frederick J. Fletcher, ed., *Reporting the Campaign: Election Coverage in Canada*. Volume 22 of the research studies of the Royal Commission on Electoral Reform and Party Financing (Ottawa: Supply and Services Canada, 1991), pp. 147–88. The quotation is from p. 181.

FURTHER READINGS

Caplan, Gerald, Michael Kirby, and Hugh Segal. *Election: The Issues, the Strategies, the Aftermath*. Scarborough, Ont.: Prentice-Hall, 1989.

Desbarats, Peter. *Guide to Canadian News Media*. Toronto: Harcourt Brace Jovanovich, 1990.

Deverell, John, and Greg Vezina. *Democracy, Eh?* Montreal: Robert Davies, 1993.

Ericson, Richard V., Patricia M. Baranek, and Janet B.L. Chan. *Visualizing Deviance: A Study of News Organizations* (1987); and, by the same authors, *Negotiating Control* (1989) and *Representing Order* (1991), all published by University of Toronto Press.

Fletcher, Frederick J. *Media, Elections and Democracy*. Volume 19 of the research studies of the Royal Commission on Electoral Reform and Party Financing. Ottawa: Supply and Services Canada, 1991.

———. *Reporting the Campaign: Election Coverage in Canada*. Volume 22 of the research studies of the Royal Commission on Electoral Reform and Party Financing. Ottawa: Supply and Services Canada, 1991.

Holmes, Helen, and David Taras, eds. *Seeing Ourselves: Media Power and Policy in Canada*. Toronto: Harcourt Brace Jovanovich, 1992.

Johnston, Richard, and André Blais, Henry E. Brady, and Jean Crête. *Letting the People Decide: Dynamics of a Canadian Election*. Montreal and Kingston: McGill-Queen's University Press, 1992, esp. chs. 3 and 7.

Laschinger, John, and Geoffrey Stevens: *Leaders and Lesser Mortals: Backroom Politics in Canada*. Toronto: Key Porter Books, 1992.

Levine, Allan. *Scrum Wars: The Prime Minister and the Media*. Toronto: Dundurn Press, 1993.

Lorimer, Roland, and Jean McNulty. *Mass Communication in Canada*. 2nd ed. Toronto: McClelland and Stewart, 1991.

Singer, Benjamin D., ed. *Communications in Canadian Society*. 4th ed. Scarborough, Ont.: Nelson Canada, 1995.

Taras, David. *The Newsmakers*. Scarborough, Ont.: Nelson Canada, 1990.

STRUCTURES

OF

CANADIAN

GOVERNMENT

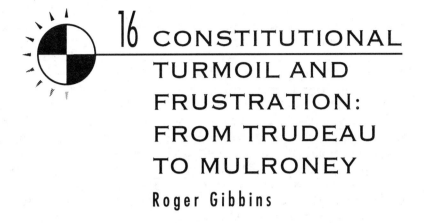

16 CONSTITUTIONAL TURMOIL AND FRUSTRATION: FROM TRUDEAU TO MULRONEY

Roger Gibbins

If we look back over the past ten to fifteen years, it is difficult to escape the conclusion that we have failed in our prolonged effort to create a new constitutional order. The political landscape is littered with innovative proposals for constitutional reform that failed to find national support. The major failures, including the final collapse of the Meech Lake Accord in June 1990 and the decisive defeat of the national constitutional referendum in October 1992, are familiar to us all. Yet along the way we have seen literally dozens of other initiatives produced by provincial governments, task forces, and research groups fall upon barren ground. Even the one apparent success during this period, the Trudeau government's patriation of the British North America Act (Constitution Act, 1867) and the proclamation of the companion Constitution Act, 1982, had embedded within it the seeds of failure to come. Rather than closing the book on constitutional reform, the 1982 act triggered a decade of constitutional turmoil and frustration. As Donald Smiley (among others) has argued, the inability to secure Quebec's formal consent to the act set in motion much of the constitutional contestation and failure that was to come in the next decade.[1]

Admittedly, Canadian constitutional failures have been of a very special kind, initially appearing in many cases as quite extraordinary successes. This was certainly the case with the Constitution Act of 1982. Its Charter of Rights and Freedoms is still seen by many as a landmark and celebratory event in the evolution of Canada's Constitution (see Chapter 17). The Meech Lake Accord also seemed to be a success in the spring of 1987 when the eleven Canadian first ministers were able to agree on a substantial set of constitutional reforms, including the recognition of Quebec as a "distinct society." The accord was supported by all of the opposition parties in the federal Parliament, editorial opinion across the land was laudatory, and public-opinion polls showed that the majority of Canadians agreed with Prime Minister Mulroney's statement that "Canada is now whole again." Three years later, the accord came within a whisker of ratification, blocked only by Elijah Harper's silent opposition in the Manitoba legislature and by Premier Clyde Wells's iconoclastic opposition in Newfoundland. So too was the 1992 Charlottetown Accord heralded as a success in many respects, even though it promptly went down to defeat in a national referendum; this accord was backed by the Government of Canada, by all ten provincial and the two territorial governments, and by representatives from four national aboriginal organizations. The line between constitutional success and failure has thus been extremely thin—and contentious, as the continuing debate over the 1982 Constitution Act demonstrates. And yet, our initial observation still holds: Canada's recent constitutional evolution has been characterized by failure rather than success.

The intent of this chapter is not to trace the path of this failure in any great detail, although some discussion of the major events is unavoidable. Rather, the intention here is to explore why the process failed and, more important, the lessons that might be learned from more than a decade of frustration. In conclusion, it will be suggested that Canadians may have been better served by failure than we realize: failure may have left us better positioned to meet the challenges of the next century than success would have done.

In making this case, this chapter attempts to show that constitutional failure stems from two sources. First, the constitutional process itself changed substantially in the years following the 1982 Constitution Act, and the nature of the change, although positive in most respects, made success more difficult to achieve than it might otherwise have been. (The Meech Lake and Charlottetown accords would have succeeded had the procedural rules of the game not changed in the intervening years.) Second, there was also a significant change in the content and character of constitutional discourse. Not only did the scope of the constitutional agenda expand dramatically, in step with an expansion in the number of players, but the perennial issues on the Canadian constitutional agenda took on more intransigent forms. This last change would have been difficult to handle even if the rules of the game had not changed. When the changes in process and substance are taken together, it is little wonder that we ended up where we did.

THE EVOLUTION OF THE CONSTITUTIONAL PROCESS

Although the Constitution itself has been changed in only minor ways since the proclamation of the Constitution Act, 1982,[2] the same cannot be said for the processes of constitutional negotiation and ratification. In this latter respect, the changes, which have been almost entirely informal, have been dramatic and of such a character as to make constitutional reform more difficult. In fact, it might be argued that we have created a process that virtually guarantees constitutional gridlock in the years to come.

Even before the proclamation of the Constitution Act, the constitutional process was beginning to change. True, the 1982 act was largely the product of conventional intergovernmental relations and of late-night negotiations held behind closed doors, the very type of negotiation that would later be so savagely attacked in the context of the subsequent Meech Lake Accord. However, there had also been extensive public discussions leading up to the closed sessions, and there would be further public forums, parliamentary debate, and legal action between the tabling of the initial deal and the final text of the 1982 act.

Thus, by the early 1980s the constitutional process was already slipping away from the hegemonic control of first ministers as it began to move outside the intergovernmental arena. This changing context was recognized in the provisions of the 1982 act that created the new amending formulas. Provincial consent to the act itself had been registered only by the premiers, or at least by nine of the premiers (Quebec excepted), who signed on behalf of their provinces. (This Alberta author's consent was conveyed by Peter Lougheed's signature; there was no public ratification, no provincial referendum, not even an act of the provincial legislature.) Section 38 (1) of the 1982 act changed this procedure by stating that future constitutional amendments would be "authorized by (a) resolutions of the Senate and House of Commons; and (b) resolutions of the legislative assemblies." Although few people at the time recognized this as a potentially monumental procedural change in Canadian constitutional life, it was to open the door to parliamentary debate and legislative committee hearings, to public forums, and, indirectly, to new forms of popular ratification. It can be argued, for example, that the failure of the Meech Lake Accord can be traced to the 1982 amending formulas, for they led directly to New Brunswick premier Frank McKenna's decision to hold public hearings on the accord. Those hearings, in turn, slowed the ratification process and gave opponents of the accord the opportunity to marshall their forces.

It should also be noted here that the collapse of the Meech Lake Accord fundamentally altered the dynamics of Canadian constitutional politics. The government of Quebec believed that Ottawa and the nine other provinces had "betrayed" it in pushing through the Constitution Act, 1982, without Quebec's assent. In Quebec's view, the provisions of the Meech Lake Accord—including recognition of its role in promoting the province's "distinct society" as well as restrictions on the federal spending power—restored enough of the Quebec state's traditional powers to enable the province to "sign on" to the post-1982 Canadian constitutional regime.

And so, when the accord was not ratified, Quebec withdrew from multilateral negotiations and waited for an "offer" from the rest of Canada. Although the government of Quebec did enter the Charlottetown negotiations in the end, the subsequent defeat of the national referendum makes it very unlikely that future Quebec governments will be again drawn into a multilateral process. We may, therefore, be left without a "national" intergovernmental process for handling constitutional negotiations. At the same time, there is little tolerance outside Quebec for bilateral negotiations between Quebec and the "rest of Canada," no matter how the latter is represented.

It may seem that the process that produced the Meech Lake Accord was a throwback to the older, if not necessarily darker, days of governmental hegemony in constitution-making. The accord was reached during a private, all-night session of first ministers, and was sprung upon Canadians with little warning. However, it was the public reaction to the Meech Lake process and the ultimate failure of the accord to be ratified that mark the more significant evolution of the constitutional process. The castigation of the "eleven white men meeting in the middle of the night in secret to re-write Canada's constitution" sharply eroded public support for intergovernmental forms of constitutional negotiation. Thus, when the Government of Canada went back to the constitutional drawing boards in the spring of 1991, one conclusion was clear: any proposal emanating from the federal government could not be presented to the Canadian people as a "seamless web," as the Meech Lake Accord had been. It would not only have to be exposed to public and parliamentary debate, but would also have to be open to amendment as a consequence. The federal government therefore embarked on an extensive and open constitutional process, which included public hearings by the Special Joint Committee of the Senate and the House of Commons (chaired by Gérald Beaudoin and Dorothy Dobbie), five national conferences hosted by groups such as the Canada West Foundation and the C.D. Howe Institute, and five months of intensive intergovernmental negotiations following the conferences.[3] Then, to cap it off, the final Charlottetown Accord was submitted to the Canadian people in a nonbinding referendum conducted under the most stringent ratification conditions, with the federal government announcing beforehand that the referendum would have to pass in every province.

The constitutional process leading up to the referendum stretched over more than a year and was by far the most open to date. Even the intergovernmental aspects of the process were more open than before, with territorial and aboriginal representatives sitting down with the provincial and federal negotiators. While the federal government may have been reluctantly driven to hold a referendum by the decision of the governments of Alberta, British Columbia, and Quebec to do so in any event, there is no question that the referendum was a critically important event in the evolution of Canada's Constitution. It seems likely that it will serve as a binding precedent for all but the most minor constitutional amendments in the future, although it is to be hoped that the unanimity provision will not be retained. Given the populist current flowing through the land, and given the strong support that both Quebec nationalists and the Reform Party will provide for constitutional referendums, it would be extraordinarily difficult to turn back the clock.

The 1992 constitutional process was also a watershed of sorts for the involvement of aboriginal peoples, although one that raises a number of problems. There is considerable doubt that any aboriginal leader, or small group of leaders, will now have the authority or legitimacy to negotiate on behalf of the broader aboriginal community. In 1992, aboriginal negotiators were able to reach with the federal, provincial, and territorial governments a wide-ranging consensus that wove aboriginal interests into the basic institutional and constitutional structures of the Canadian federal state. Sections of the accord provided, among other things, for the entrenchment of the right to self-government, for aboriginal Senate representation, and for special procedures for Supreme Court cases dealing with aboriginal interests. However, the negotiators, including Assembly of First Nations Grand Chief Ovide Mercredi, were unable to sell to their own constituents the deal they had reached. Many aboriginal communities and individuals, and quite likely a majority, rejected the Charlottetown Accord; many refused even to participate in the referendum. The dilemma for the future is that while aboriginals cannot be left out of the constitutional process, it is by no means clear how they can be included. The unfortunate reality is that there is no clear consensus within the very diverse aboriginal community to permit anything approximating intergovernmental negotiations, but neither can the multitude of individual communities be brought directly into future negotiations. Moreover, if the referendum process becomes the instrument through which Canadians address the ratification of constitutional amendments in the future, it is not an instrument that can be used to measure aboriginal consent. It would be rejected by many aboriginal communities as an infringement of their sovereign status, and because of the difficulty in identifying the off-reserve aboriginal people, it could not help us determine the preference of the full aboriginal population.[4]

Of course, the changes that occurred between 1982 and 1992 were more than ones of process. The constitutional agenda expanded dramatically to include such things as aboriginal self-government, a "Canada clause" preamble, Senate reform, and changes to the division of powers. Indeed, the scope of constitutional politics expanded to such an extent that the distinction between *constitutional* and *conventional* politics was all but erased. More important, the constitutional visions at play in the land became increasingly incompatible, and thus their reconciliation within a single constitutional framework became increasingly problematic.

To explain this last point, we need to look briefly at what happened between 1982 and 1992 in both the West and Quebec.

CHANGES IN THE WEST

The period between the 1982 Constitution Act and the 1992 constitutional referendum was a period of significant change in the western Canadian constitutional landscape. As this author has argued elsewhere,[5] the western premiers adopted a very defensive posture in the 1980–81 constitutional negotiations. Still reeling from the imposition of the National Energy Program in 1980, and deeply suspicious of a federal Liberal government virtually devoid of elected western representation,[6] the premiers sought above all else to defend the constitutional status quo with respect to the provincial ownership and control of natural resources. The amending formula included in the Constitution Act, 1982, was therefore of particular interest as a defence against confiscatory federal action in the future, as were the provisions of the act that dealt with the ownership and taxation of natural resources. What the premiers lacked was any coherent vision as to how chronic western alienation might be mollified through institutional reform. Certainly, at the time, Senate reform was not placed on the table as a potential cure.

In the following years, however, a regional vision did begin to come into focus, one that was to play a critically important role in the constitutional process during the early 1990s. This vision, anchored by a Triple-E Senate—equal, elected, and effective—was not the product of western governments, or of intergovernmental negotiations. In fact, the western premiers displayed little initial enthusiasm for Senate reform in general, and for the Triple-E model in particular. The Alberta government, for example, favoured replacing the existing Senate with a House of the Provinces in which Alberta's representatives would be nonelected and directed by the provincial government. Institutional reform was approached as a means by which the power of provincial governments and premiers would be strengthened on the national stage.

Yet as the regional discussion of Senate reform evolved, the premiers and their governments lost control of the debate. The Alberta government took its proposals for a provincially appointed Senate into public hearings across the province, uncovered not a shred of popular support, and found itself, to the dismay of Premier Lougheed, coming out in support of an elected Senate. The Senate-reform movement was increasingly driven by Bert Brown and his Committee for a Triple-E Senate, by the Canada West Foundation, and by Preston Manning and the Reform Party. It was a movement, moreover, that picked up the regional threads of populism, threads that precluded any nonelected Senate option, and that was fed by massive popular discontent with the GST. Finally, it was a movement that came to be championed by Alberta Premier Don Getty after he had been politically burned by accepting the Meech Lake Accord without having made any significant progress on Senate reform. When the accord collapsed, Getty was determined not to be burned again, and he became the primary conduit between the broader forces supporting Senate reform and the 1992 intergovernmental constitutional negotiations.[7]

The transformation of the Senate-reform movement has proved problematic in several respects for the evolution of Canadian constitutional politics. The earlier models of institutional reform, such as the House of the Provinces initially favoured by the government of Alberta, were reasonably compatible with the constitutional aspirations of Quebec. In the early 1980s, both Quebec and the West could live with institutional reform that would give provincial *governments* more clout within the national legislative process, and that would provide a strengthened line of defence for provincial powers. There was, in other words, some modicum of convergence between Quebec and western Canadian constitutional visions. However, the emergent Triple-E model of Senate reform called for the enhanced representation of provincial *electorates*, not governments, in Ottawa, and would likely undercut the status and influence of provincial governments and their premiers on the national stage. This was a reform model that had no appeal in Quebec, where the defence of the provincial state was the primary objective. In addition, the distribution of seats proposed by the Triple-E model was of no appeal to Quebec, much less to Ontario. Provincial equality in the Senate seemed to contradict the recognition of Quebec as a distinct society, given that it provided Quebec with even less representation than it would warrant on the basis of its population alone.

Finally, the Triple-E model has taken on considerable symbolic importance in the West. (Indeed, it can be argued that support for the Triple-E Senate as a symbol of the West's recognition by the national community far exceeds the support provided by those who are convinced by the institutional merits of the Triple-E design.) As a consequence, any constitutional package in the future that does not include a Senate reformed along the lines of the Triple-E model would have about as much popular appeal in the West as a new package would have in Quebec if it failed to incorporate the recognition of Quebec as a distinct society. Certainly this will be the case so long as the Reform Party maintains its electoral strength in the region. Constitutional politics are symbolic politics, and the new symbol of the Triple-E Senate can be counted on to gum up the constitutional works in the years ahead.

In summary, the transformation of the Senate-reform debate in the West, the growing coherence of a regional constitutional vision, and the aggressive promotion of that vision by the Reform Party will all work to complicate constitutional politics in the future. It is not that the western vision is right or wrong; the problem is that it is increasingly difficult for the rest of the country, and for Quebec in particular, to digest. Unfortunately, but perhaps inescapably, constitutional developments in the West are running against the tide of constitutional evolution in Quebec.

HARDENING POSITIONS IN QUEBEC

There is no clear evidence that Quebec's constitutional objectives have changed appreciably since 1982. In fact, one might argue that there is a remarkable consistency to Quebec's constitutional position that reaches back at least to the Duplessis governments in the 1950s. Quebec governments have consistently sought greater respect for the constitutional division of powers, the withdrawal of Ottawa from provincial fields of jurisdiction and taxation, and an expansion in provincial jurisdiction. However, there is little question that Quebec's position has hardened in the wake of the "betrayal" of 1982 and the collapse of the Meech Lake Accord. Even the national rejection of the 1992 referendum, which was rejected in Quebec as well, has contributed to the hardening of the provincial position.

The Quebec nationalist movement can point to more than a decade in which Canada has made no appreciable progress in addressing the constitutional concerns and aspirations of Quebec. The will to engage in multilateral negotiations (a will which revived briefly during the summer of 1992) has been all but extinguished. Given the strength of the Bloc Québécois in the House of Commons, and the strength of the Parti Québécois on the provincial stage, it is unlikely that Quebec governments in the near future will engage in conventional constitutional negotiations. Nor is there likely to be support for an accommodative stance toward the new constitutional vision in western Canada, or for entrusting Quebec's constitutional future to a Canada-wide referendum. Hence the paradox. Quebec's concerns still dominate the country's constitutional agenda, but Quebec is the province perhaps the least disposed to engage in constitutional negotiations. So what, then, does the future hold?

THE FUTURE EVOLUTION OF CONSTITUTIONAL POLITICS

In many respects, the failures of the past decade may have been fortuitous, for, as we sought to solve constitutional problems rooted in the country's past, the face of contemporary Canada was being transformed in significant and even dramatic ways. If we had succeeded in putting a new constitutional order into place, it may well have been one designed more for the 19th than the 21st century. Somewhat ironically, constitutional failure may have left us better positioned to meet the challenges of the future than constitutional success might have done.

In the negotiations surrounding the Meech Lake and Charlottetown accords, the argument was frequently made that the constitutional recognition of Quebec as a distinct society would do little more than acknowledge a historical reality, namely, that Quebec had always occupied a distinctive niche within Canada and North America. Yet while this may be true, Quebec's distinctiveness is less apparent today than it was in the past. The forces of globalization, which are stripping national and continental cultures of their distinctiveness, are at work within Quebec as they are within Canada and North America. The quest for the constitutional recognition of Quebec's distinctiveness comes at a time when Quebeckers themselves are emphatically embracing the new global order, and when Canadians are locking themselves into the new continental instruments of the FTA and NAFTA. Canadians and Quebeckers are trying at the same time to grapple constitutionally with the past and economically with the future, without fully realizing that the signposts of the past and future may well point in quite different directions.

Nor was the situation any better with respect to the West, where constitutional visions have also missed the boat in a key respect. Westerners began to wrestle with institutional cures for regional alienation just at the time when regional identities were beginning to weaken for many Canadians, or at least were being challenged by emergent nonterritorial identities based on gender, race, and religion. Just as we tried to find a way to provide effective institutional representation for people as British Columbians or Newfoundlanders, Canadians were starting to look for effective institutional representation for themselves as women, as visible minorities, and as carriers of new ideological creeds and passions that sweep across territorial boundaries.

There were also new issues that Canadians at large missed almost entirely in the constitutional negotiations. Scarcely a word was said, for instance, about environmentalism, few asked or even worried whether the new constitutional order would provide an effective vehicle for addressing the environmental challenges that Canadians will confront in the next century. To have discussed environmentalism would have disrupted the delicate negotiations to find a balance among competing constitutional claims rooted in the last century—and so the issues of the next were put aside.

Nor is it clear that we were about to create an appropriate institutional structure for aboriginal peoples. Our notions of aboriginal self-government have been framed by our perception of the largely self-contained aboriginal communities spawned by the reserve system that was established during the latter half of the 19th century. Far too little thought has been given to the fact that the bulk of the aboriginal population does not live in reserve-based communities, but rather in either a complex pattern of cultural interpenetration in the major urban centres of Canada, or in the North where they are a large component of the total population. Our views on aboriginal self-government have been based on views of aboriginal communities that have had more to do with the last century than with the next.

All of this is not to deny that there will be a political price to be paid for constitutional failure, for our inability to come to grips with outstanding constitutional issues rooted in the 19th century. Certainly the nationalist movement in Quebec has been energized by the failure of constitutional negotiations to date, although there is always the nagging thought that some of the constitutional proposals that *have* been on the table might have contributed just as much to strengthening that movement. It may also be more difficult to deal with pressing aboriginal concerns without first putting into place a more emphatic constitutional statement of recognition and inclusion. Finally, we may be left with a federal division of powers, and a more informal division of program responsibility and financing, that will not serve us well as we try to address the spiralling problems associated with the debt and deficit.

Nonetheless, it can be argued that on balance we have not been badly served by constitutional failure. We know ourselves better as a national community, even though part of that knowledge is that we have incompatible visions and dreams. Perhaps as a consequence we will have a more pragmatic view of the future; we may realize that our national life, like many of our personal lives, will be built on compromises and half-fulfilled promises. As Edward McWhinney noted in his discussion of the 1979–82 constitutional process, "The quest for a new constitution has sometimes been presented as a panacea for all our assorted national ills, as if all our problems would be resolved once and for all, and the need for imagination, courage, and the normal skills of political compromise would somehow disappear."[8] If we have learned nothing else, we should have learned that a new constitution is not a panacea. Certainly we should now know that our national community is very complex, and that it can be bent only so far to serve any one set of interests before it starts to rupture and split.

Over the past decade or more, the basic conflicts in Canadian political life have been fought from the heights of constitutional principle. We tried to address an expanding agenda of national problems through constitutional means, and we failed not because we did *not* understand one another, but because we *did*. We reached the point where we recognized that our constitutional visions were incompatible and could not be bridged easily, if at all, by innovative institutional structures cobbled together from competing principles and incompatible interests. Notions such as "special status" and "asymmetrical federalism" fell by the wayside as more sharply defined, albeit contradictory, constitutional visions came into sharper focus. Perhaps, then, we have learned that the high ground of constitutional politics is not the appropriate terrain for political contestation. Maybe it is time to ground such conflict in the more pragmatic territory of conventional public policy, and to carry out such conflict within existing federal and parliamentary institutions. In this sense, the 1993 election of large contingents of Bloc and Reform MPs may serve us well if potential constitutional conflict can be normalized by being brought into the House of Commons. There is no reason to expect that we will be less well served by a revitalized parliamentary environment than we have been by constitutional negotiations in the past. With luck, the evolution of Canada's Constitution in the future will be informal. If we again try to work through the formal processes of constitutional amendment as these have evolved over the past decade, then success will unlikely be found.

For those determined to pursue constitutional reform regardless of the odds, the past decade offers little strategic guidance. The Meech Lake debacle shows that a sequential strategy will not work. It is highly improbable that Quebec, the West, or aboriginal peoples will put aside their constitutional aspirations in order to first address the aspirations of other players. Yet if sequential strategies will not work, the Charlottetown failure shows that linkage strategies are equally problematic. A comprehensive package contains too many trade-offs, too many compromises for easy public consumption, and therefore Peter Russell is probably correct in forecasting an end to "mega-constitutional politics."[9] Perhaps the only sensible conclusion is that constitutional politics is the wrong game to be playing as Canada moves with trepidation toward the next century. The best constitutional strategy may be no strategy at all.

NOTES

1. Donald Smiley, "A Dangerous Deed: The Constitution Act, 1982," in Keith Banting and Richard Simeon, eds., *And No One Cheered: Federalism, Democracy, and the Constitution Act* (Toronto: Methuen, 1983), pp. 74–95.

2. The Constitutional Amendment Proclamation, 1983, made sight alterations to the provisions of the 1982 Act dealing with aboriginal peoples and First Ministers' Conferences relating to aboriginal peoples. A subsequent amendment extended the official languages provisions of the Charter to New Brunswick.

3. For an insightful summary of this process, see Leslie A. Pal and F. Leslie Seidle, "Constitutional Politics 1990–92: The Paradox of Participation," in Susan D. Phillips, ed., *How Ottawa Spends, 1993–1994* (Ottawa: Carleton University Press, 1993), pp. 143–202.

4. There is another and perhaps more profound problem: *should* aboriginal consent be built into the formal or informal amending formulas? If so, what would be the means by which that consent might be measured, and to what forms of constitutional amendment might an aboriginal veto apply?

5. Roger Gibbins, "Constitutional Politics and the West," in Banting and Simeon, *And No One Cheered,* pp. 119–32.

6. Only two Liberal MPs—both from Manitoba—were elected from the West in the 1980 general election. Regional cabinet representation was provided by Liberal senators.

7. Premier Getty also took more direct action by passing the Alberta Senatorial Selection Act, and orchestrating Canada's first and, to this point, only Senate election, which saw Stan Waters go to the Senate shortly before the last stage of the Meech Lake Accord negotiations. Alberta's more recent Senate appointments have been made directly by the prime minister, and the provincial legislation has not been brought into play.

8. Edward McWhinney, *Canada and the Constitution, 1979–1982* (Toronto: University of Toronto Press, 1982), p. 123.

9. Peter H. Russell, *Constitutional Odyssey*, 2nd ed. (Toronto: University of Toronto Press, 1993).

FURTHER READINGS

Bercuson, David J. and Barry Cooper. *Deconfederation: Canada without Quebec*. Toronto: Key Porter Books, 1991.

Brodie, Ian, and Neil Nevitte. "Evaluating the Citizens' Constitution Theory." *Canadian Journal of Political Science* 26, no. 2 (June 1993): 235–60.

Cairns, Alan C. *Disruptions: Constitutional Struggles from the Charter to Meech Lake*. Edited by Douglas E. Williams. Toronto: McClelland and Stewart, 1991.

————. *Charter versus Federalism: The Dilemmas of Constitutional Reform*. Montreal and Kingston: McGill-Queen's University Press, 1992.

Canadian Public Policy 14 (September 1988). Special Supplement on the Meech Lake Accord.

Gibbins, Roger, ed. *Meech Lake and Canada: Perspectives from the West*. Edmonton: Academic Printing and Publishing, 1988.

LaSelva, Samuel V. "Federalism as a Way of Life: Reflections on the Canadian Experiment." *Canadian Journal of Political Science* 26, no. 2 (June 1993): 219–34.

Romanow, Roy, John Whyte, and Howard Leeson. *Canada Notwithstanding: The Making of the Constitution, 1976–1982*. Toronto: Carswell/Methuen, 1984.

Weaver, R. Kent, ed. *The Collapse of Canada?* Washington, D.C.: The Brookings Institution, 1992.

Young, Robert, ed. *Confederation in Crisis*. Toronto: James Lorimer, 1991.

17 THE CHARTER AND THE COURTS

Radha Jhappan

It has been more than a decade since the Charter of Rights and Freedoms was enacted, yet curiously, Canadians may be more familiar with the constitutional rights of their American neighbours than with their own. Given the domination of Canadian airwaves and movie houses by American productions, it is perhaps not surprising that many Canadians believe that the U.S. Bill of Rights applies to them. They imagine, for example, that arresting officers must inform suspects that they have the right to remain silent, when in fact police in this country are not legally bound to do so.[1] It is common to invoke the American protection against self-incrimination by "taking the fifth," but invoking the fifth article of our Charter of Rights actually means calling upon Parliament and each provincial legislature to sit at least once every twelve months.[2]

This chapter examines the Canadian Charter of Rights and Freedoms with a view to distinguishing it both from the American Bill of Rights and from Canada's previous constitutional arrangements. Many have argued that the addition of the Charter to the Canadian Constitution in 1982 was the single most important event in our political development since 1867. The Charter has expanded the rights and liberties of citizens, as well as the power of judges, at the expense of governments, and hence it has changed the manner in which we conduct politics. Some regard these developments as healthy and progressive, while others worry that the Charter has done more damage than good.

The discussion that follows seeks to explain these conflicting views of the Charter's impact on Canadian politics. As the Charter's significance cannot be measured without an understanding of what came before it, the chapter begins with a brief overview of the courts' treatment of civil rights under the British North America (BNA) Act, 1867, and the 1960 Canadian Bill of Rights. After examining some of the changes implied by the adoption of entrenched civil and political rights, the chapter outlines the key provisions of the Charter, distinguishing between negative liberties and positive rights, and between individual and collective rights. This is followed by a short survey of major Charter decisions issued by the higher courts in a variety of policy areas. Finally, the chapter outlines the main debates that have developed among left- and right-wing critics about the nature of Charter rights and the enhanced role of the courts in public policy making.

CIVIL RIGHTS FROM THE BNA ACT TO THE CANADIAN BILL OF RIGHTS

Before the enactment of the Charter of Rights in 1982, the civil and political rights and freedoms of Canadians were not entrenched as the fundamental law of the land. This may partially explain why they were seldom discussed by political scientists, who, in their analysis of the constitutional system, focused instead on federalism and the 1867 BNA Act (now the Constitution Act, 1867). In fact, as Alan Cairns has observed, and as generations of students of Canadian politics can attest, the BNA Act is "a document of monumental dullness which enshrines no eternal principles and is devoid of inspirational content."[3] In contrast, almost a century before the act became the cornerstone of Canada's constitutional system, our closest neighbours had drawn up the U.S. Declaration of Independence (1776), which begins with the heady statement,

> *We hold these truths to be self-evident, that all men are created equal,*
> *that they are endowed by their Creator with certain unalienable Rights,*
> *that among these are Life, Liberty and the pursuit of Happiness. That to*
> *secure these rights, Governments are instituted among Men, deriving*
> *their just powers from the consent of the governed.*

The BNA Act begins with a less than arresting preamble declaring the creation of the Dominion "with a Constitution similar in principle to that of the United Kingdom." The union of Canada, Nova Scotia, and New Brunswick would "conduce to the Welfare of the Provinces and promote the Interests of the British Empire." Thus, whereas the Americans put the welfare and interests of citizens above all else, the BNA Act is wholly concerned with the interests of the Empire and of the federal and provincial governments. Nowhere does it endorse such ringing concepts as rights, equality, liberty, or happiness, and it certainly does not presume that the consent of the governed is required for anything at all.

Indeed, the BNA Act lacks not just impassioned lyricism, but also any mention of citizens or their relationship to the federal and provincial governments whose compositions, legislative organs, powers, and jurisdictions are so meticulously laid out. No lofty principles grace the 50 pages of the act. Of its 147 articles, only one—section 93—mentions the rights of citizens vis-à-vis governments. The section allows provinces to make laws in respect to education subject to "any Right or Privilege to Denominational Schools which any Class of Persons have by Law in the Province at the Union." The only other section that comes close to acknowledging a "right" is section 133, which declares that either English or French may be used in Parliament, the Quebec Legislature, and the courts, and provides that legislative acts and records be kept in both languages. Taken together, sections 93 and 133 hardly express a set of civil and political rights likely to arouse the sort of ideological and patriotic fervour inspired by the American Constitution.

Instead of spelling out the relationship between the governors and the governed, then, the BNA Act described the major political institutions and laid out the respective powers of the federal and provincial governments. The imported parliamentary system was founded squarely on the doctrine of parliamentary supremacy, or the unlimited power of the legislature to enact laws. The doctrine holds that current statutes always take precedence over older statutes, cabinet orders, common law, and hence common-law rights. It was tempered in the Canadian context only by the federal–provincial division of powers that constrained each level of government to legislate only within the areas of jurisdiction assigned exclusively to it under sections 91 or 92 of the BNA Act.

The division of powers and the idea of legislative supremacy meant that the courts were entrusted with a relatively modest duty in the constitutional sphere: they would be asked only whether a government, in enacting a law or policy, was acting within its proper jurisdiction. An *ultra vires* (beyond jurisdictional competence) ruling against one level of government meant only that the loser could not legislate in a given policy field. However, the power simply went to the other level of government, which was then free to delegate it back to the first. Federalism review then, was concerned only with the proper allocation of power; virtually any law with any content could be passed, as long as it was passed by the *correct* level of government. Without an entrenched bill of rights, the courts did not have to consider the wisdom or impact of legislation. This is not to say that Canadians *had* no rights, however.

Before the enactment of the Charter, the civil rights of Canadians were ostensibly protected by the body of common-law rights established over several centuries by the judiciaries of Britain, Canada, and the other Commonwealth countries. However, beyond freedom of religion and speech and legal rights such as *habeas corpus,* few civil rights were actively protected by Canadian courts. Indeed, Canadian courts could not boast a particularly distinguished record with respect to civil liberties.

A series of higher-court decisions made in the 19th century and the first half of the 20th century upheld racial segregation or exclusion in theatres, restaurants, and taverns as the acceptable exercise of the private rights of the owners.[4] On those rare occasions when the courts found in favour of a plaintiff, it was on some tangential ground. *Sparrow v. Johnson*

(1899) is a case in point: when a black couple were refused the right to take their reserved theatre seats because of their race, the court refused to decide the case on the grounds of racism, but awarded damages for breach of contract.[5] In the vast majority of cases, however, governments were able to enact racist laws with impunity. For example, in 1903 a B.C. statute that disqualified people of Chinese, Japanese, or Indian descent from voting was upheld, as was a 1914 Saskatchewan law that prohibited Chinese men from employing white women.[6] Chief Justice Duff remarked that although the legislation may have affected the civil rights of "Chinamen," it was only incidental to the main aim of protecting women and children.[7] The Supreme Court of Canada went even further in a 1939 case involving a black man who was refused service in a Montreal tavern, holding that racial discrimination was not "contrary to good morals or public order."[8] Taken together, such decisions in effect told racists within and outside government that racism and discrimination were both legal and constitutional if they were promulgated by the proper level of government.

In fact, up to 1982 Canadian courts had customarily deferred to parliamentary supremacy. Only occasionally had they ranked traditional civil liberties above that doctrine, and then only vis-à-vis provincial governments. In 1938, for example, the Supreme Court struck down a number of Social Credit laws in Alberta that, among other things, impinged upon freedom of the press.[9] Chief Justice Duff argued that there was an "implied bill of rights" in Canada, although this doctrine was never adopted by the majority of the Court (and presumably did not extend so far as to include "Chinamen"). Nevertheless, in the 1950s, on a variety of grounds the Court struck down a series of Quebec laws aimed at suppressing the activities of Jehovah's Witnesses and Communists. Yet they were just as likely to cite a violation of the division of powers as freedom of religion or equal application of the law.[10] Generally, as Christopher Manfredi points out, "the impact of legislation on civil liberties was of only secondary importance in determining its constitutionality; enactment of restrictive legislation by the proper level of government was the threshold issue."[11]

In part because of such unsatisfactory outcomes, by 1960 there was a feeling in some quarters that Canada ought to have a domestic bill of rights in keeping with the increasing international concern for civil liberties, as exemplified by the United Nations Universal Declaration of Human Rights (1948). This was the commitment of the Prairie populist prime minister, John Diefenbaker. His Progressive Conservative government enacted the Canadian Bill of Rights, which substantially resembled the first such bill in any Canadian jurisdiction, the Saskatchewan Bill of Rights (1947). The bill represented a codification of the various common law and statutory rights that had developed over the years, from the Magna Charta to its American counterpart. Of its two substantive articles, the first promised fundamental freedoms (life, liberty, security of the person, religion, speech, assembly, association, property, the press, equality before the law, and equal protection of the law). These freedoms were to be enjoyed without discrimination by reason of race, national origin, colour, religion, or sex. The second substantive article provided that laws of Canada should not be construed so as to abrogate legal rights such as *habeas corpus*, immunity from cruel and unusual punishment, the right to a fair trial, counsel, bail, and the presumption of innocence.

Unfortunately, although the Canadian Bill of Rights opened up the area of civil liberties for the courts, it was disarmed by conditional provisions. First, it was an ordinary statute rather than the fundamental, constitutional law of the land; as a result, it was subject to easy amendment, repeal, or simple override through use of its "notwithstanding" clause. Second, as a federal statute it applied only to federal legislation; the provinces were free to continue to pass laws within their jurisdictions without any particular concern for their effects on civil liberties.

Taken together, these limitations may help to explain why the courts did not use the 1960 Bill of Rights to become human-rights crusaders, correcting the violations committed by legislatures. Indeed, between 1960 and 1982, of the 34 Bill of Rights cases decided by the Supreme Court of Canada, the rights claimant won in only five cases, a success rate of under 15 percent. Moreover, only in one case did the Court defy parliamentary supremacy and strike down a law. The *Drybones* case of 1970 was the sole instance in which the Supreme Court's application of the Canadian Bill of Rights rendered a discriminatory statute inoperative. The case involved a registered Indian, Drybones, who had been found intoxicated off a reserve, contrary to an Indian Act provision that prohibited Indians from possessing or manufacturing intoxicants, or being intoxicated off a reserve, on pain of a $10–$50 fine or three months in prison. As non-Indians were not subjected to such prohibitions, five of the six judges found that Indians, because of their race, were being denied equality before the law in section 1 of the Bill of Rights.[12]

While the line of reasoning in *Drybones* seems the only logical one, the Supreme Court retreated to its traditional judicial passivism in the 1974 *Lavell* case.[13] This case also involved the Indian Act, section 12(1)(b) of which provided that an Indian woman who married a non-Indian man would lose her status under the act, as would any children of the union; hence, she and her children could not live in the reserve community, and would forfeit all other benefits associated with Indian Act status. On the other hand, if an Indian man married a non-Indian woman, not only would he *not* lose his status, but his wife and their children would gain Indian status. In a perplexing decision, five of the nine Supreme Court justices found that the section did not violate equality before the law, since all Indian women who married non-Indian men were being treated in the same way. In doing so, they were taking the "formal equality" approach, according to which there can be no inequality as long as everyone in an ascribed category is treated in the same fashion. This approach would not identify the appropriate reference group as Indian men, but rather as other Indian women; thus, it would tend to allow almost all forms of legislative discrimination. As Justice McIntyre noted fifteen years later in the *Andrews* case, the formal equality approach would justify Hitler's Nuremburg laws since "similar treatment was contemplated for all Jews."[14] The same sort of reasoning was nevertheless repeated in the *Bliss* case of 1979. This case involved a section of the Unemployment Insurance Act that stipulated a longer qualifying period for pregnant women than for others. Again, the Court found that there was no gender or other discrimination, curiously attributing the difference in treatment to nature (which has determined that only women carry children), rather than to a policy choice on the part of legislators.[15]

All in all, the Canadian Bill of Rights turned out to be rather disappointing. Its inherent limitations, together with the traditionally circumscribed role of the courts, made for some rather questionable results. In the end, the only right the courts were willing to protect under it was the right to be drunk regardless of one's race, which hardly ranks as a cardinal civil right. On the other hand, blatant examples of racism, sexism, and other forms of discrimination were all but endorsed by the courts.

WHAT THE CHARTER CHANGED

Given the courts' deference to legislatures prior to 1982, the Charter represented a watershed in terms of the power of citizens and courts vis-à-vis the power of governments. First and foremost, the Charter explicitly rejects the timeworn doctrine of parliamentary supremacy by declaring in section 52 that "the Constitution of Canada is the supreme law of Canada, and any law that is inconsistent with the provisions of the constitution is, to the extent of the inconsistency, of no force or effect." This means that governments can no longer enact virtually any legislation they like on any matter within their respective jurisdictions. Instead, the Charter requires that their legislative and policy actions not violate the rights and freedoms enshrined in it. Thus, the Charter manacles governments in a manner unprecedented in Canadian constitutional history.

A second major change wrought by the Constitution Act, 1982, concerns the much wider scope of judicial review. Under federalism review, a government on the wrong side of an *ultra vires* ruling can persuade the winning level of government simply to exercise the power on its behalf. In contrast, if a law is struck down as unconstitutional under the Charter, *neither* level of government can enact it. Moreover, Charter review is much broader in scope than federalism review because for the first time in Canadian history even executive actions are subject to judicial review.

A third and critical consequence of the 1982 reform is the fact that the Charter made it easier for some 27 million players to initiate constitutional review. Section 24 of the Charter grants a very broad right of standing to individuals in providing that "[a]nyone whose rights or freedoms, as granted by this Charter, have been infringed or denied may apply to a court of competent jurisdiction to obtain such remedy as the court considers appropriate and just in the circumstances." In fact, this clause empowers both citizens and judges, since any court may declare a statute or other executive act invalid, although, of course, Supreme Court decisions have the final authority. Because specific acts can be disputed one by one, in a sense governments are more explicitly accountable to the people than they ever were under the traditional mechanism of periodic elections.

Finally, some Canadians mistakenly believe that the Charter covers abuses of their rights by private parties. However, the Charter did *not* change this aspect of the constitutional system. In fact, it applies *only* to the actions or laws passed by federal or provincial governments and not to individual or group relations in the private sector. Rights or discrimination disputes between individuals and nongovernmental parties such as corporations, vendors, landlords, employers, neighbours, or retailers must still be routed through provincial human-rights codes.

CHARTER PROVISIONS

Although the Charter of Rights and Freedoms was itself a novel addition to Canada's Constitution, its provisions represent a collage of rights bundled together from various sources. In some cases, the phraseology is taken directly from other documents: rights such as those against "unreasonable search and seizure," "cruel and unusual punishment," or to "due process of law" are found in the American Bill of Rights, and the majority of Charter rights are found in more or less the same form in the 1960 Canadian Bill of Rights. What is new about the Charter, then, is not so much that it creates wholly new rights, but that it codifies and enshrines the rights of people vis-à-vis both levels of government.

The Charter of Rights and Freedoms consists of the first 34 clauses of the Constitution Act, 1982, though not all of them contain substantive rights. There are two critical distinctions to be made between different kinds of rights included in the Charter. First, true to Canadian tradition, the document contains a mixture of individual and collective rights. In fact, all of the substantive rights or freedoms up to section 23 are granted to "every individual," "every citizen," "everyone," "any member of the public," or "any person"—in other words, they are rights individuals can claim against the federal and provincial governments. In contrast to these individual rights, at least two sections refer to rights that are claimable only by virtue of one's membership in a group. Section 23 grants collective minority language educational rights to "Citizens of Canada" who belong to the English or French minority population in the province in which they reside. Section 25 of the Charter also acknowledges the existence of a body of collective rights, that is, the Aboriginal and treaty rights of the aboriginal peoples of Canada.

The second important distinction between the rights protected by the Charter is that between negative liberties and positive rights. Generally speaking, a negative liberty can be understood as freedom from interference by the state. Examples of negative liberties include freedom of conscience, religion, or association, where all that is required is that governments refrain from interfering with the exercise of certain facilities. On the other hand, a positive right involves a claim against another party, which in turn has a duty to provide or contribute something so that the right might be exercised. In other words, a positive right is an entitlement. Examples of positive rights would include the right to legal counsel or to state-funded education. Obviously, the key distinction between negative liberties and positive rights is that the former are in infinite supply (there is no cost attached to their observance), whereas the latter are in finite supply to the extent that resources are scarce.

Although the Charter contains, as its title suggests, both rights and freedoms, the majority of its provisions recognize negative liberties rather than extend positive entitlements. Perhaps the most important of these negative liberties are found in section 2—the "fundamental freedoms" clause—which, along with freedom of the press, guarantees everyone freedom of conscience, religion, thought, belief, opinion, expression, peaceful assembly, and association. Considered essential to democracy, these liberties are complemented in section 3 by democratic rights, defined in Charter terms as the right of citizens to vote in elections for federal and provincial legislatures, and to be qualified for membership in either. As governments assume the costs of holding elections, section 3 might be interpreted as a positive right, since the state must provide the physical requisites by which the right is to be exercised. On the other hand, the mobility provisions in section 6 guarantee citizens the right to free movement, including the right to enter, remain in, or leave Canada, and the right to move to and gain a livelihood in any province. However, no duties are imposed on governments to supply citizens with either the means of moving or their livelihoods. On the contrary, subsection 3(b) enables provincial governments to limit the receipt of publicly funded social services to those meeting certain residency requirements.

Sections 7–14 of the Charter provide for legal rights, most of which are derived from common-law practice or from statutes such as the Criminal Code, and almost all of which are negative liberties. They include the following rights: to life, liberty, and security of the person; to security against unreasonable search and seizure; to be free from arbitrary detention or imprisonment; to *habeas corpus;* to be presumed innocent until proven guilty; not to be subjected to any cruel and unusual treatment or punishment; not to be tried or punished for an offence more than once; and not to be compelled to be a witness in proceedings against oneself. On the other hand, in the mix of rights and freedoms, a few provisions in sections 7–14 imply some positive rights: for example, the authorities must provide for a fair and public hearing by an independent and impartial tribunal; a trial by jury if the maximum punishment for the offence is five or more years; and an interpreter for witnesses who are deaf or who do not understand the language in which a legal proceeding is being conducted. By granting these three rights, the state clearly assumes financial burdens. Finally, a more ambiguous right is found in section 10 (b), which declares that everyone has the right on arrest or detention to retain and instruct counsel. It is not entirely clear whether this section grants a constitutional right to state-funded legal services. In practice, however, all provinces and territories provide legal aid on a means-tested basis, so that no one charged with a criminal offence has gone without legal services.

The equality rights section of the Charter has been heralded by many as the most important and far-reaching equality guarantee in any modern democratic constitution. As section 15(1) states,

> *Every individual is equal before and under the law and has the right to the equal protection and equal benefit of the law without discrimination and, in particular, without discrimination based on race, national or ethnic origin, colour, religion, sex, age or mental or physical disability.*

It must be noted, however, that these guarantees do not fit easily into the negative liberties/positive rights distinction. At a general level, they may be understood as negative liberties, since they do not enjoin governments to ensure equality of outcomes but merely forbid governments from discriminating between groups on the listed grounds. This means that governments cannot, as a rule, single out the listed groups for less beneficial treatment than everyone else. Section 15 does not mean that laws cannot make distinctions and treat people differently for different purposes, but it does mean that governments may not impose burdens on people on the basis of irrelevant criteria. Indeed, section 15(2) allows for affirmative-action programs aimed at ameliorating the conditions of individuals or groups that are disadvantaged because of the listed attributes. However, although it insulates such programs from charges of reverse discrimination, it does not in any sense require them; in this respect, section 15(2) is a negative liberty for governments.

The most unambiguous positive rights in the Charter are undoubtedly those in sections 16–23. Apart from entrenching official bilingualism by declaring English and French the two official languages of Canada and enshrining the negative liberties to their use in all of the institutions of the Parliament and government of Canada (and New Brunswick), these sections require that statutes, records, and journals of Parliament be printed and published in both English and French. Further, section 20 stipulates that the government of Canada must provide services in both of the official languages in any head or central office, or in local offices, where numbers warrant. Similarly, section 23 grants citizens the right to have their children receive primary- and secondary-school education in the language of the English or French linguistic minority population of a province (subject to several conditions and where numbers warrant).

The remaining articles of the Charter are largely general interpretive principles or nonderogation clauses. Section 25, for example, insulates aboriginal, treaty, and land rights from certain Charter rights; section 27 provides that the Charter be interpreted "in a manner consistent with the preservation and enhancement of the multicultural heritage of Canadians"; and section 28 guarantees Charter rights and freedoms equally to male and female persons.

Finally, it must be noted that Charter rights are not absolute. The framers of the Charter attempted to accommodate the fact that rights occasionally clash with one another, as well as the possibility that governments may have legitimate policy objectives that might justify overriding some individual rights. There are three important sources of limitation in the Charter. First, some clauses contain internal or built-in qualifications. For example, as noted above, section 6 allows provincial governments to impose residency requirements for the receipt of social services. Even section 7—the right to life, liberty, and security of the person—is not absolute, as it suggests that one can be deprived of these things as long as it is "in accordance with the principles of fundamental justice."

The second vital limit on Charter rights is section 33, the notwithstanding or override clause. This section allows the federal and provincial governments to exempt legislation from sections 2 and 7–15 of the Charter for a five-year renewable period. Thus far, the section has been used in only three contexts: (1) by the Saskatchewan government in 1986 to force striking public servants back to work; (2) by the Parti Québécois government up to 1987 to exempt all Quebec legislation from what was seen by that party as the illegitimate post-1982 constitutional regime; and (3) by Premier Bourassa in 1988 after the Supreme Court struck down Quebec's French-only sign law as a violation of freedom of expression.

Despite its infrequent use, many have called for the repeal of section 33. If the Charter is to mean anything, critics argue, it should not grant rights with one hand and take them away with the other. Moreover, the section in effect creates a hierarchy of rights in which some are considered so important that governments are not allowed to override them, while others are treated as dispensable and contingent. Although it is possible to think of valid grounds for legislatures to suspend certain rights, it is not immediately apparent why equality rights and fundamental freedoms are any less important than language, mobility, or democratic rights. The third and pivotal limit on Charter rights is section 1, which states that the Charter "guarantees the rights and freedoms set out in it subject only to such reasonable limits prescribed by law as can be demonstrably justified in a free and democratic society." This clause allows governments to infringe *any* Charter right as long as they can come up with a justification that is satisfactory to the courts. It involves a two-step process in which a claimant must first show that a Charter right has been impaired by a law before the onus shifts to the government to justify the infringement. In one of its most important decisions to date, in 1986 the Supreme Court of Canada laid out what came to be called the "Oakes test."[16] Peter Hogg points out that "this judgment has taken on some of the character of holy writ," in that it is routinely used in almost all Charter cases where a rights violation has been found.[17] The two-part Oakes test holds that if a government is to limit a right, its objective must be pressing and substantial, while the means employed must be proportional to that objective. In other words, there must be a rational connection between the objective and the limit; the right must be impaired as little as possible to achieve the valid objective; and the costs of impairing the right must be proportional to the benefits.

As David Beatty argues, "section 1, not the substantive sections in which the rights and freedoms are entrenched, is where all of the action takes place,"[18] precisely because through it governments can negate any and all Charter rights. The higher courts have applied section 1 and the Oakes test with varying results, sometimes upholding legislation as meeting a pressing and substantial objective, sometimes striking laws down as unreasonable limits on Charter rights. Nevertheless, taken together, sections 1 and 33 reintroduce legislative supremacy to the constitutional system by giving governments the right to conduct legislative review of judicial review. If the courts strike down a law that violates fundamental, legal, or equality rights, the government can simply invoke section 33 and reintroduce the legislation. Alternatively, through section 1 governments can willfully violate any Charter right under the guise of wider objectives (as long as they can persuade the courts of their importance).

MAJOR CHARTER DECISIONS

The Supreme Court of Canada decided approximately 100 Charter cases between 1984 and 1989. On average, Charter cases account for just under a quarter of the Court's annual post-1982 caseload. According to Morton, Russell, and Withey, whereas rights claimants had only a 15 percent success rate under the Canadian Bill of Rights, in the first two years of Supreme Court Charter decisions claimants enjoyed a success rate of

67 percent.[19] However, this rate has declined significantly over the ensuing years, to around 18 percent generally, or under 12 percent for non-criminal cases. The decline may be explained in part by a shift in the Court's view of its role after the initial burst of activism, and in part by the fact that over time the courts come to settle certain legal and constitutional questions as well as the principles and tests by which they adjudicate them. Yet whatever the success rates for litigants, higher-court decisions have clearly had far-reaching effects on public policy, governments' spheres of decision-making, and individual and group rights.

Since 1982, the Supreme Court has made important decisions on a wide range of issues, including abortion, fetal rights,[20] mandatory retirement, strikes and secondary picketing, Sunday shopping, children's advertising, minority language education rights, French-only signs, official bilingualism, extradition, drunk driving, narcotics, breathalizer tests, refugees, nuclear weapons, assisted suicide, pornography, hate literature, political rights of public servants, constituency boundaries, dangerous offenders, sexual assault, battered women, prisoners' rights, and prostitution.

These issues have been decided under a variety of Charter provisions. Because only a limited number of categories are provided, many different issues will be argued in court under a single Charter provision. Freedom of expression, as a case in point, has incorporated very diverse issues, with the Supreme Court sometimes upholding and sometimes invalidating statutes. For example, the Court has upheld freedom of expression by striking down the French-only signs provision of Quebec's Bill 101,[21] defending trade unions' right to picket,[22] and supporting federal public servants' right to participate in election campaigns on behalf of a party or candidate.[23] On the other hand, the Court has found reasonable limits to freedom of expression in cases involving violent, "degrading and dehumanizing" pornography,[24] the dissemination of hate literature,[25] communicating for the purpose of prostitution,[26] advertizing aimed at children,[27] and bans on publishing the names of victims of sexual assault.[28]

Because the Charter is silent on some issues, litigants must sometimes squeeze round pegs into square holes. For example, because the Charter accords unions no express collective rights, they have been forced to defend rights won over many decades under the freedom-of-association clause. Generally, unions have not fared well under the Charter. While section 2(d) includes employees' right to form a union, it is nevertheless a right possessed by individuals, not associations. Freedom of association does not, according to the Supreme Court of Canada, include a right of trade unions to strike. In 1987, the Court released the so-called "labour trilogy" of cases in which it found that freedom of association was not infringed by three separate laws denying public-sector employees the right to strike, ordering striking dairy workers back to work, and imposing caps on future wage increases of public-sector employees.[29] On the other hand, a community college employee who objected to his union's use of compulsory dues to contribute to political parties lost his case to establish a right *not* to associate.[30] The *Lavigne* case was very much the exception, however.

Similarly, because the Charter is silent on economic and property rights, the business sector has been creative in its use of various Charter rights to fend off government regulation. In the *Big M Drug Mart* case, for instance, under the guise of religious rights a corporation managed to persuade the Supreme Court of Canada to strike down the federal Lord's Day Act, which prohibited commercial activity on Sunday. The Court found that the act infringed religious freedom since its purpose was "to compel the observance of the Christian Sabbath."[31] It is doubtful whether the corporation was truly interested in religious freedom, however. In a similar vein, a combines inquiry into Southam newspapers was frustrated when *The Edmonton Journal* asserted a legal right against unreasonable search and seizure vis-à-vis the search provisions of the Combines Investigation Act.[32]

Again, because Charter provisions are both few in number and very much open to interpretation, at times the same clause has been invoked to support two utterly opposing claims. Section 7, for example, was used by Henry Morgentaler to argue that a woman's life, liberty, and security of the person included her right to abort an unwanted fetus in the landmark Supreme Court decision that struck down the abortion law in 1988.[33] Joe Borowski also appealed to section 7, arguing that it was not the woman's but the *fetus's* right to life, liberty, and security of the person that should prevail.[34]

Section 7 has also been used to support a medley of other causes, usually unsuccessfully. In the *Rodriguez* case, for example, the Supreme Court upheld the Criminal Code's prohibition of assisted suicide, against a dying woman's claim that her right to life, liberty, and security of the person included her right to a doctor-assisted suicide without criminal penalties being imposed on her assistant.[35] The section was invoked, also to no avail by a coalition of groups that sought to ban the testing of American cruise missiles in Canada by arguing that the increased chances of nuclear war that would result from the testing would violate the section 7 rights of Canadians.[36] On the other hand, the *Singh* case of 1985 was an important exception where the "security of the person" and "fundamental justice" aspects of section 7 required that the government provide an oral hearing for refugee claimants whose lives could be in danger if they were deported to their countries of origin.[37]

A final observation about the fate of certain Charter provisions over the last decade concerns the fact that some have not provided much relief to the groups they were ostensibly established to assist. Section 15 (equality rights) is perhaps the best example of this trend. This is not to suggest that there have been no victories for those who have suffered discrimination on the basis of the listed characteristics (race, national or ethnic origin, colour, religion, sex, age, or mental or physical disability). For example, the gender discrimination endorsed by the *Bliss* decision (discussed above) has been rejected,[38] as has that in the Ontario Human Rights Code, which permitted single-sex sports teams, thereby denying a girl the benefit of the Code by reason of her sex.[39] Similarly, the age discrimination in the Unemployment Insurance Act, which denied benefits to persons over 65, has also been overruled by the Supreme Court.[40] On the other hand, the Court ruled that mandatory retirement is a reasonable limit on equality rights, thus allowing legislatures to discriminate on the basis of age.[41] A claim of discrimination on the basis of mental disability was also dismissed by the Court when it endorsed the Criminal Code provision that a person found not guilty by reason of insanity could nevertheless be detained indefinitely, whereas a finite sentence would have been imposed with a guilty finding.[42]

In fact, the most important (and successful) equality rights claim to date was decided by the Supreme Court in 1989. In the *Andrews* case the Court found that the B.C. Law Society's exclusion of noncitizens from the bar violated the equality rights of otherwise qualified noncitizens (in this instance, a landed immigrant from Britain who had passed his bar exams in the province).[43] The case was important because the Court indicated that it saw equality not as a procedural right, but as a substantive right. It is ironic, however, that the first significant section 15 case should have upheld the equality rights of a healthy, wealthy, white male of British origin, rather than a member of a group that has been historically disadvantaged.

Section 15, then, has not been used to great effect by the groups one might have expected. Yet issues such as abortion, pornography, prostitution, and past-sexual-history evidence, each decided under a different clause, have had just as much (if not more) impact on the equality rights of various groups. Indeed, it is possible that the selection of an appropriate provision may be the key strategic decision in Charter litigation.

CHARTER DEBATES

Although the courts have produced a mixed bag of results over the last decade, there is no question that the Charter of Rights has been embraced by the Canadian public.[44] Some have even argued that it has become a key symbol of national unity, an inviolate set of values that is now fundamental to Canadians' understanding of what it means to be Canadian. The same is not necessarily true of academic and legal circles, however. In fact, no chorus of hosannas was heard in the hallways of the courts and academies when the Charter was first proclaimed, although some were generally in favour of it. But ten years' worth of mixed results have tempered the accolades of even so-called Charterphiles. Debates now rage between those who take the position that, on balance, the Charter is an improvement over the previous regime of legislative supremacy that had permitted such flagrant violations of civil rights, and those who believe that the Charter has done us much more harm than good.

In the Charterphile camp we might include the various groups and individuals who wish to use the Charter to pursue their interests, together with many liberal and progressive academics and legal practitioners. These individuals and groups generally take the position that the Charter has expanded democracy by giving "the people" the chance to challenge government actions that they feel infringe their rights and interests. At last, there is a check on the potential excesses of majoritarian governments, and at last Canadians can enjoy a sense of national unity, secure in the knowledge that they have fundamental rights no matter where they live. Rights are good insofar as they build fences around individuals and protect them from unlimited state power. Moreover, entrenched rights can offer historically and currently disadvantaged minorities not just relief from discrimination, but affirmative action, and all of this can only enhance democracy as citizens are acknowledged and empowered by the Charter.

On the other hand, a number of scholars, lawyers, and others have become increasingly sceptical about the Charter and its impact on Canadian society. There are two major areas of contention among so-called Charterphobes. The first concerns the nature of the Charter itself and the kinds of rights it enshrines, while the second has to do with the enhanced role of the judiciary in decision-making. Curiously, quite similar critiques issue from those on the left and right of the ideological spectrum, though representatives of each are motivated by very different underlying concerns. The following discussion seeks to covey the flavour of these critiques in general terms, stressing the points of convergence and divergence between them.

THE NATURE OF CHARTER RIGHTS

To begin with, both left- and right-wing critics worry that the Charter has led to the Americanization of our legal and political systems, as well as our political culture. First, there is a concern that Canadian courts will use American precedents and approaches to rights claims, although David Beatty points out that the Supreme Court of Canada has consciously rejected the idea of relying on American precedents.[45] Second, it is feared that Canadians will become litigation-loving libertines, more concerned with individual interests and pleasures than with collective values and goods, and hence, like the Americans, more apt to sue not only governments, but one another. Rights-thinking is atomistic, conducive not to a sense of community, but to rampant self-interest. Of course, the sense of community and values to be lost differs according to the ideological persuasion of the critic. Nevertheless, it is self-evident that the Americans' unbridled individualism has torn the social fabric asunder, and the same fate awaits us if we encourage such self-oriented thinking.

Oddly enough, both right- and left-wing critics maintain that the Charter is a profoundly antidemocratic document. There is considerable anxiety that "special interests" are now able to use the Charter to win through the courts what they could not achieve by lobbying elected representatives in the normal political process. Right-wingers like Rainer Knopff and F.L. Morton believe that the courts have fallen under the influence of a so-called "court party" comprised of liberal or progressive groups (i.e., women's, gay, ethnic, and other identity-based organizations), academics, and bureaucratic and media elites.[46] As we have seen above, these groups have, among other things, used the courts to strike down the abortion law, to deny the fetus human status, to allow girls to play hockey in teams with boys, to prohibit violent and degrading pornography, and to recognize aboriginal rights,[47] all in direct opposition to the policy choices of our elected representatives. By appealing to Charter rights, then, the court party has subverted the idea of representative democracy and the electoral process.

On the other hand, leftists, who also criticize interest groups' new-found ability to circumvent democratic decision-making, worry about an entirely different set of special interests, namely, private corporations, the wealthy, and the privileged. As shown above, these interests have used the courts to roll back hard-won union rights, to deny workers a day of rest by allowing Sunday shopping, to win "equality" rights for rich noncitizen lawyers, to override the principle of "one person, one vote,"[48] and to protect free speech for white supremacists who claim that the Holocaust is a hoax concocted by international Jewish conspirators.[49] Leftists argue that the Charter is, in fact, an instrument of the advantaged—business, the wealthy, private interests, and professionals—and that the real losers must be the poor, ethnic minorities, women, workers, the unemployed, and other disadvantaged groups.[50]

Leftists point out that the Charter basically enshrines negative liberties (it protects individuals from state interference) rather than positive rights to employment, income, education, social services, health care, and so on.[51] Hence, it does not contribute to substantive equality, but at best provides only limited guarantees of equality of opportunity, and then only insofar as individual–government relations are concerned. Protection against discrimination by governments will not produce real equality because it is in the so-called private spheres of the workplace, housing, the family, and other social and economic spaces where sexism, racism, homophobia, ablism, and other forms of discrimination and disadvantage flourish. Furthermore, whereas right-wingers fret, for example, that equality rights decisions extending spousal benefits to same-sex couples will force governments to spend more and more on expensive social programs, the latter are perturbed by quite the opposite prospect. As Andrew Petter argues, the Charter is "a 19th century document let loose on a 20th century welfare state," and that the rights enshrined in it "are founded on the belief that the main enemies of freedom are not disparities in wealth nor concentrations of private power, but the state."[52] Thus, he fears, private and business interests will use the courts to attack redistributive taxation and equalization policies, social services, and state regulation.

Whereas leftists value equality over liberty, right-wing critics take the opposite tack. For them, the Charter is a dangerous document because it includes certain rights at the expense of others. They worry that it sacrifices liberty for equality—that it is a misguided attempt at "social engineering" that denies natural differences between individuals, and that will ultimately stifle the creativity and individual initiative a healthy (capitalist) economy requires. Human-rights codes and Charter provisions guaranteeing not just equal opportunity but equality of result will curtail freedom, which surely must be the fundamental aim of society.[53] This problem is compounded by the fact that there is no balancing mechanism in the Charter in the form of property rights, which means that individuals cannot control the disposition of their property against encroachments or regulation by the state. The twin facts that property rights have always been respected by the common law and that private interests have managed to use different Charter provisions to protect themselves against regulation do not seem to satisfy such critics.

THE ROLE OF THE JUDICIARY

Apart from the nature of Charter rights, the second major prong of the anti-Charter assault concerns the augmented role of the judiciary. It is generally accepted that in a democracy in which elected politicians make the law through the executive and civil servants then administer it, there must be some ultimate check at the operational stage. In theory, even a parliamentary system has some checks and balances in the policy process, as the House of Commons, the Senate, interest groups, and others assume certain roles in policy formulation. But after a policy or law is passed, some body must be able to ensure that it is properly implemented and that it does not penalize some members of society unfairly.

It is also generally accepted that a strong, independent judiciary is essential to the functioning of a democracy for several reasons. First, statutes passed by the elected representatives normally codify broad rules and principles, and hence their texts are open to interpretation. No matter how well written, statutes contain ambiguous language; they cannot cover all contingencies, nor can they guarantee impartial implementation by the various departments and agencies responsible for delivering them. Second, in a federal system such as Canada's, jurisdictional disputes between the two levels of government need to be adjudicated by a neutral body susceptible to neither bribe nor threat. Third, in states which have bills of rights enshrining the basic rights and freedoms of citizens, the courts play a critical role in determining whether government actions are respectful of those rights and fundamental values such as freedom and equality.

According to Charterphobes, however, the Charter of Rights has inflated the role and importance of judges beyond the legitimate functions of yesteryear. It has legalized politics so that instead of being decided in an open political process by elected representatives, public policy issues are now transformed into technical questions to be settled by lawyers in a closed legal process.[54] Furthermore, if the Charter has legalized politics, it has politicized the law in equal measure. To the extent that judges have the power to uphold or strike down laws they consider inconsistent with the Charter, they are in effect making and breaking public policy. Moreover, because legal language in general and constitutional provisions in particular tend to be imprecise, judges' interpretations (which may vary considerably depending on the individual judge) can either create new rights or negate rights that the framers of the Constitution intended to include. Hence, according to Knopff and Morton, judges have become "politicians in robes." They can be as activist or as deferential to Parliament as they choose, but in the meantime politicians can hide behind those spacious robes to dodge their decision-making responsibilities regarding controversial issues.

Charterphobes do not believe that judges are competent in these new spheres. For starters, judges are unelected. They are appointed by the federal government in a closed process because of their training as lawyers, not because they have any particular expertise regarding complex social, moral, economic, or political problems. It is not immediately apparent why lawyers should have ultimate decision-making authority over anyone else. In addition, there is the question of accountability. Superior-court judges have tenure until the age of 75, a measure to ensure that neither politicians nor popular pressures can compromise their judgments.[55] Protecting judges from bullying, however, also means rendering them unaccountable, either to those who appoint them (elected representatives) or to the public, the consumers of their decisions. All of this was fine when judges merely enforced the law and umpired federalism, but now that they are more significantly engaged—making and breaking public policy, deciding tricky issues, constructing fences around the individual, and putting up "no trespassing" signs against governments—their lack of accountability is at least questionable.

Leftist scholars have pointed out that judges as policy-makers are not only unaccountable, but relatively inaccessible as well. Because litigation is extremely expensive and legal aid is only automatically available for criminal matters, individuals and groups with noncriminal cases can be shut out of the courts for want of money. Whereas governments and wealthy private interests have virtually unlimited resources, time, and personnel to fight cases through trials and appeals, the "oppressed and disempowered groups who are the supposed beneficiaries of progressive Charter litigation will, because of their lack of resources, be the least likely to have genuine access to the Courts."[56] Moreover, the Charter has also forced such groups to take defensive actions against privileged parties who are using the courts to promote their interests at the expense of others, and hence they must divert their precious resources from other activities to the black hole of litigation.

Apart from the question of access, there is also concern that ideological biases might further limit the policy options of governments. The fact is, the law moves slowly over time, and one legal decision based on the particular ideological interpretation of current judges can handcuff elected representatives for a very long time, despite changes in social and economic needs. Not surprisingly, while right-wing sceptics are convinced that the legal elite is dominated by left-wing intellectuals, leftist critics argue that "legalized politics is the quintessential conservative politics."[57] This is because judges are unrepresentative of the Canadian population, and their worldviews must be biased by their privileged backgrounds.

In an earlier age, when Canada's political culture was perhaps more deferential to the authority of various elites, we were more apt to accept the mystique of the judge. He (as it was almost invariably a he) was an eminence, an omniscient luminary who dispensed justice from a high bench in a spirit of anonymous and fair-minded detachment. He symbolized something larger than himself—justice—and the exercise of his powers could be questioned by none but more senior members of the same priesthood. In Canadian politics in the 1990s, however, far from assumed, judicial objectivity is considered all but impossible.

Leftists frequently observe that Canadian judges are not representative of a cross-section of Canadian society in terms of characteristics such as class, gender, ethnicity, age, religion, marital status, and political experience. In fact, as Peter McCormick and Ian Greene point out, when judges make decisions involving discretion, they often apply the "average reasonable person" standard. The problem, however, is that "the 'average reasonable person,' as seen through the eyes of a typical judge, is likely to be a high-achieving male of British or French origin, who adheres to one of the mainline religions, approaches 60 years of age, lives in a comfortable middle-class or upper-class environment, and is active in a political party."[58] Quite apart from the constricted rules of evidence that present extremely partial accounts of those who appear before the courts, a judge with the foregoing characteristics cannot possibly appreciate the life circumstances of the disadvantaged. Because of their backgrounds, and because of a legal culture that is itself inherently conservative, judges' decisions must be infused with both conscious and unconscious biases.

While this argument makes sense at the intuitive level, it is difficult for such critics to explain those judicial decisions that have favoured disadvantaged claimants. Conversely, it is difficult for those who fear the influence of the court party to explain decisions that have favoured privileged interests. Moreover, both left- and right-wing sceptics are asking us to rely on elected representatives to make our public policies, when these individuals are not necessarily more "representative" than judges. Politicians too tend to be male, white, of British or French origin, Protestant or Catholic, middle-aged, trained in law or business, ensconced in a comfortable middle-class or upper-class environment, and, of course, active in a political party. The assumption that politicians will somehow make better policy choices than judges is suspect, given that politicians are responsible for passing the discriminatory laws that are subsequently challenged under the Charter. In addition, the argument that at least the policy-making process is democractic is also questionable, given the concentration of power in the hands of cabinets and senior (unelected) bureaucrats at the expense of ordinary elected MPs. Besides, the role of the courts is precisely to protect the rights of the casualties of majoritarian politics.

CONCLUSION

The Canadian Charter of Rights and Freedoms has undoubtedly had a significant impact on Canadian politics in the 1980s and 1990s. But must it mean the end of democracy as we have known it, as Charter sceptics maintain? In my view, the critics have overestimated the political, social, and economic impacts of both the Charter and the new role of judges. Certainly, some higher-court Charter decisions have had serious repercussions. For example, the Supreme Court decision that struck down the French-only sign law as a violation of freedom of expression led the government of Quebec to invoke the notwithstanding clause so that it could re-enact the law. The Premier of Manitoba, in turn, stopped discussion of the Meech Lake Accord in the legislature, an action that ultimately led to the unravelling of the accord, which would probably have satisfied Quebec's constitutional demands. Yet even so, if Quebec should decide to separate from the federation in the future, no one could seriously blame the Supreme Court. The decision is merely one link in a chain of complex historical events that might take an entirely different course at any time.

The anxiety among both left- and right-wing critics that the courts have been captured by the other side is also somewhat overblown. In fact, the behaviour of the courts is inconvenient to both, precisely because they do not consistently favour the advantaged over the disadvantaged or vice versa. Although there are legitimate questions to be asked about the expanded role of the courts in the Charter era, given that legal decisions rendered by nonelected, nonaccountable judges can overrule decisions made by our democratically elected representatives, a number of factors suggest that the Charter has not given courts unlimited power over legislatures. First, the fact that the Charter has three built-in sources of limitation, including sections 1 and 33, recognizes the policy-making authority of legislatures even if their policies violate Charter guarantees. Second, legal decisions cannot be considered the final and definitive pronouncements on issues. The fact of the matter is that courts must interpret the law as it stands: in *Daigle v. Tremblay* (1989) for example, the Supreme Court found that the fetus does not enjoy a right to life *under current Canadian law*. If legislatures do not like court decisions, they can change either the law or, ultimately, the Constitution that they imposed on themselves. For these reasons, legislatures are still very much in control of the policy process, with the courts acting as reviewers to ensure that policy is consistent with the fundamental values the legislatures have enshrined in the Constitution.

Third, after the initial burst of activism in the early 1980s, the success rate of Charter claims has declined dramatically. There is no reason to expect that it will suddenly shoot up again, for the simple reason that many of the issues avoided by legislatures have now been settled by the courts. After a decade, legislatures have cleaned up their acts, as it were, and are now more careful to frame legislation that will not violate the Charter.

Finally, in a context of long-term recession and a seemingly bleak economic future, if citizens are preoccupied by anything, it is certainly not the Charter or the courts. Although both will undoubtedly continue to affect the Canadian political system into the 21st century, it is more likely that they will become less rather than more controversial over time. If anything is to destroy Canadian democracy as we know it, it will not be the Charter of Rights—indeed, the Charter may well turn out to be democracy's best defence.

NOTES

1. The U.S. Supreme Court found that the Fifth Amendment required this caution in the 1966 case, *Miranda v. Arizona* (1966), 384 U.S. 436. In Canada, however, even though it has been a common law right, there is no constitutional provision to that effect. In practice, Canadian police issue a caution after informing the accused of the Criminal Code charge, of the right to retain and instruct counsel without delay, and of the right to legal assistance without charge. But whereas the "Miranda card" refers to the *right* to remain silent, the Canadian caution is less direct: "You need not say anything. You have nothing to hope from any promise or favour and nothing to fear from any threat whether or not you say anything. Anything you do say may be used as evidence."

2. In fact, the old common-law right of an accused person to refuse to answer any question on the grounds that the answer might tend to incriminate him or her has been abolished in Canada. It has been replaced by section 13 of the Charter, which provides only that the incriminating answer cannot be used against the witness in any other proceedings.

3. A.C. Cairns, "The Living Canadian Constitution," in D.E. Williams, ed., *Constitution, Government and Society in Canada: Selected Essays by Alan C. Cairns* (Toronto: McClelland and Stewart, 1988), p. 27.

4. Ian Greene describes these and other early civil-rights cases in *The Charter of Rights* (Toronto: James Lorimer, 1989), pp. 17–23.

5. Cited in Noel A. Kinsella, "Tomorrow's Rights in the Mirror of History," in G.L. Gall, ed., *Civil Liberties in Canada: Entering the 1980s* (Toronto: Butterworths, 1982), p. 32.

6. These and other cases are discussed more fully in D.A. Schmeiser, *Civil Liberties in Canada* (Toronto: Oxford University Press, 1965), pp. 258–59; and Dale Gibson, *The Law of the Charter: Equality Rights* (Toronto: Carswell, 1990), pp. 3–4.

7. *Quong-Wing v. R.*, [1914] 49 S.C.R. 440. See M.L. Berlin and W.F. Pentney, eds., *Human Rights and Freedoms in Canada: Cases, Notes and Materials* (Toronto: Butterworths, 1987), p. 12.

8. Quoted in Schmeiser, *Civil Liberties in Canada*, p. 264.

9. *Reference re Alberta Statutes*, [1938] 2 S.C.R. 100.

10. For example, in *Saumur v. Quebec*, [1953] 2 S.C.R. 299, the Supreme Court found the Quebec government's requirement that Jehovah's Witnesses obtain a permit to distribute their literature in the street violated an implied freedom of religion. In the famous *Roncarelli v. Duplessis* case ([1959] S.C.R. 121), the Court held that the principle of equal application of the law had been infringed when the Quebec government cancelled the liquor licence of a wealthy Montreal restaurateur who habitually posted bail for Jehovah's Witnesses arrested for distributing their literature. On the other hand, in *Switzman v. Elbling* ([1957] S.C.R. 285), the Court struck down Quebec's 1937 Padlock Act (under which any premises used to produce or distribute communist literature could be locked up) because it violated the federal government's jurisdiction over criminal law.

11. Christopher P. Manfredi, *Judicial Power and the Charter: Canada and the Paradox of Liberal Constitutionalism* (Toronto: McClelland and Stewart, 1993), p. 31.

12. *R. v. Drybones*, [1970] S.C.R. 282. It is interesting to note, however, that it was not until 1985 that the offence of being drunk *on* a reserve was repealed.

13. *Lavell v. A.G. Canada*, [1974] S.C.R. 1349.

14. *Andrews v. Law Society of British Columbia*, [1989] 1 S.C.R. 143.

15. *Bliss v. A.G. Canada*, [1979] 1 S.C.R. 183.

16. *R. v. Oakes*, [1986] 1 S. C. R. 103.

17. Peter Hogg, *Constitutional Law of Canada*, 3rd ed. (Toronto: Carswell, 1992), p. 866.

18. David Beatty, *Talking Heads and the Supremes: The Canadian Production of Constitutional Review* (Toronto: Carswell, 1990), p. vii.

19. F.L. Morton, P.H. Russell, and M.J. Withey, "The Supreme Court's First One Hundred Charter of Rights Decisions: A Statistical Analysis," *Osgoode Hall Law Journal* 30, no. 1 (1992): pp. 8–9.

20. *Daigle v. Tremblay*, [1989] 2 S.C.R. 530. In a civil action brought by a biological father to prevent his ex-fiancé from having an abortion, the Supreme Court of Canada found that current Canadian law neither includes a right to life for the fetus nor supports the claim of a paternal right to veto a woman's decision to have an abortion. It should be noted that this was not a Charter case, since no state action or law was involved.

21. *Ford v. Quebec (Attorney General)*, [1988] 2 S.C.R. 712.

22. *RWDSU v. Dolphin Delivery Ltd.*, [1986] 2 S.C.R. 573.

23. *Osborne v. Canada*, [1991] 2 S.C.R. 69.

24. *R. v. Butler*, [1992] 1 S.C.R. 452.

25. *R. v. Keegstra*, [1990] 3 S.C.R. 697.

26. *Re ss. 193 and 195(1) of Criminal Code (Prostitution Reference)*, [1990] 1 S.C.R. 1123.

27. *Irwin Toy Ltd. v. Quebec (Attorney General)*, [1989] 1 S.C.R. 232.

28. *Canadian Newspapers Co. v. Canada (Attorney General)*, [1988] 2 S.C.R. 122.

29. The three cases were, respectively: *Re Public Service Employees Relations Act*, [1987] 1 S.C.R. 313; *RWDSU v. Saskatchewan*, [1987] 1 S.C.R. 460; and *PSAC v. Canada*, [1987] 1 S.C.R. 424.

30. *Lavigne v. Ontario Public Service Employees Union*, [1991] 2 S.C.R. 211.

31. In *R. v. Big M Drug Mart*, [1985] 1 S.C.R. 351. However, the following year the Court upheld Ontario's Retail Business Holidays Act, since its purpose was the secular one of providing a common day of rest for retail workers. See *R. v. Edwards Books and Art*, [1986] 2 S.C.R. 713.

32. *Hunter v. Southam*, [1984] 2 S.C.R. 145.

33. *Morgentaler v. the Queen*, [1988] 1 S.C.R. 30. The Supreme Court of Canada struck down section 251 of the Criminal Code on procedural grounds—that is, the therapeutic abortion committee requirement and the fact that not all hospitals had such committees or provided abortion services meant unnecessary delays and unequal access to abortion across the country. As a result of the *Morgentaler* decision, abortion reverted back to a negative liberty, but certainly did not become a positive right.

34. *Borowski v. Canada (Attorney General)*, [1989] 1 S.C.R. 342. Borowski ultimately lost this case as it was moot, the Supreme Court having recently struck down section 251 of the Criminal Code in *Morgentaler*.

35. *Rodriguez v. British Columbia (Attorney General)*, [1993] S.C.R. (unpublished) 23476.

36. *Operation Dismantle Inc. v. the Queen*, [1985] 1 S.C.R. 441. The Court found the argument hypothetical and purely speculative, since the group could not prove the projected outcome.

37. *Singh v. the Minister of Employment and Immigration*, [1985] 1 S.C.R. 177. It was in this case that the Supreme Court found that everyone physically present in Canada enjoys Charter rights (except those that expressly require citizenship).

38. *Brooks v. Canada Safeway*, [1987] 1 S.C.R. 1219.

39. *Blainey v. Ontario Hockey Association* (1986), 54 O.R. (2d) 513 (C.A.).

40. *Tetreault-Gadoury v. Canada*, [1991] 2 S.C.R. 22.

41. *McKinney v. University of Guelph*, [1990] 3 S.C.R. 229.

42. *R. v. Swain*, [1991] 1 S.C.R. 933.

43. *Andrews v. the Law Society of British Columbia*, [1989] 1 S.C.R. 143.

44. The Parti Québécois government of René Lévesque refused to sign the Constitution Act, 1982, and it has subsequently been assumed in the rest of Canada that the Charter is regarded as illegitimate in Quebec. However, Andrew Heard has recently shown that residents of Quebec have used the Charter for a wide range of claims, much like residents of other provinces, and that Quebec courts have been willing to accept Charter claims roughly as often as courts in other provinces. See Andrew Heard, "Quebec Courts and the Canadian Charter of Rights," *International Journal of Canadian Studies* 7–8 (Spring–Fall 1993): 153–66.

45. Beatty, *Talking Heads and the Supremes*, p. 19.

46. Rainer Knopff and F.L. Morton, *Charter Politics* (Scarborough, Ont.: Nelson Canada, 1992) p. 79.

47. For an analysis of major Supreme Court of Canada decisions on aboriginal rights, see R. Jhappan, "Natural Rights v. Legal Positivism: Indians, the Courts and the New Discourse of Aboriginal Rights in Canada," *British Journal of Canadian Studies* 6, no. 1 (1991): 60–100.

48. *Re Provincial Electoral Boundaries (Saskatchewan)*, [1991] 2 S.C.R. 158. The Supreme Court upheld Saskatchewan's electoral boundaries law, which allowed a 25 percent variation in constituency size (from a rural district with 6,309 voters to an urban riding of 10,147), resulting in the overrepresentation of rural voters.

49. *R. v. Zundel* (1987), 58 O.R. (2d) 129 (C.A.). In 1987, the Ontario Court of Appeal upheld Ernst Zundel's conviction for the Criminal Code offence of spreading false news via his claim that the Holocaust was a hoax invented by Jews in an international conspiracy. However, the Supreme Court of Canada struck down the Criminal Code provision in 1992 on the grounds that freedom of expression in section 2 (b) of the Charter protects even falsehoods if there is a defence of honest belief.

50. Michael Mandel provides one of the best-known left/progressive critiques in his famous book, *The Charter of Rights and the Legalization of Politics in Canada* (Toronto: Wall and Thompson, 1989), pp. 53–54. From the other end of the ideological continuum, Morton and Knopff offer a range of critiques in *Charter Politics*.

51. Section 36 of the Constitution Act, 1982 (which is not part of the Charter, incidentally) commits the federal and provincial governments to "(a) promoting equal opportunities for the well-being of Canadians; (b) furthering economic development to reduce disparity in opportunities; and (c) providing essential public services of reasonable quality to all Canadians." It also commits the federal government to equalization payments to the provinces. However, the section is a commitment in principle rather than an actionable or justifiable clause. The social charter originally proposed by the New Democratic government of Ontario as a constitutional amendment in what became the Charlottetown Accord would have compelled governments to provide minimal levels of medicare, housing, food, and other basic necessities, and primary and secondary education, among other things. The final version of the social charter in the accord would not have been binding on governments, however, even if the accord had been passed in the national referendum of October 1992. See David Shugarman, "The Social Charter," in D. Cameron and M. Smith, eds., *Constitutional Politics* (Toronto: James Lorimer, 1992).

52. Andrew Petter, "Immaculate Deception: The Charter's Hidden Agenda," *The Advocate* 45 (1987): 857.

53. For articulations of this view, see, for example, Rainer Knopff, *Human Rights and Social Technology: The New War on Discrimination* (Ottawa: Carleton University Press, 1989).

54. See Peter Russell, "The Political Purposes of the Canadian Charter of Rights and Freedoms," *Canadian Bar Review* 61 (1983): 30–54.

55. Peter McCormick and Ian Greene describe the terms, conditions, functions, socioeconomic backgrounds, and attitudes of Canadian judges in *Judges and Judging: Inside the Canadian Judicial System* (Toronto: James Lorimer, 1990).

56. Joel Bakan, "Constitutional Interpretation and Social Change: You Can't Always Get What You Want (Nor What You Need)," in R. Devlin, ed., *Canadian Perspectives on Legal Theory* (Toronto: Emond Montgomery, 1991), pp. 449–50. On the other hand, the Court Challenges Program was instituted in 1985 to fund test-case litigation on equality rights, multiculturalism, and language issues. The program was cut in the 1991 federal budget, however, leaving many groups stranded (though it has recently been reinstated). Nevertheless, the point is that funding is not automatic, but rather depends on the government's willingness to provide it to disadvantaged groups; and unlike wealthy interests, these groups must submit themselves to rigorous bureaucratic evaluation processes.

57. Mandel, *Charter of Rights and Legalization of Politics in Canada*, p. 4.

58. McCormick and Greene, *Judges and Judging*, p. 79.

FURTHER READINGS

Bayefsky, A., and M. Eberts. *Equality and the Canadian Charter of Rights*. Toronto: Carswell, 1990.

Greene, Ian. *The Charter of Rights*. Toronto: James Lorimer, 1989.

Hogg, Peter. *Constitutional Law of Canada*. Toronto: Carswell, 1993.

Knopff, R., and F.L. Morton. *Charter Politics*. Scarborough, Ont.: Nelson Canada, 1992.

Mahoney, K.E., and S.M. Martin. *Equality and Judicial Neutrality* Toronto: Carswell, 1987.

Mandel, Michael. *The Charter of Rights and the Legalization of Politics in Canada*. 2nd. ed. Toronto: Wall and Thompson, 1993.

Manfredi, Christopher. *Judicial Power and the Charter*. Toronto: McClelland and Stewart, 1993.

McCormick, Peter and Ian Greene. *Judges and Judging*. Toronto: James Lorimer, 1990.

Monahan, Patrick. *Politics and the Constitution: The Charter, Federalism and the Supreme Court of Canada*. Toronto: Carswell, 1987.

Russell, P., R. Knopff, and F.L. Morton. *Federalism and the Charter*. Ottawa: Carleton University Press, 1989.

18 PARLIAMENTARY GOVERNMENT IN CANADA

Michael M. Atkinson

There are two fundamentally opposing perspectives on how parliamentary government in Canada should be organized.[1] In the parliament-centred view, the most important unit of parliamentary government is the individual MP, the representative of the people. The right of MPs to speak on behalf of constituents and to make personal contributions to the policies of the country is critical to democratic governance. Reforms that are premised on this view seek to enhance the ability of MPs to control Parliament's agenda, to appoint or elect its officers, and to shape the content of legislative debate. There will always be room for leadership in the parliament-centred view, but that leadership must be responsive to the will of the House, which may fluctuate as temporary majorities unite behind specific policy proposals. Political parties in the parliament-centred view become the instruments of MPs. They are useful for expressing broad programs with which MPs can associate, but they must never choke off individual expression or stand in the way of an MP's service to constituents.

In the second perspective on parliamentary government—the cabinet-centred view—strong, executive leadership is understood to be the *sine qua non* of effective government. Parliament, in this view, consists of leaders and followers. The role of parties is to provide a vehicle for communication between them and a mechanism for distributing rewards and sanctions. The use of patronage and other tested methods for rewarding supporters is considered a legitimate means of securing the authority of the parliamentary party leadership. This view of parliamentary government expects discretion on the part of leaders and deference on the part of followers. Members of Parliament are not lawmakers in anything but the formal sense of the term. Parliament is a deliberating assembly, an arena in which cabinet outlines and defends it proposals before an organized, sceptical opposition. It is the cabinet and individual ministers, acting in the name of the Crown, who exercise effective political authority, and it is the job of the House to hold these ministers accountable.

The development of the Canadian Parliament has been strongly influenced by the cabinet-centred perspective. Often referred to as the Westminster model of parliamentary government, this perspective has found favour among Canadian politicians and academics.[2] The Canadian public, on the other hand, has been alternatively confused, bemused, and offended by the practices it engenders. The first part of this chapter outlines those practices and comments critically on the capacity of the Westminster model to deliver on its promise of effective government. The second part of the chapter examines relations between cabinet and Parliament that challenge those emphasized by the Westminster model. Also discussed are the 1980s reforms, most of which embody the parliament-centred view, and the degree to which they have succeeded in achieving a workable balance, or a middle ground, between competing views of the purpose of parliamentary government.

THE FUNDAMENTALS OF THE WESTMINSTER MODEL

For those observing from the gallery of the House of Commons, the scene below is a bewildering mixture of ritual, humour, incivility, and solemnity. Most onlookers are unaware of the most important formal rules that govern procedure (the Standing Orders), let alone the established, if informal, norms that govern personal conduct. Yet a careful study of these rules and norms is not the place to begin to understand parliamentary government in Canada. The rules are important, of course, but primarily because they give expression to more profound principles and conventions upon which the Westminster model is based. In this section, two of these principles are examined. They may strike readers as so elementary that little more than a brief mention is necessary. But as we shall see, problems arise when we are forced to interpret these principles. Not only are they at odds with one another, but they often give rise to behaviour that many find inimical to good government. Moreover, these fundamental principles impose on politicians, public servants, and the electorate demands that are, in the context of the modern administrative state, quite unrealistic.

1. *The cabinet is in charge of and responsible for the conduct of parliamentary business.* During the 19th century, ordinary members of Parliament assumed much of the initiative for legislation by offering proposals in the form of private and private members' bills.[3] Even then, however, it was the government-sponsored public bill that was used to change the general laws of the country.[4] Now almost all of the bills that Parliament finally adopts are government bills; that is, they have been introduced by ministers of the Crown. Moreover, only ministers are permitted to

introduce bills that authorize the raising or spending of money. Parliamentary procedure has gradually tightened to give the government sufficient time to enact its legislative program and to curtail lengthy debates, while the Speaker is counted on to dispose of dilatory motions.

The government has responsibilities other than the sponsoring of a legislative program. Every year, on or before March 1, the government lays before the Commons a request for funds to conduct business. This request, appearing in the form of "estimates," is followed by a supply bill, which is needed to give the estimates legislative authority. Supplementary estimates and further supply bills are tabled as required during the remainder of the fiscal year. The Minister of Finance introduces a budget, usually in the spring of each year, which announces the government's overall financial plan and intended tax changes. Major policy announcements often accompany the budget.

The government House leader is responsible for orchestrating all of this activity, ensuring that deadlines are met, that important government bills are not postponed indefinitely, and that the opposition is satisfied with the time that has been made available to discuss these measures. The week-by-week and month-by-month planning of the parliamentary session is in the hands of the parliamentary party leadership. The prime minister is responsible for calling Parliament and requesting that the governor general dissolve it. From the narrowest of details to the broadest of constitutional responsibilities, the government is in charge.

How does the government acquire and retain these responsibilities? The formal (and rather uninformative) answer is that the cabinet enjoys the confidence of the House of Commons and is therefore able to offer advice to, and act on behalf of, the Crown. But behind this expression of confidence lies the machinery of the electoral process and the politics of party organization and cohesion. The support that the cabinet possesses has been garnered in the electorate, not in the House of Commons. The electorate has given one party more seats than the others. That party's leader usually (but by no means necessarily) becomes prime minister and chooses a cabinet. As individuals, members of Parliament have no special role in any of this. They seek election, of course, but the support they receive cannot easily be interpreted as a personal endorsement.

Small wonder then that once MPs arrive in Ottawa, the Westminster model assigns them a rather prosaic task. If they sit on the government side of the House, their job is to express confidence in the leadership by voting for government-sponsored measures; if they are opposition members they are expected to oppose those measures, at least if directed to do so by the opposition party leadership. The team spirit that this exercise engenders is reinforced by the "confidence convention," the erroneous notion that the defeat of any government-sponsored bill requires the government's resignation.[5] No such requirement exists, except perhaps in the minds of MPs. However, many MPs appear to be convinced that given the circumstances of their own election—namely, the role played by the party's leadership—an overt expression of independence is tantamount to a renunciation of that leadership. The result of this logic is that rigid party discipline, punctuated (on the opposition side at least) by leadership crises, is the standard behavioural dynamic in the House of Commons.

Called upon to extol the virtues of this system, one would surely point out that it concentrates authority and responsibility in the hands of elected representatives. A government created and sustained in this manner is able to act decisively and can accomplish a great deal without delaying and equivocating until problems have reached crisis proportions. Professor C.E.S. Franks has argued that medicare and the social programs to which Canadians often point with pride have emerged not because of broadly based social democratic parties, but "through the electoral dialectic of a powerful, centralized cabinet and a mass electorate."[6] The Westminster model, it appears, is better suited to the development of integrative, national programs than to the cultivation of narrow, special interests. By the same token, the concentration of responsibility implicit in this model would seem to assist in the assignment of blame. Ministers can be held responsible for their actions (or inactions), and cabinet, because it remains a cohesive political body, can presumably be sanctioned collectively for poor performance. It is not surprising that this type of system, with its focus on the effectiveness of centralized decision making, is often referred to as cabinet government.

In spite of these advantages, certain problems have arisen in the practice of cabinet government in Canada. In the first place, our single-member plurality electoral system has sometimes been unable to manufacture a majority of seats for the governing party in the House of Commons. To have the confidence of the House, the government must therefore attract and retain the support of at least some members of the opposition. Confidence motions, under these circumstances, are no longer routine demonstrations of party solidarity. Moreover, the assignment of responsibility for government actions is not as clear cut. It has been suggested, in their defence, that minority governments are likely to be sensitive to the House of Commons. What is lost in the concentration of authority is gained in a new responsiveness to Parliament. This may be true, but there is nothing to guarantee this outcome, and during the Pearson and Diefenbaker years there was very little evidence of it.[7] Minority governments have their virtues, but the point is that they are not the same as those used to justify the Westminster model.

The second problem is that of ministerial responsibility. Are cabinet ministers willing to accept responsibility for all of the actions of their departments and agencies, to the point of resigning in the face of administrative errors? Put that way, the answer is no. In Canada, no minister has ever resigned because of a mistake committed by someone in the bureaucracy.[8] Ministers retain effective responsibility for actions undertaken in accordance with their instructions or policies, but determining which actions are encompassed in this understanding can be a very difficult and contentious matter.[9] And when things go wrong, as they did in the Al-Mashat case of 1991, ministers are tempted to reverse the logic of ministerial responsibility and lay the blame at the feet of public servants.[10] In short, while the Westminster model is supposed to concentrate authority and responsibility, there is evidence that ministers are unwilling to assume all of that burden.

In their attempt to tighten up the responsibility system, MPs and others have proposed that deputy ministers (who are public servants) accept responsibility for administrative matters and politicians responsibility for questions of policy.[11] Under this proposal, deputy ministers would be required to explain and justify how departments were managed, but they would not be held responsible for the (ostensibly) neutral policy advice they give to politicians. Of course, this formula for accountability rests on the assumption that policy and administration can be neatly separated, and both observers and participants are quick to agree that complete separation is impossible.[12] Besides, the policy role of deputy ministers and other senior officials is widely acknowledged. Yet, in the Westminster model, it is ministers who accept responsibility and take the political heat in Parliament. No one questions the government's right to obtain the best advice possible, but perhaps something is amiss when some of the chief architects of government policy are able to avoid the questions of parliamentarians. Has ministerial responsibility become merely a polite subterfuge used to protect the senior officials and "superbureaucrats" who silently govern?

The answer is almost certainly no. Politicians still wield significant power, especially in the setting of priorities. On the other hand, there is ample evidence that senior bureaucrats and ministers do form a policy-making oligarchy in which the differences between them are sometimes hard to detect. Senior Canadian bureaucrats, for example, are far more tolerant of politics than their junior colleagues and they work heavily within contact networks that include only ministers and other senior public servants.[13] Under the circumstances, some politicization of the bureaucracy and some blurring of lines of responsibility is bound to occur. The Westminster model, in spite of its stress on centralized political decision-making, cannot resolve the problem of accountability.

A third problem with the cabinet-centred version of parliamentary government is that it seems unable to resist the diffusion of power in Ottawa's policy system. Although the Westminster model is supposed to supply strong executive leadership, and has been defended as the source of national programs, many observers detect a leaching of power to individual departments where technical expertise resides and interest-group contacts are frequent.[14] The resulting bureaucratic pluralism stands squarely in the way of strong central direction.

This diffusion of power within the bureaucracy is compounded by the willingness of politicians to devote large chunks of time and vast amounts of money to programs that are fashioned to meet the territorial realities of Canadian politics. The system of regional ministers has survived in spite of the efforts of Prime Ministers Trudeau and Mulroney to do without these political agents of cabinet. In addition to being responsible for patronage, regional ministers have succeeded in mobilizing their department's resources behind provincial and local projects.[15] Of course, a parliament-centred approach might make matters worse, inviting all MPs to concentrate on nothing but locally tailored programs. But it should be acknowledged that we do not have to endorse a parliament-centred view of government before we can witness the diffusion of power. It is, in many ways, already upon us.

It is not just the bureaucracy and individual politicians that have seized the policy initiative. Parliament as a whole, and the government in particular, is now obliged to share the political stage with another institutional actor, the judiciary. In Canada, the judiciary has always had a policy-making role, but the Charter of Rights and Freedoms, introduced into the Constitution in 1982, has vastly increased the capacity of the courts to scrutinize and limit both legislative and executive actions. Without the Charter, the nature and extent of the rights possessed by Canadians was made concrete only by the actions of Parliament and the provincial legislatures. With the Charter, a portion of this task has been passed over to the courts. Early fears that the Supreme Court might adopt a highly activist stance, striking down legislation in a host of policy areas, appear to be groundless. The courts have taken their place in a more expanded and delicate constitutional balance, but they have not replaced Parliament as a legislative body. Even so, it must be acknowledged that the courts have intervened in certain policy areas to strike down specific legislative and executive actions. Such interventions may be justifiable, but they weaken the capacity of the Westminster model to deliver decisive government.

The final problem with the operation of the Westminster-style cabinet government is perhaps the most important of all: this system offers individual members of Parliament very few opportunities for personal initiative and achievement. Unless MPs are fortunate enough to be elevated to cabinet, or unless they obtain special jobs such as whip or Speaker, most MPs must be content with a vicarious experience of power and the satisfaction that comes from performing countless tasks on behalf of constituents. In debating the McGrath Report on parliamentary reform, backbenchers expressed frustration with their rather confined role. They decried the chains of party discipline, severely criticized the conduct of private members' business, and described the legislative process in general as a charade. A respected MP, Keith Penner [Lib: Cochrane–Superior], summed up the mood: "We have a parliamentary system in Canada which is underdeveloped, immature, retarded and defective. ... In what other

Parliament of the world are members referred to as sheep or trained seals?"[16] In short, MPs are typically servants of their parties; they are not powerful, independent political entrepreneurs.

Political parties did not always dwarf individual MPs. Before parties secured their grip on elected representatives, responsible government in Canada meant that, if provoked, the assembly could and would dismiss a government and install another without the benefit of a general election. From 1848 (when responsible government was first introduced in British North America) to 1864 (when Confederation discussions began in earnest) a series of governments were made and unmade in this way. After Confederation, the term "responsible government" lost this meaning.[17] Between 1867 and 1873, John A. Macdonald suffered several defeats in the House of Commons but refused to resign. As political parties became cohesive in the electorate and in Parliament, the threat of defeat itself diminished considerably. And when defeat came, governments sometimes refused to treat it as a matter of confidence (February 1968, December 1983), or else called an election immediately (May 1974, December 1979). Parliament is still the site on which governments are confirmed, and when no single party has a majority in the House of Commons this is where the matter of "who governs" is largely settled. But when governments are defeated in the House, it is most often the electorate, not members of Parliament, who choose their replacement.

In the 1990s, the cabinet is responsible, through the party system, to the electorate. This does not imply that Parliament and parliamentarians are irrelevant. Parliament's chief task is to ensure that the government behaves appropriately and that ministers account for their actions. It performs this task through the political parties around which Parliament is organized. The spectacle of a vigilant House of Commons constantly questioning and criticizing the government is sufficient assurance for some that this task is being performed well. But it is the actions of political parties, including the party in power, that determine how much of this is show and how much is substance. In this respect, a great deal of emphasis is placed on the role of the opposition as an alternative government and a constant source of sceptical and critical pronouncements. We turn now to a consideration of the second principle of parliamentary government in Canada and an evaluation of the opposition's ability to hold governments accountable between elections.

2. *The opposition must have the right to criticize the government openly and the ability to make that criticism felt.* In Parliament, the government explains and justifies its action (or inaction) not to a sympathetic audience anxious to offer assistance, but to an organized, institutionalized opposition bent on demonstrating the inappropriateness and inefficiencies of government policy. Though it may never have the votes necessary to defeat the government, the opposition is nonetheless charged with ensur-

ing that the responsibility of the government to the House of Commons is more than a formality. As John Stewart has put it, "It is this public testing of governance, with the government and the opposition as institutionalized adversaries, that is the hallmark of contemporary Responsible Government."[18]

The idea of opposition was not always so compatible with parliamentary government. Parliaments in Britain were originally meetings of nobles called to offer advice to the King and, it was hoped, to support the Crown in its (mostly military) ventures. Although an offer of advice often implied criticism, outright opposition could easily be construed as treason. In the 17th and 18th centuries, by which time Parliament had made good its claim to supremacy, the idea of opposition-in-Parliament was still resisted, this time by those who saw it as divisive—an expression of greedy factionalism. But by then efforts to create governments composed of the "best men" had failed, and observers had come to recognize that, while opposition to the government might be denounced as factional, the government itself was a "party."[19] Parties, moreover, might prove advantageous if they could be used as a bulwark against the danger of concentrated power. This bulwark would take the form of a recognized and legitimate opposition eager to secure office.

With the government facing the opposition in Parliament and two teams of party leaders struggling for support in the electorate, have we at last defined the essence of responsible government? Defined perhaps, but this system has to work before anyone can feel completely satisfied, and there are several obstacles to its effective operation.

First, the opposition in Parliament, because it is not in control of the parliamentary agenda, cannot insist that significant public issues be addressed on the floor of the Commons before the government takes any action. Many important policy decisions—including the reorganization of Via Rail and the cancellation by the newly elected Liberal government of military helicopters contracts—are taken by order-in-council (i.e., by executive fiat) without the benefit of parliamentary debate. Financial matters are case in point. The tradition of budget secrecy has meant that as the Minister of Finance delivers the budget speech to Parliament, Revenue Canada is already preparing to collect taxes according to its provisions. Even though the legislation turning the speech into law remains to be enacted, governments and their officials simply assume that it will pass unamended, regardless of opposition protests.

Can anyone blame the media when they decline to take these protests seriously? Although opposition members are charged with scrutinizing government action, or deploring inaction, they cannot rely on the media to report on their efforts, especially if these do not take the form of pithy pronouncements suitable for the evening news. What is the likelihood that opposition members who engage in lonely debates in the chamber will have their ideas and reservations communicated to an alert and interested public? Even more to the point, are electoral fortunes influenced by the performance of the opposition on the floor of the House of Commons? A strong affirmative answer is impossible. In spite of the televising of Parliament (which began in 1977 and remains selective in content and distribution), there is no evidence that the electorate has an improved awareness of opposition policies and attitudes. The press gallery persists in concentrating on spectacular developments, scandals, and human-interest stories, while election campaigns continue to be contests among party leaders, not alternative ministerial teams.

A second problem is simply the quality and persuasiveness of opposition criticism. There are now several institutions capable of offering compelling critiques of government policy. Consider first the "think tanks": the C.D. Howe Institute, the Fraser Institute, the Canadian Centre for Policy Alternatives, and the Institute for Research on Public Policy, to name a few. On most occasions, these bodies are capable of supplying policy analysis that is more sophisticated and informed than that produced by the opposition. Then there are investigative journalists whose employers, including the Canadian government in the case of the CBC, have deeper pockets than opposition MPs. It is true that the opposition can use academic studies and capitalize on media revelations, but despite the more than $5 million allocated to the opposition parties for operational and research purposes, they have been unable (or unwilling) to generate their own economic analyses. The opposition is certainly without the information and expertise the government is able to marshal on virtually any specialized subject, and opposition parties appear to be convinced that the resources they do have ought to be used to exploit short-term partisan opportunities.

In addition, the opposition must also compete with institutional rivals, including the provinces and the Senate. Nowhere is the irrelevance of opposition criticism more apparent than in the realm of federal–provincial relations. For instance, because provinces own and control the development of most natural resources, debates on the floor of the Commons about the price of oil in Alberta or hydro development in Quebec have the quality of a sideshow compared to the negotiation and debate on these matters that takes place between federal and provincial officials. The major issues of centralization and decentralization in the Canadian federation are also debated outside of Parliament. Inside Parliament, the Senate has sometimes appeared more fearsome than all of the opposition parties combined. In a spectacle rich with irony, the Senate in recent times has donned the mantle of the people's protector and fought hard battles over pharmaceutical legislation and the GST. Of course, the opposition has been supportive in these matters, but the point is that the Senate has occasionally been a genuine obstacle to a government hell-bent on enacting its program. In these cases, it is the provinces and the Senate that supply the counterbalance on which the Westminster model depends.

The third problem faced by the opposition in Canada is that of achieving policy distinctiveness. The institutionalization of opposition in Parliament was originally premised on an agreement among all participants not to question the foundations of the parliamentary system. Opposition parties have added to this their tacit agreement not to question the fundamentals of the social and economic order. Securing power, therefore, became a matter of piecing together a coalition, consisting of regional and linguistic interests, sufficient to produce a majority of seats in the House of Commons. For the greatest part of Canadian history the opposition has comprised those elements left out of the governing coalition.[20] With little to unite them other than antipathy toward the government, Liberal and Conservative parties in opposition have experienced wrenching divisions over policy and leadership. They have seized opportunities, such as the free-trade debate, to distance themselves from government policy, only to experience strong pressures for conformity once the debate was over.

Until the advent of the Reform Party, only the NDP had succeeded in supplying an ideologically consistent critique of the governing parties, often (ironically perhaps) at the expense of appearing unnecessarily rigid and uncompromising. Both the Reform Party and the Bloc Québécois promise opposition of a fundamental nature. The Bloc is openly committed to the politics of regional advantage until such time as the Quebec electorate signals its willingness to dissolve the province's ties to the rest of Canada. Reform challenges many of the practices of the Westminster model, including party discipline, and many of the precepts of the interventionist state. On the surface, neither party should experience much difficulty in projecting its distinctiveness. And yet, because many policy dilemmas do not lend themselves to easy categorization, let alone easy solution, it is not clear that either of these opposition parties will be able to sustain a distinctive message across a wide range of policy problems.

The final problem emerges from this difficulty. Regardless of their true beliefs, opposition parties are expected to oppose. This understanding is fundamental to the entire edifice of adversarial politics. But many Canadians appear to have lost patience with the idea that good government requires constant criticism on the part of the opposition. They wonder whether it is best to organize a political system on the assumption that there exists nothing but conflicting interests. If Parliament is a deliberative assembly, why are there so few public examples of consensus and agreement?

These observations on the opposition in Canada should not be interpreted simply as criticisms of opposition parties, the government, or the media, whatever their shortcomings may be. The point is that the Westminster model of parliamentary government requires a great deal of the parliamentary opposition. Yet this opposition must work under severe institutional and political constraints not at all anticipated by the model.

Conclusion

In summary, the Westminster model promises decisive government, political accountability, and the open debate of legislative changes, spending decisions, and controversial government actions. It promises political stability in the form of a government-in-waiting should the present one falter. Unfortunately, as argued above, the Westminster model is unable to deliver on all of these promises. Of course, a model of parliamentary government based on a parliament-centred, rather than a cabinet-centred, approach will have liabilities as well. But this has not deterred parliamentarians from pressing for parliament-centred reforms. They recognize that the overwhelming authority of the Westminster model makes it unlikely that it will be replaced altogether. In the next section, we consider some of these reforms and relationships between cabinet and Parliament that are largely ignored in the Westminster model.

EXECUTIVE–LEGISLATIVE RELATIONS

The Westminster model rests heavily on the clash of government and opposition forces. But to expect the opposition to assume the entire burden of ensuring a responsible government is, as argued, no longer realistic. This section explores relations between the government and the House of Commons that carry us beyond government–opposition confrontation. The work of members of Parliament, either as individuals or in concert, can complement the dominant adversarial style of politics in the House and supplement the work of the opposition. In fact, the activities of Parliament should be understood as a process of conflict and concession involving the government on the one hand and, on the other, three elements: the opposition, taken as a whole; small groups of MPs, in caucus and committees; and private members, that is, MPs acting as individual representatives.

THE GOVERNMENT VERSUS THE OPPOSITION

The House of Commons has found it hard to shake its "bear-pit" image. The Chamber is still the stage on which the ritual and theatre of partisan antagonism is performed. It is the primary battleground of government and opposition forces, which usually means ministers or parliamentary secretaries, on the one hand, and members of the opposition front bench, on the other. The dominant style of debate is oratory, and backbenchers on both sides of the House are expected to provide an appreciative audience.

Three important activities that take place on the floor of the House display these combative and partisan qualities. Question Period is, by a considerable margin, the most successful, at least from the point of view of the party leadership. During the 1980s, the opposition parties developed a systematic approach to Question Period in which questions were orchestrated and ordinary backbenchers were discouraged from interrupting the flow until the front bench was finished. But this did little to improve decorum or enhance respect for the Speaker or parliamentary traditions. More than any single institution, Question Period has created the impression that the only political test of importance is survival in combat conditions on the floor of the House of Commons. Members of the media, often untutored in the ways of the House or in the substance of policy, gravitate to these stylized confrontations because they offer the sound bites demanded by radio and television. Unfortunately, this overattention to Question Period has diminished the significance of other debates and left the impression that adversarial politics is all that the Commons is about.

Of course, there are many adversarial moments. A second occasion on which opposition and government traditionally confront one another is the Second Reading stage of government-sponsored legislation. First Reading is nothing more than parliamentary approval to allow the bill to be printed and placed on the order paper. Second Reading is the stage at which Parliament debates "the principle" of the bill; no amendments to the content of the bill are permitted, and strict rules of relevance are enforced. It is here that the minister appears in the House to defend the legislation (although this task has increasingly been delegated to parliamentary secretaries) and the opposition spokesperson mounts a challenge. The government prefers to believe that once the Second Reading stage has been successfully completed, Parliament is obliged to concentrate on the details of the bill, the main battle over principles having been fought. This interpretation of Second Reading is entirely in keeping with the idea that legislation is a government–opposition affair.

A similar quality of partisanship is found in the special debates that are scattered throughout the parliamentary year. The throne speech and the budget debate are opportunities for the opposition to criticize, and for the cabinet to defend, the government's vaguely worded legislative program and its more precisely formulated tax proposals. In addition, twenty "opposition days" are set aside in each parliamentary session during which motions proposed by the opposition parties form the basis for debate. These normally take the form of general critical pronouncements on government policy.

Unfortunately, none of these debates can be considered a splendid success from anyone's perspective. Franks puts the matter bluntly: "The action is slow, the dialogue is ponderous and interminable, the scene is sparsely populated and the wit has all the subtlety but none of the force of a Mack truck."[21] In 1983, the Special Committee on Procedure (Lefebvre Committee) succeeded in persuading the House to adopt a set of reforms that have improved the circumstances of debate. There are now shorter speeches (normally twenty minutes), followed by a brief exchange; a new system has been introduced for private members' bills; and debates have been organized to avoid, as much as possible, evening sittings. In April 1991, further changes were introduced, this time to shorten the parliamentary session to a maximum of 134 days, and to shorten the amount of time devoted to opposition days and other general debates. But the essential problem of parliamentary debate—the absence of media (hence citizen) interest—remains and cannot be solved by procedural reforms. Until MPs exercise sufficient independence in their own speechmaking to attract media attention, their efforts will be lost in the larger picture of government–opposition confrontation.

That said, a great deal of parliamentary activity is conducted well away from the floor of the House of Commons or the Senate. With the growth of government activity and with annual government spending running at over $120 billion, the government has found it expedient to transfer some of its own business to parliamentary committees. In 1968, changes were made to the Standing Orders to require that detailed, clause-by-clause consideration of legislation be accomplished in standing committees. At the same time, the opposition somewhat reluctantly agreed that the scrutiny of departmental spending estimates, previously considered under the heading of "Supply" on the floor of the House, could also be transferred to the committee system. Committees hold out the prospect of conflict as well, but not always on a strictly partisan basis.

Even without these changes to parliamentary rules, it would still be a distortion to think of Parliament simply in terms of government–opposition relations. Some of the most important political activity in Parliament takes place away from the floor of the House, in the caucuses of the governing and opposition parties. It is in forums such as these—caucus and committees—that conflicts over policy are refined or redefined, that agreement is often achieved, and that truly controversial matters are subject to a measure of conciliation.

THE GOVERNMENT VERSUS CAUCUS AND COMMITTEES

For the government, one of the most important sources of criticism is the government backbench. Normally quiescent and polite in public, in private the backbench supporters of the government frequently clash with cabinet on matters of policy. Open rebellion, though rare, can take the form of abstentions on important votes, minor media campaigns, and cross-voting.

The disapproval of backbench supporters is a serious matter for the government. Occasional expressions of personal disgruntlement can be tolerated, and many potentially disruptive issues can be assuaged by appeals to party loyalty. But when backbenchers refuse to respond to threats (no trips to Europe), to inducements (the possibility of a parliamentary secretary position), or to the rallying cry of party solidarity, the viability of the government itself is at stake. The opposition preys on suspected rifts within the governing party, and while cross-votes may not lead directly to government defeats, when a government has lost the confidence of its own backbenchers then it has lost the confidence of the House of Commons.

Government members, ministers included, meet in caucus every week when Parliament is in session. Because these meetings are always held *in camera* and, because MPs are very reluctant to expose to the public any sign of divisiveness in the party, the impression is sometimes one of cabinet control and caucus deference. The reminiscences of MPs from the Diefenbaker and Pearson years have helped to confirm this image: denied any knowledge of the government's pending legislative program, MPs were forced to content themselves with issues such as parking spaces on Parliament Hill. In 1969, however, the Liberal caucus insisted that it be consulted on legislation and other expressions of government policy before these were announced in the House of Commons. A system of ad hoc caucus committees was created to implement this consultative arrangement, and since 1970 the Liberal caucus has elected its own officers, including the caucus chairperson, without the direct interference of the parliamentary party leadership. Since then, regional caucuses and caucus task forces have proven to be successful vehicles for mobilizing caucus opinion and forcing the party leadership to be responsive to its backbench supporters.

Caucus meetings are as closed as ever, but the noise of battle can occasionally be heard in spite of the secrecy. There is no doubt, for example, that many members of the Liberal caucus strongly opposed changes to the Unemployment Insurance Commission throughout the 1970s. Several amendments to the Liberal government's Crow Rate legislation in 1983 were accomplished at the insistence of caucus. During their period in opposition (1984–1993), the Liberals continued to divide in private and unite (sometimes only partially) in public over such matters as the Free Trade Agreement and the Constitution.

On the Conservative side, Brian Mulroney enjoyed a reputation for being successful at mediating caucus divisions, but even he had problems. Division over amendments to the Official Languages Act forced Mulroney to fire one of his parliamentary secretaries, whose opposition to the government's measures had aroused the party's Quebec caucus. The passage of the GST saw perhaps the most heated policy division, with MPs such as David Kilgour and Alex Kindy driven from caucus because of their unwillingness to endorse the tax.

As these cases illustrate, the government must attempt to anticipate and answer caucus opinion. Caucus is not a decision-making body, however, and the outcomes of caucus meetings are frequently a mystery even to participants. The committee systems do not always work, regional input does not always find expression in national caucus decisions, and the party leadership almost always has the last word.[22] Despite these structural problems, a veteran of the Liberal caucus, Mark MacGuigan, came to the following (perhaps overly emphatic) conclusion: "From the beginning of my years in Parliament it has been apparent that strong caucus opposition to any government proposal imposes an absolute veto on the proposal."[23]

Like the meetings of caucus, committees of the Commons are means by which smaller groups of MPs acting in concert can influence the direction of government policy. The potential of committees in this regard lies primarily in their ability to study specific topics in depth and offer detached, and sometimes nonpartisan, assessments. Unlike caucus, however, Commons committees comprise representatives from all parties and, with some exceptions, conduct their hearings in public. The present committee system is the product of two and a half decades of reform, most of it aimed at enhancing the role of private members of Parliament and much of it inspired by the parliament-centred view of parliamentary government. The last comprehensive set of reforms, contained in the McGrath Committee report of 1985,[24] was the most dramatic and has set the stage for a much stronger system of parliamentary committees.

There are now four types of committees: legislative committees, created to give clause-by-clause consideration to bills that have passed Second Reading; standing committees, which give continuous consideration to broad policy areas and review the departmental estimates; special committees, which normally have a specific task and seldom last beyond a session; and joint committees (either standing or special) composed of senators as well as MPs.

Legislative committees are a relatively new innovation, and at the moment they rest on rather shaky ground. The McGrath Committee wanted all legislation reviewed by legislative committees. These would be ad hoc committees dedicated to technically sound legislation, but having no subject-matter specialty and no permanent chair. For the first few years after the McGrath report was tabled, all legislation went to these committees. But as early as 1989, standing committees began to reassert themselves, arguing that they should receive the legislation because they were familiar with the subject matter. In the last few years, this argument has gathered steam, with more and more legislation being referred to standing rather than legislative committees. Regardless of which committee reviews legislation, MPs normally respect party lines, and if changes are made they usually have the support of the sponsoring minister.[25]

Standing committees, of which there are about twenty, are organized around subject-matter areas, many of which parallel the responsibilities of government departments. Since the McGrath reforms, these committees have been free to frame their own agendas and study those matters that appeal to them. Except for a few committees that have special jobs (e.g., Public Accounts), the only regular task of standing committees is to scrutinize departmental spending estimates. However, because estimates can only be reduced (something that happens very rarely, and hardly ever during a majority Parliament), committees have begun to devote less and less time to what many regard as a pointless exercise. They have turned instead to broad problem areas where the partisan mould can often be broken and where committee members can begin to act as a unit.

Using Standing Order 108(2), which permits the initiation of studies, standing committees in the 34th Parliament (1988–1993) produced reports on a wide variety of issues, including child poverty, disabled persons and the media, energy and the environment, and regulatory reform. These investigations have been made more effective by the McGrath Committee reforms. Most standing committees are now relatively small (between seven and fourteen members); are increasingly using subcommittees for special tasks; and are able to hire research staff (although they want more freedom in this regard). Furthermore, the government must eventually respond to their reports (although not necessarily in writing).

Governments are ambivalent about the launching of general investigations by parliamentary committees. On the positive side (from the government's point of view), public inquiries give the appearance of action, without the substance. They ascertain the reactions of interest groups to government proposals without requiring that a formal commitment be made to introduce changes. Moreover, in the 1990s governments have been increasingly tempted to ask committees for their advice. Thus, MPs (particularly government backbenchers) are kept busy and all members are given an opportunity to prove themselves.

On the negative side (again, from the government's point of view), committees eventually present reports, and committee members, not surprisingly, are usually eager to have their proposals discussed. Moreover, these reports are not always what the government wants to see. The Standing Committee on Finance and Economic Affairs, chaired by Don Blenkarn (PC: Mississauga South), produced a report on bank charges that was highly critical of the banking community, and another on tax reform that suggested the middle class would bear the brunt of the tax changes. If reports are tabled with the unanimous approval of committee members, the government will be facing a small body of informed opinion, usually supported by interest groups, that it might find difficult to ignore.

Despite the problems that committees pose for traditional government–opposition confrontation as sanctified in the Westminster model, it is safe to predict that throughout the 1990s governments will be called upon to respond to the studies and recommendations of parliamentary committees. And if, as seems likely,[26] more and more legislation is referred to committee *before* Second Reading, the scope for committee intervention will increase rather than decrease. How far can this be permitted to go? Critics of an expanded committee system have warned that once committees cease behaving as little replicas of the Commons, we can look forward to the decline of parliamentary traditions and a weakening of party ties, which can culminate only in congressionalism. In short, the Westminster model will ultimately be undermined.

It is not at all clear, however, that this is the only path that Parliament must tread. Several years after the McGrath Committee reforms, the government does not appear to have lost control of Parliament. Cross-voting has not increased, and government MPs are as loathe as ever to criticize party policy in public. One of the reasons for politics as usual is that committees continue to have their problems: high turnover remains an obstacle to the development of expertise or feelings of solidarity; the leadership of standing committees is still in the hands of the governing party; the government continues to ignore many committee reports; committees can only review (not reject) order-in-council appointments; and the public service often treats MPs as naive interlopers.[27]

On the other hand, MPs are now better able to make a timely contribution to the government's policy agenda, and parliamentarians on both sides of the House have acquired a measure of control over the procedures, personnel, and precincts of Parliament. Developments like these suggest that there is another dimension to responsible government. The responsibility of a vigilant assembly to monitor closely the actions of a government need not be borne exclusively by the united opposition. Other groups of MPs, including the government caucus, standing committees, and task forces of MPs, can reasonably be expected to share that responsibility.

THE GOVERNMENT VERSUS THE PRIVATE MEMBER OF PARLIAMENT

On September 30, 1986, the House of Commons, for the first time, met to elect a Speaker. At 3:00 a.m. the next day, twelve hours and eleven ballots later, John Fraser, a former Conservative cabinet minister, emerged victorious. It was a remarkable event.[28] Previous Speakers had been chosen by the prime minister in consultation with the leaders of the opposition parties. Dissatisfaction with that procedure had been brewing for years, but it took the bell-ringing incident of 1982 (in which Parliament was effectively suspended for two weeks), and the resultant demands for reform, to finally make the Speaker the choice of the House of Commons. Early in

1994, Parliament used the same procedure for a second time to select a new Speaker, Gilbert Parent, for the 34th Parliament.

The election of a Speaker was one of a number of reforms introduced in the 1980s to provide MPs with greater control over the internal affairs of the House of Commons. Indeed, as we have already suggested, the 1980s was a reform decade. Did any of these reforms genuinely enhance the role of MPs? Probably not. In a government that spends enormous sums of money and employs hundreds of thousands of people, the private member of Parliament cuts a lonely figure. The vast majority of MPs owe their electoral victory to regional and national trends in the popularity of their party and its leaders. The machinery of party politics is such that very few of them will have made a critical contribution to their own election.[29] Many of them, moreover, will enjoy only a short stay in Ottawa before the electorate returns them to private life or before they voluntarily relinquish an often frustrating and demanding job.[30]

Those who establish longer careers in Parliament still have the privileges earned by their predecessors in the British House of Commons, but on their own they can never be a serious source of legislation. A few hours every week are set aside for the consideration of private members' business, but attendance is generally poor and, until recently, the vast majority of private members' bills were not voted on at Second Reading. The arrival of cohesive political parties and the government-sponsored public bill long ago set the stage for the departure of the private member as lawmaker.

But neither the House of Commons as a whole nor private members should be judged as initiators of policy. While it is true that many items in the government's legislative program have, as their precursors, private members' bills, the task of private members, like that of the opposition and groups of MPs, is to prod, encourage, question, and occasionally castigate the government with the intention of forcing it to justify in public its actions or inactions. For a certain range of matters, the private member is in an excellent position to do just that.

Each member of Parliament represents, on average, about 70,000 electors. Representation implies, among other things, responsiveness to the needs of individual constituents, and many MPs spend most of their working time attending to their constituency caseload. This includes unemployment insurance problems, immigration cases, and countless other instances in which the personal intervention of a member of Parliament is requested. While some MPs come to resent this combined role of social worker and ombudsperson, a 1983 Gallup poll showed that over 60 percent of respondents believed that looking after constituents should be the first priority of the MP. Moreover, this type of activity keeps members in touch with the concerns and problems of their constituents. For people who feel aggrieved in some fashion, the government *is* the post office that has curtailed its service, or the unemployment insurance official who refuses a claim. The tendency to judge members of Parliament solely on the strength of their ability to affect the broad strokes of policy does a disservice to those MPs who labour to make sure that their constituents receive justice at the hands of the federal bureaucracy.

There are, in addition, those MPs who wage personal campaigns to secure a particular policy objective. Bill Domm (PC: Peterborough) worked tirelessly for the restoration of capital punishment in Canada, and the name of Jed Baldwin (PC: Peace River) will always be associated with the battle for freedom-of-information legislation. The efforts of these MPs have been assisted by the introduction of a new system for handling private members' bills. Thirty such bills or motions are chosen at random at the beginning of a session, and an all-party committee selects ten for debate in the House. These ten are permitted to come to a vote at Second Reading. It was through this procedure that Lynn McDonald (NDP: Broadview–Greenwood), in 1988, successfully sponsored a bill to eliminate smoking in all federally regulated buildings.

Anthony King has described these personal campaigns as the "private members' mode" of executive–legislative relations. MPs who adopt it, in his words, "come to see themselves simply as backbench Members of Parliament, concerned with investigating the quality of the performance of the executive (of whichever party), with protecting the rights of the citizen against the executive (of whichever party) and with asserting the prerogatives of backbench MPs (irrespective of party)."[31] Very few MPs can stand up to the demands imposed by this style of operation. Parliament is about political parties, not private members. Nonetheless, members of Parliament frequently feel the need to make manifest their legislative aspirations, sometimes to fulfill a personal mission, sometimes to demonstrate their political talents. For these reasons alone, the government will always be confronted by the private member of Parliament.

CONCLUSION

The importance of Parliament does not lie in its capacity to be a centre for the detailed construction of public policy, for this capacity is meagre indeed. Parliament is, instead, a forum where the ideas and concerns of the government, the opposition, and groups of MPs and individual representatives meet. According to the cabinet-centred view, the government should always be in charge: its ideas and policies should form the basis for the most important debates. But the government must also listen. To be out of touch with the sentiments of backbench supporters or the opposition is to court disaster.

Reform proposals inspired by the parliament-centred view will continue to find articulate supporters on both sides of the House. If the norms and rules that underpin responsible government continue to grow in complexity, and Parliament is strengthened in its ability to question and prod, governments will have to listen more closely to MPs. This will undoubtedly occasion some loss of flexibility, and pressures on governments to inform and explain will tax ministerial and bureaucratic resources. But it is surely not too much to ask that a government that listens so closely to the pronouncements of the provinces, interest groups, GATT, and Washington also remain in touch with the country's elected representatives.

It is essential, however, that these representatives have something to say that merits attention. While strengthening Parliament's side in each of the relationships discussed above will help, it will also be necessary to challenge the fundamental principles of the Westminster model with a view to guiding its evolution. If ordinary MPs remain in splendid isolation, entirely neutralized by strictures of party discipline that very few Canadians understand, Parliament will increasingly become an irrelevant and obscure institution.

NOTES

1. For excellent discussions of the history of these perspectives and their contemporary relevance, see Gordon T. Stewart, *The Origins of Canadian Politics: A Comparative Approach* (Vancouver: University of British Columbia Press, 1986); and C.E.S. Franks, *The Parliament of Canada* (Toronto: University of Toronto Press, 1987), esp. ch. 1.

2. For the argument that academic infatuation with this view is the product of a colonial mind-set, see Mark Sproule-Jones, "The Enduring Colony?: Political Institutions and Political Science in Canada," *Publius* 14 (Winter 1984): 93–108.

3. On the various types of bills and the distinction between private bills and private members' bills, see Robert J. Jackson and Michael M. Atkinson, *The Canadian Legislative System,* 2nd rev. ed. (Toronto: Gage, 1980), pp. 89–92.

4. John B. Stewart, *The Canadian House of Commons: Procedure and Reform* (Montreal and Kingston: McGill-Queen's University Press, 1977), p. 201.

5. Eugene Forsey and Graham Eglinton, "Twenty-Five Fairy Tales About Parliamentary Government," in Paul W. Fox and Graham White, eds., *Politics: Canada,* 6th ed. (Toronto: McGraw-Hill Ryerson, 1987), pp. 507–13.

6. Franks, *The Parliament of Canada,* p. 260.

7. Linda Geller-Schwartz, "Minority Governments Reconsidered," *Journal of Canadian Studies* 14 (Summer 1979): 67–79.

8. Sharon Sutherland, "Responsible Government and Ministerial Responsibility," *Canadian Journal of Political Science* 24 (March 1991): 91–120.

9. Kenneth Kernaghan, "Power, Parliament and Public Servants in Canada," in Harold Clarke et al., eds., *Parliament, Policy and Representation* (Toronto: Methuen, 1980), pp. 128–29.

10. Sharon Sutherland, "The Al-Mashat Affair: Administrative Responsibility in Parliamentary Institutions," *Canadian Public Administration* 34 (Winter 1991): 573–603.

11. Thomas d'Aquino, G. Bruce Doern, and Cassandra Blair, *Parliamentary Democracy in Canada: Issues for Reform* (Toronto: Methuen, 1983), pp. 45–46;

and Canada, Royal Commission on Financial Management and Accountability, *Final Report* (Ottawa: Supply and Services, 1979), p. 374.

12. Colin Campbell and B. Guy Peters, "The Politics/Administration Dichotomy: Death or Merely Change?" *Governance* 1 (January 1988): 79–99.

13. Michael M. Atkinson and William D. Coleman, "Bureaucracy and Politicians in Canada: An Examination of the Political Administration Model," *Comparative Political Studies* 18 (April 1985): 58–80.

14. A. Paul Pross, "Parliamentary Influence and the Diffusion of Power," *Canadian Journal of Political Science* 18 (June 1985): 235–66; and Michael M. Atkinson and William D. Coleman, *State and Industry: Growth and Decline in the Canadian Economy* (Toronto: University of Toronto Press, 1989), ch. 3.

15. Herman Bakvis, *Regional Ministers: Power and Influence in the Canadian Cabinet* (Toronto: University of Toronto Press, 1991).

16. *Debates* (December 4, 1985), p. 9157.

17. The transition is outlined in Thomas A. Hockin, "Flexible and Structured Parliamentarism," *Journal of Canadian Studies* 14 (Summer 1979): 8–17.

18. Stewart, *The Canadian House of Commons*, p. 21.

19. Ghita Ionescu and Isabel de Madariaga, *Opposition* (Harmondsworth: Penguin, 1972), ch. 2.

20. Franks, *The Parliament of Canada*, pp. 40–44.

21. Ibid., p. 155.

22. Paul G. Thomas, "The Role of National Party Caucuses," in Peter Aucoin, ed., *Party Government and Regional Representation in Canada*, collected research studies of the Royal Commission on the Economic Union and Development Prospects for Canada (Toronto: University of Toronto Press, 1985), pp. 69–136.

23. Mark MacGuigan, "Parliamentary Reform: Impediments to an Enlarged Role for the Backbencher," *Legislative Studies Quarterly* 3 (November 1978): 676.

24. House of Commons, *Report of the Special Committee on Reform of the House of Commons* (Ottawa: Queen's Printer, 1985).

25. Paul G. Thomas, "The Influence of Standing Committees of Parliament on Government Legislation," *Legislative Studies Quarterly* 3 (November 1978): 683–704.

26. See, for example, House of Commons, Standing Committee on House Management, *Report on Parliamentary Reform* (Ottawa: April 1993).

27. For a review of committee problems and some suggestions for improvement, see Report of the Liaison Committee on Committee Effectiveness, *Parliamentary Government*, no. 43 (June 1993).

28. See Gary Levy, "A Night to Remember: The First Election of a Speaker by Secret Ballot," *Canadian Parliamentary Review* 9 (Winter 1986-87).

29. William Irvine, "Does the Candidate Make a Difference?: The Macro-Politics and the Micro-Politics of Getting Elected," *Canadian Journal of Political Science* 15 (December 1982): 755–82.

30. Michael M. Atkinson and David C. Docherty, "Moving Right Along: The Roots of Amateurism in the Canadian House of Commons," *Canadian Journal of Political Science* 35 (June 1992): 295–318.

31. Anthony King, "Modes of Executive–Legislative Relations: Great Britain, France and West Germany," *Legislative Studies Quarterly* 1 (February 1976): 11–36.

FURTHER READINGS

Some of our difficulties in understanding the contemporary Canadian Parliament stem from inattention to the origins of the parliamentary system. On this subject consult Gordon T. Stewart, *The Origins of Canadian Politics* (Vancouver: University of British Columbia Press, 1986); Philip Resnick, *The Masks of Proteus* (Montreal and Kingston: McGill-Queen's University Press, 1990); and Janet Ajzenstat, *The Political Thought of Lord Durham* (Montreal and Kingston: McGill–Queen's University Press, 1988).

On the present-day Parliament, the best single source is C.E.S. Franks, *The Parliament of Canada* (Toronto: University of Toronto Press, 1987), but useful perspectives can be found in Robert J. Jackson and Michael M. Atkinson, *The Canadian Legislative System: Politicians and Policymaking*, 2nd ed. (Toronto: Macmillan, 1980); and John B. Stewart, *The Canadian House of Commons: Procedure and Reform* (Montreal and Kingston: McGill-Queen's University Press, 1977). There are very few books on the attitudes and behaviour of MPs and ministers, but see Allan Kornberg and William Mishler, *Influence in Parliament: Canada* (Durham, N.C.: Duke University Press, 1977).

For chapters on specific topics of parliamentary government, consult Peter Aucoin, ed., *Institutional Reforms for Representative Government*, the collected research studies of the Royal Commission on the Economic Union and Development Prospects for Canada (Toronto: University of Toronto Press, 1985); and John C. Courtney, ed. *The Canadian House of Commons* (Calgary: University of Calgary Press, 1985). On the subject of ministerial responsibility, there are a number of useful chapters and articles scattered about, but the best place to start is with the work of Sharon Sutherland cited above.

Those interested principally in organizational and procedural matters should see John A. Frazer, *The House of Commons at Work* (Montreal: Les Editions de la Chenelière, 1993); and Table Research Branch, *Précis of Procedure*, 4th ed. (Ottawa: House of Commons, 1991). Beware, however, that procedures change frequently and it is wise to consult the reports of procedural committees such as the Standing Committee on House Management.

An evaluation of research on the Canadian Parliament can be found in Michael M. Atkinson and Paul G. Thomas, "Studying the Canadian Parliament," *Legislative Studies Quarterly* 18 (August 1993): 423–51. It contains, among other things, the message that there is still plenty of interesting work to do on this topic.

19 THE FEDERAL CABINET IN CANADIAN POLITICS

David E. Smith

In the year of Confederation, Walter Bagehot described the cabinet as "a combining committee—a *hyphen* which joins, a *buckle* which fastens the legislative part of the state to the executive part of the state." Buckle and hyphen have proved durable metaphors with which to open discussions of cabinet government, despite the fact that the functions and structure of modern cabinets are significantly different from those of Bagehot's time. The executive he had in mind, the Crown, has faded into obscurity in the public consciousness. For most Canadians, the cabinet's central importance lies in its *governing and representative* functions, while its role as adviser to the Crown is seldom considered and, when it is regarded, scarcely understood. Nevertheless, we should keep in mind that the cabinet, through the prime minister, still formally advises the chief executive officer—the governor general—who almost always takes that advice, for not to take it would create a constitutional crisis.

Metaphors like Bagehot's are attractive when facts are hard to find, and, with notable exceptions, studies of the federal cabinet are rare. There is no encyclopedic Canadian work comparable to Sir Ivor Jenning's *Cabinet Government* in Great Britain, nor are there many less ambitious exercises.[1] Personal accounts of those in command at the cabinet table go unwritten; to date, of nineteen former prime ministers, only three (Diefenbaker, Pearson, and Trudeau) have published their own memoirs, and these tell disappointingly little about cabinet decision-making or about the respective influences on cabinet business of the bureaucracy, interest groups, political parties or the Parliamentary opposition.[2] In the twenty years since Lester Pearson formed a government, just two Liberal ministers (Walter Gordon and Judy LaMarsh) wrote memoirs, though the revelations of cabinet business contained in them are cause for regret that other ministers did not follow suit. Unfortunately, recent accounts written by former Trudeau and Mulroney ministers do not meet this earlier standard.[3] This reticence to "talk" on the part of past ministers is not new. Mackenzie King's extraordinary 22-year tenure as prime minister proved no more productive in terms of the number of published accounts that followed it. If Pearson is excluded, only one of King's 73 other ministers dictated his memoirs.[4] In the first half-century of Confederation, when cabinets were smaller and responsibilities less extensive, the selection is no better.[5]

The absence of memoirs is more than unfortunate for academics or citizens who would like to know how government works. However, it also points to a political system that produces politicians who are uncommunicative and incurious, and who, according to Norman Ward and David Hoffman in their study *Bilingualism and Biculturalism in the Canadian House of Commons,* also lack ambition: "Only 24 percent [of the backbench MPs interviewed in a 1964–65 survey] indicated that they would be interested in a cabinet post at some time in the future; 50 percent said that they had no interest in any public office(s) in the future."[6] This reign of political silence and passivity stands in marked contrast to the situation in Great Britain, where a former Prime Minister, Harold Wilson, once had to resort to the courts to try to stop his ministers from publishing their memoirs, although some cynics suggested the prohibition had less to do with alleged violations of the Official Secrets Act than with allowing the Prime Minister to publish first!).

Thus, while we may not know as much as we might like about the inner operation of the cabinet, we can begin our investigation by locating the process of cabinet government within the context of the Canadian political tradition. This will prepare us for a subsequent examination of the role of cabinet according to its two principal and historic functions: as an instrument of government and as a vehicle for representation.

CABINET AND THE CANADIAN POLITICAL TRADITION

PRAGMATIC POLITICS

Whatever label might be applied to the two political parties that have formed Canada's federal governments, "doctrinaire" is not one of them. Debates between these parties in Parliament and in the country do not reflect differences of principle so much as differences over how to implement policies of economic growth or social security (in this respect, the single issue "free-trade" election of 1988 was unusual). Within cabinet as well, this value consensus generally holds, and only very occasionally are there intraparty divisions in which the alignment of sympathies is as clear as it was between economic nationalists and continentalists in the Liberal Party in the 1960s and the early 1980s. Significantly, one of the rare ex-ministerial authors of memoirs was Walter Gordon, the gadfly of economic nationalism who held several portfolios in the Pearson government of the 1960s.

Walter Gordon was unusual less for the policy he advocated than for the arguments he used. He urged economic nationalism for its long-run concrete benefits, but promoted it first as a principle. From such studies of cabinet that do exist, the impression gained is that ministers are normally pragmatic in the positions they take. While pragmatism might seem inevitable in a country as large and diverse as Canada, one must be careful not to underestimate the latent importance of values in Canadian politics. Walter Gordon was distinctive not so much because he had firm principles but because he publicized his position. Most ministers do not, and in fact they may act embarrassed when it is suggested that they hold an ideological stance on some issue. But the Liberal leadership contest in 1990 and the PC leadership contest in 1993 demonstrate, for instance, that candidates *are* forced to declare their positions on such ideologically charged questions as medicare, privatization, and bilingualism. Nevertheless, it is clear that at least one reason Canadians are not used to thinking ideologically about subjects is that their politicians have been reluctant to treat them this way.

The absence of a doctrinaire approach within the old political parties is revealed paradoxically enough in the resignations of ministers from the federal cabinet. Not only do few resignations occur, but those that do are seldom attributed to policy differences. There are exceptions, of course. For example, Israel Tarte (Public Works) was ejected from Laurier's cabinet in 1902 for publicly disagreeing with the government's tariff policy; Clifford Sifton (Interior) resigned in 1905 from the same government because he dissented from the original educational provisions of the Alberta and Saskatchewan acts; J.L. Ralston (National Defence) was fired by Mackenzie King in 1944 for advocating military conscription for overseas service before King, who long resisted this policy, was ready to accept it; and Douglas Harkness (National Defence) resigned from the Diefenbaker Government in 1963 because he supported the arming of BOMARC missiles with nuclear warheads, and his leader did not.

But even in instances such as these, the effect of the resignations has never been to extend the political debate very far or for very long.[7] Much more typical is a resignation like that of John Turner's (Finance) from the Trudeau government in 1975, which was publicly described as being for "personal reasons." Although Turner was subsequently labelled as more conservative than Trudeau on economic and social issues, and although he was even then widely viewed as a major contender for the Liberal leadership when Trudeau retired, his resignation prompted little public debate over political principle either inside or outside the party. Certainly there was no massing of Liberal support behind competing interpretations of liberalism.

To conclude, one consequence of this reluctance to inject policy differences into public debate or cabinet is to discourage political discussion within political parties and within the country, to the detriment of politics as an educative activity. In its place, the cult of personality seizes the attention of the media, the public and the politicians, and this is not, as we shall next see, an attitude conducive to the growth of professionalism in politics.[8]

AVOCATIONAL POLITICS

Arguably, political debate is pragmatic because the politicians who take part in it are not professionals. Thirty years ago, in *The Vertical Mosaic*, John Porter wrote that a model political career implies

> *a professionalizing of political roles where the individual devotes his life to politics and in the process develops a "love" for political institutions. ... [But] where the political career is unstable and taken up for an interstitial period only, during a career devoted to something else, the political system will probably be strong in administration and weak in creativity.*[9]

In the period he studied, Porter discovered that life at the top was peopled by ministers who had been co-opted from other careers (e.g., business or the public service), or whose experience in the House of Commons had been brief, and that in either case their period in cabinet was surprisingly short. In 1960, 47 percent of the ministers had served for less than six years. Porter's findings were confirmed in a 1973 study by Dennis Olsen which found that 52 percent had served for five years or less and that 95 percent had served fewer than eleven years.[10] Moreover, given a House of Commons where the turnover rate per election is usually around 40 percent (over 70 percent in 1993, largely because of the success of Reform and Bloc candidates), and where, generally, another 20–35 percent of the MPs have less than five years' experience, cabinet "timber" nurtured in a parliamentary environment is never a commodity in great supply when a prime minister sets about constructing a government.

There are other reasons why the cabinet is deficient in political experience. The most important is the imperative of sectional representation, which will be discussed in more detail later in this chapter. At this point, it is enough to say that the practice of ensuring representation from all the provinces in cabinet (with the occasional exception of Prince Edward Island, as occurred following the 1993 election) is now so strong—it is a convention, or binding rule, of prime-ministerial behaviour—that it overrides considerations of political experience whenever the two criteria conflict. The depressing effect of this practice on those MPs who aspire to ministerial office, but who are excluded for geographic reasons, needs to be recognized when explaining why Porter's model political career is infrequently seen in Canada. Conversely, the size of recent cabinets (between 35 and 40 until 1993, when Kim Campbell and subsequently Jean Chrétien reduced the number to 25 and 23, respectively) increases the problem of finding sufficient personnel with satisfactory parliamentary experience.

One final word on the absence of professionals in federal politics concerns the party leaders themselves. Jean Chrétien is the first Liberal leader since Laurier to have experienced life for any length of time on the backbenches (1963–67); King had less than a year, St. Laurent none, Pearson none, and Trudeau seventeen months, fifteen of them as a parliamentary secretary. Norman Ward once wrote that "one excellent way of ensuring that one will not rise to the top of the Liberal party is to start at the bottom."[11] One effect of leadership conventions has been to favour nonparliamentary experience over parliamentary experience, and this is almost as true of Progressive Conservatives as it is of Liberals. Since 1942 and John Bracken's selection, the PCs have had seven leaders, four of whom have had no parliamentary background. Kim Campbell was first elected to the House of Commons in November 1988; she joined the cabinet in January 1989.

Thus, the cabinet is not the kindergarten of political leadership in Canada that it is in Great Britain. (While no one knows, for example, who will succeed John Major, the probability that he or she will come out of the cabinet's ranks is extremely high.) This fact, coupled with the pragmatic nature of Canadian politics already alluded to, helps to explain the nature of cabinet government in Canada. But there is a third factor, related to those already mentioned, that needs to be considered, and that is the process by which major interests reach agreement through bargaining—brokerage politics.

BROKERAGE POLITICS

Brokerage theory, which has dominated Canadian political science, argues that national political parties must encompass all the essential interests in the country if both a majority is to be secured and minority rights guaranteed. The theory is both empirical and prescriptive. It purports to describe how parties actually practise their art, and it defends that practice. Parties, it is believed, are supposed to act as agents of consensus and as aggregators of interests rather than as instruments of choice. But despite its hegemony, the theory has its critics, none more pertinent than John Porter, who charged brokerage politics with stultifying "creative" political debate. The search for the middle ground in politics, Porter argued, too often excluded rather than included interests. The result was that parties and governments seemed always to pay undue attention to professional, commercial, middle-class concerns. "Seemed" was the operative verb, for as he noted, "We have in fact very little information about what interests political leaders take into consideration in making up cabinets."[12]

Unfortunately, we still lack the concrete information necessary to confirm Porter's judgment on the mechanisms of cabinet selection.[13] But the belief that interests must be balanced—traditionally regional ones— remains strong and can be seen currently in support for proposals to reform the electoral system or the upper house so as to bring to the centre a greater range of regional interests. More will be said of these proposals later in the chapter. At this point, it need only be stated that institutional reformers assume the validity and utility of brokerage politics, and, in the case of proponents of proportional representation, believe it would strengthen the cabinet by presenting the prime minister with more choices when selecting ministers.

Brokerage politics cannot really be fully discussed in this chapter, for the scope of the discussion would go far beyond its effect on the cabinet. However, it is necessary to recognize what its assumptions imply for a study of the cabinet. Inevitably, they suggest an analysis of the cabinet in terms of how faithfully its members reflect the "elemental" divisions of the country. It is for this reason that so much research on the cabinet presents in detail the geographic and socioeconomic characteristics of its members. But it is also the case that very few of these same studies explain why such "representation" is significant. Instead, it is assumed rather than demonstrated that *balanced Cabinet representation leads to balanced policies*.

An alternative theory to appear recently in Canadian political discourse is the theory of *consociational democracy*, developed in small European countries where the interests of strong subcultures require accommodation if national unity is to exist.[14] In the European experience, accommodation takes place at the elite levels and requires for its success integrated subcultures with clear patterns of leadership. From this brief description, the appeal of consociational democracy in Canada can be appreciated, especially since the 1960s, when the Canadian polity became increasingly fragmented as the Quiet Revolution spread in Quebec and as the other provinces increased their demands on Ottawa for greater financial and political control over economic and social policies. In addition, consociational democracy as a theory of bargaining among elites gave new respectability to brokerage politics. However, in the past, political party elites had been the brokers, while in the modern period governmental elites, under the rubric of executive federalism, have gained the upper hand.[15]

Having mapped out the essential topography of the federal cabinet process within the Canadian political tradition according to its pragmatic, avocational, and brokerage boundaries, we are now ready for a closer examination of the evolution of its governing and representative functions. Because the history of the federal cabinet is the history of Canada's evolution as an independent parliamentary democracy, we must now trace the changing role of the cabinet, beginning with the achievement of responsible government in the 1840s.

CABINET AS AN INSTRUMENT OF GOVERNMENT

A COLONIAL AND IMPERIAL PAST

Colonial origins and imperial models determined the evolution of cabinet government. The idea that the Crown should heed the advice of those who command the support of the popularly elected chamber (which in the United Canadas was recognized in 1848 by Lord Elgin's acceptance of the Rebellion Losses Bill) implied more than a new parliamentary democratic value, as important as that was; it also signified a new organizing principle for the British Empire. Lord Durham's recommendation a decade earlier that colonies should be responsible for their internal affairs was now to be implemented. The importance of this development for Canada cannot be underestimated. The conflict between Parliament and the King which had seen Parliament prevail in Great Britain a century before, was now to be repeated in the colonies, with the same result. However, there was something more here as well. To the extent that colonial Parliament prevailed over the King's representative, so did Canada prevail over Great Britain—responsible government thus ultimately led to independent government.

All of this is history, but it is history with a point as far as the development of the Canadian cabinet is concerned. It would be misleading to discuss the federal cabinet's growth solely in terms of domestic politics, for the cabinet and its leaders also gained strength and unity from the colonial situation. Not only did external matters occupy cabinet attention (especially military questions and their effect on domestic harmony—the Boer War and Laurier, the First World War and Borden, the Second World War and King), but the evolution of the Empire into the Commonwealth was accompanied by a transfer of power from imperial to Canadian authorities (in such forms, for example, as the power to make treaties, to declare war, and, finally, to amend the Constitution at home). Questions of status—colonial, dominion, national, and international—have traditionally bulked large for prime ministers because of their implications for Canada's developing autonomy and prestige. This explains why, until 1946, the prime minister acted as his own Secretary of State for External Affairs, and why even afterward, in contrast to their British counterparts, Canadian prime ministers continued to play a leading role in foreign affairs.

If over time Canada's developing colonial status conferred new responsibilities on its cabinet and enhanced the power of its prime minister, there were other influences derived from its colonial origins that affected the cabinet right from the start. Indeed, some of these were pronounced well before Confederation. Responsible government arrived in the St. Lawrence lowlands when the Canadas, united since 1840 by a single set of political institutions and little else, were already an embryonic federal system. In order to operate this unwieldy structure, practical adjustments were necessary, and from early on the cabinet proved especially useful as a mechanism for accommodating the social diversities of the colony. There were several reasons for this development. The myriad interests—religious, linguistic, legal, economic, and military, among others—that jockeyed for attention in the colony evolved through a period when they looked to the executive (the governor and his council) to protect them. And there were no modern disciplined political parties. Instead, factions based on regional or social groupings were in a seemingly continuous process of formation and dissolution. The result was a series of coalition governments, throughout the history of the United Canadas, whose authority was frequently rejected by the elected legislators, but who could look to their executive power as the Crown's advisers to give them the legitimacy they needed.

OLD TRADITIONS AND MODERN PRACTICE

From the outset, Canadian cabinets were large because of the number of interests to be accommodated in a culturally bifurcated society, and because of the breadth of territory to be represented. The pressure to include rather than exclude affected the conduct of business. From colonial days, the preferred practice was to confer rule-making power on the council and not on individual ministers. In the modern era of expanded delegation from Parliament to the executive, the same is true, for to do otherwise would favour with power or information some ministers over others—an act of discrimination that the sectional dimension of cabinet membership particularly discourages. As an indicator of the volume of administrative matters delegated to the cabinet, in 1976 there were 3,326 orders-in-council, of which the three largest categories concerned appointments (22.5 percent), regulations (19.6 percent), and property transactions (14.5 percent).[16]

A related effect has been to minimize traditional British distinctions, for example, between cabinet and council or between cabinet and ministry. In Great Britain, where rank is one of life's organizing principles, such distinctions are accepted, but in Canada, where society is both more open and more heterogeneous, they are not. Or they *were* not, for, as will be discussed below, Jean Chrétien in 1993 made a clear distinction between the ministry and the cabinet. Here the governor's old Executive Council (after July 1, 1867, it was called the Privy Council) evolved into cabinet, with minimal distinction between the two. (By convention, membership in the council is retained for life, along with the designation "Honourable," but even for ceremonial purposes the council rarely convenes.) The cabinet as a Committee of Council is a "masquerade," according to R. MacGregor Dawson, which it adopts "when it desires to assume formal powers."[17]

It is only since the Second World War, and particularly after Trudeau became prime minister, that the Privy Council Office began to have a life of its own. Although there has been a Clerk of the Privy Council since Confederation, from Laurier through Diefenbaker the office was (with rare exceptions) seen as the fiefdom of the prime minister. Since Pearson's time, the Privy Council Office itself has become one of the so-called central agencies whose influence is derived from its position in the decision-making process.[18]

There was a similar reluctance, and for the same reasons, to follow British precedent and distinguish between cabinet and ministry. For although the number of ministers has always appeared large in comparison to the needs of a relatively small population, any attempt to introduce efficiency by streamlining structures (which usually has meant reducing numbers) has been resisted because of its exclusionary effect. In Great Britain, the ministry may be in excess of 100 members and the cabinet a quarter that number. By contrast, in Canada, *all* members of the ministry have, with rare exceptions, been members of the cabinet. Moreover, while the Priorities and Planning Committee, introduced by Trudeau in the early 1970s, has functioned as a de facto inner cabinet, only in 1993 did the new prime minister, Jean Chrétien, actually create an outer circle of junior ministers (eight secretaries of state) around his comparatively small cabinet of 23 ministers. Junior ministers have specific responsibilities and report directly to senior ministers; they are paid less than ministers, and have smaller staffs and fewer perks. It should be noted that the new secretaries of state are distinct from the parliamentary secretaries who have existed on a regular basis since the 1940s (when they were called parliamentary assistants), but who have never been considered part of the ministry.

In 1993, financial restraint, combined with the desire of government to appear sensitive to public concern about debt and deficit, allowed Kim Campbell and Jean Chrétien to break with tradition when they set about selecting ministers. Smaller cabinets (there were 40 members in Brian Mulroney's government in 1984) had voter appeal. Yet the need to balance categories of representation persisted, and was evident in the senior and junior ministerial appointments Chrétien made. Those categories (women and Natives are two of them) continue to multiply and modify the age-old Canadian concern for accommodating English–French dualism.

The principal functions of the federal cabinet are to direct the business of Parliament, to administer the individual departments of government, to formulate and discuss policy, and to pass orders-in-council. The cabinet's most important function is "to furnish initiative and leadership" for the country and Parliament.[19] Essentially, this is a joint enterprise of the cabinet and the prime minister, but how well it is done and what character it assumes is the responsibility of the prime minister alone. In the Canadian system, the prime minister enjoys inordinate powers by tradition and as a result of innovations in technology (e.g., television) and institutions (e.g., leadership conventions), which elevate the position vis-à-vis the cabinet to the point where the oft-repeated claim that the prime minister is *primus inter pares* (first among equals) is no more descriptive of the position than Bagehot's buckle-and-hyphen metaphor is of the cabinet.[20]

THREE MODELS OF POLITICAL LEADERSHIP

The Canadian system of government is party government, or more precisely party-in-government. The telescoping of these two features confers exceptional power on the leader of the legislative party that controls the House of Commons, but how that power is used is at his or her discretion. It is possible to identify three broad approaches to political leadership since Confederation, each of which has not only implied a different role and function for the cabinet, but also has affected the image Canadians have of themselves. For brevity's sake, the three models may be labelled as the personal, the accommodative, and the pan-Canadian approaches. In sequence, they dominated the following major eras of Canadian history: Confederation to First World War (personal) interwar and immediate post–Second World War (accommodative), and mid-1950s to the present (pan-Canadian).

The personal approach, in place up to the First World War, can be identified with the leadership of Macdonald and Laurier. Although of different political parties, each was concerned with national expansion: Macdonald basically with rounding out the Union by incorporating new provinces and territories, and by welding the whole into one economic unit through his National Policy, with its protective tariff, transcontinental railway, and accelerated immigration; and Laurier by furthering that expansion through more aggressive immigration and settlement of the West. But though their policies were national, their political practices were local. As Gordon Stewart has shown, they pioneered patronage politics to create a national party system that was intensely local in its interests and profoundly personal in its management by the party leader.[21]

Under Macdonald and Laurier the cabinet became a collective through which to channel gifts in the form of jobs and contracts from the government, which in this period was among the largest businesses (in terms of expenditure and employment) in the country. Unlike the United States, Canada had no giant capitalist corporations of national breadth, except perhaps the Canadian Pacific Railway, itself scarcely independent of the federal government. In the process, Macdonald and Laurier created an "effective party structure" but not a "modern" one, and the First World War, with its economic and social dislocations, revealed just how inadequate the system was in adjusting to change. The rise of a strong third party in the form of the Progressives, who captured 65 of 235 seats in the 1921 election, vividly demonstrated the need for a new political response. That response had to come from the cabinet and its leader, for among the functions of the cabinet not listed earlier, but of crucial significance to Canadian politics, is its role as the "managing committee for the party in power."[22]

The new accommodative approach initiated by Mackenzie King became the hallmark of his long tenure as party leader and prime minister (as well as of Louis St. Laurent's prime ministership), and differed from the Macdonald–Laurier style in several important respects. King was unusually alive to the divisive forces in Canadian society, in part because of his experience as a labour conciliator and in part because of two events that preceded and accompanied his rise to office: (1) the conflict in English–French relations from 1890 onward, culminating in the conscription crisis in Quebec; and (2) the farmers' revolt in the Prairies, which up to 1917 had represented safe Liberal territory. These factors and others, such as the civil-service reforms of the former (Union) government— which moderated patronage in federal politics and thus conformed more closely to King's personal disposition and political decision to be less directly involved in these matters than Laurier—help explain the source of King's consensual approach to leadership.

There is no dispute that King had no peer in the art of accommodation or compromise. Nor is there any doubt that he used the cabinet as one of his instruments and was supremely skilled in its use. He deflected the Progressives in the 1920s, in part by co-opting two of their leaders (Forke and Crerar), and similarly blunted the CCF threat by taking in Labour spokesperson Humphrey Mitchell. Further, he defused a Quebec explosion over conscription by seeking assistance from his Quebec ministers (two of whom eventually resigned over this drawn-out question), and by dismissing the Minister of National Defence (not from Quebec), who advocated conscription for overseas service before King believed the country was ready for it.

Under King and St. Laurent, the cabinet became not only the locus for resolving domestic tensions, but the directing arm of the Liberal Party. The ministers, when they were not former partisan opponents, were the chief Liberals of the day. A former provincial premier like J.G. Gardiner from Saskatchewan, for example, was as close to being a "pro-consul" in that province—and, on occasion, in the neighbouring Prairie provinces—as could be found in Canadian political history. King and St. Laurent respected departmental autonomy, and thus their ministers gained unprecedented independence at the same time as the growth of the Canadian government's activities and responsibilities increased their powers. But with power came costs. In the period of Macdonald and Laurier, the party had penetrated the bureaucracy through patronage, and now the bureaucracy penetrated the party by transmitting its values, objectives, and procedures to the politician. In the end, the Liberals became what Reginald Whitaker has called "the government party."[23] And if the parties and governments of Macdonald and Laurier grew out of touch with national economic and social trends, the Liberal Party and governments of King and St. Laurent followed suit, this time by failing to comprehend the growth of regionalism.

The pan-Canadian approach to leadership represented a response to this rise in regionalism, first by creating federal programs and departments to deal specifically with regional questions, and then, more distinctively, by promoting pan-Canadian policies—that is, policies that overarched constituency or group interests and touched individual Canadians wherever they might live in Canada. John Diefenbaker's "One Canada," his appeal to "unhyphenated Canadianism," his Bill of Rights, his national social policies (such as hospitalization), and other responses in the late 1950s and early 1960s took as their premise "equal rights for all, privileges for none." It was Diefenbaker who used the prime minister's appointment power to "recognize" distinctive groups in society by placing the first woman and the first Canadian of Ukrainian origin in the cabinet, and by appointing the first Indian to the Senate and the first French Canadian as governor general.

But this initial attempt at a pan-Canadian approach of governing was cut short by the Quiet Revolution, for Diefenbaker's vision of his country did not sanction treating Quebeckers any differently from the rest of Canadians. However, the vision of his successors, Lester Pearson and Pierre Trudeau, did accept as a first principle that Canada was composed of two founding peoples. From this premise flowed a host of policies aimed at touching all Canadians through the medium of one or other of two official languages. Diefenbaker never accepted this Liberal view of Canada and, indeed, continued to fight it all of his political life, in part because of what he interpreted as its anti-British connotations. But he did accept the implementation of other pan-Canadian policies, applauding, for instance, the federal government's national medical care and pension plans. With its

National Energy Program, constitutional reforms, and entrenchment of a Charter of Rights and Freedoms, Trudeau's government went further than either Diefenbaker's or Pearson's in breaking the consensual mould of national politics created by Mackenzie King. One cost of this approach for the Liberals was the loss for over two decades of major electoral support in the West, a region of the country where there had once been significant Liberal sympathy. The long-run implications for Canada of these policies remain disputed (some critics blame them for the rise of both the Reform Party and the Bloc Québécois).[24] But in the short run, the benefits to French Canadians of broadening the institutions of the federal government are substantial. Nowhere else was this clearer than in the cabinet itself. Under Pearson and Trudeau, the number of French-Canadian ministers rose, as did the importance of the portfolios they held. In this century until 1963, the proportion of cabinet ministers of French ethnic origin never exceeded 30 percent; after 1963, it stood consistently above 40 percent, and while as late as 1970 it could be said that no French Canadian had ever held the Finance, Trade and Commerce, or Labour portfolios, by 1984 French Canadians either did hold or had held all three.

Significantly, the election of a Progressive Conservative majority government in 1984 and 1988 did not lead to abandonment of this most recent approach to leadership, although the constitutional initiatives it sponsored—the Meech Lake and Charlottetown accords—eventually failed. On the one hand, Mulroney sought to reduce conflict with the provinces by emphasizing conciliation over confrontation, going so far in the Meech Lake agreement as to tolerate ambiguity between Charter guarantees and recognition of Quebec as a "distinct society." On the other hand, the PC prime minister aggressively promoted official bilingualism, vigorously used his appointment power to bring representatives of visible minorities onto national boards and commissions, and tirelessly sought to promote the careers of prominent francophones within the Tory Party, especially in his cabinet. In this last regard, Mulroney's efforts were initially frustrated not because of lack of will, but because of the low calibre of some of the 57 first-time members of his party from Quebec who were swept to victory in the PC tidal wave of 1984.

This summary of models of leadership indicates not only the importance of political personality but also the different uses to which the cabinet can be put, for, as an instrument of government, it is more than a body that passes orders-in-council or that superintends the administration of government. Because it combines political and governmental power, it occupies a unique position from which a leader can initiate and direct policies. This is true even when a prime minister is new and untested: on the day Kim Campbell became prime minister, she instituted the most far-reaching reorganization of government structures and operations in recent memory (one that Jean Chrétien has largely continued). What policies are chosen and how they are implemented is a function of many variables, but crucial among them is that leaders depend on the power they possess at the head of a disciplined party, caucus, and cabinet.

CABINET AS A VEHICLE FOR REPRESENTATION

The cabinet is the pre-eminent institution of sectional representation in the Canadian parliamentary system. In practice that has meant the representation of the provinces and the historic linguistic and religious communities of Canada. Other minorities have been present in the cabinet, but the term "sectional representation" customarily refers to the foregoing interests. Whatever the expectations of the Fathers of Confederation, the Senate has never played this role. Appointment by governor-in-council, allocation of equal numbers of senators by regions and not provinces, separation from the executive that sat in the lower house, and infrequent membership in the cabinet all saw to that. A province or group (e.g., the English-speaking Protestants of Quebec or the Irish Catholics of either Quebec or Ontario) that wanted to take part in the decisions of the day or to protect its special interests had to be represented in the cabinet. Of course, there was not equal representation there either, since generally two-thirds of the ministers came from Ontario and Quebec, but a seat at the cabinet table was believed to be more influential than any other federal office.

THE TRADITIONAL CABINET: A FEDERAL STRUCTURE

The conviction that provinces must be represented was shared by leaders as well as followers, and the history of cabinet-building by any prime minister reveals the strength of this particularly Canadian article of faith. When the electorate of a province was thoughtless enough to return to Parliament no members from the party that formed the government, then the prime minister had to become a political gymnast, twisting his way around an inconvenient election result in order to fulfill one of the first commandments of cabinet-making—that all parts of the whole must, if at all possible, be represented in the finished product. Generally speaking, he has had two alternatives: (1) to run those who cannot get elected in their home province in a safe seat elsewhere (when the Liberals were shut out of Alberta in the 1921 election, Mackenzie King brought the former Liberal premier of that province, Charles Stewart, into the cabinet as Minister of the Interior by opening a Quebec seat for him); (2) or to resort to the Senate route, where there are usually several cabinet aspirants per province.

The former route is out of fashion today, although it was used in Canadian history to bring into cabinet such outstanding ministers as Charles Dunning (Finance) and Angus MacDonald (Naval Services), who were not electoral liabilities by any stretch of the imagination, but for whom a federal seat elsewhere than in their home province was at the time convenient to them and the prime minister. The latter route is the preferred modern method (in 1980, Trudeau took in three senators from the three most western provinces, where no Liberals had been elected), though it has little to recommend it other than its simplicity. While the Senate continues to do some fine investigative work, it is not an institution in which the principle of democratic accountability is strong, and its members as cabinet ministers experience and cause frustration. Senators are appointed to cabinet to represent those regions where the governing party is weakest in electoral favour, yet the process does nothing to build the party and can, indeed, divide it by creating antagonisms and jealousies. The fact that recent prime ministers have resorted to this alternative in spite of its disadvantages is evidence of the strength of the convention that cabinet must encompass representation from all provinces.

Sectional representation is not an abstract notion of symbolic value only, though this is not an unimportant consideration. In regard to certain matters, ministers *from* individual provinces are seen as ministers *for* those provinces. This is true particularly with respect to appointments, but also to discussions of policy and its potential effect on provincial interests. It is misleading to depict the cabinet as no more than a collection of sectional "veto groups"—some policies, labelled above as "pan-Canadian," are less regionally specific than others, and therefore less susceptible to regional bargaining—but it is equally erroneous to ignore the durable effect of a federalized cabinet on policy formulation.[25] Canada is still a country of sharply defined regions, with geographic and cultural boundaries that enclose distinctive ways of life, and the cabinet continues to reflect this fact.

For much of the country's history, particular portfolios were identified with particular regions or provinces. With the opening of the West, responsibility for agriculture went to a Westerner until 1965. But the Liberals' dismal electoral record in that region altered this tradition, and in only four of the next twenty years did a Westerner hold that portfolio. (The Mulroney government appointed a Westerner only after the 1988 election, a practice Chrétien continued in 1993.) As compensation, responsibility for the Canadian Wheat Board, the agency in charge of the Prairies' staple industry, was assigned either to a western minister with another portfolio or to a Minister of State who was a senator. The old Department of the Interior, which disappeared shortly after the transfer of the Prairie provinces' natural resources from the federal government in 1930, was even more closely identified with that region's settlement and expansion. The prominence of that endeavour, which has been described as the most "far-reaching activity" in this century except for the prosecution of the wars, is indicated by the high calibre of those who held the portfolio, among them Edgar Dewdney, Clifford Sifton, Frank Oliver, Arthur Meighen, Sir James Lougheed, Charles Stewart, and T.A. Crerar.[26] Contrarily, Transport is seen as a portfolio associated with any province but Ontario. George Hees, who was given this portfolio in 1957 by John Diefenbaker, has commented that "a central Ontarian is not very much interested in Transport," and the list of ministers who have had this responsibility in the last half-century would bear him out. Transport has been the bailiwick of Quebec, and of the eastern and western hinterlands.

The above comments concern portfolios that have a specific regional impact; there are others (Fisheries is an example) of which the same could be said. But there are more portfolios, including the great departments of state—Finance, Trade and Commerce (and its modern equivalents), Justice, and External Affairs—that are marked by their lack of obvious geographic specificity. And yet these too have historically been allocated to ministers who are distinctive for their provincial origins but also for their language group. Finance until very recently has always gone to an English-speaking minister, and more often than not to one from Ontario, but sometimes from Quebec and occasionally from elsewhere. Justice, on the other hand, has tended (though not since 1984) to go to French-speaking Quebeckers. The concentration of the business community in Toronto and Montreal and the dual legal systems of Canada help to explain this distribution of portfolios in the same way that other reasons can be found for additional discernible patterns of portfolio allocation. What is perhaps most significant in the last two decades, however, is the decline in the boldness of geographic and cultural patterns. Sectional representation remains an indelible part of Canadian political practice; the allocation of portfolios to specific types of ministers does not.

THE MODERN CABINET: A NATIONAL INSTITUTION

The politics of the federal cabinet, like the politics of the country, are more national than they once were. Ministers are less likely to be the party chiefs in their provinces than used to be the case in the time of Mackenzie King and St. Laurent, and one looks in vain to find a cabinet minister who can play the role of pro-consul, as J.G. Gardiner did in Saskatchewan, or Stewart Garson in Manitoba, or Angus MacDonald in Nova Scotia. Canadian federalism has witnessed major changes since those days, none more significant than the growing separation between federal and provincial politics in the last quarter-century. The effect on political parties has been immense, not least on their claim to be institutions of national integration. The old structures of federated parties—

national leaders dependent on a provincial base—require reform, and the Liberals more than the others (because, by 1984, they were in power in no province) experimented with pan-Canadian structures to conform to their pan-Canadian policies. The cabinet may remain the managing committee of the party, but the party it manages looks very different than it once did.

Federal–provincial relations are less a matter to be resolved through intraparty bargaining and more a subject for negotiation among governments. All ministers, but particularly the prime minister, find themselves meeting on a regular basis with their provincial counterparts. This was true of first ministers as well, but the collapse of the Meech Lake Accord in 1990 and the failure of the 1992 referendum to support the government-negotiated Charlottetown Accord has placed a brake on these kinds of negotiations. The description of cabinet as party-in-government is still true, but in the federal–provincial realm the emphasis continues today be placed more on the government side of this unique entity than on the party side. It is for this reason that federal governments in the modern period are so particularly concerned to have within their ranks authoritative spokespersons for the provinces with which they must negotiate. But it is because of the deterioration of the old party structures that they regularly find themselves deprived of this representation in some parts of the country. Here is the attraction of proportional representation, for under whatever guise it was implemented it would in all probability produce from each province at least a minimum of one popularly elected member of Parliament who, once admitted to the cabinet, would confer on that body the imprimatur of a national government. Proportional representation was once promoted as a system of election preferable to plurality voting because it would facilitate the representation of multiple interests in national legislatures. The national legislature would become a congress of more varied opinion than is produced by the system of election that Canada at the federal level has always had. It is a measure of the strength of the belief in cabinet—as an instrument of government and as a vehicle for sectional representation—that proportional representation has been turned on its head, such that it is advocated not to make Parliament more diverse in the interests it embraces, but to make cabinet more powerful for its task of governing Canada.

CONCLUSION

Political attitudes and practices affect the operation of political institutions. In this chapter, three attitudes and practices have been singled out for attention as regards the cabinet: a reluctance to inject ideology into politics; an inclination to view politics not as a career in itself, but rather as a temporary occupation into and out of which significant numbers of key personnel move; and a belief that the primary aim of politics is to balance conflicting geographic and cultural interests. As an instrument of government, the cabinet has been crucially influenced as well by Canada's history, especially its colonial origins. By tradition, the cabinet as a collective body has been favoured by tradition over its ministerial parts, a fact that in turn has made Canadians place a great premium on leadership. At different times, different models of leadership have dominated. In chronological sequence, these have been identified as personal, accommodative, and pan-Canadian models. But while the cabinet might be seen over time to have adjusted to a succession of leadership styles, at all times it has been expected to function as a vehicle of sectional representation, although here too an evolution in practice has occurred. Whereas once the cabinet was pre-eminently a federalized structure, more recently this guise has been subsumed by a new emphasis on the cabinet as a national institution.

NOTES

1. The most useful Canadian sources are Thomas A. Hockin, ed., *Apex of Power: The Prime Minister and Political Leadership in Canada* (Scarborough, Ont.: Prentice-Hall Canada, 1971); and W.A. Matheson, *The Prime Minister and the Cabinet* (Toronto: Methuen, 1976).

2. From this count are excluded biographies, "life and times" studies, Henry Borden, ed., *Robert Laird Borden: His Memoirs*, 2 vols. (Toronto: Macmillan, 1938), and Mackenzie King's mammoth diary. Extracts of the latter constitute the four-volume *The Mackenzie King Record* (Toronto: University of Toronto Press), which covers the period 1939 to 1948. Volume 1 is edited by J.W. Pickersgill; the remaining volumes are jointly edited by him and D.F. Forster.

3. See Walter L. Gordon, *A Political Memoir* (Toronto: McClelland and Stewart, 1977); Judy LaMarsh, *Memoirs of a Bird in a Gilded Cage* (Toronto: McClelland and Stewart, 1968); Eugene Whelan (with Rick Archbold), *Whelan: The Man in the Green Stetson* (Toronto: Irwin, 1986); and Erik Nielsen, *The House Is Not a Home* (Toronto: Macmillan, 1989).

4. Norman Ward, ed., *A Party Politician: The Memoirs of Chubby Power* (Toronto: Macmillan, 1966).

5. The best is Sir Richard Cartwright, *Reminiscences* (Toronto: William Briggs, 1912).

6. David Hoffman and Norman Ward, *Bilingualism and Biculturalism in the Canadian House of Commons*, Royal Commission on Bilingualism and Biculturalism, Study No. 3 (Ottawa: Queen's Printer, 1970), p. 125.

7. Two exceptions to this generalization should be mentioned; in each a defector more ideological than his leader formed a new party and campaigned against his old colleagues. In 1935, H.H. Stevens resigned from R.B. Bennett's cabinet (because he believed Bennett was too soft on capitalists) and formed the Reconstruction Party. In 1990, Lucien Bouchard deserted Brian Mulroney over the terms of the Meech Lake Accord and founded the Bloc Québécois. Stevens won one seat in the 1935 election, Bouchard 54 in 1993. See J.R.H. Wilbur, *H.H. Stevens*

(Toronto: University of Toronto Press, 1977); and Jeffrey Simpson, *Faultlines: Struggling for a Canadian Vision* (Toronto: HarperCollins, 1993), 270–311.

8. "In the adversary confrontation of the floor of the House, psychological issues may be more important than substantive ones." J.R. Mallory, "The Two Clerks: Parliamentary Discussion of the Role of the Privy Council Office," *Canadian Journal of Political Science* 10 (March 1977): 18.

9. John Porter, *The Vertical Mosaic* (Toronto: University of Toronto Press, 1965), pp. 405–6.

10. Dennis Olsen, *The State Elite* (Toronto: McClelland and Stewart, 1980), p. 130.

11. Norman Ward, "The Liberals in Convention: Unrevised and Unrepentant," *Queen's Quarterly* 45 (Spring 1958): 1.

12. Porter, *The Vertical Mosaic*, p. 397.

13. An exception with a specific focus is Frederick W. Gibson, ed., *Cabinet Formation and Bicultural Relations: Seven Case Studies,* Royal Commission on Bilingualism and Biculturalism, Study No. 6 (Ottawa: Queen's Printer, 1970).

14. See Kenneth D. McRae, ed., *Consociational Democracy: Political Accommodation in Segmented Societies* (Toronto: McClelland and Stewart, 1974).

15. The literature on executive federalism is large. The best place to start is Richard Simeon, *Federal-Provincial Diplomacy: The Making of Recent Policy in Canada* (Toronto: University of Toronto Press, 1972).

16. House of Commons, *Debates* (October 17, 1977), p. 8259. The durability of this practice is confirmed in Canada, House of Commons, *Third Report of the Special Committee on Statutory Instruments* (1968–69) pp. 35–37; though, as the *Fourth Report of the Standing Joint Committee on Regulations and Other Statutory Instruments* notes: "Very few draft regulations are actually considered by the Cabinet as a deliberative body. By far the greater number ... is recommended ... by the Special Committee of Council which consists of ten Ministers with a quorum of four." Senate, *Debates* (July 7, 1980), p. 757–91 at 761.

17. R.M. Dawson, *The Government of Canada* (Toronto: University of Toronto Press, 1947), p. 201, quoted in J.R. Mallory, "Cabinets and Councils in Canada," *Public Law* 2 (Autumn 1957): 244.

18. See Colin Campbell, *Governments Under Stress: Political Executives and Key Bureaucrats in Washington, London, and Ottawa* (Toronto: University of Toronto Press, 1983), pp. 83–90.

19. Dawson, *The Government of Canada*, p. 233.

20. The prime minister's extensive powers are codified to some extent in a minute of the Privy Council (P.C. 3374, October 25, 1935), reprinted in Paul Fox, ed., *Politics: Canada*, 3rd ed. (Toronto: McGraw-Hill, 1970). These include, among others, the calling of cabinet meetings, recommendations for the dissolution and summoning of Parliament, and recommendations for the appointment of such offices as cabinet minister, lieutenant-governor, and senator.

21. "Political Patronage Under Macdonald and Laurier, 1878–1911," in *American Review of Canadian Studies* 10 (1980): 3–12; and "John A. Macdonald's Greatest Triumph," *Canadian Historical Review* 43 (March 1982): 3–33.

22. Richard Van Loon, *The Structure and Membership of the Canadian Cabinet* (Internal Research Project of the Royal Commission on Bilingualism and Biculturalism, October 1966), p. 27.

23. Reginald Whitaker, *The Government Party: Organizing and Financing the Liberal Party of Canada, 1930–58* (Toronto: University of Toronto Press, 1977).
24. See David J. Bercuson and Barry Cooper, *Deconfederation: Canada without Quebec* (Toronto: Key Porter Books, 1991).
25. The idea of the veto group is taken from Mallory, "The Two Clerks," 240.
26. Chester Martin, *"Dominion Lands" Policy,* ed. with introduction by Lewis H. Thomas (Toronto: McClelland and Stewart, 1973), p. xiv.

FURTHER READINGS

Aucoin, Peter. "Trudeau and Mulroney: Rationalism and Brokerage as Prime Ministerial Leadership Styles," *Canadian Journal of Political Science* 19, no. 1 (March 1986).

Bakvis, Herman. *Regional Ministers: Power and Influence in the Canadian Cabinet.* Toronto: University of Toronto Press, 1991.

Foster, Sir George. "Getting into the Cabinet." From *The Memoirs of the Rt. Hon. Sir George Foster, P.C., G.C.M.G.,* edited by W.S. Wallace, *Politics: Canada,* 4th ed., edited by Paul Fox. Toronto: McGraw-Hill, 1977.

Fox, Paul. "The Representative Nature of the Canadian Cabinet." In Paul Fox, ed., *Politics: Canada,* 4th ed. Toronto: McGraw-Hill, 1977.

Guide to Canadian Ministries Since Confederation, July 1, 1867—February 1, 1982. Public Archives of Canada. Ottawa: Supply and Services, 1982.

Presthus, Robert. *Elite Accommodation in Canadian Politics.* Toronto: Macmillan, 1973.

Rogers, Normal McL. "The Introduction of Cabinet Government in Canada," "Federal Influences on the Canadian Cabinet," and "Evolution and Reform of the Canadian Cabinet." *Canadian Bar Review* 11 (January, February, and April 1933).

20 FEDERALISM AND INTER-GOVERNMENTAL RELATIONS

Garth Stevenson

Federalism is one of the most obvious characteristics of the Canadian political system, and federal–provincial controversy seems to pervade most aspects of Canadian life. The joke about the Canadian who was asked to write an essay on the elephant, and who chose to explore the question of whether the animal fell under federal or provincial jurisdiction, is now more than a quarter-century old. The seemingly interminable efforts during the last three decades to modify Canada's formal Constitution (see Chapter 16) have helped to focus our attention on the politics of federalism. Although John A. Macdonald hoped, and some 20th-century social scientists have predicted, that our preoccupation with federalism, regionalism, and provincialism would decline in the course of economic and political modernization, up to the present this prediction has proved erroneous.

Federal–provincial relations in Canada are by no means confined to constitutional politics. In fact, modern federalism, wherever it exists, seems inevitably to produce a complex pattern of intergovernmental relations involving many aspects of public policy. It would be fair to say, however, that in the most successful and stable federations, like Australia, Germany, Switzerland, or the United States, intergovernmental relations are less conflictual and less controversial than they are in Canada.

The importance of intergovernmental relations may seem paradoxical given that formal definitions of federalism suggest that the two levels of government have totally distinct and mutually exclusive areas of responsibility, so that little or no interaction between them should logically be expected. In fact, a celebrated judicial interpretation of Canada's Constitution once referred to the "watertight compartments" that supposedly confined the federal and provincial governments within their respective fields of jurisdiction.[1] From this perspective, it might seem that, assuming a suitable distribution of responsibilities at the outset, each level of government could then act unilaterally within its own sphere and ignore the activities of the other level. At most, the two levels might require a Supreme Court with the authority to interpret the Constitution, to settle jurisdictional disputes, and to prevent one level of government from trespassing on the jurisdictional turf of the other.

This is not, of course, how Canadian government really works, but to a large extent the Constitution Act of 1867 did attempt to follow this model. Parallel institutions of government were established, insofar as they did not already exist, at the federal and provincial levels. Each was given access to certain sources of revenue. The types of laws that could be made by Parliament and the provincial legislatures were listed in exhaustive detail, with no less than 48 enumerated categories. All but three of the 48 categories were assigned exclusively to one level of government or the other. According to the Colonial Laws Validity Act of 1865, neither Parliament nor the legislatures could legislate contrary to the terms of any imperial statute applying to them, and since the BNA Act was an imperial statute, this meant in practice that the Judicial Committee of the Privy Council would act as an arbiter in cases of disputed jurisdiction.

Insofar as the Constitution Act of 1867 deviated from this model, it did so by enabling the federal government to exercise power over provincial governments, even if the latter remained within their own fields of jurisdiction. Thus, the federal government appoints the judges to provincial superior and county courts, and also appoints the lieutenant-governor, who is formally the chief executive officer at the provincial level. In the early days of Canadian federalism, lieutenant-governors exercised real power: sometimes dismissing their ministerial advisers, refusing their assent to acts of the legislature, or reserving such acts for a final decision by the federal government on whether they would be allowed to come into law. In addition, the federal government can disallow any provincial act within a year of its adoption, although this power was used very rarely after 1911 and has not been used at all since 1943. Parliament can unilaterally assume jurisdiction over "works and undertakings" within a province, although this power also has fallen into disuse. The federal government can interfere with provincial jurisdiction over education to protect the rights of certain minorities, but the one attempt to exercise this power in 1896 probably demonstrated that it was unusable in practice.

These admitted departures from the pure theory of federalism have little importance for modern intergovernmental relations. The powers of disallowance and reservation are unlikely ever again to be used. While provincial governments certainly complain loudly and frequently about federal "intrusions" into what they regard as their exclusive spheres of authority, it is usually the federal government's economic and fiscal policies that give offence, not the appointment of judges and lieutenant-governors. Moreover, and in complete contrast to the centralist preferences of the Fathers of Confederation, the provincial governments themselves now possess impressive means of complicating, frustrating, and interfering with policy-making at the federal level, means that they are far less hesitant to employ than the federal government is to employ its virtually abandoned power of disallowance. Finally, a variety of intergovernmental institutional devices not provided in the formal Constitution have been developed to facilitate interaction between the two levels of government.

Much of the change accommodated by the Constitution has been in the direction of increasing the power and importance of provincial governments, the larger of which now exercise powers that would be the envy of many supposedly sovereign members of the United Nations. Admittedly, while the power and importance of the federal government has expanded enormously as it performs functions that it was not expected to perform a century ago, the growth of provincial power is clearly more striking.

The growth of the state is a ubiquitous phenomenon in the modern world, but Canada is unusual and perhaps unique in the extent to which that growth has taken place at the subnational level. Economic development and external relations, considered the most important state functions in 1867 (and probably still today), were originally placed mostly beyond the reach of provincial jurisdiction, yet today the provincial governments seek, with some success, to influence federal policies in these areas and, with even greater success, to conduct policies of their own.

Provincialists will respond that this change is counterbalanced by increasing federal involvement in such areas as health and welfare, environmental policies, and the protection of consumers, but this response is unconvincing for two reasons. In the first place, these functions were not so much left to the provinces in 1867 as they were left to the private sector, so that the expansion of federal government activity in these fields has not really been at the expense of provincial states. Second, while these functions are certainly important, most observers would still consider them less fundamental to the *raison d'être* of the modern state than the more traditional functions of developing the economy and managing relations with the rest of the world. It is the performance of those traditional functions partly at the provincial level and partly at the federal level that seems to distinguish Canada from most other modern states. The involvement of the central government in policies related to health, welfare, and the "quality of life," while it too contributes to the complex pattern of Canadian intergovernmental relations, is a phenomenon not unique to Canada.

Neither the increased importance of the provincial governments nor the increased complexity of intergovernmental relations is the result of formal amendments to the Constitution. Until 1982, formal amendments were usually of a minor character, and the more significant ones, providing for unemployment insurance in 1940 and for pensions in 1951, increased the powers of the federal Parliament rather than those of the provincial legislatures. The changes made by the Constitution Act of 1982 were more substantial, but their impact on federal–provincial relations was limited and somewhat ambiguous. The Charter of Rights and Freedoms restricted the powers of both levels of government while increasing the influence and importance of the judiciary. The new amending formula entrenched what was already accepted practice, namely, the involvement of the provincial governments in the amending process. Provincial powers over natural resources were increased to some extent, and the poorer provinces secured constitutional entrenchment of the equalization payments they had been receiving from the federal government since 1957. Yet important as these changes were, they were less important than the nonconstitutional developments that have transformed Canadian federalism in the 20th century.

CAUSES OF DECENTRALIZATION

Although John A. Macdonald's hope that the provincial governments would dwindle away into insignificance was shown to be fallacious within a decade after Confederation, it is only since about 1960 that the growth of provincial powers and the relatively limited capacity (or willingness) of the central government to act unilaterally in most areas of public policy have appeared to distinguish Canada from other modern federations. During this period, various Canadian political scientists (including the present writer) have attempted to explain these phenomena, but no real consensus has been achieved. Some observers, particularly in Quebec, continue to deny that the Canadian central government is weaker than those of other federal countries. Even among those who recognize that it is, opinions differ as to the most significant reasons for why this is so. Probably few would argue that any single explanation is adequate. The following is a summary of the main categories of explanatory factors that have been suggested.

INSTITUTIONAL

Some observers attach primary importance to certain features of Canada's federal Constitution as explanations for the growth of provincial power, even though the Fathers of Confederation apparently designed it with quite a different intention. There are a number of specific explanations within this category. The adoption of British parliamentary government and an appointed upper house, rather than institutions based on the American pattern, limited the ability of the central government to accommodate provincial interests and thus encouraged the growth of strong provincial governments to speak for such interests. The explicit enumeration of provincial legislative powers, although designed to limit them, actually facilitated their expansion in practice by provincial governments and the judiciary, particularly since they included such broad categories as "property and civil rights." The very fact of having provincial governments at all facilitated "province-building" and the development of separate identities. Provincial ownership of natural resources, although considered insignificant in 1867, strengthened provincial governments, most obviously in Alberta but in other provinces as well. Health, education, and welfare, all entrusted to some extent to the provincial governments, proved to be more important areas of public policy than had been anticipated.

GEOPOLITICAL

Mackenzie King once observed that Canada has "too much geography."[2] Although sometimes taken for granted, Canada's vast size, small and scattered population, and geographical barriers such as the Laurentian Shield, the Rocky Mountains, and the Gulf of St. Lawrence tend to inhibit national integration and encourage emphasis on the provincial level of government as a supplier of services. Also of significance in this regard are the relatively small number of provinces in contrast to the 50 American states; the large populations of Quebec and Ontario, which enable them to challenge federal power if they so desire; and the absence of metropolitan areas (apart from the national capital region) that spill across provincial boundaries.

SOCIOCULTURAL

Particularly in recent years, the literature on Canadian federalism has tended to emphasize, and often to celebrate, the allegedly distinctive cultural "identities" of Canadians in the different provinces. It is said that Canadians in different provinces are objectively different in terms of such categories as ethnicity and religion, and also that they are subjectively different in that they feel attachments to their respective provinces or "regions" more strongly than to Canada as a whole. According to this view, the provincial governments are strong in Canada because Canadians have distinctive needs and interests that cannot be accommodated within a single national government, and also because Canadians actually prefer strong provincial governments and a relatively weak federal one. This belief is often used as an explanation for the present state of Canadian federalism, but also as an argument for further weakening the central government through formal constitutional change.

In his classic analysis of Canadian society, *The Vertical Mosaic*, John Porter described the belief that the provinces had distinctive cultures as "hallowed nonsense" unsupported by any evidence, except perhaps in the case of Quebec.[3] Even if it were true, it would not necessarily explain the power exercised by provincial governments; American states are at least as culturally distinctive as Canadian provinces, but American federalism has evolved in quite a different direction.

Quebec, however, is undoubtedly a special case (see Chapter 5). Not only is it large enough to have a considerable influence on Canadian federalism, but it has most of the characteristics of a distinct nation. In particular, it is the only part of North America where French is the predominant language. The legal system, the schools, and even financial institutions in Quebec are quite different from those elsewhere. Although there are important ethnic minorities, most Quebeckers are descended from French settlers who came to the province during the reign of Louis XIV, and the overwhelming majority of persons born in Quebec remain there throughout their lives. Quebec nationalism has grown more intense since Confederation, partly in response to the ungenerous treatment of francophone minorities in the other provinces and, in more recent decades, out of resentment against the anglophone domination of Quebec's economy. Public-opinion polls consistently show more support in Quebec than elsewhere for the view that provincial powers should be increased. The referendum of 1980 suggested that 40 percent of Quebec's population were inclined to support political independence if economic ties with Canada could be retained. Thus, some observers believe that the existence of Quebec is a sufficient explanation for Canada's failure to develop a more centralized form of government. The fact that the centrifugal tendency in Canadian federalism became most apparent after 1960, when Quebec was undergoing a process of social, economic, and political change known as the Quiet Revolution, gives some credence to the argument.

POLITICAL

While it may be more a symptom than a cause of the difficulties of Canadian federalism, the peculiar character of the party system seems to be associated with them. Parties in a federal system are supposed to accommodate all the divergent interests of the provinces and regions, but Canadian parties have considerable difficulty in doing so. The Conservative Party has not contested a Quebec provincial election since 1935, and the Alberta Liberals have not held office since 1921. On the other hand, exclusively provincial parties, like Social Credit in British Columbia or the Parti Québécois in Quebec, have sometimes been strong enough to win office. In several provinces, the provincial and federal wings of the Liberal Party are completely separate from one another. Quebec's Liberal premier, Robert Bourassa, even gave tacit support to the Progressive Conservatives in the federal election of 1988. The weak links between federal and provincial politics have the consequence that very few politicians with provincial experience seek election to the federal House of Commons. Federal and provincial politicians live throughout their careers in separate environments, interacting only in the formal, and usually conflictual, setting of a federal–provincial conference.

Another aspect of Canada's fragmented party system is the fact that the strength of the federal parties is very unevenly distributed across the country. The New Democrats have only once won a seat in Quebec. The Liberals have been weak in Saskatchewan and Alberta since the rise of John Diefenbaker more than 35 years ago. The Conservatives were weak in Quebec for most of the 20th century, although their fortunes there dramatically improved under Brian Mulroney. The federal election of 1993 left only one major national party in existence, and even its support was unevenly distributed. The victorious Liberals dominated Ontario, Manitoba, and the Atlantic provinces. The Bloc Québécois gained the role of official Opposition by winning 54 seats in Quebec, although it presented no candidates outside that province. The Reform Party won most of the ridings in Alberta and British Columbia, but performed poorly elsewhere and presented no candidates in Quebec. The danger of unevenly distributed support is that a federal government with little support in a province may lack legitimacy there, and may even have difficulty in giving that province its usual quota of representation in the cabinet. This in turn may give credence to claims by the provincial government that only it can speak for provincial interests. Some observers have suggested that proportional representation, either in the House of Commons or in an elected Senate, might overcome this problem. Under the present electoral system, a party that receives 20 percent of the vote in a province may elect no members at all from that province.

ECONOMIC

Many features of Canadian economic development might help to account for the relative weakness of the federal level of government and the corresponding strength of the provincial level. Mainly for natural reasons, but perhaps partly because of federal economic policies, the provinces differ considerably from one another in the structure of their economies, the predominance of particular industries, and the nature and extent of their trading and investment ties with foreign countries. Business interests concentrated in a particular province may encourage the strengthening of that province's government and the weakening of the federal government. Interprovincial disparities of wealth and income are very pronounced, and the rank ordering of the provinces in this regard has changed very little since the 1920s. The importance of mining, petroleum, and forestry in the

Canadian economy reinforces the provincial level of government, which owns and controls these resources in accordance with the Constitution. The relatively slow and limited development of manufacturing has restricted the mobility of population and thus reinforced provincialist sentiments. The dominant influence of the United States over the Canadian economy has weakened the effectiveness of, and lessened the support for, the Canadian federal government. The domination of Quebec's economy by anglophones, at least until recently, stimulated Quebec nationalism and caused resentment to be directed against the federal government. The influence exercised over the federal government by financial, mercantile, and transportation interests caused businesspeople associated with other industries to prefer the provincial level of government. Social and economic changes in Quebec and Alberta have produced in those provinces new and powerful classes dedicated to strengthening the provincial level of government at the expense of the federal level.

All of these types of explanations are of some value, although all have their weaknesses. The institutional and geopolitical explanations fail to explain why Canadian federalism has developed so differently since 1960 from the way it operated previously. The sociocultural explanation is undermined by the important diversities that exist *within* the individual provinces, and by the increasingly homogeneous character of Canadian society, including, to some extent, Quebec. At the very time when demands for more power to the provinces are most strident, the fact is that, except in Quebec, provincial politicians appear far more committed to provincial autonomy than does the general public. The latter fact should be disconcerting to supporters of the sociocultural explanation, for the politicians, unlike the general public, are predominantly urban, upper middle class, Protestant, and of British ancestry. Finally, the economic explanations, while the present writer finds them the most persuasive, are sometimes guilty of circular reasoning or of surreptitiously borrowing arguments from the other explanations.

In any event, and regardless of which explanations are preferred, the provincial level of government is clearly strong enough to deny the central government uncontested supremacy, even within many of the fields of jurisdiction explicitly assigned to the latter under the Constitution. The federal government apparently cannot disregard the provincial governments, and must bargain with them almost continuously in order to achieve its own objectives. The curious expression "the eleven senior governments," which has recently found its way into Canadian political discourse, is symptomatic of this factual equality of bargaining power, whatever the Constitution may say to the contrary. We next describe the actual (as opposed to formal) division of responsibilities between the two levels, the areas of conflict, and the mechanisms of interaction, and conclude the chapter with an evaluation and critique of the system.

AREAS OF CONFLICT

As an aid to understanding how responsibilities are actually divided between the two levels of government, the Constitution Act of 1867, with its detailed and seemingly precise division of jurisdictions, is of very limited value for several reasons: the categories overlap considerably; many subjects that preoccupy governments in the latter part of the 20th century are not listed at all; and both levels of government have expanded their activities without much regard for the Constitution.

The actual functional areas of public policy can be classified into three areas: those occupied exclusively by one level of government with little or no objection from the other; those where both levels of government are active but apparently without much conflict; and those that give rise to federal–provincial conflict. The last category includes areas that the Constitution Act of 1867 assigns primarily to the federal level, areas that it assigns primarily to the provincial level, and areas that it does not assign at all because they were insignificant or unknown at the time of Confederation. Of course, the extent to which particular subjects are shared or give rise to conflict changes over time; the emphasis here will be placed mainly on the situation at the time of writing.

An examination of the names of departments in the federal and provincial governments suggests what further investigation confirms: very few areas of policy are now occupied exclusively by one level of government. The only exclusively federal areas appear to be military defence, veterans' affairs, and monetary policy. The only exclusively provincial areas appear to be municipal institutions, elementary and secondary education, and some areas of law related to property and other noncriminal matters.

Some fields of jurisdiction are partially occupied by both levels of government, but are not areas of serious conflict, at least for the moment. These include agriculture and immigration, both of which the Constitution says either level can legislate, and pensions, which were placed in the same position by subsequent amendments. Both immigration and pensions were the source of serious conflicts between the federal and Quebec governments in the not too distant past, but both seem now to have been resolved. Other areas of harmoniously shared jurisdiction, not mentioned explicitly in the federal Constitution, include scientific research, cultural and recreational activities, tourism, and protection of the environment.

A number of areas assigned to federal jurisdiction have become sources of federal–provincial controversy, either because provincial governments have succeeded in becoming involved in them or because some of them are dissatisfied with federal policies and would like to do so. Freight rates and other aspects of railway transport policy have always been controversial in the hinterlands of Canada; the governments of Manitoba, Saskatchewan, and Alberta took vociferous, although not identical, positions on the Western Grain Transportation Act of 1983, which revised the so-called Crow rate. More recently, several provinces have expressed concern about the abandonment of railway branch lines, which has been encouraged by the federal policy of deregulation. The government of Newfoundland received generous financial compensation in return for withdrawing its objection to the termination of railway service on the island in 1988. Prince Edward Island demanded similar compensation for the demise of its railway service, a year later, but without success.

Trade and commerce, including the external aspects of commercial policy, is another field of federal jurisdiction that has seen increasing provincial involvement and intergovernmental controversy. Provinces have established a variety of informal barriers to interprovincial trade (a few of which have been struck down by the Supreme Court), and have tried to become involved in foreign trade policy by influencing the federal government or even, on occasion, by dealing directly with foreign governments. When the Mulroney government, in 1986, began to negotiate a comprehensive free-trade agreement with the United States, several provincial governments expressed concern that the agreement might affect areas of provincial jurisdiction. However, most withdrew their objections because they supported the general aims of the negotiations, and because the federal government was careful to keep them informed as the negotiations progressed. Ontario's Liberal government, both before and after the agreement was concluded, suggested on various occasions that the federal government might lack the legal authority to conclude an agreement that would bind the province. These remarks caused some concern in Washington, but Ontario did not actually do anything to block the agreement, perhaps because its legal case was weak and because the Ontario business community generally supported free trade with the United States.

The provinces have also become interested in macroeconomic policy, particularly since the temporary imposition of wage controls by the Trudeau government in 1975. Although that initiative was supported by the provincial governments, which cooperated by limiting wage increases in their own bureaucracies, the price of their acquiescence was a federal commitment to convene First Ministers' Conferences on the management of the economy, a useless practice that has continued long after its original justification disappeared. On these occasions, which have been annual since 1984, provincial premiers can be counted on to seek easy popularity by irresponsible demands for lower interest rates. They can offer this unsolicited advice knowing that it will probably not be adopted, and that, even if it were, the resulting inflation would be the federal government's problem.

Some intergovernmental conflict involves clashes over jurisdiction. Federal responsibilities for the aboriginal peoples, and for trade and commerce in sources of energy, conflict with provincial ownership and control of public lands and natural resources south of the sixtieth parallel. The administration of justice, a responsibility shared in a somewhat ambiguous but usually effective way between the two levels of government, has led to conflict over federal efforts to prosecute offences under the Narcotics Control Act, the Combines Investigation Act, and the Food and Drugs Act. The provinces, which prosecute ordinary criminal offences, argued that the federal government was trespassing on their jurisdiction, but the Supreme Court ruled that it was not.[4]

Some of the most intractable areas of federal–provincial conflict are fields of jurisdiction that were not envisaged in 1867. A leading example would be the complex and arcane matter of "communications," which has grown increasingly contentious as technological change has blurred the once-familiar distinctions between telephones, telegraphs, and broadcasting while at the same time adding new and anomalous categories such as cable and pay television. The situation is complicated by provincial ownership of some telephone systems, the use of broadcasting (declared a federal responsibility by the Judicial Committee of the Privy Council in 1932) for purposes of education, and Quebec's desire to protect its language and culture.

Another increasingly controversial field in which both levels of government claim jurisdiction is occupational and vocational training, which is closely associated both with federal responsibility for unemployment insurance and with provincial responsibility for education. Responsibility for this area has been shared between the two levels since at least 1960. The subject has gained prominence in recent years because of growing concerns about the international competitiveness of Canadian industry, and because the traditional Keynesian belief that full employment can be secured by increasing the level of aggregate demand in the economy has been largely discredited. While many Canadians believe that the federal government should implement a national training strategy, as the central governments in some European countries have done, Quebec has grown increasingly strident in its claim that the area falls under provincial jurisdiction. In the summer of 1993, Prime Minister Kim Campbell agreed to transfer responsibility for training to Quebec, without a formal constitutional amendment. The agreement drew criticism from anglophone Canadians (particularly the Premier of Ontario), some of whom pointed out that it would implement an important part of the Charlottetown Accord, which the voters had rejected in a referendum less than a year ago.

A particularly important area of intergovernmental conflict, and one that exists to some extent in all federal countries, is that of finance and taxation. The Constitution allows the federal government to impose any kind of taxation, while the provinces are restricted to "direct" taxation and to revenues from their natural resources. The Constitution Act of 1867 also provided for modest federal subsidies to provincial governments, but while these are still paid they have been overshadowed since 1957 by massive "equalization" payments to provinces with below-average ability to raise revenue, a program whose annual cost to the federal treasury now exceeds $8 billion. Since 1982, the obligation to make these payments has been entrenched in the Constitution.

Because both levels of government have constantly increasing needs for revenue, and because both ultimately rely on the same taxpayers to provide it, the need for coordination and the scope for conflict are obvious. Apart from its obvious purpose of providing revenue, taxation is now viewed by governments as a tool for manipulating, regulating, and stimulating the economy. Moreover, tax concessions to both individuals and corporations are important means of winning and keeping political support. Thus, the "stakes" in financial negotiations are high.

Since the Second World War, elaborate arrangements have been devised (and modified at five-year intervals) for sharing revenue from personal and corporation income taxes, which are now the most important sources of revenue. While these arrangements have been reasonably successful, there have been some eruptions of conflict, particularly involving the larger provinces, in the course of negotiating the five-year agreements. Although the federal government collects personal income tax on behalf of every province except Quebec, and corporation tax on behalf of all except Quebec, Ontario, and Alberta, provinces occasionally threaten to discontinue these arrangements. To prevent them from doing so, the federal government has agreed to so many interprovincial variations that there are now ten different versions of the income-tax return form, one for each province. Further conflict erupted over the federal Goods and Services Tax (GST), which replaced the old Manufacturers' Sales Tax (MST) in 1991. Some provinces appeared to believe that sales taxes should be exclusively provincial, while Alberta, perhaps as a legacy of its Social Credit past, was ideologically opposed to any tax on consumption. By 1993, only Quebec and Saskatchewan had taken any steps to harmonize their own sales taxes with the federal tax.

Intergovernmental conflicts over energy resources between 1973 and 1984 had important financial implications, although there were other issues as well. As oil and gas prices rose, both levels of government tried to capture the economic rents that resulted by imposing taxes or, in the provincial case, by increasing the royalties that the province collected as the owner of the resource. The producing provinces claimed that their ownership rights entitled them to reap the financial benefits of higher prices, while the federal government argued that its powers to regulate trade and commerce entitled it to control domestic prices and to tax exports to the United States. An additional problem was that increasing resource revenues in a few provinces increased the federal government's obligation to make equalization payments. By 1977, even Ontario would have received equalization had not the formula hastily been changed to preclude this possibility.

Another source of controversy, particularly with the governments of Quebec and Ontario, has been federal spending in the areas of health, education, and welfare, all of which fall under provincial jurisdiction. The federal government initially offered to share the costs of certain programs in an effort to encourage provinces to establish them. After the programs were established, and as their costs began to escalate, the federal government would try to impose a ceiling on its own expenditure or even withdraw from the field altogether. Provincial governments argued that these conditional grants put pressure on them to alter their spending priorities (precisely the federal government's intention), that the terms and conditions of federal support prevented them from designing programs that fitted their own needs, and that subsequent federal efforts to restrict federal spending placed an unfair burden on the provinces.

These issues have become increasingly complex over the years and have become entangled with the issues of tax sharing as discussed above. In 1965, Quebec was allowed to "opt out" of certain programs, meaning that federal grants and federal taxes were both reduced, allowing Quebec to increase its own taxes and run the programs without federal interference. In 1977, all provinces were given a combination of cash payments and additional tax room in place of the payments previously received in support of health insurance and postsecondary education, an innovation known as Established Programs Financing (EPF). In 1984, strict federal conditions regarding the design of health-insurance programs were reimposed by the Canada Health Act. Although supported by all three parties in Parliament, this measure was resented by most provincial governments. Quebec in particular continues to call for restrictions on the federal power to spend in areas of provincial jurisdiction.

In recent years, the fiscal crisis of the Canadian state has cast a long shadow over federal–provincial fiscal relations. Discussions of the federal "spending power" have become somewhat academic when interest on the public debt is the largest single item of federal expenditure, and when federal tax revenues cover only about three-fourths of federal expenditures. During the 1980s, the financial situation of most provincial governments was far more favourable than that of the federal government, a consequence of the disastrous fiscal policies pursued by federal governments between 1973 and 1979. Not unreasonably in the circumstances, the Mulroney government responded to its own fiscal crisis by cutting back its expenditures, including payments to the provinces, and then by imposing a new tax, the GST. Both actions were resented by the provinces. The three richest, Ontario, Alberta, and British Columbia, took the federal government to court in 1990 when it announced measures to limit its payments to them for postsecondary education, health, and welfare. The Supreme Court ruled in 1991 that the federal government was entitled to control its own budget. However, the federal government still has a gigantic annual deficit, and several provinces, including Ontario, are also in desperate financial straits.

In resisting or opposing federal initiatives, provincial governments make use of the following arguments: the provincial level of government is "closer to the people" and better able to understand their needs; the federal government is seeking to impose "bureaucracy," centralization, and excessive spending; their province's allegedly distinctive "way of life" is in danger; and (more rarely in recent years) the terms of the Constitution are being violated. Western provincial governments often argue that federal policies discriminate in favour of Ontario and Quebec, while Quebec governments argue that federal policies discriminate in favour of Ontario and the West. As the great economic historian Harold Innis commented in 1946,

> The hatreds between regions in Canada have become important vested interests. Montreal exploits the hatred of Toronto and Regina that of Winnipeg and so one might go through the list. A native of Ontario may appear restive at being charged with exploitation by those who systematically exploit him with their charges of exploitation, but even the right to complain is denied to him.[5]

Behind the rhetoric, the interests at stake are often more specific than would appear at first glance. Provincial politicians may need votes to win an election, or provincial officials may want to expand the budget and clientele of their own "shop" by excluding the federal government from a contested field of policy. Interests in the private sector are also influential. Alberta's demands for higher oil prices and natural gas exports reflect the interests of the petroleum industry as well as the government. The Ontario government often lobbies against federal initiatives that are opposed by secondary manufacturing firms, such as tougher restraints on corporate mergers and combines, an initiative contemplated in the 1970s. The differing positions of Alberta and Saskatchewan regarding the Crow's Nest freight rates reflected the predominance of ranchers in the former province and of grain farmers in the latter. Prior to the deregulation of air transport, several provinces supported locally based regional air carriers, in opposition to federal policies that were perceived to favour Air Canada. Federalism provides regionally concentrated interests with a powerful defence against the possibility of being overridden by a national majority.

The intensity of federal–provincial conflict, of course, varies over time, and from province to province. Newly elected federal governments seem to enjoy a "honeymoon" in their relations with the provinces, but after they have been in office four or five years, relations typically deteriorate. The parliamentary Opposition then blames the federal government for the situation and promises to do better, but when the Opposition party eventually wins office the same cycle repeats itself. Heads of government may also differ in their preferred approach to federal–provincial relations. Prime Minister Trudeau favoured a more formal and structured approach while Prime Minister Mulroney preferred to make "deals" with political allies such as Robert Bourassa of Quebec or Grant Devine of Saskatchewan. The provinces themselves may vary in their behaviour over time, depending on economic conditions, partisanship, and even the personality of the premier. On the other hand, there are certain continuities in their behaviour. Quebec is always the most sensitive to any restrictions on its autonomy, with Alberta not far behind. Some of the smaller provinces are traditionally quite passive and accommodating in their dealings with the federal government.

INTERGOVERNMENTAL MECHANISMS

Because of the many ways in which the two levels of government affect one another's freedom of action, a variety of mechanisms and processes have developed for coordinating policies and resolving conflicts. A common characteristic of these mechanisms and processes is that none of them are provided for in the Constitution. Those institutions that were provided for—the lieutenant-governors and possibly the Senate—have proven to be ineffectual as means of facilitating intergovernmental coordination.

As in most other federations, the judiciary is an important mechanism for resolving questions of jurisdiction. Established in 1875, the Supreme Court of Canada did not actually become the highest court of appeal until 1949, when Parliament abolished the right of appeal to the Judicial Committee of the Privy Council (JCPC) in London. The JCPC's interpretations of Canada's Constitution, because they had tended to restrict the powers of the central government and to enhance the status of the provinces, were deplored by Canadian nationalists. For two decades after the abolition of appeals, the Supreme Court did not strike down any federal statutes, and it was also quite permissive in regard to provincial statutes, so that it attracted little controversy. From about 1973 onward, the Supreme Court was much more in the limelight as it struck down provincial statutes relating to agricultural marketing, taxation and management of natural resources, and Quebec's efforts to regulate cable television.[6] Critics, particularly in Quebec and the Prairie provinces, charged that the Court had a "centralist" bias, perhaps because its justices were appointed by the federal government. In 1978, Saskatchewan's governing political party won re-election largely by campaigning against Chief Justice Bora Laskin, one of the most distinguished persons ever to sit on a Canadian court. The critics, however, ignored the fact that the Supreme Court struck down a number of federal statutes in the same period. Even its decision upholding federal wage controls in 1976 did so on such narrow grounds that the scope of federal power was arguably diminished.[7] In 1979, the Supreme Court also ruled that the reform of the Senate involved provincial rights and was thus not within the powers of Parliament.[8]

The Supreme Court's interpretations of the Constitution may arise out of litigation in which an individual or a corporation challenges the constitutionality of a federal or provincial statute. Until the Charter of Rights and Freedoms was enacted in 1982, such a challenge could be made only on the grounds that the statute trespassed on the powers of the other level of government. Judicial interpretations may also arise out of reference cases, in which a government seeks an advisory opinion on a question of constitutional law. A government may do this either to forestall litigation directed against its own legislation (as a means of challenging another government's legislation) or simply to clarify an uncertain situation. The federal government can submit reference cases directly to the Supreme Court. Provincial governments can submit them to their own high courts, whose decisions can be appealed to the Supreme Court of Canada. Governments that are not directly involved frequently intervene in important constitutional cases, whether these arise as references or as ordinary litigation.

Politicians generally prefer political solutions—in which they can split the difference and provide partial satisfaction to both sides—to the clear-cut, "either/or" decisions produced by the judicial process. For some provincial politicians, this preference is reinforced by the belief that the Supreme Court has a centralist bias. In fact, a great variety of informal political mechanisms for arriving at solutions are available: federal and provincial governments interact at a number of different levels; bilateral contacts between the federal government and one provincial government are a part of the process; and there are also interprovincial relations not involving the federal government.

During the two decades that followed the Second World War, as the two levels of government began to have a greater and greater impact on one another's activities, there was a rapid development of collaborative relationships, including semiformal and semipermanent committees with representatives of both levels. Most of these involved officials, sometimes of relatively junior rank. Most were concerned with a few functional areas of policy in which there was a large amount of intergovernmental interaction: finance, health, welfare, agriculture, renewable resources, and statistics. This pattern of intergovernmental relations came to be designated by the term "cooperative federalism." In many cases, it was related to programs that were jointly financed by the two levels of government, though primarily administered by the provincial. It was characterized by a fragmentation of intergovernmental relations within each government, since departments with specific responsibilities were largely given a free hand to conduct their own relations with counterpart departments in other governments. Most of the officials involved were more concerned with resolving problems and running effective programs than they were with scoring points for their level of government in relation to the other level. In fact, it is not easy to be certain, even in retrospect, whether cooperative federalism was centralizing or decentralizing in its overall impact. At the time, no one much cared.

Beginning in the 1960s, and continuing in the 1970s, this pattern of intergovernmental relations was transformed into a new pattern for which the term "executive federalism" is appropriate. Conditional grants, in which the federal government pays a fixed percentage of the cost of provincially administered programs that meet federally determined criteria, became unpopular as both levels of government sought to tighten control over their expenditures. Central agencies such as the Privy Council Office and its offshoot, the Federal–Provincial Relations Office, began to play a greater role in intergovernmental relations, riding hard on the activities of the functional departments. Political leaders, as opposed to appointed officials, also played an increasingly prominent role. For all of these reasons, there was an increasing tendency among both federal and provincial participants to assign the prestige and power of "their" level of government a higher priority than the resolution of conflicts or the success of programs in delivering services to the public.

These changes were partly associated with the growth of Quebec separatism and with the energy crisis, developments that led to more conflict and less collaboration in federal–provincial relations. They were also encouraged by the popularity of "rational" approaches to decision-making which were based on the premise that each government could and should arrange its "priorities" in a centralized fashion and exercise a tight grip over its expenditures. Central agencies and elected politicians are more inclined than specialists in health, welfare, or resource development to think in terms of maximizing their government's power or prestige in relation to other governments.

A characteristically Canadian institution that has assumed great prominence is the First Ministers' Conference (FMC), which brings together the federal prime minister and the ten premiers, assisted by numerous officials. Until the 1960s, FMCs occurred only occasionally, usually in connection with proposed amendments to the Constitution or major changes in fiscal arrangements between the two levels of government. Since 1963, there has been at least one such meeting in most years, and in some years more.

Despite all the advance preparation, expense, and ballyhoo, the record of FMCs in reaching agreements or solving problems is poor; in fact, it would be difficult to devise a worse way to carry on the nation's business. Provincial premiers often have no strong incentive to reach an agreement, and may even gain popularity by being as unreasonable and intransigent as possible. The federal prime minister, on the other hand, is expected both to defend the national interest and to satisfy the demands of all the provinces, two objectives that may be totally incompatible. He or she, rather than the premiers, will be blamed if an agreement is not concluded, and the temptation is therefore strong to sacrifice the national interest to provincial demands.

A majority vote at a FMC would have little meaning, because the prime minister represents Canadians in every province and should logically have as many votes as all of the premiers combined. The premiers themselves are not equal except in a formal sense. Ontario's population is 73 times that of Prince Edward Island and almost equal to the total of all the western and Atlantic provinces combined. Only Alberta can cut off the nation's supply of oil and gas, and only Quebec can plausibly threaten to secede from Canada and become a sovereign nation. All of the Atlantic provinces depend on federal grants to maintain even a semblance of provincial status. Thus, agreement must be on a basis of consensus or, at the very least, must include the federal government and eight or nine provinces. (Some constitutional amendments can be made by seven provinces, including either Ontario or Quebec, but the provinces that did not agree would have the right to opt out if the amendment affected any of their "rights or privileges.")[9] Consensus, whether on constitutional amendments or on more mundane matters, is not easily achieved among governments representing different regions, political parties, and jurisdictional interests. If it is achieved, it will probably be because the prime minister has given the premiers everything they asked for. Parliament, not to mention the provincial legislatures, will then be told that it must give automatic approval to the agreement or else run the risk of a dire threat to national unity. This, of course, makes a mockery of responsible government. In any event, opposition parties in the House of Commons are often reluctant to criticize intergovernmental agreements involving premiers with whom they share a party label, or agreements popular in a province where they hope to win votes.

While FMCs, particularly those dealing with the Constitution, are the most publicized aspect of executive federalism, there are also frequent meetings at the ministerial level that involve almost every field of public policy. Other meetings include nonelected officials, rather than politicians, and may be designed to prepare for the executive sessions, to implement agreements concluded by the politicians, or simply to exchange information. Since 1960, the provincial premiers have also held an annual meeting with the prime minister not present, followed by a communiqué that usually criticizes an assortment of federal policies and initiatives. From 1980 to 1984, when no provincial government had the same party label as the federal government, these communiqués were exceptionally strident and hostile in tone. More typically, they are toned down in deference to the sentiments of premiers who may be political allies of the prime minister.

CONCLUSION

While Canada's problems may be slight compared to those of many other countries, and while the federal state has survived through a number of decades in which its future appeared less than assured, there is nonetheless some cause for concern about its present situation and prospects. Contrary to the myth propagated in some provincial capitals, the picture that Canada presents to the outside world is that of an increasingly loose collection of semisovereign provinces, with a central government unable or unwilling to exercise much control over the economy or to carry out coherent policies even within its own fields of jurisdiction. Compared with almost any other modern federation, or with Canada itself as recently as the 1950s, the extent of provincial power and the political and financial weakness of the central government are remarkable.

The conspicuous and frequent intergovernmental conferences since the early 1960s have possibly accustomed many Canadians to regard the central government as only one government among eleven that are more or less equal in status—a serious misreading both of Canada's Constitution and of the requirements of a healthy political system. Harold Innis once wrote that provincial control over lands and resources was a survival of "feudalism" and a source of weakness for Canada.[10] Certainly the effort that the central government must devote to bargaining with quasi-independent provincial potentates both lessens its ability to function effectively and undermines its authority in the eyes of the public. The federal–provincial conference resembles a meeting between a medieval king and his feudal barons more than it does the government of a modern state. The implicit assumption that regional divisions and interests are the most significant ones in Canada, and that only the provincial governments are capable of representing them, calls into question the authority and usefulness of the federal Parliament, which must often rubber-stamp the results of intergovernmental agreements, and which is prevented from legislating—even in the areas assigned to its jurisdiction—without interference by the provinces.

Particularly in Quebec and Alberta, some persons continue to propagate what former federal cabinet minister Jim Fleming once called "the myth of the power-hungry centralizers," and to argue that the provincial governments should be given more influence over federal policies and more freedom to pursue their own.[11] The reality is that Canada is already the most decentralized country in the industrialized world. Provincial revenues have been greater than federal revenues in every year since 1977, although they were only half as large as federal revenues in 1960.[12] Federal powers have been whittled away by judicial interpretation, or have simply fallen into disuse; the power to declare works and undertakings for the general advantage of Canada has not been used since 1961. Labour relations (apart from those of the railways and airlines), postsecondary education, highway transport, and the regulation of trading in securities have become exclusively provincial fields of jurisdiction de facto. Since 1974, the provinces have distributed family allowances according to their own criteria, although the federal government provides all the funds. Some provinces even maintain permanent diplomatic missions in foreign countries, although Ontario closed its foreign offices as an economy measure in 1993.

Contrary to a widespread belief that is incongruously shared by its opponents and by many of its supporters, the Constitution Act of 1982 did not give the federal government any additional powers, either in theory or in practice. The Charter of Rights and Freedoms limits provincial powers in certain respects, but most of its provisions can be overridden by the "notwithstanding" clause, to which two provinces have already resorted. The bizarre amending formula, originally devised by the Alberta government, makes it easier to transfer federal powers to the provinces than vice versa. The Canada–United States Free Trade Agreement, which came into effect at the beginning of 1989, weakens federal powers over energy, foreign investment, financial institutions, regional development, industrial strategy, and various other areas, as well as the whole rationale for having a federal government at all. It is surely significant that former Alberta premier Peter Lougheed and Parti Québécois leader Jacques Parizeau were among the most fervent supporters of the Free Trade Agreement, both arguing that it would make their provinces more independent of the federal government. The fact that Quebec's pro-business Liberal Party now supports a radical reduction of federal powers, as proposed by the party's constitutional committee headed by Jean Allaire, may be in part a consequence of the Free Trade Agreement.[13]

Outside of Quebec, on the other hand, there are signs of resistance to further decentralization of Canadian federalism. The strident behaviour of the western provinces during the so-called energy crisis has noticeably moderated in recent years. The Charter of Rights and Freedoms has focused attention on social cleavages of gender, ethnicity, and so forth, rather than on regionalism. Widespread opposition to both the Meech Lake Accord of 1987 and the Charlottetown Accord of 1992 was based, in part, on the belief that the federal government should not surrender any more powers to the provinces.

Canada is a relatively small industrialized country in a world where most of its competitors are larger, stronger, and more centralized. If it is to survive in this environment, and to overcome the divisive effects of its geographical barriers and its closeness to the United States, it may require a stronger central government than it has enjoyed in recent years, and a corresponding reduction in the powers of provincial governments. More-over, a lessening of the Canadian obsession with provincial interests and jurisdictional controversies might direct attention to more significant is-sues, such as industrial competitiveness, the fiscal crisis, and the unequal distribution of wealth, power, and opportunity among the population.

NOTES

1. Lord Atkin in *A.G. Canada v. A.G. Ontario* (1937), A.C. 327.
2. Canada, House of Commons, *Debates,* Session 1936, p. 3868.
3. John Porter, *The Vertical Mosaic* (Toronto: University of Toronto Press, 1965), p. 382.
4. *R. v. Hauser,* [1979] 1 S.C.R. 984; *A.G. Canada v. CN and CP Transport,* [1983] 2 S.C.R. 206; *R. v. Wetmore,* [1983] 2 S.C.R. 284.
5. Harold A. Innis, *Political Economy in the Modern State* (Toronto: Ryerson, 1946), p. xi.
6. *Burns Foods Ltd. v. A.G. Manitoba,* [1975] 1 S.C.R. 494; *CIGOL v. Saskatchewan,* [1978] 2 S.C.R. 545; *Central Canada Potash v. Saskatchewan,* [1979] 1 S.C.R. 42; *Dionne v. Public Service Board of Quebec,* [1978] 2 S.C.R. 191.
7. *Reference re Anti-inflation Act,* [1976] 2 S.C.R. 373.
8. *Reference re Legal Authority of Parliament to Alter or Replace the Senate,* [1980] 1 S.C.R. 54.
9. Constitution Act, 1982, section 38.
10. Harold A. Innis, *Essays in Canadian Economic History* (Toronto: Univer-sity of Toronto Press, 1956), pp. 277–78.
11. Jim Fleming, "The Myth of the Power-Hungry Centralizers," address to the Empire Club, Toronto, February 19, 1981.
12. Canadian Tax Foundation, *The National Finances, 1992* (Toronto: 1992), table 3.11.
13. See its report, *A Quebec Free to Choose,* released on January 28, 1991.

FURTHER READINGS

Banting, Keith G. *The Welfare State and Canadian Federalism.* 2nd ed. Montreal and Kingston: McGill-Queen's University Press, 1987.

Black, Edwin R. *Divided Loyalties: Canadian Concepts of Federalism.* Montreal and Kingston: McGill-Queen's University Press, 1975.

Cairns, Alan C. *Constitution, Government and Society in Canada: Selected Essays.* Toronto: McClelland and Stewart, 1988.

Leslie, Peter. *Federal State, National Economy.* Toronto: University of Toronto Press, 1987.

Milne, David A. *Tug of War: Ottawa and the Provinces under Trudeau and Mul-roney.* Toronto: James Lorimer, 1986.

Simeon, Richard, ed. *Intergovernmental Relations.* Toronto: University of Toronto Press in cooperation with the Royal Commission on the Economic Union and Development Prospects for Canada, 1985.

Simeon, Richard, and Robinson, Ian. *State, Society, and the Development of Cana-dian Federalism.* Toronto: University of Toronto Press in cooperation with the Royal Commission on the Economic Union and Development Prospects for Canada, 1990.

Smiley, Donald V. *The Federal Condition in Canada.* Toronto: McGraw-Hill Ryerson, 1987.

Stevenson, Garth. *Unfulfilled Union: Canadian Federalism and National Unity.* 3rd ed. Toronto: Gage, 1989.

21 POLITICIANS AND BUREAUCRATS IN THE POLICY PROCESS

Reginald A. Whitaker

In liberal-democratic states, there has always been, and no doubt always will be, tension between politicians and bureaucrats over their respective roles in making public policy. The reason for this is straightforward, even if the practice is anything but: it has proved impossible to define decisively the division of responsibilities between ministers and their senior bureaucrats. This relationship is constantly in a state of redefinition and renegotiation, from government to government and from minister to minister in the same government. One thing, however, is sure: bureaucrats inevitably have an important role in the policy process, while it is the politicians who are ultimately responsible to the public.

THE POLITICS/ADMINISTRATION DICHOTOMY

The simple theory of responsible democratic government is that the people choose among competing political parties at election time. Once a government is elected, it has a mandate from the people to enact the policies it has proposed. The bureaucrats are civil *servants*, whose task is to execute the will of the people's elected representatives in implementing and administering the government's policies. The problem with this theory is that it is too simple.

In the earlier part of this century, there was a prevalent theory among students of public administration that reflected this simple approach. This was referred to as the *politics/administration dichotomy*. Politics is politics, and administration is administration. Politics is about setting policy, inevitably a partisan and controversial matter. Administration, on the other hand, is technical and nonpartisan. There is no overlap.

This principle was argued both as a statement of fact and as an ethical guide for politicians and bureaucrats.

No reputable scholar of public administration and public policy would be prepared today to defend the politics/administration dichotomy, at least in its pristine form. As a statement of fact, it is obviously erroneous, as we shall see. As an ethical guide, however, it still informs some of the basic elements of our administrative institutions, such as the *merit principle* as the basis for appointment to the public service, and the protection against *political patronage* built into the process in the selection of public servants. It is generally believed to be a good thing that bureaucrats are shielded from undue political interference with their duties. At the same time, the idea that secretive, unaccountable bureaucrats may be shaping public policy behind the scenes is widely viewed as a dangerously undemocratic practice. A popular (and very clever) British TV sitcom—*Yes, Prime Minister*—was premised upon the crafty ways in which senior civil servants in Whitehall baffle and manipulate the politicians they are supposed to serve. One might sum up public attitudes as follows: politics and administration *ought to be* separate, watertight compartments, but in fact the bureaucracy is to some extent out of control. Unfortunately, when politicians seek to extend their influence, they are politicizing administration, and this is just as bad as a bureaucracy out of political control. Obviously, there is no satisfactory "solution" to this dilemma given that the tension is structural. The question is whether this tension can be creative rather than debilitating.

The original impetus behind the politics/administration dichotomy came from a desire to banish political influence from the administrative process. This was not surprising considering the prevalence of political patronage in North America in the 19th and early 20th centuries. Especially in the United States, but to a considerable extent in Canada as well, politicians had used patronage appointments to the civil service as a useful political resource (jobs for votes, in effect), and as the most appropriate means of maintaining control over the administration. A strong reaction to the old order came with the progressive reform movements in national and local politics in the early 20th century. These largely middle-class movements sought to diminish the influence of the political bosses and their machines by, among other things, freeing the administration of government from partisan political control. The creation of nonpartisan boards and commissions—out of the direct reach of politicians—to administer various functions of government was one approach. Another was to replace patronage with a merit system of appointment to the regular civil service. Patronage was associated with corruption and inefficiency. The professionalization of the civil service was seen as a necessary step toward putting government on a more businesslike basis—not to mention offering career avenues for the educated middle-class people who supported reform.

It is interesting to note that the crucial step toward reducing the patronage system in the federal civil service came when a group of prominent Ontario businessmen made a proposal to the then leader of the Opposition, Conservative Robert Borden, during the 1911 election. They offered their support, financial and otherwise, to the Conservative campaign if Borden would pledge himself to a number of policies they had enumerated, among them the institution of a merit system of appointment to the civil service. Since they also wanted a stronger role for the federal government in promoting Canadian trade around the world, they obviously saw a merit-based administration as the prerequisite to a more effective government that could act in their interests. Borden did win that election. Civil-service reform finally came in 1918 when a wartime Union government composed of Conservatives and Liberals proved incapable of dividing patronage. The Civil Service Act of 1918 took a good proportion, although not all, of the federal civil service out of the range of patronage and ushered in a new regime of merit selection, with written examinations for entry and specific qualifications for particular positions. All this was to be guaranteed by the Civil Service Commission (later the Public Service Commission), an appointed and nominally independent body that would act as a watchdog against any recurrence of patronage. Thus was born the modern system of professional administration.

Despite some ups and downs over the years, the reforms of 1918 proved irreversible, so much so that when a special committee appointed by the federal government reported in 1979, it found the likelihood of a return to patronage "about nil."[1] Political patronage continues to exist for a range of senior appointments: judges to federal and provincial courts, senators, ambassadors, heads of Crown corporations, and chairs of a host of special boards, commissions, and regulatory agencies. But with the sole exception of deputy ministers (an exception to which we will return shortly), appointments and promotions within the permanent federal public service are on a competitive merit basis. Political interference in these matters is considered quite inappropriate. Thus, the institutional structures still tend to reflect the politics/administration dichotomy. Administrators are supposed to be divorced from politics, and politicians restrained from interfering with administration.

One of the problems with this situation is the ambivalence we display in democratic countries toward "politics." On the one hand, politics is often viewed as a less than exemplary process typically involving deception, if not downright dishonesty. Not only are politicians held in low social repute, but disdain for politics enters everyday life, as in the term "office politics" to describe manipulative behaviour by fellow workers. On the other hand, politics are the means through which the people can assert their public policy preferences, the very mechanism of democracy. Thus, political interference with administration is a double-edged sword: the dark side is inefficiency and corruption through the introduction of partisan considerations into the neutral world of administration; the good side is a party with a mandate from the electorate seeking to direct the bureaucrats to fulfil the will of the people. The democratic side of politics can be glimpsed in the public reaction to administrators so insulated from political control that they act autonomously. "Faceless bureaucrats" are denounced for imposing an Orwellian state on the people. It is precisely the lack of direct accountability that leads people to fear unchecked bureaucracy. After all, people can always get back at the politicians in the next election, but the bureaucrats do not have to submit themselves to the electorate.

THE CHANGING ROLE OF THE DEPUTY MINISTER

The notion of direct political control over the work of government departments focuses on the office of deputy minister. Deputy ministers, the chief executive officers of government departments, are appointed "at pleasure," which means that they do not have security of tenure. Deputy ministers have a double role (some would call it an ambiguous role) in that they represent the department to the minister and the minister to the department. As such, they are the crucial link between the elected politicians and the permanent bureaucracy. It is through the deputy ministers that governments can seek to impose their policy directions on the huge and often unwieldy apparatus of government. Following an election, it is up to the new government to reappoint (or not reappoint) deputy ministers. Moreover, a prime minister can at any time move or remove deputy ministers. Appointment of people from outside government to deputy ministerial positions is a prime-ministerial prerogative and is not normally deemed to constitute political patronage. If a deputy minister were unqualified for the post except for partisan political credentials, no doubt a cry would be raised, but this rarely if ever happens. On the other hand, it is a legitimate interest of governments that deputy ministers share their general ideological and policy orientations, or at least not be actively hostile toward them.

When one party remains in office for a long period, there is a tendency for the ministers and the senior civil servants to grow close together in orientation. But when another party comes to office for the first time, or after long years in opposition, tension is almost inevitable. The Liberals ran Ottawa from 1935 to 1957, an era that has since been dubbed the "golden age of the civil service mandarins." A small number of deputy ministers became extremely powerful and influential figures in Ottawa, due to considerable technical knowledge of their departments and policy fields, and the years of experience they had accumulated in the Ottawa environment. They indeed became the chief source of policy input and ideas to the Liberal governments they served. This relationship became so close, if not symbiotic, that the Liberals of this era have been dubbed the "Government party," and the civil-service mandarins were widely seen as "liberals," if not Liberals.

In 1957, this cosy relationship was broken with the unexpected electoral victory of the Progressive Conservatives under a Prairie outsider, John Diefenbaker. Diefenbaker harboured considerable suspicions and misgivings about the Liberal mandarins, but he also grudgingly respected their expertise and experience. Instead of replacing them with a new generation of deputy ministers more attuned to Tory policy directions, Diefenbaker by and large left the incumbents in place. However, due to his innate mistrust of their political tendencies, he failed to utilize them effectively on behalf of his government. There was some justification for his mistrust: when the Liberals under Lester Pearson returned to national office in 1963, their first cabinet was graced with a half-dozen former senior civil servants who had abandoned the bureaucracy for Liberal political careers—including the prime minister himself, a former Undersecretary of State for External Affairs.

Although the Liberals remained in office from 1963 to 1984 (with one nine-month blip in 1979–80), there was not another golden age of the mandarinate, Liberal or otherwise. The era of centralization in Ottawa was coming to a close. Regional tensions were on the rise; "province-building" emerged, in the form of competitive provincial state bureaucracies, first in Quebec, then in Ontario and the wealthier western provinces. The Ottawa civil service no longer dominated the field. Moreover, as government became far more extensive and complex in its interventions in the society, as it did in the 1960s and 1970s, the capacity of individual deputy ministers to command all the detail and expertise in their increasingly large, and often technically specialized, departments became more questionable. Nor could a small number of deputy ministers gain a wide grasp of the business of government as a whole through relatively intimate informal gatherings of senior colleagues, as they had in the past. Communication between departments became much more formal and unwieldy as the size and complexity of government grew. Deputy ministers themselves were shuffled from department to department as often as ministers, and were encouraged to move in and out of the public and private sectors to gain wider experience. In effect, deputy ministers were becoming senior managers whose skills lay in managing large and complex organizations, public or private, and who tended to leave the technical expertise to the people hired for their technical qualifications.

Even with the relative decline of the once-commanding figure of the deputy minister, questions about the influence of bureaucrats in the policy process persist. The very technical specialization inherent in the complex interventions in the private sector of the contemporary state strategically position the bureaucrats to influence the policy process. One of the weakest links in the politics/administration dichotomy is the idea that victorious parties come out of an election with a clear policy mandate to implement. In the age of professionally packaged image politics, parties tend to avoid specific policy commitments for fear of alienating potential voters. Policy, it is often argued, is too complex to be intelligently argued during the heat of an election campaign. In any case, over the four- to five-year mandate of a government, the speed with which events move often compels governments to undertake policy initiatives that were unforeseen during the election campaign. In recent years, three of the most significant policy initiatives of the former Conservative government—the Canada–U.S. Free Trade Agreement, the foiled Meech Lake constitutional accord, and the GST—were not even mentioned in the preceeding election campaigns, let alone debated. Although general policy directions may emanate from a ruling party (for instance, the former Conservative government was predisposed to market-driven solutions and to reducing state intervention in the private sector), specific policy is most often worked out by the politicians in close conjunction with their bureaucrats and the major interested groups in the society.

The bureaucrats command *information*, a key resource in the policy process—even if that command is now less concentrated at the top. Politicians are always at a disadvantage when confronting officials with greater technical knowledge. There is never any question that the elected politicians have the right to set policy directions, and that bureaucrats have no business attempting to interpose their own policy preferences (directly or openly, that is). However, when it comes time to present ministers with detailed policy *options*, the way in which alternate routes to achieving the policy goal are presented can have a powerful effect on how a policy actually takes shape. *Evaluating* the possible effects of a policy change can have similarly dramatic effects on a proposed change. Finally, the way in which a policy is actually *implemented* has a powerful impact on the policy itself; moreover, implementation is a bureaucratic prerogative usually done in the absence of political attention (that attention having wandered on to other things).

In each case, it is the permanent officials who normally have greater access to information resources. Ministers, after all, are also MPs and party politicians who spend much of their time giving speeches, travelling, attending political functions, and engaging in other activities quite remote from the business of their ministerial portfolios. In many cases, they have no previous training or experience in the policy fields of their departments, little time to gain such knowledge while there, and a relatively short span in one portfolio before they move on (or out). The bureaucracy, on the other hand, was there before, and will be there long after. Moreover, there is a considerable amount of highly specialized knowledge that can be marshalled by the organization—that is, after all, what modern complex organizations are supposed to do. But the result is that bureaucrats do have input into the policy process that cannot simply be seen as neutral.

Bureaucratic control over information has if anything increased in recent years with the development of what students of interest groups call *policy communities*. Policy communities include all actors who have an interest in a policy area, who share a common policy focus, and who help shape policy outcomes.[2] Increasingly, such "communities" have grown up around particular policy areas involving bureaucrats from the federal government, their counterparts in the provincial bureaucracies, and the interested private-sector organizations, including companies, trade associations, and pressure groups. For instance, in the energy resource field, the policy community would include officials from the federal energy department, their counterparts in such energy-producing provinces as Alberta and British Columbia, the resource corporations, and the various producer groups. In effect, such communities expand access to relevant information and establish external bases of potential support for specialized bureaucrats in their policy fields.

Given these kinds of dynamics, no serious student of the policy process would argue that current public policy is not positively affected by both politicians and bureaucrats. Nor would anyone seriously argue that policy could, or should, be entirely divorced from bureaucratic input. To do so would be impracticable and undesirable. The relative balance of inputs is more debatable. Politicians have become more restive in recent years about the extent of bureaucratic input, and have sought various devices to recover ground they believe they have lost. There are a number of reasons for this, and all of them point in the direction of placing on the bureaucrats greater restrictions and stronger mechanisms of political accountability.

THE RISE OF THE CENTRAL AGENCIES

For the past quarter-century or so, federal governments have shown concern about what politicians have seen as an undue degree of influence exercised by bureaucrats in the policy process. When Pierre Trudeau took over as prime minister in 1968, he indicated a strong desire to establish "counterweights" to the traditional channels of advice from the bureaucracy. One counterweight was sought in a beefed-up Prime Minister's Office (PMO) that would offer *political* policy advice to match the voices offering bureaucratic advice. Although Trudeau was much criticized for "presidentializing" the prime ministership, the PMO never functioned effectively as a policy counterweight to the permanent officialdom. This was not surprising given the lack of expertise among the PMO's often young and relatively inexperienced "politicos" recruited from the party. Nevertheless, the PMO has remained a relatively large and at least sporadically active player in the Ottawa policy process ever since, right through the nine years of the Mulroney government. The PMO functions both as a channel for specifically party-based political input, and as an extension of prime-ministerial influence, not only over the policy process generally, but over cabinet ministers as well.

The main method adopted by Trudeau to counter the bureaucracy was, paradoxically, to use the bureaucracy itself. It was in the Trudeau years, especially the early 1970s, that the role of the *central agencies* in the policy process became a preoccupation of Ottawa decision-makers. The central agencies are those parts of the bureaucracy whose leading purpose is to support the decision-making activities of cabinet. There are four main central agencies, all of which, unlike the PMO, are part of the permanent civil service: the Privy Council Office (PCO), the Department of Finance, the Treasury Board Secretariat (TBS), and the Federal–Provincial Relations Office (FPRO). Two other central agencies—the Ministry of State for Economic and Regional Development and the Ministry of State for Social Development—existed from 1980 to 1984, when they were abolished by the incoming Liberal prime minister John Turner and not revived by subsequent Tory governments.

The PCO is, in effect, the department in charge of the civil service, and the Clerk of the PCO is the head of the permanent civil service. The PCO is the official record-keeper for cabinet (the Clerk of the PCO attends cabinet meetings and all important cabinet committee meetings). But above all, the PCO coordinates policy planning within the bureaucracy and keeps watch over the machinery and process of government from the point of view of policy development. Finance, also a department of government with its own functionally specific policy field, exercises general authority over policy that has a macroeconomic impact on the Canadian economy, which is to say, virtually all policy that matters. The finance department plays a key role in the budgetary process, especially in terms of revenue sources for financing government programs. TBS supports the Treasury Board—a statutory committee of cabinet—and exercises hands-on intervention in all matters of expenditure control. TBS personifies government as "management" when it comes to bargaining with organized civil servants on matters of pay and conditions of work. Finally, the FPRO coordinates policy from the perspective of federalism or intergovernmental affairs. The FPRO is generally considered to be the weakest and least important of the central agencies (the other three are widely seen as powerful actors).

The emergence of the central agencies as key players in the policy process cannot be separated from two other developments in the Trudeau years: the cabinet committee system and the theory of rational policy management. Regarding the committee structure, it was apparent by the end of the 1960s that the old-style cabinet, which met as a whole to deliberate and make decisions, could no longer continue. The problem was one of size. Cabinets had grown, from sixteen in Diefenbaker's 1957 cabinet (a number unchanged from the 1920s) to 28 in Trudeau's cabinet after the 1968 election. This tendency continued to accelerate, reaching the all-time record for bloatedness—40 ministers—in Brian Mulroney's 1984 cabinet.

An elaborate system of cabinet committees, most devoted to particular policy areas, grew up to replace the now nonfunctional and largely ceremonial full cabinet. By 1979, the Trudeau cabinet had five committees that dealt with broad policy areas (economic policy, social policy, external affairs, and defence, etc.), a number of ad hoc committees struck for specific purposes; and four committees with wide mandates for policy in general: Priorities and Planning (P&P), treasury board, government operations, and legislation and house planning. In theory, all four committees funnelled into the full cabinet, but the latter was effectively limited to rubber-stamping matters already decided by the relevant committee. The central agencies were supportive of the cabinet committees, but particularly of the four with wide mandates for policy. The P&P committee, chaired by the PM and supported by the PCO, was by far the most influential. The logical culmination of these developments was the creation, during Joe Clark's short-lived government of 1979–80, of a smaller "inner cabinet" to which the various committees reported. In 1980, the returning Liberals discontinued the inner cabinet (it had attracted much political flack from regions that felt themselves underrepresented in the smaller body) and simply made the P&P committee the effective inner cabinet. Later, in the Mulroney years, P&P itself grew so large (nineteen members at one point) that a smaller committee, Government Operations, became the effective "inner" P&P—and the real power centre of cabinet. This proliferation and differentiation of cabinet committees required still more specialized bureaucratic agencies to support their activities.

The other factor that gave a decisive push to the central agencies in the Trudeau years was the craze for "rational policy planning" that swept Ottawa and other Western capitals in the late 1960s and early 1970s. In an era still characterized by the seemingly inevitable expansion of government, a technocratic approach to policy took hold. In the new age, it was argued, public policy was a matter of *information* and *information processing*. If all the relevant data could be loaded into policy machinery scientifically designed for processing, the theory went, the "right" answer would appear at the other end. Trudeau himself was somewhat obsessive about applying rational principles to government (he had adopted as his personal slogan "Reason over Passion"). Various management fads, tagged by a bewildering variety of acronyms, were applied to the bureaucratic process in successive attempts to rationally organize the technical and intellectual resources of the public service. None of these schemes achieved much success before being abandoned for a newer fad with a trendier acronym. The problem with the rationalist approach was that it tried to "assume away" politics, and to imagine that the policy process in the real world could approximate an abstract technocratic model of inputs and outputs. In the end, a gathering economic and fiscal crisis of the state demonstrated that the model did not work well in the real world. Two byproducts of the 1970s were an enhancement of the role of the bureaucrat and a continuing preoccupation with experimenting with the machinery of government, especially at the level of the central agencies.

APPROACHES TO BUREAUCRACY: FROM MULRONEY TO CHRÉTIEN

When the Mulroney Conservatives took over in 1984, they undertook a number of changes in direction that significantly altered the balance between politicians and bureaucrats. Two in particular require examination. First, the suspicion with which the Tories viewed models of bureaucratic rationality translated into a shift to a more openly "political" approach to policy and process. Second, the Mulroney Tories, like the "Thatcherite" Tories in Britain and the "Reaganite" Republicans in Washington, viewed government as inherently inefficient and wasteful, and favoured extending the scope of the private sector and the principles of the free market. These two tendencies, are, in fact, interrelated.

To the Tories, "bureaucratic rationality" was a self-evident oxymoron. Government had grown far too big and far too intrusive in Canadian society. The Trudeau approach of extending bureaucracy to control bureaucracy was little more than a rationalization of out-of-control growth and out-of-control costs. According to the Tories, the real way to control government was to downsize it. One of the first things they did upon assuming office was to appoint a special task force under Deputy Prime Minister Erik Nielson to review government expenditures and programs. The task-force studies were done by teams that included people from the private sector. This exercise matched similar external reviews by conservative governments in Britain and the United States. In each case, principles of private-sector management were applied to government, and the latter was found wanting. In line with the British Tories and the U.S. Republicans, the Canadian Conservatives also launched programs of privatization and deregulation designed to downsize government and reduce the level of intervention in the private sector. Much of this was consistent with the traditional Conservative emphasis on deficit reduction, at least at the rhetorical level (Tory government performance in deficit reduction was considerably less impressive than the rhetoric). But it also implied that markets were far better regulators of efficiency than were bureaucratic mechanisms. Such thinking led to a sharp decline in the prestige of senior bureaucrats and a pervasive sense in Tory Ottawa that achieving bureaucratic "effectiveness" meant reducing the numbers of bureaucrats and limiting the policy influence of those that remained.

The new conservatism did not necessarily translate into less bureaucracy, just as a rhetorical emphasis on deficit reduction did not necessarily translate into actual deficit reduction. Privatization did proceed apace, as many public enterprises were moved out of the public sector. But deregulation proved difficult to actually effect, for the regulatory regime was not reduced, at least as measured by the number of regulatory instruments that continued to be enacted each year. Government cost-cutting initiatives did not start with Brian Mulroney. Ad hoc attempts to cut back expenditure and the size of the civil service had sporadically convulsed the Trudeau governments. On one memorable occasion in the late 1970s, Trudeau returned from an official European trip imbued with a newfound missionary zeal for fiscal restraint and ordered a $2.5 billion cut to federal expenditures. Chaos reigned in Ottawa as programs were axed with little underlying logic or planning informing the process. With the Mulroney governments, however, restraint became a consistent watchword and leading standard to be applied to the evaluation of bureaucratic performance, even if the mechanisms for putting this standard into practice were elusive.

One of the results of restraint-mindedness was that the machinery for central control of bureaucratic activity, which had been built up by the previous Trudeau governments, found new life under the Tories. Among the central agencies, Finance and Treasury Board in particular retained important influence over the departments in overseeing expenditure control and checking the all-important economic implications of policy. The PCO, as the "department of the civil service," also retained a leading role in coordinating the downsizing of government and its reorganization along more businesslike lines. Mulroney's cabinet committee structure increasingly emphasized expenditure controls, but to do this effectively required effective support from the central agencies. A central paradox of the new conservatism was that the goal of cutting down bureaucracy itself required more bureaucracy to do the job. For politicians dedicated to restraint, this presented a real problem. The Tories felt that they had a mandate to reduce bureaucracy, but could the bureaucrats not, in effect, swallow up the politicians even while talking the new line?

It was considerations like this, along with a perhaps understandable mistrust of a bureaucracy that had had such long and close relations with their Liberal rivals, that led the Mulroney Tories to emphasize a more "political" approach to the relations between ministers and their senior bureaucrats. The Tories instituted "chiefs of staff" for each minister. These were political appointments intended to offer the ministers a political arm in dealing with their departments.[3] The theory was that partisan political input could serve to balance the apolitical advice ministers receive from their departments, and that chiefs of staff could offer a minister independent management assistance in running the ministers' offices. Senior bureaucrats were not, on the whole, happy with this innovation. Deputy ministers could not be expected to welcome a political figure interposed between them and their ministers. But the frequency of complaints about inexperience and lack of understanding of the technical details of departmental work on the part of some chiefs of staff suggests that recruitment from the ranks of party service was no guarantee of competence at this high level of policy and administration. By the end of the Mulroney years, resentment of the "politicos" had become a major theme of bureaucratic complaint.

Another ground for friction between politician and bureaucrat lay in the Tory suspicion (not always unfounded, it should be acknowledged) that bureaucrats could use their superior command of information to blunt or undermine the policy directions the ruling party was seeking to impose. To reduce this risk and to stamp their own imprint on the process as firmly as possible, the Tories took to discouraging departments from presenting the kind of detailed policy option papers that the Trudeau government had encouraged. "Don't give us a dozen reasons why we shouldn't do what we want to do," the Tory ministers in effect instructed their departments, "just tell us *how* you intend to do what we want you to do." In one sense, this represented the not unreasonable desire of a democratically elected government to make the unelected bureaucracy fully accountable, to ensure that the civil servants really are *servants* of the peoples' representatives. But there were problems with this approach. Policy options are not always devices for undermining the political will of the politicians. The bureaucrats have the knowledge and experience to point to pitfalls and traps that the politicians have not considered. Bureaucrats pride themselves on keeping their political masters out of trouble, but persistent snubbing of their efforts may create an adversarial situation where one did not previously exist. Moreover, senior and even upper-middle-range bureaucrats in the Mulroney years sometimes felt that their professionalism was being put in question; morale suffered as a consequence.

REORGANIZATION AND THE RETURN OF THE LIBERALS, 1993

Bureaucrats and Tories were on a collision course that culminated in the summer of 1993, which happened also to be the last days of the Conservatives in office. But the course was set at least a year earlier, when Prime

Minister Mulroney appointed Glen Shortliffe Clerk of the Privy Council. Shortliffe was widely viewed as a willing instrument for the further politicization of the civil service;[4] this appointment caused consternation that only deepened when it became known that, as boss of the civil service, Shortliffe would preside over the most serious overhaul and reorganization of government structure ever mounted. In fact, a reorganization project under a Tory cabinet minister, Robert de Cotret, had called in four former senior civil servants as consultants, and already had a preliminary report on the prime minister's desk when the Shortliffe appointment was announced. Pressed politically by the rise of the restraint-minded Reform Party among traditional Tory voters, the Tories decided to radically downsize government. The de Cotret study offered a blueprint, and Shortliffe was to oversee its implementation.

This reorganization involved not only downsizing the bureaucracy, but also reducing the unwieldy cabinet and cabinet committee system. This latter required some political courage on the part of the prime minister. The cabinet, and thus the number of ministries, had grown as a result of the rising expectations of regions and special-interest groups that there would be an ever increasing number of ministers, ministries, and programs to "represent" them. Any ruthless cutback of these "representatives" would be sure to attract potentially damaging political criticism. And from within, actual elimination of senior bureaucratic positions, and thus the dismissal of senior civil servants, would inevitably rouse a storm of bureaucratic resistance. Mulroney, perhaps not too surprisingly, chose not to stir these hornets' nests before his retirement from office. It was thus left to his successor, Kim Campbell, to bite the bullet. This she did when she named her cabinet in June 1993. It comprised only 25 ministers, a sharp reduction from the Mulroney pattern. She also reduced the number of cabinet committees from eleven to five. Under Campbell's plan, which closely reflected the recommendations of the de Cotret group, the number of ministries was reduced from 32 to 23. Many were merged or amalgamated, and overlapping functions were eliminated. A small number of "superministries" (as they were inevitably dubbed by the press) emerged, while other departments were either downgraded or eliminated altogether.

With fewer ministers and a smaller number of cabinet committees, some observers detected a shift of power back to a bureaucracy where decisions would more likely be made in the absence of detailed ministerial scrutiny.[5] This perception was at some odds with the view that the Tories were "politicizing" the bureaucracy, but in such matters the intended consequences of changes are not always at one with the unintended consequences. Once again, there is the paradox of a government resorting to bureaucratic means to reduce the size of the bureaucracy. Certainly, two civil servants in the central agencies—Shortliffe at PCO and Ian Clark, Secretary to the Treasury Board—now had extremely powerful positions in Ottawa as they shepherded the reorganization into place. It was Shortliffe who effectively held the fate of senior civil servants in his hands, as it was essentially on his recommendation that senior civil servants were reshuffled to fit the new top slots in the reorganized bureaucracy—and in some cases shuffled right out of the picture.

The seriousness of the situation was made clear little more than a month after the Campbell cabinet was sworn in. The axe fell on the assistant deputy minister (ADM) level, a category that had risen greatly in Ottawa over recent years, to reach 319. These numbers were reduced by 17 percent, for a new total of 266. This left 53 ADMs out of a job. Moreover, normal personnel processes (through the individual departments and the Public Service Commission) were sidetracked in the reorganization. Instead, a small committee of deputy ministers, and Glen Shortliffe, decided their fates. Those terminated, many of whom had 25 to 30 years of service in government, had no right of appeal. This was an unprecedented shakeup of the upper range of the bureaucracy; never before had executive firings on a mass scale been effected in Ottawa. Needless to say, this had severe repercussions on the morale of the civil service as a whole. Particular criticism was directed from women, both inside and outside government, who noted that senior female administrators suffered the worst setbacks, both in terms of failure to achieve any of the highest ranks in the reorganized service, and in terms of the proportion of those demoted or terminated. That this had been done under the first woman prime minister (and a self-described feminist) seemed particularly hard to take.

Previous Tory governments had shied away from frontal attacks for fear of stirring large conflicts within their own administration. The political situation in the summer of 1993 was such that the "optics" had apparently changed. A press report from Ottawa acknowledged that the "cuts have created a climate of fear within the civil service," but went on to point out that "Ms. Campbell and her ministers are primarily concerned with the political signal they hope the cuts will send—a picture of the bureaucrats in Ottawa experiencing some of the same pain that people in the private sector have felt during the recession."[6] With the Reform Party snapping at Tory heels, and an election pledge to eliminate the deficit in five years without raising taxes, the Tories had reached the point where they not only wanted to reduce and restrain the public sector, but wanted to be *seen* to be doing so, at whatever cost to the morale of their administrators. The fact that, under the new regime, some bureaucrats would actually have *more* power and influence on the policy process than before only adds irony to the situation.

It is difficult to evaluate what effect, if any, the Tory adversarial stance against the bureaucracy had on the election of 1993. The Conservatives were not only swept out of power, but were virtually eliminated as an active force in federal politics. Reform, with its strong anti-government, pro–free market principles, replaced the Conservatives as the main opposition party in English Canada. The emergence of the Bloc Québécois as the official Opposition in Parliament offers the prospect of a party that, if successful in its *raison d'être* (the sovereignty of Quebec), will cause the most wrenching turbulence in the bureaucracy, especially among francophone civil servants. The spectacular emergence of these two new parties presages future storm clouds over the relationship between politicians and bureaucrats.

More immediately significant, however, is the return of the Liberals to office with a majority government. The Liberals made it clear that they wish to avoid an adversarial relationship with their bureaucrats, and have set as a priority the rebuilding of morale among the senior civil service. David Zussman, a former senior bureaucrat-turned-academic who has written sympathetically of the problems of morale in public-sector management,[7] was made head of the Liberal transition team. The Tory innovation of ministerial chiefs of staff has been scrapped. A former Clerk of the Privy Council, Marcel Massé, who had resigned in protest over what he deemed the politicization of the civil service under the Tories, resurfaced as a star Liberal candidate and, following the election, as the Minister for Federal–Provincial Relations. Massé delivered to the Public Service Alliance a speech that was reassuring to the bureaucracy. "Good government requires a close and congenial relationship between public servants of every level and politicians," he said, calling for a new partnership. He criticized the Tory reorganization not only for creating "uncertainty and destabilization," but for undertaking cutbacks before determining what the role of government should be and what services it should provide: "How can you decide the shape and size of the instrument without deciding what you want it to do?"[8]

The Liberals have not reversed the main thrust of the reorganization initiated under the Tories. Prime Minister Jean Chrétien's first cabinet is even smaller than Kim Campbell's. At 23 members, Chrétien's cabinet is the smallest in three decades, returning to the size of the Pearson cabinets in the mid-1960s. The standing cabinet committees are reduced from Campbell's simplified structure—from five to four. This, together with the Liberal strictures against the Tory "war" on bureaucrats, would seem to indicate that Ottawa under Chrétien may be returning to the departmentalized-style policy-making of old, with less emphasis on the central control agencies and less enforcement of political directives from above.

CONCLUSION

While tensions between politicians and bureaucrats may be less acute than they were during the nine years of Tory rule, it is doubtful that Ottawa is entering a new golden age of the mandarinate. The conditions under which governments operate in the 1990s have changed drastically since the 1940s and 1950s, and with them the relationship between politics and administration. All governments in this decade labour under the burden of a public debt that is seen as a powerful constraint on positive governmental activity. In an age of fiscal restraint, bureaucrats face severe structural limitations on their actions; politicians, whatever their ideology and whatever their basic attitudes toward bureaucrats, will seek to tightly control the bureaucracy, motivated by political self-preservation if nothing else.

We are now in an age when the very definition of the boundaries between the public and the private sectors is in fundamental question, and when the role of government is constantly being redefined in the face of such factors as economic globalization and new challenges to the legitimacy of the state. In the former case, the toolbox of economic policy available to national governments has been depleted, leaving citizens angry and dissatisfied about the apparent impotence of their policy-makers. In the latter case, the new populism that has swept through Western democracies (dramatically exemplified in Canada by Reform, but hardly limited to that party) demands greater accountability on the part of political elites. This insistence on political accountability forces politicians to tighten the reins on their bureaucrats, and will probably, before the movement has run its course, force previously insulated and secretive areas of administration under more direct public scrutiny. After all, as bureaucracy has penetrated civil society (the growth of complex interventions in, and regulations of, "private behaviour," and the emergence of policy communities), it should hardly be surprising that demands for greater transparency of the state should emerge from the society.

Superficially, the return of the Liberals to office with a majority government might seem to signal a return to the past in the relations between politicians and bureaucrats. It is more likely that the characteristic tension between the two roles (a tension that could not be eliminated even under the best of circumstances) will resurface in the 1990s in ways that, though not entirely predictable, are inevitable—and under circumstances far from favourable.

NOTES

1. Guy D'Avignon, *Report of the Special Committee on the Review of Personnel Management and the Merit Principle* (Ottawa 1979).

2. Definition drawn from William D. Coleman and Grace Skogstad, "Policy Communities and Policy Networks: A Structural Approach," in Coleman and Skogstad, eds., *Policy Communities and Public Policies in Canada: A Structural Approach* (Toronto: Copp Clark Pitman, 1990), p. 26.

3. The chief of staff is precisely the opposite of the British institution of the private secretary to ministers. In the British case, private secretaries are permanent civil servants who are appointed to head each minister's private office. It has often been argued that this offers the bureaucrats a window on the ministers; the chief

of staff was designed, on the other hand, to offer the ministers a window on the bureaucrats.

4. Shortliffe had gained considerable notoriety in 1991 when he had engineered what many regarded as the offloading of blame from politicians onto senior civil servants in the Al-Mashat scandal at External Affairs (Mashat was an Iraqi diplomat given political asylum, an action that caused great political embarrassment).

5. See, for instance, Hugh Winsor, "Slim cabinet fattens mandarins," *The Globe and Mail* (July 5, 1993).

6. Hugh Winsor, "Axe to fall on more top bureaucrats," *The Globe and Mail* (August 6, 1993).

7. See David Zussman and Jak Jabes, *The Vertical Solitude: Managing in the Public Sector* (Halifax: Institute for Research on Public Policy, 1989).

8. Hugh Winsor, "Liberals seeking to improve relations with civil servants," *The Globe and Mail* (October 29, 1993).

FURTHER READINGS

Aucoin, P., and H. Bakvis. *The Centralization–Decentralization Conundrum: Organization and Management in the Canadian Government.* Halifax: Institute for Research on Public Policy, 1988.

Boyle, C. "The 'Irrationality' of the State: The Nielson Report." *Studies in Political Economy* 27 (Autumn 1988): 53–85.

Doern, B., and P. Aucoin. *Public Policy in Canada.* Toronto: Macmillan, 1979.

Dwivedi, O.P., ed. *The Administrative State in Canada: Essays in Honour of J.E. Hodgetts.* Toronto: University of Toronto Press, 1981.

French, R. *How Ottawa Decides.* Toronto: James Lorimer, 1984.

Hockin, T., ed. *Apex of Power.* 2nd ed. Scarborough, Ont.: Prentice-Hall Canada, 1977.

How Ottawa Spends, annual volumes from 1983, various editors.

Osbaldeston, G. *Keeping Deputy Ministers Accountable.* Toronto: McGraw-Hill Ryerson, 1992.

Phidd, R., and B. Doern. *The Politics and Management of Canadian Economic Policy.* Toronto: Macmillan, 1978.

Sutherland, S.L., and B. Doern. *Bureaucracy in Canada: Control and Reform.* Toronto: University of Toronto Press, 1985.

Van Loon, R., and M.S. Whittington. "Kaleidoscope in Grey: The Policy Process in Ottawa." In Michael S. Whittington and Glen Williams, eds., *Canadian Politics in the 1990s.* 3rd ed. Scarborough, Ont.: Nelson Canada, 1990, pp. 448–67.

Wilson, V.S. *Canadian Public Policy and Administration: Theory and Environment.* Toronto: McGraw-Hill Ryerson, 1981.

INDEX

Democracy in Alberta, 160
Deputy ministers, 364, 427–30
Deregulation, 282, 434
Deutsch, Karl, 120
Devine, Grant, 416
Devoir, Le, 88
Dewdney, Edgar, 397
Diasporan communities, 204–5
Dickson, Brian, 181
Diefenbaker, John, 29, 226, 233, 338, 363, 382, 384, 393, 397, 408, 428
Difference (ethnic/racial), 192
Disaffecteds, 111–12
Dobbie, Dorothy, 326
Domestic workers, 206
Domm, Bill, 378
Dorman, Christopher, 313
Douglas, Tommy, 228
Dunning, Charles, 396
Duplessis, Maurice, 87–89, 227, 330
Durham, Lord, 388
Durham Report, 85

Easton, David, 106
Economic summits, 49
Economy
  Quebec, 87
  U.S. control of, 30–31, 59
Edmonton Journal, The, 347
Education
  and political participation, 137, 138–39, 140, 141, 150n.9
  in Quebec, 87, 88, 90–91, 95
Election Expenses Act (1974), 225
Elections. *See also* Voting
  in antiquity, 238
  campaigns, 244
  effectiveness of, 144, 147, 249–50
  functions of, 238–39
  interest in, 133, 134
  issues in, 240–42, 248
  mass media and, 309–12
  origins of, 222
  and political participation, 130, 134

voter turnout in, 132–33
  and voting behaviour, 239–44
Electoral conversion, 244–47
Electoral replacement, 244–47
Elgin, Lord, 388
Elite-pluralism, 154–56
Elites
  analysis of, 154–60
  behaviour of, 152–53
  Clement's view of, 156
  defined, 152
  and environment, 153
  Francis's view of, 157
  McQuaig's view of, 157–58
  and media, 156, 296
  Olsen's view of, 157
  Porter's view of, 154–56
  Presthus's view of, 157
Elkins, David, 111–12
Employment equity, 194
Employment Equity Program, 209
Employment growth
  in G7, 60
  in public sector, 65
Energy resources, 413
Environmental issues
  and the constitutional process, 331
  and political culture, 121
  and pressure groups, 261, 262
Equalization payments, 71, 413
Ericson, Richard, 295
Established Programs Financing (EPF), 71, 414
Ethnicity. *See also* Race
  and Canadian foreign policy, 205
  concept of, 193–94
  and homeland politics, 204–5
  and political participation, 139, 199–204
  and skin colour, 194
  and social movements, 205–6
  as term, 213–14n.16
Ethos theory, 112–13, 126n.15
Eugenics, 197
European Community, 49, 59

To the owner of this book

We hope that you have enjoyed *Canadian Politics in the 1990s* and we would like to know as much about your experiences with it as you would care to offer. Only through your comments and those of others can we learn how to make this a better text for future readers.

School _____ Your instructor's name _____

Course _____ Was the text required? _____ Recommended? _____

1. What did you like the most about *Canadian Politics in the 1990s?*

_____

_____

_____

2. How useful was this text for your course?

_____

_____

_____

3. Do you have any recommendations for ways to improve the next edition of this text?

_____

_____

_____

4. In the space below or in a separate letter, please write any other comments you have about the book. (For example, please feel free to comment on reading level, writing style, terminology, design features, and learning aids.)

_____

_____

_____

Optional

Your
name _____ Date _____

May Nelson Canada quote you, either in promotion for *Canadian Politics in the 1990s* or in future publishing ventures?

Yes _____ No _____

Thanks!

- FOLD HERE - - - - - - - - - - - - - -

MAIL ⤳ POSTE
Canada Post Corporation / Société canadienne des postes

Postage paid
if mailed in Canada

Port payé
si posté au Canada

Business Reply

Réponse d'affaires

0107077099   01

TAPE SHUT

TAPE SHUT

0107077099-M1K5G4-BR01

Nelson Canada
College Editorial Department
1120 Birchmount Rd.
Scarborough, ON M1K 9Z9

Nelson

PLEASE TAPE SHUT. DO NOT STAPLE.